PATERNOSTER BIBLICAL MONOGRAPHS

'But God Raised Him from the Dead'

The Theology of Jesus' Resurrection in Luke-Acts

PATERNOSTER BIBLICAL MONOGRAPHS

A full listing of titles in this series and
Paternoster Theological Monographs
will be found at the close of this book.

PATERNOSTER BIBLICAL MONOGRAPHS

'But God Raised Him from the Dead'

The Theology of Jesus' Resurrection in Luke-Acts

Kevin L. Anderson

Wipf & Stock
PUBLISHERS
Eugene, Oregon

Wipf and Stock Publishers
199 W 8th Ave, Suite 3
Eugene, OR 97401

"But God Raised Him from the Dead"
The Theology of Jesus's Resurrection in Luke-Acts
By Anderson, Kevin L.
Copyright©2006 Paternoster
ISBN 13: 978-1-55635-237-9
ISBN 10: 1-55635-237-9
Publication date 1/31/2007
Previously published by Paternoster, 2006

This Edition Published by Wipf and Stock Publishers by arrangement with Paternoster

Paternoster
9 Holdom Avenue
Bletchley
Milton Keyes, MK1 1QR
Great Britain

Unless otherwise noted, biblical quotations
will be translated by the Author or from the
HOLY BIBLE, NEW REVISED STANDARD VERSION
Copyright © 1989 by the Division of Christian Education of the
National Council of the Churches of Christ in the United States of
America. All rights reserved. Used by permission of
Zondervan Publishing House, Grand Rapids, Michigan

PATERNOSTER BIBLICAL MONOGRAPHS

Series Preface

One of the major objectives of Paternoster is to serve biblical scholarship by providing a channel for the publication of theses and other monographs of high quality at affordable prices. Paternoster stands within the broad evangelical tradition of Christianity. Our authors would describe themselves as Christians who recognise the authority of the Bible, maintain the centrality of the gospel message and assent to the classical credal statements of Christian belief. There is diversity within this constituency; advances in scholarship are possible only if there is freedom for frank debate on controversial issues and for the publication of new and sometimes provocative proposals. What is offered in this series is the best of writing by committed Christians who are concerned to develop well-founded biblical scholarship in a spirit of loyalty to the historic faith.

Series Editors

I. Howard Marshall, Honorary Research Professor of New Testament, University of Aberdeen, Scotland, UK

Richard J. Bauckham, Professor of New Testament Studies and Bishop Wardlaw Professor, University of St Andrews, Scotland, UK

Craig Blomberg, Distinguished Professor of New Testament, Denver Seminary, Colorado, USA

Robert P. Gordon, Regius Professor of Hebrew, University of Cambridge, UK

Tremper Longman III, Robert H. Gundry Professor and Chair of the Department of Biblical Studies, Westmont College, Santa Barbara, California, USA

*For my father, Charles L. Anderson (1934–2000)
and father-in-law, Daniel L. Hanna (1938–1989)*

*Two men 'worthy to attain to that age and
the resurrection from the dead' (Luke 20:35)*

Contents

Preface	xvii
Abbreviations	xix

Chapter 1
The Resurrection of Jesus in Luke-Acts:
Twentieth-Century Research and
the Need for Current Study — 1
1.1　Paucity of Studies on the Resurrection of Jesus in Luke-Acts　1
1.1.1　*Dominance of Tradition-Historical Research*　4
1.1.2　*Disproportionate Attention to the Ascension Accounts*　5
1.1.3　*Lack of Consensus on Research Methodology*　10
1.1.4　*Purpose of Luke-Acts*　11
1.2　The Resurrection of Jesus and the Hope of Israel:
　　A Current Approach　13
1.2.1　*Scope of the Study*　13
1.2.2　*Principal Issues*　14
1.2.2.1　THE RESURRECTION OF JESUS
　　　　AND THE THEME OF SALVATION　14
1.2.2.2　NATURE AND SIGNIFICANCE OF RESURRECTION　15
1.2.2.3　RELATIONSHIP OF RESURRECTION,
　　　　ASCENSION, AND EXALTATION　15
1.2.3　*Methodology: An Authorial Audience to the Resurrection*　16

Chapter 2
Salvation and Resurrection:
Theme and Focus in Luke-Acts — 22
2.1　Salvation in Luke-Acts　22
2.1.1　*Salvation as the Theme of Luke-Acts*　22
2.1.2　*The Meaning of Salvation in Luke-Acts*　26

2.2	The Resurrection of Jesus as Theological Focus	30
2.2.1	*The Prominence of the Resurrection of Jesus in Luke-Acts*	32
2.2.2	*The Death of Jesus in Luke-Acts*	37
2.2.3	*The Ascension of Jesus in Luke-Acts*	41
2.3	Prospect: Jesus' Resurrection and Lukan Soteriology	47

Chapter 3
Resurrection in Second Temple Judaism — 48

3.1	Resurrection in Ancient Judaism	49
3.1.1	*Pre-Maccabean and Maccabean Period*	52
3.1.1.1	HOSEA 6:1–3 AND EZEKIEL 37:1–14: PRECURSORS TO RESURRECTION FAITH IN ISRAEL	52
3.1.1.2	ISAIAH 26:19 AND DANIEL 12:1–3: EARLY WITNESSES TO RESURRECTION	55
3.1.2	*From the Maccabean Period to the Dawn of Christianity (pre-70 A.D.)*	61
3.1.2.1	SECOND MACCABEES: THE HOPE OF PHYSICAL RESURRECTION	63
3.1.2.2	THE RESURRECTION IN *FIRST ENOCH*	69
3.1.2.3	OTHER RESURRECTION PASSAGES	73
3.1.3	*From the Destruction of Jerusalem (A.D. 70) to the End of the First Century*	74
3.1.3.1	*FOURTH EZRA*: RESURRECTION, RE-CREATION, AND REWARD	75
3.1.3.2	*SECOND BARUCH*: PHYSICAL RESURRECTION AND SALVATION, EXALTATION, AND VINDICATION	78
3.1.3.3	RESURRECTION IN THE *TESTAMENTS OF THE TWELVE PATRIARCHS*	81
3.1.3.4	JOSEPHUS AND THE JEWISH 'PHILOSOPHICAL SCHOOLS'	85
3.2	Summary and Conclusions	90

Chapter 4
Resurrection in the Hellenistic World — 92

4.1	A Synopsis of Hellenistic Conceptions of the Afterlife	93
4.1.1	*The Tomb as the Residence for the Dead*	93
4.1.2	*Hades: The House of Death*	94

4.1.3	*Variations and Departures from the Homeric Vision of the Afterlife*	96
4.1.4	*Summary*	98
4.2	Reactions to Resurrection in the Greco-Roman World	99
4.2.1	*General Attitudes toward Resurrection*	99
4.2.2	*The Earliest Imaginative Representations of 'Resurrection'*	100
4.2.3	*Cave-Dwelling, Astral Projection, and 'Resurrection'*	101
4.2.4	*The 'Second Chance' and Scientific Demonstrations of 'Resurrection'*	104
4.2.5	*'Death' and 'Resurrection' in the Hellenistic Novels*	108
4.2.5.1	SIMILAR SITUATIONS AND LANGUAGE	109
4.2.5.2	NATURAL EXPLANATIONS AND HIGH ADVENTURE	110
4.2.6	*Epicureans, Stoics, and the Resurrection*	112
4.3	Summary and Conclusions	113
	Excursus on the Definitions of Resurrection and Resuscitation	114

Chapter 5
Resurrection in Luke-Acts: Miracle, Contention, and Hope for the People of God — 118

5.1	The Resurrection Miracles in Luke-Acts	119
5.1.1	*The Miracles of Resurrection*	119
5.1.1.1	PROPHETIC AGENTS OF RESURRECTION	119
5.1.1.2	REALITY OF RESURRECTION IN LUKE-ACTS	122
5.1.1.3	THEOLOGICAL MEANING OF RESURRECTION	125
5.1.2	*The Miracles of Resurrection and the Resurrection of Jesus*	127
5.1.2.1	JESUS' RESURRECTION, A DIRECT ACT OF GOD	127
5.1.2.2	THE REALITY OF JESUS' DEATH AND RESURRECTION	127
5.1.2.3	THE RISEN JESUS AND THE RESTORATION OF THE PEOPLE OF GOD	128
5.1.3	*Conclusions*	128
5.2	Resurrection in Contention	129
5.2.1	*The Issue of Resurrection among Jews*	129

5.2.1.1	THE SADDUCEES AND JESUS ON RESURRECTION (LUKE 20:27–40)	130
5.2.1.1.1	The Sadducees' Conundrum (Luke 20:27–33)	131
5.2.1.1.2	Jesus' Response—Part 1 (Luke 20:34–36)	132
5.2.1.1.3	Jesus' Response—Part 2 (Luke 20:37–38)	136
5.2.1.2	PHARISEES VERSUS SADDUCEES ON RESURRECTION (ACTS 23:8)	139
5.3	Gentile Perceptions of the Resurrection	143
5.4	Conclusion: The Resurrection as the Hope of Israel	144

Chapter 6   **146**
Reading with the End in Mind (1):
The Resurrection of Jesus and the Hope of Israel (Luke 24)   **146**

6.1	Closure in Ancient Narrative	146
6.1.1	*Defining Narrative Closure*	147
6.1.2	*Analyzing Narrative Closure*	149
6.1.3	*Closure in Hellenistic Historiography*	151
6.1.3.1	MACRO-LEVEL CLOSURE	152
6.1.3.2	MICRO-LEVEL CLOSURE	154
6.1.3.3	CONCLUSION	155
6.2	Defining Beginnings and Endings in Luke-Acts	156
6.2.1	*Literary Planning and Luke-Acts*	156
6.2.2	*The Parameters and Structure of the End of Luke*	157
6.3	Resurrection and the Hope of Israel at the End of Luke's Gospel	160
6.3.1	*The Empty Tomb (Luke 24:1–12)*	160
6.3.1.1	CIRCULARITY	161
6.3.1.2	PARALLELISM	163
6.3.1.3	INCOMPLETION	164
6.3.2	*The Way to Emmaus (Luke 24:13–32)*	166
6.3.2.1	CIRCULARITY	167
6.3.2.2	PARALLELISM	169
6.3.2.2.1	The Transfiguration and the Emmaus Scene	172
6.3.2.2.2	The Feeding of the Five Thousand and the Emmaus Scene	179
6.3.2.3	INCOMPLETION	181
6.3.3	*The Final Appearance of the Risen Jesus (Luke 24:36–53)*	181
6.3.3.1	CIRCULARITY	183

Contents xiii

6.3.3.1.1	Extension of Salvation to All Nations	183
6.3.3.1.2	Devout People Awaiting God's Salvific Action	185
6.3.3.2	PARALLELISM	185
6.3.3.3	LINKAGE	188
6.3.3.3.1	Jesus' Post-Resurrection Appearances	188
6.3.3.3.2	The Universal Reach of the Message of Salvation	193
6.3.3.3.3	Witnesses Appointed Whose Activity Originates in Jerusalem	193
6.3.3.3.4	The Promise of the Father	194
6.3.3.3.5	The Ascension of Jesus	195
6.4	Conclusion	195

Chapter 7
Peter's Resurrection Speeches (Acts 2–3)   197

7.1	The Speeches in Acts and the Resurrection of Jesus	197
7.1.1	*The Resurrection of Jesus: A Unifying Element in the Speeches*	197
7.1.2	*The Resurrection of Jesus and Particular Narrative Settings*	198
7.2	Peter's Speech at Pentecost (Acts 2:14–36)	200
7.2.1	*The Speech in Its Narrative Setting*	200
7.2.2	*The Structure of the Speech*	201
7.2.3	*The Eschatological Breakthrough of Jesus' Resurrection (Acts 2:22–28)*	202
7.2.3.1	THE CHRISTOLOGICAL KERYGMA (2:22–24)	202
7.2.3.2	'HAVING BROUGHT THE BIRTH PANGS OF DEATH TO AN END' (2:24)	203
7.2.3.3	THE QUOTATION FROM 'DAVID' (2:25–28)	208
7.2.4	*Jesus Enthroned as Lord and Messiah (2:29–36)*	209
7.2.4.1	JESUS' INSTALLMENT ON DAVID'S THRONE (2:29–32)	209
7.2.4.2	THE EXALTED JESUS POURS OUT THE HOLY SPIRIT (2:33–35)	213
7.2.4.3	GOD HAS MADE JESUS BOTH LORD AND MESSIAH (2:36)	218
7.3	Peter's Speech at Solomon's Portico (Acts 13:12–26)	219
7.3.1	*The Speech in Its Narrative Setting*	219
7.3.2	*The Structure of the Speech*	221
7.3.3	*Resurrection, Repentance, and Restoration in Peter's Temple Speech (Acts 3:12–26)*	222

7.3.3.1	THE RESURRECTIONAL FRAME OF THE SPEECH (3:13, 26)	222
7.3.3.2	JESUS THE AUTHOR/LEADER OF LIFE (3:15)	224
7.3.3.3	JESUS' RESURRECTION, REPENTANCE, AND ISRAEL'S RESTORATION	226
7.3.3.3.1	Repentance and Israel's Resurrection and Restoration (3:20–21)	226
7.3.3.3.2	Resurrected Prophet Like Moses and Israel's Repentance (3:22–26)	231
7.4	Conclusion	233

Chapter 8
Paul's Resurrection Speech at Pisidian Antioch (Acts 13) — 234

8.1	The Resurrection of Jesus in Paul's Speeches	234
8.2	Setting and Structure of Paul's Speech at Pisidian Antioch (Acts 13:16–41)	235
8.2.1	*The Narrative Setting of the Speech*	235
8.2.2	*The Structure of the Speech*	238
8.3	Paul's Resurrection Speech at Pisidian Antioch (Acts 13:16–41)	239
8.3.1	Narratio *(13:16b–25): Historical Survey Culminating in Israel's Saviour, Jesus*	239
8.3.2	Argumentatio *(13:26–37): Kerygma and Scriptural Proof*	242
8.3.2.1	THE CHRISTIAN KERYGMA (13:27–31)	242
8.3.2.2	DEMONSTRATION FROM THE SCRIPTURES (13:32–37)	244
8.3.2.2.1	The First Scriptural Witness: Psalm 2:7 (Acts 13:33b)	247
8.3.2.2.2	The Second Scriptural Witness: Isaiah 55:3 (Acts 13:34)	249
8.3.2.2.3	The Third Scriptural Witness: Ps 15:10 LXX (13:35)	254
8.3.2	Peroratio *(13:38–41): Options of Belief or Unbelief in the Risen One*	255
8.4	Conclusion	259

Chapter 9
Reading with the End in Mind (2):
The Resurrection of Jesus and
the Hope of Israel (Acts 28) — 261

9.1	The Parameters of the Ending, Middle, and Beginning in Acts	262

9.2	Hope of Israel, Resurrection, and Jesus at the End of Acts	266
9.2.1	*Circularity between the End and Beginning of Acts*	266
9.2.2	*Parallelism between the End of Acts and Earlier Passages*	269
9.2.2.1	THE SCRIPTURAL PROMISE OF HOPE AND RESURRECTION	278
9.2.2.2	THE KEY FULFILMENT OF THE PROMISE: THE RESURRECTION OF JESUS	279
9.2.2.3	THE RESURRECTION OF JESUS AND THE RESURRECTION OF THE DEAD	280
9.2.2.3.1	Proclaiming 'in Jesus the Resurrection of the Dead' (Acts 4:2)	281
9.2.2.3.2	Proclaiming 'Jesus and Anastasis' (Acts 17:18)	284
9.2.3	*Incompletion in Acts 28*	285
9.3	The Focus of Paul's Apology: Hope of Israel, the Resurrection, and Jesus' Resurrection	286
9.4	Conclusion	291

Bibliography	**293**
1. Commentaries on Luke and Acts	293
2. Texts and Translations	295
3. Reference Works	296
4. Other Works	296
Index of Modern Authors	**324**
Index of Ancient Literature and Scripture	**330**
1. Classical and Hellenistic Writings	330
2. Old Testament Pseudepigrapha	333
3. Dead Sea Scrolls	335
4. Josephus	335
5. Philo	335
6. Rabbinic Texts	336
7. Apostolic Fathers and Church Fathers	336
8. New Testament Apocrypha and Pseudepigrapha	337
9. Old Testament	337
10. Apocrypha	340
11. New Testament	341

PREFACE

This work is a slight revision of my dissertation 'The Resurrection of Jesus in Luke-Acts,' presented for the Ph.D. in New Testament at London School of Theology in 2001. The genesis of the project is of some interest. As a research assistant during my post-graduate studies at the Graduate Theological Union (Berkeley, Calif.), I was assigned the task of gathering bibliographical material on the resurrection in Luke-Acts. To my great surprise, there was no avalanche of research on the subject, as I had expected. On account of that providential experience, I was privileged to embark upon a doctoral research topic of such grand importance and interest, rather than something perhaps more arcane and specialized. My hope is that, despite how unequal to the task I have often felt, I have been able to offer a substantive contribution to a greater understanding of St. Luke's two-volume history addressed to Theophilus.

All scholarship stands on the shoulders of others. I have benefited from professors who have influenced me tremendously by their teaching and scholarship. I was introduced to the exciting world of biblical scholarship by James D. Hernando while he was a professor of Bible and theology at Trinity Bible College (Ellendale, N. Dak.). My exegetical skills and faith were deepened by my professors at Nazarene Theological Seminary (Kansas City, Mo.), but especially New Testament professors Alex R. G. Deasley and Morris A. Weigelt. Above all, I am indebted to my *Doktorvater*, Joel B. Green, Professor of New Testament Interpretation at Asbury Theological Seminary (Wilmore, Ky.). His wise counsel and encouragement have been of immense help to me throughout my doctoral studies and beyond.

The research and writing for this work would not have been possible without the assistance of many people. I would like to thank particularly Barbara Pfeifle and her staff at Bosworth Memorial Library (Lexington Theological Seminary, Lexington, Ky.), in whose quiet space I wrote the lion's share of the manuscript. I am grateful to the interlibrary loan librarian, Dot James, at B. L. Fisher Library (Asbury Theological Seminary, Wilmore, Ky.), who procured for me many difficult-to-find titles. As drafts of chapters were written, I was also challenged and supported by members of a doctoral seminar that met at Asbury Theological Seminary in the late

1990s, where I was introduced to some dear colleagues, not least being David Smith (Indiana Wesleyan University, Marion, Ind.) and Jason Borders (Huntingdon College, Montgomery, Ala.).

I would also like to thank those who urged this work toward publication, beginning with my examiners, I. Howard Marshall and Steve Walton. Others include my doctoral advisor, Joel Green; professors at London School of Theology, especially Max Turner and Tony Lane, whose warm and hospitable spirits I shall never forget; Robin Parry, commissioning editor at Paternoster; and David Rightmire, chair of the Bible and Theology department at Asbury College (Wilmore, Ky.). I would like to extend a special thanks to that veritable master of St. Luke's resurrection theology, Robert F. O'Toole, S. J., who kindly agreed to review the manuscript. I should also mention the assistance of Seth Maislin, president of the American Society of Indexers, who initiated me into the mysteries of indexing during the final stages of preparing the manuscript for publication. Last, but certainly not least, I have had my wife, Sandi, by my side through this entire process. I cannot adequately express my appreciation for her technical expertise in desktop publishing, her uncommon wisdom, and above all, her love.

Kevin L. Anderson
Asbury College
Wilmore, Kentucky

ABBREVIATIONS

Abbreviations (apart from those listed below) conform to Patrick H. Alexander et al., eds., *The SBL Handbook of Style for Ancient Near Eastern, Biblical, and Early Christian Studies* (Peabody, Mass.: Hendrickson, 1999), and in the case of some classical references, Simon Hornblower and Antony Spawforth, *Oxford Classical Dictionary* (3d ed.; Oxford and New York: Oxford, 1996).

A1CS	The Book of Acts in Its First Century Setting
BC	*The Beginnings of Christianity.* Edited by Jackson F. J. Foakes and Kirsopp Lake. 5 vols. London, 1920–1933
BRS	Biblical Resource Series
BU	Biblische Untersuchungen
ExpBC	*Expositor's Bible Commentary.* Edited by Frank Gaebelein. 12 vols. Grand Rapids, 1976–1992
IBRB	Institute for Biblical Research Bibliographies
FilNT	*Filologia Neotestamentaria*
ITS	Innsbrucker theologische Studien
JHC	*Journal of Higher Criticism*
JPTMS	Journal of Pentecostal Theology Monograph Series
LII	Luke the Interpreter of Israel
McMNTS	McMaster New Testament Studies
OTM	Old Testament Message
PRStSSS	Perspectives in Religious Studies, Special Studies Series
TCGNT	Bruce W. Metzger, *A Textual Commentary on the Greek New Testament.* 2d ed., Stuttgart, 1994
TCSPCK	Theological Collections (Society for Promoting Christian Knowledge)
ThInq	Theological Inquiries
UBSHT	UBS Helps for Translators
WSTR	Walberberger Studien, Theologische Reihe

Chapter 1

The Resurrection of Jesus in Luke-Acts: Twentieth-Century Research and the Need for Current Study

An anecdote that circulated among Harvard students of the pioneering Luke-Acts scholar, Henry Joel Cadbury, stated that he earned his doctorate by wresting Luke's away from him.[1] Cadbury may also be credited for forging the hyphen between Luke and Acts, regarding the two volumes as a unity, and arguing that Luke 1:1–4 functions as the preface to both volumes.[2] Yet there is another first that may be ascribed to Cadbury that is never recognized. He appears to be the first twentieth-century NT scholar to articulate the singular importance of the resurrection in Luke-Acts vis-à-vis the rest of the NT. Cadbury observed, 'No New Testament writer more often refers to the resurrection as predicted in Scripture or cites more texts in its support than does Luke.'[3] He further asserted: 'It is plain that for this writer [sc. Luke] the resurrection of Jesus is the distinguishing article of faith for Christians over against the Jew.'[4] Unfortunately, although Cadbury and others have recognized the importance of Jesus' resurrection for Luke, none has undertaken a comprehensive study of the resurrection of Jesus in Luke-Acts.

1.1 Paucity of Studies on the Resurrection of Jesus in Luke-Acts

A perusal of the vast array of research on Luke-Acts reveals a startling lacuna: not one monograph has been devoted to the subject of the resurrec-

---

[1] Amos N. Wilder, 'In Memoriam: Henry Joel Cadbury, 1883–1974,' *NTS* 21 (1975): 314. Ernst Haenchen (*Die Apostelgeschichte* [12th ed.; Göttingen: Vandenhoeck & Ruprecht, 1959], 41) called Cadbury 'Der Altmeister angelsächsischer Actaforschung.'

[2] Henry J. Cadbury, 'Appendix C: Commentary on the Preface of Luke,' *BC* 2:491–92; idem, *The Making of Luke-Acts* (2d ed.; London: SPCK, 1959; repr., Peabody, Mass.: Hendrickson, 1999), 194–98.

[3] Cadbury, *Making of Luke-Acts*, 279.

[4] Cadbury, *Making of Luke-Acts*, 278.

tion in Luke-Acts as a whole,[5] and relatively few essays have been devoted to the subject.[6] Things have not changed dramatically since 1978 when Richard Dillon lamented the dearth of study on Luke 24 from a *redaktionsgeschichtliche* perspective, and was thereupon forced to forego the exercise of writing a *Forschungsbericht*.[7] The following year, Robert O'Toole offered the first summary of resurrection-ascension-exaltation-*Forschung*, in which he outlined a modest number of interpretations, suggested solutions to lingering problems, and recommended a methodology that attends to all the Lukan data and to the entire Lukan schema of salvation history.[8] On the heels of his doctoral dissertation, *The Christological Climax of Paul's*

---

[5] A possible exception is Jean-Marie Guillaume (*Luc Interprète des anciennes traditions sur la résurrection de Jésus* [Ebib; Paris: Librairie Lecoffre, 1979]), but this study deals only marginally with material outside of Luke 24 and Acts 1.

[6] Günter Kegel (*Auferstehung Jesu—Auferstehung der Toten: Eine traditionsgeschichtliche Untersuchung zum Neuen Testament* [Gütersloh: Gerd Mohn, 1970], 81–100) approaches the resurrection in Luke-Acts as Luke's own 'Thematisierung' and takes a sweeping look at the Lukan data related to the resurrection of Jesus and to the resurrection of the dead generally. According to Kegel, Luke is interested in establishing the facticity ('Faktizität') of both Jesus' resurrection and the general resurrection in the course of dialogue with sceptics such as Sadducees, Hellenistic philosophers, and a Gentile public. Daniel P. Fuller (*Easter Faith and History* [Grand Rapids: Eerdmans, 1965], 188–261) devotes two chapters to Jesus' resurrection in Acts, but with a view toward questions of historicity. Marshall has contributed two instalments in defence of the historicity of the resurrection traditions in Luke-Acts: I. Howard Marshall, 'The Resurrection of Jesus in Luke,' *TynBul* 24 (1973): 55–98; idem, 'The Resurrection in the Acts of the Apostles,' in *Apostolic History and the Gospel* (eds. W. Ward Gasque and Ralph P. Martin; Grand Rapids: Eerdmans, 1970), 92–107.

[7] Richard J. Dillon, *From Eye-Witnesses to Ministers of the Word: Tradition and Composition in Luke 24* (AnBib 82; Rome: Biblical Institute, 1978), vii–viii. Dillon pointed to only a handful of essays—chief among them Paul Schubert's oft-cited 'The Structure and Significance of Luke 24' (in *Neutestamentliche Studien für Rudolf Bultmann, zu seinem siebzigsten Geburtstag am 20. August 1954* [ed. Walther Eltester; BZNW 21; Berlin: Töpelmann, 1954], 165–86) and Max Brändle's 'Auferstehung Jesu nach Lukas,' *Orientierung* 24 (1960): 85–89—and only one monograph on a specific pericope in Luke 24, Joachim Wanke, *Die Emmauserzählung: Eine redaktionsgeschichtliche Untersuchung zu Lk 24,13–35* (ETS 31; Leipzig: St. Benno-Verlag, 1973). My own research has confirmed Dillon's observation that, despite the bulk of general studies on resurrection in the NT, the Lukan voice can hardly be heard above the cacophony of resurrection *Überlieferungen* and the din of Easter *Historie* reconstruction (viii).

[8] Robert F. O'Toole, 'Luke's Understanding of Jesus' Resurrection-Ascension-Exaltation,' *BTB* 9 (1979): 106–14. Positions on the interrelation of resurrection-ascension-exaltation are sketched in greater detail in A.W. Zwiep, *The Ascension of the Messiah in Lukan Christology* (NovTSup 77; Leiden: Brill, 1997), 1–35.

Defense, he emerged as one of the few Lukan scholars who is attentive to the theological significance of Jesus' resurrection in Luke-Acts.[9] A prominent theme in O'Toole's interpretation is that Jesus' resurrection makes it possible for him to continue his saving activity in the life of the church as recorded in the Book of Acts. More recently, Charles Talbert has profiled the resurrection within the complex of Luke's theology.[10] He discussed Jesus' resurrection in relation to Luke's theology, Christology, soteriology, ecclesiology, and missiology. Joel Green has made a fresh contribution to our understanding of the resurrection as the embodiment of God's salvific purpose in Jesus and its outworking in the communal life and mission of the church in Acts.[11] Luke Timothy Johnson includes a chapter in *Living Jesus* that builds upon his earlier emphasis on the risen Jesus as the prophet like Moses who initiates the restoration of Israel.[12] The most insightful study to date is Daniel Marguerat's 'Luc-Actes: La résurrection à l'œuvre dans l'histoire.'[13] His thesis is that Luke-Acts not only offers an account of the resurrection, but is itself a testimony to the resurrection. The resurrection of Jesus is the hermeneutical key to Luke's construction of a Christian view of salvation history. All of these contributions are valuable, but each falls short of providing a full-scale study of how the resurrection of Jesus functions within Luke's entire narrative project, and therefore within his overall vision of salvation.

There is, of course, a myriad of commentary on Jesus' resurrection strewn throughout the plethora of literature on Luke-Acts; but because

---

[9] Robert F. O'Toole, *The Christological Climax of Paul's Defense (Ac 22:1—26:32)* (AnBib 78; Rome: Biblical Institute, 1978); idem, 'Christ's Resurrection in Acts 13,13–52,' *Bib* 60 (1979): 361–72; idem, 'Some Observations on *anistēmi* 'I Raise,' in Acts 3:22, 26,' *ScEs* 31 (1979): 85–92; idem, 'Activity of the Risen Jesus in Luke-Acts,' *Bib* 62 (1981): 471–98; idem, *The Unity of Luke's Theology: An Analysis of Luke-Acts* (GNS 9; Wilmington, Del.: Michael Glazier, 1984), 38–61.

[10] Charles H. Talbert, 'The Place of the Resurrection in the Theology of Luke,' *Int* 46 (1992): 19–30.

[11] Joel B. Green, '"Witnesses of His Resurrection": Salvation, Discipleship, and Resurrection in the Acts of the Apostles,' in *Life in the Face of Death: The Resurrection Message of the New Testament* (ed. Richard N. Longenecker; McMNTS; Grand Rapids: Eerdmans, 1998), 227–46. The bibliography for Green's essay underscores the dearth of concentrated research on our topic.

[12] Luke Timothy Johnson, *Living Jesus: Learning the Heart of the Gospel* (San Francisco: HarperSanFrancisco, 1999), 159–75; cf. idem, *The Literary Function of Possessions in Luke-Acts* (SBLDS 39; Missoula, Mont.: Scholars Press, 1977), 60–78.

[13] Daniel Marguerat, 'Luc-Actes: La résurrection à l'œuvre dans l'histoire,' in *Résurrection: L'àpres-mort dans la monde ancient et le Nouveau Testament* (eds. Odette Mainville and Daniel Marguerat; *MdB* 45; Montreal: Médiaspaul; Geneva: Labor et Fides, 2001), 195–214.

sustained, meaningful discussions are sparse, one cannot help but be wary of their pedigree, thoughtfulness, or consistency. Then there is the extensive research in NT Christology, as well as the multitude of works devoted to the NT teaching on the resurrection of Jesus,[14] each including obligatory treatments of Lukan pericopae. Not only do these bodies of work defy neat summarization, but they are of limited value for our study. Our primary interest is not to fit Luke's presentation of the risen Jesus within the stream of early Christian tradition, but to discover how the resurrection of Jesus functions in the Lukan narrative itself as it would have been read within the conceptual framework of Jewish and/or Hellenistic understandings of death and resurrection. It is this focus on Luke's portrayal of the resurrection of Jesus within his first-century world that has been heretofore neglected.

Four factors have contributed to the want of intensive study into Luke's conception of Jesus' resurrection, and which may help to distinguish some of the boundaries for our own investigation.

1.1.1 Dominance of Tradition-Historical Research

Twentieth-century research into the resurrection of Jesus has been concerned in large part with tracing resurrection traditions within early Christianity. Most simply characterized, some scholars have attempted to demonstrate that traditions about Jesus' resurrection may be classified according to their respective positions within a line of developments and accretions to the earliest kerygma, while others have attempted to discern continuity between the NT authors and the earliest, historic Christian traditions.[15] In either case the Lukan material is given short shrift. Tradition-

---

[14] For a concise overview of scholarship, see John M. G. Barclay, 'The Resurrection in Contemporary New Testament Scholarship,' in *Resurrection Reconsidered* (ed. Gavin D'Costa; Oxford: Oneworld, 1996), 13–30.

[15] The idea of an evolutionary development of resurrection traditions that were illustrative or supplemental to the kerygma is often associated with the German form critics: Martin Dibelius, *From Tradition to Gospel* (trans. Bertram Lee Woolf; London: Iver Nicholson and Watson, 1934), 18–22, 178, 199; Rudolf Bultmann, *History of the Synoptic Tradition* (rev. ed.; trans. John Marsh; Oxford: Basil Blackwell, 1963), 284–91. That the Easter traditions are dependent upon (therefore subsidiary to) the kerygma has been challenged by Leonhard Goppelt, 'The Easter Kerygma in the New Testament,' in Leonhard Goppelt, Helmut Thielicke, and Hans-Rudolf Müller-Schwefe, *The Easter Message Today* (London: Thomas Nelson, 1964), 27–58; Leonhard Goppelt, *Theology of the New Testament* (2 vols.; trans. John Alsup; Grand Rapids: Eerdmans, 1981), 1:240–42; John E. Alsup, *The Post-Resurrection Appearance Stories of the Gospel-Tradition* (Calwer theologische Monographien 5; London: SPCK, 1975); Pheme

critical analyses atomistically compare portions of Luke 24, Acts 1, or the missionary speeches in Acts with other NT (or extra-canonical) witnesses, all the while downplaying (wittingly or unwittingly) the distinctive presentation of Jesus' resurrection within Luke's narrative. Luke's theological portrait of the risen Jesus is obscured or blunted on the one hand by endeavours to harmonize it with that of other New Testament writers, or discounted on the other by those who regard Luke's work as late and theologically tendentious.[16] Our own view, influenced by narrative-critical and canonical concerns, is that tradition-criticism ought not to form the heart of a study of Jesus' resurrection in Luke-Acts. One must first duly attend to the theological message of Luke's representation of Jesus' resurrection within his entire narrative project. Only then should one set oneself to the task of comparing Luke's resurrection theology with that of other NT writers.[17]

1.1.2 Disproportionate Attention to the Ascension Accounts

One factor that casts its shadow over the study of the resurrection in Luke-Acts is the tremendous interest scholars have taken in Luke's double

---

Perkins, *Resurrection: New Testament Witness and Contemporary Reflection* (Garden City, N.Y.: Doubleday, 1984), 113–14; cf. 90–91.

[16] The tradition history normally runs thus: Paul, then the Markan resurrection story, followed by an intermediate stage of development represented by Matthew and Luke, with John belonging to an even later stage; cf. Kirsopp Lake, *The Historical Evidence for the Resurrection of Jesus Christ* (New York: G. P. Putnam's Sons, 1907), 206–27; P. Gardner-Smith, *The Narratives of the Resurrection* (London: Methuen, 1926), 140–70; Hans Graß, *Ostergeschehen und Osterberichte* (Göttingen: Vandenhoeck & Ruprecht, 1964), 113–27. The prevalence of this view may be observed at a glance in the tables of contents to works such as Reginald H. Fuller, *The Formation of the Resurrection Narratives* (New York: Macmillan, 1971); and C. F. Evans, *Resurrection and the New Testament* (SBT 12; London: SCM, 1970). This classic paradigm has now been ably demolished by N. T. Wright, *The Resurrection of the Son of God* (Minneapolis: Fortress, 2003).

[17] Thus, while we shall take side-glances at the teaching about the resurrection of Jesus in other NT authors, we shall not pursue an exhaustive comparison of their teaching with Luke-Acts. Our reasons for this include at least three factors, related, e.g., to a comparative study with Paul: (a) Such an undertaking would be gargantuan, and would require us to navigate through manifold questions related to Paul's resurrection theology, to which we could not do proper justice. (b) The comparison would open up questions concerning Lukan authorship, and the relationship of the author to Paul and his NT letters—answers to which are speculative. (c) Accurate comparisons and contrasts between Luke and Paul are more likely to be fruitful only after each has been independently investigated against a wider common background in Second Temple Judaism.

accounting of the ascension (Luke 24:50–53; Acts 1:9–11) and its attendant textual, literary, historical, and theological problems.[18] To be sure, the resurrection receives tangential treatment within this context, since the ascension is in both instances the conclusion to post-resurrection appearances. Yet the baseline for investigation has continued to be the ascension, and the lines of questioning have frequently been governed by inquiry into the literary and historical relationships of the resurrection to the ascension or its theological import (or lack thereof) vis-à-vis the ascension. Five general positions have been set forth:

(1) The resurrection and ascension occurred precisely as Luke recorded them. This is the traditional view, which has virtually no support among current NT scholars.[19]

(2) The resurrection of Jesus took place on Easter morning and his ascension-exaltation on Easter evening. Though not without ancient precedent,[20] this view was championed by J. G. Davies, and has garnered little support.[21]

(3) The resurrection of Jesus was spiritual and coincided with his actual ascension, but evolving traditions increasingly represented these as separate occurrences, complete with the legend of an empty tomb and physical appearances.[22] The accounts in Luke-Acts are representative of an

---

[18] Whereas there is a paltry amount of literature devoted to the resurrection in Luke-Acts, the literature on the ascension is voluminous. A. W. Zwiep (*Ascension of the Messiah*, 200–15) lists 394 entries in his bibliography on the ascension (Luke 24:50–53; Acts 1:1–12) for the years 1900–1996.

[19] According to Peter Toon ('Resurrected and Ascended: The Exalted Jesus,' *BSac* 140 [1983], 204) this view, which was the predominant view in the nineteenth century, was held by Bruce M. Metzger ('The Ascension of Christ,' in *Historical and Literary Studies* [NTTS 8; Grand Rapids: Eerdmans, 1968], 77–87, but see p. 85 which reads very much like view [4] below) and William Barclay (*Crucified and Crowned* [London: SCM, 1961], 171–78; see also A. W. Argyle, 'The Ascension,' *ExpTim* 66 [1954/55], 240–42).

[20] Mark 16:2 (codex *k*); 16:19; *Barn.* 15:8–9; Aristides, *Apol.* 15; *Ep. Apos.* 51; *Gos. Pet.* 13.56.

[21] J. G. Davies, *He Ascended into Heaven: A Study in the History of Doctrine* (London: Lutterworth, 1958); idem, 'The Prefigurement of the Ascension in the Third Gospel,' *JTS* 6 (1955): 229–33. This view was adopted by C. K. Barrett, *Luke the Historian in Recent Study* (FBBS 24; Philadelphia: Fortress, 1970), 55–57.

[22] This view is traceable to David F. Strauss, *The Life of Jesus Critically Examined* (trans. George Eliot; Lives of Jesus Series; Philadelphia: Fortress, 1972), 745–56. For a synopsis of the variations on Strauss's understanding, see Pierre Benoit, 'The Ascension,' in *Jesus and the Gospel* (2 vols.; trans. Benet Weatherhead; New York: Herder and Herder, 1973), 1:222–26. A discussion of the development of Strauss's ascension myth by A. Harnack and E. Meyer may be found in Zwiep, *Ascension of the Messiah*, 4–

advanced stage of corporealizing the resurrection and ascension, as well as placing the events within a temporal (forty days) and spatial (Jerusalem, Mount of Olives) framework in the service of an apologetic against Docetic or Hellenistic interpretations. Gerhard Lohfink's view falls under this category, since he characterizes the ascension accounts as historicizing or concretizing ('historisiert' or 'konkretisiert') an a-historical event.[23] In doing so, claims Lohfink, Luke has radically altered the primitive *Erhöhungskerygma* ('exaltation kerygma') attested to by other NT witnesses. Luke has appropriated elements from the *Entrückungserzählungen* ('rapture stories') familiar in the Greco-Roman world, but especially their Jewish counterparts such as the Elijah rapture story, in order to graphically depict the exaltation.[24] Luke has thus reinterpreted the exaltation kerygma. What had been an invisible, transcendent conception was expressed as a concrete, historical occurrence visible to human witnesses. The inherent unity of resurrection and exaltation was broken, since now the point of exaltation was conceived of as an entirely separate moment from resurrection: an ascension preceded by an intervening period of forty days.[25] Eric Franklin holds a comparable position, assigning to Jesus' ascension-exaltation (over against resurrection) a central place in Luke's theology.[26]

---

6. Exponents of this view include Lake, *Historical Evidence*, 166–239; E. Bickermann, 'Das leere Grab,' *ZNW* 23 (1924): 281–92; G. Bertram, 'Die Himmelfahrt Jesu vom Kreuz aus und der Glaube an seine Auferstehung,' in *Festgabe für Adolf Deissmann zum 60. Geburtstag* (ed. K. L. Schmidt; Tübingen: Mohr-Siebeck, 1927): 187–217; Amos N. Wilder, 'Variant Traditions of the Resurrection in Acts,' *JBL* 62 (1943): 307–18, esp. 309; and, of course, the heir *par excellence* to Strauss, Rudolf Bultmann, who writes (*History of the Synoptic Tradition*, 290): 'Paul knows nothing about the empty tomb, which does not imply that the story was not yet in existence, but most probably that it was a subordinate theme with no significance for the official Kerygma. The same point is suggested by the speeches in Acts. That is finally established by the fact that originally there was no difference between the Resurrection of Jesus and his Ascension; this distinction first arose as a consequence of the Easter legends, which eventually necessitated a special story of an ascension with heaven as an end of the risen Lord's earthly sojourn. But the story of the empty tomb has its place right in the middle of this development, for in it the original idea of exaltation is modified already.'

[23] Gerhard Lohfink, *Die Himmelfahrt Jesu: Untersuchungen zu den Himmelfahrts- und Erhöhungstexten bei Lukas* (SANT 26; Munich: Kösel-Verlag, 1971), 244, 276–83.

[24] Lohfink, *Himmelfahrt Jesu*, 270.

[25] Lohfink, *Himmelfahrt Jesu*, 239–50.

[26] Eric Franklin, *Christ the Lord: A Study in the Purpose and Theology of Luke-Acts* (Philadelphia: Westminster, 1975), 30–45; idem, 'The Ascension and the Eschatology of Luke-Acts,' *SJT* 23 (1970): 191–200; see also Eugene A. LaVerdiere, 'The Ascension of the Risen Lord,' *TBT* 95 (1978): 1553–59. Emmeram Kränkl (*Jesus der Knecht*

(4) The resurrection, ascension, and exaltation of Jesus occurred on Easter morning, followed by a series of appearances from heaven, concluding with Jesus' final leave-taking. This is a view commonly held among Roman Catholics and conservative scholars.[27] According to this view, Luke 24 and Acts 1 are to be interpreted in line with the prevailing NT conception that Jesus' exaltation is intimately associated with his resurrection.[28] The resurrection was not a reanimation of Jesus' physical body and a return to terrestrial life like other 'resurrection' miracles.[29] Rather, at his resurrection Jesus was exalted and translated into a glorious, celestial (even spiritual[30]) existence. This was to be expected, given his promise of para-

---

Gottes: Die heilsgeschichtliche Stellung Jesu in den Reden der Apostelgeschichte [BU 8; Regensburg: Pustet, 1972]) holds a position similar to Franklin's; see the summary and critique in François Bovon, *Luke the Theologian: Thirty-Three Years of Research (1950–1983)* (PTMS 12; trans. Ken McKinney; Allison Park, Pa.: Pickwick, 1987; originally *Luc le théologien. Vingt-cinq ans de recherches (1950–1975)* [Neuchâtel: Delachaux; Paris: Niestlé, 1978]), 131–35.

[27] The representative Roman Catholics include one of the earliest proponents of this view, Pierre Benoit, 'L'Ascension,' *RB* 56 (1949): 161–203 (English trans. in *Jesus and the Gospel*, 1:222–26); and Joseph A. Fitzmyer, 'The Ascension of Christ and Pentecost,' in *To Advance the Gospel: New Testament Studies* (2d ed.; BRS; Grand Rapids: Eerdmans; Livonia, Mich.: Dove Booksellers, 1998), 265–94; idem, 'The Resurrection of Jesus According to the New Testament,' in *To Advance the Gospel*, 378–80. Conservative scholars include F. F. Bruce, *The Acts of the Apostles: Greek Text with Introduction and Commentary* (3d rev. and enl. ed.; Grand Rapids: Eerdmans, 1990), 103; Kevin Giles, 'Ascension," *DJG* 48–50; Murray J. Harris, *Raised Immortal: Resurrection and Immortality in the New Testament* (Grand Rapids: Eerdmans, 1983), 72–94; George Eldon Ladd, *I Believe in the Resurrection of Jesus* (Grand Rapids: Eerdmans, 1975), 127–29; J. F. Maile, 'The Ascension in Luke-Acts,' *TynBul* 37 (1986): 29–59; Grant R. Osborne, *The Resurrection Narratives: A Redactional Study* (Grand Rapids: Baker, 1984), 266–70; A. Michael Ramsey, 'What Was the Ascension?' *SNTS Bulletin* 2 (1951): 43–50, reprinted in *Historicity and Chronology in the New Testament* (TCSPCK 6; eds. D. E. Nineham et al.; London: SPCK, 1965), 135–44; Peter Toon, 'Resurrected and Ascended,' 203–4; idem, *The Ascension of Our Lord* (Nashville: Thomas Nelson, 1984), 121–23; Zwiep, *Ascension of the Messiah*, 145–66.

[28] 1 Thess 1:10; 4:16; 2 Thess 1:7; Phil 3:20; 1 Cor 4:5; 15:47; Rom 8:34; Col 3:1; Eph 1:3, 20; 2:6; 6:9; 1 Tim 4:18; 1 Pet 3:22; Acts 2:33; 5:30–31; 7:55; Heb 1:3, 13; 8:1; 9:12, 24; 10:12–13; 12:2; Rev 1:12–18; 3:21; 6:1–7; 7:17.

[29] Miracles of resurrection include those effected through Elijah and Elisha (1 Kgs 17:17–24; 2 Kgs 4:32–37; 13:21; cp. Sir 48:13–14), Jesus (the widow's son at Nain [Luke 7:11–17]; Jairus's daughter [Mark 5:21–24, 35–43; Matt 9:18–19, 23–26; Luke 8:40–42, 49–56]; Lazarus [John 11:43–44; 12:1–2]), Peter (Tabitha, Acts 9:36–43), and Paul (Eutychus, Acts 20:9–10).

[30] Benoit dissents here, arguing that *all* of the appearances of Jesus (even to Paul on the road to Damascus) were equally physical in nature. Jesus' body was 'transfigured by

dise to the thief on the cross (Luke 23:43).[31] The risen Christ appears to his disciples *from heaven* after having ascended there secretly and invisibly at his resurrection. This might be hinted at in Jesus' words to the two disciples travelling to Emmaus: 'Was it not necessary that the Messiah should suffer these things and then enter into his glory?' (Luke 24:26). Therefore, the 'ascension' of Luke 24:50-53 and Acts 1:9-11, in Fitzmyer's words, 'is nothing more than *the* appearance from glory in which Christ took his final leave from the assembled followers.' It marks the conclusion of the period in which Jesus would be visibly present to his followers 'in their corporate unity.'[32] The clouds and angel-interpreters of Acts 1:9-11 may only be 'apocalyptic stage props' accompanying Jesus' final leave-taking,[33] or they may indicate a visible manifestation, dramatization, or confirmation of the exaltation Jesus had already experienced at his resurrection.[34] In any event, the visible ascension may be viewed either as divine condescension to human sensibilities, or Luke's historicizing and periodizing the 'paschal mystery.'[35]

(5) The death, resurrection, and ascension comprise Jesus' entire movement from suffering to glory. P. A. van Stempvoort set forth this view

---

the Spirit,' yet no less corporeal ('Ascension,' 226-35); see also Fitzmyer, 'Resurrection of Jesus Christ,' 379. Murray Harris, on the other hand, has become notorious among certain evangelicals for his view that Jesus' resurrected state was one of 'invisibility and therefore immateriality' (*Raised Immortal*, 53-57); idem, *From Grave to Glory: Resurrection in the New Testament* (Grand Rapids: Zondervan, 1990). For responses to Harris, see Norman L. Geisler, *The Battle for the Resurrection* (Nashville: Thomas Nelson, 1989); idem, *In Defense of the Resurrection* (Lynchburg, Va.: Quest, 1991); Robert H. Gundry, 'The Essential Physicality of Jesus' Resurrection According to the New Testament,' in *Jesus of Nazareth: Lord and Christ. Essays on the Historical Jesus and New Testament Christology* (eds. Joel B. Green and Max Turner; Grand Rapids: Eerdmans, 1994), 204-19.

[31] Joseph A. Fitzmyer, '"Today You Shall Be with Me in Paradise" (Luke 23:43),' in *Luke the Theologian: Aspects of His Teaching* (New York and Mahwah, N.J.: Paulist, 1989), 203-33; see also Hans-Joachim Eckstein, 'Bodily Resurrection in Luke,' in *Resurrection: Theological and Scientific Assessments* (eds. Ted Peters, Robert John Russell, and Michael Welker; Grand Rapids: Eerdmans, 2002), 120-21. Eckstein, however, deals with Luke 23:43 in terms of Luke's dichotomous anthropology, not any historical revision of the paschal sequence of events.

[32] Fitzmyer, 'Ascension of Christ and Pentecost,' 275.

[33] Fitzmyer, 'Ascension of Christ and Pentecost,' 273.

[34] Benoit, 'Ascension,' 248-52; Harris, *Raised Immortal*, 92; Maile, 'Ascension in Luke-Acts,' 55.

[35] Fitzmyer, 'Ascension of Christ and Pentecost,' 276.

in an important article on the ascension.³⁶ He sought to demonstrate that the words ἀνάλημψις and ἀναλαμβάνομαι were used in Luke's time to mean 'to die, to be taken up in the sense of to pass away, removal out of this world.'³⁷ After providing a number of examples, he concluded that in Luke 9:51 (ἀναλήμψεως) and Acts 1:2 (ἀνελήμφθη) Luke refers to 'the whole process of his passing away and being taken up in the wide sense.'³⁸ Stempvoort's view has been adopted and refined by Mikeal Parsons to apply to a death-resurrection-ascension complex. According to Parsons, Luke does not equate Jesus' exaltation with the ascension. Jesus is exalted through his 'entire journey back to God' (death, resurrection, and ascension).³⁹

The last three views command the largest following. Yet a canvass of the literature on Luke-Acts would reveal that, especially within recent scholarship, there is relatively little clarity on this issue.⁴⁰ Variations of the last view seem to be the most popular. Throughout the literature one finds hyphenated descriptors—death-resurrection-ascension, death-resurrection-exaltation, resurrection-ascension, resurrection-ascension-exaltation—that give the impression of a fuzziness or lack of definition either in this aggregative view, Luke's representation itself, or perhaps both.

1.1.3 Lack of Consensus on Research Methodology

Prior to the mid-1970s the biblical guild was dominated by historical-critical or diachronic research methods. Studies in Luke-Acts were no exception. This was followed by tectonic shifts in biblical research methodology during the last twenty-five years of the twentieth century.⁴¹ During

---

³⁶ P. A. van Stempvoort, 'The Interpretation of the Ascension in Luke and Acts,' *NTS* 5 (1958): 30–42.

³⁷ Stempvoort, 'Ascension,' 32.

³⁸ Stempvoort, 'Ascension,' 33.

³⁹ Mikeal C. Parsons, *The Departure of Jesus in Luke-Acts: The Ascension Narratives in Context* (JSNTSup 21; Sheffield: JSOT Press, 1987), 130–33 (quote is from 133).

⁴⁰ We know of only one full-length study devoted to this issue: John G. Lygre, 'Exaltation: Considered with Reference to the Resurrection and Ascension in Luke-Acts' (Ph.D. dissertation; Princeton Theological Seminary, 1975).

⁴¹ Major transitions in Luke-Acts studies were perceptively observed and fostered by Charles H. Talbert, 'Shifting Sands: The Recent Study of the Gospel of Luke,' *Int* 30 (1976): 381–95. Talbert (in a review of Joseph A. Fitzmyer, *The Gospel According to Luke (X–XXIV)*, *CBQ* 48 [1986]: 336–38) pointed to the year 1974 as the dividing line between an earlier diachronic approach and an emerging synchronic one, and viewed

this period studies in Luke-Acts were enriched by literary analyses, ancient and new. There has been a marked emphasis on reading Luke's narrative within its Hellenistic literary milieu, and an appropriation of newer methods such as narrative, reader-response, and social-scientific criticisms.[42] A proliferation of methods has eclipsed the common historical-critical platform upon which earlier scholars engaged in study after study of the resurrection of Jesus in the NT. While no comprehensive approach to the study of Jesus' resurrection in Luke-Acts has been set forth as of yet, it should be noted that the first fruits of such investigation have been produced by scholars who have a methodological kinship. Scholars like Green, Johnson, O'Toole, Talbert, Marguerat, and even Cadbury view Luke-Acts as a unified literary and theological work in narrative form.[43]

1.1.4 Purpose of Luke-Acts

A lack of agreement regarding the purpose of Luke-Acts presents a major hurdle for any inquiry related to the Lukan narrative,[44] but this issue acutely affects Luke's theology of resurrection. For example, the resurrection of

---

Fitzmyer's commentary on Luke as belonging methodologically to the close of that earlier era of research (1954–1974).

[42] For a discussion of the shifts in Gospel studies, see Stephen D. Moore, *Literary Criticism and the Gospels: The Theoretical Challenge* (New Haven and London: Yale University Press, 1989). For statements on newer methodology, see Robert C. Tannehill, *The Narrative Unity of Luke-Acts: A Literary Interpretation* (2 vols.; FF; Philadelphia: Fortress, 1986), 1:1–12; 2:1–8; William S. Kurz, *Reading Luke-Acts: Dynamics of Biblical Narrative* (Louisville, Ky.: Westminster/John Knox, 1993), 1–6 and passim; Joel B. Green, *The Gospel of Luke* (NICNT; Grand Rapids: Eerdmans, 1997), 1–21; Gunter Wasserberg, *Aus Israels Mitte—Heil für die Welt* (BZNW 92; Berlin and New York: Walter de Gruyter, 1998), 31–67; Jerome H. Neyrey, ed., *The Social World of Luke-Acts: Models for Interpretation* (Peabody, Mass.: Hendrickson, 1991); Jack Dean Kingsbury, ed., *Gospel Interpretation: Narrative-Critical and Social Scientific Interpretation* (Harrisburg, Pa.: Trinity Press International, 1997), 124–77.

[43] Green, Johnson, Talbert, and Marguerat are clearly influenced by narratology, while O'Toole employs composition criticism. As for Cadbury, observe how he reserves discussion of authorship, date, and provenance for the very end of *The Making of Luke-Acts*, where he sounds strikingly like a New Critic in his approach (353).

[44] On the purpose of Luke-Acts, see Gerhard Schneider, 'Der Zweck des lukanischen Doppelwerks,' *BZ* 21 (1977): 45–66; Robert F. O'Toole, 'Why Did Luke Write Acts (Lk-Acts)?' *BTB* 7 (1977): 66–76; Robert Maddox, *The Purpose of Luke-Acts* (Göttingen: Vandenhoeck & Ruprecht, 1982); Mark Allan Powell, 'Luke's Second Volume: Three Basic Issues in Contemporary Studies of Acts,' *Trinity Seminary Review* 13 (1991): 74–78; I. Howard Marshall, *The Acts of the Apostles* (NTG; Sheffield: Sheffield Academic Press, 1992; repr. 1997), 31–46.

Jesus means one thing if the purpose of Luke's narrative is to present an apology to the Roman authorities on behalf of the burgeoning Christian movement—namely, it means that Jesus' resurrection is a specimen of the hope for resurrection shared by the Jews (particularly Pharisaic Jews), who are a protected religious group within the Roman empire. Hence, Jesus' resurrection would do little more than provide Christians with a theological basis for political 'cover.'[45] It means quite another thing if Luke-Acts is aimed at persuading Jews to embrace the Way as the true embodiment of ancient Judaism, or alternatively, at repudiating ethnic Jews on account of their rejection of Jesus and offering the Christian message of salvation to Gentiles instead—namely, it means that the resurrection of Jesus is the pivotal moment in the history of God's saving action toward humankind.

This leads us into one of the thorniest problems in Lukan research: What is Luke's view of the people of Israel vis-à-vis the Christ-event and the Christian movement? This may in itself provide a clue to why an overall approach to studying the resurrection of Jesus in Luke-Acts has not been forthcoming. The resurrection of Jesus is inextricably bound up with the question of Israel, and the latter has been one of the most contested issues in Lukan scholarship. However, our study appears at a time when there seems to be an emerging consensus regarding the purpose of Luke-Acts and, to a lesser degree, the Israel question. This is evident in two recent compendia. First, in the introductory essay to *Witness to the Gospel*, I. Howard Marshall represents more than a score of scholars who share the following understanding of the theology of Acts: 'We believe that Acts is primarily about God's action in offering salvation through Jesus Christ to both Jews and Gentiles and thereby creating a new people.'[46] Second, David Moessner and David Tiede introduce the volume *Jesus and the Heritage of Israel* as the outgrowth of 'an amazing sea change of opinion' regarding the tenor of Luke's narrative project: 'A new consensus is emerging that Luke as the interpreter of Israel presents a carefully crafted argument *in two parts* to lay claim to a culmination of Israel's traditions in Jesus of Nazareth, Messiah of Israel.'[47] There is no time like the present to explore Luke's portrayal of Jesus' resurrection in light of the hope of Israel.

---

[45] This is the view of Ernst Haenchen, 'Judentum und Christentum in der Apostelgeschichte,' *ZNW* 54 (1963): 157–58, 182, 187 n. 44.

[46] I. Howard Marshall, 'How Does One Write on the Theology of Acts?' in *Witness to the Gospel: The Theology of Acts* (eds. I. Howard Marshall and David Peterson; Grand Rapids: Eerdmans, 1998), 16.

[47] David P. Moessner and David L. Tiede, 'Introduction: *Two* Books but *One* Story?' in *Jesus and the Heritage of Israel: Luke's Narrative Claim upon Israel's Legacy* (LII 1; ed. David P. Moessner; Harrisburg, Pa.: Trinity Press International, 1999), 2–3.

1.2 The Resurrection of Jesus and the Hope of Israel: A Current Approach

Our contention is that the resurrection of Jesus in Luke-Acts constitutes the pivotal act of God in the salvation of Israel and the whole world, and it is consequently the focus of the Lukan message of salvation. *Theologically*, the resurrection of Jesus is part of God's purpose for Israel and the world. *Christologically*, the resurrection of Jesus establishes him as the definitive leader of the people of God and the agent of God's covenant blessings of salvation. *Ecclesiologically*, Jesus' resurrection is the inaugural action of God in the promised restoration of Israel. The resurrection of Jesus, by initiating the restoration of Israel, effects both a division within Israel and an expansion of the people of God among the nations. Jesus, not only as Israel's Messiah, but as universal Lord, grants repentance and forgiveness of sins to people from all nations in view of the day of judgment when he will act as the appointed judge; and these facts are undergirded by divine proof: Jesus' resurrection from the dead. *Eschatologically*, the resurrection of Jesus adumbrates and guarantees the culmination of God's salvation of his people and the full realization of the kingdom of God among humankind. The resurrection of Jesus, as the first installment of the eschatological resurrection of the dead, is comprised not only of his being raised up out of the tomb, but being raised up to the right hand of God. These four theological categories, which outline the contours of Lukan soteriology, will be explored in Chapter 2.

Since we possess no comprehensive exemplar of how to approach the subject of Jesus' resurrection in Luke-Acts, we shall have to fashion our own. In the following introduction we will outline the scope of our work, the principal issues involved, and some points about methodology.

1.2.1 Scope of the Study

If we are to conduct a study of Luke's narrative presentation of Jesus' resurrection, then we will do well to consider all of the relevant data impinging on the subject. The study ought to take into account the story and commentary about Jesus' resurrection found in Luke 24, Acts 1, and in the speeches in Acts. These texts must be viewed, not in isolation, but in relationship to the flow of Luke's larger narrative. However, it is clear that Luke-Acts was not written in a vacuum, and the resurrection of Jesus, though singular in importance, is not foisted upon readers as a radically novel development within God's plan. The resurrection of Jesus takes place in accordance with the ancient purposes of God expressed in the Scriptures of Israel. Therefore, a preliminary step toward understanding the Lukan conception of Jesus' resurrection entails a discussion of the background against which the idea of 'the resurrection of the dead' might be maximally understood. This will be undertaken in three phases. First, in Chapter 3 we shall deal at length with the conception of resurrection in Second Temple Judaism. Second, in Chapter 4 we shall outline Greco-Roman notions about individuals returning from the dead in order to provide a wider Hellenistic backdrop for Luke's material on resurrection. Third, in Chapter 5 we will take a wide-angle view of Luke's conception of resurrection generally, first by looking at the 'resurrection' miracles in his work, and then by studying the relevant passages in which the resurrection of the dead is a topic of controversy or where specific reactions to the idea of resurrection are reported. Our discussion of the resurrection in Luke-Acts is unique in its provision of this broader conceptual framework.

This spadework will be followed by Chapters 6–9, in which we shall explore how Jesus' resurrection is integral to Luke's salvation message. In Chapter 6 we will explore how Luke 24, as the close of Luke's first volume, features the resurrection of Jesus as one of the climactic events in Luke's narrative. Chapters 7 and 8 will focus upon the 'resurrection speeches' of Peter and Paul in Acts 2–3 and 13. These speeches represent the authorized interpretation of Jesus' resurrection as the key fulfilment of God's salvific promises to Israel. Chapter 9 will investigate how the witness to Jesus' resurrection is related to the hope of Israel, which Paul proclaims in the final episode of Acts. We will discover that there is an intimate association between belief in the hope of Israel, the final resurrection of the dead, and Jesus' resurrection.

1.2.2 Principal Issues

There are three fundamental aspects of our study that need to be highlighted.

1.2.2.1 THE RESURRECTION OF JESUS AND THE THEME OF SALVATION

We concur with a growing number of scholars who view the overarching theme of Luke's two-volume work to be God's salvific action for and through Israel to the world. In Chapter 2 we will sketch our own understanding of Luke's soteriology, and we will show how the resurrection of Jesus is the theological focus of Luke's message of salvation. For Luke, salvation takes place on a theological grid. God is the source of every act of deliverance, liberation, restoration, or forgiveness. But God's saving activity is always executed through a designated agent and on behalf of persons with whom God wants to establish a covenant relationship. These soteriological factors form two axes: one christological, the other ecclesiological. Salvation is brought about through the Messiah (christological axis) for those who will become members of the people of God (ecclesiological axis). At the intersection of these two axes is the resurrection of Jesus from the dead, by which God both adumbrates and inaugurates the promised restoration of Israel, and hence the (re-)establishment of a covenant people who will extend the message about his salvation and kingdom to all the inhabitants of the world. Jesus' resurrection is pivotal to the outworking of God's plan of salvation. It is a critical event within the eschatological fulfilment of Israel's restoration, as it decisively sets in motion both a division within Israel and an extension of the people of God among the Gentiles.

1.2.2.2 NATURE AND SIGNIFICANCE OF RESURRECTION

Absolutely fundamental to any discussion is the definition of terms. 'Resurrection' needs to be defined not only in terms of its nature (spiritual, corporeal?) but its theological significance. In the course of our investigation we will discover that resurrection from the dead was conceived of by many who claimed to be partakers of Israel's heritage—Luke included—as the concrete act by which God raises up, restores, and exalts his covenant people. The resurrection is indissolubly linked to the establishment of God's kingdom and to the people of God's participation in his reign. In Chapter 3 we will trace a theological pattern in Jewish understanding in which resurrection is accompanied by three elements: new creation, covenant renewal, and exaltation or enthronement. There is virtually no support for the notion of resurrection as merely a spiritual reality or a theological metaphor. The retrieval of Israel's existence as a living, breathing, liberated people of God is promised as God's concrete, eschatological act of saving his righteous ones from death by literally raising them up out of their tombs, enlivening them, and exalting them as sons and daughters of the living God. Since Jesus is the first to be raised up in the eschatological resurrection of the dead, his resurrection stands as a guarantee of the complete fulfilment of God's saving action for his people at the final resurrection of the dead.

1.2.2.3 RELATIONSHIP OF RESURRECTION, ASCENSION, AND EXALTATION

Extrapolating from the conception of resurrection within Second Temple Judaism, one may infer that Jesus' resurrection would be closely associated with exaltation, enthronement, and participation in the new creation under God's universal reign. This obtains for statements about resurrection in biblical and intertestamental Jewish literature as well as in extra-Lukan pronouncements regarding Jesus' resurrection in the NT. Yet Luke's distinctive narration of a separate, observable ascension requires explanation. Did Luke re-interpret the exaltation kerygma and transfer the theological centre of gravity from resurrection to ascension? Or is the visible ascension merely a dramatization of the invisible ascension-exaltation coincident with his resurrection on Easter morning? Or should we be satisfied with an ill-defined reference to Jesus' death-resurrection-ascension-exaltation? Our approach to this issue will proceed from two criteria stemming from narrative and audience-oriented criticisms. An explanation of the Lukan view of the relationship between Jesus' resurrection, ascension, and exaltation must take into consideration both the flow of Luke's narrative and the explanations of the Christ-event by Jesus himself in the Gospel and by the apostles in the speeches in Acts. First, an interpretation must not do violence to the flow of Luke's narrative. Second, any theological inferences drawn from Luke's sequencing of events must be augmented or corrected by the statements made by Jesus himself in the Gospel or by his witnesses in Acts. These statements serve as authorized commentary on the narrated events.

1.2.3 Methodology: An Authorial Audience to the Resurrection

Prior to our comments on method, we must declare two assumptions that underlie our study. First, we assume that the NT books of Luke and Acts form a unity (Luke-Acts). This unity is authorial, literary, and theological. Although Mikeal Parsons and Richard Pervo have called into question the unity of Luke and Acts on the latter two counts,[48] their challenge has been met by an even more forceful defence of the unity of Luke's two-volume work.[49] Second, we assume that Luke-Acts belongs within the broad generic category of ancient historiography.[50]

Our study will be informed by insights from ancient literary theory and practice as well as modern narrative theory. Specific methodological discussions about narrative closure and the interpretation of speeches need not detain us here, but may await treatment in chapters 6 and 7. However, some general comments about our approach to Luke's narrative are in order.

At this point we need to address the preliminary question of how we shall approach an ancient text such as Luke-Acts. The *actual audience* of Luke-Acts consists of a countless number of readers who span hundreds of years, languages, and cultures. Individual readers are also distinguished

---

[48] Mikeal C. Parsons and Richard I. Pervo, *Rethinking the Unity of Luke and Acts* (Minneapolis: Fortress, 1993).

[49] Cf. I. Howard Marshall, '"Israel" and the Story of Salvation: One Theme in Two Parts,' in *Jesus and the Heritage of Israel: Luke's Narrative Claim upon Israel's Legacy* (LII 1; ed. David P. Moessner; Harrisburg, Pa.: Trinity Press International, 1999), 340–57; as well as the collection of essays in Joseph Verheyden, ed., *The Unity of Luke-Acts* (BETL 142; Leuven: Leuven University Press, 1999).

[50] The genre question is exceedingly large and cannot be pursued here. For an entrée into the issue, see Joel B. Green, 'Acts of the Apostles," *DLNT* 7–8; Joel B. Green and Michael C. McKeever, *Luke-Acts and New Testament Historiography* (IBRB 8; Grand Rapids: Baker, 1994).

from one another by variations in class, race, sex, age, personality, geographical location, and life experience. No author, Luke included, can tailor his or her writing to communicate effectively with every conceivable reader in such an expansive audience. Therefore, authors usually begin writing with a set of conscious or unconscious assumptions about their prospective readers' beliefs, knowledge, and familiarity with conventions. These assumptions are fundamentally bound up with an author's choice of genre. C. S. Lewis, for example, has a different audience in mind for his children's fantasy series *The Chronicles of Narnia* than for his works of Christian apologetic such as *Mere Christianity*. So authors generally direct their writing toward a projected or hypothetical audience, which Peter Rabinowitz has termed the *authorial audience*.[51] Readers will have an adequate understanding or will satisfactorily experience a work's intended rhetorical effect only to the extent that they are able to bridge the gap that exists between a writing's actual and authorial audience. Flesh-and-blood readers, to be sure, have the option of approaching texts much like Humpty-Dumpty did in *Through the Looking-Glass*, believing that words mean anything one wants them to mean. But most readers, whether they are reading Shakespeare or Star Trek novels, do not attempt to produce idiosyncratic readings, but rather readings they can share with others and that may be identified as fair representations of the works they have read.[52] A modern reader of Shakespeare, for example, who trips over archaisms, historical references, and social conventions that are unfamiliar to her, and simply interprets them according to her fancy, cannot, strictly speaking, be said to be 'reading Shakespeare.' Stated differently, she is not functioning as an authentic Shakespeare reader, because she is not even trying to read the bard's text in a publicly accessible fashion. Subjectivity and misunderstanding are bound to enter into any reading, but the task of responsible and faithful reading begins with a respect for the work of the author, and is evidenced in a serious attempt to identify as closely as possible with the authorial audience of the text. This is what may be called *authorial reading*.

---

[51] Peter J. Rabinowitz, *Before Reading: Narrative Conventions and the Politics of Interpretation* (Ithaca, N.Y. and London: Cornell University Press, 1987) 15–46; idem, 'Reader-Response Theory and Criticism,' in *The Johns Hopkins Guide to Literary Theory and Criticism* (eds. Michael Groden and Martin Kreiswirth; Baltimore and London: Johns Hopkins University Press, 1994) 606–9; Peter J. Rabinowitz and Michael W. Smith, *Authorizing Readers: Resistance and Respect in the Teaching of Literature* (New York and London: Teachers College Press, 1998), esp. the first chapter by Rabinowitz, 'Where We Are When We Read,' 1–28.

[52] Even the father of deconstruction, Derrida, has been caught in the self-contradiction of chiding one of his critics, John Searle, for misconstruing his writing; see John M. Ellis, *Against Deconstruction* (Princeton: Princeton University Press, 1989) 13–14.

What is meant by the authorial audience may be clarified by contrasting it with other literary concepts. The authorial audience, while related to authorial intention, is not identical to it. This is because the authorial audience of a text does not exist solely in the mind of the author, but is a matter of social convention, and hence a guiding factor in both the composition and subsequent reading of a work. Rabinowitz explains the importance of distinguishing between the author's intention as a matter of individual psychology and the authorial audience as a social convention:

> In other words, my perspective allows us to treat the reader's attempt to read as the author intended, not as a search for the author's private psyche, but rather as the joining of a particular social/interpretive community; that is, the acceptance of the author's invitation to read in a particular socially constituted way that is shared by the author and his or her expected readers.[53]

By 'authorial audience' we refer to 'publicly available social practice rather than to private mental processes.'[54] The authorial audience is also different from the text-immanent 'implied reader' so often spoken of by narrative critics. First, the authorial audience is not reducible to a cognitive component, since it embraces ethical and aesthetic dimensions (and for scriptural texts, spiritual and theological dimensions, too). Second, it is not a purely textual feature.[55] The authorial audience is *presumed by* the text, not inscribed in it. The authorial audience, finally, is not the same as Stanley Fish's interpretive communities, which are the basis for stable readings among an infinite number of possible interpretations for any given text.[56] The authorial audience of a specific text is accessible, however imperfectly, to readers of diverse backgrounds and cultures, so that they are able to encounter new information and differing perspectives from their own within texts. Under Fish's solipsistic theory, the indeterminacy of texts would render it impossible for readers to be challenged by or offer critiques of the works they read, since their readings could only be mirror images of their own community's ideology. When an actual reader attempts to identify with the authorial audience of a text, she does not have to personally adopt the attitudes, commitments, and prejudices of the piece's intended readership (e.g., the authorial audience of a racist pamphlet); but she cannot reject the ideology of a text if it is impossible to discover it in the first place. Authorial reading is therefore privileged in the pursuit of a faithful interpretation, not evaluation, of a text.

---

[53] Rabinowitz, *Before Reading*, 22.
[54] Rabinowitz, 'Where We Are When We Read,' 8.
[55] Rabinowitz, 'Where We Are When We Read,' 7, 9.
[56] Stanley Fish, *Is There a Text in This Class? The Authority of Interpretive Communities* (Cambridge, Mass.: Harvard University Press, 1980).

How, then, does one go about closing the gap between the actual and authorial audience? The task is difficult enough when reading modern fiction, and can be nearly impossible with respect to many ancient texts (the Nag Hammadi scrolls come to mind). According to Rabinowitz, joining the authorial audience of a text involves three interpretive moves.[57] First, reading texts demands generic expertise. For example, an audience will apprehend Jesus' teaching only if they understand how parables function in the first place. Second, understanding requires not only a formal understanding of genre, but of how a particular specimen functions within a larger cultural matrix. One is reminded of the form critics' attempt to situate Gospel material into appropriate *Sitze im Leben*. We may understand how parables work, but be unclear about the point of the particular parable that contrasts the prayers of a Pharisee and a tax collector. Third, a text requires that we understand the values that it anticipates in its audience. Even if we do understand who Pharisees and tax collectors are (e.g., within the social context of first-century Palestine), we cannot understand the aforementioned parable without knowing what stance the text presumes its audience will or should take toward them. A modern example would be an immigrant's inability to 'get' a joke deprecating lawyers, because she is unaware of the common sentiment toward persons who practice law in the United States. Thus, a reader can identify with the authorial audience of a text by recognizing the sort of literary competencies and social conventions presupposed for its adequate decoding.

Joining the authorial audience of an ancient text is complicated by its having been written in a language, time-period, and cultural milieu that is foreign to modern readers. Matching an authorial audience to Luke-Acts is a lot like searching for the exact puzzle piece that will interlock with another piece. However, the Lukan text provides a number of clues regarding the shape of its authorial audience. Luke-Acts is addressed to a specific reader, Theophilus (Luke 1:3; Acts 2:1), who has already received instruction in the truth that is being rehearsed and buttressed in Luke's narrative (Luke 1:4). Luke's narrative, therefore, presupposes a familiarity with the story of Jesus and the early Christian movement. The existence of a preface at the beginning of Luke and Acts, as well as the appearance of historical synchronisms (Luke 2:1–2; 3:1–2; Acts 11:28; 18:2), presume an audience's facility with Greco-Roman literary conventions. Essential to the authorial audience's 'extratextual repertoire' is knowledge of the Septua-

---

[57] Rabinowitz, 'Where We Are When We Read,' 13–14. The following examples from biblical studies are my own.

gint.[58] These and other textual and extratextual factors have been used as a 'window' into Luke's 'original' audience or community, which is subject to the pitfalls of mirror reading.[59] While we are sceptical about any quest for the historical 'Lukan community,' our focus on the resurrection of Jesus in Luke-Acts compels us to search for common denominators characterizing the authorial audience of Luke-Acts that transcend variables such as social location.[60] In Chapter 5 we attempt to show that Luke's theology of resurrection may be maximally understood only by an audience who has an acquaintance with the Jewish hope of resurrection. Typically, Gentiles within Luke's narrative who have had little or no exposure to Jewish faith find the concept of resurrection incomprehensible, if not open to ridicule. Moreover, the resurrection from the dead is specifically identified as Israel's hope, and discussion about the resurrection is related in terms of intra-Jewish debate that incorporates arguments grounded in the Scriptures of Israel. At the same time there are assumptions about Jewish eschatology that are not made explicit in Luke's narrative. For this reason, the nature and significance of resurrection generally and of Jesus' resurrection in particular are likely to be illuminated by aspects related to our subject that are common within Judaic thought. This likelihood is increased if we can trace a consistent and widespread theological pattern in Jewish thinking about resurrection that seems to be taken for granted in Luke's two-volume work.

---

[58] John Darr, *Herod the Fox: Audience Criticism and Lukan Characterization* (JSNTSup 163; Sheffield: Sheffield Academic Press, 1998), 61–63.

[59] Luke Timothy Johnson, 'On Finding the Lukan Community: A Cautious Cautionary Essay,' *SBL Seminar Papers, 1979* (2 vols.; SBLSP 16; Missoula, Mont.: Scholars Press, 1979), 1:87–100. We are sympathetic to the view that the Gospels were written for a general Christian audience and not specific communities; see Richard Bauckham, ed., *The Gospels for All Christians: Rethinking the Gospel Audiences* (Grand Rapids and Cambridge, UK: Eerdmans, 1998), esp. Stephen C. Barton, 'Can We Identify the Gospel Audiences?' 186–89.

[60] For an experimental study of two readers who occupy different social locations, see Robert C. Tannehill, '"Cornelius" and "Tabitha" Encounter Luke's Jesus,' in *Gospel Interpretation: Narrative-Critical and Social-Scientific Approaches* (ed. Jack Dean Kingsbury; Harrisburg, Pa.: Trinity Press International, 1997), 132–41. Tannehill contrasts his work with John Darr's (see n. 58 above), who is concerned only with a composite description of the 'implied reader.' We prefer Darr's focus insofar as it intersects with ours, but find both Tannehill's and Darr's privileging of the sequential, temporal, first-time reading of Luke-Acts to be unsuitable for our analysis. We are concerned with the literary competencies and familiarity with conventions that are presumed of the authorial audience *before* reading, and may be refined *after* reading. We do not presume to offer a virginal reading of Luke-Acts, but instead build our study upon what Rabinowitz calls 'reading against memory,' i.e., re-readings of the text ('"A Thousand Times and Never Like": Re-Reading for Class,' in *Authorizing Readers*, 88–102).

In sum, our study depends upon a close reading of the Lukan data on both the general resurrection of the dead and the resurrection of Jesus. The Lukan conception of Jesus' resurrection will be explored by looking at these data within the context of God's plan of salvation in Luke-Acts, as well as within a wider ancient context. What we mean by the 'Lukan' conception of Jesus' resurrection is not identical to the author's intention, but the authorial audience's publicly accessible knowledge about the nature and significance of resurrection that is both assumed and adjusted within the Lukan presentation of Jesus' resurrection.

Chapter 2

Salvation and Resurrection: Theme and Focus in Luke-Acts

Luke-Acts is above all a narrative about salvation. From the opening infancy scenes to the final portrait of Paul preaching at Rome, Luke's is a story about God's covenant promises to Israel's ancestors—first of all to Abraham, and then more specifically to David—concerning the salvation of the people of God and the extension of that salvation to all nations. Integral to the theme of salvation in Luke-Acts is the promise concerning a Messiah who will be Israel's saviour and the designated leader over all in God's kingdom. The purpose of this chapter is to explore God's salvation as the theme of Luke-Acts, and then to look at how Jesus' resurrection emerges as the focus of Luke's salvation message.

2.1 Salvation in Luke-Acts

2.1.1 Salvation as the Theme of Luke-Acts

A lengthy debate has raged among interpreters concerning Luke's view of salvation history. The complicated array of issues involved in that discussion need not detain us here.[1] The important point is that salvation—however it has been defined or related to interpretations, e.g., of Lukan history or eschatology—has long been regarded as a significant component of Lukan theology. The view taken here may be counted within an emerging consensus of scholarship that perceives Luke-Acts as a narrative primarily occupied with the salvific action of God in Jesus Christ. In the words of W. C. van Unnik, salvation is 'the leading idea' in Luke-Acts.[2]

Two lines of evidence support the thematic primacy of salvation in Luke-Acts.[3] First is the high incidence of soteriological vocabulary. The

---

[1] For a summary, see Bovon, *Luke the Theologian*, 1–77.

[2] W. C. van Unnik, 'The "Book of Acts" the Confirmation of the Gospel,' in *Sparsa Collecta: The Collected Essays of W. C. van Unnik* (part 1: *Evangelia, Paulina, Acta*; NovTSup 29; Leiden: Brill, 1973), 363.

[3] Studies of Lukan soteriology include: François Bovon, 'Le salut dans les écrits de Luc,' *RTP* 23 (1973): 296–307; M. Dömer, *Das Heil Gottes: Studien zur Theologie des*

prevalence and distribution of σῴζω and its derivatives in Luke-Acts are well known. These terms are employed more often in Luke-Acts than in any of the other Gospels.[4] But Luke's lexicon of salvation extends beyond one word group. Additional phraseology reveals vital elements of salvation. Luke-Acts refers to salvation in terms of the redemption (λύτρωσις/ λυτρόω) of God's people (Luke 1:68; cf. 21:28), Jerusalem (2:38), or Israel (24:21). It is viewed as divine visitation (ἐπισκέπτομαι, Luke 1:68, 78; 7:16; Acts 15:14; ἐπισκοπή, Luke 19:44). Peace is another important component of salvation (Luke 1:79; 2:14; 19:38, 42; Acts 10:36), and Simeon's expectation of 'the consolation of Israel' (παράκλησιν τοῦ Ἰσραήλ, Luke 2:25) is

---

lukanischen Doppelwerkes (BBB 51; Köln and Bonn: Peter Hanstein, 1978); Augustin George, 'Le vocabulaire de salut,' in *Études sur l'œuvre de Luc* (SB; Paris: Gabalda, 1978), 307–20; Richard Glöckner, *Die Verkündigung des Heils beim Evangelisten Lukas* (WSTR 9; Mainz: Matthias-Grünewald, 1975); Neal Flanagan, 'The What and How of Salvation in Luke-Acts,' in *Sin, Salvation, and the Spirit* (ed. Daniel Durken; Collegeville, Minn.: Liturgical, 1979), 203–13; Kevin Giles, 'Salvation in Lukan Theology (1)' and 'Salvation in Lukan Theology (2),' *RTR* 42 (1983): 10–16, 45–49; Joel B. Green, 'The Message of Salvation in Luke-Acts,' *Ex Auditu* 5 (1989): 21–34; G. Mangatt, 'The Gospel of Salvation,' *BiBh* 2 (1976): 60–80; I. Howard Marshall, *Luke: Historian and Theologian* (New Testament Profiles; 3d ed.; Downers Grove, Ill.: IVP, 1988); Ralph P. Martin, 'Salvation and Discipleship in Luke's Gospel,' *Int* 30 (1976): 366–80; O'Toole, *Unity of Luke's Theology*, passim; Mark Allan Powell, 'Salvation in Luke-Acts,' *WW* 12 (1992): 5–10; Walter Radl, *Das Lukas-Evangelium* (EdF 261; Darmstadt: Wissenschaftliche, 1988), 105–11; B. H. Throckmorton, 'Σῴζειν, σωτηρία in Luke-Acts,' *SE* 6 (1973): 515–26; W. C. van Unnik, 'L'Usage de ΣΩΖΕΙΝ "sauver" et des dérivés dans les Évangiles synoptiques,' in *Sparsa Collecta: The Collected Essays of W. C. van Unnik* (part 1: *Evangelia, Paulina, Acta*; NovTSup 29; Leiden: Brill, 1973), 16–34. Cf. chs. 2–8 in Marshall and Peterson, *Witness to the Gospel*; Robert C. Tannehill, 'The Story of Israel within the Lukan Narrative,' in *Jesus and the Heritage of Israel*, 325–39; and I. Howard Marshall, '"Israel" and the Story of Salvation: One Theme in Two Parts,' in *Jesus and the Heritage of Israel*, 340–57.

[4] σῴζω (28x—17x Luke; 13x Acts; cp. 15x Matthew; 15x Mark; 6x John); διασῴζω (6x—Luke 7:3; Acts 23:24; 27:43, 44; 28:1, 4; only 2x elsewhere in the NT: Mark 14:36; 1 Pet 3:20); σωτήρ (4x—Luke 1:47; 2:11; Acts 5:31; 13:23; in the other Gospels only 1x in John 4:42); σωτήριον (3x—Luke 2:30; 3:6; Acts 28:28; never in the other Gospels); σωτηρία (10x—Luke 1:69, 71, 77; 19:9; Acts 4:12; 7:25; 13:26, 47; 16:17; 27:34; in the other Gospels only 1x in John 4:22). For lexical studies, see *EDNT* 2:319–21, 325–29; *TDNT* 7:965–1024; *NIDNTT* 3:205–23. A helpful tabulation appears in George, 'Vocabulaire,' 307. Powell charts the usage of σῴζω, σωτηρία, and σωτήριον in Luke-Act in two tables ('Salvation in Luke-Acts,' 6–7). For a comparison of the usage of σῴζω vocabulary among the Synoptics, see van Unnik ('L'Usage de ΣΩΖΕΙΝ'), who concludes from the frequent and striking salvation terminology (32): 'La σωτηρία se trouve donc au centre de l'évangile de Luc, elle constitue l'idée dominante de sa prédication. Les Actes, eux aussi, restent fidèles à cette ligne de pensée.'

related to this idea.⁵ All of these descriptions of salvation have deep roots in the faith of the Hebrew people.⁶ Luke also envisions salvation as 'the hope of Israel' (Acts 28:20). Especially in the Book of Acts, this 'hope' is closely associated with the resurrection of dead (23:6; 24:15; 26:6–7), and its fulfilment is inaugurated in the resurrection of Jesus (26:8–9, 23; cf. Luke 24:21; Acts 2:26).

Second, the theme of salvation is featured at pivotal points in the narrative. (1) In the very beginning of the Gospel the twin narrative cycles relating the births of John the Baptist and Jesus (Luke 1:5–2:52) inaugurate the theme of salvation.

(a) The language, literary structure, and cast of characters reverberate with the ancient salvific action of God among the people of Israel. The language itself is evocative of the Septuagint, and there are numerous echoes from the Hebrew Scriptures. The appropriation of literary forms, like the annunciation type-scene (or commissioning story) and hymnic response, as well as the descriptions of characters, are reminiscent of a collage of Old Testament stories about patriarchs, prophets, and deliverers through whom Yahweh worked mightily. Abraham and Sarah (Gen 15:1–18:15), Hannah (1 Sam 1:1–2:11), Elijah (Mal 3:1; 4:5–6), and David (2 Sam 7:4–17) are given particular volume.⁷

(b) Specific expressions regarding the fulfilment of divine promises of salvation appear repeatedly throughout Luke 1–2. Mary's joyful response 'to God my Saviour' (Luke 1:47) celebrates the gracious⁸ and merciful action of God toward those who have a claim to Abrahamic promises

---

⁵ Cp. Luke 2:29 with Acts 9:31.

⁶ Redemption is especially related to the memory of Israel's exodus (Exod 6:6; 15:13; Deut 7:8; 9:26; 13:15; 15:15; 24:18; 2 Sam 7:23; 1 Chr 17:21; Neh 1:10; Ps 77:16; Isa 43:1; 51:10; Mic 6:4). Divine visitation embraces the bestowal of blessing or deliverance for God's people (Ruth 1:6; 1 Sam 2:21; Pss 65:10; 106:4; Jer 27:22; 29:10) and judgment on those who oppose them (Jer 15:15; Wis 14:11; Sir 16:18; 4 Mac 10:21; 2 Esdr 9:2). Peace (exemplified in life under vine and fig tree, 1 Kgs 4:25; 2 Kgs 18:31; Isa 36:16; Mic 4:4; Zech 3:10) is ubiquitous in the Hebrew Scriptures, but its prominence in Isaiah will suffice as documentation (52:7; 53:5; 54:10, 13; 57:2, 19; 59:8; 60:17; 66:12). Consolation, too, derives from Isaianic prophecies concerning Israel's return from exile (Isa 40:1, 2, 11; 41:27; 49:10, 13; 51:3; 12, 18, 19; 57:18; 61:2; 66:11–13; see also Ps 125:1 LXX).

⁷ For more on the literary structure and scriptural echoes in Luke 1–2, see Green, *Gospel of Luke*, 47–58; Tannehill, *Narrative Unity*, 1:35–41. Tannehill (*Luke*, 40) refers to the 'primacy effect' in narrative, where initial events provide thematic orientation for the remainder of the story.

⁸ The language of grace had already appeared in Gabriel's annunciation: 'Greetings, favoured one (κεχαριτωμένη).... Do not be afraid, Mary, for you have found favour (χάριν) with God' (Luke 1:28, 30).

(1:55). Zechariah prophetically declares that God 'has raised up a horn of salvation in the house of his servant David' (1:69); that he has provided 'salvation from our enemies and from the hand of all who hate us' (1:71). The preparatory role of John the Baptist is oriented toward the aim of God 'to give knowledge of salvation to his people by the forgiveness of their sins' (1:77). The angels announce to the shepherds 'that today in the city of David there has been born to you a Saviour who is Christ the Lord' (2:11). Simeon, recognizing in the Christ-child the fulfilment of the promise given to him that he would see the Messiah before he died, exclaims, 'my eyes have seen your salvation' (2:30). These are only a few of the notes heard in this overture to Luke's 'symphony of salvation.'[9]

There are four more pivotal points where the salvific thrust of Luke's narrative comes to the fore:

(2) Jesus' programmatic appearance in Nazareth previews his Spirit-filled ministry as the bringing of good news to the poor and release for captives (Luke 4:16–30). The element of 'release' (ἄφεσις) is underlined through the splicing of a phrase from Isa 58:6 into Jesus' reading of Isa 61:1–2, and sounds one of the prominent notes in Lukan soteriology: the forgiveness of sins.[10]

(3) The thread of salvation runs through Peter's Pentecost speech (Acts 2:14–36). The closing of a citation from the prophet Joel (Acts 2:21: 'and it shall be that everyone who calls upon the name of the Lord shall be saved') is picked up in the culmination of the sermon, in which Peter argues that Jesus' resurrection has demonstrated his rightful position as Lord and Messiah (2:36). The prescribed response to the speech is that all Israel repent, be baptized in the name of Jesus for the forgiveness of sins, receive the gift of the Holy Spirit, and so 'be saved from this perverse generation.' (2:38–40).

(4) Paul's inaugural sermon in Antioch of Pisidia is punctuated with the theme of salvation (Acts 13:16–41). Israel's history is rehearsed up to the period of David, at which point Paul announces Jesus as Israel's promised Saviour (13:23). The promise of salvation, coming to its initial realization in the resurrection of Jesus, is designated 'the message of this salvation' (13:26) and the proclamation of the good news that was promised to Israel's ancestors (13:32). The outcome of this salvation is forgiveness of

---

[9] Marshall, *Luke: Historian and Theologian*, 97; cf. Fearghus Ó Fearghail, *The Introduction to Luke-Acts: A Study of the Role of Lk 1,1–4,44 in the Composition of Luke's Two-Volume Work* (AnBib 126; Rome: Biblical Institute, 1991).

[10] ἄφεσις is used of forgiveness sins elsewhere: Luke 1:77; 3:3; 24:47; Acts 2:38; 5:31; 10:43; 13:38; 26:18; ἀφίημι is used thus in Luke 5:20–24; 7:47–49; 11:4; 12:10; 17:3–4; 23:34; Acts 8:22.

sins and freedom from everything which people could not be freed by the Mosaic law (13:38-39).

(5) The final recorded words of Paul in Acts are a declaration that 'this salvation of God has been sent to the Gentiles' (28:28).

2.1.2 The Meaning of Salvation in Luke-Acts

Luke has not provided us with a logical series of propositions constitutive of his soteriology. Rather, he has written a narrative showing the continuation of Israel's redemptive story in the life of Jesus and his followers. Therefore, any schematization of Luke's soteriology will be in some measure artificial. We will briefly analyze salvation in Luke-Acts under four theological categories.

(1) *Theology*. Salvation is fundamentally *theo*logical for Luke. Twice salvation is explicitly designated as *'God's* salvation' (Luke 3:6; Acts 28:28; cf. 16:17), and one of the first titles applied to God is 'Saviour' (Luke 1:47). Two indicators reveal a pervasive divine stamp on salvation. (a) The message of salvation proclaimed by Jesus is described as the good news about 'the kingdom of God' (Luke 4:43; 6:20; 7:28; 8:1, etc.). (b) All of history, according to Luke, proceeds under divine control (Acts 1:7; 17:26; cf. Luke 1:1; 21:24). The course of events is determined by God's βουλή (Acts 2:23; 4:28), which may be served (13:36; cf. 13:22; 21:14) or opposed (Luke 7:30), but never thwarted (Acts 5:38). Human beings may even unwittingly fulfil God's purposes, despite their own ignorance (3:17; 13:27; 14:15-17; 17:30). Events that are coming to pass in Luke's narrative follow historical trajectories that have been destined 'from of old' or 'long ago,' just as the ancient prophets had announced (3:21; 15:7, 18, 21; cf. Luke 1:70; Acts 3:24). God's plan has been articulated in the Hebrew Scriptures, and events are often said to take place in fulfilment of the Scriptures (e.g., Luke 4:21; 21:22; 22:37; 24:44; Acts 1:16; 3:18; 13:27, 33). The salvific orientation of God's purpose is illustrated well in Paul's farewell speech to the Ephesian elders. In describing how he has faithfully discharged his ministry, Paul says he has 'testified to the good news of God's grace' (Acts 20:24) and has gone about 'preaching the kingdom' (20:25), all of which he sums up as his 'declaring the whole purpose of God (πᾶσαν τὴν βουλὴν τοῦ θεοῦ)' (20:27).[11] So Luke represents saving events in history as occurring on a theological grid. But the saving action of God is executed through two axes on that grid: one, christological; the other, eccle-

---

[11] On the purpose of God as a major theme in Luke-Acts, see John T. Squires, *The Plan of God in Luke-Acts* (SNTSMS 76; Cambridge: Cambridge University Press, 1993).

siological. This leads us on to the second theological component of salvation.

(2) *Christology*. Throughout Israel's history God raised up leaders or deliverers for his people. Of special significance throughout Luke's work is first of all, Abraham, through whom God initiated his covenant relationship with the people of Israel (Luke 1:55, 73; Acts 3:25; 7:2, 8, 32). Then there is Moses, who was Israel's first great ruler and liberator (7:27, 35), and whose name, coupled with the prophets, represents the authoritative communication of God's will in the Scriptures (Luke 16:29, 31; 24:27, 44; Acts 26:22; 28:23). Finally, Israel's greatest king, David, represents the zenith and ideal for God's rule over Israel, as a man after God's own heart (Acts 13:22; cf. 7:45–46). The name of David is also associated closely with the composition of the Scriptures, since he was thought to be the writer of the book of Psalms (Luke 20:42; Acts 1:16; 2:25, 31, 34; 4:25).

These chosen leaders and spokespersons from Israel's ancient past provide a pattern for the divine action of salvation that has now appeared in the person of Jesus. The help that God is extending toward Israel, which Mary sees in the announcement of the coming birth of the Messiah, is celebrated as the remembrance of God's mercy communicated to 'our ancestors,' beginning with Abraham (Luke 1:55). Zechariah, too, exults in the fact that God has raised up a mighty saviour, which demonstrates the mercy he promised to 'our ancestors' and the remembrance of his sacred covenant, that is, 'the oath' that he swore to 'our ancestor, Abraham' (1:73; see 1:69–75). Peter, in his temple speech in Acts 3, announces that 'the God of Abraham, the God of Isaac, the God of Jacob, the God of our ancestors' glorified Jesus (Acts 3:13); and Peter reminds his listeners that they are heirs of the covenant that God made with Abraham, which is why the risen Jesus has been sent to them first, to offer them the opportunity for repentance and covenant renewal (3:25–26). In this same speech, Peter identifies Jesus as the anticipated prophet like Moses (3:22). The risen Jesus' status as ἀρχηγός and σωτήρ (3:15; 5:31) is reminiscent of Moses as 'ruler' (ἄρχων) and 'liberator' (7:27, 35). Most of all, Jesus' appearance as God's 'horn of salvation' (Luke 1:69) or Israel's 'saviour' (2:11) has to do with God's keeping his covenant promises to David. Jesus is from the house of David (1:27, 69; 2:4), and he is destined to reign forever on the throne of his father, David (1:32), as Messiah and Lord (2:11; 20:41–44; Acts 2:36). Particularly important for our study is the fact that Jesus' identity as the Davidic messianic king is confirmed by God's action of raising him up from the dead (Acts 2:24–36; 13:32–37). God's saving purposes, according to Luke's narrative, have always been accomplished via human agents through whom God brings deliverance, establishes a covenant relationship, and conveys his will and promises to his people. This pattern comes to its peak in the person of Messiah-Jesus. Salvation, therefore, is inextricably christological. God the Saviour (Luke 1:47) acts in covenant fidelity toward his people by bringing to Israel 'a Saviour, Jesus, according to promise' (Acts 13:23).[12]

(3) *Ecclesiology*. The objects or recipients of God's salvation who immediately come into view in Luke's narrative are the people of Israel. At the announcement of the Messiah's birth, Mary rejoices that God has helped 'his servant Israel' and that he is remembering the covenant promise he made with 'Abraham and his descendants forever' (Luke 1:54–55). Previously, an angel had informed Zechariah that the Messiah's forerunner has come to 'turn many of the people of Israel to the Lord their God' and 'prepare a people fit for the Lord' (1:16–17). Zechariah himself says later that 'the Lord God of Israel' has visited and brought redemption 'to his people' (1:68). Like Mary, he declares that God has shown mercy to 'our ancestors' and has remembered the sacred covenant that he had sworn on oath to 'our ancestor Abraham' (1:72–73). The benefits of God's introduction of a saviour for his people include 'salvation from our enemies' (1:71)—deliverance designed to create a peaceable environment for Israel to worship God 'in holiness and righteousness all our days' (1:74–75). But the experience of this salvation (γνῶσιν σωτηρίας) will be effected only through release from or forgiveness of the people's sins (1:77). An angel announced to the shepherds that the Messiah's birth was joyous news 'for all the people' (παντὶ τῷ λαῷ, 2:10), undoubtedly an announcement for the people of Israel. The proclamation of God's salvation, therefore, is directed first of all to the covenant people of Israel. The presentation of Jesus in the Jerusalem temple, the symbolic centre of Israel's worship, vividly exemplifies the commencement of God's salvific action in the midst of Israel. There we meet not only Simeon, whose expectation for 'the consolation of Israel' (2:25) is matched by a revelation from the Spirit that he would not die until he had beheld the Lord's Messiah (2:26), but the devoted prophetess, Anna, who begins to speak about the newborn Jesus to 'all who were expecting the redemption of Jerusalem' (2:38).

However, the Holy Spirit announces a startling development through Simeon. Simeon takes the baby Jesus in his arms and blesses God that he has seen 'your salvation, which you have prepared in the presence of all peoples (πάντων τῶν λαῶν)' (2:30–31; cp. παντὶ τῷ λαῷ, 2:10). The contradistinction between the 'peoples' (the Gentiles) and the 'people' (Israel) is clarified in a couplet describing the Messiah as 'light for revelation of Gentiles' as well as 'the glory of your people Israel' (2:32). Simeon also re-

---

[12] A further recognition of the christological dimension of salvation in Luke-Acts is in Marshall's observation that Jesus is both the Proclaimer and the Proclaimed ('"Israel" and the Story of Salvation,' 347–49).

veals that Jesus will be destined to bring about 'the falling and rising of many in Israel' and will be a 'sign opposed' (2:34). Thus, early on in Luke's narrative, the priority of the people of Israel as recipients of salvation is underlined. But it is also disclosed that their response to God's salvation will be divided, with some (perhaps many) rejecting the Lord's Messiah. Alongside the achievement of Israel's glory through Jesus, is the expansion of God's salvation among 'all peoples' through the light of the Christ's revelation. 'And all flesh will see the salvation of God' (3:6).

(4) *Eschatology*. In keeping with the visualization of salvation as two axes (christological and ecclesiological) on a theological grid, we shall propose that the intersection of these two axes is a monumental conjunction in the history of salvation. The life, ministry, death, and resurrection of Jesus inaugurate the final epoch of salvation history.[13] Jesus told his disciples: 'Blessed are the eyes that see what you see! For I tell you that many prophets and kings desired to see what you see, but did not see it, and to hear what you hear, but did not hear it' (Luke 10:23–24). The time of Jesus is not 'die Mitte der Zeit.' It is rather the beginning of the end. The two recitals of Israel's history in Acts 7:1–53 and 13:17–25 depict the appearance of Jesus at the culmination of Israel's history. The appearance of Jesus marks a decisive shift in world history, in which all men and women are called to repentance, in view of the coming judgment (17:30–31) and the completion of God's saving work in the restoration of all things (3:20–21). The days of salvation foreseen by the prophets of old are coming to pass through Jesus (3:24), and the covenant promises made to Israel's ancestors are being fulfilled. Israel's past is the overture to what God is now accomplishing through Messiah-Jesus to fully establish his kingdom in Israel and the whole world.

God's initiative and timing, therefore, bring the opportunity for salvation to the people of Israel through the person of Jesus. Jesus' ministry includes (a) preaching about the kingdom of God and (b) healing (Luke 4:40–43; 7:22; 8:1–3; 9:2, 11; 10:9; 11:20; cf. Acts 1:3; 10:38). Jesus' ministry reaches persons who would otherwise be excluded from the people of God (e.g., Luke 19:9–10), and his acts of healing not only reverse physical abnormalities, but make possible the (re-)incorporation of persons into communal life, and therefore into the people of God (8:43–48; 13:10–17; 17:12–19).[14] Jesus is confronted by mounting opposition, climaxing with

---

[13] The notion of salvation history in mind here parallels that of Jacob Jervell, 'The Future of the Past: Luke's Vision of Salvation History and Its Bearing on His Writing of History,' in *History, Literature, and Society in the Book of Acts* (ed. Ben Witherington III; Cambridge: Cambridge University Press, 1996), 104–26.

[14] We reject the view that healing is only emblematic of a superior and spiritual salvation; *contra* Bovon, 'La salut dans les écrits de Luc,' 303; Flanagan, 'What and How

his trial and execution. While there are signs of remorse among the people about Jesus' crucifixion (23:27, 48), his death leaves his followers disappointed about the prospect that Israel's hope for restoration would come to pass (24:21). Appearances of the resurrected Jesus rekindle this hope, and begin a decisive phase in salvation history. The resurrection of Jesus is the pivotal act of God for the salvation of Israel and the whole world, and hence the focus of the Lukan message of salvation.

2.2 The Resurrection of Jesus as Theological Focus

The claim that the resurrection of Jesus is at the heart of the Lukan message of salvation may appear as a truism. Indeed, one need not look very far to find assertions about the centrality of Jesus' resurrection in Luke-Acts.[15]

---

of Salvation,' 211; Giles, 'Salvation,' 10–11; Marshall, *Luke: Historian and Theologian*, 95–96. Witherington, too, has succumbed to this false dichotomy, pointing out that σωτήρ, σωτηρία, and σωτήριον do not occur in stories about healing: 'It is as though Luke has basically reserved these nouns to refer to something of more enduring and eternal significance'; Ben Witherington III, 'Salvation and Health in Christian Antiquity: The Soteriology of Luke-Acts in Its First Century Setting,' in *Witness to the Gospel: The Theology of Acts* (eds. I. Howard Marshall and David Peterson; Grand Rapids: Eerdmans, 1998), 153–54. First, Witherington's assertion about Luke's use of salvation vocabulary is not accurate. Luke writes about the lame man in Acts 3–4 as someone who was sick (ἀνθρώπου ἀσθενοῦς) but now is saved (σέσωται, 4:9), restored to health (ὁλοκληρίαν, 3:16; παρέστηκεν ἐνώπιον ὑμῶν ὑγιής, 4:10), or healed (τεθεραπευμένον, 4:14; cf. τὸ σημεῖον τοῦτο τῆς ἰάσεως, 4:22) by the name of Jesus, this name being the exclusive means of *salvation* (ἡ σωτηρία, 4:12). Second, it is true that 'the full-orbed Good News about salvation could not be proclaimed until after the death and resurrection of Jesus' (165), but not because there is a distinction between a 'mundane' and a 'fuller and more spiritual sense' of salvation (154, 165), but because the resurrection of Jesus initiates his exalted position as the new leader over Israel whose restoration he has inaugurated (Acts 2:36; 4:15, 22–23; 5:31). For more on the significance of healing in Luke-Acts, see John J. Pilch, 'Sickness and Healing in Luke-Acts,' in *The Social World of Luke-Acts: Models for Interpretation* (ed. Jerome Neyrey; Peabody, Mass.: Hendrickson, 1991), 181–209. On the relation of healing to incorporation into the people of God, see John T. Carroll, 'Jesus as Healer in Luke-Acts,' *SBL Seminar Papers, 1994* (SBLSP 33; Atlanta: Scholars Press, 1994), 269–85, esp. 282, 284; Luke Timothy Johnson, 'The Social Dimension of *Sōtēria* in Luke-Acts and Paul,' *SBL Seminar Papers, 1993* (SBLSP 32; Atlanta: Scholars Press, 1993), 520–36, esp. 525–26, 528–29.

[15] Bovon claims, 'la résurrection est le cœur du message'; François Bovon, *Luc le théologien. Vignt-cinq ans de recherches (1950–1975)* (2d ed.; *MdB* 5; Geneva: Labor et Fides, 1988), 132. George writes, 'Il faut donc dire que, dans le schéma lucanien de l'Histoire du salut, la résurrection de Jésus est l'évenement décisif qui ouvre une période nouvelle'; Augustin George, 'Le sens de la mort de Jésus,' in *Études sur l'œuvre de Luc* (SB; Paris: Gabalda, 1978), 210. Green claims that the resurrection of Jesus is 'the cen-

Yet others, as we shall see, demur or offer qualifications to this claim. There are two poles operating like magnetic forces to tug in diametrically opposite directions from the focus on resurrection. The first is a greater emphasis on the role of Jesus' suffering and death in Luke-Acts, and is a reaction to the notion that Luke's is a theology of glory. The second is an emphasis upon Jesus' ascension as the moment of his exaltation-enthronement. Before we look at these countervailing positions, it is necessary to point out that the idea of any particular event as the centre of Luke's soteriology is perhaps flawed from the start. Luke's narrative about God's salvation is too richly textured to yield to such reductionism. Jesus' ministry, death, resurrection, ascension, outpouring of the Spirit at Pentecost, and continued ministry through his witnesses are all significant developments within the entire movement of salvation history. In order to be as precise as possible, we would like to propose that the resurrection of Jesus occupies, not the centre, but the *focus* of Lukan soteriology. It must be admitted that there are a number of arguably decisive events in Luke-Acts,[16] none of which marginalizes the others—especially since all of these events have taken place in accordance with God's plan. The narrator,

---

tral affirmation of the Christian message in the Acts of the Apostles,' 'the centerpiece' of the proclamation by Jesus' followers ('Witnesses of His Resurrection,' 227, 245). Marguerat ('Luc-Actes: La résurrection à l'œuvre dans l'histoire,' 195) notes how Jesus' resurrection underlies all christological reflection in the NT, then adds: 'Or, surprenante, un seul écrit en a fait le thème fondamental de son discours: Luc-Acts.' Later, he refers to Jesus' resurrection as the 'clef du voûte' (204) and 'la clef herméneutique de l'histoire de Dieu avec son peuple' (205). Marshall ('Resurrection in the Acts of the Apostles,' 92; cf. idem, *Luke: Historian and Theologian*, 176–77) thinks it is accorded 'the fundamental place in salvation history.' O'Toole ('Resurrection-Ascension-Exaltation,' 111) asserts that 'the salvific event of Jesus' life which dominates Luke-Acts proves to be his resurrection, not his ascension nor his exaltation.' Wilckens could not be more emphatic: 'If one allow Luke himself to speak, then it is obvious that the centre of his scheme is the idea that in Jesus the fullness of God's salvation was truly present and was for all time established by the resurrection'; Ulrich Wilckens, 'Interpreting Luke-Acts in a Period of Existentialist Theology,' in *Studies in Luke-Acts* (eds. Leander E. Keck and J. Louis Martyn; Nashville: Abingdon, 1966), 66. See also Zwiep, *Ascension of the Messiah*, 146–47.

[16] The difficulty of defining the centre of Lukan soteriology is illustrated by Conzelmann's confusing attempt to demarcate the boundary between his second and third epochs of salvation history (*Theology of St. Luke*, [trans. Geoffrey Buswell; London: Faber and Faber, 1960]). Does the turning point occur at Luke 22:36 (16), the passion (16), the complex of resurrection-ascension-Pentecost (179), the ascension (204; cf. Ernst Haenchen, *The Acts of the Apostles: A Commentary* [Philadelphia: Westminster; Oxford: Basil Blackwell, 1971], 96), the exaltation (179), or Pentecost (204)? Cf. Bovon, *Luke the Theologian*, 14.

however, has chosen to theologically focus upon the significance of the resurrection of Jesus in salvation history. This theological focus is what we shall attempt to demonstrate in succeeding chapters. Presently, we will survey the data indicating the prominence of Jesus' resurrection within Luke-Acts. Then we will discuss the place of the passion and the ascension in Luke's theology.

2.2.1 The Prominence of the Resurrection of Jesus in Luke-Acts

(1) *The incidence of references to Jesus' resurrection in Luke-Acts.* The prominence of the resurrection of Jesus in Luke-Acts is indicated first of all by the number of references to it. (a) Luke refers explicitly to the resurrection of Jesus more than any of the other Evangelists, and is rivalled only by Paul in the frequency of references. The verb ἀνίστημι, used in reference to Jesus' resurrection, appears 4x in Luke and an additional 8x in Acts.[17] By contrast, other NT writers use this verb less frequently when referring to Jesus' resurrection: never in Matthew, 5x in Mark, 2x in John, and only 1x in Paul.[18] The cognate noun ἀνάστασις occurs in none of the Gospels to refer to Jesus' resurrection (but see John 11:25); however, it does appear repeatedly so in Acts (4x directly, and 5x by implication[19]), 3x in Paul, and 2x in Peter.[20] The verb ἐγείρω is used the most liberally in the NT to refer to Jesus' resurrection. Luke uses it thus 3x in his Gospel and 7x in Acts, as opposed to 9x in Matthew, 2x in Mark, and 3x in John. No one uses this verb more abundantly of Jesus' resurrection than Paul (24x).[21] Luke also refers to the resurrected Jesus as 'alive' (4x),[22] a designation unparalleled in the other Gospels (with the possible exceptions of John 6:57 and 14:19). The 'aliveness' of the resurrected Jesus is pointed out elsewhere in the NT,[23] but in Luke-Acts it is tied more directly to his physical

---

[17] Luke 16:31; 18:33; 24:7, 46; Acts 2:24, 32; 3:26; 10:41; 13:33, 34; 17:3, 31.

[18] Mark 8:31; 9:9, 10, 31; 10:34; John 6:39; 20:9; 1 Thess 4:4.

[19] Directly: Acts 1:22; 2:31; 4:33; 26:23; by implication: Acts 4:2; 17:18, 32; 23:6; 24:21. In the last two instances, note that the general resurrection is not specifically at issue, but rather Jesus' resurrection (cf. 25:19).

[20] Paul: Rom 1:4; 6:5; Phil 3:10. Paul also uses ἀνάστασις to refer to the resurrection of the dead in 1 Cor 15, but in connection with Jesus' resurrection (15:12, 13, 21, 42). Peter: 1 Pet 1:3; 3:21.

[21] Rom 4:24, 25; 6:4, 9; 7:4; 8:11, 34; 10:9; 1 Cor 6:14; 15:4, 12, 13, 14, 15, 16, 17, 20; 2 Cor 4:14; 5:15; Gal 1:1; Eph 1:20; Col 2:12; 1 Thess 1:10; 2 Tim 2:8. The only other such NT reference is in 1 Pet 1:21.

[22] Luke 24:5, 23; Acts 1:3; 25:19. The verb employed is ζάω.

[23] Rom 6:10 (2x); 14:9; 2 Cor 13:4; Heb 7:25; 1 Pet 2:4; Rev 1:18; 2:8.

revivification after death,[24] as a comparison between the presentation of the resurrected Jesus and the resurrected Tabitha shows:

Acts 1:3: [Jesus] παρέστησεν ἑαυτὸν ζῶντα
Acts 9:41: [Peter] παρέστησεν αὐτὴν ζῶσαν

Compare also the resurrection of Eutychus:

Acts 20:12: ἤγαγον δὲ τὸν παῖδα ζῶντα

The Emmaus disciples report how the women were told by angels that Jesus was alive (λέγουσιν αὐτὸν ζῆν, Luke 24:23; cf. 24:5), but after the women were unable to find his body (Luke 24:23; cf. 24:3). This aspect of Jesus' resurrection is underlined in Acts by repeated references to his body not being subject to decomposition (Acts 2:27, 31; 13:34, 35, 36, 37). This concern is not explicitly shared by any of the other Evangelists. Paul and Peter, however, mention the incorruption of resurrected bodies.[25]

(b) The resurrection of Jesus is prominent narratively in Luke-Acts. As in the other Synoptics, in Luke's Gospel there are explicit predictions[26] as well as allusions[27] to the resurrection of Jesus. But Luke devotes more space to the post-resurrection appearances than the other Synoptics. Only John in its canonical form outdoes Luke in this regard.[28] Nevertheless, Luke ultimately outperforms John, too, since he includes a recapitulation of Jesus' post-resurrection appearances at the beginning of his second volume

---

[24] This linkage (viz., resurrection of *mortal* bodies) is not unknown to Paul (Rom 8:11; 2 Cor 4:10; Phil 3:21); see also Rev 1:18; 2:8.

[25] 1 Cor 15:42, 50, 52, 53, 54; 1 Pet 1:4.

[26] Luke 9:22 // Matt 16:21 // Mark 8:31; Luke 18:31-33 // Matt 20:18-19 // Mark 10:33-34. There are, however, additional statements regarding Jesus' future resurrection in Matthew (17:9, 23; 26:32; 27:63-64) and Mark (Mark 9:9-10, 31; 14:28). See Hans F. Bayer, *Jesus' Predictions of Vindication and Resurrection* (WUNT 20; Tübingen: Mohr-Siebeck, 1986).

[27] In addition to the Synoptic parallels (Luke 20:17 // Matt 21:42 and Mark 12:10; Luke 22:18 // Matt 26:29 and Mark 14:25; Luke 11:29-30 // Matt 12:39-40) Luke has Abraham's provocative declaration about the rich man's five brothers: 'they will not be convinced even if someone were to rise from the dead' (Luke 16:31).

[28] The percentage of each Gospel devoted to post-resurrection events breaks down as follows: Matthew (28:1-20—329 words out of 18,346—1.79%); Mark (16:1-8—136 words out of 11,099—1.23%); Luke (24:1-53—818 words out of 19,482—4.20%); John (20:1-21:25—1,162 words out of 15,635—7.43%). This statistical comparison was inspired by Edwyn Clement Hoskyns and Francis Noel Davey (*Crucifixion-Resurrection: The Pattern of the Theology and Ethics of the New Testament* [London: SPCK, 1981], 281) who conclude that 'the consistent increase...suggests that the authors of Luke and John were dissatisfied with such a small proportion.'

(Acts 1:3–8) and significant references or extended discussion of the resurrection of Jesus in nearly every major speech in Acts.[29]

(2) *The resurrection of Jesus is the primary object of witness.* This is not the place to delve into all the particulars of the witness-motif in (Luke-)Acts.[30] The task here is to show that Luke's deployment of this motif is directed especially toward one object: the resurrection of Jesus. One may isolate twenty-four instances where witness terminology[31] is used with respect to apostolic testimony to either the message of salvation (in various forms) or Jesus (in general and more specific terms).[32] (a) In several instances the object of witness is the message of salvation. Peter and John are said to have 'testified and spoken the word of the Lord' to the Samaritans (Acts 8:25). Paul relates his proclamation and teaching at Ephesus (Acts 20:20) in terms of 'testifying to both Jews and Gentiles about repentance toward God and faith toward our Lord Jesus Christ' (Acts 20:21). So his ministry may be summed up as a 'testifying to the good news of God's grace' (Acts 20:24) or 'testifying about the kingdom of God,' which entails persuasion about Jesus from the Law and the Prophets (Acts 28:23). All of the prophets do indeed testify that everyone who believes in Jesus may receive forgiveness of sins (Acts 10:43; cf. Luke 24:47).

(b) In most cases Jesus is the object of testimony (and he is referenced, too, in several of the aforementioned instances). Jesus himself alerted his disciples that they would be arraigned in synagogues and before kings and

---

[29] In Peter's speeches in Acts 2–5 and 10 (2:24, 32; 3:15, 26; 4:10; 5:30; 10:41); in Paul's speeches in Acts 13, 17, 21–26, and 28 (13:30, 33, 34, 37; 17:3, 18, 31, 32; 23:6; 24:15, 21; 26:8, 23).

[30] See Peter G. Bolt, 'Mission and Witness,' in *Witness to the Gospel: The Theology of Acts* (eds. I. Howard Marshall and David Peterson; Grand Rapids: Eerdmans, 1998), 191–214; Robert P. Casey, 'Note V. Μάρτυς," *BC* 5:30–37; L. Cerfaux, 'Témoins du Christ d'après le livre des Actes,' *Ang* 20 (1943): 166–83; Andrew Clark, 'Role of the Apostles,' in *Witness to the Gospel: The Theology of Acts* (eds. I. Howard Marshall and David Peterson; Grand Rapids: Eerdmans, 1998), 169–90; Marshall, *Acts of the Apostles* (NTG), 55–60; Philippe H. Menoud, 'Jesus and His Witnesses: Observations on the Unity of the Work of Luke,' in *Jesus Christ and Faith* (trans. Eunice M. Paul; Pittsburgh: Pickwick, 1978), 149–66; E. Nellessen, *Zeugnis für Jesus und das Wort. Exegetische Untersuchungen zum lukanischen Zeugnisbegriff* (Köln: Peter Hanstein, 1976); A. Rétif, 'Témoinage et prédication missionaire dans les Actes des Apôtres,' *NRTh* 73 (1951): 152–65; Strathmann, 'μάρτυς, κτλ.,' *TDNT* 4:474–514, esp. 492–94; Allison A. Trites, *The New Testament Concept of Witness* (SNTSMS 31; Cambridge: Cambridge University Press, 1977), 128–53; Charles H. Talbert, *Luke and the Gnostics* (Nashville: Abingdon, 1966), 17–32.

[31] μαρτυρέω, μαρτύρομαι, διαμαρτύρομαι, μάρτυς, μαρτύριον, μαρτυρία.

[32] The natural division of the data into these two categories itself serves as an indication of the linkage between salvation and Jesus' resurrection in Luke-Acts.

governors 'on account of my name' (Luke 21:12), which would afford them opportunities to testify (ἀποβήσεται ὑμῖν εἰς μαρτύριον, Luke 21:13). Apostolic testimony about Jesus in Acts sometimes follows this broad conception. Peter, the spokesman for the twelve,[33] declares: 'We are witnesses (μάρτυρες) to all that he did both in Judea and in Jerusalem' (Acts 10:39). The risen Jesus instructs Paul that he is to bear testimony 'about me' (περὶ ἐμοῦ, Acts 22:18; 23:11). Jesus' witnesses, especially the Twelve, testify concerning the entire career of Jesus. More specific testimony about Jesus may relate to his messiahship (Acts 18:5; cf. 2:36; 3:18; 5:42; 8:5; 9:22; 17:3; 18:28) or his future role as universal judge (10:42; cf. 17:31; 24:24–25). These claims, however, are grounded in the apostolic witness to the climactic events of Jesus' life—his death, resurrection, and ascension. The death of Jesus is included within specific statements of apostolic testimony at least four times (Luke 24:46–48; Acts 3:14–15; Acts 5:30–32; 26:22–23).[34] The burial of Jesus (Acts 13:29–31) and his exaltation (Acts 5:31–32; cf. 2:33) are each mentioned once in direct connection with the apostolic witness. But it is the resurrection of Jesus that is most often the object of testimony (9x: Acts 1:22; 2:32; 3:15; 4:33; 5:32; 10:40–41; 13:31; 22:15; 26:16). The apostolic witness, then, encompasses the whole of Jesus' career, and concentrates on the climactic series of events in Jesus' life (death, resurrection, and ascension), but primarily on his resurrection.[35]

The broader testimony about Jesus' ministry, beginning in Galilee after his baptism by John, itself buttresses the apostolic witness to Jesus' resurrection. This is apparent in Luke 24, where the angelic announcement of Jesus' resurrection harks back to his Galilean predictions (24:6–7; cf. Acts 1:11). Only those who had been with him during his Galilean ministry could vouch for the fact that the same person had indeed risen from the dead according to his own prophecies (see Luke 8:1; 23:49, 55; Acts 10:37–41; 13:31).[36] The totality of the apostolic witness, brought to focus upon the resurrection of Jesus, is particularly clear in the first chapter of Acts (1:1–3, 22).

(3) *The resurrection of Jesus receives divine confirmation.* The apostolic witness to Jesus' resurrection is insufficient apart from divine forms of cor-

---

[33] On Peter as the representative of the Twelve, see Clark, 'Role of the Apostles,' 172–73.

[34] Of course, the death of Jesus is mentioned more often than this in Luke-Acts. See below for further discussion about the significance of the death of Jesus.

[35] The above analysis and conclusion is in keeping with Talbert, *Luke and the Gnostics*, 29; cf. Casey, 'Μάρτυς,' 32; Trites, *Concept of Witness*, 144.

[36] The *anabasis* from Galilee has often been noticed as one of the fundamental bases for the apostolic witness; see Dillon, *Eye-Witnesses*, 9; Talbert, *Luke and the Gnostics*, 24–30.

roboration. (a) The apostolic testimony includes insight into the scriptural witness to the resurrection of Jesus. This was imparted to the disciples by Jesus himself, who disclosed to them the import of the Scriptures concerning his death and resurrection (Luke 24:27, 44–48; cf. 18:31–33). Thus, in the programmatic speeches of Peter and Paul (Acts 2 and 13) the citation of Scripture is integral to the testimony to the resurrection of Jesus. No other author in the NT refers to the resurrection as the fulfilment of scriptural prophecy as often as Luke does.[37]

(b) The power of the Holy Spirit is an important component in the validation of Jesus' resurrection. This is so in at least two ways. First, the occasion of Jesus' outpouring of the Spirit, with all of its visual and aural manifestations (Acts 2:1–13), is itself an indication that Jesus has risen and ascended to the right hand of God, for he has received the promised Holy Spirit and 'has poured out this which you both see and hear' (2:32–33). Later, in speaking of the apostolic witness to Jesus' death and resurrection, Peter adds, 'and so is the Holy Spirit whom God has given to those who obey him' (Acts 5:32). It should come as no surprise, then, that Stephen is filled with the Holy Spirit before beholding the risen Jesus standing at the right hand of God (Acts 7:55–56—hence, Stephen is a witness to the risen Jesus, cf. 22:20), or that the gift of the Spirit should be given to Cornelius's household even while Peter is preaching about the lordship of Jesus by virtue of his resurrection (Acts 10:34–44; cf. 11:15–17; 15:8).

Secondly, the witness of the apostles cannot and does not commence until they have been 'clothed with power from on high' (Luke 24:49; cf. Acts 1:4–5, 8). Only then do they replicate the powerful ministry of Jesus through the performance of signs and wonders (2:22; 4:30; 5:12; 6:8; 8:6, 13; 14:3; 15:12). For what purpose? So that 'with great power' they may give testimony to the resurrection of the Lord Jesus (Acts 4:33).[38] This is dramatically realized in the healing of the lame man at the Beautiful Gate. The healing itself is figurative of Jesus' resurrection: Peter 'raises up' the lame man (3:6–7) in the name of Jesus Christ of Nazareth, whom God 'raised up' from the dead (3:15; 4:10).[39] Peter begins his sermon by informing his listeners that the man has been healed not by the apostles' own 'power or piety' (3:12), but precisely through the name of Jesus, the one

---

[37] Bayer, *Jesus' Predictions*, 116–17; Cadbury, *Making of Luke-Acts*, 279.

[38] Turner notes that 'in this case the Spirit would evidently be *presumed* to be the source of the "great power" with which the apostles gave their testimony (4.33; cf. Lk. 24.49; Acts 1.8)'; Max Turner, *Power from on High: The Spirit in Israel's Restoration and Witness in Luke-Acts* (JPTMS 9; Sheffield: Sheffield Academic Press, 1996), 414.

[39] Marguerat concludes ('Luc-Actes: La résurrection à l'œuvre dans l'histoire,' 208): 'Bref, le miracle de guérison actualise dans le présent le miracle par excellence: Pâques.'

whom God raised from the dead (3:14–16). Again, this linkage is underscored when Peter and John have been arrested for preaching 'that in Jesus there is the resurrection of the dead' (4:2). Peter declares that the lame man has been healed by the name of Jesus, 'whom you crucified, whom God raised from the dead' (4:10). The authorities are stymied by two important observations: that Peter and John had been 'with Jesus' (which qualifies them as witnesses, cf. 1:21–22), and that the lame man had obviously been cured (4:14; before all Israel, 4:10!). The episode closes with Peter and John refusing to abide by an official proscription upon their speaking in the name of Jesus, 'for we cannot refrain from speaking about what we have seen and heard' (4:20). The authorities cannot enforce their prohibition because of the notable sign of healing (4:21–22; cf. 4:16). And so the healing power of Jesus and the bold testimony of the apostles to his resurrection are mutually authenticating (cf. 4:29–30).[40]

In sum, the frequent and strategic incidence of references, the main object of the apostolic witness, and the forms of divine confirmation all underscore the importance of the resurrection in Luke-Acts. It is necessary, though, to inquire about the significance of Jesus' resurrection vis-à-vis his death and ascension in order to confirm or disconfirm the role of the resurrection as the theological focus of the Lukan message of salvation.

2.2.2 The Death of Jesus in Luke-Acts

It has become commonplace among NT scholars to assert that Luke has no atonement theology.[41] Three lines of evidence are usually called upon in support of this contention. (1) In Luke the debate over greatness in the kingdom (Luke 22:24–27) is set within a different context and does not contain the so-called 'ransom saying' that concludes the parallels in Mark 10:41–45 and Matt 20:24–28. (2) The apostolic speeches in Acts, to be sure, mention the necessity of Jesus' death within salvation history, but no direct link exists between Jesus' death and forgiveness of sins. (3) The fourth Servant Song (Isa 52:13–53:12), a veritable seedbed for NT teaching on the atoning death of Jesus, is cited from on two occasions (Isa 53:12 in Luke 22:37 and Isa 53:7–8 in Acts 8:32–33), but without capitalizing on the expiatory elements close at hand in the Song (e.g., the final words of Isa

---

[40] Such mutual authentication has also been noted by Green ('Witnesses of His Resurrection,' 240–41) and Trites (*Concept of Witness*, 149–53).

[41] F. F. Bruce, *The Time is Fulfilled: Five Aspects of the Fulfillment of the Old Testament in the New* (Grand Rapids: Eerdmans, 1978), 31 n. 34; Cadbury, *Making of Luke-Acts*, 280–81; Conzelmann, *Theology of St. Luke*, 201; Ernst Käsemann, 'Das Problem des historischen Jesus,' *ZTK* 51 (1954): 137; for further references, see Dillon, *Eye-Witnesses*, 29 n. 84.

53:6: 'the LORD has laid on him the iniquity of us all').[42] As for the two places in Luke-Acts where the death of Jesus is ostensibly portrayed in sacrificial terms (Luke 22:19-20; Acts 20:28), the atoning significance of Jesus' death in these verses seems undeniable,[43] but both passages may be instances where Luke has transmitted traditional formulae resistant to alteration though not integral to his overall theology.[44] An earlier generation of scholars concluded that in Luke-Acts, Jesus' death was merely that of an innocent martyr.[45] According to Ernst Käsemann, Luke has deliberately replaced a *theologia crucis* with a *theologia gloriae*, thus robbing the cross of any salvific significance.[46] The death of Jesus—'das Ärgernis des Kreuzes Jesu' which Luke does not fully comprehend, since he portrays Jesus' death as a peaceful martyrdom—is due to the ignorance and misunderstanding of the Jews. The resurrection emerges as the divine fix for Israel's misdeed.[47]

During the last three decades of the twentieth century there was a reaction to the negative assessment of Luke's understanding of the death of Jesus (particularly in its extreme Käsemannian form). This was aided by changes in methodology and approach. Methodologically, the more atomistic tendency of redaction critics to draw conclusions from the slightest modifications (or omissions) detected in Luke has given way to more holistic perspectives of the Lukan narrative, hence providing a broader base for apprehending Luke's soteriology. A significant change in approach eschews measuring Luke's soteriology against Paul's. No, Luke does not emphasize the expiatory value of the cross like Paul does, but that does not mean that the cross is devoid of salvific significance for Luke. At the very least, the death of Jesus should be viewed as a *sine qua non* for his

---

[42] For more on this threefold evidence, see Green, 'Message of Salvation,' 23; Jerome Kodell, 'Luke's Theology of the Death of Jesus,' in *Sin, Salvation, and the Spirit* (ed. Daniel Durken; Collegeville, Minn.: Liturgical, 1979), 222.

[43] In the case of Luke 22:19-20, however, it has been contended that the sacrificial language here may be indicative less of an atoning sacrifice than a 'covenant-founding sacrifice'; so Robert C. Tannehill, *Luke* (ANTC; Nashville: Abingdon, 1996), 315.

[44] For an attempt to counter this line of thinking, see Reginald H. Fuller, 'Luke and the Theologia Crucis,' in *Sin, Salvation, and the Spirit* (ed. Daniel Durken; Collegeville, Minn.: Liturgical, 1979), 214-20.

[45] Cf. Talbert, *Luke and the Gnostics*, 71-76.

[46] Ernst Käsemann, 'Ministry and Community in the New Testament,' in *Essays on New Testament Themes* (London: SCM, 1964), 91-94.

[47] Ernst Käsemann, *Der Ruf der Freiheit* (5th ed.; Tübingen: Mohr-Siebeck, 1972), 218-19: 'Gott hat zu Ostern diese weltgeschichtliche Panne wieder in Ordnung gebracht, wie er alles zu seiner Zeit in Ordnung bringt.'

resurrection and exaltation.[48] Others have sought to detect soteriological models constitutive of a more substantive role for Jesus' death in salvation history—beyond simply its divine necessity (Luke 9:22; 13:33; 17:25; 18:31–33; 22:22, 37; 24:6–7, 26, 44; Acts 2:23; 3:18; 17:3; 26:23). Richard Glöckner has located Jesus' death within the larger Lukan conception of salvation as the raising up of the lowly.[49] Robert Karris has highlighted Jesus as the innocent suffering righteous one whose death is exemplary of his faith, and to whom God in turn is faithful in raising him up from the dead.[50] Jerome Neyrey believes Luke has employed an Adam-Jesus Christology in which Jesus, the new Adam, exhibits his faithfulness and obedience to God even to the extent of death on a cross, and thus becomes the head of a new people of God.[51] Susan Garrett has propounded a model in which Jesus as the prophet like Moses leads an exodus from satanic bondage through his death and resurrection.[52] David Moessner has developed a similar model in much of his work, but on the basis of a Deuteronomic typology.[53]

---

[48] George, 'La mort de Jésus,' 209–11; Richard Zehnle, 'The Salvific Character of Jesus' Death in Lucan Soteriology,' *TS* 30 (1969): 420–44. Dillon (*Eye-Witnesses*, 30–31) regards the death of Jesus as a 'station' or 'intermediate, now finished phase of the journey of Jesus into glory.' Yet the death of Jesus is a *positive* aspect of Jesus' prophetic course in accordance with the divine will (289–90).

[49] Glöckner, *Verkündigung*, 155–95. An excellent précis appears in Kodell, 'Luke's Theology of the Death of Jesus,' 226–28.

[50] Robert J. Karris, *Luke: Artist and Theologian. Luke's Passion Account as Literature* (ThInq; New York: Paulist, 1985). A similar view is taken up by Peter Doble, who thinks that the crucifixion and resurrection are framed within a sapiential model of paradoxical salvation (*The Paradox of Salvation* [SNTSMS 87; Cambridge: Cambridge University Press, 1996]).

[51] Jerome Neyrey, *The Passion According to Luke: A Redaction Study of Luke's Soteriology* (ThInq; New York: Paulist, 1985).

[52] Susan R. Garrett, 'The Meaning of Jesus' Death in Luke,' *WW* 12 (1992): 11–16; idem, 'Exodus from Bondage: Luke 9:31 and Acts 12:1–24,' *CBQ* 52 (1990): 656–80.

[53] David P. Moessner, '"The Christ Must Suffer": New Light on the Jesus–Peter, Stephen, Paul Parallels in Luke-Acts,' *NovT* 28 (1986): 220–56; idem, *Lord of the Banquet: The Literary and Theological Significance of the Lukan Travel Narrative* (Harrison, Pa.: Trinity Press International, 1989); idem, 'Good News for the "Wilderness Generation": The Death of the Prophet Like Moses According to Luke,' in *Good News in History: Essays in Honor of Bo Reicke* (ed. Ed. L. Miller; Atlanta: Scholars Press, 1993), 1–34; idem, 'The "Script" of the Scriptures in Acts: Suffering as God's "Plan" (βουλή) for the World for the "Release of Sins,"' in *History, Literature, and Society in the Book of Acts* (ed. Ben Witherington III; Cambridge: Cambridge University Press, 1996), 218–50.

A major element of Moessner's thesis that sets it apart from all of the previous models is his contention that not only is the suffering of Jesus a necessary part of God's plan, but it constitutes an atoning sacrifice. Even as Moses had to die for the sins of the people, so also does Jesus, the prophet like Moses. However, the data fall short of substantiating Moessner's assertion about the redemptive nature of suffering in Luke-Acts. For one, neither Deuteronomy nor Luke-Acts represents the death of Moses as a vicarious sacrifice for the sins of the people. Indeed, Deut 32:48–51 indicates that Moses died outside the Promised Land on account of his own sin. And although Moessner appropriately accents the role of suffering within God's plan of salvation, both in the suffering Jesus and his suffering witnesses, he is not successful in drawing a direct line between such suffering and release from sins. He also tends to diminish the significance of the resurrection of Jesus in Luke-Acts.[54] Finally, as Garrett has suggested, the exodus motif (explicit in Luke 9:31) summons images of liberation rather than atonement.[55]

Clearly, most recent interpreters agree that the suffering and death of Jesus are vital to Lukan soteriology, but not in the same way as in Paul. Luke does not focus on the death of Jesus as atonement for sin. Rather, Jesus' death is itself an act of sin against him. This is repeatedly underlined in the contrast scheme between the ignominy of Jesus' death and God's vindication of Jesus by raising him from the dead (Acts 2:23–24; 3:14–15; 4:10; 5:30; 10:39–40; 13:27–30). The death of Jesus must happen—'the Messiah must suffer' (Luke 24:26, 46; Acts 3:18; 17:3; 26:23)—but God must also reverse his death if salvation is to be offered to Israel and the world.[56] This reversal is only possible for one who fulfils the prophetic role of the Suffering Servant, the Righteous One (Acts 3:14; 7:52; 22:14), who dies innocently and in humiliation and is consequently glorified by God (Acts 3:13–16).[57] The locus of salvation is not to be found in the rejection

---

[54] See Moessner, 'Wilderness Generation,' 31–33; idem, '"Script" of the Scriptures,' 239.

[55] Garrett, 'Exodus from Bondage,' 658. For a critique of Moessner, see Turner, *Power from on High*, 246 n. 100; Mark L. Strauss, *The Davidic Messiah in Luke-Acts: The Promise and Its Fulfillment in Lukan Christology* (JSNTSup 110; Sheffield: Sheffield Academic Press, 1995), 276–84.

[56] George ('La mort de Jésus,' 210) has pointed out that the death of Jesus is nearly always tied to his resurrection, the exception being Luke 9:44. Cf. also the 'saved Saviour' aspect of Jesus' death and resurrection explicated by Neyrey (*Passion According to Luke*, ch. 5).

[57] Echoes from the Servant Songs are unmistakeable: ἐδόξασεν τὸν παῖδα αὐτοῦ (Acts 3:13; cf. ὁ παῖς μου...δοξασθήσεται σφόδρα, Isa 52:13); παρεδώκατε (3:13; cf Isa 53:6, 12); δίκαιον (3:14; Isa 53:11). On the role of Jesus as the Suffering Servant, see

of Jesus by Israel, but in his resurrection by God. God's purpose is fulfilled when Jesus dies, but particularly in the *manner* of his death as a righteous victim. The execution of Jesus stands as a past fulfilment of God's design (Acts 2:23; 4:27–28), even though it was carried out in ignorance (Acts 3:17–18; 13:27, 29). Both the death and resurrection of Jesus fall under divine necessity (Luke 24:26; Acts 17:3), but only the latter has a lasting salvific effect. The divine plan was fulfilled when Jesus was put to death (aorist tense: ἐπλήρωσαν...ἐτέλεσαν πάντα τὰ περὶ αὐτοῦ γεγραμμένα, Acts 13:27, 29; cf. 3:18), but the resurrection of Jesus continues as an enduring fulfilment of God's promises of salvation for Israel (perfect tense: ὅτι ταύτην ὁ θεὸς ἐκπεπλήρωκεν τοῖς τέκνοις αὐτῶν ἡμῖν ἀναστήσας Ἰησοῦν, 13:33)![58] This understanding of the death and resurrection of Jesus comports well with what we have already proposed concerning Lukan soteriology. Each of these events is crucial to salvation history, but the resurrection of Jesus stands as the focal point in the salvation message.

2.2.3 The Ascension of Jesus in Luke-Acts

There is little clarity or unanimity among scholars about the function of the ascension in Luke-Acts vis-à-vis Jesus' resurrection. In Chapter 1 we surveyed five perspectives of this issue. Three of these enjoy the most critical support. One view, associated with such names as Lohfink and Franklin, asserts that the ascension is for Luke the pivotal moment in salvation history. This event is identical to Jesus' exaltation and is deliberately distinguished from Jesus' resurrection. A second view, supported notably by Fitzmyer and Zwiep, equates Jesus' resurrection with his ascension. The post-resurrection appearances are appearances of the ascended Jesus, and the 'ascension' should be interpreted simply as Jesus' final departure. A view that commands the most assent, perhaps by default, does not carefully define the relationship between the climactic events of Jesus' earthly life, but speaks of them as a hyphenated series, such as death-resurrection-ascension/exaltation. We believe the question of how Jesus' resurrection and ascension are related to his exaltation should keep two hermeneutical criteria in mind: (a) any proposed solution should not complicate the reading of Luke's narrative; and (b) any proposed solution should be consistent with the authoritative interpretation of the Christ-event found in

---

Joel B. Green, 'The Death of Jesus, God's Servant,' in *Reimaging the Death of the Lukan Jesus* (BBB 73; ed. Dennis D. Sylva; Frankfurt am Main: Anton Hain, 1990), 20–21; Strauss, *Davidic Messiah*, 324–33, esp. 330–32; and Robert F. O'Toole, 'How Does Luke Portray Jesus as Servant of YHWH?' *Bib* 81 (2000): 328–46.

[58] Dillon, *Eye-Witnesses*, 30–31.

the speeches of Acts. These criteria lead us to the conclusion that Luke has portrayed both the resurrection and ascension of Jesus within a continuum of exaltation, but that the resurrection is the theological focus of the message of salvation.

(1) The first position may be framed as follows. Luke is the only NT author to narrate a visible ascension of Jesus, separable from the resurrection.[59] The extra-Lukan authors of the NT, according to Lohfink, hold together the resurrection and exaltation of Jesus as a unity.[60] For Lohfink, the early church's exaltation kerygma was a secondary, interpretative development of the Easter experience. With the aid of scriptural texts, the NT writers expressed the significance of the resurrection in terms of exaltation or enthronement. Exaltation was the conceptualization of an invisible occurrence coterminous with Jesus' resurrection, which was itself an unseen event. The exaltation kerygma of the NT may therefore be schematized: death → resurrection-exaltation → *sessio ad dexteram*. According to Lohfink, Luke has modified this schema. The fundamental alteration consists of his *historicizing* or *concretizing* ('historisiert' or 'konkretisiert') the exaltation.[61] Luke appropriated elements from the *Entrückungserzählungen* familiar in the Greco-Roman world, but especially their Jewish counterparts (such as the Elijah rapture story),[62] in order to depict the exaltation graphically. In so doing, Luke reinterpreted the exaltation kerygma. What had been an invisible, transcendent conception was expressed as a concrete, historical occurrence visible to human witnesses. The inherent unity of resurrection and exaltation was broken, for now the point of exaltation was conceived of as an entirely separate moment from resurrection: an ascension preceded by an intervening period of forty days. The resultant schema: death → resurrection → appearances over forty days → ascension (rapture) → *sessio ad dexteram*.

Lohfink has accurately identified Luke's casting of the ascension in the form of a rapture story. This precise form is unique to the Lukan *Doppelwerk*, and belief in the ascension is not similarly expressed until the time of Justin Martyr and Irenaeus.[63] But Lohfink has exaggerated the uniqueness

---

[59] Mark 16:19 perhaps does not qualify as an exception. Lohfink thinks the longer ending is dependent upon the post-resurrection appearance stories of Matthew, John, and especially Luke (*Himmelfahrt Jesu*, 119–21).

[60] Lohfink, *Himmelfahrt Jesu*, 80–98, esp. 94–98.

[61] Lohfink, *Himmelfahrt Jesu*, 244.

[62] Lohfink, *Himmelfahrt Jesu*, 270. Lohfink also thinks that Luke was the heir to an exaltation kerygma that had already undergone modification through the influence of a cosmic Christology that began to attach more independent value to the ascension aspect of the exaltation (245–50).

[63] Lohfink, *Himmelfahrt Jesu*, 109–12.

of the Lukan perspective of the ascension in comparison to other NT writings. He has minimized the importance of Jesus' elevation to heaven for the theology of the Gospel of John and the Epistle to the Hebrews.[64] The writer to the Hebrews makes explicit mention of the resurrection of Jesus only at 13:20-21, and an implicit reference only at 7:16; but the fact that Jesus has 'passed through the heavens' (4:14; cf. 7:26; 8:1; 9:24) is central to his Christology.[65] Is this a purely independent adaptation of the exaltation kerygma that happens to focus on the exaltation of Jesus as an ascension into heaven? Mikeal Parsons has shed some doubt on Lohfink's argument concerning the originality and exclusivity of a Lukan development of the exaltation kerygma. It is open to question whether the ascension accounts in the longer reading of Mark (16:19) and in *Barnabas* (15:9) are directly dependent upon the Lukan narrative.[66] We are especially sceptical of the nineteenth-century evolutionary model underlying Lohfink's assumption, stating that the earliest Christians must have thought of Jesus' resurrection abstractly as an invisible, supramundane event, not subject to empirical verification. We are then expected to believe that Luke has unilaterally revised and reinterpreted the primitive exaltation kerygma by narrating the resurrection and ascension/exaltation of Jesus as concrete and distinguishable historical events.

Lohfink's claim that Luke has reinterpreted the exaltation kerygma depends upon Luke's differentiation between the resurrection and the exaltation, on one hand, and his identification of the ascension and the exaltation, on the other. However, in light of such passages as Luke 24:26 and Acts 13:33, resurrection is not so easily separated from exaltation,[67] and Acts 2:33 and 5:31 comprise a slender basis for the equation of ascension and exaltation. Additionally, if Luke has so deliberately modified the exaltation kerygma, his avoidance of omniscient narration in the ascension accounts—by employing the earth-bound perspective of the rapture story form—is puzzling, because it creates a lack of narrative precision concerning the connection of Jesus' ascension to his exaltation (contrast Mark

---

[64] See the criticism by Bovon, *Luke the Theologian*, 176-77.

[65] For the identification of explicit and implicit references to the resurrection of Jesus in Hebrews, see William L. Lane, 'Living a Life of Faith in the Face of Death: The Witness of Hebrews,' in *Life in the Face of Death: The Resurrection Message in the New Testament* (McMNTS; ed. Richard N. Longenecker; Grand Rapids: Eerdmans, 1998), 264-68.

[66] Parsons, *Departure*, 140-49. We think this is more likely in the latter case than in the former.

[67] Lohfink (*Himmelfahrt Jesu*, 235-39) interprets both of these passages as expressions related to the resurrection only. But we see the regal motif of exaltation tightly bound up with the resurrection in these passages, as well as in Acts 2:30-31.

16:19).⁶⁸ As a matter of fact, neither Jesus' exit from the tomb or his actual installation at the right hand of God is narrated in Luke-Acts.

There is a further argument for the centrality of the ascension in Luke's theology that must be considered. Eric Franklin contends, 'Luke described the event twice because he put such great weight upon it.' The repeated account of the ascension indicates its importance over and above the resurrection: 'Without it, even with the resurrection—at least as Luke describes it—he [i.e., Jesus] would not have been other than one of the prophets.'⁶⁹ Robert Maddox reinforces Franklin's argument by calling attention to Luke's technique of retelling events that are of particular theological importance.⁷⁰ The repetition of the ascension is all the more emphatic due to its placement at both the end of volume one and the beginning of volume two.⁷¹ This is a formidable argument that cannot be taken lightly, but is not as strong as it seems at first. First, as both Franklin and Maddox note, the double ascension accounts serve as a bridge between the two volumes. This supports the idea that the ascension accounts function as a 'continuous linkage' rather than a 'watershed.'⁷² Second, the repeated accounts do not buttress the same theological point as in the other cited cases of repetition, and this variation is carried out by way of different language and tone (Luke 24:50–53 evokes worship; Acts 1:9–11 has an eschatological orientation).⁷³ Third, the argument from repetition is vitiated by the fact that Acts 1:1–11 functions as a recapitulation or retrospective summary of Luke's first volume.⁷⁴ The post-resurrection appearances of Jesus are also summarized in

---

⁶⁸ On the earthbound vantage point common in rapture stories, see Lohfink, *Himmelfahrt Jesu*, 273. Note Lohfink's comment (14): 'Daß die Himmelfahrt die Erhöhung Jesu zur Rechtung Gottes sei, hat Lukas in seinen beiden Himmelfahrtserzählungen nicht gesagt, wenigstens nicht direkt und ausdrücklich.'

⁶⁹ Franklin, *Christ the Lord*, 35. I cannot comprehend the force of Franklin's argument, given Jesus' solidarity with the prophets in Luke-Acts. Precisely the opposite conclusion is logical. There were other prophets who had ascended into heaven (like Elijah), but who had not been raised from the dead like Jesus. Jesus transcends the prophets of old because he was raised from the dead *and* exalted (cf. Acts 2:29–36; 13:36–37).

⁷⁰ Conversion of Gentiles: Acts 10, 11, and 15; Paul's Damascus road experience: Acts 9, 22, and 26.

⁷¹ Maddox, *Purpose of Luke-Acts*, 10.

⁷² Lygre, 'Exaltation,' 192.

⁷³ Cf. Stempvoort, 'Interpretation of the Ascension in Luke-Acts,' 30–42; Kurz, *Reading Luke-Acts*, 21–22.

⁷⁴ The so-called ἀνακεφαλαίωσις was designed to assist in reading multi-volume works that could not be read in their entirety on one occasion, e.g., the introductions to Books 2, 3, 4, 5, and 7 in Xenophon's *Anabasis*; Josephus, *Ag. Ap.* 2.1 §1; Chariton, *Callirhoe* 5.1.1–2. See Henry J. Cadbury, 'Appendix C: Commentary on the Preface of

this passage (1:3). Finally, if repetition is a deciding factor for theological focus, then the frequency of references to the resurrection compared to the paucity of references to the ascension outside of Luke 24:50–53 and Acts 1:1–11 should give one pause.[75] Franklin sees Acts 2:32–35 as the only other instance when the ascension is treated separately from the resurrection, but he sees this as proof of the artificiality of the Lukan scheme through which everything else in Luke-Acts is to be interpreted.[76] This assessment originates from a flawed method of discerning the theology of Luke-Acts, in which Luke's narration of events trumps the authoritative witness and interpretation of those events in the speeches. If the speeches in Acts are purely Lukan compositions, then why do they not more clearly reflect the Lukan scheme that Franklin thinks is so prominent? On the other hand, if Luke has been constrained to reproduce the kerygma of the early church in the speeches, then why has he freely composed scenes within the narrative that flagrantly contradict it? It is possible that the perspective of Luke-Acts on this subject is muddled, but that does not redound in Franklin's favour. Lohfink and Franklin's position does not contravene our first criterion, because it does no violence to Luke's narrative, but it does not account satisfactorily for the great stress placed upon Jesus' resurrection in the speeches.

(2) The second view falls into difficulties with respect to both of our criteria. First, it frustrates the reading of Luke's narrative. For example, are we really expected to think (as Fitzmyer suggests) that Jesus' words to the Emmaus pair in Luke 24:26 ('Was it not necessary that the Messiah should suffer these things and then enter into his glory?') were designed to castigate them for not realizing that he had already ascended into heaven?[77] The flow of the narrative itself works against this view. Jesus was crucified, buried, raised up on the third day, then appeared to his disciples and ascended into heaven. The only reasonable point at which he could have been exalted (spatially) to the right hand of God, *in terms of the narrative*, is at the ascension. A corollary to the view that Jesus' exaltation is coincident with his resurrection is that he subsequently appeared to his disciples as the already-ascended Lord. So the ascension accounts in Luke-Acts

---

Luke," *BC* 2:491–92; Unnik, 'Book of Acts,' 344; Loveday C. A. Alexander, 'The Preface to Acts and the Historians,' in *History, Literature, and Society in the Book of Acts* (ed. Ben Witherington III; Cambridge: Cambridge University Press, 1996), 79–82.

[75] O'Toole, 'Resurrection-Ascension-Exaltation,' 111; idem, 'Acts 2:30 and the Davidic Covenant of Pentecost,' *JBL* 102 (1983): 249. Even Lohfink (*Himmelfahrt Jesu*, 243) observes: 'Der geschlossene Erzählzusammenhang ist beidemale erstaunlich klein.'

[76] Franklin, *Christ the Lord*, 33, 193 n. 51.

[77] Fitzmyer, 'Ascension of Christ and Pentecost,' 275; idem, 'Resurrection of Jesus Christ,' 378.

represent only Jesus' final departure, not his exaltation. Zwiep admits, 'Exegetical indications in the text itself to corroborate this hypothesis are few, if any.'[78] He asserts that Luke's anti-docetic tendency to accent the physicality of the resurrection erases exactly those elements that would indicate appearances from heaven.[79] Yet he concludes that since the appearance stories follow the pattern of anthropomorphic theophanies there is no 'principal objection' to interpreting them as appearances from heaven. Secondly, this view not only contravenes the sense of the narrative, but the speeches in Acts. Acts 10:40–43 and 13:30–31 easily mirror Luke's narrative sequence. The resurrection of Jesus is followed by appearances to his disciples, without any hint of an intervening 'ascension-exaltation.' The latter text (ὅς ὤφθη ἐπὶ ἡμέρας πλείους, 13:31) harmonizes nicely with the forty-day time period indicated in Acts 1:3. Acts 2:32–35 may reflect the same narrative sequence: resurrection—appearances (='of which we are all witnesses')—ascension.

(3) A form of the third perspective, which views the resurrection and ascension of Jesus as part of a continuum, is to be preferred. Jesus' resurrection and ascension stand in functional unity, despite their temporal and spatial separation. The ascension is the extension and enactment of the risen Jesus' exalted status as the new leader of Israel. This functional unity allows Luke to include the ascension of Jesus within the ken of apostolic witness, yet explicitly zero in on the resurrection of Jesus as the target of that witness. In Acts 1:21–22 the requirements for becoming one of the Twelve include exposure to the entire life of Jesus, from the beginning of his ministry to his ascension, in order to qualify as a 'witness to his resurrection.' This functional unity is also evident from the fact that the resurrection, ascension, and exaltation of Jesus are referred to interchangeably in Luke's work. In Acts 2:30–31 the resurrection of Jesus is viewed as enthronement, while exaltation and ascension are paired in 2:33–34. In Acts 3:14–15 the deadly rejection of Jesus is followed by his resurrection as ἀρχηγός, while in Acts 5:30–31 deadly rejection is followed by exaltation to the right hand of God as ἀρχηγός and σωτήρ. One is not forced to see either the resurrection or ascension as more significant than the other, while permitting greater focus upon the resurrection of Jesus throughout the apostolic preaching.[80] Resurrection and ascension are not theologically

---

[78] Zwiep, *Ascension of the Messiah*, 161.

[79] Zwiep, *Ascension of the Messiah*, 162–63.

[80] For comparable interpretations, see J. Bradley Chance, *Jerusalem, the Temple, and the Salvation of Israel* (Macon, Ga.: Mercer University Press, 1988), 64–65; Lygre, 'Exaltation,' passim. Note also Tannehill's comment on Paul's Pisidian Antioch speech (Acts 13): 'The narrator distinguishes between the resurrection and exaltation of Jesus in Acts 1 in order to emphasize Jesus' careful instruction of the apostles. However, when

competitive, but complementary. Jesus was not merely 'raised up' in the sense of being revivified, but also 'raised up' in the sense of entering into exalted status (Luke 24:26) and being exalted spatially to God's right hand.

2.3 Prospect: Jesus' Resurrection and Lukan Soteriology

In the remainder of this book (especially Chapters 5–9) we will support in more detail our claim that the resurrection of Jesus is the theological focus of the message of salvation in Luke-Acts. This may be outlined according to several theological rubrics. *Theologically*, the resurrection of Jesus is part of God's purpose for Israel and the world. *Christologically*, it confirms his position as the definitive leader of the people of God and the agent of God's covenant blessings of salvation. *Ecclesiologically*, it is the inaugural action of God in his promised restoration of Israel. The resurrection of Jesus, in initiating the restoration of Israel, effects both a division within Israel and an expansion of the people of God among the nations. Jesus, not only as Israel's Messiah, but as universal Lord, grants repentance and forgiveness of sins to people from all nations in view of the day of judgment when he will act as the appointed judge. The decisive challenge of the message of salvation is supported by the divine proof of Jesus' being raised from the dead. *Eschatologically*, the resurrection of Jesus adumbrates and guarantees the culmination of God's salvation of his people and the full realization of the kingdom of God among humankind.

Jesus' messianic enthronement is the main concern, this distinction can be ignored'; Robert C. Tannehill, 'Rejection by Jews and Turning to Gentiles: The Pattern of Paul's Mission in Acts,' in *Luke-Acts and the Jewish People* (ed. Joseph B. Tyson; Minneapolis: Augsburg, 1988), 150 n. 6.

Chapter 3

Resurrection in Second Temple Judaism

The aim of this chapter and the next is to sketch the conceptual background against which the Lukan conception of resurrection may be interpreted. Since in Luke-Acts faith in the resurrection is grounded in the Scriptures (Luke 20:37–38) and in the deep-seated hopes of the Hebrew people (Acts 24:14–15; 26:6–8), the natural starting-point will be ancient Jewish texts that attest to resurrection from the dead. Yet the Lukan narrative was heard in a world swirling with competing notions regarding the afterlife, both in and outside of Judaism. Indeed, Luke-Acts itself testifies to how controversial the issue of resurrection could be, whether in Jerusalem on the temple mount (Luke 20:27–40 [cf. 19:47]; Acts 4:1–2) or in the Sanhedrin (Acts 23:6–10), or in Athens at the agora (Acts 17:16–18) or on the Areopagus (Acts 17:19–34). The unsettled and fragmentary nature of the discussions regarding the afterlife in antiquity frustrates any attempt to delineate *the* view of the afterlife in any of the cultural spheres of the Greco-Roman world, least of all Second Temple Judaism. Nevertheless, it is desirable as well as possible to discern the contours of thought regarding death and the afterlife in Judaism and in the wider Hellenistic world within which Luke-Acts positioned itself.

Because this study is particularly concerned with the resurrection of Jesus in Luke-Acts, the background data will be approached with two foci in mind. First, we will be concerned with how resurrection was understood in antiquity. This includes not only the issue of definition, about how resurrection was conceived (corporeal, spiritual, some kind of transformative experience?), but the issue of its acceptance or non-acceptance in antiquity. What factors—social, economic, or philosophical—cohere to positions for and against one conception or another of resurrection? The latter issue is entangled with our second focus, the theological significance of resurrection. Among Jews who believed in resurrection, for example, what did the resurrection mean in terms of national hope, or in relation to the nation's covenant identity and destiny under Yahweh? Among Greeks, what significance would be attached to a person who had (purportedly) returned from the dead? Would that person be labelled a god, charlatan, outcast? And how would these conceptions and reactions impact readings of the Lukan presentation of Jesus' resurrection? So the *nature* and *theology* of resurrection will be the foci. This chapter will take up the subject of the resurrection within Judaism, beginning with its emergence in the Hebrew Scriptures and other Jewish texts, and concluding with its more mature form in late Second Temple Judaism. Then, in the next chapter, we will outline a number of perspectives regarding the afterlife that will assist us in viewing the Lukan resurrection message along the Greco-Roman landscape.

3.1 Resurrection in Ancient Judaism

A number of caveats are in order before surveying texts that relate ancient Jewish views concerning the resurrection. (1) Although the following discussion will generally follow a chronological scheme, it must be emphasized that there will be no attempt to trace the genealogical development of the doctrine of the resurrection in Judaism. The relevant texts are sometimes composite (or fragmentary), often impossible to date precisely, and subject to varying assessments by scholars. Apart from the pitfalls involved in such an endeavour, determining the precise origins and development of the Israelite belief in resurrection is simply not germane to this study.[1] (2) The texts are scattered helter-skelter along a timeline which reaches back to just before the exile of the northern kingdom and extends three or four decades beyond the time of Jerusalem's destruction by the Romans. In addition to biblical texts, we will be dealing with a number of Jewish pseudepigraphal texts. Later rabbinic texts will concern us only as occasional sources of collateral data, as there are well-known doubts about their value as representatives of first-century Jewish beliefs. (3) Because our focus will be on resurrection, our analysis of texts will necessarily be selective. While remaining aware of the diverse options within Judaism, we will give only cursory attention to texts that repudiate life after death (e.g., Ben Sirach) or speak of the afterlife in terms of the immortality of the soul (e.g., 4 Maccabees). More comprehensive studies of the Jewish views of the

---

[1] More than a generation ago the predominant view was that Israel borrowed the belief in resurrection from the Persians, and this inference was based upon the role resurrection played in Zoroastrianism, as well as upon testimony to such belief among the Persians by the Greek writers Theopompus (cited in Plut. *Is. Os.* 47 and Diog. Laert. 1.9) and Herodotus 3.62. Cf. H. Lesêtre, 'Résurrection de la chair,' *DB* 5:1066; T. H. Gaster, 'Resurrection,' *IDB* 4:40–41; Bernhard Lang, 'Afterlife—Ancient Israel's Changing Vision of the World Beyond,' *BRev* 4 (1988): 12–23. Arguing for an earlier expectation of a 'beatific afterlife' in Israel were Mitchell Dahood, *Psalms* (AB; 3 vols.; New York: Doubleday, 1970), 1:xxxvi, 91, 99; 3:xli–lii; and Klaas Spronk, *Beatific Afterlife in Ancient Israel and in the Ancient Near East* (AOAT 219; Neukirchen-Vluyn: Neukirchener, 1986). A prudent view discerns outside influences (e.g., Near Eastern ideas about astral immortality) while affirming unique developments in Israel's faith through reflection upon the Hebrew Scriptures; so John J. Collins, *Daniel* (Hermeneia; Minneapolis: Fortress, 1993), 396–97.

afterlife are already available.² (4) Finally, a word about terminology: there is a difficulty in choosing English terms to denote the various ancient interpretations of the phenomenon roughly described as persons returning from the dead. It is problematic to employ the term 'resurrection' with a preconceived definition, while at the same time exploring what 'resurrection' means. Therefore, in this chapter and the next, the term 'resurrection' will be employed generically to refer to the return of persons from the dead. Then, after we have completed our study of ancient views regarding persons returning from the dead, we will be in a better position to locate more precisely the denotation of words like 'resurrection' or 'resuscitation.'³

In this survey we will discover, with respect to the nature of resurrection, that most Jews who expressed a definite hope in resurrection thought of it as the raising up of entire human persons from the dead, out of their tombs. This is commonly referred to as a belief in 'bodily resurrection,' but this did not necessitate—though could include—a body-soul duality, since many of its earliest expositors viewed the nature of human beings along the lines of classical Hebrew monism.

The theological meaning of resurrection among ancient Jews was multi-faceted. First of all, resurrection was intimately tied to the Hebrew worldview, which cherished the nation's divinely selected position among all other nations as God's covenant people. Yahweh, the Creator of the world,

---

² The principal studies are H. C. C. Cavallin, *Life After Death: Paul's Argument for the Resurrection of the Dead in 1 Cor 15*, part 1, *An Enquiry into the Jewish Background* (ConBNT 7:1; Lund: Gleerup, 1974); Günter Stemberger, *Der Leib der Auferstehung* (AnBib 56; Rome: Pontifical Biblical Institute, 1972); and George W. E. Nickelsburg, Jr., *Resurrection, Immortality, and Eternal Life in Intertestamental Judaism* (HTS 26; Cambridge, Mass.: Harvard University Press, 1972). One may also consult the historical works: George Foot Moore, *Judaism in the First Centuries of the Christian Era: The Age of Tannaim* (Cambridge, Mass.: Harvard University Press, 1927–1930; repr., Peabody, Ma.: Hendrickson, 1997), 2:279–322; Emil Schürer, *The History of the Jewish People in the Age of Jesus Christ (175 B.C.–A.D. 135)* (eds. Geza Vermes, Fergus Millar, and Matthew Black; Edinburgh: T. & T. Clark, 1979), 2:539–44; Wright, *Resurrection of the Son of God*, 85–206. Concise surveys may be found in Hermann Lichtenberger, 'Resurrection in the Intertestamental Literature and Rabbinic Theology,' in *Reincarnation or Resurrection?* (eds. Hermann Häring and Johann-Baptist Metz; Concilium 5; London: SCM, 1993), 23–31; John P. Mason, *The Resurrection According to Paul* (Lewiston, N.Y.: Edwin Mellen, 1993), 11–34; Christopher A. Davis, *The Structure of Paul's Theology: 'The Truth Which Is the Gospel'* (Lewiston, N.Y.: Edwin Mellen, 1995), 165–96. Of value, as well, is the popular work by Neil Gillman, *The Death of Death: Resurrection and Immortality in Jewish Thought* (Woodstock, Vt.: Jewish Lights, 1997).

³ See our 'Excursus on the Definitions of Resurrection and Resuscitation' below in Chapter 4, beginning on p. 114 below.

entered into a covenant relationship with Israel, and the nation was behoved to relate to Yahweh under the terms of that agreement, because Yahweh had made gracious promises to the nation's patriarchs and had delivered the nation from Egyptian slavery. Obedience would result in life, prosperity, peace, and national sovereignty—a nation of kings and priests in God's land of promise. Disobedience spelled death, destitution, subjection to tyranny, and exile. Yet the covenant provided for opportunities to have this second state of affairs reversed if the nation repented of its covenant violations. We shall see that as early as the eighth-century prophet Hosea the covenantal status of the nation vis-à-vis these life and death outcomes could already be articulated in the language of death and resurrection.

Second, during the Maccabean period the nation experienced a critical reinforcement of the covenant idea in response to the political and cultural upheaval of that era and through a newfound hope in the resurrection. When many Israelites were persecuted and killed *because of* their covenant loyalty, it was felt that these individuals would not be deprived of the covenant blessings due them. The sufferings of the martyrs could be viewed as a paradigm for the nation's salvation and reinstatement into covenant relationship with God after the exile. The martyrs represented the nation suffering the consequences for its sins and reasserting its covenantal allegiance to God, while there was further hope for a share in the covenant blessings beyond death. In accordance with an emerging apocalyptic vision, there would be a resurrection of God's faithful from the dead. This would coincide with the ultimate establishment of theocratic dominion in a cosmos totally renovated by the Creator, a new creation and kingdom intended for God's people. Resurrection, then, was securely bound up with national hope in the creative power of God, the triumph of the kingdom of God, and Israel's participation in that realm of supremacy and blessing on the basis of her covenant fidelity.

Finally, we will observe that the powerless, poor, and oppressed often clung to the hope of resurrection. Hence, the images of the exodus and the restoration of Israel from the exile were powerful symbols of salvation that were entwined with hope in the resurrection. Yahweh is the God who 'raises up,' both in the sense of exalting the widowed, orphaned, or enslaved, and in causing the dead to live. Those who have been oppressed because of their covenant faithfulness, Yahweh will enthrone before the eyes of their oppressors. Correspondingly, their wealthy, powerful, and godless persecutors will be cast down from their thrones. Thus, four terms sum up the theology outlined above: (new) creation, covenant, exaltation, and resurrection. These four pieces are critical to the theological mosaic of Israel's hope for salvation.

The following survey will be arranged into three general time periods. The first period encompasses those texts written before and up to the time of the Maccabees. The second period ranges from the time of the Maccabees to the destruction of Jerusalem in A.D. 70. The third period concerns those texts written after the fall of Jerusalem to around the end of the first century A.D.

3.1.1 Pre-Maccabean and Maccabean Period

Belief in the resurrection of the dead belongs to the later frontiers of ancient Israelite religion.[4] The dominant Old Testament view of the afterlife described how the dead were deposited in the sepulchres of their ancestors (e.g., Gen 50:13; Josh 24:32; 1 Kgs 2:10; 11:43), but also envisioned the dead continuing in a shadowy (non)existence in a common, subterranean grave called *Sheol*.[5] There are only three examples of actual resurrection in the Hebrew Bible, all of them connected with the prophets Elijah and Elisha (1 Kgs 17:17–24; 2 Kgs 4:32–37; 13:21; cp. Sir 48:13–14). The first undisputed reference to the hope of resurrection in the Old Testament appears in Dan 12:1–3, although earlier glimmers of the concept may be encountered.

3.1.1.1 HOSEA 6:1–3 AND EZEKIEL 37:1–14: PRECURSORS TO RESURRECTION FAITH IN ISRAEL

The eighth-century prophet Hosea writes about the prospect of Israel's revival (6:1–3):

> 'Come, let us return to the LORD;
>   for it is he who has torn, and he will heal us;
>   he has struck down, and he will bind us up.
> After two days he will *revive* us (יְחַיֵּנוּ);
>   on the third day he will *raise us up* (יְקִמֵנוּ),
>   that we may live before him.

---

[4] Otto Kaiser has written that belief in the resurrection from the dead appears only 'at the limits of the Old Testament' (*Isaiah 13–39* [OTL; Philadelphia: Westminster, 1974], 218), while Gerhard von Rad writes: 'The prediction that God will provide a resurrection from the dead of his own people is found in it only peripherally (Is. XXVI. 19; Dan. XII. 2)' (*Old Testament Theology* [2 vols.; San Francisco: Harper & Row, 1965], 2:350).

[5] See Gerhard von Rad, 'Life and Death in the OT,' *TDNT* 2:46–49; Robert Martin-Achard, *From Death to Life: A Study of the Development of the Doctrine of the Resurrection in the Old Testament* (Edinburgh and London: Oliver and Boyd, 1960), 36–46; Edmund F. Sutcliffe, *The Old Testament and the Future Life* (2d ed.; London: Burns Oates & Washbourne, 1947), 36–57. One of the most thorough treatments to date is that of Nicholas J. Tromp, *Primitive Conceptions of Death and the Nether World in the Old Testament* (BibOr 21; Rome: Pontifical Biblical Institute, 1969).

> Let us know, let us press on to know the LORD;
>   his appearing is as sure as the dawn;
>   he will come to us like the showers,
>   like the spring rains that water the earth.'

The Targum explained this passage as a depiction of the eschatological resurrection of Israel,[6] and a number of Church Fathers seized upon it as a prophecy of Jesus' resurrection on the third day.[7] Modern interpreters reject these explanations, but are not united as to whether the passage reflects death and resurrection imagery at all, but rather recovery from sickness, or whether the notion of death and resurrection mirrors that of Canaanite fertility cults.[8] The language is admittedly metaphorical, but its exact function was not satisfactorily identified until J. Wijngaards proposed that the language of death and resurrection falls squarely amongst *covenantal terminology*. Wijngaards demonstrated from a number of ancient Near Eastern texts that it was not uncommon to describe the deposing of a king in terms of killing.[9] 'Killing a king' meant deposing him, and the expression may or may not indicate that the ruler had been physically put to death, as well.[10]

---

[6] *Tg. Neb.* Hos 6:2 reads: 'He will give us life *in the days of consolation that will come; on the day of the resurrection of the dead* he will raise us up and we shall live before him,' in Kevin J. Cathcart and Robert P. Gordon, *The Targum of the Minor Prophets: Translated, with a Critical Introduction, Apparatus, and Notes* (The Aramaic Bible 14; Wilmington, Del.: Michael Glazier, 1989), 41. The omission of any reference to 'the third day' may have been due to anti-Christian polemic.

[7] Tertullian, *Marc.* 4.43.1; Cyprian, *Treatises* 3.2.25; *Test.* 2.25; Lactantius, *Inst.* 4.29; *Epit.* 47; cf. Selby Vernon McCasland, 'The Scripture Basis of "On the Third Day,"' *JBL* 48 (1929): 124–37.

[8] (a) Resurrection: David Allan Hubbard, *Hosea: An Introduction and Commentary* (TOTC 22a; Downers Grove, Ill.: InterVarsity Press, 1989), 125–26; Douglas Stuart, *Hosea-Jonah* (WBC 31; Waco, TX: Word, 1987), 108. (b) Recovery from illness: Hans Walter Wolff, *Hosea* (Hermeneia; Philadelphia: Fortress, 1974), 117; A. A. MacIntosh, *Hosea* (ICC; Edinburgh: T. & T. Clark, 1997), 220–24. (c) Reflective of Canaanite fertility cults: Edmond Jacob, Carl-A. Keller, and Samuel Amsler, *Osée, Joël, Amos, Abdias, Jonas* (3d ed.; CAT 11a; Genève: Labor et Fides, 1992), 51–52; Henry McKeating, *The Books of Amos, Hosea, and Micah* (CBC; Cambridge: Cambridge University Press, 1971), 109.

[9] J. Wijngaards, 'Death and Resurrection in Covenantal Context (Hos. VI 2),' *VT* 17 (1967): 230–32. For example: 'You, Manapa Dattaš, were left by your father as a minor and you were only a boy....Your brothers tried to kill (you) frequently *and they did kill you* (but you) escaped and (they drove you) out of the (land of the River Şeha)' (230, italics are Wijngaards').

[10] Wijngaards ('Death and Resurrection,' 232) notes that 'killing' is an apt descriptor for the deposition of a king: 'The actual death of a king or his military defeat are, of course, so intimately linked with his official dethronement, that it is difficult to draw a

Apropos of the Hosea text are instances when a vassal breaks treaty with his suzerain and is therefore 'killed' (i.e., dethroned) by the latter, but later 'raised to life' (i.e., reinstated as vassal).[11] The pattern is replicated in Hosea. In the Syro-Ephraimitic war, instead of calling upon Yahweh for help, Israel sought the assistance of Tiglath-Pileser: 'When Ephraim saw his sickness, and Judah his wound, then Ephraim went to Assyria, and sent to the great king[12]' (Hos 5:13). As a result, Yahweh ravages Israel like a lion (5:14).[13] Only when Israel acknowledges her treason (5:15), returns to the Lord, and renews her covenant faithfulness will she 'know the Lord' and experience the concomitant covenantal blessings (6:3). Wijngaards suggests that the time markers, 'after two days ...on the third day' (6:2), derive from the practice of solemnizing the covenant 'in the morning on the third day.'[14] Christoph Barth augments this suggestion by pointing to the enactment of the covenant in Exodus 19–20 'on the third day' (19:11, 15–16; cf. 24:4; 34:2, 4).[15]

Hosea 6:1–3 does not substantiate a pre-exilic belief in physical resurrection from the dead,[16] but if the studies of Wijngaards and Barth are correct, the triumvirate of covenant-renewal, enthronement, and resurrection were by this time established in Israelite religious understanding and ritual

---

clear-cut line of distinction between them.' The origin of the expression might have indeed originated from the violent action required to dethrone a king.

[11] A salient example is that of Mattiwaza who requests reinstatement under the king of Hatti: '*If you, my Lord, raise me to life* and the gods come to my support, may then the Suzerain, king of Hatti land...not change Artatama from the throne of his kingdom. But I want to put myself under (the Suzerain's) service and govern the Mitanni land.' Subsequently, the king of Hatti issues the pronouncement: 'I, the Suzerain, king of Hatti, *the dead country Mitanni I raise to life*; I restore it to its old position' (Wijngaards, 'Death and Resurrection,' 233–34, italics his). Notably, both the vassal and the country over which he is to rule are said to be 'raised to life.'

[12] The MT reads מֶלֶךְ יָרֵב ('a king who will contend'), but BHS conjectures רָב (י- being an old nominative termination, see 'יָרֵב,' BDB 937) or מֶלֶךְ רָב ('the great king'; or 'suzerain' as Wijngaards tenders ['Death and Resurrection,' 236]; cf. Hos 10:6; Ps 48:3 MT).

[13] Other passages use more direct language of killing or death: 2:3; 6:5; 9:16; 13:1; esp. 13:14: 'Shall I ransom them from the power of Sheol? Shall I redeem them from Death?'

[14] Wijngaards, 'Death and Resurrection,' 237; cf. Walter Brueggemann, 'Amos iv 4–13 and Israel's Covenant Worship,' *VT* 15 (1965): 1–15.

[15] Christoph Barth, 'Theophanie, Bundschließung und neuer Anfang am dritten Tage,' *EvT* 28 (1968): 521–33, esp. 530–33.

[16] Robert Martin-Achard, however, maintains that Hos 6:2 permits us to affirm that the Israelites were already aware of this idea in the eighth century ('Résurrection dans l'Ancien Testament et le Judaïsme,' *DBSup* 10:445, 469).

practice. Walter Brueggemann has expanded the trio to a quartet by correlating the formula of enthronement in 1 Kgs 16:2–3 (and 1 Sam 2:6–8 and Ps 113:7) with the creation formulas of Gen 2:7 and 3:19.[17] He tracks the intersection of covenant restoration with the 'dust' imagery of royal exaltation and creation in a series of Old Testament texts. The salvation of Israel is effected by the Creator, Yahweh, who can kill as well as bring to life, who brings down to Sheol and raises up from the dust, and who requires a loyal regent in covenant relationship to him.

The creation motif is vividly appropriated in Ezekiel's vision of the restoration of Israel (Ezek 37:1–14). The vision of Israel's reconstitution in the valley of dry bones recalls the creation of Adam from the dust of the ground when God breathed into him and he became a living being (cp. Ezek 37:5–6, 8–10 with Gen 2:7). Although the vision is expressly figurative (see Ezek 37:11), its graphic depiction of resurrection ('I am going to bring you up from your graves,' 37:12–13) accounts for later Jewish and Christian interpretations of it as a prophecy regarding a general resurrection,[18] and may indicate that a familiarity with the concrete notion of physical resurrection underlies the metaphor.[19] The import of the vision, however, is in line with the ensuing promise that Yahweh will return and consolidate both the northern and southern tribes in their land as one Israelite nation, united under a Davidic monarch, cleansed and conscientious of Yahweh's everlasting covenant with them (37:15–28). The pre-exilic and exilic presence of resurrection imagery in Hosea and Ezekiel, then, belongs among the interlocking motifs of creation, covenant-renewal, and exaltation under Yahweh's lordship that form a framework for envisioning God's ultimate salvation/restoration of the people of Israel.

3.1.1.2 ISAIAH 26:19 AND DANIEL 12:1–3:
EARLY WITNESSES TO RESURRECTION

Most scholars can agree on Dan 12:1–3 as the first uncontested reference to future physical resurrection in the Hebrew canon. Others point to Isa 26:19 as the premier reference:

---

[17] Walter Brueggemann, 'From Dust to Kingship,' *ZAW* 84 (1972): 1–18.

[18] Cf. 4Q Second Ezekiel; *Liv. Pro.* 3:12. On rabbinic and patristic interpretations, see Martin-Achard, *From Death to Life*, 93–94. A vivid representation of Ezekiel 37 appears in the paintings of the Dura-Europos synagogue. There it is not bones but dismembered corpses that are rearticulated and then revivified by winged figures resembling Psyches; see Rachel Hachlili, *Ancient Jewish Art and Archaeology in the Diaspora* (HO 1.35; Leiden: Brill, 1998), 124–27 and colour plates III–18, III–19, III–20.

[19] An observation made also by G. Grogan, 'Isaiah,' *ExpBC* 6:167; cf. Ben C. Ollenburger, 'If Mortals Die, Will They Live Again? The Old Testament and Resurrection,' *Ex Auditu* 9 (1993): 37.

> Your dead shall live, their corpses shall rise.
> O dwellers in the dust, awake and sing for joy!
> For your dew is a radiant dew,
> and the earth will give birth to those long dead.

Isaiah 26:19 appears in the so-called 'Apocalypse of Isaiah' (chs. 24–27), which has been the focus of critical disagreements with regard to its date, structure, and perspective (past or futuristic?).[20] Dates ranging from the eighth to the second century B.C. were proposed in the past,[21] but the present range has been narrowed to the sixth and fifth centuries.[22] For our purposes it is needful only to concur with the consensus view that Isaiah 24–27 pre-dates Daniel.

Isaiah 26:19 is interpreted either metaphorically or non-metaphorically. The metaphorical reading of the verse apprehends resurrection as a graphic figure for Israel's return from exile.[23] Two factors typically contribute to this line of interpretation: First, the date of Isa 26:19 (earlier or later) correlates to its metaphorical or non-metaphorical interpretation. As a rule, only a later dating will yield a non-metaphorical interpretation, since it is often asserted that the idea of individual, physical resurrection could not have come to expression in Israel until the emergence of apocalyptic (as in Dan 12:2).[24] Second, the use of the resurrection motif here is often com-

---

[20] For a concise overview of the critical discussions, see Dan G. Johnson, *From Chaos to Restoration: An Integrative Reading of Isaiah 24–27* (JSOTSup 61; Sheffield: Sheffield Academic Press, 1988), 11–17.

[21] On the dating of the 'Isaiah Apocalypse,' see Gerhard F. Hasel, 'Resurrection in the Theology of Old Testament Apocalyptic,' *ZAW* 92 (1980): 268–69; John N. Oswalt, *The Book of Isaiah: Chapters 1–39* (NICOT; Grand Rapids: Eerdmans, 1986), 441–42.

[22] Johnson, *From Chaos to Restoration*, 14. The extremes of the range have been lopped off: an eighth century date linking the prophecy to the historical Isaiah has long been dismissed by critical scholars, and the radical proposal of a late second century date has been eliminated by the discovery of 1QIsa^a.

[23] Commentators who espouse a metaphorical interpretation: P. Auvray, *Isaïe 1–39* (SB; Paris: Gabalda, 1972), 237; Ronald E. Clements, *Isaiah 1–39* (NCB; Grand Rapids: Eerdmans, 1980), 216–17; Georg Fohrer, *Das Buch Jesaja* (2d ed.; ZBK; Zürich and Stuttgart: Zwingli, 1967), 2:31–32; Hans Wildberger, *Jesaja 13–27* (BKAT 10.2; Neukirchen-Vluyn: Neukirchener, 1978), 995; Johnson, *From Chaos to Restoration*, 80.

[24] For example, Otto Kaiser is able to interpret Isa 25:8a and 26:19 non-metaphorically, but only by positing that they are Maccabean interpolations (*Isaiah 13–39*, 218–20). The principal exception, of course, is conservative scholarship that holds to eighth-century, Isaianic authorship *and* a literal reference to physical resurrection in Isa 26:19, e.g., Grogan, 'Isaiah,' *ExpBC* 167; John Mauchline, *Isaiah 1–39: Introduction and Commentary* (TBC; New York: Macmillan, 1962), 193; Alec Motyer, *The Prophecy of Isaiah: An Introduction and Commentary* (Downers Grove, Ill.: InterVarsity Press,

pared to its deployment in Ezek 37:1-14 as a metaphor for the restoration of Israel.

The strongest case for a non-metaphorical reading has been set forth by Gerhard Hasel.[25] Hasel's case is fourfold. (a) The non-metaphorical reading is supported in the co-text of chapter 26. In particular, a metaphorical interpretation does not take into account the eschatologically destined 'righteous' (26:7) and the non-eschatologically destined 'wicked' (26:10). (b) The contrast between the 'righteous' and the 'wicked,' as well as the reference to the entire earth (26:21; see also 26:9), support the universal outlook of the unit. (c) The following verses (26:20-21) do not harmonize well with an interpretation of 26:19 in terms of national or political renaissance. That 'the earth will disclose the blood shed on it, and will no longer cover its slain' (26:21) is in marked contrast to the hope of resurrection in 26:19. (d) Another contrast exists with 26:14:

Isa 26:14   The dead (מֵתִים) do not live (יִחְיוּ);
            shades (רְפָאִים) do not rise (יָקֻמוּ)

Isa 26:19   Your dead (מֵתֶיךָ) shall live (יִחְיוּ),
            their corpses (נְבֵלָתָם)[26] shall rise (יְקוּמוּן)...
            and the earth will give birth
            to those long dead (רְפָאִים).

The natural course of death will overtake the wicked (26:14) but will be mightily overturned on behalf of the righteous (i.e., Yahweh's dead, 26:19). A corroborative piece of evidence is the promise of Isa 25:7 that Yahweh 'will swallow up death forever.'

Hasel makes a compelling case for a non-metaphorical interpretation of Isa 26:19. Arguments (c) and (d) are particularly forceful. The heaping up of vocabulary (noted in parentheses in the above citation)—and signally the use of the word 'corpses'—may alone lead one to the verdict of John Sawyer: 'This is a reference to the resurrection of the dead which no-one but a Sadducee, ancient or modern, could possibly misconstrue.'[27] Yet Hasel goes too far in militating against a metaphorical reading by attempting to obliterate any hint of national restoration in Isaiah 26 and by magnifying the universal thrust of the Isaiah Apocalypse. References to

---

1993), 219-20; Oswalt, *Isaiah*, 441; Edward J. Young, *The Book of Isaiah* (3 vols.; NICOT; Grand Rapids: Eerdmans, 1969), 2:226-27.

[25] Hasel, 'Resurrection in the Theology of OT Apocalyptic,' 271-76.

[26] MT reads נִבְלָתִי, 'my corpse,' which some take as a collective (Kaiser, *Isaiah 1-39*, 215); but modern translators (e.g., NRSV, NASB, NAB, NEB, NLT) normally follow BHS (נִבְלָתָם, 'their corpses').

[27] John F. A. Sawyer, 'Hebrew Words for the Resurrection of the Dead,' *VT* 23 (1973): 234.

'inhabitants of the earth' (26:9, 21) do not erase the special concern of Yahweh for his people. The inhabitants of the earth are in fact pitted against the nation that awaits God's judgment on her enemies (26:7–15). The contrast between the righteous and the wicked in 26:9–10 is clearly a contrast between the righteous of the nation and their unrighteous foes ('we,' 'us' vs. 'they,' 'them' is evident throughout 26:7–15); and this is pointedly brought out in 26:20–21 where 'my people' is juxtaposed with 'the inhabitants of the earth.' Flashes of national interest may be seen in the mention of Yahweh's 'zeal for the people' (26:11) and his enlargement of the nation (26:15). The note of covenant relationship, coupled with what we already know about the Old Testament linkage between the language of resurrection, enthronement, and creation, may point to Isaiah 26 as a victorious song about Israel's exaltation above the nations.[28] While opposing a 'purely hyperbolic'[29] view of this passage, we must not rob it of theological significance. As Günter Stemberger suggests, it is a false dichotomy to separate national restoration from 'a concrete resurrection' in Isa 26:19.[30] The latter functions as the ultimate fulfilment of the former, and this way of thinking has already been paved by Ezekiel (37:1–14). Resurrection is one of the means by which God restores, exalts, and brings Israel into the full realization of his covenant blessings.

Daniel 12:1–3 comprises the climax to the revelation which began in 11:2 regarding a succession of rulers, and Antiochus Epiphanes IV in particular (11:21–45), who pose a threat to the nation of Israel. The appearance of the angelic champion, Michael (12:1), who stands to execute judgment on behalf of God's people, signals the final triumph of Israel over her enemies. After the most monumental distress in the nation's history—akin to Jeremiah's characterization of the exile (Jer 30:7)—Israel will finally experience definitive salvation. But it is not all Israel who will be delivered, but only those registered in 'the book,'[31] that is to say, those who may be accounted as the genuine covenantal people of God (see 11:32).

The passage is woven together with intertextual threads from the prophecy of Isaiah. The first of these is from Isa 26:19:

---

[28] Brueggemann ('From Dust to Kingship,' 11–13) points out the appearance of the 'dust' motif in the only two Old Testament texts which clearly affirm resurrection (Isa 26:19; Dan 12:2) and concludes that *the resurrection of Israel is in fact the enthronement of Israel* among the nations' (13).

[29] T. H. Gaster ('Resurrection,' *IDB* 4:40) thus identifies Isa 26:19.

[30] Günter Stemberger, 'Auferstehung, I/2. Judentum,' *TRE* 4:444 lines 19–23; cf. Ollenburger, 'If Mortals Die,' 39.

[31] This is, no doubt, the 'book of life' (Exod 32:32–33; Ps 69:29; Isa 4:3; Mal 3:16–18), although it is probably associated with the 'books' of judgment in Dan 7:10 and the 'book of truth' in 10:21. A remarkable parallel to Daniel appears in 4QDibHam^a.

Resurrection in Second Temple Judaism

Dan 12:2   Many of those who sleep (מִיְּשֵׁנֵי) in the dust of the earth (עֲפָר־אַדְמַת) shall awake (יָקִיצוּ).

Isa 26:19   O dwellers (שֹׁכְנֵי) in the dust (עָפָר), awake (הָקִיצוּ).

There is virtual unanimity among modern scholars that an actual resurrection is intended in Dan 12:2, due to the additional mention of everlasting destinies: 'some to everlasting life, and some to shame and everlasting contempt.'[32] Whereas in Isa 26:19 there was a resurrection for righteous Israel alone, here it is expanded to include wicked individuals as well.[33]

A second intertextual thread supports the idea of a physical resurrection.[34] The Hebrew term דְּרָאוֹן ('abhorrence, contempt') occurs elsewhere in the Hebrew Bible only at Isa 66:24. There the idyllic life of Israel (in 'the new heavens and the new earth') is contrasted with the final lot of those who sinned against Yahweh: 'And they shall go out and look at the dead bodies of the people who have rebelled against me; for their worm shall not die, their fire shall not be quenched, and they shall be an abhorrence (דֵּרָאוֹן) to all flesh.' The phrasing in Daniel may be drawing upon this scene in which the corpses of the wicked are consigned to the Valley of Hinnom. The nature of resurrection life, however, is not so much the focus in Daniel as is the vindication of God's righteous servants over against the ignominious end for their opponents.[35]

This leads to the third Isaianic thread. Daniel turns his attention toward the fate of those who were martyred under Antiochus Epiphanes IV. The case of the martyrs was a thorny one for the classical Hebrew conception of justice. Acting in covenant-loyalty did not bring them blessing and prosperity (Deut 7:12–26; 11:1–25), but rather sword and flame, captivity and plunder (Dan 11:32–33). Meanwhile, the archenemy of Yahweh exalted himself above every other god (11:36–38), and granted wealth, power, and land to those who acknowledged him (11:39). The injustice of this state of

---

[32] Collins, *Daniel*, 392. Collins also notes that the image of 'awaking from sleep' is used of resurrection in the Pseudepigrapha (*1 En.* 91:10; 92:3; *T. Jud.* 25:4) and later tradition; cf. Sawyer, 'Hebrew Words,' 223–24.

[33] The terseness of the prophecy makes it difficult to determine the scope of Daniel's resurrection: a universal resurrection, a general Israelite resurrection (righteous and unrighteous), a resurrection of righteous Israel as well as Israelite apostates and foreign archenemies, the resurrection of Israel's martyrs and their murderers? See Hasel, 'Resurrection in the Theology of OT Apocalyptic,' 277–80. Here it is only necessary to observe that resurrection is a vehicle for the vindication of faithful Israel and the condemnation of her opponents, however broad or narrow these classifications may be.

[34] So Cavallin, *Life After Death*, 27; Nickelsburg, *Resurrection*, 23; but see Collins, *Daniel*, 393.

[35] Nickelsburg (*Resurrection*, 21–22) has shown this parallel concern in Isa 66:14 and *Jub.* 23:30–31.

affairs must not stand. The martyrs are thus cast in the form of Isaiah's Suffering Servant (Isa 52–53).[36] The martyrs are known as 'the wise' (*maś-kilîm*, מַשְׂכִּלִים; cf. Dan 11:33, 35) and 'those who lead many to righteousness' (מַצְדִּיקֵי הָרַבִּים). Striking parallels occur in the fourth Servant Song, where it is said of the servant, 'Behold, my servant shall prosper (יַשְׂכִּיל[37])' (Isa 52:13a) and, 'The righteous one, my servant, shall make many righteous (וַיַּצְדִּיק צַדִּיק עַבְדִּי לָרַבִּים)' (53:11). Identification with the servant gives credence to the hope that the *maśkilîm* will indeed be rewarded for their devotion. Having been condemned to death in a human court, they will be vindicated in the divine court. Like the servant, they will be exalted ('he shall be exalted and lifted up, and shall be very high,' Isa 52:13b): they shall 'shine like the brightness of the sky...like the stars forever and ever' (Dan 12:3). Stars were associated with heavenly beings or angels (Dan 8:10; cf. Judg 5:20; Job 38:7), and so the eternal life of the martyrs is described as an angel-like existence (as in *1 En.* 39:5; 104:2–6; *2 Bar.* 51:10–11; *T. Mos.* 10:99; cf. *4 Ezra* 7:[97], 55 [125]). Although not impossible, an actual celestial transformation is probably not in view.[38] The use of simile (with the preposition כְּ) may be pressed to yield a figurative meaning,[39] and this is all the more likely in light of the use of star imagery to indicate royal position.[40] In any event, the restoration and triumph of righteous Israel and her 'best and brightest' (cf. Dan 11:35) are effected in part through resurrection, and the astral imagery is doubtless evocative of

---

[36] Scholars generally agree that Daniel has embraced the Suffering Servant figure in his portrayal of the *maśkilîm*; see Cavallin, *Life After Death*, 27; M. Delcor, *Le Livre de Daniel* (SB; Paris: Gabalda, 1971), 256; Collins, *Daniel*, 393; Martin-Achard, *From Death to Life*, 143–44; Nickelsburg, *Resurrection*, 24–26; H. L. Ginsberg, 'The Oldest Interpretation of the Suffering Servant,' *VT* 3 (1953): 401–4.

[37] Lit. 'act with insight, devotion, piety,' see 'I שָׂכַל," in *A Concise Hebrew and Aramaic Lexicon of the Old Testament* (ed. William L. Holladay; Leiden: Brill, 1988), 352. LXX translates συνήσει. Martin-Achard remarks: 'The connexion between wisdom in all its aspects—cleverness, acumen, understanding (practical rather than intellectual), not excluding the fear of God—and prosperity is one of the favourite themes of Wisdom thought in Israel; but here the stress must be laid on the success which is the consequence of wisdom, and the glory which is its outcome' (*From Death to Life*, 109 n. 21).

[38] *Pace* Cavallin (*Life After Death*, 27) and Collins (*Daniel*, 393–94).

[39] Nickelsburg, *Resurrection*, 26; John E. Goldingay, *Daniel* (WBC 30; Dallas, Tex.: Word, 1989), 308–9. Goldingay, following Walter Wifall ('The Status of "Man" as Resurrection,' *ZAW* 90 [1978]: 382–94), sees the *maśkilîm* as obtaining what pre-exilic tribal chieftains were thought to have possessed: a noble position in Yahweh's council.

[40] Num 24:17; Judg 5:20; Isa 14:12–14; Dan 8:10; Wis 13:2; 2 Macc 9:10. Exaltation to the heavens has an analogous function, see Gen 11:9; Jer 51:53; Lam 2:1; Dan 4:11, 20, 22; 7:13.

enthronement (Isa 14:12–14; *Pss. Sol.* 1:5; *T. Levi* 18:3; *T. Jud.* 24:1). Daniel himself is counted among those who will participate in the resurrection to eternal life. The prophecy closes with a heavenly injunction to him: 'But you, go your way, and rest; you shall rise for your reward at the end of the days' (12:13).

In sum, Isa 26:19 and Dan 12:1–3 contain the interrelated motifs of resurrection, covenant-loyalty, and enthronement/exaltation that we have detected in Hosea 6 and Ezekiel 37. The raising up of bodies from the dust of the earth also echoes the motif of creation. Resurrection belongs within the context of eschatological judgment when the righteous are raised and vindicated in the presence of their foes—whether that means the wicked do not rise at all (Isa 26:14, 20–21) or are raised only to be consigned to endless shame and abhorrence (Dan 12:2). In short, resurrection from the dead is instrumental in the definitive salvation of the nation of Israel, or at least of a remnant that is faithful to Yahweh. The resurrection is expressed as the hope of the oppressed and persecuted people of God who long for the realization of God's kingdom when their wicked oppressors will be judged and destroyed. As for the nature of resurrection, in Isa 26:19 it is likely corporeal, although this may not be determinative on the basis of the MT alone. The LXX, however, quite clearly renders it as a prophecy concerning physical resurrection from the dead: ἀναστήσονται οἱ νεκροί καὶ ἐγερθήσονται οἱ ἐν τοῖς μνημείοις. The Daniel text even more clearly relates a corporeal resurrection. If we can be less sure about the nature of resurrection represented in the earliest texts (Hos 6:1–3 and Ezek 37:1–14), we can be certain that the theological meaning of resurrection that we have been outlining is securely and consistently grounded in all of the Scriptures we have looked at thus far.[41]

3.1.2 From the Maccabean Period to the Dawn of Christianity (pre-70 A.D.)

From the time Alexander the Great hurtled Palestine into the Hellenistic Age, forms of Greek thought had a profound effect upon Second Temple

---

[41] Cf. N. T. Wright, *The New Testament and the People of God* (Minneapolis: Fortress, 1992) 322. A wide-sweeping study of the overarching theme of Israel's exile (=death) and restoration (=resurrection) in the OT prophetic books would enrich our own study, but it is impossible to pursue within the compass of this chapter, which is focused upon resurrection texts per se. Moreover, such a study has already been undertaken by Donald E. Gowan, *Theology of the Prophetic Books: The Death and Resurrection of Israel* (Louisville, Ky.: Westminster John Knox, 1998).

Judaism.⁴² The effect was no less felt in the domain of thought regarding the afterlife. The book of *Jubilees* may reflect a dualistic view of the human person due to Hellenistic influence (23:31):

> And their bones will rest in the earth,
> and their spirits will increase joy,
> and they will know that the Lord is an executor of judgment.

Some think this text envisages a spiritual resurrection of sorts,⁴³ while others think it reflects the Greek concept of the immortality of the soul.⁴⁴ Other Jews chafed at Hellenistic conceptions of the afterlife. Qoheleth dismissed the popular Greek notion that a deceased person's soul soared to the heavens, into the aether, the habitation of the gods (3:19–21).⁴⁵ Rather, it is merely human 'breath' that returns to the Creator who gave it (12:7). Ben Sirach, too, held tenaciously to a classical Hebrew anthropology. Human beings were created from the earth, and that is where they return when they die (Sir 16:30; 17:1; 40:1, 11; 41:10); death is inevitable for them (14:12–19); they should be true to the Lord and experience his blessings while they are alive (17:27–30; 28:6; 41:4), for their lot is 'maggots and vermin and worms' (10:11); thus they are definitely not immortal (ἀθάνατος, 17:30; cf. 44:9). In addition to countering the notion of an immortal soul, Ben Sirach may have disputed the idea of resurrection (38:21).⁴⁶ During the course of hellenization in Palestine, the Hebrew understanding of the afterlife seems to have undergone a process of modification, and was the subject of lively debate. At the risk of oversimplification, one may say that the classical Hebrew position championed by Ben Sirach was pulled in one of two directions: (a) toward belief in resurrection from the dead; or (b) belief in the immortality of the soul.⁴⁷ It is the first of these directions that interests us.

---

⁴² For an overview, see Martin Hengel, *Judaism and Hellenism: Studies in Their Encounter in Palestine during the Early Hellenistic Period* (2 vols.; Minneapolis: Fortress Press, 1974).

⁴³ Hengel, *Judaism and Hellenism*, 1:198–99; Nickelsburg, *Resurrection*, 32.

⁴⁴ Cavallin, *Life After Death*, 38.

⁴⁵ Hengel, *Judaism and Hellenism*, 1:123–24.

⁴⁶ See Gabriele Boccaccini, *Middle Judaism: Jewish Thought, 300 B.C.E. to 200 B.C.E.* (Minneapolis: Fortress, 1991), 120. However, Sirach does make explicit mention of the resurrection performed by Elijah (48:5; see also 48:14).

⁴⁷ We speak of oversimplification because, as we shall see, these two options are not always mutually exclusive in the sources that have come down to us. The fundamental defect of Oscar Cullmann's controversial study (*Immortality of the Soul or Resurrection of the Dead? The Witness of the New Testament* [London: Epworth, 1958]) was precisely his assumption that there existed a definitive Jewish or Christian view of the afterlife that was somehow hermetically sealed from Hellenistic influences. The intertestamental and NT data do not yield easily to Cullmann's imposition of purity and

3.1.2.1 SECOND MACCABEES: THE HOPE OF PHYSICAL RESURRECTION

If Ben Sirach has offered something of an apology for the classical Hebrew view of the afterlife, then in 2 Maccabees[48] we have an apologetic concern for hope in the resurrection. Belief in the resurrection of the dead is most forcefully and repeatedly expressed in the centrepiece of the book, the account of the martyrdom of seven brothers and their mother (7:1–42).[49] The martyrdom of the seven brothers is preceded by the exemplary martyrdom of the aged Eleazar (6:18–31; esp. 6:28, 31); and the two martyrdom sequences are joined to the foregoing account of atrocities against pious Jews (6:1–11) by an explanation of such calamities as divine discipline for the nation's sins (6:12–17). After the dramatic martyrdom of the seven brothers is concluded, the successful revolt of Judas Maccabeus commences in chapter eight, after 'the wrath of the Lord had turned to mercy' (8:5).

The seven brothers and their mother are brought before Antiochus Epiphanes IV and compelled to eat swine's flesh, but all of them rebuff him and are subsequently slaughtered in a variety of grisly forms. The serial martyrdoms are punctuated with statements of hope in the resurrection from the dead. The second brother rails against Antiochus (7:9):

> 'You accursed wretch, you dismiss us from this present life (ἐκ τοῦ παρόντος... ζῆν), but the King of the universe will raise us up to an everlasting renewal of life (εἰς αἰώνιον ἀναβίωσιν ζωῆς ἡμᾶς ἀναστήσει), because we have died for his laws.'

The third brother bravely puts out his tongue and extends his hands (7:11):

---

logical consistency. See Nickelsburg's critique, 'Appendix: Some Presuppositions of Cullmann's Essay on *Immortality of the Soul or Resurrection of the Dead*,' in *Resurrection*, 177–80.

[48] 2 Maccabees may have been written during the first half of the first century B.C., but it is an epitome of the five-volume work of Jason of Cyrene (cf. 2:19–32) who perhaps wrote contemporaneously with or soon after the events recounted. There is no unanimity regarding its date of composition: (a) the last quarter of the second century B.C.—John J. Collins, *Daniel, First Maccabees, Second Maccabees with an Excursus on the Apocalyptic Genre* (OTM 16; Wilmington, Del.: Michael Glazier, 1981), 261–63; (b) first century B.C.—John R. Bartlett, *The First and Second Books of the Maccabees* (CBC; Cambridge: Cambridge University Press, 1973), 215; (c) between 78/7 and 63 B.C.—Jonathan A. Goldstein, *II Maccabees* (AB 41a; Garden City, N.Y.: Doubleday, 1983), 71–83; (d) early first century A.D.—Solomon Zeitlin, ed., *The Second Book of Maccabees* (JAL; New York: Harper & Brothers, 1954), 27–30.

[49] Although resurrection is mentioned in a couple other passages (12:44–45; 14:45–46). According to Stemberger (*Leib*, 14–15) hope in the resurrection is implicit, too, in the account of Eleazar's martyrdom (6:18–31).

'I got these (ταῦτα) from Heaven, and because of his laws I disdain them (ταῦτα), and from him I hope (ἐλπίζω) to get them (ταῦτα) back again.'

The fourth brother contrasts the fate of the martyrs with that of the king (7:14):

'One cannot but choose to die at the hands of mortals and to cherish the hope (τὰς...ἐλπίδας) God gives of being raised again by him (πάλιν ἀναστήσεσθαι ὑπ' αὐτοῦ). But for you there will be no resurrection to life (ἀνάστασις εἰς ζωήν)!'

Before the seventh brother is martyred, the mother offers a speech in which the theological rationale for resurrection is presented (7:22–23). She expresses the mystery of birth and creation known only to the Creator who gives breath and life (τὸ πνεῦμα καὶ τὴν ζωήν) and who, she is confident, will restore her sons to life because of their covenant loyalty. The mother reinforces the seventh brother's courage to die nobly in allegiance to God's law, using similar creational language (7:27–29). Finally, before his death the seventh brother expresses hope in the resurrection (7:36):

'For our brothers after enduring a brief suffering have inherited eternal life,[50] under God's covenant (ἀενάου ζωῆς ὑπὸ διαθήκην θεοῦ πεπτώκασιν); but you, by the judgment of God, will receive just punishment for your arrogance.'

A detailed exegesis of 2 Maccabees 7 is impossible within the compass of this chapter. Yet a series of observations is in order under our two points of investigation regarding (1) the nature and (2) the theological significance of resurrection.

(1) As to the nature of resurrection, 2 Maccabees conceives of it as a post-mortem embodied existence.

---

[50] Here we have varied from the NRSV's 'have drunk of ever-flowing life,' which is based upon the emendation πεπώκασιν ('they have drunk') instead of πεπτώκασιν ('they have fallen'); cf. Bartlett (*First and Second Books of the Maccabees*, 276), Félix Marie Abel (*Les Livres des Maccabées* [Ebib; Paris: Gabalda, 1949], 380), NEB, NAB, and REB who all favour this emendation. Translators have struggled, as well, with how to construe the genitive phrase ἀενάου ζωῆς: (a) with the preceding clause (as in the NEB; H. Bückers, 'Das "ewige Leben" in 2 Makk 7:36,' *Bib* 21 [1940]: 406–12; and Stemberger, *Leib*, 22); or (b) with the following clause (NRSV; NEB margin; NAB; and Sidney Tedesche's translation in Zeitlin, *Second Book of Maccabees*, 169). The Greek MSS have no variants that warrant emendation; and the Latin Vulgate, other Latin versions, and Jossipon follow the latter construal of ἀενάου ζωῆς (Zeitlin, *Second Book of Maccabees*, 168). Goldstein (*II Maccabees*, 317) holds (a) that the genitive may be used with verbs of inheritance (following Raphael Kühner and Bernhard Gerth, *Ausführliche Grammatik der griechischen Sprache* [Hannover and Leipzig: Hahn, 1898–1900], 1:349–40); (b) that πεπτώκασιν means 'they have fallen heir to' (cf. 'πίπτω,' B, V, 1 and 3 in LSJ 1407); and (c) translates, 'My brothers, having borne pain for a short while, now have inherited eternal life under the terms of God's covenant' (291).

(a) The resurrection of the martyrs is depicted in crudely physical terms. The third brother's statement (7:11), with the thrice-repeated ταῦτα[51] referring to his dismembered tongue and extremities, is echoed later during the suicide of Razis, who hurls his entrails into a crowd, 'calling upon the Lord of life and spirit[52] to give them (ταῦτα) back to him again' (14:46).

(b) 2 Maccabees 7 has drawn from Dan 12:2 LXX at two points. The second brother's statement reflects the language of Daniel, but with the pleonastic inclusion of the term ἀναβίωσις ('revivification,' 7:9). The fourth brother, too, recalls Dan 12:2 in his exclusion of the king from ἀνάστασις εἰς ζωήν (7:14). The import of these allusions is not to indicate a resurrection only for the martyrs or righteous Israel, but to hint at the Danielic *kinds* of resurrection that both they and the king may expect.[53] The fact that 2 Maccabees draws from Daniel points to the resurrection as a decisive future event, and this is further reflected in the language of expectation (προσδοκάω, 7:14; 12:44) and hope (ἐλπίζω, 7:11; ἐλπις, 7:14, 20) of being 'raised again' (πάλιν ἀναστήσεσθαι, 7:14), as well as in the second brother's contrast between 'this present life' and the resurrection 'to an everlasting renewal of life' (7:9).[54]

(c) The mother invokes the power of God as Creator of the world and giver of life in the womb. Her use of the expression 'life and breath' (7:22, 23; cf. 14:46) surely harks back to Gen 2:7 (cf. 6:17; 7:15, 22; see also Job 10:8–12). The phrasing may additionally be designed to counter the sort of scepticism in Qoheleth 12:7. The mother's words advance the *a fortiori*

---

[51] Abel (*Maccabées*, 374) notes: 'La répétition de ταῦτα est voulue pour exprimer l'identité du corps mortel et de celui qui sera reconstitué à la résurrection.'

[52] NRSV has 'life and spirit' here, while it translates the same expression (more appropriately, we think) as 'life and breath' in 2 Macc 7:22, 23.

[53] Abel, *Maccabées*, 374–75; Goldstein, *II Maccabees*, 305–6.

[54] Note the careful parallelism in the second brother's statement:
σὺ μέν ἀλάστωρ

ἐκ τοῦ παρόντος	ἡμᾶς ζῆν	ἀπολύεις
ὁ δὲ τοῦ κόσμου βασιλεὺς	ἀποθανόντας ἡμᾶς ὑπὲρ τῶν αὐτοῦ νόμων	
εἰς αἰώνιον ἀναβίωσιν	ζωῆς ἡμᾶς	ἀναστήσει.

This twofold delineation juxtaposes the present dismissal from life by the wicked king (note the present tense participle παρόντος and verb ἀπολύεις) with the future resurrection (future tense ἀναστήσει) and eternal state (εἰς αἰώνιον ἀναβίωσιν ζωῆς) initiated by the King of the universe. There is nothing in 2 Maccabees to support Ulrich Kellermann's contention that upon death the martyrs are immediately taken into heaven (*Auferstanden in den Himmel* [SBS 95; Stuttgart: Katholisches Bibelwerk, 1979], 63–73). Martin-Achard ('Résurrection,' 461–62) thinks the timing of the resurrection cannot be determined from 2 Maccabees, and that 'la date de l'événement dont il veut fonder la certitude sur la doctrine du Dieu créateur est moins importante que le fait lui-même' (464).

argument that if God is able to create the world *ex nihilo*, then how much more conceivable is it that God can reconstitute a human being, who once existed, from the dead!⁵⁵

(d) Finally, it may be observed that the author of 4 Maccabees, who utilized 2 Maccabees 7 as the principal source for his own expanded account of the seven martyrs, has assiduously avoided the resurrectional orientation of 2 Maccabees.⁵⁶ In its place is a pronounced belief in the immortality of the soul.⁵⁷ Eleazar's martyrdom is depicted in nautical terms as his having

---

⁵⁵ Goldstein, *II Maccabees*, 307-11. Stemberger (*Leib*, 19-20, 24) puts great emphasis upon the mother's analogy of creation, and believes that resurrection is thereby presented as an entirely new creation and not as the revivification of corpses. Yet the literalistic language of 7:11 and 14:46, the indebtedness to Dan 12:2 (which speaks of an awakening of 'those who sleep in the dust of the earth'), as well as the mother's own words of expectation about the resurrection of her sons (7:23, 29) indicate a continuity between dead and resurrected bodies, however crude that may appear to us. The only instances of actual resurrection recounted in the Old Testament support this concrete manner of description (1 Kgs 17:17-24; 2 Kgs 4:32-37; 13:21; cp. Sir 48:13-14). We have already pointed out the graphic depiction of Yahweh opening tombs and bringing Israelites up out of them in Ezekiel 37—a passage which also reverberates with the creation motif. The mother trusts that God will 'give back again' her sons' 'life and breath' (N.B. the redundant phrase, πάλιν ἀποδίδωσιν, employed also by Razis in 14:46 [πάλιν ἀποδοῦναι] regarding the recovery of his entrails from 'the Lord of life and breath.') Equally telling is her expectation that she will 'get back' her sons (7:29). The verb used here is κομίζω, and it may be used generally in the sense of getting something back (as in 7:11), but its collocation with death here evokes the image of dead bodies being carried off to be buried (cf. 2 Macc 9:8, 10, 29; 12:39; Luke 7:12; Herodotus 4.71; see 'κομίζω,' II, 1 in LSJ 975). The mother views the funeral procession in reverse, receiving her sons back from the dead. Another observation should be made about Judas's concern that pagan talismans were found on the bodies of his fallen warriors, and that prayers and sacrifices be offered for them on account of the resurrection (2 Macc 12:39-45). The narrator of 2 Maccabees comments on this action: 'For if he were not expecting that those who had fallen would rise again (εἰ μὴ γὰρ τοὺς προπεπτωκότας ἀναστῆναι προσεδόκα), it would have been superfluous and foolish to pray for the dead' (12:44). Judas's focus is said to have been upon 'those who had fallen' (12:44), 'those who had died' (τῶν τεθνηκότων, 12:40, 45), or 'the dead' (νεκρῶν, 'corpses,' 12:44).

⁵⁶ On 2 Maccabees as a source for 4 Maccabees, see Jan Willem van Henten, *The Maccabean Martyrs as Saviours of the Jewish People: A Study of 2 and 4 Maccabees* (JSJSup 57; Leiden: Brill, 1997), 70-73, and the literature cited there.

⁵⁷ There is a catena of what might be called 'resurrection proof-texts' (including Ezek 37:2-3 and Deut 32:39) in 4 Macc 18:13-19, but they are offered without commentary and do not necessitate an interpretation in terms of bodily resurrection (see Cavallin, *Life After Death*,122-23). Additionally, there is a question about the textual integrity of 18:6-19; see Stephen D. Moore and Janice Capel Anderson, 'Taking It Like a Man: Masculinity in 4 Maccabees,' *JBL* 117 (1998): 270 n. 61.

'sailed into the haven of immortal victory (ἐπὶ τὸν τῆς ἀθανάτου νίκης λιμένα)' (4 Macc 7:3). The commentary upon the gruesome torture of the first brother is that he was 'as though transformed by fire into immortality (εἰς ἀφθαρσίαν)' (9:22). The seven youths are pictured 'as though running the course toward immortality (ὥσπερ ἐπ' ἀθανασίας ὁδόν)' (14:4–5). The conclusion to the book underscores this view of the afterlife (16:23–24):

> But the sons of Abraham with their victorious mother are gathered together into the chorus of the fathers, and have received pure and immortal souls (ψυχὰς ἁγνὰς καὶ ἀθανάτους) from God, to whom be glory forever and ever. Amen.

Interestingly, the vocabulary of immortality is shared in the Alexandrian canon (LXX) almost exclusively by the Wisdom of Solomon and 4 Maccabees.[58] The narrator of 4 Maccabees, evidently, has deliberately rejected the belief in physical resurrection set forth in 2 Maccabees.

(2) As to the theological significance of resurrection in 2 Maccabees:

(a) This may be approached first by discussing the identity of the mother and the seven brothers. That they are a stylized cast of characters is apparent from the existence of comparable tales, such as that of Taxo and his seven sons (*T. Mos.* 9:1–7), that of a Hebrew who slew his wife, seven children, and himself to escape enslavement (Josephus, *Ant.* 14.15.5 §429), among others.[59] Moreover, 'seven sons' indicates the ideal number and gender of progeny in the Hebrew Bible (Ruth 4:15; Job 1:2; 42:13; 1 Sam 2:5; Jer 15:9). In 2 Maccabees the seven brothers stand for the entire nation of Israel. As already noted, the martyrdoms are introduced by a statement explaining their function in God's discipline of the nation for its sins (6:12–17). The martyrdom of Eleazar follows as the frontispiece for the martyrdom of the seven. His death is regarded as paradigmatic 'to the great body of his nation' (6:31). Then the story of the seven brothers and their mother is recounted, and all throughout it there is an awareness that what is of concern is God's relationship, not simply with an isolated family, but with an entire people (7:6, 16, 18–19, 30–38).

---

[58] The terms ἀθανασία / ἀθάνατος occur only in 4 Macc (14:5; 16:13 / 7:3; 14:6; 18:23), Wis (3:4; 4:1; 8:13, 17; 15:3 / 1:15), and Sir (/ 17:30, but only to deny immortality). Likewise, the occurrences of ἀφθαρσία are isolated to 4 Macc (9:22; 17:12) and Wis (2:23; 6:18, 19; ἄφθαρτος also occurs at 12:1; 18:4). For more on the conception of immortality in the Wisdom of Solomon, see James M. Reese, *Hellenistic Influence on the Book of Wisdom and Its Consequences* (AnBib 41; Rome: Pontifical Biblical Institute, 1970), 62–71; and Michael Kolarcik, *The Ambiguity of Death in the Book of Wisdom 1–6: A Study of Literary Structure and Interpretation* (AnBib 127; Rome: Pontifical Biblical Institute, 1991), 144–46, 149–51.

[59] See Collins, *Daniel, 1–2 Maccabees*, 310; van Henten, *Maccabean Martyrs*, 4 n. 12.

(b) Israel's covenant relationship with God forms the core of the story. The first brother quotes from the 'Song of Moses' (or the 'song that bore witness against the people' [7:6], a title derived from Deut 31:21), but the brief citation from Deut 32:36 serves to recollect the whole song's flow of thought recapitulated in 2 Maccabees 7.[60] The song sounds out faith in God's creation/birthing and election of Israel (Deut 32:4–9, 18; cp. 2 Macc 7:23, 28); his punishment of its waywardness (Deut 32:19–26; 2 Macc 6:12–17; 7:32–33); his concern that Israel's enemies will misconstrue his judgments upon the nation as their own triumph (Deut 32:27–33; 2 Macc 7:18–19, 34); and his consequent vengeance against Israel's enemies (Deut 32:35, 40–43; 2 Macc 7:16–17, 19, 31, 35–36) and vindication of his people (Deut 32:36–39; 2 Macc 7:6, 9, 14, 16–17, 33, 36–38). In 2 Maccabees the vindication is called for because the martyrs are dying for God's laws (6:23, 28; 7:2, 9, 11, 23, 30, 36–37). But the blessings of the covenant that are due to God's servants, with whom he will once again be reconciled (7:33; cf. 1:5), will be realized only through resurrection from the dead (7:9, 14, 23, 29, 36). Perhaps it is not coincidental that in the 'Song of Moses' Yahweh declares, 'I kill and I make alive' (Deut 32:39).[61] Equally apropos is the admonition of Moses that obedience to the law is no trivial matter, but it is 'your life,' and through it long life in the land is made possible (Deut 32:47). And so the martyrs in 2 Maccabees, who have died for God's laws, will be raised up to 'an everlasting renewal of life' (7:9), and 'after enduring brief suffering have inherited eternal life, under God's covenant' (7:36).

(c) Finally, the connection of resurrection with the notion of 'Sin-Exile-Return' is close at hand. This may be seen most clearly in the speeches of the mother (2 Macc 7:22–23, 27–29) which bear a resemblance to the words of Mother Zion in Baruch (4:11, 19, 21–23). Both mothers lament over their exiled children. They speak of giving birth to them and nurturing them. They encourage them as they fall into the clutches of foreign oppressors,[62] and hope to receive them back in accordance with God's mercy.[63] Paradoxically, the brothers say that they are not only dying for God's laws, but 'on our own account, because of our sins against our own God' (2 Macc 7:18; cf. 7:32). The death of the seven brothers, therefore, dramatizes how the wrath of God is at last spent on a nation that has strayed from God's

---

[60] The *Testament of Moses* likewise recasts Deut 31–34; cf. Nickelsburg, *Resurrection*, 29, 97.

[61] Cf. also the Song of Hannah, esp. 1 Sam 2:5b–6: 'The barren has borne seven.... The Lord kills and brings to life; he brings down to Sheol and raises up.'

[62] The language difference between Antiochus and the Hebrews is highlighted in 2 Macc 7:21, 27; cp. Bar 4:15.

[63] Nickelsburg, *Resurrection*, 106–107.

covenant, is now bearing the punishment for its sins (as though yet in exile), and will ultimately be restored through the mercies of a God who has not forsaken his people (6:16; 7:16).[64] The compassion extended to God's servants and the promises of the divine covenant are not forfeited by cruel torture and death. At the resurrection God's covenant blessings will be realized everlastingly in a renewed creation.[65]

In sum, 2 Maccabees views the resurrection as a decisive future event, much like Daniel envisioned it. It is conceived of in quite literal, physical terms—to the extent of presuming continuity between the dead and resurrected body, down to specific parts of the body, even the viscera. The seven brothers are typical of the entire nation of Israel. Resurrection from the dead carries with it the ultimate fulfilment of God's covenant blessings for Israel, and its theological significance is expressed under the figures of God's creation and election of the nation and her restoration from exile. Second Maccabees 7 fits well within the theological framework of creation, covenant, exaltation, and resurrection.

3.1.2.2 THE RESURRECTION IN *FIRST ENOCH*

One of the earliest extant witnesses to Jewish belief in the resurrection of individuals is in *1 Enoch* 22.[66] Enoch is shown the various chambers into which the dead are separated, and he is informed that at the day of judgment those sinners who have already been recompensed for their sins 'shall be together with (other) criminals who are like them, (whose) souls will not be killed on the day of judgment but will not rise from there' (22:13b).[67]

---

[64] Second Maccabees does not explicitly present the martyrdoms of the seven brothers as vicarious atonement for the sins of the nation. The interpretation of their deaths as 'an atoning sacrifice' is distinctly set forth in 4 Macc 17:21–22 (cf. 1:11; 6:28–29).

[65] Nickelsburg traces the post-exilic hopes of Baruch to Second and Third Isaiah. There the return from exile is paired with the vision of a new creation (*Resurrection*, 107). Less convincing is Nickelsburg's attempt to establish a conceptual linkage between 2 Maccabees 7 and the Servant of Isaiah (and the parallel tradition of Wis 2, 4–5). Glaringly absent from 2 Maccabees 7, as Nickelsburg admits (104), is the mention of the seven brothers being exalted. Furthermore, the brothers are not represented as innocent victims, for they express their own solidarity with the nation in its sins.

[66] *1 En.* 1–36 comprises a subunit known as 'The Book of Watchers' which may be dated at least to the first half of the second century B.C., since the mid-second century *Jubilees* presupposes it; see Albert-Marie Denis, *Introduction aux pseudépigraphes grecs d'Ancien Testament* (SVTP 1; Leiden: Brill, 1970), 26; John J. Collins, *The Apocalyptic Imagination: An Introduction to Jewish Apocalyptic Literature* (BRS; 2d ed.; Grand Rapids: Eerdmans, 1998), 47.

[67] This section is extant in Greek, which at this location reads, '...but will not rise (μετεγέρθωσιν) from there' (see Cavallin, *Life After Death*, 41).

We may presume that the righteous dead *will be* resurrected. Some scholars believe that a spiritual resurrection is intended,[68] but it is more likely that the 'old nondualistic view' is at work here.[69] The shades of the dead are emerging from a cavernous Sheol. The passage is significant in that it associates resurrection with the final destiny of individuals on the great day of judgment.

There are two references to the resurrection in *1 Enoch* that are clearly dependent upon Dan 12:2–3. In the midst of a passage in which the way of righteousness is encouraged and the way of wrongdoing is said to be doomed to destruction, we read (91:10):[70]

> And the righteous shall arise from their sleep,
> And wisdom shall arise and be given unto them.

In the 'Epistle of Enoch' the righteous are offered hope in tumultuous times (92:3–55):

> And the righteous shall awake from sleep,
> He shall arise and proceed in the ways of righteousness,
> And all his paths and conversation shall be in eternal goodness and grace
> And he (the great Holy One) will be gracious to the righteous and give him eternal uprightness,
> And he will give him power so that he shall execute judgement with goodness and righteousness,
> And he shall walk in eternal light.
> And sin shall perish in darkness for ever,
> And shall no more then appear from that day for evermore.

In both of these passages the echoes of Dan 12:2–3 are clearly discernible, and so we may safely presume that a corporeal resurrection is in mind. Both passages reserve resurrection for the righteous. The latter text describes a state of eternal righteousness in which the resurrected are granted authority to rule.

---

[68] Cavallin, *Life After Death*, 41–42.

[69] Richard Bauckham, 'Life, Death, and the Afterlife in Second Temple Judaism,' in *Life in the Face of Death: The Resurrection Message in the New Testament* (McMNTS; ed. Richard N. Longenecker; Grand Rapids: Eerdmans, 1998), 88; A. J. M. Wedderburn, *Baptism and Resurrection: Studies in Pauline Theology against Its Graeco-Roman Background* (WUNT 44; Tübingen: Mohr-Siebeck, 1987), 173–76. This finds support in Martinez's conclusion that the eschatology of *1 En.* 22 developed 'prior to the hellenisation of Palestine' and was 'detached from the body of problems typical of the 2nd century B.C.'; Florentino Garcia Martinez, *Qumran and Apocalyptic: Studies on the Aramaic Texts from Qumran* (STDJ 9; Leiden: Brill, 1992), 71–72.

[70] The translations of 1 Enoch are from Matthew Black, *The Book of Enoch or 1 Enoch: A New English Edition with Commentary and Textual Notes* (SVTP 7; Leiden: Brill, 1985).

The 'Similitudes of Enoch' (37–71) are of a different complexion than the rest of *1 Enoch*,[71] and contain tantalizing eschatological information for our investigation of the resurrection in Luke-Acts. The first reference to resurrection is in 51:1:

> And in those days shall the earth give back that which has been entrusted to it,
> And Sheol shall give back that which has been committed to it,
> And Abaddon shall repay that which it owes.

The synonymous parallelism reiterates the understanding that resurrection will involve the dead coming up out of the ground.[72] The resurrection is an eschatological event, taking place 'in those days,' and comprises a key component in the definitive salvation of the righteous (51:2):

> And he shall choose the righteous and holy from among them,
> For the day has drawn nigh that they should be saved.

The resurrection seems to be universal, thus requiring such a selection of the righteous.[73] The appearance of the Elect One is central to this scene, and to the execution of divine judgment throughout the Similitudes. Here he is said to have been designated and glorified by the Lord of spirits to sit on a throne (51:3). The celebration of salvation resonates with the sounds of the exodus and the entrance (or return from exile) into the promised land (51:4–5):

> And in those days shall the mountains leap like rams,
> And the hills also shall skip like lambs satisfied with milk,[74]
> And all will become angels in heaven.
> Their faces will shine with joy, for in those days the Elect one shall arise and the earth shall rejoice.
> And the righteous shall dwell upon it and the elect shall go and walk thereon.[75]

The note that 'all will become angels in heaven' (51:4c) likely functions as an expression of the regal authority in which the righteous will share, rather than as an indication of celestial metamorphosis, given a co-text with the

---

[71] The scholarly consensus at the *SNTS* Pseudepigrapha Seminar in Tübingen (1977) and Paris (1978) considered the Similitudes as Jewish and dated them to the first century A.D.; see E. Isaac, '1 (Ethiopic Apocalypse of) Enoch," *OTP* 1:7. George W. E. Nickelsburg ('Enoch, First Book of," *ABD* 2:512–13) states that most scholars date the Similitudes to the first half of the first century B.C. or the first three quarters of the first century A.D.

[72] Cavallin, *Life After Death*, 45.

[73] However, *1 En.* 46:6 might mean that the powerful will be barred from resurrection.

[74] Cf. Ps 114:4, 6; Wis 19:9.

[75] Cf. Gen 13:17; Deut 5:33; 8:1; 11:9; 12:1, 10; 30:16, 20; 32:47; etc. See also Isa 35:9–10; Bar 5:5–9; Pss 37:29; 69:36.

accompanying similes of leaping mountains and skipping hills. The image is carried forward through a reference to luminous joy.[76] The scene, moreover, is otherwise manifestly terrestrial.

The most provocative aspect of the Similitudes is the role of the Elect One, known also as the Son of Man, the Righteous One, and the Messiah.[77] The complex of titles displays a montage of messianism patterned after the elect Servant of Isaiah (Isa 42:1), the Danielic 'son of man' (Daniel 7), and the righteous Davidic messiah-king (Isa 11:1–9; cp. *1 En.* 49:3; 62:2).[78] He is the appointed executor of divine judgment in support of the righteous and in opposition to the rich and powerful rulers who oppress them (*1 En.* 46:4–8; 48:8–10). According to 61:5 the righteous are resurrected to witness the judgment meted out by the Elect One, and they include those who have not been properly buried:

> Those who have been destroyed by the desert,
> And those who have been devoured by the fish of the sea and by wild beasts,
> That they will return and stay themselves on the day of the Elect One.

The judgment against the rulers is relentless in 62:1–12 (cf. 63:1–12), whereas 'the righteous and the elect shall be saved on that day' (62:13). The continuing life of the righteous is then described in 62:14–16:

> And the Lord of spirits shall abide by them,
> And with that Son of Man they shall eat,
> And lie down and rise up for ever and ever.
> And the righteous and elect shall be raised up from the earth,

---

[76] *Contra* Cavallin, *Life After Death*, 45; Stemberger, *Leib*, 51.

[77] Elect One (*1 En.* 39:6; 40:6; 45:5; 49:2, 4; 51:3, 5; 52:6, 9; 53:6; 55:4 ('my Elect One'); 61:5, 8, 10; 62:1–2), Son of Man (46:3–4; 48:2; 62:7, 9, 14; 63:11; 69:27–29; 71:14 [identified as Enoch], 17), Righteous One (38:2–3; 53:6), Messiah (48:10; 52:4). Curiously, this complex of titles is shared only by Luke-Acts, although the title 'Son of Man' occurs in the other Gospels: Elect One (Luke 9:35, 'my Chosen' [cp. *1 En.* 55:4]; Luke 23:35); Son of Man (Luke 5:24; 6:5, 22; 7:34; 9:22, 26, 44, 58; 11:30; 12:8, 10, 40; 17:22, 24, 26, 30; 18:8, 31; 19:10; 21:27, 36; 22:22, 28; 69; 24:7; Acts 7:56); Righteous One (Acts 3:14; 7:52; 22:14); and Messiah (Luke 2:11, 26; 3:15; 4:41; 9:20; 20:41; 22:67; 23:2, 35, 39; 24:26, 46; Acts 2:31, 36; 3:18, 20; 4:26; 5:42; 8:5; 9:22; 17:3; 18:5, 28; 26:23). This is a somewhat facile observation, but its significance is enhanced when it is observed how these titles, as in the Similitudes, are used interchangeably, as evidenced by a proximity of usage in certain passages: Messiah and Elect One (Luke 23:35); Son of Man (Luke 24:7) and Messiah (Luke 24:26, 46); Righteous One (Acts 3:14) and Messiah (Acts 3:18, 20); Righteous One (Acts 7:52) and Son of Man (Acts 7:56). Paul calls Jesus the Righteous One (Acts 22:14) and the Messiah (17:3; 18:5, 28; 26:23). We are not suggesting that Luke had read the Similitudes of Enoch, but that this strain of messianism was 'in the air' in the first century A.D.

[78] Black, *Book of Enoch*, 188–89; Nickelsburg, 'Enoch,' *ABD* 2:512.

> And they shall cease to be of downcast countenance;
> They shall be clothed with garments of glory,
> And this shall be your garment, a garment of life from the Lord of spirits,
> And your garments shall not grow old, nor your glory pass away before the Lord of Spirits.

The miraculous clothing of Israel's forty-year wilderness experience stands behind the promise of a garment of eternal life (Deut 8:4; 29:5; contrast Sir 14:17).[79] In light of the Lukan interest in table-fellowship as an eschatological motif (see esp. Luke 13:29; 14:15; 22:16, 30), the comment about eating with the Son of Man is provocative. It reinforces the image of the righteous poor experiencing the delight and ease of divine paradise while their wealthy overlords go down to destruction.

The First Book of Enoch does not present a monochrome view of the resurrection. The earliest stratum of the composite work obliquely refers to a resurrection of souls (perhaps meaning independent 'spirits,' but more likely whole persons) from the chambers of the dead (*1 En.* 22). Later references to the resurrection in 91:10 and 92:3–5 are dependent upon Dan 12:2 and focus upon the righteous rising up with royal authority. The Similitudes speak of resurrection within the context of a decisive administration of justice on behalf of the righteous. Resurrection is a means by which the righteous dead are brought to a final realization of salvation. The mysterious Elect One punishes the rich and powerful despots, and thenceforth the righteous dwell with him and the Lord of spirits in eternal blessedness on earth. The resurrection of the righteous is apparently physical (given the earthly setting and references to eating and resting), and will include even those who have not been properly buried. Yet their life will be angelic in the sense that they will no longer be mortal and will participate in the authority and glory of the Lord of spirits and his Elect One. Images of Israel's salvation abound amongst these scenes of resurrection and judgment: images of the exodus, new creation, and co-regency with God's appointed ruler. Again, the theology of creation, covenant, exaltation, and resurrection appears. But no other text thus far so forcefully displays the possession of eternal glory for the righteous poor, or so vigorously enunciates the fate of their wealthy oppressors.

3.1.2.3 OTHER RESURRECTION PASSAGES

There are passages from this period that we need only mention in passing, because they do not substantially add to or subtract from the general portrait of the resurrection that we have looked at thus far. The *Psalms of*

---

[79] For more about the putting on of garments, see Isa 52:1; 61:10; Bar 5:1; *4 Ezra* 2:39.

Solomon contain only one explicit reference to the resurrection (3:10–12), but the poetic form of this passage makes its interpretation difficult. Pseudo-Phocylides, writing at the turn of the common era,[80] contains one of the most literalistic descriptions of bodily resurrection (102–103), but juxtaposes this with expressions of belief in the immortality of the soul (105–108, 115) *and* the classical Hebrew idea of the afterlife in Sheol (111–14), creating arguably the most confusing picture of the afterlife of any ancient writer. In two of the *Sibylline Oracles* there are even more explicit representations of physical resurrection (2:221–26; 4:180–84), but the theological significance of the resurrection is not expanded beyond its function as a prelude to the final judgment.

Of the texts within this time period, we may note that 2 Maccabees 7 and the Similitudes of Enoch are the most conformable to the theological pattern wherein resurrection is integrated with the concepts of covenant faithfulness, creation, and exaltation. The pattern is certainly implicit within other texts, such as in the *Psalms of Solomon*. It is not as observable in Pseudo-Phocylides or the *Sibylline Oracles*, but this is not unexpected. In these latter texts there is a stronger tendency to adapt Jewish eschatology to Hellenistic modes of thinking. Nevertheless, even here the nature of resurrection is distinctively Jewish in its concreteness.

3.1.3 From the Destruction of Jerusalem (A.D. 70) to the End of the First Century

The remaining sources that we will investigate were written after the destruction of Jerusalem in A.D. 70, but most of them incorporate traditions that were probably circulating at the beginning of the first century. There is one chronological exception, the *Testaments of the Twelve Patriarchs*, whose compositional history and dating are highly debated.

---

[80] There is wide agreement that Pseudo-Phocylides should be dated within the range between 200 B.C. and A.D. 200, but P. W. van der Horst (*The Sentences of Pseudo-Phocylides with Introduction and Commentary* [SVTP 4; Leiden: Brill, 1978], 81–83; idem, 'Pseudo-Phocylides," *OTP* 2:567–68), with the support of linguistic criteria, matters of cultural influence, and historical probability has narrowed the date to the period between 30 B.C. and A.D. 40.

3.1.3.1 *FOURTH EZRA*: RESURRECTION, RE-CREATION, AND REWARD

There are several incidental references to the resurrection in *4 Ezra*.[81] One is in 4:33–43 where Ezra sees the righteous souls in their chambers crying out, 'How long are we to remain here? When will come the harvest of our reward?' (4:35).[82] The angel Jeremiel replies that God 'will not move or arouse them'[83] until the measure of times is full (4:37). The resurrection of the righteous, therefore, is correlated with the time when they will receive their reward. This correlation occurs as well in chapter 14 as the conclusion to a retrospective sketch of Israel's history. Ezra recounts how the patriarchs lived as aliens in Egypt until they were delivered from there (14:29). They received the Law of life, but they did not obey it, as is the case for Ezra's contemporaries (14:30). The penalty for this was a loss of their land and deportation (14:31–33). Ezra therefore urges obedience to the Law in order to receive life and mercy (14:34). 'For after death the judgment will come, when we shall live again; and then the names of the righteous will become manifest, and the deeds of the ungodly will be disclosed' (14:35). Of special note is how the resurrection can be so naturally expressed as one of the sequelae in a clearly discernible Sin-Exile-Return pattern.[84] For Ezra the outcome of keeping 'the Law of life' is to experience the covenant blessing of life in the land (cf. Deut 5:33; 8:1; 11:9; 30:6, 15–20), both now (*4 Ezra* 14:34) and after death (14:35; cf. 7:[129–30]). This blessing is reserved for God's elect, whose names will be revealed (14:35).[85] In 10:16

---

[81] *4 Ezra* was written in the last decade of the first century A.D.; see Michael E. Stone, 'Esdras, Second Book of," *ABD* 2:611–12. It is extant in Latin, Syriac, Ethiopic, Georgian, Armenian, and Arabic versions (there are also Coptic and Greek fragments) which are all thought to be dependent upon a Greek translation of a Hebrew exemplar, both of which are lost.

[82] Translation is that of B. M. Metzger, 'The Fourth Book of Ezra,' *OTP* 1:516–59.

[83] On this phrasing as a reference to resurrection, see Michael E. Stone, *Features of the Eschatology of IV Ezra* (HSS 35; Atlanta: Scholars Press, 1989), 269 n. 386.

[84] The whole book of *4 Ezra* is built upon the assumption that Israel is presently in a state of exile. The text purports to have been written thirty years after Nebuchadnezzar's destruction of Jerusalem (3:1), and there is no mention of events after 587 B.C.—apart from the Eagle Vision which refers to the Roman Empire; see Michael A. Knibb, 'The Exile in Intertestamental Literature,' *HeyJ* 17 (1976): 268–69; Michael E. Stone, 'Reactions to Destructions of the Second Temple,' *JSJ* 12 (1981): 195–204; James C. VanderKam, 'Exile in Jewish Apocalyptic Literature,' in *Exile: Old Testament, Jewish, and Christian Conceptions* (ed. James M. Scott; JSJSup 56; Leiden: Brill, 1997), 89–109, esp. 107–9.

[85] On naming as an indicator of divine election, see the commentary on 10:57 and 14:35 in Michael E. Stone, *Fourth Ezra: A Commentary on the Book of Fourth Ezra* (Hermeneia; Minneapolis: Fortress, 1990), 341, 436.

mother Zion, who is wailing over her dead son (10:1), is promised that 'you will receive your son back.'[86] We may point out the affinity of *4 Ezra* 10:16 with the words of the mother in 2 Macc 7:29. The co-texts of both passages bear striking resemblances. In both we find a mother (=Zion) who is losing her son(s) (=Israel) and who conducts herself bravely throughout the ordeal (*4 Ezra* 10:15; 2 Macc 7:21). In both we find the motifs of childbearing and creation invoked in support of the hope of resurrection (*4 Ezra* 10:14, 16; 2 Macc 7:22–23, 28). God's responsibility for the creation, birth, and nurturing of human beings is detailed in *4 Ezra* 8:4–12 as well, followed by another reference to resurrection, 'You will take away his life, for he is your creation; and you will make him live, for he is your work' (8:13). All of these passing references to the resurrection are important since they frame resurrection within the context of Israel's creation and election by God, and within the Deuteronomic sanctions of Yahweh's covenant with the nation.[87]

The most substantive reference to the resurrection occurs in an overtly eschatological section in chapter seven. The third vision contains a scene which pictures the end of the age (7:26–[44]).[88] The time when the predicted signs of 6:20–24, leading up to 'my salvation and the end of the world' (6:25), is now being revealed. A complex of events occurs in preparation for the manifestation of a radically new world. The messianic era will be inaugurated with the appearance of 'the city which now is not seen,' the heavenly Jerusalem,[89] and the 'land which is now hidden,' the land promised to Israel (7:26).[90] Then 'my son (or servant) the Messiah' will

---

[86] Stone (*Fourth Ezra*, 323) cites 2 Esdr (5 Ezra) 2:15–17 as a fitting exposition of this passage (cf. 2 Esdr 2:23, 29–31).

[87] Although part of a later Christian addition, *4 Ezra* 2:1–32 speaks of the resurrection within the same context of Israel's history: deliverance from bondage and disobedience to the prophets (2:1); exile and loss of kingdom (2:2–14); but salvation for the covenant faithful who have died—'And I will raise up the dead from their places, and will bring them out from their tombs, because I recognize my name in them' (2:16); '...when you find any who are dead, commit them to the grave and mark it, and I will give you the first place in my resurrection' (2:23); 'Remember your sons that sleep, because I will bring them out of the hiding places of the earth, and will show mercy to them' (2:31).

[88] Cf. *4 Ezra* 4:26; 7:43 [113], 49 [119].

[89] Cf. the mother (=Zion) who is transformed into an 'established city' (*4 Ezra* 10:27, 42, 44, 54; see also 8:52; 13:36).

[90] Cf. *4 Ezra* 5:24; 14:41; *2 Bar.* 44:5–9; 85:3–5; Gal 4:25–27. On the unseen city and hidden land, see Stone, *Fourth Ezra*, 213–14. In Pseudo-Philo, as in *4 Ezra*, the promised land is transmuted into a heaven-like place. For example, Moses is told before his death that he will not enter the land in 'this age' (*L.A.B.* 19:7), but he will sleep until he is awakened (=resurrected) with the fathers in 'the immortal dwelling place that is not

appear for a period of 400 years, after which time he, along with every other human being, will die. What follows is a seven-day period of primeval silence (7:30) before the new world emerges (7:31–32):

> And after seven days the world, which is not yet awake, shall be roused, and that which is corruptible shall perish. And the earth shall give up those who are asleep in it; and the chambers shall give up the souls which have been committed to them.

After this ostensibly universal resurrection,[91] the 'day of judgment' ensues (7:[38]), when the Most High will apply the standard of the Law ('commandments,' 7:[37]; 'covenant,' 7:[46]) to people's righteous and unrighteous deeds (7:35).[92] The righteous will receive their 'reward' (7:35) in a 'Paradise of delight' (7:[37]), while the unrighteous receive 'recompense' (7:35) in the 'pit of torment' or the 'furnace of Hell' (7:[36]). The righteous will from then on shine like the sun and stars because they will be immortal (7:[97], 55 [125] ; cf. 8:54), living in an eternal world from which corruption has passed away (7:[113]; cf. 7:31). This scenario is entirely consonant with the passages that have incidental references to the resurrection. Images of creation (seven days), the exodus (400 years,[93] the land), and the return from exile (restoration of Zion) are skilfully brought together to envision the transition between 'the end of this age and the beginning of the immortal age to come' (7:[43] [113]).

The resurrection in *4 Ezra* is associated with a rich network of ideas pertaining to the covenant relationship between God and Israel. The pattern of covenant renewal, resurrection, (re-)creation, and exaltation could not be more evident. The weight of the resurrection's theological significance can be measured by its occurrence at pivotal junctures in the book's thought (e.g., as a key event preceding the final judgment) and structure (e.g., as a key element in Ezra's interchange with the grieving mother).[94] As to the nature of resurrection in *4 Ezra*, it seems to be defined as the body of the

---

subject to time' (19:12) or 'the place of sanctification I showed you' (19:13), i.e., the temple, and perhaps the land; see Betsy Halpern-Amaru, *Rewriting the Bible: Land and Covenant in Postbiblical Jewish Literature* (Valley Forge, Pa.: Trinity Press International, 1994), 92.

[91] It is a cosmic rousing; cf. 7:[37] which speaks of 'the nations that have been raised from the dead.'

[92] This is 'the time of threshing' (4:30, 39) when the righteous will get the 'harvest' of their reward (4:35).

[93] Cf. Gen 15:13; Exod 12:40–41; Acts 7:6; Gal 3:17; and cp. Ps 90:15. See Stone, *Fourth Ezra*, 215.

[94] See our comments on 10:16 above. The fourth vision (*4 Ezra* 10) is a crucial division within the book; see Earl Breech, 'These Fragments I Have Shored against My Ruins: The Form and Function of 4 Ezra,' *JBL* 92 (1973): 267–74, esp. 272.

deceased being raised up from the earth and reunited, in the case of the righteous, with the soul that has been inhabiting a chamber in the treasury of souls (cf. 4:35, 40–42; 7:[75]), or in the case of the unrighteous, with the soul that has been wandering about in torment (7:[80]). The reintegration of body and soul may be apprehended from the fact that the resurrection is described in a way reminiscent of Dan 12:2 (viz., as an awakening from the earth), as well as in a way that coheres with the description of death as the soul leaving the body (7:[78]) and existing in one of the two intermediate states just mentioned (for the righteous or unrighteous).[95]

3.1.3.2 *SECOND BARUCH*: PHYSICAL RESURRECTION AND SALVATION, EXALTATION, AND VINDICATION

The *Syriac Apocalypse of Baruch* describes an earthly messianic kingdom which precedes 'the consummation of time' (*2 Bar.* 29:8; cf. 30:3).[96] The Anointed One will be revealed, who will usher in a period of great plenty and justice for Israel and its allies (29:1–8; 72:1–74:4). This will be a period that is 'far away from the evil things and near to those which do not die' (74:4), for after the end of the Messiah's appearance he will return to glory and the resurrection will take place (30:1–2a):

> And it will happen after these things when the time of the appearance of the Anointed One has been fulfilled and he returns with glory,[97] that then all who sleep in hope of him will rise. And it will happen at that time that those treasuries will be opened in which the number of the souls of the righteous were kept....

Of particular importance for the study of the resurrection of the Christ in Luke-Acts is the direct linkage in *2 Baruch* between the Anointed One's departure into glory and the resurrection hope of 'all who sleep.' Here is the clearest indication in intertestamental Jewish texts of the resurrection of the

---

[95] Cavallin, *Life After Death*, 82–83; Stone, *Features*, 141, 143. Stemberger (*Leib*, 84) refrains from being categorical: 'Die Auferstehung ist noch nicht direkt als Wiedervereinigung von Leib und Seele gedacht, aber diese Vorstellung ist schon sehr nahe.'

[96] A number of parallels exist between *L.A.B.*, *4 Ezra*, and *2 Bar.*, and they may have been written in that chronological sequence; see James H. Charlesworth, 'Baruch, Book of 2 (Syriac),' *ABD* 1:621. *Second Baruch* was written perhaps a decade or two after A.D. 100; see A. F. J. Klijn, '2 (Syriac Apocalypse of) Baruch,' *OTP* 1:166–67, whose translation will be utilized in citations. Recently, however, an interpretation of the time reckoning in *2 Bar.* 28:2 has been used to propose a *terminus ad quem* of A.D. 99; Nicolae Roddy, '"Two Parts: Weeks of Seven Weeks": The End of the Age as Terminus ad Quem for *2 Baruch*,' *JSP* 14 (1996): 3–14.

[97] R. H. Charles (*The Apocalypse of Baruch* [London: Adam and Charles Black, 1896], 56) insists: 'This can have only one meaning, and this is that, at the close of His reign, the Messiah will return in glory to heaven.' Cf. Cavallin, *Life After Death*, 90–91; Stemberger, *Leib*, 92–94

dead as a messianic hope, though without any explicit mention of the Messiah's own resurrection. The concept of souls being kept in treasuries has been encountered before (*1 En.* 22; *4 Ezra* 4:41; 7:32, [80], [95]), but in *2 Baruch* the chambers are tantamount to Sheol, and (unlike *4 Ezra*) there is no distinction drawn between body and soul (see 11:4, 6).[98] Despite its classical Hebrew monism, a devaluation of somatic existence is evident in the question put before God about the nature of the resurrection body: 'In which shape will the living live in your day? Or how will remain their splendor which will be after that? Will they, perhaps, take again this present form, and will they put on the chained members[99] which are in evil and by which evils are accomplished? Or will you perhaps change these things which have been in the world, as also the world itself?' (49:2–3). What follows in chapters 50–51 is the most detailed description of the resurrection that we possess in Second Temple Jewish literature.

The resurrected state is described in two phases. (1) First, there is the resurrection itself which is undoubtedly a raising up of corpses out of the earth (50:2–4):

> For the earth will surely give back the dead at that time; it receives them now in order to keep them, not changing anything in their form. But as it has received them so it will give them back. And as I have delivered them to it so it will raise them. For then it will be necessary to show those who live that the dead are living again, and that those who went away have come back. And it will be that when they have recognized each other, those who know each other at this moment, then my judgment will be strong, and those things which have been spoken of before will come.

The continuity between bodies in their dead and resurrected states is necessary for the identification of the resurrected and is a prerequisite for the coming judgment phase.[100] (2) The judgment phase involves the transformation of both the righteous and the unrighteous. The unrighteous, who have been found 'guilty' (51:1), will be changed into forms 'more evil' than at present (51:2), 'into startling visions and horrible shapes' (51:5). 'They will waste away even more' (51:5; cf. 48:6), i.e., they will experience corruption (see 42:7; 85:13) and destruction (52:3; 54:14, 17; 85:15). They will be

---

[98] Stemberger, *Leib*, 87.

[99] Charles (*Apocalypse of Baruch*, 81) translates 'entrammeling members' and notes that the phrase is literally 'members of bonds.' This question, and its degradation of present physical existence, resembles 1 Cor 15:35, 50.

[100] Precisely the same concern may be found in *Tanh.*, Wayiggash, 104b, in which the physically impaired are not healed until *after* the resurrection so that the wicked will recognize that they have indeed been resurrected; C. G. Montefiore and H. Loewe, *A Rabbinic Anthology* (Cleveland, Ohio: Meridian, 1963), 593. Cf. *b. Sanh.* 91b; *Gen. Rab.* 95.1.

barred from 'glory' (51:16) and will 'go away to be tormented' (51:6; cf. 51:2, 16).[101] The transformation of the righteous, in contrast, will at once constitute their salvation, exaltation, and vindication.

(a) *Salvation* consists of an inheritance of Paradise (51:11) and the requisite metamorphosis to live forever in that future world that is presently invisible (51:8; cf. *4 Ezra* 7:26). The faces of the righteous will be transfigured 'into the light of their beauty so that they may acquire and receive the undying world which is promised them' (51:3). This transformation means that 'they have been saved from this world of affliction and have put down the burden of anguishes' (51:14), and they will never again grow old (51:9, 16). These wonders will be experienced by those who have been 'saved because of their works' (51:7) or have been 'proved to be righteous on account of my law' (51:3; cf. 51:1). The link between resurrection hope and covenant fidelity was forged earlier, when release for those within the treasuries of souls was promised particularly to those who follow in the steps of Israel's patriarchs: 'For as many years have passed as those which passed since the days of Abraham, Isaac, and Jacob and all those who were like them, who sleep in the earth—those on whose account you have said you have created the world' (21:24; cf. 57:1–2).

(b) The transformation of the righteous is also expressed as *exaltation*. They will be 'glorified and exalted into the splendor of angels' (51:5).

> For they will live in the heights of that world and they will be like angels and be equal to the stars. And they will be changed into any shape which they wished, from beauty to loveliness, and from light to the splendor of glory (51:10).

They will have access to all of Paradise, they will behold the living beings under the throne, and they will see all the hosts of angels (51:11). Indeed, 'the excellence of the righteous will be greater than that of the angels' (51:12).[102]

(c) Finally, the transformation of the righteous will mark their *vindication* in the presence of the wicked.[103] Those who obeyed the Law will not only be marvellously changed into immortal beings, but those who despised the Law 'will see that those over whom they are exalted now will then be more exalted and glorified than they,' while they themselves are twisted into hideous shapes and waste away at the sight (51:4–6).[104] It is a grand

---

[101] Elsewhere God is said to 'blot out' the wicked from his own people (*2 Bar.* 54:22) and exclude apostates from the world to come (83:8).

[102] Cf. 1 Cor 6:1–4; 1 Pet 1:12; Heb 2:16.

[103] 52:6–7 indicates that the righteous are suffering because of their faithfulness.

[104] Nickelsburg, *Resurrection*, 84–85. The earlier continuity between dead and resurrected bodies becomes essential at this point, because after the transformation takes

reversal akin to that in Dan 12:2-3 in which the righteous are exalted over the unrighteous to a status equivalent to the glory of the angels or stars. They are thereby given inheritance of and ascendancy over virtually all of that renewed creation (*2 Bar.* 32:6; 44:8-15; 49:3).

The *Apocalypse of Baruch* contributes to an expanding portrait of the resurrection as a key component in the salvation of those who are in covenant faithfulness to Israel's God.[105] We have sufficiently outlined the theological significance of resurrection under the rubrics of salvation, exaltation, and vindication. One can see how this is conformable to the fourfold pattern of resurrection theology we have been tracing. Especially significant, too, is the identification of the resurrection in *2 Baruch* as a distinctively messianic hope. The nature of resurrection in *2 Baruch* is twofold, as we have seen. First, there is a literal raising up of corpses out of the ground for the purposes of identification and subsequent judgment/ vindication; but then, secondly, there is a transformation of the dead into forms corresponding to their moral states. The righteous in particular transcend the limitations of present physical life which is tainted by evil and corruptibility.[106] And so Baruch combines the concept of a physical resurrection with hope for an angel-like and immortal life that will no longer be 'chained' (49:3) to a present bodily existence encumbered by sin and mortal corruption. This does not mean an entirely incorporeal life, since people will take on 'shapes,' but it will in any case be a life adapted to the new world that will be revealed.

3.1.3.3 RESURRECTION IN THE *TESTAMENTS OF THE TWELVE PATRIARCHS*

The *Testaments of the Twelve Patriarchs* (hereafter *T. 12 Patr.*) will be taken up at this point, despite the fact that they could be dated either much earlier or later. There is still no agreement regarding their date, composition (Jewish or Christian), or the original language in which they were written.[107] It is certain, though, that their final form exhibits signs of Christian

---

place, as Stemberger (*Leib*, 90) notes, 'die Identität der Auferstandenen nicht mehr feststellen könnte.'

[105] For more on the role of obedience to the Mosaic Law in *2 Baruch*, see Davis, *Structure of Paul's Theology*, 187-88.

[106] Paul's teaching is comparable (1 Cor 15:42-44, 50-53).

[107] There are three principal views: (a) The *T. 12 Patr.* was originally a Jewish work written in a Semitic language (second century B.C.), which underwent further redaction, including a final Christian redaction. Opinions vary regarding the exact stages of redaction, with the exception that the Christian interpolations are often thought to be readily identifiable and separable from the earlier Jewish *Grundschrift*. (b) It was originally a Christian work arising around A.D. 200. While probably dependent upon Jewish (pre-Christian) materials, it originated in Greek, and so sifting out Christian elements from an

influence, recognized as discernible interpolations or (as de Jonge contends) a thoroughgoing redaction.[108] Not of little significance for our discussion is Klaus Baltzer's landmark work on the covenant formulary. Baltzer has demonstrated the formal similarity between the covenant formulary in the Hebrew Bible and the testamentary form, and this lends support to the view that *T. 12 Patr.* has a Jewish background, if not a Jewish origin.[109] As it is impossible to cut the Gordian knot of such literary-critical questions, we shall have to be satisfied with the value of Baltzer's analysis for the interpretation of the *T. 12 Patr.* In particular, where one would find a section of blessings and curses in the covenant formulary, one finds an eschatological section in *T. 12 Patr.* These sections are commonly dubbed S. E. R. (Sin-Exile-Return) passages, since exile is the predominant curse mentioned.[110] Four elements occur in them: (1) a statement of the relationship to God and his commandments; (2) a list of consequences of the curses, exile being foremost; (3) repentance; and (4) the promise of salvation.[111] The resurrection is mentioned within this context of the covenant renewal and future salvation of Israel.

The resurrection is briefly mentioned in two passages. In the eschatological section of *T. Sim.* 5:4–7:3 the patriarch foretells the downfall and glorious restoration of his tribe. The tribe must eschew envy and stiff-neckedness if it is to prosper (6:2), and if Shem (=Israel) is to be glorified, humankind saved, and all evil spirits vanquished (6:5–6). Simeon an-

---

'original' Jewish document is impossible. This view is vigorously advocated by M. de Jonge. (c) The discovery at Qumran of Aramaic fragments resembling *T. Levi* chs. 6, 8–13 and a Hebrew fragment resembling *T. Naph.* 1:6–12 has led some scholars to identify the *T. 12 Patr.* as an Essene work, dating from ca. 150 B.C. when the Dead Sea Sect flourished. See Collins, *Apocalyptic Imagination*, 133–34; Marinus de Jonge, 'Patriarchs, Testaments of the Twelve,' *ABD* 5:182–84; H. C. Kee, 'Testaments of the Twelve Patriarchs,' *OTP* 1:776–78.

[108] It is universally agreed that Christian interpolations can no longer be excised on the basis of textual criticism (M. de Jonge *contra* R. H. Charles); see John J. Collins, 'Testaments,' in *Jewish Writings of the Second Temple Period: Apocrypha, Pseudepigrapha, Qumran Sectarian Writings, Philo, Josephus* (CRINT 2; ed. Michael E. Stone; Assen: Van Gorcum, 1984), 332. But this is only one means of identifying Christian interpolations, and to abandon all hope of identifying them is 'unwarranted and unnecessary' (Kee, 'Testaments,' 777).

[109] Klaus Baltzer, *The Covenant Formulary in Old Testament, Jewish, and Early Christian Writings* (trans. David E. Green; Oxford: Basil Blackwell, 1971), 141–63.

[110] The identification of S. E. R. passages was first made by M. de Jonge and has since been universally acknowledged; see H. W. Hollander and M. de Jonge, *The Testaments of the Twelve Patriarchs: A Commentary* (SVTP 8; Leiden: Brill, 1985), 7, 39–41.

[111] Baltzer, *Covenant Formulary*, 155–61.

nounces: 'Then I shall arise in joy (ἀναστήσομαι...ἐν εὐφροσύνῃ) and I shall bless the Most High because of his marvellous works' (6:7).[112] The patriarch Zebulun, in a similar co-text (see *T. Zeb.* 9:1–9), utters the same declaration with greater specificity: 'For I shall rise again (ἀναστήσομαι) in the midst of you as a ruler in the midst of his sons, and I shall rejoice (εὐφρανθήσομαι) in the midst of my tribe[,] as many as have kept the law of the Lord and the commandments of Zebulun their father' (*T. Zeb.* 10:2). These passages reveal several points about the resurrection: (1) Resurrection is a vital component in the eschatological salvation of Israel, whose antecedents are the disobedience and punishment of the nation[113] and their subsequent repentance.[114] As we might expect, the resurrection fits squarely within the restoration element of the S. E. R. sequence. (2) Resurrection pertains to Israel, and eminently to the patriarchs. The 'rising up' of the patriarchs not only indicates their 'resurrection' (without defining its precise mode) but their re-installment as rulers over Israel. The linkage of resurrection with covenant renewal and enthronement was well-established in our earliest references to resurrection (e.g., Hos 6:3; Dan 12:3), and this is particularly apropos here, given the testamentary variation on the ancient covenant formulary. (3) The accompanying 'joy' is reminiscent of the Isaianic reference to resurrection: ἀναστήσονται οἱ νεκροί...καὶ εὐφρανθήσονται οἱ ἐν τῇ γῇ (Isa 26:19 LXX; cf. 25:6, 8–9).[115] While the resurrection is not explicitly mentioned in *T. Levi* 18:14, the idyllic future of Israel described within that co-text involves Abraham, Isaac, Jacob, and all the saints rejoicing.

There are two rather extensive references to the resurrection. The first is in *T. Jud.* 25:1, 3–5:

And after these things Abraham and Isaac and Jacob will arise (ἀναστήσεται)
unto life (εἰς ζωήν),
and I and my brothers will be chiefs of our tribes in Israel:
Levi first, I second, Joseph third, Benjamin fourth, Simeon fifth,
Issachar sixth, and so all in order.

And there will be one people of the Lord and one tongue;
and there will be no longer any spirit of deceit of Beliar,
because it will be cast into the fire for ever and ever.

---

[112] Translations are from Hollander and de Jonge, *Testaments of the Twelve Patriarchs*.

[113] Cf. *T. Sim.* 5:4–6; *T. Zeb.* 9:5–6; cf. *T. Ash.* 7:2; *T. Reu.* 6:5; *T. Dan* 5:4–7; *T. Levi* 14–17.

[114] Cf. *T. Sim.* 5:2–3; 6:2; *T. Zeb.* 9:7; cf. *T. Iss.* 6:3–4; *T. Dan* 5:9; *T. Naph.* 4:3; *T. Ash.* 7:7.

[115] Hollander and de Jonge, *Testaments of the Twelve Patriarchs*, 125. See also *1 En.* 25:6; 51:5; *Jub.* 23:31; *2 Bar.* 30:2.

> And those who have died in grief will arise in joy
> and those who were in poverty for the Lord's sake will be made rich
> and those who were in want will be fed
> and those who were in weakness will be strong
> and those who died for the Lord's sake
>   will awake to life (ἐξυπνισθήσονται εἰς ζωήν).
> And the deer of Jacob will run in joyfulness
> and the eagles of Israel will fly in gladness;
> but the godly will lament
> and the sinners weep;
> and all the peoples will glorify the Lord for ever.

The observations made in the previous paragraph concerning *T. Sim.* 6:7 and *T. Zeb.* 10:2 apply here as well. But the function of the resurrection for the reconstitution of Israel is further elaborated upon. (1) The forefathers Abraham, Isaac, and Jacob will be raised up first, followed by the twelve patriarchs and their tribes. From then on one unified (Israelite) government will reign over the world. (2) Israel will be triumphant over her enemies: (a) the forces of evil ('any spirit of deceit of Beliar') will be eliminated; and (b) the oppressed will be vindicated on account of their faithfulness to God. The time of resurrection will entail a great reversal of fortunes for the poor and powerless, echoing the contrasts in Hannah's song where Yahweh's power over death is expressly stated (1 Sam 2:6–10; cf. Luke 1:51–55).[116] The resurrection of 'those who died in grief' and 'those who died for the Lord's sake' (*T. Jud.* 25:4) perhaps singles out for vindication those who were executed because of their loyalty to Yahweh. The corollary to their ultimate bliss is the final despair of the wicked (25:5). (3) Hints of Danielic descriptions of the resurrection, then, are not unusual within such a context of righteous judgment and vindication: Abraham et al. will be raised 'unto life' (εἰς ζωήν, 25:1) and those who died for the Lord 'will awake to life' (ἐξυπνισθήσονται εἰς ζωήν, 26:4; cp. Dan 12:2 LXX).[117]

Finally, resurrection is integral to Israel's restoration in *T. Benj.* 10:6–9:

> Then you will see Enoch, Noah, and Shem and Abraham and Isaac and Jacob
>   rising on the right hand (ἀνασταμένους ἐκ δεξιῶν)
> in gladness (ἐν ἀγαλλιάσει).
> Then we also will rise (ἀναστησόμεθα) each one over our tribe,
>   worshipping the king of heaven....
> Then also all men will rise,
>   some unto glory (οἱ μὲν εἰς δόξαν)
>   and some unto shame (οἱ δὲ εἰς ἀτιμίαν).

---

[116] Nickelsburg, *Resurrection*, 34 n. 111.

[117] Cavallin, *Life After Death*, 53–54. Note also this verb form in John 11:11.

While the focus of this passage, as in previous passages, is on the resurgence of Yahweh's sovereignty through Israel, it more clearly presents a universal resurrection ('all men will rise'). That there will be a resurrection 'unto glory' as well as 'unto shame' is allusive of Dan 12:2. One should not overlook how this picture of rising *from the dead* (employing the verb ἀνίστημι) is coupled with the idea of rising *at the right hand*. Resurrection from the dead and regal exaltation before God go together like hand in glove.

In nuce, the resurrection of the dead in the *T. 12 Patr.* is intimately related to the revival of an ideal, primeval leadership over a fully restored Israel. This fits within a pattern of God's covenant relationship with his people, wherein the latter apostatized and so must repent in order for the covenantal blessings to be reinstated in accordance with the ancient promises made to the fathers. So the concept of covenant renewal is quite in the forefront, along with the exaltation of Israel among the nations. With the future paradisiacal conditions of Israel's existence there is the implicit idea of new creation. The fourfold theology of creation, covenant, exaltation, and resurrection is thus firmly in place. Little can be discerned about the nature or location of the resurrection in *T. 12 Patr.*, so that while Stemberger presumes a terrestrial conceptualization (despite *T. Ash.* 6:5–6),[118] Cavallin sees the 'rising on the right hand' as an expression of 'the heavenly and transcendent character of this resurrection.'[119]

3.1.3.4 JOSEPHUS AND THE JEWISH 'PHILOSOPHICAL SCHOOLS'

Josephus's testimony about Jewish beliefs concerning the afterlife is significant because he was a contemporary observer and participant of Judaism in Palestine prior to the destruction of Jerusalem in A.D. 70.[120] Josephus is the only first-century author who gives a profile of what all of the Jewish sects were like around the time of Jesus. Josephus's first exhibition of Judaism's three philosophical schools appears in *Jewish War* 2.8.2 §§119–66. He has an additional section on the three schools in his *Jewish Antiquities*, to which we shall refer. His descriptions of the three philosophical schools deal with three areas of comparative study: philosophy, social standing (or political

---

[118] Stemberger, *Leib*, 69.

[119] Cavallin, *Life After Death*, 53; but see Joel F. Drinkard, Jr., 'Right, Right Hand,' *ABD* 5:724.

[120] Josephus's first work, the *Jewish War*, was drafted in Aramaic and translated into Greek five to ten years after A.D. 70; his *Jewish Antiquities* appeared another decade later; his *Life* and *Against Apion* were published not long before his death ca. A.D. 100. Cf. Louis H. Feldman, 'Josephus,' *ABD* 3:982.

influence), and way of life.¹²¹ The area of philosophy will concern us here, and of the three philosophical issues (fate, free will, and immortality) the third item will of course occupy our attention.

Although Josephus deals with them last, it will be simplest for us to take up the Sadducees first, since they hold to a negative position: 'As for the persistence of the soul after death (ψυχῆς...τὴν διαμονήν), penalties in the underworld, and rewards, they will have none of them' (*J. W.* 2.8.14 §165). In the supplementary material in *Jewish Antiquities*, the Sadducees are said to 'hold that the soul perishes along with the body' (τὰς ψυχὰς...συναφανίζει τοῖς σώμασι, 18.1.4 §16). An explanation for their rejection of an afterlife may be found in their repudiation of any traditions other than are found in the Mosaic Law (*Ant.* 18.1.4 §16). We can only speculate that their position resembled the classical Hebrew view of Ben Sirach: the only immortality one may aspire to is the continuance of one's name and honour through posterity (Sir 39:9; 41:13; 44:8–14; 46:12).¹²² Josephus's statements about the Sadducees vis-à-vis the afterlife are comparable to those in the NT (Matt 22:23–33; Mark 12:18–27; Luke 20:27–40; Acts 4:1–2; 23:6–8). Later the rabbis excluded from the world to come those groups who did not believe that the resurrection of the dead was taught in the Torah (*y. Sanh.* 10.1d; *b. Sanh.* 90a).¹²³

The teachings of the Pharisees concerning the afterlife are presented concisely (*J. W.* 2.8.14 §163):

ψυχήν τε πᾶσαν μὲν ἄφθαρτον, μεταβαίνειν δὲ εἰς ἕτερον σῶμα τὴν ἀγαθῶν μόνην, τὰς δὲ τῶν φαύλων ἀϊδίῳ τιμωρίᾳ κολάζεσθαι.

---

¹²¹ The headings for this delineation are those of Shaye J. D. Cohen, *From the Maccabees to the Mishnah* (LEC 7; ed. Wayne A. Meeks; Philadelphia: Westminster, 1987), 144.

¹²² The books of the Sadducees and the book of Ben Sirach were excluded by the rabbis from the canon in virtually the same breath, *b. Sanh.* 100b; cf. *y. Sanh.* 10.1d, 8a–b. Ben Sirach was once thought to be a Sadducean work (Kaufmann Kohler, 'Sadducees,' *Jewish Encyclopedia* 10:632), and indeed the rabbis may have presumed this identification because of the similarity of its teaching to that of the Sadducees; see Jean Le Moyne, *Les Sadducées* (Paris: Gabalda, 1972), 67–73; Alexander A. Di Lella, 'Wisdom of Ben-Sira,' *ABD* 6:934.

¹²³ The targets of this interdiction were the Samaritans and the Sadducees, who were in this respect classed among the Epicureans. See also ʾ*Abot R. Nat.* 5 on the exclusion of the Sadducees from the world to come. According to *b. Ber.* 54a the benedictions recited in the temple closed with the phrase 'forever,' (*min ha-ʿolam*), but this was changed to 'from age to age' (*min ha-ʿolam we-ʿad ha-ʿolam*) on account of the Sadducean assertion that there is only one world.

> Every soul, they maintain, is imperishable, but the soul of the good alone passes into another body, while the souls of the wicked suffer eternal punishment.

Again, it is profitable to compare the supplementary statement found in *Jewish Antiquities* (18.1.3 §14):

> They believe that souls have power to survive death (ἀθανατόν...ἰσχὺν ταῖς ψυχαῖς) and that there are rewards and punishments under the earth for those who have lives of virtue or vice: eternal imprisonment is the lot of evil souls, while the good souls receive an easy passage to a new life (ῥᾳστώνην τοῦ ἀναβιοῦν).

Three common elements recur: (1) the soul is immortal; (2) the souls of the wicked will be punished eternally; and (3) good souls will 'live again' (ἀναβιοῦν) or be re-embodied (μεταβαίνειν...εἰς ἕτερον σῶμα). It is the last proposition that is most tantalizing, because of its similarity to the Greek notion of metempsychosis.[124] This raises questions as to whether Josephus (a) has properly represented the Pharisees as believing in a form of reincarnation; (b) has misrepresented the Pharisaic belief in bodily resurrection attested to elsewhere; or (c) has in mind the concept of bodily resurrection, but has adapted his depiction of it to be more agreeable to his Greco-Roman listeners. The answer to this inquiry will have to await further comparative study. After we have considered the teaching of the Essenes about the afterlife according to Josephus, we shall look at the statements from Josephus that seem to indicate his own view of the matter.

Josephus's account of the Essene 'theology concerning the soul' (*J. W.* 2.8.11 §158) is more detailed. The Essenes were said to have been extraordinarily intrepid in the face of death (2.8.10 §151). Their gallantry was due to their beliefs concerning the afterlife (2.8.11 §§154–55):

> For it is a fixed belief of theirs that the body is corruptible and its constituent matter impermanent (φθαρτὰ μὲν εἶναι τὰ σώματα καὶ τὴν ὕλην οὐ μόνιμον αὐτῶν), but that the soul is immortal and imperishable (τὰς δέ ψυχὰς ἀθανάτους ἀεὶ διαμένειν). Emanating from the finest ether, these souls become entangled, as it were, in the prison-house of the body, to which they are dragged down by a sort of natural spell; but when once they are released from the bonds of the flesh (τῶν κατὰ σάρκα δεσμῶν), then, as though liberated from a long servitude, they rejoice and are borne aloft. Sharing the belief of the sons of Greece, they maintain that for virtuous souls there is reserved an abode beyond the ocean, a place which is not oppressed by rain or snow or heat, but is refreshed by the ever gentle breath of the west wind coming in from ocean; while they relegate base souls to a murky and tempestuous dungeon, big with never-ending punishments.

---

[124] This has often been observed; see Thackeray's note on *J. W.* 2.8.14 §163; F. F. Bruce, 'Paul on Immortality,' *SJT* 24 (1971): 458; Günter Stemberger, *Jewish Contemporaries of Jesus: Pharisees, Sadducees, Essenes* (trans. Allan W. Mahnke; Minneapolis: Fortress, 1995), 72.

Josephus further compares this portrait of the afterlife with the Greek conceptions of the Isles of the Blessed, reserved for their men of valour, and the torments of Hades for the wicked (2.8.10 §156). He is impressed by the utility of this set of beliefs for promoting virtuous living, and concludes that such views 'irresistibly attract all who have once tasted their philosophy' (2.8.10 §157). The three components of Pharisaic belief are mirrored here, with one variation. The Essenes believe in the immortality of the soul and in the everlasting punishment of sinners; but instead of the righteous 'passing into another body,' they are, so it seems, forever emancipated from the imprisonment of the flesh and are transported to the Isles of the Blessed.

Josephus's own perspective on the afterlife is illuminating, and the following texts are illustrative.[125] Josephus delivered a speech against suicide to his beleaguered comrades at Jotapata (*J. W.* 3.8.5 §§372–75):

> All of us, it is true, have mortal bodies (σώματα θνητά), composed of perishable matter (φθαρτῆς ὕλης), but the soul lives forever, immortal (ψυχὴ δὲ ἀθάνατος ἀεί): it is a portion of Deity housed in our bodies.... Know you not that they who depart this life in accordance with the law of nature and repay the loan which they received from God, when he who lent is pleased to reclaim it, win eternal renown;...that their souls, remaining spotless and obedient, are allotted the most holy place in heaven (χῶρον οὐράνιον λαχοῦσαι τὸν ἁγιώτατον), whence, in the revolution of the ages (ἐκ περιτροπῆς αἰώνων), they return to find in chaste bodies a new habitation (ἁγνοῖς πάλιν ἀντενοικίζονται σώμασιν)? But as for those who have laid mad hands upon themselves, the darker regions of the nether world receive their souls....

In his *Jewish Antiquities* he relates the curious story of a woman whose dead husband appeared to her in a dream and castigated her for being twice remarried. A few days later the woman died (*Ant.* 17.8.4 §§349–53). Josephus defends the inclusion of this and similar tales as 'instances (παραδείγματα)...bearing on the immortality of the soul and of the way in which God's providence embraces the affairs of man' (17.8.5 §354).[126] In another passage Josephus grounds his beliefs regarding the afterlife in the testimony of the Mosaic Law (*Ag. Ap.* 2.30 §§217–18):

> For those...who live in accordance with our laws the prize is not silver or gold, no crown of wild olive or of parsley.... No; each individual, relying on the witness of his own conscience and the lawgiver's prophecy, confirmed by the sure testimony of God, is firmly persuaded that to those who observe the laws and, if they must

---

[125] My analysis of Josephus at this point is indebted to that of Steve Mason, *Flavius Josephus on the Pharisees: A Composition-Critical Study* (StPB 39; Leiden: Brill, 1991), 158–70.

[126] There are other references to immortality in Josephus that do not necessarily reflect his own point of view: *J. W.* 1.2.4 §58 (cp. 2.8.10 §151); 1.33.2 §650; 6.1.5 §§46–48; 7.8.7 §§341–57.

needs die for them, willingly meet death, God has granted a renewed existence (δέδωκεν ὁ θεὸς γενέσθαι πάλιν) and in the revolution of the ages (ἐκ περιτροπῆς) the gift of a better life (βίον ἀμείνω λαβεῖν).

Josephus's personal statements are in agreement with his descriptions of both the Pharisaic and Essene beliefs about the afterlife on two points: the immortality of the soul and the existence of post-mortem rewards and punishments. His statements are more in line with the Essenes—both verbally and conceptually—with regard to his anthropology and his understanding of the destination of righteous souls after death. He agrees with the Essenes that upon death righteous souls 'inherit a most sacred, heavenly place' (χῶρον οὐράνιον λαχοῦσαι τὸν ἁγιώτατον, *J. W.* 3.8.5 §374; my translation), a place easily identifiable with the Isles of the Blessed and described as a location with perfect climatic conditions (*J. W.* 2.8.11 §155). But for Josephus this is only an interim residence, since 'in the revolution of the ages, they return to find in chaste bodies a new habitation' (*J. W.* 3.8.5 §374). This 'renewed existence' or 'better life' (*Ag. Ap.* 2.30 §218) coincides with his description of the Pharisaic belief that 'the soul of the good alone passes into another body' (*J. W.* 2.8.14 §163). The expressions employed by Josephus would have connoted a form of reincarnation to the educated Hellenistic reader. The idea of metempsychosis was expressed by means of virtually identical phraseology. Plato designated the process as παλιγγενεσία,[127] for the immortal soul 'becomes again' (πάλιν γίγνεσθαι)[128] or 'lives again' (τὸ ἀναβιώσεσθαι).[129] Yet Josephus's view differs in two crucial ways. (1) He does not subscribe to the notion of a cyclical process of transmigration. The 'reincarnation' of which he speaks is of singular, eschatological import. It will occur 'in the revolution of the ages,' in keeping with Jewish two-age theology. (2) This re-embodiment does not fall along a relative scale of enlightenment, but is rather part and parcel with the ultimate 'reward' experienced by the righteous. Returning to 'find in chaste bodies a new habitation' stands over against the eternal punishment of the wicked under the earth. The eschatological and ethical bent to Josephus's conception of re-embodiment leads one to suspect that he is portraying the Jewish idea of bodily resurrection, but in Greek dress. Indeed, there is some precedent for this re-appropriation. In 2 Maccabees we have already seen not only how the resurrection could be conceived within the context of Yahweh's creative activity in the womb as well as in the cosmos, but that it could be denominated αἰώνιον ἀναβίωσιν ζωῆς (2 Macc 7:9; cf.

---

[127] Plato, *Meno* 81b–c; *Phaedr.* 80e, 81e, 114c, 107c, 133d.
[128] Plato, *Meno* 81b; *Phaed.* 70c, 72a.
[129] Plato, *Phaed.* 71e.

Josephus's ῥᾳστώνην τοῦ ἀναβιοῦν).[130] Because Josephus has ingeniously adapted Greek reincarnational terminology, it is difficult to determine whether he saw continuity between dead and resurrected bodies. It is possible that the otherness of the resurrected body is not being pressed by him (ἕτερον σῶμα) so much as its sanctity (ἁγνοῖς σώμασιν) which makes it fit for the new world.[131]

Even in Josephus's Hellenized version of Jewish eschatology, some of the distinctives of Jewish resurrection theology are not lost. First of all, Josephus mentions rewards and punishments that are contingent upon one's obedience to the Law. This connotes covenant relationship, and its consequent sanctions, effective in the afterlife. This would not have derived from nor been shared by his intellectual peers in the Greco-Roman world. Second, he seems to hold to a final judgment, resurrection, and age to come, all of which are masked in Hellenistic language. If Josephus does not provide the kinds of rich theological metaphors that we have found elsewhere in Jewish literature, that is understandable. Josephus appears to have consciously adapted his work with Hellenistic listeners in mind.

3.2 Summary and Conclusions

Beginning with the earliest references to the resurrection in the Hebrew Bible, a complex of ideas coalesced around faith in Yahweh as the one who raises the dead. These expressions of the *theological significance* of the resurrection spring from Israel's realization that he is bound in covenant to the God who has created and chosen him, and that he is presently suffering under the negative sanctions of that agreement because of apostasy and sin. He in one way or another does not have full possession of the Promised Land, and is therefore in exile. He has fallen from a position of sovereignty, and is instead oppressed and enslaved. It is out of this context that a hope in the resurrection emerges—a hope that his wicked oppressors will be laid low and that he will once again be 'raised up.' Resurrection is conditioned upon Israel's repentance and covenant-renewal, and comprises a key component in the nation's subsequent re-installment into vice-regency with Yahweh over his new creation. This pattern is clearly visible in most of the texts we have surveyed, even if each detail is not spelled out in every case (Hos 6:1–3; Ezek 37:1–14; Isa 26:19; Dan 12:1–3; 2 Macc 7; Similitudes of Enoch; *4 Ezra*; *2 Bar.*; *T. 12 Patr.*). In other texts where the pattern is not nearly as explicit, or virtually nonexistent (*Sib. Or.*; Ps-Phoc.; Josephus), this is explainable by the fact that Jewish eschatological hopes have been

---

[130] See Feldman's note c on *Ant.* 18.1.3 §14 (LCL).

[131] Mason, *Josephus on the Pharisees*, 169.

Resurrection in Second Temple Judaism 91

overshadowed in the interest of accommodating Hellenistic listeners. Even in these cases, however, the distinctive Jewish understanding of the *nature* of resurrection as the raising up of the dead out of the earth (*Sib. Or.*; Ps-Phoc.)—or at least as a form of re-embodiment (Josephus)—remains. This concrete representation of the resurrection appears in most of the literature, although we have seen that it can also be accompanied by a belief in the immortality of the soul (e.g., *4 Ezra*; Josephus) or the idea that the human status, if not the human body itself, is transformed to be like the stars or the angels of heaven (Dan 12:3; *1 En.*; *4 Ezra*; *2 Bar.*). In the final analysis, the nature and theology of resurrection are not abstracted from each other. Resurrection is never simply a matter of indicating the physical resuscitation or reconstitution of the human body. Indeed, the 'physics' of resurrection is never defined as clearly as we would like (except in *2 Bar.*, and of course in later rabbinic literature). At a minimum, resurrection is coupled with the idea of a final judgment, and it is even more often linked to a theological complex that envisions Israel's covenant-renewal, national restoration, and exaltation in the new creation and dominion of Yahweh. We may conclude that the resurrection of the dead is a key aspect of Israel's hope for restoration as the covenant people of God.

Chapter 4

Resurrection in the Hellenistic World

The purpose of this chapter is to take into consideration the Hellenistic interpretations of the phenomenon of persons returning from the dead. Once our survey of both Jewish and Hellenistic ideas is complete, then we will be able to determine, in Chapter 5, how Luke-Acts is positioned against this conceptual background. Ideally, only a detailed study of the Greek and Roman views of the afterlife could demonstrate the astonishing variety of Hellenistic beliefs regarding the fate of the departed. Since the documentary, epigraphical, and archaeological evidence is vast, and as there are many fine studies already in existence,[1] we will do well to limit ourselves to a 'bird's-eye view' of the subject. After providing a synopsis of what may qualify as mainstream ideas about the afterlife leading up to the Hellenistic era, we will focus upon indicators of how people in the Greco-

---

[1] The standard is the classic work, Erwin Rohde, *Psyche: The Cult of Souls and Belief in Immortality among the Ancient Greeks* (trans. by W. B. Hillis; 8th ed.; of 1925; repr., Chicago: Ares, 1985). A wealth of epigraphical data is accessible in Richmond Lattimore, *Themes in Greek and Latin Epitaphs* (Illinois Studies in Language and Literature 28.1–2; Urbana, Ill.: University of Illinois Press, 1942); and *The Greek Anthology* (LCL) Book 7. An anthology of excerpts from primary sources appears in John Ferguson, *Greek and Roman Religion: A Source Book* (Noyes Classical Studies; Park Ridge, N.J.: Noyes, 1980), 140–56. An updated treatment of Greek beliefs is in Robert Garland, *The Greek Way of Death* (Ithaca, N.Y.: Cornell University Press, 1985), and for Roman beliefs see J. M. C. Toynbee, *Death and Burial in the Roman World* (Aspects of Greek and Roman Life; Ithaca, N.Y.: Cornell University Press, 1971). W. F. Jackson Knight's otherwise useful survey (*Elysion* [New York: Barnes & Noble, 1970]) is marred by the author's preoccupation with viewing ancient conceptions of the afterlife through the lens of modern-day spiritualism. Excellent overviews include, N. J. Richardson, 'Early Greek Views about Life after Death,' in *Greek Religion and Society* (eds. P. E. Easterling and J. V. Muir; Cambridge: Cambridge University Press, 1985), 50–66; Emily Vermeule, 'The Afterlife: Greece,' in *Civilization of the Ancient Mediterranean: Greece and Rome* (eds. Michael Grant and Rachel Kitzinger; 3 vols.; New York: Charles Scribner's Sons, 1988), 2:987–96; John A. North, 'The Afterlife: Rome,' in *Civilization of the Ancient Mediterranean*, 2:997–1007; Robert S. J. Garland and John Scheid, 'Death, Attitudes to,' *OCD* 433–34. Surveys focusing on the data impinging on the subject of resurrection: Gregory J. Riley, *Resurrection Reconsidered: Thomas and John in Controversy* (Minneapolis: Fortress, 1995), 23–68; Wright, *Resurrection of the Son of God*, 32–84.

Roman world interpreted the phenomenon, whether real or imagined, of persons coming back from the dead.

4.1 A Synopsis of Hellenistic Conceptions of the Afterlife

An evolutionary history of the ancient Greek and Roman ideas regarding life after death is impossible to write with any precision, yet general lines of development can be traced, if only for heuristic purposes. In the Hellenistic period it was common for various—often conflicting—conceptions of the afterlife to appear side-by-side. Nevertheless, three general stages will be outlined in the following discussion.[2]

4.1.1 The Tomb as the Residence for the Dead

The most ancient conception perceived the dead as somehow existing in or around the tomb. The Etruscan tombs, with their vivid paintings of the deceased as feasting, playing music, dancing, engaging in sport (including acts of love), and which contain the accoutrements of daily life such as toilet articles, culinary implements, weapons, armour, etc., bespeak an existence of the dead that is an extension of present life.[3] From ancient times up through the Hellenistic period, the practice of feeding the dead was practiced throughout the Greco-Roman world.[4] Many tombs were built with channels reaching into the space where the remains rested so that blood, food, or drink offerings could be piped in.[5] Ancients believed that the spinal cord of the deceased could be transformed into a serpent and appear at the

---

[2] For a comparable threefold delineation, see Peter G. Bolt, 'Life, Death, and the Afterlife in the Greco-Roman World,' in *Life in the Face of Death: The Resurrection Message in the New Testament* (McMNTS; ed. Richard N. Longenecker; Grand Rapids: Eerdmans, 1998), 66.

[3] Toynbee, *Death and Burial in the Roman World*, 11–12.

[4] The practice has continued even into modern times among the Greek Orthodox, and was common in the West, too, until the great fourth-century bishop Ambrose famously forbade Augustine's mother, Monica, from engaging in such cemetery ritual. Augustine would follow suit in North Africa, seeing the practice as 'pagan'; see James J. O'Donnell, *Augustine: A New Biography* (New York: HarperCollins, 2005), 150.

[5] Garland, *Greek Way of Death*, 110–15; Toynbee, *Death and Burial in the Roman World*, 37. Toynbee (50–51) reports that there were even mausolea equipped with kitchens; cf. Pausanias, *Descr.* 10.4.10: 'The Phocians bring sacrificial animals and pour the blood into the grave through a hole, but the meat they themselves customarily consume on site.' On Jewish aversion to the Gentile practice of sacrifices to the dead and eating in tombs, cf. *Jub.* 22:17.

grave site, perhaps to lick up libations.[6] Epigraphical evidence, too, points to the dead as residing in or about the tomb. The deceased, by way of epitaphs, often address passers-by in the first or second person.[7] There is also the wish, common in both Greek and Latin epitaphs, that the earth would lie lightly upon the dead person.[8] Funerary stelae of the fifth and fourth centuries B.C. often portray the dead personably shaking hands with loved ones or gazing in a serious or tranquil pose,[9] and Attic oil flasks are decorated with winged *psychai* hovering above grave-monuments.[10]

4.1.2 Hades: The House of Death

A second stage, which had an enormous impact upon the Hellenistic vision of the afterlife, encompasses the imaginative, literary descriptions of Hades found in the ancient poetic literature of Greece. Lucian asserted that the public or laity 'trust Homer and Hesiod and other myth-makers in these matters' (*Luct.* 2). Plutarch wrote of 'the doctrine and fabulous argument of mothers and nurses' (*Mor.* 1105b), Cicero of 'the monstrous fictions of poets and painters' (*Tusc.* 1.11), and Seneca rejected such 'fancies of poets' (*Marc.* 19.1). These high-minded comments only serve to underline the extensive hold that the Homeric representation of the underworld had on the religious imagination of everyday people in the Roman world. Ironically, while Lucian claims that only the ἰδιῶται cling to such beliefs, the popularity of these ideas can be attributed to the fact that Homer and Hesiod formed part of the core educational curriculum in the Roman empire.[11] In order to lampoon popular ideas about the realm of the dead, Lucian satirically rehearses each rich detail in *On Funerals* (2–9) and his *Dialogues of*

---

[6] Plutarch, *Cleom.* 39; Aelian, *Nat. an.* 1.51; Pliny the Elder, *Nat.* 10.86; Ovid, *Metam.* 15.389–90; Servius, *Aen.* 5.95; Origen, *Cels.* 4.57; see Walter Burkert, *Greek Religion: Archaic and Classical* (trans. John Raffan; Oxford: Basil Blackwell, 1985), 195.

[7] This, however, is not decisive since epitaphs which mock the idea of an afterlife are also written according to form; see Lattimore, *Themes in Greek and Latin Epitaphs*, 74–82.

[8] Lattimore, *Themes in Greek and Latin Epitaphs*, 65–74. The Latin expression is commonly abbreviated s(*it*) t(*ibi*) t(*erra*) l(*evis*).

[9] Vermeule, 'Afterlife: Greece,' 994; on the 'handshake' motif see Garland, *Greek Way of Death*, 65.

[10] Rohde, *Psyche*, 170.

[11] Stanley F. Bonner, *Education in Ancient Rome: From the Elder Cato to the Younger Pliny* (Berkeley: University of California Press, 1977), 212–13; William V. Harris, *Ancient Literacy* (Cambridge, Mass.: Harvard University Press, 1989), 61–62, 126, 137, 227.

the Dead, surely aware that nearly any common citizen could grasp the slightest turn of sarcasm. Homer, in the *Iliad*[12] and in Books 11 and 24 of the *Odyssey*, depicts the underworld as a dark, murky underground expanse (*Il.* 21.56; 22.482; *Od.* 11.57, 155; 20.356.).[13] Like Sheol in the Hebrew Bible, Hades is the common lot of every human being, which no one may escape. The souls in Hades lack both strength and wits, and are only shadows or images of their former selves.[14] The underworld is ruled by the god Hades (*Il.* 15.184–93) and his queen Persephone; his nephew Aeachus is the commander of the guard; and souls are escorted there by Hermes Psychopompus. Later, other details would be added, such as the three-headed watchdog Cerberus (Hes. *Theog.* 311, 770–73)[15] and the ferryman Charon who transports shades across the water toward Hades' gates (Ar. *Ran.* 180–270), culminating with a developed portrait like that in Book 6 of Virgil's *Aeneid*. The seriousness with which people took these descriptions of what one could expect to encounter after death is evidenced in many epitaphs[16] as well as in the practice, reported by Lucian (*Luct.* 10) and confirmed by

---

[12] *Il.* 1.3; 3.322, 646; 6.284, 422, 487–89; 7.131, 330; 8.367–70; 16.856; 23.71–76; etc.

[13] For more on the afterlife in Homer, see Christiane Sourvinou-Inwood, 'To Die and Enter the House of Hades: Homer, Before and After,' in *Mirrors of Mortality: Studies in the Social History of Death* (Social History of Human Experience; ed. Joachim Whaley; New York: St. Martin's, 1981), 15–39.

[14] They are 'strengthless' (ἀμενηνός, *Od.* 10.521, 536; 11.29, 49, 393) and without 'wits' (φρένες, *Il.* 23.104); cf. Garland, *Greek Way of Death*, 1, 133. The exceptional case is Teiresias, the Theban prophet who remains in command of his mental faculties (*Od.* 10.492–94); but even he must drink blood to gain strength to address Odysseus (11.96–99). The soul is an 'image' (εἴδωλον, *Il.* 23.72; *Od.* 11.83, 213, 476; 20.355; 24.14) or 'shadow' (σκία, *Od.* 10.495; 11.207) that looks exactly like the person at the time of death. In *Il.* 23.104–17 Achilles tries to grasp the *psychē* of Patroclus, but it vanishes away like smoke. Achilles realizes that it was only the image of Patroclus, but he remarks how it looked 'wondrously like his very self.' There are vivid images of the battle-wounded in Hades, still wearing their bloody armour (*Il.* 11.41; cp. the embattled Hector with blood-clotted hair and death wounds in Virgil, *Aen.* 2.272–73, 277–79, or the ghost of Clytemnestra who displays her death-wounds in Aeschylus, *Eum.*, 94–105). The *psychai* of valiant Achaean warriors that enter into Hades are distinguished from their 'selves' (αὐτούς) that are left as carrion for dogs and birds (*Il.* 1.3–4). See Jan Bremmer, *The Early Greek Concept of the Soul* (Princeton: Princeton University Press, 1983), 78–79; Vermeule, 'Afterlife: Greece,' 988–89.

[15] The hound of Hades is known to Homer (*Il.* 8.368), but he is as yet unnamed and is not an established figure in Homer's two *Nekyiai*.

[16] Lattimore, *Themes in Greek and Latin Epitaphs*, 87–90, 95–96, 147; *Greek Anthology* 7.57–59, 63–70, 365, 600, 603, 671.

modern archaeology, of placing an obol in the mouth of the deceased in order to pay fare to Charon.

4.1.3 Variations and Departures from the Homeric Vision of the Afterlife

The ancient Greek poets consigned all of the dead to an equally uninviting afterlife in Hades. There were flickers of a pleasant life in the Elysian Fields (Hom. *Od.* 4.561–68) or Isles of the Blessed (Hes. *Op.* 171; Pind. *Thren.* 6, frag. 129; *Ol.* 2.68–84), but those ports of call were reserved for heroes or other men of renown who were brought there before death. Conversely, only the desperately wicked Titans were plunged into the darker regions of Tartarus (Hom. *Il.* 8.13–16, 481; Hes. *Theog.* 119, 721–35), while those who had challenged the honour of the gods—Sisyphus, Tantalus, and Tityus—received tedious punishment in Hades (Hom. *Od.* 11.582–600). Eventually, Elysium was opened up to a wider range of virtuous people,[17] and the threat of punishment in Hades was extended to more common criminals.[18] Escape from the terrors of Hades was promised to those initiated into the mysteries, but it is questionable whether this implied belief in retributive justice applied on the basis of ethical behaviour, as we find in Plato (*Phaed.* 111c–114c). Pausanius describes paintings by Polygnotus at Delphi which depict the uninitiated in Hades performing repetitive tasks right alongside Tityus, Sisyphus, and Tantalus, such as Oknos ('Sloth') who is plaiting a rope that a donkey next to him is eating (10.29.1–2) or women who are carrying leaky water-pots (10.31.9–11).

Whereas in Homer the world of the dead was located under the earth, attention was later directed toward the celestial spheres.[19] By the Classical period, many Greeks believed that the *psychē* consisted of aether and that at death it returned to its ethereal source in the heavens.[20] This could mean no more than that a person's 'breath' had left the body and returned into the

---

[17] Rohde, *Psyche*, 536–37; Vermeule, 'Afterlife: Greece,' 993.

[18] Plautus, *Capt.* 5.4.1–2; Virgil, *Aen.* 6.548–627; Lucian, *Luct.* 7–8. According to Lucian (9), however, the greater part of the dead were 'of the middle way in life' who simply wander about as shadows.

[19] This coincided with the shift from the ancient cosmological model of an egg-shaped, three-story universe to the Ptolemaic model of a fixed sphere central to a number of concentric heavenly spheres; see Riley, *Resurrection Reconsidered*, 27–28; Luther H. Martin, *Hellenistic Religions: An Introduction* (New York and Oxford: Oxford University Press, 1987), 6–8.

[20] In the British Museum there is an inscription from Athens commemorating the warriors who died at the Potidaea in 432 B.C., and it includes the line: αἰθὴρ μὲν φσυχὰς ὑπεδέχατο, σώ[ματα δὲ χθών] (*IG* I,2 945.6, cited in Rohde, *Psyche*, 461 n. 149; cf. Lattimore, *Themes in Greek and Latin Epitaphs*, 31).

upper atmosphere.[21] Diogenes of Apollonia believed that the air humans and animals breathe is essentially their soul and mind; it is the primal substance of all living things, regarded by him as θεός.[22] A theological corollary to this cosmological theory was the expression of a kind of impersonal immortality, as in Euripides: 'The mind of those who have died, blown into the immortal air (ἀθάνατον αἰθέρ), immortally has knowledge, though all life is gone' (*Hel.* 1014–15).[23] The *psychē* could be said to enter into the realm of the divine, since the aether is the atmosphere in which gods and stars reside.[24] Beginning with Aristophanes' question as to whether it is really the case that when people die they become stars in the sky (*Pax* 832–33), we know of a belief in astral immortality that was widely held by the imperial period.[25] This is abundantly attested to in epitaphs;[26] its most systematic expression was traced to the philosophical thought of Pythagoras and Plato;[27] and it was pressed into imperial service

---

[21] See the epitaphs which speak of the soul fluttering away or vanishing like the wind in Lattimore, *Themes in Greek and Latin Epitaphs*, 29.

[22] W. K. C. Guthrie, *The Greeks and Their Gods* (Boston: Beacon, 1962), 135–36; cf. Rohde, *Psyche*, 437–38.

[23] In David Grene and Richmond Lattimore, eds., *The Complete Greek Tragedies* (4 vols.; Chicago: University of Chicago Press, 1992), 3:458. Cf. πνεῦμα μὲν πρὸς αἰθέρα τὸ σῶμα δ᾽ἐς γῆν (Euripides, *Suppl.* 533–34) and Euripides, frag. 971, in August Nauck, ed., *Tragicorum Graecorum Fragmenta* (Hildesheim: Georg Olms, 1964), 674.

[24] Guthrie, *Greeks and Their Gods*, 208–9, 263. In Lucian, *Icar.* 1, Menippus soars into heaven in three stages (reminding one of Paul's reference to being caught up into the third heaven, 2 Cor 12:2): from the earth to the moon; the moon to the sun; and from the sun into heaven itself, 'the citadel of Zeus.'

[25] Rohde (*Psyche*, 541) writes: 'For many individuals the hope is expressed or the certainty announced that after death they will have their dwelling in the sky—in the shining *Aether*, among the stars. This belief in the elevation of the disembodied soul to the regions above the earth is so frequently repeated in various forms in this late period that we must suppose that among those who entertained precise conceptions of the things of the next world this was the most popular and widely held conviction.'

[26] Lattimore, *Themes in Greek and Latin Epitaphs*, 32–35; e.g., 'Mother, do not weep for me. What is the use? You ought rather to reverence me, for I have become an evening star, among the gods' (35).

[27] The idea that good souls inhabit the upper world of air while the bad are incarcerated in Hades was ascribed to Pythagoras (Diog. Laert. 8.31–32). Cicero says that the first recorded person to espouse that human souls are immortal was Pherecydes of Syria, and that this opinion was further advanced by his pupil Pythagoras. In turn, Plato went to Italy where he learned the doctrine of the Pythagoreans (*Tusc.* 1.17.38–39). For more on Pherecydes and Pythagoras, see Rohde, *Psyche*, 376, 399 n. 51. According to Pausanias, the Chaldeans and Indian sages were the first to say that the human soul is immortal, and they were followed by some of the Greeks, especially Plato (*Descr.*

to depict the apotheosis of the Roman emperors.[28] In popular thought (in contradistinction to the learned disdain for underworld mythology and greater acceptance of philosophical speculation about the ascent of the soul into the divine realm[29]) poetic images were freely combined with the notion of celestial immortality: the god Hades may assist one, not into the house of the dead, but into the realm above;[30] and the Elysian Fields may be construed on the one hand with the underworld, or on the other with the aether.[31]

4.1.4 Summary

Even if it had been possible to engage in a wider-range study of the Greco-Roman beliefs regarding the afterlife, we would have still ended up with a painting more pointillist than realist. However, we have seen enough dots to discern a basic outline, beginning with the earliest view that the dead live near their tombs, proceeding to the poetic vision of the underworld, and concluding with philosophical views of the fate of souls. In reality, the Greco-Roman views of the afterlife were an amalgam of disparate ideas that accumulated over centuries, and both mythical and philosophical conceptions were often enmeshed in popular thought without any awareness of contradiction. With this picture in mind, we are now prepared to look more closely at those aspects of ancient thought that may have constituted part of an interpretive grid for contemplating the idea of resurrection from a Greco-Roman perspective.

4.32.4). Plato (*Resp.* 621b) represents souls as darting like shooting stars in every direction as they return to earth for rebirth.

[28] The appearance of a comet was believed to be a star, signifying the soul of Caesar entering into the midst of the immortal gods (Pliny the Elder, *Nat.* 2.23.94). The myth of Romulus's apotheosis during an eclipse was also used as a pattern for describing the divination of the emperors; see Bolt, 'Life, Death, and the Afterlife in the Greco-Roman World,' 71–72.

[29] Cicero, *Tusc.* 1.10–11, 37–44.

[30] 'Stand before the tomb and behold young Choro, unwedded daughter of Diognetus. Hades has set her in the seventh circle' (Lattimore, *Themes in Greek and Roman Epitaphs*, 34). The seventh circle is the lunar sphere in the Ptolemaic model of the cosmos.

[31] The location of Elysian Fields (or the Isles of the Blessed) is located variously: under the earth, in the sky, in tracts of the moon, or unspecified (Lattimore, *Themes in Greek and Roman Epitaphs*, 40–42). A part of one epitaph reads: 'you made haste to join the immortals, purifying your body with the stars of heaven…. Farewell, and be glad in Elysium' (50). Another epitaph claims that the remains of the deceased lie beneath the inscription, but 'if thou seekest Menander himself thou shalt find him in the abode of Zeus or in the Islands of the Blest' (*Greek Anthology*, 7.370).

4.2 Reactions to Resurrection in the Greco-Roman World

4.2.1 General Attitudes toward Resurrection

The idea of resurrection was not altogether foreign to the ancient Greeks, but was regarded as either impossible or, if possible, divinely forbidden and highly undesirable. The first sentiment was epitomized by the god Apollos in Aeschylus's *Eumenides*: 'But when the dust hath drained the blood of man, once he is slain, there is no return to life (ἅπαξ θάνοντος, οὔτις ἔστ' ἀνάστασις)' (647–48). Zeus, he explains, can do anything else without any effort at all, but this is a thing for which no curative spells are available (649–51).[32] Yet Pindar relates to us that Asclepius once brought back a man from the dead, and when Zeus found out, he struck down both the healer and his patient with a thunderbolt (*Pyth.* 3.54–58). Only the gods, who are immortal, may die and be reborn. There were exceptions, as we shall see, but they do not detract from the general observation that most people who imbibed the Greek way of life were not congenial toward the prospect of perpetual bodily existence after death.[33] Indeed, the notion of bodily resurrection would have been abhorrent to those who subscribed to the Orphic dictum, σῶμα σῆμα, 'the body is a tomb.'[34] The vitriolic reaction of Celsus toward the Christian doctrine of resurrection, although heightened by polemic, no doubt expressed a typical Hellenistic reflex—at least among intellectuals of late antiquity.[35] Celsus thought that the idea of returning to life in the same body in which one had died was not only preposterous but repulsive: 'This is simply the hope of worms. For what sort of human soul would have any further desire for a body that has rotted?'[36]

---

[32] Other instances of this sentiment: Homer, *Il.* 21.56; 24.551, 736.; Herodotus 3.62; Aeschylus, *Ag.* 1360–61; Sophocles, *El.* 137–45; see A. Oepke, 'Auferstehung II (des Menschen),' *RAC* 1.931; Wright, *Resurrection of the Son of God*, 32–35.

[33] Being immortalized *before* death, as in the case of heroes translated to the Isles of the Blest, was apparently another matter (cf. Rohde, *Psyche*, 536–37). Recall Calypso's offer of immortality to Odysseus (Homer, *Od.* 5.1–268).

[34] On the Orphic origin of this expression, see Plato, *Crat.* 400c.

[35] 'Resurrection in the flesh appeared a startling, distasteful idea, at odds with everything that passed for wisdom among the educated'; so Ramsay MacMullen, *Christianizing the Roman Empire (A.D. 100–400)* (New Haven: Yale University Press, 1984), 12. See also, John G. Cook, 'Some Hellenistic Responses to the Gospels and Gospel Traditions,' *ZNW* 84 (1993): 237–38, 241, 247–48, 252.

[36] Origen, *Cel.* 5.14. Celsus further quotes a statement from Heraclitus: 'corpses ought to be thrown away as worse than dung' (cf. Heraclitus, frag. 86).

4.2.2 The Earliest Imaginative Representations of 'Resurrection'

Revulsion and fascination, however, are often not far removed from each other. Some ancient poets were not reticent to play with the notion of resurrection.[37] In Aristophanes' *Frogs* (*Ran.* 170–80), two characters are on their way to the underworld when they meet up with a corpse being carried on a litter in a funeral cortège. The corpse sits up and speaks. The two men ask him if he would be willing to take along their luggage to Hades, a task for which the corpse demands two drachmas. Considering this too pricey, they offer nine obols. The corpse replies, 'I'd sooner live again!' (ἀναβιῴην νῦν πάλιν, 178).[38] A more sublime example is in Euripides' *Alcestis*. When the life of Admetus is required of him, he is able to find no one—not even his aged parents—to die in his place. Ultimately his wife Alcestis willingly dies for him, but she is retrieved from the grave by Heracles. Admetus is dumbstruck when Heracles presents Alcestis to him alive. He thinks it is only a trick of the gods (*Alc.* 1123–25), and when Heracles assures him that it is really her, he responds: 'Be careful she is not some phantom (φάσμα) from the depths... Do I see my wife, whom I was laying in the grave?' (1127, 1129). Despite further incredulity ('May I touch her, and speak to her, as my living wife?' [1131]), it is confirmed to Admetus that it is really his beloved who has been brought back from the dead. The play closes with the chorus chanting about the unpredictable possibilities in life that the supernatural world springs upon us (1159–63). Another celebrated instance of resurrection is in Plato's myth of Er (*Resp.* 614b–621d). Er was a brave warrior who was killed in action and was left on the battlefield for ten days. When the bodies of those who had fallen were collected, Er's corpse had resisted putrefaction. He was transported home, and on the twelfth day after his death, just as his funeral was beginning and he was lying on the pyre, he came back to life (ἀνεβίω). Er recounts his journey in the afterlife, wherein the cyclical process of reincarnation was revealed to him, as well as how one might eventually escape the cycle through wisdom and virtue.

These imaginative presentations are provocative because each of them expresses resurrection as the human person returning to life from the dead. In Aristophanes, the deceased makes his facetious comment about coming back to life during his *ekphora* or funeral procession, while Alcestis had actually been buried, and Er had been dead for twelve days. As remarkable as this may be, several points should be kept in mind about these examples.

---

[37] The idea that Greek poets could 'have fun with the notion' of resurrection is suggested by J. Duncan M. Derrett, *The Anastasis: The Resurrection of Jesus as an Historical Event* (Warwickshire, England: P. Drinkwater, 1982), 19.

[38] My translation; Greek text: Alan H. Sommerstein, ed., *The Comedies of Aristophanes* (10 vols.; Warminster, England: Aris and Phillips, 1996).

First, all of these examples may be categorized as mythological stories, and in the case of Aristophanes, the playfulness of the reference to resurrection is transparent. Second, these are exceptional cases. To what extent these stories were based upon actual reports of what are now called 'near death experiences' is impossible to determine. Third, especially with regard to the first two cases, it must be observed that resurrection from the dead is not singled out as an object of belief or philosophical speculation. The story of Alcestis is presented as a quirk of fate, and later Plutarch reverts to this tale in his 'Dialogue on Love' as an illustration of love's superiority over death. He likens the story to that of Protesilaus or of Orpheus,[39] and asserts that celebrants of Love's mysteries have a higher place in Hades than even those who have been initiated into the Eleusinian mysteries (*Mor.* 761e–762a). In the third instance, the resurrection of Er was employed by Plato as a vehicle to secure a report about the afterlife, and to buttress his theory about the transmigration of souls. Yet we are nowhere near to the belief among Jews in a final judgment and general resurrection of the dead. Curiously, nonetheless, it is easy to see from this Platonic example how someone like Josephus could appropriate reincarnational terminology to speak of resurrection, or how Celsus could accuse Christians of talking about the resurrection out of a misunderstanding of the doctrine of reincarnation (Origen, *Cels.* 7.32).

4.2.3 Cave-Dwelling, Astral Projection, and 'Resurrection'

Resurrection from the dead, as we have already seen, was usually not itself the object of inquiry. Rather, its occurrence—real or imagined—was the occasion for discussions of other lofty subjects like the triumph of love or, more commonly, the nature of human beings. Incredulity was registered about the possibility of resurrection, particularly by natural scientists and materialists.[40] The latter introduced more refined definition, for they interpreted the phenomenon of persons returning from the dead as a matter of

---

[39] Protesilaus was a Thessalian, and the first Achaean to be struck down in the Trojan War (Homer, *Il.* 2.698–702). He was only a youth, 'and his wife was left tearing her cheeks and his house half-built.' He was awarded hero status (Herodotus 9.116–20), and the Homeric details of his story underwent expansion, e.g., it is said his wife mourned so excessively for him that the gods allowed him to return to visit her for a few hours (Andrew L. Brown, 'Protesilaus,' *OCD* 1265). Orpheus, of course, was the mythical singer who was given permission by the chthonian gods to retrieve his lover Eurydice from Hades.

[40] Democritus, however, took into account the ἀναβιώσεις of the apparently dead in his atomic theory; see Rohde, *Psyche*, 408 n. 103.

resuscitation, rather than resurrection from the dead (see the excursus at the end of this chapter).

A number of reports of 'resurrection' appear in antiquity. One of the earliest is Herodotus's unflattering account of Zalmoxis. Zalmoxis was a god of the Getae in Thrace (4.94), for whom Herodotus supplies a euhemeristic version of his divinization (4.95–96). Zalmoxis was a slave of Pythagoras in Samos. He was later freed, and after accruing great wealth, returned to his native Thrace. There he began to attract followers through his hospitality, as well as with his teaching that whoever kept company with him would become immortal. One day he vanished. He had retreated into a subterranean chamber he had prepared for himself. His followers mourned for him as dead, and he remained hidden for three years. On the fourth year, he reappeared to a credulous public who now embraced his method for gaining immortality.

Hermippus of Smyrna's sardonic account of Pythagoras's own staged 'resurrection' is preserved by Diogenes Laertius (8.41):

> Hermippus gives another anecdote. Pythagoras, on coming to Italy, made a subterranean dwelling and enjoined on his mother to mark and record all that passed, and at what hour, and to send her notes down to him until he should ascend. She did so. Pythagoras some time afterwards[41] came up withered and looking like a skeleton, then went into the assembly and declared he had been down to Hades, and even read out his experiences to them. They were so affected that they wept and wailed and looked upon him as divine, going so far as to send their wives to him in hopes that they would learn some of his doctrines; and so they were called Pythagorean women. Thus far Hermippus.

The Cretan priest, Epimenides, had a 'Rip van Winkle' experience when as a boy he escaped the heat and fatigue by sleeping in a cave, only to wake up 57 years later.[42] These cavernous adventures probably had mantic or shamanistic importance as initiatory rituals.[43] Whatever their elaborate religious symbolism may have been, it is clear that these 'death' and 'resurrection' experiences lent authority to the holy men who underwent them, and indicated to immediate observers that these persons possessed esoteric wisdom regarding the supernatural world. Later narrators such as Herodo-

---

[41] Tertullian tells us it was seven years later (*An*. 28).

[42] Diog. Laert. 1.109; Pliny the Elder, *Nat*. 7.52.175; Plutarch, *Mor*. 784a; cf. Lucian *Philops*. 26.

[43] On the religious and symbolic significance of underground caves for chthonic initiations, see Mircea Eliade, *Zalmoxis, the Vanishing God: Comparative Studies in the Religions and Folklore of Dacia and Eastern Europe* (trans. Willard R. Trask; Chicago: University of Chicago Press, 1972), 21–75.

tus, Hermippus,[44] and Pliny (not to mention Lucian!) were not as nearly convinced.

Religious and philosophical insights into the nature of reality afforded such wise men the capacity to experience and exploit that reality with increased adeptness. They were able to have out-of-body experiences and ascertain prophetic knowledge. These acts required a kind of resurrection, but yielded findings superior to the resurrection itself. The overriding concern in nearly every retelling of such experiences was the demonstration of the nature of human beings, with special emphasis upon the Pythagorean (or Platonic) conception of the immortality of the soul. Hermotimus of Clazomenae was known in antiquity as a seer whose soul left his body for long periods to return with prophecies of impending natural disasters. He would place his wife under orders to ensure that his 'corpse' was unmolested until his soul had returned and reanimated his body. On one occasion, his wife was persuaded to allow some men into the house. They found his body lying naked and motionless on the floor, brought fire and burned it, and thus deprived the man's soul of its 'sheath.'[45] Other versions of this tale were told within the context of discussing bodily resuscitations or the nature of the soul.[46] Herodotus (4.15) relates the story of a certain Aristeas of Proconnesus who entered a fuller's shop and died. The fuller locked up his workshop and rushed to the family to inform them of the death. The word of Aristeas's death filled the city, but was vehemently disputed by a visitor who insisted that he had just seen him on his way into town. The family proceeded to the fuller's shop with all of the necessary burial preparations, but when the shop was opened, Aristeas was nowhere to be found. Aristeas reappeared seven years later and composed a famous poem, *Arimaspea*, which told of a curious one-eyed people living in the far north where he had presumably visited. Then he suddenly vanished again, and rematerialized in southern Italy 240 years later (4.15).[47] Again, whatever

---

[44] Hermippus seems to have specialized in sensational fabrications, especially death scenes; see Robert William Sharples, 'Hermippus (2),' *OCD* 692.

[45] Apollonius, *Mir.* 3.

[46] Plutarch, *Mor.* 592c–d; Pliny the Elder, *Nat.* 7.52.174. Lucian writes with tongue in cheek, as usual, of how when ashes are sprinkled on a dead fly 'she revives (ἀνίσταται) and has a second birth (παλιγγενεσία) and a new life from the beginning (βίος ἄλλος ἐξ ὑπαρχῆς). This confirms that the fly's soul is immortal like ours, and gives credence to the story of Hermotimus, whose soul would often leave and then return to his body and restore (ἀνίστα) him to life' (*Musc. Laud.* 7). Here the target is obviously the Platonic doctrine of the transmigration of immortal souls.

[47] Pliny the Elder (*Nat.* 7.52.174) mentions Aristeas as flying out of his own mouth in the form of a raven. On Aristeas, see J. D. P. Bolton, *Aristeas of Proconnesus* (Oxford: Clarendon, 1962); Bremmer, *Early Greek Concept of the Soul*, 25–27.

these purported experiences meant within their local and historical contexts (e.g., within the ecstatic Dionysian religion of Thrace), later reports associated them with Pythagorean (or Platonic) certification of the separability and immortality of the soul.[48]

4.2.4 The 'Second Chance' and Scientific Demonstrations of 'Resurrection'

'Resurrections' of a more common sort occurred frequently enough in antiquity, or at least warranted considerable attention, so that those who had experienced them required a proper designation. They were called *deuteropotmoi*, 'the second-fated.' The term appears in Hesychius's *Alphabetical Collection of All Words*, and although the famed lexicographer wrote in the fifth century A.D., we know that he relied on much earlier lexica;[49] and with respect to the term under consideration, his definitions are confirmed by Plutarch who wrote in the first century. Hesychius's entry for *deuteropotmos* is reproduced here in full:[50]

> δευτερόποτμος· ὁ ὑπὸ τινων ὑστερόποτμος. οὕτω δὲ ἔλεγον, ὁπόταν τινὶ ὡς τεθνεῶτι τὰ νομιζόμενα ἐγένετο, καὶ ὕστερον ἀνεφάνη ζῶν. ὁ δὲ Πολέμων καὶ ἀπειρῆσθαι τοῖς τοιούτοις εἰσιέναι εἰς τὸ ἱερὸν τῶν Σεμνῶν φησι Θεῶν. ἢ ὁ φημισθεὶς ἐπὶ ξένης τετελευτηκώς, ἔπειτα ἐπανελθών. ἢ ὁ δεύτερον διὰ γυναικείου κόλπου διαδύς· ὡς ἔθος ἦν παρὰ 'Αθηναίοις ἐκ δευτέρου γεννᾶσθαι.

> *deuteropotmos* ['second-fated']: according to some, *hysteropotmos* ['later-fated']. It is, as they say, when someone is reputed to have died, and later appears alive. Polemon says that such persons are forbidden to enter into the temple of the Sacred Gods. Or the one who has reportedly died in a foreign land, then shows up again. Or one who passes through the fold of a woman's garment a second time,[51] as was the custom among Athenians to be born a second time.

---

[48] Rohde, *Psyche*, 299–303, esp. 301.

[49] From as early as the second century B.C.; see Peter Barr Reid Forbes and Robert Browning, 'Hesychius,' *OCD* 701–2.

[50] My translation; Greek text: Kurt Latte, ed., *Hesychii Alexandrini Lexicon* (3 vols.; Hauniae: Ejnar Munksgaard, 1953).

[51] The significance of ὁ δεύτερον διὰ γυναικείου κόλπου διαδύς is not immediately apparent. It is possible that literal rebirth is intended, taking γυναικείου κόλπου as a reference either to the womb or the vaginal canal (=αἰδοῖον, s.v. 'γυναικείος,' LSJ 363). But this is unlikely: (a) there are clearer ways of expressing rebirth (cf. Nicodemus's query in John 3:4), and the telltale Platonic vocabulary of rebirth is absent; (b) physical rebirth would totally obliterate the need for a separate classification of *deuteropotmoi*, since virtually anyone could have been reborn (that is, in accordance with a belief in metempsychosis); and (c) finally, the subsequent clause refers to a customary practice in Athens, not a natural process. The expression makes good sense as we have translated it,

Plutarch discusses both Roman and Greek customs related to those who had purportedly died and later returned to their former sphere of life. His discussion confirms Hesychius's definitions at every point, and additionally illustrates how the reality of (assumed) death and recovery necessitated certain adjustments in order to preserve the balance of cultural perceptions about human existence. 'Why is it,' asks Plutarch, 'that those who are falsely reported to have died in a foreign country (τοὺς τεθνάναι φημισθέντας ἐπὶ ξένης ψευδῶς), even if they return (κἂν ἐπανέλθωσιν), men do not admit by the door, but mount upon the roof-tiles and let them down inside?' (*Mor.* 264d–e).[52] There follows an account of a number of men who were falsely reported to have died in a naval battle in the Sicilian war, and all but one of them died (τελευτῆσαι) in their attempt to return home (ἐπανελθόντας). When this sole survivor approached his home, the doors automatically shut him out, so he lay down in front of the threshold and fell asleep. He beheld a vision in which he was instructed to climb up to the roof and let himself down into the house. Thus he did, and lived a long and prosperous life (264d–e). Plutarch then compares this Roman practice with Greek customs. Any person, once she has been carried in a funeral procession and has been buried as though dead (οἷς ἐκφορὰ γεγόνει καὶ τάφος ὡς τεθνηκόσι), is regarded by the Greeks as impure, shunned by her family, and not permitted to approach temples (264f).[53] One such victim of this superstition, Aristinus, inquired of the Delphic oracle about how he might extricate himself from this impossible situation. He complied with the oracle by becoming like a newborn babe, committing himself into the hands of women to be washed, wrapped in swaddling clothes, and suckled. This procedure was followed by all others who were designated as *hysteropotmoi* (264f–265a).[54] Plutarch concludes that it is not odd, then, that the

---

and if this be correct, then it likely refers to slipping through the fold of a woman's garment for the purpose of being suckled as though one were an infant again (cf. Plutarch's discussion of *hysteropotmoi* which follows).

[52] Compare the language: Plutarch—τοὺς τεθνάναι φημισθέντας ἐπὶ ξένης, κἂν ἐπανέλθωσιν // Hesychius—ὁ φημισθεὶς ἐπὶ ξένης τετελευτηκώς, ἔπειτα ἐπανελθών.

[53] Again, compare Hesychius: 'such persons are forbidden to enter into the temple of the Sacred Gods.'

[54] These actions were performed perhaps because the *deuteropotmos* was thought to have been rejected by the underworld, yet no longer connected to the living, and whose only chance of being reintegrated into social life was through a ritual process of rebirth; see Garland, *Greek Way of Death*, 101. Garland (164) surmises that Alcestis is unable to speak for three days after her return from the dead because she has to undergo a similar ritual. North observes how earlier in the drama, Death (*Thanatos*) dedicated Alcestis to the gods below by cutting off a lock of her hair (*Alc.* 71–76). After her return she had to remain silent until she had been 'deconsecrated'; see Helen F. North, 'Death and After-

Romans do not admit through the door 'those who are thought to have been buried once and for all (δοκοῦσιν ἅπαξ τεθάφθαι) and to belong to the company of the departed (γεγονέναι τῆς τῶν φθιτῶν μερίδος),' but instead permit them to descend from the open air into the inner courtyard. Whereas Romans pass in and out of the door to offer sacrifices, Plutarch explains, they perform rites of purification under the open sky (265a–b).

The first-century Latin writers Valerius Maximus and Pliny the Elder record numerous instances of persons who revived before the completion of funeral ceremonies.[55] For example, both of them relate two cases, that of ex-consul Aviola and of ex-praetor Lucius Lamia, who cried out from atop the burning funeral pyre. Pliny includes two tales about individuals who mistakenly died instead of someone else.[56] Pliny and others, instead of focusing upon the societal reaction to these occurrences (as in Plutarch), explain the phenomenon itself. Two general classes of explanation may be delineated: (1) a philosophical explanation in which the phenomenon is cited to illustrate the immortality of the soul; and (2) a natural scientific explanation in which the phenomenon is described in terms of some kind of physical anomaly.

Both types of explanation were supported by documented cases. Under the first class of explanations is Empedocles' resuscitation of a woman who had been dead for seven days. Heraclides (fourth century B.C.) devoted an entire essay to this incident, a work that only survives in fragments, but is referenced by a number of ancient writers.[57] The fundamental argument of this essay seems to have been that Empedocles was able to revive the woman, after her physicians had failed, because of his insight regarding the separability and immortality of the soul.[58] A fragment from Clearchus

---

life in Greek Tragedy and Plato,' in *Death and Afterlife: Perspectives of World Religions* (ed. Hiroshi Obayashi; New York: Praeger, 1992), 55–56.

[55] Val. Max. 1.8.12; Pliny the Elder, *Nat.* 7.52.173–79.

[56] The appeal of this kind of story is evidenced by similar stories repeated (or fabricated) by other authors, as in Plutarch (Περὶ ψυχῆς, frag. 176) or Lucian (*Philops.* 25).

[57] Diog. Laert. 8.60–61, 67; Pliny the Elder, *Nat.* 7.52.175; Origen, *Cels.* 2.16; Galen, *De loc. aff.* 6.5; cf. Suidas, s.v. 'ἄπνους.' The precise title of this essay is uncertain. R. D. Hicks, the Loeb translator of Diogenes Laertius, suggests that the incident formed a part of Heraclides' Περὶ τῶν ἐν ᾅδου, one of the titles listed by Diogenes (5.87). It is more likely that Diogenes referred to the actual title later: τὰ περὶ τῆς ἄπνου, 'The Story of the Woman in a Trance' (8.67). Fragments of this work have been assembled in Fritz Wehrli, ed., *Die Schule des Aristoteles: Texte und Kommentar* (Basel: Benno Schwabe, 1953), 7:27–32.

[58] This may be inferred from the fact that authors mention Heraclides' account in conjunction with the myth of Er (Origen, *Cels.* 2.16) or with Hermotimus, Aristeas, and Epimenides (Pliny the Elder, *Nat.* 7.52.174–75); see H. B. Gottschalk, *Heraclides of*

recounts a psychic experiment at which he and his teacher Aristotle were present. A young boy had his soul drawn out of his body with a wand suited for that purpose. The boy's body was motionless and unresponsive to manhandling during the soul's absence. When touched with the wand again, the boy's soul returned, and all of the observers, including Aristotle himself, were impressed by this demonstration of the separability of the soul from the body.[59] In his treatise *On the Soul,* Plutarch recounts the story of an individual who was taken ill and diagnosed as near death. After emerging from a trance the man stated that he had died, but learned that it was not he but a certain Nicandas who was supposed to die. Nicandas came down with a fever and died two days later.[60] From other fragments of this work we know that one of Plutarch's aims was to establish belief in the immortality of the soul.[61] In previous sections we have seen a number of other accounts that were appropriated to demonstrate the immortality of the soul.

The phenomenon could also be accounted for in naturalistic terms. Pliny suggested that it was a more common occurrence among women, due to a contortion of the uterus that could interrupt respiration (*Nat.* 7.52.175).[62] It must be kept in mind that Pliny's discussion of resuscitations follows upon a section dealing with the signs of approaching death (7.51.171–72), and he flatly dismisses purported instances of persons appearing after burial, since his subject is 'works of nature, not prodigies' (1.52.179).[63] Aulus Cornelius Celsus, a physician who lived during the reign of Tiberius, attributed the majority of such cases to an inexpert recognition of life signs. A person

---

Pontus (Oxford: Clarendon, 1980), 18–19; Bremmer, *Early Greek Concept of the Soul,* 49.

[59] The fragment appears in Wehrli, *Die Schule des Aristoteles,* 3:11; cf. Bremmer, *Early Greek Concept of the Soul,* 50. The story is apocryphal, but Aristotle himself thought it possible 'for a soul which has left the body to enter in again; and upon this would follow the possibility of resurrection for animals which are dead (τούτῳ δ' ἔποιτ' ἂν τὸ ἀνίστασθαι τὰ τεθνεῶτα τῶν ζῴων)' (*De an.* 406b 4–5).

[60] Plutarch, Περὶ ψυχῆς, frag. 176.

[61] E.g., Plutarch, Περὶ ψυχῆς, frag. 177. Eusebius, who is our source for frag. 176, considered this story from Plutarch similar to that of Plato's account of Er (*Praep. ev.* 9.35).

[62] This idea finds some basis in Plato (*Tim.* 91c). It is not impossible that Heraclides, too, proposed such a physiological cause, because Pliny follows up this explanation with the words: 'To this subject belongs the essay of Heraclides, well known in Greece, about the woman recalled to life after being dead seven days.' This would suggest that philosophical and naturalistic hypotheses were not mutually exclusive. However, Gottschalk (*Heraclides of Pontus,* 19) believes it is not easy to determine a match between this proposal and Heraclides' work, since Pliny seems to have drawn from a multiplicity of sources.

[63] Pliny's own view of the afterlife was Epicurean (*Nat.* 7.55.188–90).

truly proficient in medicine will not err in apprehending the indicators of life and death. Celsus offers the example of an experienced practitioner, Asclepiades, who met a funeral procession and recognized that the man who was being carried was actually alive. Yet Celsus is willing to admit that one case in a thousand may be less than clear-cut (*Med.* 2.6.13–16). Philostratus takes an ambiguous stance concerning Apollonius of Tyana's resuscitation of a young woman in Rome (*Vit. Apoll.* 4.45). He records on the one hand that the young woman was 'seemingly dead' (τοῦ δοκοῦντος θανάτου), but on the other that she woke up 'just as Alcestis did when she was brought back to life by Hercules.' He is unsure of whether Apollonius 'detected some spark of life in her'—since some noticed a vapour that went up from her face—or whether her life had been extinguished, then returned through the warmth of touch.[64] In Philostratus there seems to be a mingling of the philosophical and naturalistic explanations that we have delineated. However, for any instance of 'resurrection' we can see that there were not only a number of precedents for comparison, but definite interpretative options for explaining them.[65]

4.2.5 'Death' and 'Resurrection' in the Hellenistic Novels

Fascination with the phenomenon of persons reviving from death seems to have had an explosion of growth around the middle of the first century A.D. This is nowhere more in evidence than in the ancient Greek novels. With the arrival of this new genre, the plot-twist of apparent death and resurrection also appeared abruptly. To be sure, there were earlier exemplars that have been touched upon above, but these cannot be compared with an entire genre identified in part by the stock motif of 'apparent death' (*Scheintod*). Moreover, never before had scenes in fiction been as similar to the Gospel accounts of Jesus' entombment and later reunion with his followers, and in a period coincident with the origins of Christianity. The esteemed classicist G. W. Bowersock has deliberated concerning the probability that this burst of interest in resurrection among the novelists was sparked by the extraordinary stories originating in Palestine and circulating throughout the empire.[66]

---

[64] Eusebius (*Hier.* 26) exploits Philostratus's ambivalence and questions the credibility of the account.

[65] Celsus (the pagan antagonist of Christianity) enumerates the stories about Zalmoxis, Pythagoras, Protesilaus et al., all of which he regards as specimens of chicanery and legend (Origen, *Cels.* 11.55).

[66] G. W. Bowersock, *Fiction as History: Nero to Julian* (Berkeley: University of California Press, 1994), 119; and see his whole chapter on resurrection, 99–119. The novelists' obsession with tomb robbery probably had an origin in reality, and may have had a connection to early Christianity. A Judean inscription dating from the middle or

Regardless of the precise genesis of this common motif, the Greek novels present astonishing parallels as well as profound differences with the NT portrayals of Jesus' resurrection. On one side of the ledger, the novels contain language and situations that are evocative of the resurrection accounts in the Gospels—particularly Luke. On the other side, death and resurrection are narrated from a natural (or scientific) perspective, enhancing the 'realism' of the events. The function of apparent deaths within the overarching plot and ethos of the novels differs substantially from Luke's vision of the death and resurrection of Jesus.

4.2.5.1 SIMILAR SITUATIONS AND LANGUAGE

In Chariton's *Callirhoe,* the title-character is kicked in the stomach by her newlywed husband, Chaereas. She collapses, and her maidservants lay her upon a bed. 'So Callirhoe lay without speech or breath (ἄφωνος καὶ ἄπνους), presenting to all the appearance of death (νεκρᾶς εἰκόνα)' (1.5.1).[67] Callirhoe is given a grandiose funeral and buried in her father's magnificent tomb by the sea. Theron, the cunning freebooter, hatches a scheme to loot the cache of treasure, while Callirhoe is reviving inside the tomb (1.8.1):

> But as for Callirhoe, she experienced a second return to life (δευτέραν ἄλλην ἐλάμβανε παλιγγενεσίαν). When lack of food had led to some loosening of her blocked respiration, she slowly and gradually regained her breath. Then she began to stir, limb by limb, and opening her eyes she regained consciousness as though waking from sleep, and called Chaereas, thinking he was asleep at her side.

Feeling the funeral wreaths and ribbons, hearing the clinking of gold and silver, and smelling the redolence of spices (ἀρώματα), she realizes she has been buried alive. Then the sound of crowbars and hammers alerts her to the presence of tomb-robbing pirates who have come to steal the treasure—and her—away. Later, when Chaereas visits the tomb to perform some funeral rites, he discovers that the pirates have left the entrance to the tomb wide open. At this point there are several parallels with Luke. When Chaereas arrived at the tomb, 'he discovered that the stones had been moved' (εὗρε τοὺς λίθους κεκινημένους, 3.3.1; cp. Luke 24:2). He 'was astonished' (ἐξεπλάγη) and 'overcome by fearful perplexity' (ὑπὸ δεινῆς

---

late first century records an imperial edict prohibiting body-snatching and tomb desecration (*Fiction as History*, 116–17). For the Greek text, translation, and brief commentary, see P. W. van der Horst, *Ancient Jewish Epitaphs* (Kampen: Kok Pharos, 1991), 159–60.

[67] The translation used here: Chariton, *Callirhoe*, (LCL 481; ed. and trans. G. P. Goold; Cambridge, Mass.: Harvard University Press, 1995). For other ancient Greek novels, see the English translations in B. P. Reardon, ed., *Collected Ancient Greek Novels* (Berkeley: University of California Press, 1989).

ἀπορίας κατείχετο, 3.3.2; cp. ἀπορεῖσθαι, Luke 24:4; θαυμάζων, 24:12; ἐξέστησαν, 24:22). In both Chariton and Luke the tomb is searched in two phases. In Chariton no one is brave enough to venture into the vault, so finally someone is commanded to do so. The response to the first search report is one of disbelief: 'It seems unbelievable that not even the corpse was lying there' (ἄπιστον ἐδόκει τὸ μηδὲ τὴν νεκρὰν κεῖσθαι, 3.3.3; cp. ἠπίστουν αὐταῖς, Luke 24:11). So Chaereas goes in to see for himself (cp. Peter's rush to the tomb, Luke 24:12), and is able to find nothing (οὐδὲν εὑρεῖν ἠδύνατο, 3.3.4; cp. Luke 24:3, 23).

Many other instances of apparent death occur in the ancient novels, and they are often characterized in terms of death and resurrection. Callirhoe's experience, we have already seen, is described as a 'second return to life,' and she later reflects upon the fact that she has died and been buried (τέθνηκα καὶ κεκήδευμαι, Chariton 5.5.2), she has died and lives again (τέθνηκα, ἀνέζηκα, 3.8.9). Death and resurrection language is most prevalent in Achilles Tatius's *Leucippe and Clitophon*. There Clitophon decides to commit suicide when Leucippe is presumed dead for the third time. Those other deaths were staged (τοῖς ψευδέσι θανάτοις), he confesses, but now she has died doubly—body and soul (νῦν δὲ τέθνηκας θάνατον διπλοῦν, ψυχῆς καὶ σώματος, 7.5.3). His companion reassures him, 'Who knows whether she is alive this time too? Hasn't she died many times before? Hasn't she often been resurrected?' (Τίς γὰρ οἶδεν, εἰ ζῇ πάλιν; Μὴ γὰρ οὐ πολλάκις τέθνηκε; Μὴ γὰρ οὐ πολλάκις ἀνεβίω; 7.6.2). Earlier, after Leucippe's first 'death,' her coffin was opened and she was presented to Clitophon with the announcement, 'Leucippe will now come to life again' (Λευκίππη δέ σοι νῦν ἀναβιώσεται, 3.17.4). After her second 'death,' Leucippe reveals to Clitophon in a letter that she has died twice (τέθνηκα ἤδη δεύτερον, 5.18.4). Clitophon responds to the letter by querying, Λευκίππη πάλιν ἀνεβίω; (5.19.2).

4.2.5.2 NATURAL EXPLANATIONS AND HIGH ADVENTURE

The death and resurrection motif within the ancient novels is very believable for readers, however, because no real death or resurrection ever takes place.[68] At some point in the novel the reader is made aware of the fact that the death was only apparent (cf. Chariton 1.5.1; Xenophon, *Ephesian Tale* 3.7.1; Achilles Tatius 7.5.3). Additionally, the novelist may provide a natural explanation for the apparent death, such as noting that a sleeping potion

---

[68] The fictional strategies for realistic portrayal in ancient novels are explored in J. R. Morgan, 'Make-Believe and Make Believe: The Fictionality of the Greek Novels,' in *Lies and Fiction in the Ancient World* (eds. Christopher Gill and T. P. Wiseman; Austin, Tex: University of Texas Press, 1993), 175–229; on *Scheintod* see 203–5.

instead of poison had actually been ingested (Xenophon 3.5.11). The explanations can be possessed of the seriousness of natural science as, for example, when Callirhoe's condition is diagnosed as an obstruction of her breathing, or when an astute medical student (who would make the physician Celsus proud) detects signs of life in the apparently dead wife of King Apollonius and restores her breathing (*Historia Apollonii* 26–27).[69] Alternatively, the event can take on the proportions of the macabre or farcical. In Achilles Tatius, Leucippe 'dies' no less than three times, and in two instances the apparent death is revealed as a kind of shocking stage trick. In the first instance, instead of Leucippe having been carved up as a human sacrifice, the hierophant had actually plunged a retractable knife into a false-stomach filled with animal entrails that had been attached to her (3.15–21). Her second 'death' involved a fake decapitation (5.7.4).[70]

Simulated death serves a far different function within the overall plot of the ancient Greek novels and expresses a different ethos than do the death and resurrection of Jesus in Luke-Acts. In the Greek novels, *Scheintod* stands alongside a host of other elements of high adventure (e.g., ship-wrecks, abductions, imprisonments, harrowing escapes) that function as complications to the plot. Even in Chariton, where the empty tomb forms 'the first overture' from which all other events take their departure,[71] it is nevertheless part of a finely woven fabric of other adventurous threads.[72] The essential ethos of the ancient novel comes to expression in apparent deaths, and this, too, varies from Luke's rendering of Jesus' death and resurrection. In the novels the protagonists struggle against the ravages of *tychē*, not only for personal survival, but to secure life's true meaning and fulfilment found in love. The apparent death, usually of the heroine, is the supreme obstacle to fulfilment, and the reunion of the lovers marks the

---

[69] In both of these cases the explanations are akin to that offered by Pliny (*Nat.* 7.52.175). Apuleius (*Flor.* 19) recounts the story of Asclepiades (perhaps the same physician named by Celsus, *Med.* 2.6.13–16) who stopped a funeral procession, detected signs of life, and revived the dead person with drugs.

[70] Plutarch reveals the use of *Scheintod* in first-century dramatic performances in his eyewitness account of a pantomime in Rome in which a trained dog feigned death and recovery (*Mor.* 973e–974a).

[71] Roland Kany, 'Der lukanische Bericht von Tod und Auferstehung Jesu aus der Sicht eines hellenistischen Romanlesers,' *NovT* 28 (1986): 87: 'Bei Chariton bildet das leere Grab eigentlich erst die Ouvertüre, von hier nehmen die Ereignisse ihren Ausgang.'

[72] On the function of Callirhoe's apparent death within Chariton's plot, see Elizabeth Hazelton Haight, *Essays on the Greek Romances* (Port Washington, N.Y.: Kennikat, 1943), 29; B. P. Reardon, *The Form of Greek Romance* (Princeton: Princeton University Press, 1991), 109.

satisfying reinvestment of life with meaning.[73] By contrast, Jesus' death and resurrection constitute the climax to Luke's Gospel. The death of Jesus is not a complication, but rather part of the dénouement of his life. Jesus' actions are not aimed at achieving life-meaning in the face of fateful threats to survival, and none of the events of his life, least of all his death and resurrection, are portrayed as adventurous.[74] The only significant journey that Jesus takes in Luke's Gospel is on a long, winding route to Jerusalem. There the plot of Jesus' life is resolved in his death and resurrection as the accomplishment of the divine will foretold in the Hebrew Scriptures (Luke 24:26–27, 44–47). Jesus' death and resurrection, indeed, stand in direct opposition to the function of apparent death in the ancient Greek novels: the pattern for life is not an enterprising survival amid the forces of chance, or the establishment of a sense of personal identity or fulfilment, even through love of another. It is relinquishing one's own life and devoting oneself supremely in obedience to God's will, trusting in the One who raises the dead.

4.2.6 *Epicureans, Stoics, and the Resurrection*

Two philosophical movements whose perspectives on the afterlife deserve special comment are the Epicureans and the Stoics. Luke mentions the reaction of some Epicureans and Stoics to Paul's preaching of the resurrection at Athens. At first they mistook Paul's message to be about two foreign deities, Jesus and Anastasis (Acts 17:18). After giving him a hearing, however, the reactions to his words about the resurrection of the dead separated along party lines: some—presumably Epicureans—mocked; others—Stoics—responded, 'We will hear you again about this' (17:32).[75] These reactions are in accord with what we know about these philosophical schools. Epicurean physics held that the soul was a substance of fine particles or atoms that dissipated at death.[76] All sensation occurs in bodies animated by souls, and therefore death is nothing to be feared, since it results in experiencing nothing at all.[77] Such disbelief in an afterlife was expressed in the epitaph,

---

[73] For this analysis of apparent deaths in the ancient Greek novels, see Suzanne MacAlister, *Dreams and Suicides: The Greek Novel from Antiquity to the Byzantine Empire* (London: Routledge, 1996), 24–25, 29.

[74] Kany, 'Tod und Auferstehung,' 89–90.

[75] On the Epicurean and Stoic response to the preaching of the resurrection, see N. Clayton Croy, 'Hellenistic Philosophies and the Preaching of the Resurrection (Acts 17:18, 32),' *NovT* 39 (1997): 21–39; cf. Riley, *Resurrection Reconsidered*, 37–41 and the literature cited there.

[76] Diog. Laert. 10.63–67.

[77] Diog. Laert. 10.124–25, 139; Lucr. 3.624–33.

'I wasn't, I was, I am not, I don't care,'[78] which appeared often in abbreviated form. Stoic views of the afterlife are more difficult to summarize. There was no settled position on the matter, as there was among Epicureans, and (especially the later) Stoics were preoccupied with ethics rather than physics. Many Stoics seem to have believed that human souls could survive for an indefinite period after death,[79] but there was a question as to whether all, or only certain wise souls, would endure until the ἐκπύρωσις.[80] It is impossible to tell precisely what any given Stoic would have made of Paul's preaching concerning the resurrection—although few if any would have found *bodily* resurrection acceptable—but Stoic views of the afterlife seem to have been open to Platonic influences.[81] Thus, Luke plausibly represents them as being curious about this new doctrine of the resurrection, whereas the Epicureans would have nothing to do with it.

4.3 Summary and Conclusions

An estimation of the Greco-Roman reactions to the Christian proclamation of Jesus and the resurrection of the dead must begin with the question of definition. Reactions can only be based upon interpretation, and it is apparent that there were numerous understandings of 'resurrection.' We have seen that there were ancient instances when it was believed that persons were quite literally raised from the dead to return to their former bodily existence. However, these were imaginative representations (e.g., Alcestis), or they concerned gods or heroes (e.g., Orpheus and Eurydice, or Protesilaus). They were exceptional cases that may be categorized as mythical. The general position toward the concept of bodily resurrection in the Hellenistic period, particularly among the educated, was negative. However, we know of mantics whose souls soared in search of prophetic insight, leaving their bodies in a lifeless state. Some of these individuals, who were hailed as gods by those who followed them, were later suspected of being tricksters. We know also that there were enough extraordinary cases of 'resurrection'—during an *ekphora,* under the aegis of philosophical or quasi-scientific experimentation, or under the care of a physician—to warrant explanation. The two predominant explanations included either pointing to such instances as demonstrations of the separability and immor-

---

[78] *Non fui, fui, non sum, non desidero.* For this and other epitaphs of similar sentiment, see Lattimore, *Themes in Greek and Latin Epitaphs,* 74–86.
[79] Cicero, *Tusc.* 1.31.7; Diog. Laert. 7.156.
[80] Eusebius, *Praep. ev.* 15.20.6; Diog. Laert. 7.157.
[81] Note, for example, the Platonic/Orphic themes in Cicero's 'Dream of Scipio' (*Resp.* 6.9–26), or Seneca's statements about post-mortem heavenly existence (*Marc.* 26.1–6).

tality of the soul, or providing a naturalistic or medical rationale for the phenomenon. Popular reactions criss-crossed mythical, philosophical, and scientific lines. Both among Greeks and Romans traditions arose to cope with the disruption caused by the appearance of the *deuteropotmoi*. Those who had supposedly died and returned to life were regarded as extremely taboo and had to undergo a ritualistic reintroduction into society. The ancient Greek novels bear witness to a burst of interest in death and resurrection beginning in the early first century A.D., and the motif of *Scheintod* was raised to a *topos* in that genre of literature. Resurrection was explained 'realistically' in naturalistic terms (viz., as resuscitation), and was employed to enhance the adventurous and romantic appeal of the novels. So resurrection in the Jewish sense of the dead being supernaturally reanimated and coming forth from their graves would have sounded at once strange and fascinating to nearly any first-century Greco-Roman ear. The possibility would have been rejected out of hand by some—like the Epicureans—but it would have elicited curiosity and further discussion amongst others—such as some Stoics. It remains to be seen how Luke-Acts is positioned amongst both the Jewish and Greco-Roman visions of the afterlife in its proclamation of the resurrection of the dead. We shall turn to that task in our next chapter.

Excursus on the Definitions of Resurrection and Resuscitation

The subject of resurrection is fraught with a complex terminological problem involving both Greek and English usage. There is a fundamental problem with the choice of terms to label the afterlife phenomena as they have been variously understood in antiquity. Up to this point we have considered a range of phenomena under such terms as 'resurrection' (ἀνάστασις and the verbs ἀνίστημι and ἐγείρω), 'resuscitation,' and 'revivification' or 'reanimation' (ἀναβιώσις and the verbs ἀναβιόω and ἀναζάω). We have noted the phenomena and have employed these various terms to refer generically to instances when dead persons were reported to have returned from the dead. Now, after surveying the ancient evidence, we are in a position to define our terms more closely. The use of these terms can be misleading in at least two directions: (1) any given term may not adequately convey the ancient understanding; and (2) the term may be misunderstood by the contemporary reader, who has a modern scientific conception of death under neatly defined categories such as biological and clinical death. Specific definitions of the variegated vocabulary are determined not only by the co-texts in which they are used, but also by the speaker, character, or author who is using them, and the reader or auditor who is attempting to decode what is being communicated. For example, the ἀναβιώσις of an individual will mean one thing for a Pythagorean, another thing for an Epicurean, then yet again something entirely different for Josephus or the author of 2 Maccabees.

We shall continue to use the English terms 'revivification' or 'reanimation' to refer generally to a return from the dead, without specifying anything further than a *coming back to life*. The terms 'resurrection' and 'resuscitation,' however, may be more closely defined in light of our discussion in Chapters 3 and 4. The term 'resurrection' is used in three ways:

resurrection$_1$ a dead individual (a human corpse) being revived or coming back to life in the same body

resurrection$_2$ a dead individual being brought back to life in a transformed body

resurrection$_3$ a dead individual entering into a new state of existence in another body

The term 'resuscitation' is used in two ways:

resuscitation$_1$ an individual is revived after a potential (or perhaps temporary) death

resuscitation$_2$ an individual is only apparently dead (e.g., has swooned or is in a coma) and later regains consciousness

The term 'resurrection' may be used in one of the three ways delineated above. 'Resurrection' may be diametrically opposite to the popular Hellenistic belief in the immortality of the soul when it is understood in conjunction with anthropological monism (e.g., 2 Maccabees [versus 4 Maccabees]), or the two ideas may coalesce in authors who hold to a form of anthropological dualism (e.g., Pseudo-Phocylides, Josephus). The defining characteristic of any understanding of resurrection involves some kind of post-mortem *somatic* existence, whether this is understood as fleshly, celestial, or whatever. It must be noted that *resurrection*$_3$ does not appear to have wide support and, as we have argued in the case of Josephus, seems to represent an adaptation suited to Hellenistic sentiments. All three definitions may involve individuals who have been interred (or who should have been) and whose bodies have suffered the ravages of decomposition, while *resurrection*$_1$ may also involve individuals who are known to be dead but have not yet been buried. 'Resurrection' under any of these definitions is to be distinguished from translation, ascension, or apotheosis in that it involves the prior *death* of the individual. Observe also that 'the resurrection,' that is '*the* resurrection from the dead' associated with the day of judgment, may involve any one of the definitions above, but refers to the final eschatological resurrection of either the righteous or of all humankind. Examples of the various distinctions in definition are:

*resurrection*₁	the miracles of resurrection under Elijah and Elisha; references in Isa 26:19 and Dan 12:3; the Maccabean martyrs (2 Macc 7); the Sibylline Oracles
*resurrection*₂	*2 Bar.* 50–51 (although here we observed *resurrection*₁ and *resurrection*₂ employed in succession); Paul (1 Cor 15)
*resurrection*₃	this definition comes to the fore in Josephus, whose explanation of re-embodiment employs Platonic expressions used in connection with the transmigration of souls

The two senses of 'resuscitation' are distinguished from each other in their conceptions of the nature of death. In *resuscitation*₁ death may be regarded as real, but incomplete or transitory. This view is consonant with a Pythagorean or Platonic explanation of death as the separation of a personal soul from an individual's body. The death is temporary, and is reversed when the individual's soul re-enters his or her body (either spontaneously, as in the case of the mantics, or through the agency of a philosopher-healer). Death becomes permanent for an individual if the soul never returns to the body, or, if while the soul is absent, the body is destroyed (as in the case of Hermotimus). *Resuscitation*₂ is usually associated with a materialistic or naturalistic view of life and death. Under this definition the death is only apparent. It is a phenomenon that can be diagnosed and remedied by a skilled physician, or may occur and be reversed spontaneously (e.g., Callirhoe's obstructed breathing).

The two clusters of ideas may be identified respectively with Jewish conceptions of the afterlife on the one hand (resurrection), and Greco-Roman conceptions on the other (resuscitation), although there is some cross-fertilization.[82] It is difficult, for example, in the case of the revival of a dead individual (whether s/he be Alcestis or the Shunnamite woman's son), to clearly distinguish between *resurrection*₁ and *resuscitation*₁ ₒᵣ ₂. The distinction, however, lies in the fact that resurrection presumes the radical finality of death, over which only God has control, while resuscitation views death as a quirk of nature, or as flexible and responsive to manipulation by some-

---

[82] Our study invalidates Porter's attempt to argue that the concept of bodily resurrection originated not from the Jewish but from the Greco-Roman milieu; Stanley E. Porter, 'Resurrection, the Greeks and the New Testament,' in *Resurrection* (eds. Stanley E. Porter, Michael A. Hayes, and David Tombs; JSNTSup 186; Sheffield: Sheffield Academic Press, 1999), 52–81. Porter's argument is largely built upon the exceptional case of Euripides' *Alcestis*. However, this instance was imaginative or mythical in nature, and did not prevail against what appears to have been a widespread incredulity, or even disgust, within the Hellenistic world toward the concept of bodily resurrection, to which Luke's narrative itself attests. For further refutation of Porter, see Wright, *Resurrection of the Son of God*, 35, 66 n. 195, 68 n. 202, 178 n. 207, and 201 n. 306.

one who possesses wisdom about its operation. The distinction primarily concerns different theological perspectives on death. Resuscitation is a philosophically or scientifically explicable occurrence that may be understood or even effected by someone who is wise concerning the workings of life and death. Resurrection is the result of divine intervention, when deliverance from death is granted as a free act of God.

Chapter 5

Resurrection in Luke-Acts:
Miracle, Contention, and Hope for the People of God

The point of departure for understanding the resurrection of Jesus in Luke-Acts has traditionally been Luke 24. Alternatively, an appropriate starting point might be Jesus' passion/resurrection predictions. The missionary speeches in Acts, particularly those in chapters 2 and 13, present the most substantive statements about the resurrection of Jesus, and would provide a suitable entrée into Luke's 'theology of resurrection.' However, in keeping with our procedure thus far of working from the larger milieu down to the specific contribution of Luke-Acts, our starting point will be to establish a broader framework for understanding the Lukan conception of resurrection generally, before investigating Luke's theology of Jesus' resurrection more particularly.

Luke's portrayal of other resurrections in his two-volume work may provide us with a proper introduction to his resurrectional conceptions. Before a word is spoken about the death and resurrection of the Son of Man, the Lukan narrative recounts two resurrection miracles performed at the hands of Jesus. There are also two resurrections that occur in Acts under the ministries of Peter and Paul respectively. These accounts are useful in several ways. First, they assist us in determining the basic orientation of Luke's conceptualization of resurrection. They help answer the question: How does the narrator position himself amidst the varying ideas about resurrection that we explored in chapters 3 and 4? Second, they will reveal some of the theological significance of resurrection within the Lukan universe of thought. Finally, a preliminary comparison of these miracles with the resurrection of Jesus will point up the singularity and importance of Jesus' resurrection. In the course of this chapter, we want to pursue two other interrelated issues: namely, the particular intellectual environment in which Luke seems to anticipate discussion and debate about resurrection, and how this provides a foundation for understanding what the theological significance of resurrection is in his two-volume work. We will discover that Luke-Acts assumes that the resurrection from the dead may only be meaningfully discussed by those who are within the orbit of Judaism. Those who are outside the bounds of Judaism in general, and 'the Way' in particular, are incapable of understanding fully either the nature or theological bearing of resurrection. This is because, in Luke's narrative, the resurrec-

Miracle, Contention, and Hope for the People of God

tion from the dead is fundamental to Israel's hope for eschatological salvation.

5.1 The Resurrection Miracles in Luke-Acts

Apart from the resurrection of the Christ in Luke 24, there are four other instances of resurrection in Luke-Acts. Two in the Gospel are Jesus' raising up of a widow's son at Nain (Luke 7:11–17) and of Jairus's daughter (8:41–42, 49–56). In Acts there is the raising of Tabitha after the prayer and command of Peter (Acts 9:36–42) and the raising up of Eutychus after the embrace of Paul (20:7–12). It will not suit our purpose to engage in a full-scale exegesis of these passages seriatim. The miracles bear enough resemblances to one another to warrant a number of general remarks regarding all four of them as a group. First, we shall enumerate several observations about these resurrection accounts. Next, we will draw some initial comparisons and contrasts between these accounts and the presentation of Jesus' resurrection in Luke-Acts.

5.1.1 The Miracles of Resurrection

Three observations can be made about the resurrection miracles in Luke-Acts:

5.1.1.1 PROPHETIC AGENTS OF RESURRECTION

In each of them there is an agent of God (Jesus, the apostle Peter, Paul) who is instrumental in the resurrection. What is striking is that in each case the agent is cast in such a way as to resemble the prophets Elijah or Elisha, the only figures in the Hebrew Bible who were known to have raised the dead.[1] The first resurrection miracle in Luke-Acts, the raising up of the widow's son at Nain, resonates with key details from Elijah's raising up of the son of the widow of Zarephath (1 Kgs 17:8–24). Like Elijah, Jesus comes to a town and meets a widow at the gate (1 Kgs 17:10); he restores the widow's dead son to life (1 Kgs 17:22); and finally, the identical verbal expression from 1 Kgs 17:23 is found in Luke 7:15: καὶ ἔδωκεν αὐτὸν τῇ μητρὶ αὐτοῦ.[2] The Elijan character of this resurrection is carried forward in the

---

[1] This is noted by commentators, but see esp. François Bovon, *Das Evangelium nach Lukas* (EKKNT 3; Zurich: Benziger; Neukirchen-Vluyn: Neukirchener, 1989), 1:357–58; Augustin George, 'Les récits de miracles. Caractéristiques lucaniennes,' in *Études sur l'œuvre de Luc* (SB; Paris: Gabalda, 1978), 79–82.

[2] See Thomas L. Brodie, 'Towards Unravelling Luke's Use of the Old Testament: Luke 7.11–17 as an *Imitatio* of 1 Kings 17.17–24,' *NTS* 32 (1986): 241–67; Leopold Sabourin, 'The Miracles of Jesus (III): Healings, Resuscitations, Nature Miracles,' *BTB*

raising of Jairus's 'only' daughter (Luke 8:42; cf. 7:12), whose spirit returns at Jesus' command (Luke 8:55; cf. 1 Kgs 17:17, 21). These stories set the tone for the remaining two resurrection miracles in Acts. It is fitting that, whereas Jesus' resurrection miracles resemble that of Elijah, Peter and Paul are involved in miracles reminiscent of Elisha's raising up of the Shunammite woman's son. The resurrection of Tabitha takes place in an upper room (Acts 9:37, 39; cf. 2 Kgs 4:10–11, 21; see also 1 Kgs 17:19, 23), and Peter, who is in another location, is summoned there (Acts 9:38; cf. 2 Kgs 4:22–25). As in Elisha's raising up of the Shunammite's son (cf. Luke 8:51), the door is closed and Peter privately prays and issues his charge to the corpse (Acts 9:40; cf. 2 Kgs 4:33). That Tabitha has been restored to life is indicated by her opening her eyes (Acts 9:40; cf. 2 Kgs 4:35). In the resurrection of Eutychus an upper room is also involved (Acts 20:8), although in this instance a scriptural linkage is more tenuous. The raising up of Eutychus involves a greater physical component than in the other resurrection miracles in Luke-Acts: Paul 'fell upon' the lad and 'embraced' him (Acts 20:10; cf. 2 Kgs 4:34–35).[3]

These parallels with the resurrections under Elijah and Elisha are not vitiated by features that coincide with Hellenistic accounts of the revival of dead persons. The most celebrated parallel to Luke 7:11–17 is Apollonius of Tyana's resuscitation of a Roman maiden (Philostratus, *Vit. Apoll.* 4.45). Our discussion in chapter 4 of revivifications in the Greco-Roman world would indicate that the similarities between these two stories are easily explained by the prominence of this motif in first-century literature (there is only a limited number of ways to tell such a story). But when interpreting Luke 7:11–17, one has to take into account the inherent *differences* between Luke and Philostratus. We have already noted Philostratus's ambivalent appraisal of what had actually transpired.[4] Luke, as we shall see, does not abide with such ambiguity. There is also a crucial difference in how the miracles are performed, to wit: the magical nature of Apollonius's incantation over the girl versus Jesus' direct command. Then, finally, there are the

---

5 (1975): 146–200. The Elijan parallels are strengthened by the previous Elijah-like miracle story with which this story is coupled (see Green, *Luke*, 289), as well as by the characterization of Jesus' ministry in terms of the ministries of Elijah and Elisha in the programmatic Nazareth sermon (Luke 4:16–30).

[3] Is it possible that the raising up of Eutychus functions typologically as a kind of re-enactment of the resurrection of Jesus? The event takes place after Passover (20:6), in the midst of breaking bread and conversing on the first day of the week (20:7; cp. Luke 24:1, 13 and the ensuing Emmaus account), and Eutychus falls down *three* floors (// Jesus raised on the *third* day?). For this type of interpretation, see M. D. Goulder, *Type and History in Acts* (London: SPCK, 1964), 50.

[4] See p. 108 above.

manifest intertextual cues from 1 Kings 17 in Luke's account, whereas in Philostratus the occurrence is explicitly likened to the revival of Alcestis by Heracles. Luke's frame of reference is not primarily the Hellenistic tales of resuscitation, but Yahweh's mighty acts of resurrection performed through his prophets as narrated in the Scriptures.[5]

There is, however, a fascinating intertextual relationship between the story of Eutychus and Homer's tale of a certain young man named Elpenor who fell from a roof after waking from a drunken slumber. Homer's story was probably available to Luke, for it was actively appropriated by other authors near the time of Luke's writing. Dennis MacDonald believes Luke is employing a literary strategy that Gérard Genette labelled 'hypertextual transvaluation.'[6] This is a useful analytical tool, but MacDonald concentrates on the 'hypertextual' correspondences between the two stories without elucidating the Lukan 'transvaluation.' Both the original Homeric tale and later renditions of it capitalize on Elpenor's misfortune, so it is significant that in Luke's variation the plummeting victim is fortunate (hence the name, Eutychus). This can hardly exhaust Luke's transvaluation of Homer's story. The Lukan imitation is not intended as a humorous or entertaining vignette.[7] It is a parabolic lesson about apostasy and restoration that

---

[5] These points weigh against the proposal that there is a literary relationship between Luke and Philostratus; *contra* Paul J. Achtemeier, 'The Lukan Perspective on the Miracles of Jesus: A Preliminary Sketch,' in *Perspectives on Luke-Acts* (ed. Charles H. Talbert; PRStSSS 5; Danville, Va.: Association of Baptist Professors of Religion, 1978), 166. On the differentiation between the two accounts, see Joseph A. Fitzmyer, *The Gospel According to Luke* (2 vols.; AB 28–28a; Garden City, N.Y.: Doubleday, 1981), 1:656-57.

[6] Dennis R. MacDonald, 'Luke's Eutychus and Homer's Elpenor: Acts 20:7–12 and *Odyssey* 10–12,' *JHC* 1 (1994): 4–24.

[7] *Contra* Ben Witherington III, *The Acts of the Apostles: A Socio-Rhetorical Commentary* (Grand Rapids: Eerdmans; Cambridge: Paternoster, 1998), 607, esp. n. 199; James D. G. Dunn, *The Acts of the Apostles* (Narrative Commentaries; Valley Forge, Pa.: Trinity Press International, 1996), 268, who calls this a 'tragi-comic episode'; but esp. Richard I. Pervo, *Profit with Delight: The Literary Genre of the Acts of the Apostles* (Minneapolis: Fortress, 1987), 65–66—and these represent a wide range of scholarly and homiletical opinion. Why would the narrator or his readers consider it humorous or entertaining that a young lad was inattentive to Paul's late-night discussion and fell to his death? Plutarch regarded it as 'general and common requirements' to pay careful attention even to the worst speakers, and insisted that the listener sit up straight 'without any lounging or sprawling,' and forbade inattentive gestures such as 'sleepy yawns' or 'bowing down the head' ('On Listening to Lectures,' *Mor.* 45c-d). Surely, falling dead away asleep out of a window would have been a faux pas in the extreme. The amusement of falling asleep during a long, boring homily is an anachronistic imposition upon the text. Paul was passing through on a farewell tour, and so the Christians at Troas

fits in well with the Pauline itinerary, which involved the 'encouragement' of believers along his way to Jerusalem (παρακαλέω, cp. Acts 20:12 with 20:1–2) and warnings about defection from faith in Jesus (Acts 20:28–32).[8] Eutychus was the recipient of more than just good fortune, but great grace (cf. Acts 4:33; 14:3; 20:24, 32). Elpenor had appeared as a spectre before Odysseus, begging for a proper burial so that he could gain entry to the house of Hades. But Eutychus was delivered from Pluto's domain altogether, and he was rejoined to those who attend to the word and to the breaking of bread, which proclaim and betoken the hope of resurrection that is in Jesus (20:7, 11; cf. Luke 24:30–35; Acts 2:42–47). Like Odysseus, Paul is a traveller who is passing through Troas (=Troy); but the comparison stops there. Paul does not leave Eutychus to die, only later to encounter his *psychē* at the gates of Hades. He acts like the prophet of old, Elisha, and the prophet *par excellence*, Jesus, by being instrumental in keeping death from taking its full course. Instead of letting the *psychē* of Eutychus slip down to Hades (like Elpenor's did), the actions of Paul were undertaken to insure that 'his *psychē* is in him' (Acts 20:10). Luke has traded the values of the underworld for the powerful witness to the resurrection of Jesus and to the hope of resurrection for those who follow in the Way (Acts 4:2, 33; 17: 31; 24:14–15). So there was a resurrection instead of a funeral at Troas.

The present point to bear in mind is that in these resurrection miracles there is a prophetic agent of God who is instrumental in the concrete working out of the divine plan of salvation. A corollary that will be enlarged on as we proceed is that the salvation program exemplified in the ministries of Elijah and Elisha, and ultimately in Jesus, and the way in which resurrection contributes to it, proceeds within a scripturally charged environment of late Second Temple Judaism that is not directly translatable into many spheres of Greco-Roman thought.

5.1.1.2 REALITY OF RESURRECTION IN LUKE-ACTS

If the resurrection miracles in Luke-Acts are viewed with a wide-angle Greco-Roman lens, there is bound to be some ambiguity about their nature. For example, even though the widow's son is called a *nekros*, a corpse (Luke 7:15), many Hellene auditors, realizing that the phenomenon occurred during the young man's *ekphora* (funeral procession), would infer that it may be explained, for example, as an instance of Jesus' medical or

---

would presumably want to spend as much time with the apostle as possible, and vice versa. In addition, if Luke's story were meant to echo Homer, it must be kept in mind that the Elpenor incident was not humorous, but haunting.

[8] For similar symbolical readings, see Bernard Trémel, 'À propos d'Actes 20,7–12: Puissance du thaumaturge ou du témoin?' *RTP* 112 (1980): 359–69; Tannehill, *Narrative Unity*, 2:247–51.

philosophical acumen, on the one hand, or on the other, as a deceptive stage trick. The raising of Tabitha would be equally subject to speculation since the incident occurred during the *prothesis* (the laying out of the body after it has been washed, anointed, and clothed, and before the *ekphora* and interment); and this would be the case *a fortiori* for Jairus's daughter and Eutychus, who were both restored to life soon after death.[9] This is why the interpretative horizon of the Scriptures is so important for Luke in apprehending the nature and meaning of these resurrection miracles. Notwithstanding, the narrator is aware of the capacity for ambiguity in these stories and is able to exploit or dispel it. This is best illustrated in the case of Jairus's daughter. Unlike Mark's rendering of the story, where Jesus' declaration, 'The child is not dead but sleeping,' casts a shadow of ambivalence over the scene (Mark 5:22-24, 35-43), Luke clarifies that the household responded to this statement with scornful laughter, 'knowing that she was dead' (Luke 8:53). Thus, the authoritative words of Jesus are counterpoised by the narrator's report of the facts as they are known to Jairus's household. These facts are further supported by the narrator's note that after Jesus ordered the girl to arise 'her πνεῦμα returned' (8:55).[10] The words of Jesus are thus not a commentary on what is transpiring, but a riddle. Those who are laughing outside the house are left to wonder whether the girl had only been asleep or had actually come back from the dead.[11] Those inside heard Jesus' command, 'Child, arise (ἔγειρε)!' and watched the girl get up (ἀνέστη). The vocabulary suggests not only resurrection, but the effortlessness of waking someone from sleep, thus capitalizing on the polyvalence of the expressions.[12] The astonishment of the girl's parents is determinative

---

[9] Dibelius suggests, with regard to the raising up of Eutychus, that it is 'uncertain as to whether Paul is seen as a worker of miracles or a doctor'; Martin Dibelius, *Studies in the Acts of the Apostles* (London: SCM; New York: Charles Scribner's Sons, 1956), 18.

[10] We shall not exercise ourselves over the precise nature of πνεῦμα in this verse. Many commentators believe it to be only a vital principle, e.g., C. F. Evans, *Saint Luke* (TPINTC; London: SCM; Philadelphia: Trinity Press International, 1990), 393; and E. Earle Ellis, *The Gospel of Luke* (rev. ed.; NCB; Grand Rapids: Eerdmans, 1975), 130. Walter Grundmann (*Das Evangelium nach Lukas* [THKNT 3. Berlin: Evangelische, 1971], 183–84) and Bovon (*Lukas*, 1:452) believe that 'spirit' here is equivalent to 'soul' (ψυχή), and George ('Les récits de miracles,' 80) hears an echo from 1 Kgs 17:21. John Nolland (*Luke* [3 vols. WBC 35a–c. Dallas, Tex.: Word, 1989–1993], 1:422) remains agnostic on the matter. In any case, the absence of 'spirit' or 'soul' from the body indicates death (cf. Jas 2:26).

[11] The narrative leaves some question as to who was inside and outside the house, but see Nolland, *Luke*, 1:421; Green, *Luke*, 350.

[12] See Tannehill, *Narrative Unity*, 1:150. Tannehill and many other commentators mention the use of 'sleep' as a Christian euphemism for death (cf. its appearance in the Hebrew Bible: 1 Kgs 1:21; 2:10; 11:21, 43; 14:20; Ps 13:4; 22:30; Jer 51:39, 57; etc.).

(Luke 8:56), since they surely would not have marvelled at a rabbi waking their daughter from a nap. Hence, Luke is able to exploit the polyvalence present in the vocabulary, while at the same time clarifying that an actual resurrection has taken place.

The important point to be made here is that Luke's narrative precludes the notion that only an apparent death has occurred. This is so even for Eutychus.[13] First, it is misleading to translate Acts 20:9 as saying the lad was 'picked up *as* dead' or 'picked up *for* dead,'[14] as though he was only *assumed* to be dead. This could have been easily expressed by ἤρθη ὡς νεκρός instead of what we find here: καὶ ἤρθη νεκρός.[15] The narrator recounts that the boy was dead, not that he was assumed to be dead. Secondly, Paul's exclamation to call off mourning (Μὴ θορυβεῖσθε; cf. Mark 5:39), 'for his *psychē* is in him,' is not a diagnosis, but a prognosis (='he is going to live') after he had fallen upon the lad and embraced him. Paul does not say, 'his *psychē* is *still* in him.'[16] As Meyer has pointed out, 'The young man had, in fact, been but now ἄψυχος.'[17] Moreover, Paul's action and its

---

[13] Tannehill (*Narrative Unity*, 2:248–49) believes that Luke's account of Eutychus is ambiguous concerning whether the boy had died or not. It is difficult to see how ambiguity in this instance serves the Lukan portrayal of the providential itinerary and miraculous ministry of Paul.

[14] The latter rendering is Fitzmyer's; Joseph A. Fitzmyer, *The Acts of the Apostles: A New Translation with Introduction and Commentary* (AB 31; Garden City, N.Y.: Doubleday, 1998), 667. Nevertheless, he takes the phrase to mean that Eutychus was dead (669).

[15] Rev 1:17; Matt 28:4; Mark 9:26; cf. Kirsopp Lake and Henry Joel Cadbury, *The Acts of the Apostles*, BC 4:256–57. The same expression καὶ ἤρθη νεκρός appears in *T. Jud.* 9:3, where it refers to actual death. Luke characteristically uses ὡς (e.g., Luke 3:22; 10:3, 18; Acts 10:11) and esp. ὡσεί (e.g., Luke 22:44; 24:11; Acts 2:3; 6:15) to draw comparisons or approximations; cf. John C. Hawkins, *Horae Synopticae* (Oxford: Clarendon, 1909), 23; Lloyd Gaston, *Horae Synopticae Electronicae: Word Statistics of the Synoptic Gospels* (SBLSBS 3; Missoula, Mont.: SBL, 1973), 84. The absence of this feature here is significant. There is also the incident at Lystra in which Paul was stoned and presumed dead (νομίζοντες αὐτὸν τεθνηκέναι, Acts 14:19). Luke, therefore, is perfectly capable of distinguishing between real and assumed death.

[16] In this we agree with Haenchen (*Acts*, 585) and earlier scholars cited by him.

[17] Heinrich August Wilhelm Meyer, *Critical and Exegetical Handbook to the Acts of the Apostles* (translated from the 4th ed. by Paton J. Gloag; rev. and ed. William P. Dickson; New York: Funk & Wagnalls, 1889), 386. It must be granted that the absence of *psychē* could be associated with swooning in the Hellenistic world (see Bremmer, *Early Greek Concept of the Soul*, 15). For instance, when a man was cast down upon the deck of a ship and passed out, Thucydides called it *lipopsycheō*, a 'leaving of the *psychē*' (4.12). But it is quite another thing to fall three stories down. Henry J. Cadbury points to a parallel in the Oxyrhynchus papyri (3.475) in which a young boy fell from a

Miracle, Contention, and Hope for the People of God   125

result may be a mimesis of Elisha's: 'and while he lay bent over him, the flesh of the child became warm' (2 Kgs 4:34).[18] Finally, the scene closes with the report that Eutychus was led away 'alive' (Acts 20:12) in contradistinction to his earlier state of death.[19] The situation under any other circumstances, without the presence of the Elisha- and Jesus-like Paul, would have had a tragic ending. The narrator of Luke-Acts is cognizant of the ambiguity that can exist in telling stories about revivification, but he is able to dispel ambivalence, as well as use it to his own advantage. Less uncertainty is involved in apprehending such stories to be about actual resurrections given their Elijan cast.[20]

5.1.1.3 THEOLOGICAL MEANING OF RESURRECTION

In each case an important statement about the meaning of resurrection emerges. Notice how in every instance the individual is returned to his or her kinship group (Luke 7:15; 8:55–56; Acts 9:41; 20:11–12).[21] This

---

rooftop to his death (*The Book of Acts in History* [London: Adam and Charles Black, 1955], 9).

[18] Ivoni Richter Reimer (*Women in the Acts of the Apostles: A Feminist Liberation Perspective* [trans. Linda M. Maloney; Minneapolis: Fortress, 1995], 53) suggests but then rejects this mimetic line of interpretation. Reimer (49–53, 61) also contends that all of the 'resurrection stories' cannot relate anything other than 'reawakenings' or 'resuscitations.' They cannot be instances of the 'eschatological resurrection' because the recipients of such miracles are not resurrected into a new world. On this latter point we must agree, but it does not follow that these miracles are therefore not resurrections. The rabbinic text she quotes (53) actually buttresses our own position: the sons who were brought back to life under Elijah and Elisha are viewed as instances of causing 'the resurrection of the dead to come before its time' (*Midr. Song of Songs* 2.5 [98a]). The anomaly is not the supernatural occurrence itself—it is not a biological 'hiccup,' as in some Hellenistic understandings of resuscitation—but its timing. Later, the matter of permanence or immortality will be seen to figure into the difference between resurrection miracles and the eschatological resurrection.

[19] Note the similarity in language for the resurrected Jesus (Luke 24:23; Acts 1:3; 25:19) and Tabitha (Acts 9:41; see p. 33 above for this comparison). Another factor in favour of taking this as an account of an actual resurrection is Luke's use of parallelism between the miracles of Peter and Paul; so George, 'Les récits de miracles,' 82.

[20] Later, concern heightened among early Christians to demonstrate the authenticity of the apostles' miracles of resurrection as opposed to the deceptive tricks of false teachers, e.g., see the contest between Peter and Simon in *Acts of Peter* 28 (J. K. Elliott, *Apocryphal New Testament* [Oxford: Clarendon, 1993], 418–21).

[21] The note about eating in the case of Jairus's daughter (and perhaps also Eutychus) is important not only because it was a symbolic act of familial or social union, but because the death of a loved one began a period of fasting for the survivors among Jews (e.g., 1:12; 31:31; 2 Sam 12:16–23; 1 Chron 10:11; *4 Ezra* 10:4; 3 Macc 7:15–16; Jdt

reincorporation into one's family is a pervading element in resurrection. This element, too, has an Elijah pedigree (cf. 1 Kgs 17:23; 2 Kgs 4:36), but it belongs also to the nature of healing miracles in the Gospels and Acts, whose saving significance involves the restoration of community just as much as the amelioration or elimination of physical suffering. There is in this connection a distinct contrast with Hellenistic attitudes regarding the return of persons from the dead. Despite the fear or amazement caused by the resurrection itself (e.g., Luke 7:16; 8:56), the resurrected person is not shunned or regarded as taboo. Unlike Plutarch's report concerning the Greek and Roman responses to the so-called *deuteropotmoi*,[22] among Jews resurrected individuals were freely welcomed into their former social associations (especially Tabitha, who was an indispensable benefactress to the widows in her community).[23] This is due to a fundamental theological disparity between the Greco-Roman and Judaic perspectives. For the Greco-Roman it seems that the *deuteropotmos* has been rejected by the chthonian gods, whereas for the Jew the resurrected person is a testament to the power of Yahweh over death and his watchcare over the people of God (Luke 7:16).[24]

8:6) and Greeks (for three days, see Garland, *Greek Way of Death*, 39). For the hitherto deceased, to eat with family or friends would be a powerful experience of reintegration into the social world of the living.

[22] See our discussion of Plutarch and the *deuteropotmoi*, beginning on p. 105 above.

[23] For a more extensive discussion of resurrection stories within the widow tradition, see Robert M. Price, *The Widow Traditions in Luke-Acts: A Feminist-Critical Scrutiny* (SBLDS 155; Atlanta: Scholars Press, 1997), 83–100. On the renewal of communal life, see Reimer, *Women in the Acts of the Apostles*, 61–62.

[24] Lest it be objected that we have chosen merely one testimony to Greco-Roman reaction to returns from the dead (viz., Plutarch's, but note also Hesychius), while ignoring the striking parallel in Philostratus (*Vit. Apoll.* 4.45) where the revived girl returns to her father's house, let it be observed: (a) Philostratus is writing long after Luke (third century A.D.), and it is probable that this story has been affected by Christian attitudes toward resurrection (cf. the accounts in the apocryphal Acts, wherein there is competition between Christians and pagan miracle workers precisely on this count: resurrection; see Price, *Widow Traditions*, 83–100); (b) perhaps a rite of purification or a waiting period before the maiden's re-entry into her household is simply not mentioned; (c) or, since Philostratus clearly leaves open the possibility that this is only an apparent death that is reversed before the girl has been buried (contrast Plutarch who speaks of both the funeral procession *and* burial [*Mor.* 264f]), a taboo rule may simply not apply. Curiously, although the model for this miracle is specified as Euripides' Alcestis, Apollonius of Tyana's patient is unlike Alcestis in two important respects. First, the girl is revived before she is buried, whereas Alcestis was dead, buried, and then brought back from the grave by Heracles. Secondly, the girl immediately spoke out loud (a sure sign of her having been revived), whereas Alcestis was not allowed to speak for three days.

5.1.2 The Miracles of Resurrection and the Resurrection of Jesus

Next, let us draw a preliminary comparison between these miracle accounts of resurrection and the resurrection of Jesus in Luke-Acts.

5.1.2.1 JESUS' RESURRECTION, A DIRECT ACT OF GOD

First, it will be observed that the former resurrection accounts are indeed miracle stories. Of course, the outcome of Jesus' resurrection is itself presented in Luke's Gospel through a series of miracle stories, usually classified as epiphanies or appearances. The actual event of Jesus' resurrection, however, is not narrated by Luke, or any of the other canonical Evangelists.[25] This points up a principal distinction between the resurrection miracles and Jesus' resurrection. In the former, as we have seen, there is always an agent or mediator involved in the dead person's recovery. In Jesus' resurrection there is no such intermediary—no one touching the funeral bier or standing before the sepulchre, no one summoning the corpse to come forth from the tomb (cf. John 11:38–44). Luke consistently attributes the raising up of Jesus to God alone.[26] Human (and diabolical) instrumentality applies with respect to his death, but it is only God who raised up Jesus from the dead.[27]

5.1.2.2 THE REALITY OF JESUS' DEATH AND RESURRECTION

The Lukan account of Jesus' crucifixion and burial leaves no doubt regarding the death of Jesus. Notice that the women *saw* the tomb and how his body was laid in it (Luke 23:49, 55).[28] Jesus, unlike any of the other resurrected individuals, is actually entombed. The resurrection of Jesus does not happen during the *prothesis* (like Tabitha) or the *ekphora* (like the widow's son at Nain) or even around the time of his interment. It is noted repeatedly that his resurrection occurred 'on the third day' after his burial.[29] Also, unlike the ancient Greek novelist Chariton before him, Luke does not provide an omniscient view inside the tomb to behold the workings of a perfectly explainable resuscitation.[30] To the contrary, Jesus had died, and hence Luke stresses the fact that after his death and entombment he was 'alive.' But the

---

[25] Contrast *Gos. Pet.* 10.39.

[26] Never in Luke-Acts is Jesus said to 'rise' from the dead; but always he 'is raised' by God (Marguerat, 'Luc-Actes: La résurrection à l'œuvre dans l'histoire,' 206–7).

[27] Acts 2:23–24; 3:13–15; 5:30; 10:39–40; 13:27–30.

[28] There is a concentration of verbs of sight in these verses; see Green, *Luke*, 826, 831.

[29] Luke 9:22; 18:33; 24:7, 21, 46; Acts 10:40.

[30] This difference in narrative technique has been pointed out by Kany, 'Tod und Auferstehung,' 83–85.

'aliveness' of Jesus is infinitely more enduring than that of the beneficiaries of the other resurrection miracles. Jesus' body, it is explained by both Peter and Paul, was not allowed to suffer decay (Acts 2:27, 31; 13:34–37). This does not mean only that his body had not yet begun to decompose. That was clearly the case for the others as well. They were restored to life before even being buried. Rather, this refers to Jesus' 'indestructible life,' to echo the preacher to the Hebrews (Heb 7:16). The others were raised up, and returned to their former sphere of existence, only to die again.[31] Jesus was raised up, never to die again, and exalted to the right hand of God. He was installed as the ruler and judge over a renewed people of God as 'Leader of life' and Saviour (Acts 3:15; 5:31). Jesus' resurrection, we shall demonstrate later, is in Luke-Acts the premier instance of the eschatological resurrection of the dead.

5.1.2.3 THE RISEN JESUS AND THE RESTORATION OF THE PEOPLE OF GOD

While the other miracles of resurrection demonstrate the purpose of God to restore individuals into relationships that had been fractured by death, Jesus' resurrection is itself a pivotal moment for the restoration of God's people. Since this strikes upon a major point that needs to be substantiated in succeeding chapters, we can only baldly state the proposition here. Jesus' resurrection does not merely renew his contact with his followers, but it confirms his position as God's righteous servant, Messiah and deliverer of Israel, as well as universal Lord.

5.1.3 Conclusions

What conclusions, in light of the comparisons above, may be drawn (at least provisionally) regarding the Lukan view of resurrection? First, as to the nature of resurrection, we may conclude that in Luke-Acts the various instances of revivification are conceived of as the raising to life of truly dead individuals. The essential difference between the resurrection miracles and the resurrection of Jesus relates to the permanence of the resurrection. Second, theologically, resurrection is one of God's concrete saving acts. God graciously effects resurrection, whether directly or through an intermediary. It surpasses a modernist focus upon it as a reversal of the physical process of death. Resurrection is a means whereby the Creator brings restoration and healing to the people of God. In the resurrection miracles, the

---

[31] In the apocryphal *Acts of Peter* (28) the distinction between future eternal life and the temporal effects of a resurrection miracle are stated by Peter in a brief speech: 'Romans, thus the dead are awakened, thus they speak, thus they walk when they are raised; they live for so long as it pleases God' (Elliott, *Apocryphal New Testament*, 420).

Miracle, Contention, and Hope for the People of God 129

dead person is reintegrated as a son, daughter, or generous benefactor in the social network to which he or she belonged. Because of the resurrection of Jesus, the way is made possible for the people of Israel, and indeed people from the entire world, to be (re)incorporated or (re)instated among the people of God.

5.2 Resurrection in Contention

The narrator of Luke-Acts assumes that the resurrection of the dead is not a universal dogma that can be successfully deployed in any discourse setting. Rather, the resurrection is a contested topic, open to differing interpretations, misunderstanding, or outright rejection both in and outside of Judaism. It is with this awareness that Luke-Acts advocates the people of God's hope in the resurrection of the dead. The proper and authoritative view of the matter is presented in Luke-Acts through the reported revelation of scriptural truth by Jesus and his witnesses. According to Luke, the Scriptures are the bedrock for the belief in resurrection, as they are the foundation for comprehending every divinely ordained event in salvation history. Yet the revelatory value of the Scriptures cannot be separated from the particular (and for Luke, legitimate) interpretive legacy bequeathed by Messiah-Jesus. The resurrection can be optimally grasped only by those who have not only encountered the scriptural texts, but who have obtained the key to their interpretation in the Christ-event. The ideal recipient of the gospel message would be someone like the Ethiopian eunuch who, when asked whether he understood the passage from Isaiah he was reading, responded, 'How can I, unless someone guides me?' (Acts 8:31). Philip then explained the text by proclaiming the good news about Jesus (8:35). The notion of the resurrection of the dead is comprehensible only within the bounds of Jewish belief, and more particularly by way of tutelage in 'the Way.'

5.2.1 The Issue of Resurrection among Jews

According to Luke-Acts, Jewish debate regarding the resurrection would typically take place among two religious sects, the Pharisees and Sadducees. As in the other Synoptics, the Sadducees are recognized for their opposition to the idea of resurrection (Matt 22:23; Mark 12:18).[32] Indeed, as characters in the Lukan narrative, the Sadducees are almost exclusively

---

[32] Matthew, however, tends to indiscriminately lump together the Pharisees and Sadducees (Matt 3:7; 16:1, 6, 11–12), except in the pericope in which the Sadducees present their resurrection riddle to Jesus (see 22:34).

identified by their anti-resurrection stance.[33] The first time they appear in the narrative, they are described as 'those who say there is no resurrection' (Luke 20:27). In Acts 4:1-2 they reappear along with the temple authorities,[34] and are perturbed at the apostolic proclamation 'that in Jesus there is the resurrection of the dead.' Finally, in Acts 23:6-8 Paul creates pandemonium in the Jerusalem Sanhedrin by raising the issue of the resurrection, over which the Pharisees and Sadducees are deeply divided. It is in the first and last encounters with the Sadducees in Luke-Acts that we are given brief but precious information about the substance of the resurrection debate within Judaism that the narrator has deemed necessary to convey.

5.2.1.1 THE SADDUCEES AND JESUS ON RESURRECTION (LUKE 20:27-40)

While the Sadducees' confrontation with Jesus in Luke 20:27-40 bears independent value as a source of information regarding the Jewish resurrection debate, its function within the immediate and wider co-texts of the Lukan *Doppelwerk* cannot be neglected. First, this passage falls within a series of confrontations between Jesus and the temple leaders in which Jesus' authority is being questioned (20:1-40).[35] The setting and characters in this struggle are introduced in 19:45-48, where Jesus clears the sellers from the temple and begins a daily teaching ministry. The chief priests, scribes, and leaders of the people (19:47; cf. 20:1, 19, 39) seek a way to destroy Jesus, but they are unable to because the people are hanging on Jesus' every word (19:48; cf. 20:1, 6, 9, 19, 26). At issue is the validity of Jesus' proclamation, on temple grounds, of the in-breaking of the kingdom of God (cf. 20:1; 21:37-38). The temple authorities attempt to undercut Jesus' credibility with the people by striking at the more fundamental issue of who has the divine authority to wield influence over the people: the temple leaders, whose authority is legitimized by their positions of power vis-à-vis the Jerusalem temple, or Jesus, whose whole ministry of teaching and healing has been characterized as divinely authoritative (Luke 4:32, 36; 5:24; 9:1; 10:19; Acts 2:22; 10:38)?[36] The Sadducees' poser about the resurrection (Luke 20:27-40) is the last in a series of abortive attempts to invalidate Jesus' investiture of divine authority. Jesus' response to this final question closes down any further questioning (20:40), and Jesus launches a

---

[33] Cf. Robert L. Brawley, *Luke-Acts and the Jews: Conflict, Apology, and Conciliation* (SBLMS 33; Atlanta: Scholars Press, 1987), 115.

[34] The high priest and those with him are closely associated with the Sadducees in Acts 5:17. On the Saducean and high-priestly coalition in Luke-Acts, see Brawley, *Luke-Acts and the Jews*, 107-17.

[35] For how this whole section operates as a literary unit, see James M. Dawsey, 'Confrontation in the Temple: Luke 19:45-20:47,' *PRSt* 11 (1984): 153-65.

[36] Green, *Luke*, 696-97.

scriptural question of his own (left unanswered, 20:41-44) and an indictment of the unjust conduct of those whose connection to the temple is used to elevate themselves at the expense of the less privileged (20:45-21:4).

Second, Luke 20:27-40 is an important backdrop for the controversy that takes place later in Acts 3-4 between the temple authorities (including Sadducees) and the apostles over the resurrection of Jesus and the authoritative teaching and healing by the apostles in Jesus' name. It is also appropriate that Luke 20:27-40 is followed by Jesus' question about how the Messiah can be David's son, since David calls him 'Lord' (20:41-44). Only later will the reader learn that the two issues, resurrection and the Messiah's lordship, are indissolubly bound together. How can the Messiah be the son of David, yet also his Lord? By virtue of his resurrection from the dead in accordance with prophecy (Acts 2:22-36)![37] The resurrection from the dead, therefore, does not merely constitute a fine point of theology over which Jewish teachers squabble. It plays a significant role in the Lukan understanding of the Christ and the salvation of God's people. With this broader framework in mind, we will investigate the subject of resurrection in Luke 20:27-40.

5.2.1.1.1 The Sadducees' Conundrum (Luke 20:27-33)

The Sadducees formulate a question that pits the authority of Moses against that of Jesus. They cite the Mosaic legislation regarding levirate marriage (20:28 = Deut 25:5; Gen 38:8), and then tell a tale of serial levirate marriages which, in their estimation, precludes the viability of any resurrection from the dead. Seven brothers, one by one, marry the same woman and all of them, as well as the woman herself, die without bearing any offspring.[38]

---

[37] Charles H. Talbert, *Reading Luke: A Literary and Theological Commentary on the Third Gospel* (New York: Crossroad, 1982), 195-96; Dawsey, 'Confrontation in the Temple,' 164; Green, *Luke*, 724.

[38] In the search for the literary origins of this story, several possible contributing sources have been singled out. The mention of seven brothers has been regarded as a possible echo of the (Pharisaic?) martyrology in 2 Maccabees 7; see Le Moyne, *Les Sadducéens*, 126-27. True, the exemplary piety of the seven Maccabean martyrs continued to be lauded in the first-century book of 4 Maccabees; but stories using the number seven (perhaps as a symbol of perfection, cf. Le Moyne, 126 n. 10) were common enough, and were not usually associated with resurrection (e.g., *T. Mos.* 9:1). The attempt by Peter Bolt to trace this story to the book of Tobit may have some merit ('What Were the Sadducees Reading? An Enquiry into the Literary Background of Mark 12:18-23,' *TynBul* 45 [1994]: 369-94), for there is a similar situation of sevenfold levirate marriage; but the linkage with resurrection is simply not as strong as Bolt contends. The real question is not what the Sadducees were reading, but what Luke's *listeners* were

The story is a clever repudiation of the resurrection, apparently on the basis of an alternative understanding of what 'resurrection' really is: the 'raising up' of children (ἐξαναστήσῃ σπέρμα, 20:28; contrast ἐν τῇ ἀναστάσει, 20:33).[39] The story is dominated by successive deaths and childlessness.[40] This, as we shall see, is important for Jesus' unravelling of the Sadducees' argument.

5.2.1.1.2 Jesus' Response—Part 1 (Luke 20:34-36)

Jesus responds to the Pharisees in reverse order to how they presented their puzzle. He first takes up the point of their story (20:34-36), and then he addresses the purported Mosaic authority of their negation of the resurrection (20:37-38). The general drift of the first part of his response is easy to grasp. Jesus' vision of the resurrection is rooted in apocalypticism, which divides human history into two ages: this age and the age to come. He speaks of how 'the sons of this age' marry and are given in marriage (20:34), whereas the participants in 'that age' (i.e., the age to come, 20:35) do not.[41] The reason for this difference is that the resurrected are no longer able to die (20:36). This strikes at the heart of the Sadducees' objection; for if there is no death, then there is no longer any need to perpetuate one's life or name through the reproduction of offspring.

There are two sets of details in Jesus' response that require further clarification. The first is Jesus' statement about 'those have been accounted worthy to experience that age and the resurrection from the dead' (20:35). It is true that the participle καταξιωθέντες ('accounted worthy') is a divine passive, as commentators have observed;[42] but little or nothing is normally

---

hearing. Would they have immediately detected an allusion to the book of Tobit? Probably not.

[39] Green, *Luke*, 719-20. For an interpretation of the Markan parallel which draws attention to the faithfulness of Yahweh (the God of Abraham et al.) in insuring the birth of progeny for the patriarchs in impossible or complicated circumstances, and how this ancestral story of sterility and subsequent fertility debunks the Sadducean hermeneutic, see J. Gerald Janzen, 'Resurrection and Hermeneutics: On Exodus 3.6 in Mark 12.26,' *JSNT* 23 (1985): 43-58.

[40] The verb ἀποθνῄσκω appears 4x in this section (20:28, 29, 31, 32); the adjective ἄτεκνος, 2x (20:28, 29); and the expression οὐ κατέλιπον τέκνα, 1x (20:31).

[41] Kilgallen's attempt to limit the marriage in this passage to '*repeated* marrying' and 'being *repeatedly* given in marriage' (or 'being made [by the Law] to marry') is, in his own words, 'hypothetical'; John J. Kilgallen, 'The Sadducees and Resurrection from the Dead: Luke 20,27-40,' *Bib* 67 (1986): 479, 484 n. 16.

[42] E.g., Fitzmyer, *Luke*, 1305.

written about the meaning of this expression.[43] A ready answer to the question of who may be regarded as worthy of the resurrection may be found in Jesus' symposium discourse in Luke 14.[44] There Jesus advocates a social ethic that is counter to the prevailing notions of social stratification and standards of reciprocity by urging wealthy hosts to invite, not those who are of similar status and wealth and who are able to return the favour, but the poor, crippled, blind, and lame (14:13, 21). This instruction is given in two back-to-back passages: the first countering the customary honour-seeking practices in a banquet setting (14:7–14), and the second being an illustration of someone who has broken from the constraints of status-maintenance in order to follow the kingdom ethic of open giving to society's marginalized (14:15–24). The two passages are hinged together with a statement by Jesus in 14:14, and a response from one of the guests in 14:15, which provide an eschatological framework for Jesus' teaching. Jesus' rationale for instructing the host to invite the underprivileged to feast with him is that 'you will be blessed, because they cannot repay you, for you will be repaid at the resurrection of the righteous.' In our treatment of the resurrection in Second Temple Judaism we observed that the resurrection is often associated with the righteous poor, oppressed, or exiled who will be exalted or rewarded in the face of their wealthy, powerful oppressors who will be cast down (e.g., Dan 11–12; *1 En.* 62:14–16; *T. Jud.* 25:3–5; *4 Ezra* 4:35; 7:35). One of the guests at the table wants to soften the severity of this eschatological reversal by offering a universal macarism: 'Blessed is *anyone* who will eat bread in the kingdom of God!' But Jesus urges his wealthy tablemates, by way of a parable, to conduct themselves in such a way as to avoid this dramatic reversal (cf. Luke 14:24). The paradox is that those who tout their Abrahamic pedigree, who collude in safeguarding a network of reciprocal relationships among members of their high-status group, who are preoccupied with their own wealth, and who exclude the less-deserving and 'sinners' from their social intercourse—these have a sense of worthiness about their position before God (Luke 16:14–15; 18:11–12); but in fact they have disqualified themselves from having a place at the banquet table in the kingdom of God (13:28–29). Because they have barred others from the kingdom, while jockeying for their own

---

[43] Perhaps this is because, as Marshall notes aptly, the specifics of the matter are not mentioned here; I. Howard Marshall, *The Gospel of Luke* (NIGTC; Exeter: Paternoster; Grand Rapids: Eerdmans, 1978), 741.

[44] On Luke 14, see Willi Braun, *Feasting and Social Rhetoric in Luke 14* (SNTSMS 85; Cambridge: Cambridge University Press, 1995); Robert C. Tannehill, 'The Lukan Discourse on Invitations (Luke 14,7–24),' in *The Four Gospels 1992: Festschrift Frans Neirynck* (eds. F. Van Segbroeck et al; 3 vols.; BETL 100; Leuven: Leuven University Press, 1992), 2:1603–16.

position, they have ironically judged themselves 'unworthy' of eternal life (cf. Acts 13:46). Conversely, those who are social outcasts and 'sinners' may become the very ones who are fit for the kingdom of God, although proclaiming themselves 'unworthy' of being God's children (Luke 15:18–19, 21; cf. 18:13), but aligning their lives with the purpose of God (i.e., 'repenting') and acting in ways 'worthy' of repentance (Luke 3:8; Acts 26:20; cf. Luke 7:29–30). These are the lost who have been found, and the dead who have come to life (Luke 15:24, 32); they are the last who will become first (13:30); and the humble who will be exalted (14:11; 18:14). They are the ones who will be accounted worthy of that age and the resurrection from the dead.[45]

A second set of details concerns the glorious, deathless future of those who have been deemed worthy of the resurrection. Jesus says that they will no longer be able to die, 'because they are like angels and are children of God, being children of the resurrection' (Luke 20:26). Many scholars rightly dismiss Fitzmyer's suggestion that the resurrected will be like the angels in that they are 'disembodied spirits who do not marry.'[46] The rare term ἰσάγγελος, by analogy to other words compounded with ἴσος (such as ἰσοβασιλεύς or ἰσόθεός), denotes an equivalence in function or attributes, not ontological identity. The choice of terms rules out any notion that the resurrected will become angels, but rather invites a comparison between the two.[47] Here the comparison pivots around immortality and the non-necessity of marriage (hence, procreation), not incorporeality.

The exalted, angel-like status of the resurrected is further expressed in the statement that they are 'children of God' (lit. 'sons of God') and 'children of the resurrection' (lit. 'sons of the resurrection'). What is meant by the expression 'sons of God'? How is divine sonship related to angel-likeness? And what is the relationship between being 'sons of God' and

---

[45] On the motif of reversal in Luke, see John O. York, *The Last Shall Be First: The Rhetoric of Reversal in Luke* (JSNTSup 46; Sheffield: Sheffield Academic Press, 1991). Later in Luke's work the early Christian community is depicted as a society that embodies the social ethic of Luke 14 (Acts 2:44–46; 4:32, 34–35) *and* is grounded in the apostolic testimony to the resurrection of Jesus (4:33); cf. Green, 'Witnesses of His Resurrection,' 241.

[46] Fitzmyer, *Luke*, 2:1305, cf. Philo, *Sacr.* 1 §5. In Luke the comparison concerns immortality, not anthropology; so Kilgallen, 'Sadducees and Resurrection,'485 n. 17; Ellis, *Luke*, 237; Nolland, *Luke*, 3:966; Charles A. Kimball, *Jesus' Exposition of the Old Testament in Luke's Gospel* (JSNTSup 94; Sheffield: Sheffield Academic Press, 1994), 171 n. 89.

[47] Frederick W. Danker, *Jesus and the New Age: A Commentary on St. Luke's Gospel* (rev. ed.; Philadelphia: Fortress, 1988), 323.

'sons of the resurrection,' i.e., is one determinative of the other?[48] Since the idea of sonship is not frequently allied with the Lukan conception of the people of God (cf. Luke 6:35–36), it will be fruitful to read this manifestly Semitic expression ('sons of God') as it was employed during the Second Temple period. The only extensive study of the 'sonship of God' in the intertestamental literature (excluding, of course, the plethora of works on 'son of God' as a messianic title) is that of Brendan Byrne.[49] Byrne studies the term 'sons of God' under three categories of usage: (a) 'heavenly beings'; (b) 'Israelite' sonship of God; and (c) 'royal' sonship of God. He draws three conclusions about the sonship of God in the intertestamental literature, all of which cast light upon its appearance in Luke.[50] First, sonship of God is often expressed as the sole privilege of Israel, dependent upon Yahweh's election and calling. The sonship of God is often employed to sharply distinguish Israel from other nations, and so the expression 'sons of God' often functions as a virtual synonym for 'the people of God' or 'Israel.'[51] Second, the sonship of God motif 'occurs with considerable frequency in eschatological contexts, suggesting that it was an epithet to be particularly applicable to the ideal Israel of the end-time, the holy and purified people of God, the citizens of his eternal kingdom.'[52] In these contexts the righteous are *recognized* as sons of God. Third, the sonship of God is often associated with the idea of rescue from death or destruction. The pattern of reversal often appears in this connection, in which the righteous are ultimately granted immunity from the death and suffering inflicted upon them, and their oppressors are forced to recognize and confess the sonship status of those they have oppressed.[53] These points are particularly apposite

---

[48] There is disagreement regarding this last question. Marshall, for example, thinks that persons become sons of God (a status ascribed also to angels) by virtue of the resurrection (*Luke*, 742), whereas Kilgallen emphatically reverses the relationship ('Sadducees and Resurrection,' 486).

[49] Brendan Byrne, *'Sons of God'—'Seed of Abraham': A Study of the Idea of the Sonship of God of All Christians in Paul against the Jewish Background* (AnBib 83; Rome: Biblical Institute, 1979), 18–70; idem, 'Sons of God,' *ABD* 6:156–59.

[50] For what follows, see Byrne, *Sons of God*, 62–63.

[51] 4QDibHam^a 3:4–6; Sir 36:17; *Pss. Sol.* 17:30; *Jub.* 1:25–28; 2:20; *4 Ezra* 5:28; 6:58; Jdt 9:4, 13; Tob 13:4; *2 Bar.* 13:9; *L.A.B.* 32:10; *T. Mos.* 10:3; 3 Macc 5:7; 6:3, 8, 28; 7:6; Wis 11–19; Add Esth 16:14–16.

[52] *Jub.* 1:25–28; *Pss. Sol.* 17:30; *Sib. Or.* 3:702–4; 5:248–50; *T. Levi* 18:13.

[53] Wis 2–5; 13–18; Add Esth 16:14–16; 3 Macc 6:28; 7:6–7.

to Luke 20:36, and lend support to the position that 'being sons of the resurrection' indicates a moment when the true 'sons of God' are revealed.[54]

What of the collocation of 'sons of God' with 'angel-equals'? Was there in the Second Temple period a conflation of the idea of 'sons of God' as angelic beings (cf. Gen 6:1–4) with that of 'sons of God' as the people of Israel? Byrne points out that only rarely can one find a total fusion of the two concepts (e.g., *Prayer of Joseph* A). Typically, the 'Israelite' usage is not absorbed by the 'angelic,' and indeed the distinction between the two is essential to drawing a comparison between them. In the Wisdom of Solomon, as an example, in which the divine sonship of the righteous is crucially significant (cf. Wis 2:13, 16), the righteous are numbered among the 'sons of God' and have a lot among 'the holy ones' (i.e., angels, 5:5). The two concepts interpenetrate at one critical point: the Israelite 'sons of God' will be like the angelic 'sons of God' in that the latter are characteristically immortal (*1 En.* 69:11; *2 Bar.* 51:3, 5, 9–10, 12).[55] This is precisely the relationship expressed in Luke 20:36. The 'sons of God' are the genuine people of God who experience resurrection and life eternal. They become like the angels in that they are given the privilege of dwelling in the divine presence forever.

5.2.1.1.3 Jesus' Response—Part 2 (Luke 20:37–38)

The second part of Jesus' response deploys a quotation from the Torah (Exod 3:6) to indicate that the authority of Moses is in fact aligned with Jesus' own position that God will raise the dead. There is no precedent for Jesus' selection of this particular text to argue for resurrection.[56] It is significant for two reasons. First, it is drawn from a foundational passage in Israel's history. The scene is the call of Moses 'at the bush' (ἐπὶ τῆς βάτου).[57] Second, the scriptural words comprise none other than the covenantal formula of the God of Israel: 'the Lord, the God of Abraham and the

---

[54] Cf. Evans, *Luke*, 717–18; Ellis, *Luke*, 237; Kilgallen, 'Sadducees and Resurrection,' 485–86; *pace* Marshall, *Luke*, 742; Robert H. Stein, *Luke* (NAC 24; Nashville: Broadman, 1992), 503.

[55] Byrne, *Sons of God,* 64–67. Recall our discussion of the conception of the resurrection in the Second Temple period in which the exalted, post-resurrection status of the righteous can be described as angelic or astral.

[56] That his form of argumentation is also unprecedented within rabbinic tradition has been argued by D. M. Cohn-Sherbok, 'Jesus' Defense of the Resurrection of the Dead,' *JSNT* 11 (1981): 64–73; but see Kimball, *Jesus' Exposition*, 174–77.

[57] On the significance of this scene for the history of Israel's deliverance out of Egyptian bondage, cf. Acts 7:30–36.

God of Isaac and the God of Jacob' (cf. Exod 3:6, 15–16).[58] Standing behind this citation, then, is the enormous shadow of Yahweh who delivered Israel out of Egypt with a mighty arm, in keeping with his covenantal promises to the patriarchs. Jesus is citing the charter of God's chosen people, Israel, as a promise of resurrection. The two parts of Jesus' response to the Sadducees thus form two sides of the same coin. They both convey the promise of salvation for God's people via resurrection. The repetition of the word 'God' in this covenant formula is brought forward into an emphatic position in Jesus' subsequent comment: θεὸς δὲ οὐκ ἔστιν νεκρῶν ἀλλὰ ζώντων.[59] Having dismissed the Sadducees' casuistic example of levirate marriage, Jesus now focuses on the theological basis for the hope in resurrection. The God of Israel, the living God, does not maintain a covenant relationship with corpses, but with living persons. How then can the three great patriarchs be dead? But this begs the question: In what sense are they alive?

The brief explanatory clause that closes Jesus' reply to the Sadducees (πάντες γὰρ αὐτῷ ζῶσιν) is the most difficult part of this passage to interpret. Nearly every word in this clause has been debated. Luke's predilection for the word 'all' throughout his two-volume work may commend a universalistic understanding of πάντες. The antecedent could then be all of the living and the dead just previously mentioned.[60] But this cannot be so, since the contention being sustained is that the Lord is God of the living, not the dead.[61] The 'all' here must therefore be qualified. A likely referent would be the three mentioned patriarchs ('all of them' as the NRSV translates). Or perhaps the 'all' refers to everyone who has entered into covenant relationship with God even as Abraham, Isaac, and Jacob have.[62] But what is meant

---

[58] A study of this covenant formula that is still of immense value is that of F. Dreyfus, 'L'argument scripturaire de Jésus en faveur de la résurrection des morts (Marc, XII, 26–27),' *RB* 66 (1959): 213–24.

[59] Contrast οὐκ ἔστιν [ὁ] θεὸς νεκρῶν ἀλλὰ ζώντων (Matt 22:32; Mark 12:27); cf. Fitzmyer, *Luke*, 2:1306; Kilgallen, 'Sadducees and Resurrection,' 490–91.

[60] '[P]*antes* means "all people regardless of their being alive or dead,"' according to J. Reiling and J. L. Swellengrebel, *A Translator's Handbook on the Gospel of Luke* (UBSHT 10; Leiden: Brill, 1971), 655.

[61] It is one thing to be the Lord over (Rom 14:9) or to judge the living and the dead (Acts 10:42; 2 Tim 4:1; 1 Pet 4:5), but quite another thing to be the God of corpses. The latter is unthinkable for a Sadducee, who likely held to a classical Hebrew view of the afterlife in which the dead in Sheol are forever cut off from the land of the living, and therefore from continued relationship with or worship of Yahweh (Num 16:30, 33; Pss 6:6; 17:4–6; 88:3–12; 115:17; Isa 38:10–11, 18; Sir 17:27–28; Bar 2:17).

[62] So, e.g., Evans, *Luke*, 719; Marshall, *Luke*, 743; but esp. Alfred Plummer, *A Critical and Exegetical Commentary on the Gospel According to St. Luke* (ICC; New York:

by the assertion that they 'live to him [i.e., God]'? Two explanations have been set forth.[63] (1) The traditional view is that the patriarchs enjoy a post-mortem, spiritual existence in that they have been granted immortality.[64] (2) There are several construals of this clause that are intended to counter the traditional view with its inherent basis in a body-soul dualism and the immortality of the soul. Nolland, for example, takes the αὐτῷ as an indicator of perspective: they live 'as far as God is concerned.'[65] Ellis interprets it in terms of Paul's conception of mystical union with Christ.[66] Green states that patriarchs are given life by God 'in some sense.'[67]

Several points should be kept in mind regarding the interpretation of this phrase. First, although the phrase bears a striking resemblance to 4 Macc 7:19 and 16:25, a direct literary relationship is uncertain. We do not know whether this phrase was unique to 4 Maccabees, or if it also appeared elsewhere within the context of articulating hope in the resurrection. Therefore, it is rash to import from 4 Maccabees the notion of post-mortem existence as immortal souls, let alone assume that Luke's readers would have called this to mind at the utterance of these four little words.[68] Second, the Lukan co-text must be the primary determiner of the meaning of this phrase. We have already learned that it is in 'that age,' when the resurrection of the dead takes place, when the children of God will realize an angel-like, immortal existence. The introduction to Jesus' citation of the covenant formula, moreover, speaks of Moses' revelation concerning the resurrection of the dead, not of life in an intermediate state.[69] Finally, the idea of 'living' or

---

Charles Scribner's Sons, 1901), 471: 'The πάντες need not be restricted to the three patriarchs: it includes all who are mentioned in *vv.* 35, 36.'

[63] See Kimball, *Jesus' Exposition*, 173 n. 95.

[64] Fitzmyer, *Luke*, 2:1301–2; Evans, *Luke*, 719.

[65] Nolland, *Luke*, 3:967.

[66] Ellis, *Luke*, 237; idem, 'Jesus, the Sadducees and Qumran,' *NTS* 10 (1964): 274–76; similarly, Eduard Schweizer, *The Good News According to Luke* (trans. David E. Green; Atlanta: John Knox, 1984), 307. Ellis's view has been roundly criticized by Fitzmyer (*Luke*, 2:1301, 1307).

[67] Green, *Luke*, 722.

[68] *Pace* Fitzmyer, *Luke*, 2:1307.

[69] Only Luke 16:19–31 could substantiate a similarity in thought with 4 Maccabees; but here, as Bauckham has pointed out, the prospect of discovering information about life beyond the grave is subverted by the parable itself, since the persuasive power of a resurrected witness who could attest to the conditions of the underworld is negated, and instead the sufficiency of existing scriptural revelation is affirmed; see Richard Bauckham, 'The Rich Man and Lazarus: The Parable and the Parallels,' *NTS* 37 (1991): 244–46; idem, 'Visiting the Places of the Dead in the Extra-Canonical Apocalypses,' *PIBA* 18 (1995): 93. Luke, therefore, is not particularly interested in the question of life after death 'in this age.' The patriarchs are mentioned in Luke 13:28, but this is in connection

being 'alive' is repeatedly associated with resurrection in Luke-Acts (Luke 24:23; Acts 1:3; 9:41; 20:12; 25:19; cf. Luke 15:24, 32). So whether it is thought that the patriarchs were already enjoying resurrection life (as the present tense ζῶσιν might indicate), or that they would be resurrected at the end of the age, resurrection is in any case at the heart of the matter. More importantly, the life of the patriarchs is contingent upon their covenant relationship with God. They live 'to him,' without whom they would assuredly remain among the dead. Later it is the same covenant God of Israel who exalts his servant, Jesus, by raising him from the dead (Acts 3:13; 5:30).

Jesus' confrontation with the Sadducees reveals a remarkable continuity with the theological contours that we discovered in Second Temple Judaic thought on resurrection. The resurrection is viewed as intimately linked to a new creation. This is part and parcel with the two-age theology evident in this passage. The motif of exaltation is prominent, too. Those who are deemed worthy of the resurrection will become angel-like, and will transcend the vagaries of human existence, particularly the cycle of procreation and death. Resurrection, finally, is a covenant blessing. It is a revelation of those who are the bona fide people of God, those who live within the parameters of God's covenant, and who are the rightful heirs to the promise of resurrection inherent in the patriarchal covenant formula.

5.2.1.2 PHARISEES VERSUS SADDUCEES ON RESURRECTION (ACTS 23:8)

During Paul's hearing before the Jerusalem Sanhedrin he was aware of the party separation between the Sadducees and Pharisees within the council, and cried out, 'Brothers, I am a Pharisee, a son of Pharisees. I am on trial concerning the hope of the resurrection of the dead' (Acts 23:6). This was not simply a clever ploy to exploit a rift between the two sects. Paul is not being portrayed as disingenuous in his claim that at issue was the hope of the resurrection of the dead. After all, Paul had been a member of that strictest of Jewish sects, Pharisaism (26:5). And in hearing after hearing he would continue to maintain that he was on trial on account of the hope of the resurrection of the dead (24:15, 20–21; 26:6–8). The salient points of contention between the Pharisees and Sadducees are presented in 23:8:

Σαδδουκαῖοι μὲν γὰρ λέγουσιν μὴ εἶναι ἀνάστασιν μήτε ἄγγελον μήτε πνεῦμα, Φαρισαῖοι δὲ ὁμολογοῦσιν τὰ ἀμφότερα.

Yet the issues involved are more opaque than at first glance. First, there is the question of how the items ἀνάστασιν, ἄγγελον, and πνεῦμα are to be delineated. There are three things rejected by the Sadducees, but the Pharisees are said to acknowledge 'both' of them. Second, there is the concomitant

---

with the eschatological banquet which will presumably take place at the time of the resurrection (13:29; cf. 14:14–15).

matter of how the three things are related to one another. Specifically, we are concerned with whether or not, and if so, how 'resurrection' is related to the other two items.

This passage has not given rise to an enormous amount of discussion.[70] Most translators and commentators appear to see little difficulty in parsing the three terms or interpreting what is at issue. As to translation, most English versions simply list the three negated items in the first clause, and then render τὰ ἀμφότερα in the second clause as a reference to 'all' of them.[71] This translation is grammatically possible, although the more inclusive usage of ἀμφότεροι is not attested to until the second century A.D.[72] A common interpretation of the passage is that the Sadducees denied the future resurrection as well as the existence of angels or spirits. The purported Sadducean denial of angels or spirits, despite not being paralleled elsewhere among ancient writers, is thought to be consonant with Josephus's report that the Sadducees repudiated the idea of the survival of the *psychē* beyond death (*J. W.* 2.8.14 §165; *Ant.* 18.1.4 §16).

The difficulties with this view are essentially twofold. First, with the loose delineation of the three items and the free translation of τὰ ἀμφότερα, the Gordian knot is perhaps too hastily cut. There may well be more precision in Luke's statement than this view allows. Second, there is a historical problem with the conclusion that the Sadducees categorically denied the existence of angels. Josephus's description of the Sadducees in terms closely matching the Epicureans may be a stylization of them, along with the Essenes and Pharisees, in order to demonstrate how they approximate Hellenistic philosophical schools. Josephus also says that the Sadducees adhered to the traditions in the Mosaic Law (*Ant.* 18.1.4 §16). Angels play significant roles at key points in the Torah (e.g., the Akedah; Jacob's wrestling match and naming; Moses and the burning bush; the direction of Israel through the wilderness) as well as throughout the rest of the

---

[70] For a recent critical survey of research, see Floyd Parker, 'The Terms "Angel" and "Spirit" in Acts 23,8,' *Bib* 84 (2003): 344–65

[71] Cf. ESV, NAB, NASB, NRSV, REB, TEV, MOFFATT. The notable exception is the KJV: 'but the Pharisees confess both' (cf. also Luther and Louis Segond). NEB glosses over the difficulty by translating: 'but the Pharisees accept them.'

[72] 'ἀμφότεροι, αι, α,' BDAG 55; LSJ 95. The free usage of ἀμφότεροι appears in Acts 19:16, but note that in the Majority text it is replaced by αὐτῶν. JB translates 19:16: 'and the man with the evil spirit hurled himself at them and overpowered first one and then another.' JB's marginal reading is 'both' in the sense of 'two of their number.' For various attempts to explain Acts 19:16, see John B. Polhill, *Acts* (NAC 26; Nashville: Broadman, 1992), 404 n. 23; Bruce, *Acts of the Apostles*, 411.

Tanakh.⁷³ How could the Sadducees have rejected a belief in angels? This question has been addressed in the pages of *JBL* in two pairs of articles during the last half of the twentieth century. The earlier discussion in the 1960s is not particularly helpful.⁷⁴ In the early 1990s, however, two provocative critical notes appeared, one under the name of David Daube, and another under the names of Benedict Viviano and Justin Taylor.⁷⁵ Both of these notes share a common set of premises: (1) that there is a historical difficulty with the notion that the Sadducees did not believe in the existence of angels; (2) that τὰ ἀμφότερα ought to be taken in its restricted, dyadic sense ('both'); and (3) that the first term in the series ('resurrection') stands in relationship to the final two ('angel' and 'spirit'). The divergence between Daube and Viviano/Taylor concerns the nature of the relationship between resurrection and angels or spirits.

Daube proposes a creative interpretation that understands Acts 23:8 as the synopsis of a controversy over the fate of individuals in the afterlife.⁷⁶ 'Both' issues may be delineated as follows: (1) the final resurrection of the dead; and (2) the state of the dead in the interim between death and resurrection 'in the realm or mode of angel or spirit.'⁷⁷ Daube finds support for this interpretation in Josephus's report of the Pharisaic belief in the continued existence of ψυχαί after death (interim) as well as their re-embodiment at the revolution of the ages (resurrection). He cites *1 En.* 39:5 and 54:1–2 as references to both the interim dwelling of the righteous among the angels and at the resurrection. Daube also thinks that in Luke's version of the res-

---

⁷³ The common assertion that the Sadducees only accepted the Torah as canonical has not been documented. The issue between the Pharisees and Sadducees that Josephus mentions does not reflect a debate over canon, but over the authority of oral laws that are extraneous to the Torah itself; see Wayne O. McCready, 'Sadducees and Ancient Sectarianism,' *RelStTh* 12 (1992): 89–91.

⁷⁴ Bernard Bamberger, 'The Sadducees and Belief in Angels,' *JBL* 82 (1963): 433–35; Solomon Zeitlin, 'The Sadducees and the Belief in Angels,' *JBL* 83 (1964): 67–71. Bamberger (435) suggested that the Sadducees believed in the existence of angels, but denied that they were agents of revelation (cf. 23:9); but this is hardly defensible. Zeitlin (71), too, is far from compelling when he argues that the Sadducees did not believe in angels because, since the advent of the prophets, their function as spokespersons for God had been discontinued.

⁷⁵ David Daube, 'On Acts 23: Sadducees and Angels,' *JBL* 109 (1990): 493–97; Benedict T. Viviano and Justin Taylor, 'Sadducees, Angels, and Resurrection (Acts 23:8–9), *JBL* 111 (1992): 496–98.

⁷⁶ Yet this view is not novel, as Daube suggests. A nearly identical argument was already advanced by Augustin George, 'Les anges,' in *Études sur l'œuvre de Luc* (SB; Paris: Gabalda, 1978), 165–68 (following Adolf Schlatter et al.); and Le Moyne, *Les Sadducéens*, 131–34.

⁷⁷ Daube, 'On Acts 23,' 493.

urrection debate with the Sadducees, Jesus more closely identifies the resurrected with angels by use of the term ἰσάγγελοι. So in Acts 23:9 some of the scribes from among the Pharisees understand Paul's Damascus experience (cf. 22:6–10, 17–21) as an audition of the angel or spirit of Jesus. Their assessment of Paul's experience is inaccurate in light of the larger Lukan narrative, but its frame of reference is understandable. For example, the disciples mistake the risen Jesus for a 'spirit' in Luke 24:37, 39. And after Peter's miraculous release from prison, the assembled Christians cannot believe it is he, but that it is 'his angel' (Acts 12:15). The expectation is that a deceased person could appear as a spirit or angel.[78]

Viviano and Taylor also hold that Acts 23:8 refers to beliefs about the afterlife, but they delineate the three terms differently. Instead of Daube's delineation of the resurrection on the one hand and the angelic or spiritual interim state on the other, they see the terms 'angel' and 'spirit' as two different modifiers of 'resurrection.'[79] Resurrection in the form of an angel corresponds with how the resurrected are depicted in various texts (e.g., Dan 12:2–3; Matt 22:30 par.). This type of resurrection presupposes a monistic anthropology in which the deceased human person becomes like an angel. Resurrection in the form of a spirit is based upon a dualistic anthropology. In this type of resurrection, the spirit survives the body but later passes into 'another body' (as per Josephus, *Ant.* 18.1.3 §14; *J.W.* 2.8.14 §163).

The view espoused by Viviano and Taylor is easily dispensed with. Although theoretically possible, it is difficult to believe that Acts 23:8 is an effort to convey two subtle variations of Pharisaic teaching on resurrection. This would be the only ancient reference to the resurrection to treat the subject with such sophistication (with the prominent exception of *2 Bar.* 50–51). There are, however, simpler syntactical reasons for rejecting this interpretation. First, Acts 23:9 confirms that 'angel' and 'spirit' are being paired (not contrasted) in 23:8. Second, if 'angel' and 'spirit' were in a correlative expression qualifying 'resurrection,' they would naturally be in the genitive case: ἀνάστασιν μήτε ἀγγέλου μήτε πνεύματος. The view of Daube has much to commend it. Under this interpretation, the comments of certain scribes in 23:9 comprise a fitting Pharisaic reading of Paul's Damascus encounter with Jesus. Since the final resurrection had not yet taken place, the appearance of Jesus to Paul in the interim as an angel or spirit would

---

[78] Among recent commentators, Daube's view has been endorsed by Witherington, *Acts*, 692; see also Wright, *Resurrection of the Son of God*, 133.

[79] Fitzmyer (*Acts*, 719), who accepts Viviano and Taylor's position, states that the 'double *mēte* phrase should most likely be taken as an appositive to the noun *anastasin*, "resurrection," specifying a mode of it.'

seem appropriate. The corroboration of Luke 24:37, 39 evidences the explanatory power of this interpretation. The weakness of this position, however, is in its failure to establish that there was a belief that deceased persons *become* angels. Matt 22:30 and Mark 12:25 assert that they will become *like* angels, and Luke 20:36 (as we have argued above, p. 134) strengthens this comparative aspect. Importantly, this transformation into an angel-like existence is usually associated with the resurrection, instead of with an interim period as Daube asserts. In addition, it is not clear that when Peter's companions mistook him for an angel in Acts 12:15 that they were assuming he had died and was appearing to them in spiritual form. There is more evidence for the notion of a guardian or representative angel than Daube admits.[80] A more fundamental objection to both Daube and Viviano/Taylor concerns the question of why one has to posit a relationship between 'resurrection' and 'angel' or 'spirit' in the first place. The Saducean dismissal of the second issue need not refer to a blanket rejection of the existence of angels. The Sadducees must have believed in angels, but they may have been insistent upon a biblical view of them as impersonal extensions of the divine presence ('angel of the Lord'). The designation 'angel or spirit' could be a shorthand expression for an elaborate, highly developed angelology. According to this angelology there was a spiritual world filled with an array of angels or spirits who each possess individual personalities and are morally responsible for their actions (hence, there are righteous as well as evil spirits).[81] The Sadducees, then, would have rejected the Pharisaic views on resurrection and angelology as fanciful and unbiblical.

5.3 Gentile Perceptions of the Resurrection

There are only a few instances of Gentile reaction to the idea of the resurrection of the dead in Acts, and in every case there is a lack of understanding when the concept is pursued outside of the Jewish belief system. In Chapter 4 we have already looked at the reaction to Paul's declaration of

---

[80] J. H. Moulton, '"It Is His Angel,"' *JTS* 3 (1902): 514–27; *TDNT* 1:86; W. D. Davies and Dale C. Allison, *The Gospel According to Matthew* (3 vols.; ICC; Edinburgh: T. & T. Clark, 1988–1991), 2:770–72 (on Matt 18:10); Parker, '"Angel" and "Spirit,"' 351.

[81] For this explanation, see Louis Finkelstein, 'The Pharisees: Their Origin and Their Philosophy,' *HTR* 22 (1929): 238–40. A similar view is taken by Bruce, *Acts of the Apostles*, 466. Parker ('"Angel" and "Spirit,"' 360–62, 365) posits two reasons for Sadducean rejection of angelology: (a) the connection of angels to an apocalyptic worldview, which they rejected; and (b) their service in administering divine predestination or providence.

the resurrection of Jesus before the Areopagus. Some (presumably Epicureans) scoffed, while others (perhaps Stoics) were curious to hear more about the matter on another occasion (Acts 17:32). Paul's preaching in Athens yielded only a limited, positive response (17:34). The Roman governor, Felix, was stricken with fear at Paul's discussion of righteousness, self-control, and the coming judgment (24:25), so we may assume that he had some understanding of the resurrection of the dead. The narrator tells us that Felix 'knows the things of the Way more accurately' (24:22) and that his wife, Drusilla, was Jewish (24:24); and this follows directly after Paul has stated that he is on trial on account of the resurrection of the dead (24:21). Any understanding that Felix has of the resurrection is thus mediated to him through a more intimate knowledge of the Way. Felix's successor, Festus, by contrast, finds Paul's claim about the resurrection of Jesus to be incomprehensible (25:19–20). Paul is eager to get a full hearing from the visiting King Agrippa who (unlike Festus) has a superior command of Jewish customs and controversies (26:2–3).[82] Paul's preaching that the Messiah must suffer and be the first to rise from the dead (26:23) elicits from Festus the opinion that Paul is crazy (26:24). Paul, in turn, appeals to Agrippa's familiarity with the Way and his acceptance of the prophets (26:26–27), and the king appears to find Paul to be somewhat persuasive (26:28). These examples indicate that in Luke-Acts the resurrection of the dead is truly intelligible only within the confines of Judaism. Gentiles who are unfamiliar with Jewish issues in general, or with the Way in particular, cannot enter into meaningful discussion about the resurrection, since it is nonsensical to them.

5.4 Conclusion: The Resurrection as the Hope of Israel

In this chapter we have seen that the resurrection, whether viewed as a miracle at the hands of a divine agent, the singular event of Jesus' resurrection, or the final resurrection of the dead, is a proprietary belief within Second Temple Judaism. The resurrection miracles bear the stamp of Elijah/Elisha resurrection traditions, which provide a frame of reference for their interpretation. Luke gives no indication that resurrection can be accurately understood beyond the ken of Jewish thought. To the contrary, Gentiles generally react negatively to the idea, unless, like Felix, they have been

---

[82] O'Toole (*Christological Climax*, 40) refers to the resurrection of Jesus 'as just another dispute among the Jews of no interest to the Romans.' Note the appearance of the word ζητημάτων in 23:29; 25:19; and 26:3, as well as in the sharp ruling of Gallio concerning the irrelevance of Jewish ζητήματα, which are in Roman eyes only semantic garble (18:14–15).

adequately exposed to matters of Jewish faith. The controversy over resurrection between the Pharisees and Sadducees, as well as Agrippa's ability to follow Paul's preaching concerning the resurrection because of his expert knowledge of Jewish issues, are testaments to its status as an intra-Jewish controversy. Jesus' argument for the resurrection is based upon Israel's covenantal foundation. Those Israelites who affirm the resurrection of the dead are not merely expressing a theory about the afterlife. The resurrection is an integral part of an expectation that Israel will be fully restored in accordance with the covenant promises of Yahweh. A major question to be answered in the remainder of this dissertation is how Jesus' resurrection is conceived in Luke-Acts in relation to Israel's hope of resurrection. We shall begin to discuss this in our next chapter.

Chapter 6

Reading with the End in Mind (1): The Resurrection of Jesus and the Hope of Israel (Luke 24)

Having completed the broader task of viewing interpretations of resurrection within the ancient world—both in Second Temple Judaism and in Greco-Roman culture, as well as in Luke-Acts generally—we are now prepared to focus more closely on the function of Jesus' resurrection within Luke's twin work. Two literary components are employed in Luke-Acts to feature Jesus' resurrection from the dead. The first is the Lukan narrative itself, or more precisely, the way the narrative is crafted so as to bring the Gospel to a dramatic dénouement centred on the resurrected Christ. The expansion of the Christian mission in Acts, then, is initiated by and focused on the risen Jesus. The second component is the speeches in Acts, which provide an authoritative interpretation of the Christ-event, especially Jesus' resurrection from the dead. This chapter concerns the 'resurrection chapter' (Luke 24) that closes Luke's first volume. In Chapter 9 we will return to the subject of how the resurrection of Jesus plays a part in Acts 28, and therefore in the closure of Luke's entire two-volume work. Intervening chapters will look at the 'resurrection' speeches of the two principal characters in Acts, Peter and Paul. Before we consider the function of Luke 24 in the closure of Luke's Gospel, we shall first look at the dynamics of narrative closure itself.

6.1 Closure in Ancient Narrative

Both Luke 24:1–53 and Acts 28:16–31 are arguably the most important interpretative touchpoints in the Lukan narrative.[1] Each of these passages

---

[1] Richard J. Dillon has called Luke 24 'the literary and thematic intersection of his two volumes' and an 'axis in the structure of the sweeping history told to Theophilus' ('Easter Revelation and Mission Program in Luke 24:46–48,' in *Sin, Salvation, and the Spirit* [ed. Daniel Durkin; Collegeville, Minn.: Liturgical, 1979], 240). More recently, Wasserberg (*Aus Israels Mitte—Heil für die Welt*, 71) has written about 'die Schlußperikope Act 28,16–31 als hermeneutischer Schlüssel zum Gesamtverständnis von Lk-Act.' But few interpreters have attempted to advance the stereoscopic agenda set forth by Paul Schubert in his landmark essay ('Structure and Significance of Luke 24,'

The Resurrection of Jesus and the Hope of Israel (Luke 24)

brings its respective volume to a close. The importance of the ending for an historical work is expressed well by Carolyn Dewald:

> The historian's choice of ending is crucial to our overall interpretation of the work, because it is (as in any narrative) the ending that sets the capstone on the plot and so determines the final shape of a history's story line. It is the historian's choice of an ending (and thus of plot) that sets the reader some basic limits on the meanings the historian sees in the plethora of data belonging within the chosen limits of his or her investigation, and it is for this reason a particularly important pointer to the patterns and underlying coherence of the work and to the individual and idiosyncratic understanding of the historian who wrote it.[2]

This statement anticipates a number of points that need to be made about narrative closure. In this section we shall discuss the definition of narrative closure, the factors involved in its analysis, as well as the legitimacy of applying a modern literary model of narrative closure to an ancient historiographical work such as Luke-Acts.

6.1.1. Defining Narrative Closure

Don Fowler has distinguished five senses in which closure may be understood in modern literary criticism:

(1) The concluding section of a literary work;
(2) The process by which the reader of a work comes to see the end as satisfyingly final;
(3) The degree to which an ending is satisfyingly final;
(4) The degree to which the questions posed in the work are answered, tensions released, conflicts resolved;
(5) The degree to which the work allows new critical readings.[3]

166–67), which inquired about the literary function of *both* Luke 24 and Acts 28: 'More precisely the question is whether these two final chapters of the two parts of the whole work constitute anything which may or should be regarded as a conscious literary conclusion and as a theological climax. Is it that the excusable preoccupation with the "prologue" and the "transition" have prevented interpreters from asking this question? Or is it that there are here no literary conclusions or theological climaxes? Or is it that conclusions and climaxes are of such a nature as to affect the modern interpreter as inconclusive and as anti-climactic?'

[2] Carolyn Dewald, 'Wanton Kings, Pickled Heroes, and Gnomic Founding Fathers: Strategies of Meaning at the End of Herodotus's *Histories*,' in *Classical Closure: Reading the End in Greek and Latin Literature* (eds. Deborah H. Roberts, Francis M. Dunn, and Don Fowler; Princeton: Princeton University Press, 1997), 76.

[3] Don Fowler, 'Second Thoughts on Closure,' in *Classical Closure: Reading the End in Greek and Latin Literature* (eds. Deborah H. Roberts, Francis M. Dunn, and Don Fowler; Princeton: Princeton University Press, 1997), 3.

Fowler thinks all of these definitions of closure interpenetrate. For example, if the concluding section of a work (1), does not answer questions, release tensions, or resolve conflicts (4), the reader will hardly sense that the ending is satisfyingly final (2 and 3), and will thus have difficulty offering a new critical reading of the work (5).[4]

The most enduring closural model is that of Marianna Torgovnick.[5] Her model focuses on 'the process by which a novel reaches an adequate and appropriate conclusion or, at least, what the author hopes or believes is an adequate, appropriate conclusion.' Closure encompasses the 'integrity' or 'completeness' of a work—'a sense that nothing necessary has been omitted from a work.'[6] Torgovnick offers this general description of the function of endings:

> In any narrative, 'what happens next' ceases to be a pertinent question only at the conclusion, and the word 'end' in a novel consequently carries with it not just the notion of the turnable last page, but also that of the 'goal' of reading, the finish-line toward which our bookmarks aim. In long works of fiction, endings are important for another commonplace but true reason: it is difficult to recall *all* of a work after a completed reading; but climactic moments, dramatic scenes, and beginnings and endings remain in the memory and decisively shape our sense of a novel as a whole.[7]

Therefore, the concluding section of a literary work draws together elements from the 'high points' in a narrative (beginnings, climactic moments, dramatic scenes) in order to forge the connectedness and unity of the story and to invite reflection on the meaning of the entire piece. Torgovnick's definition of narrative closure varies from Fowler's in one crucial way. She does not wish to tie closure to a flesh-and-blood reader's 'sense' that all of the issues and themes raised in a work have been definitively brought to a conclusion. 'The test is the honesty and the appropriateness of the ending's relationship to beginning and middle, not the degree of finality or resolution achieved by the ending.'[8] As such, Torgovnick's model is aimed at analyzing the textual features of a narrative, even of a putatively 'anti-closural'

---

[4] Fowler, 'Second Thoughts on Closure,' 4.

[5] Marianna Torgovnick, *Closure in the Novel* (Princeton: Princeton University Press, 1981). Parsons in his seminal work on closure in Luke's Gospel fortuitously chose Torgovnick's study as a primary methodological guide; Mikeal C. Parsons, 'Narrative Closure and Openness in the Plot of the Third Gospel: The Sense of an Ending in Luke 24:50–53,' *SBL Seminar Papers, 1986* (SBLSP 25; Atlanta: Scholars Press, 1986), 201–23; idem, *Departure*, 69–113. Torgovnick's stamp can be seen throughout the compendium on closure in ancient Greek and Latin literature, *Classical Closure*.

[6] Torgovnick, *Closure in the Novel*, 6.

[7] Torgovnick, *Closure in the Novel*, 3–4.

[8] Torgovnick, *Closure in the Novel*, 6.

or 'open' narrative, which reveal a work's closural strategies and organic unity.

6.1.2 Analyzing Narrative Closure

Torgovnick's model of narrative closure has at its foundation the analysis of the relationships between a work's ending and its beginning and middle. She provides a précis of her procedure for analyzing narrative closure:

> To study closure and the shape of fictions, we begin with the ending, but evaluate its success as part of an artistic whole, as the final element in a particular structure of words and meanings. The discussion of closure indicates the discussion of aesthetic shape—verbal, metaphorical, gestural, and other formal patterns. It also includes the study of the themes and ideas embodied in the text and of relevant extratextual contexts that help form those themes and ideas, contexts including the author's life, his times, and his or her culture's beliefs about human experience.

This description contains several important elements: (1) a particular structure of words and meanings (lexical); (2) verbal, metaphorical, gestural, and other formal patterns (aesthetic shape, such as literary structure); (3) themes and ideas in the text (conceptual); and (4) the contexts that help shape those themes and ideas (extratext). The final element is notable for our study of the resurrection of Jesus in Luke-Acts, since it brings into play how resurrection was interpreted within Luke's cultural environment.

Torgovnick has developed a taxonomy for the identification of various relationships that can exist between narrative beginnings, middles, and endings. She has introduced simple and elegant descriptive terms for these relationships. First, there is *circularity*, when the ending of a narrative 'recalls the beginning in language, in situation, in the grouping of characters, or in several ways.' Second, *parallelism* occurs when 'language, situation, or the grouping of characters refers not just to the beginning of the work but to a series of points in the text .' Third, *incompletion* is when the ending 'includes many aspects that suggest circular or parallel closure, but omits one or more crucial elements necessary for full circularity or parallelism.'[9] Incompletion may occur as a result of authorial deliberation, on the one hand, or oversight, on the other. Finally, *linkage* is when the ending of a narrative is linked, not to its own beginning or middle, but to another work.[10] Torgovnick perceives linkage largely in terms of multi-volume works or sequels, and this is apropos of features in Luke 24 that point to Acts 1.

---

[9] Torgovnick, *Closure in the Novel*, 13.
[10] Torgovnick, *Closure in the Novel*, 14.

Torgovnick's identification of closural patterns is not intended as a universal poetics of narrative closure. Rather, her model is intended as a set of analytical tools one may use for 'entering into the complexities of individual texts.'[11] Three factors are crucial for discerning the movements toward closure in Luke-Acts. First, there is the matter of *segmentation*. What are the divisions within the narrative, and how are they sequenced? This is an important consideration for Luke, and one that is explicitly mentioned in his preface (Luke 1:3).[12] Segmentation involves the explicit transitions and progressions on the discourse level, as well as the sequencing that emerges with respect to the story level, but is in any case discernible through temporal, spatial/ geographical, and textual (or narratological) ordering. The endpoint of Luke's Gospel and its interplay with the beginning of Acts is in itself a good example of the importance of segmentation. A second factor involves the inclusion of *previews and reviews* in the text.[13] Pivotal future events, utterances, actions, or characters in (or beyond) the narrative can be previewed or foreshadowed, while important past occurrences can be reviewed or recapitulated, thereby alerting the reader to elements within the narrative that are of especial interpretative value. The repetition of reviews or previews is an effective technique for signalling points within the text that are critically important for narrative closure. Even when narratives do not draw formal or explicit comparisons between situations or statements, certain scenes or actions may be so dramatic and memorable as to cast their light forward or backward over the narrative landscape. In Luke-Acts this is accomplished through various *revelatory benchmarks* or divine disclosures. Mnemonic power and legitimating authority are self-evident in events such as the angelic proclamations in the prologue, the heavenly voice at Jesus' baptism, scriptural citations, the transfiguration, or the visions of Stephen, Paul, and Peter in Acts. Since these and like occurrences within the narrative mark specific instances when the divine purpose is being dramatically manifested, they cannot but capture the

---

[11] Torgovnick, *Closure in the Novel*, 198.

[12] See David P. Moessner, 'The Appeal and Power of Poetics: Luke's Superior Credentials (παρακολουθηκότι), Narrative Sequence (καθεξῆς), and Firmness of Understanding (ἡ ἀσφάλεια) for the Reader,' in *Jesus and the Heritage of Israel: Luke's Narrative Claim upon Israel's Legacy* (ed. David P. Moessner; LII 1; Harrisburg, Pa.: Trinity Press International, 1999), 84–123. For further theoretical discussion of segmentation, see Fowler, 'Second Thoughts on Closure,' 13–14.

[13] Technically, *prolepses* and *analepses*, terms coined by Gérard Genette, *Narrative Discourse: An Essay in Method* (trans. Jane E. Lewin; Ithaca, N.Y.: Cornell University Press, 1980), 40. The nomenclature, 'previews and reviews,' is that of Robert C. Tannehill, 'Israel in Luke-Acts: A Tragic Story,' *JBL* 104 (1985): 69; idem, *Narrative Unity*, 1:2, 21, 61, and passim.

attention of the reader, as well as possess unimpeachable hermeneutical authority over preceding or succeeding scenes.

These three features are important for discerning movement toward narrative closure because they aid the reader in tracing the connections that unify and elucidate the overall meaning and impact of the work. They assist the reader in searching for 'retrospective patterning' in the narrative.[14] We think the retrospective patterning within a text may be best discovered through multiple readings. We do not hold any pretensions of capturing a virginal or pristine reading of the text. Many ancient readers, in fact, would not have been able to apprehend all of the linkages and patterns woven throughout a text such as Luke-Acts after experiencing only one performance. Moreover, since authors usually put a whole lot more into their works than many readers can draw out of them in an initial (or sometimes secondary or tertiary) reading, it is only natural that re-reading is the way to perceive maximally the complexity and intricacy of a literary work. Only in re-reading does the reader gain greater awareness of the make-up of the plot ('how things are taking place'), whereas in the initial reading one is caught up in the suspense of the plot ('what will happen next').[15]

6.1.3 Closure in Hellenistic Historiography

We shall now turn to the question of whether a contemporary literary model of narrative closure such as Torgovnick's may be legitimately applied to ancient literature.[16] The subject of closure in ancient prose narrative has received only scant attention, and there is no extended treatment of closure in ancient historiography generally.[17] It is beyond the bounds of this study to hazard a full-blown analysis of the poetics of closure in ancient literature. Therefore, the following discussion will be confined to a set of observations about the closural strategies used by Hellenistic historians. This limitation is serendipitous in two significant ways. First, it is our position that Luke-

---

[14] Torgovnick, *Closure in the Novel*, 5. The expression 'retrospective patterning' was coined by Barbara Herrnstein Smith, *Poetic Closure: A Study of How Poems End* (Chicago: University of Chicago Press, 1968).

[15] Torgovnick, *Closure in the Novel*, 8.

[16] Torgovnick touts the suitability of her method for narratives of 'all periods' (*Closure in the Novel*, 202).

[17] Cf. the annotations prefacing the bibliography in *Classical Closure*, 276–77. In this same volume there are two essays, one dealing narrowly with an ancient historian (Carolyn Dewald, 'Wanton Kings, Pickled Heroes, and Gnomic Founding Fathers: Strategies of Meaning at the End of Herodotus's *Histories*,' 62–82), the other with an ancient biographer (Christopher Pelling, 'Is Death the End? Closure in Plutarch's *Lives*,' 228–50).

Acts shares a large proportion of generic affinities with Hellenistic historiography. Second, Hellenistic historians such as Diodorus Siculus, Polybius, and Dionysius of Halicarnassus are the most loquacious of historians with respect to how they think the historiographical process should be executed literarily. Closure in Hellenistic historiography can be examined on two levels: on the macro-level, dealing with the integrity and unity of historical works as wholes; and on the micro-level, dealing with the closure of scenes, chapters, or entire books within a larger narrative.

6.1.3.1 MACRO-LEVEL CLOSURE

All of the Hellenistic historians with whom we are concerned seem to have been of one mind concerning the necessity of structuring an historical narrative in accordance with an overarching scheme. Diodorus Siculus is capable of listing the number of books in his *Library of History*, describing their basic character, and summarizing 'the general plan of the history' (τὴν ὅλην ἐπιβολὴν τῆς ἱστορίας).[18] In Polybius's *Histories*, as well as in Josephus's *Antiquities of the Jews*, each historian's command of an overall plan, scope, and purpose is equally borne out.[19] What is striking is that Polybius and Josephus close their histories by distinctly pointing out that the completed form of the narrative corresponds to what was outlined at the *beginning* of the work.[20] This is important for our study of closure since it evidences a sensitivity about achieving organic unity and completeness for the whole history.

We are fortunate that Dionysius of Halicarnassus has written explicitly about historiographical procedure and the achievement of closure in history

---

[18] Diodorus Siculus, *Library*, 40.8.1. In 1.1–5 Diodorus provides a precise outline in order to inform his readers about 'the project as a whole' (τῆς ὅλης προθέσεως, 1.5.2). Diodorus refers to his universal history as the recording of the entire history of the world in 'one narrative' (μιᾶς συντάξεως, 1.3.3; 1.3.8) as though it concerned the affairs of a 'single city' (1.3.5).

[19] Polybius summarizes his historical project (*Histories*, 3.1.4–10), which he thinks should be viewed as 'a single whole' (3.1.4). The grand scope of the work is revisited at its end (39.8.3–8). Josephus offers a synopsis of his *Antiquities* (20.12.1 §§259–67) and emphasizes that he has drawn up 'the whole story in full and accurate detail' (20.12.1 §260). Regrettably, the conclusion to Dionysius of Halicarnassus's *Roman Antiquities* is not extant, and therefore we cannot know whether he included a similar recapitulation. Dionysius does, however, summarize his project (1.8.1–2) before commencing the history (1.8.4).

[20] Polybius, *Histories*, 39.8.3–4; 39.8.8; Josephus, *Ant.* 20.12.1 §261 (cp. Proem 2–4 §§5–26); *J. W.* 7.11.5 §454 (cp. Proem 6–12 §§17–26). In *Ant.* Proem 2 §7, Josephus indicates that he has made the *War* into a separate volume 'with its own beginning and end' (ταῖς ἰδίαις ἀρχαῖς αὐτοῦ καὶ τῷ τέλει).

writing. In his *Letter to Pompeius* he delineates the historian's duty as, first, 'to choose a beautiful subject, pleasant to the readers' (3.767), and second, to determine 'where to begin' and 'how far one must go' (3.769).[21] Herodotus is cited as a model of how the thematic unity of a history ought to be secured by tying together the end and the beginning of the work (3.767).[22] Thucydides, that 'most distinguished of the historians,' is criticized by Dionysius on this very count (*Thuc.* 10):

> Some critics also find fault with the order of his history, complaining that he neither chose the right beginning for it (ὡς οὔτε ἀρχὴν τῆς ἱστορίας εἰλοφότος ἦν ἐχρῆν) nor a fitting place to end it (οὔτε τέλος ἐφηρμοκότος αὐτῇ τὸ πρέπον). They say that by no means the least important aspect of good arrangement is that a work should begin where nothing can be imagined as preceding it (ἀρχήν τε λαβεῖν, ἧς οὐκ ἂν εἴη τι πρότερον), and end where nothing further is felt to be required (καὶ τέλει περιλαβεῖν τὴν πραγματείαν ᾧ δόξει μηδὲν ἐνδεῖν); and they claim that Thucydides has not paid due attention to either of these considerations.[23]

Dionysius expresses a preference for circularity, or thematic *inclusio*, and points out an exemplar of this procedure in Xenophon: for 'everywhere, he has begun and ended in the most suitable and appropriate manner' (*Pomp.* 4.778). Polybius espoused the same compositional rule, building upon Aristotle's noted discussion of plot, since he took great pains to demonstrate that his history is a unified narrative about how the known world was subjugated by Rome and 'should be viewed as a single whole, with a recognized beginning, a fixed duration, and an end which is not a matter of dispute' (*Histories*, 3.1.4–5). In concluding his history, Polybius points out how his summary of its contents establishes 'both in general and particular the connexion between the beginning and the end' (39.83–84).

---

[21] We were apprised of Dionysius's discussion of closure via Daniel Marguerat, 'The Enigma of the Silent Closing of Acts (28:16–31),' in *Jesus and the Heritage of Israel: Luke's Narrative Claim upon Israel's Legacy* (ed. David P. Moessner; LII 1; Harrisburg, Pa.: Trinity Press International, 1999), 290–92.

[22] This is itself problematical, since many other readers of Herodotus do not concur that there is an appropriateness or sense of closure at the end of the *Histories*; see Marguerat, 'Enigma of the Silent Closing,' 291–92; Dewald, 'End of Herodotus's *Histories*,' 62–82.

[23] Dionysius is obviously mirroring Aristotle's discussion of plot (*Poet.* 7.21–35) in which the end is defined as 'that which is inevitably or, as a rule, the natural result of something else but from which nothing else follows…. Well-constructed plots must not therefore begin and end at random, but embody the formulae we have stated.' Cf. *On Thucydides* 12, where Dionysius castigates Thucydides for not providing a full enough account, in violation of his intention expressed in the introduction to the work.

6.1.3.2 MICRO-LEVEL CLOSURE

A perusal of Hellenistic histories reveals that ancient historians sought unity and closure on the micro-level, as well. This includes marking the conclusions to scenes, explanatory digressions, chapters, books, or other narrative units. In the case of Josephus, for example, various literary formulae are deployed to create narrative pauses at the ends of scenes or chapters.[24] Closure at the ends of books is not always desirable or achievable in multivolume works—since aperture is necessary for the narrative thread to be picked up in the succeeding book—yet Josephus often attempts to close whole books with 'bookend' statements such as, 'So ended Herod's reign' (*J. W.* 1.33.9 §673) or 'Thus ended the siege of Jerusalem' (6.10.1 §442),[25] or through the report of a major figure's death.[26] Diodorus Siculus far more rigorously attempts to achieve thematic unity and closure for each of the books in his *Library of History*. Nearly all of his fully preserved books close with a direct reference to the fact that the present book has come to fulfil the promise enunciated at the beginning of the book.[27] Diodorus articulates the rationale for this procedure as follows (16.1.1–2):

> In all systematic historical treatises it behooves the historian to include in his books actions of states or of kings which are complete in themselves from beginning to end (αὐτοτελεῖς ἀπ' ἀρχῆς μέχρι τοῦ τέλους); for in this manner I conceive history to be most easy to remember and most intelligible to the reader. Now incomplete (ἡμιτελεῖς) actions, the conclusion of which is unconnected with the beginning, interrupt the interest of the curious reader, whereas if the actions embrace a continuity of development culminating naturally, the narrative of events will achieve a well-rounded perfection. Whenever the natural pattern of events itself harmonizes with the task of the historian, from that point on he must not deviate at all from this principle. Consequently, now that I have reached the actions of Philip son of Amyntas, I shall endeavor to include the deeds performed by this king within the compass of the present Book.

---

[24] This has been documented extensively by Pere Villalba I. Varneda, *The Historical Method of Flavius Josephus* (ALGHJ 19; Leiden: Brill, 1986), 157–88.

[25] Cf. *J. W.* 2.22.1 §654; *Ant.* 6.14.9 §378; 7.15.3 §394; 8.15.6 §420; 11.8.7 §347; 12.11.2 §434; 13.16.6 §432; 14.16.4 §491; 15.11.7 §425; 18.9.9 §379.

[26] Cf. *Ant.* 1.22.1 §346; 4.8.49 §331; 11.8.7 §346; 12.11.2 §§432–33; 13.16.6 §432.

[27] Diodorus Siculus, *Library of History* 1.98.10 (cf. 1.4.6); 2.60.3 (cf. 2.1.3); 3.74.6 (cf. 3.1.3); 4.85.7 (cf. 4.1.5); 11.92.5 (cf. 11.1.1); 12.84.4 (cf. 12.2.3); 13.114.3 (cf. 13.1.3); 14.117.9 (cf. 14.2.4); 15.95.4 (cf. 15.1.6); 16.95.5 (cf. 16.1.1–3); 17.118.4 (cf. 17.1.2); 18.74.3 (cf. 18.1.5); 19.110.5 (cf. 19.1.9–10); 20.113.5 (cf. 20.2.3). Diodorus also quite regularly forms a link to the preceding book (or series of books) by beginning many books with an ἀνακεφαλαίωσις: 2.1.1; 3.1.1–2; 4.1.5; 11.1.1; 12.2.3; 14.2.4; 15.1.6; 17.1.1; 18.1.6; 19.1.10; 20.2.3.

The Resurrection of Jesus and the Hope of Israel (Luke 24)

Here Diodorus states as a principle that individual books within a history should possess a topical unity. Each book should narrate a complete set of actions without remainder.[28] The actions should form a series, constituting a circuit in which the beginning is brought to its own conclusion. This procedure yields two benefits for the reader: (a) the contents of the book are more easily remembered; and (b) an unbroken chain of narrative evolvement will maintain the reader's interest.[29] Noteworthy is Diodorus's awareness that most historical actions are not inherently conducive to this procedure. Historical events do not usually conform neatly to the historian's design to narrate them in accordance with an organizing principle or theme. For example, a single king's activities may warrant no more than a narrative aside in one instance, but in another would be coterminous with a chronology spanning several books and touching upon a variety of themes. However, in the case of Philip of Macedon, and of his son, Alexander the Great, each ruler's actions naturally work together with the historian's topical approach. Diodorus's approach includes not only topical unity, but continuity or connectedness,[30] appropriate chronology,[31] as well as brevity and proportion.[32] Evidently, an accounting of the reigns of Philip and Alexander coincided nicely with all of these concerns, and each could therefore occupy an individual book.

6.1.3.3 CONCLUSION

We may safely conclude that among Hellenistic historians, ideally if not in practice, an historiographical project had to proceed with an overall design in mind. The purpose, scope, and plan of the work ought to issue in a unified narrative. The organic unity and integrity of a history was conceived of in Aristotelian terms of emplotment, in which there is an appropriate beginning, middle, and end. Most importantly, narrative closure should be

---

[28] Diodorus wrote at some length earlier about his preference for the topical arrangement of books (5.1.1–2.1).

[29] All of these points are succinctly stated again at the beginning of Book 17: 'This is the best method, I think, of ensuring that the events will be remembered, for thus the material is arranged topically (κεφαλαιωδῶς τεθείσας), and each story is told without interruption (καὶ συνεχὲς ἐχούσας ταῖς ἀρχαῖς τὸ τέλος—lit. "and continually holding the end in the beginnings")' (17.1.2).

[30] Cf. 1.3.1–8. Diodorus's predilection for continuous narrative leads him to criticize the practice of inserting lengthy speeches into an historical work (20.1.1–5).

[31] Cf. 1.3.4; 1.3.8; 5.84.4.

[32] Diodorus divides Book 1 into two volumes in conformity with his principle of proportionality (1.42.1–2). For the sake of brevity he truncates his discussion of the flooding of the Nile (1.41.10; cf. 1.6.1) and deliberately forgoes prefixing lengthy introductions to his books (13.1.1–3).

effected by establishing a connection between the beginning and end. This can take a number of forms, such as a closing scene that draws out the singular theme of the work, or an explicit declaration that the plan outlined at the beginning of the history has been fully executed as the narrative reaches its conclusion. Historians could also aim for thematic unity and *autotelic* connectedness between beginnings and endings in smaller narrative units, such as scenes, chapters, or entire books. The literary technique of Hellenistic historians appears to cultivate fertile ground for an analytical model of narrative closure such as Torgovnick's, since both are concerned with the plotting of interconnections between beginnings, middles, and ends.

6.2 Defining Beginnings and Endings in Luke-Acts

6.2.1 Literary Planning and Luke-Acts

In its infancy the text of Luke-Acts most likely occupied two papyrus rolls, one for the Gospel and the other for Acts. Both volumes are roughly equivalent in length, as is the case for most other ancient multi-volume works, and, perhaps not coincidentally, are of nearly equal length to the Gospel of Matthew.[33] The material limitations of scroll length would have dictated the extent of economy and proportion required in ancient book writing. Writers would do well to work within these physical limits and produce volumes which—even though part of a larger, continuous narrative—possess an integrity and perfection all their own, as Diodorus Siculus advocated. This, in turn, would facilitate the reading experience. The division of Luke-Acts into two volumes would lend itself well to reading the narrative in two sessions, perhaps at the sort of symposia Jesus attended in the Gospel.[34] The strong closural features in Luke 24, such as promise-fulfilment, dusk, journey's end, recognition, and final departure,[35] signal the terminus of Jesus' earthly assignment as well as a fitting place to bring the first volume to a close. At the opening of volume two, and presumably for the second reading session, the contents of volume one are conveniently recapitulated

---

[33] Cadbury, *Making of Luke-Acts*, 324.

[34] The reading of Luke-Acts would have taken one or two sittings; so F. Gerald Downing, 'Theophilus' First Reading of Luke-Acts,' in *Luke's Literary Achievement: Collected Essays* (ed. C. M. Tuckett; JSNTS 116; Sheffield: Sheffield Academic Press, 1995), 92.

[35] Pelling ('Is Death the End?' 230) lists deaths, dusks, departures, journey's ends, winters, and old age as 'natural' ends frequently appearing in ancient poetry and novels.

(Acts 1:1–2),[36] followed by a 'progymnastic' re-performance of the post-resurrection activity of Jesus related at the end of the Gospel (Acts 1:3–11).[37] Yet Luke 24 contains prominent elements of openness such as the incomplete number of apostles (the Eleven), their commission from Jesus, and the promise of the Spirit. These apertures foster anticipation for a continuation of the narrative thread. Luke 24 is a masterful literary conclusion to the first volume of Luke-Acts because of its fine dialectical balance between closure and aperture.

In the following discussion we shall concern ourselves with the closural features appearing at the end of volume one (Luke 24) and their relationships to the beginning and middle of that volume (Luke) and linkages to volume two (Acts). We shall not be able to capture all of the complexity of Luke's conclusion that an exhaustive exegesis of Luke 24 would reveal. However, by focusing on the resurrection of Jesus and its connection to the hope of Israel, we shall unearth the taproot of Luke's theology: the fulfilment in the risen Jesus of the ancient promises of salvation for the people of Israel and the whole world. Our discussion will begin with a consideration of the parameters and structure of the conclusion to Luke's Gospel.

6.2.2 The Parameters and Structure of the End of Luke

Before the conclusion to Luke's Gospel can be studied, its boundaries must first be surveyed. Since Luke 24:53 contains the final words of the Gospel, it of course marks a hard break in Luke's two-volume narrative. Therefore, the issue involves determining where the end of Luke begins.[38] In many ways it is more difficult to pinpoint where the ending of a work begins than to discover where its beginning ends. Although closural signals customarily

---

[36] A contemporary example of a work written in a manner conducive to being read in two sittings is Chariton's *Callirhoe*, whose Book 5 appears to have opened a new scroll and begins with a recapitulation of the whole plot-line up to that point—presumably to jog the memory or perhaps to acquaint those who have only begun to listen at the second reading session (5.1.1–2). For more on recapitulations, see Alexander, 'Preface to Acts and the Historians,' 89–92.

[37] See Vernon K. Robbins, 'The Claims of the Prologues and Greco-Roman Rhetoric: The Prefaces to Luke and Acts in Light of Greco-Roman Rhetorical Strategies,' in *Jesus and the Heritage of Israel: Luke's Narrative Claim upon Israel's Legacy* (ed. David P. Moessner; LII 1; Harrisburg, Pa.: Trinity Press International, 1999), 76–82.

[38] This is a reversal of the issue of determining where Luke's beginning ends, both in Luke (see Morna D. Hooker, *Beginnings: Keys that Open the Gospels* [Harrisburg, Pa.: Trinity Press International, 1997], 43–63) and Acts (Steve Walton, 'Where Does the Beginning of Acts End?' in *The Unity of Luke-Acts* [ed. Joseph Verheyden; BETL 142; Leuven: Leuven University Press], 447–67).

start to accumulate toward the end of a work, 'toward the end' may indeed be rather close to the beginning.[39] Perhaps it will be most advantageous, then, to work backwards from the end of Luke. Luke 24:50-53 is a crisp summary of Jesus' ascension and the disciples' continuance in Jerusalem, but it can hardly tie up many of the narrative threads woven throughout the Gospel.[40] It is in fact the culmination of the preceding post-resurrection scenes, which are carefully interconnected, as we shall see below. The first of these scenes (Luke 24:1-12) is closely associated with the preceding burial scene (23:50-56) through temporal markers (Sabbath, 23:54, 56; first day of the week, 24:1), identical characters (the women who had followed Jesus from Galilee, 23:55; 24:6, 10), burial spices preparation (23:56; 24:1), and tomb inspection activity (23:55; 24:2-3). Nevertheless, 23:50-56 is clearly a bridge between Luke's account of Jesus' death and resurrection.[41] Therefore, Luke 24:1-53 will be regarded as the 'end' of Luke's Gospel in this study since all of the scenes in this unit relate to Jesus' resurrection from the dead.

The three scenes in Luke 24 are structurally linked together with time markers, spatial movements, and intercommunication. The Easter events are presented within the time frame of a single day (24:1, 13, 33, 36).[42] An accent falls on the fact that the events are transpiring 'on the third day' after Jesus' death (24:7, 21, 29, 46). The scenes progress from one to another by way of spatial movement. At the end of the first scene we see the women 'returning' from the tomb' (24:9), and Peter running to the tomb and leaving in amazement (24:12); then in the second scene a pair of disciples are 'going' to Emmaus (24:13; cf. 24:17, 28). At the end of the second scene the Emmaus disciples 'return' to Jerusalem (24:33), and the third scene commences with Jesus standing in the midst of the conversing believers (24:36). This scene is concluded with movement from Jerusalem to Bethany (24:50), Jesus' movement upwards into heaven (24:51), and the disciples' 'return' to Jerusalem (24:53). In the three scenes such movements facilitate intercommunication between the characters in the scenes. At the end of the first scene the women relate to the disciples what they had experienced at the tomb (24:10). This communication is recalled in the second scene by the Emmaus pair (24:24), and these two share their own

---

[39] Fowler, 'Second Thoughts on Closure,' 21.

[40] This is why Parsons ('Narrative Closure and Openness,' 205), although focusing on the ascension pericope (Luke 24:50-53), finds it necessary to extend his discussion to 24:36-39 and 24:1-53.

[41] It is tenuous to see 23:56b and 24:53 as forming an *inclusio*, as Talbert does (*Reading Luke*, 226).

[42] The final summary (24:50-53) may not be tightly entailed in this chronology (Green, *Luke*, 835).

report about the risen Jesus upon their return to Jerusalem (24:35), as do the Eleven and those with them concerning an earlier, unnarrated appearance to Simon (24:34).

These ligatures unite the separate scenes into one continuous narrative series, while at the same time maintaining the independent character of each revelatory experience. Luke uses a similar technique in Acts when recounting Paul's commission (Acts 9, 22, 26) and the salvation of Cornelius (Acts 10–11). Separate revelatory encounters criss-cross, converge, and cross-check one another to forge an impressive verification of the fact that God is at work to accomplish his salvific plan. The progression toward the third scene, with its physical demonstrations and scriptural disclosures, does not depreciate the value of previous revelations (such as to the women at the tomb), but rather buttresses the direct and personal *apostolic* witness to the resurrection of Jesus.[43] The scenes are structured to produce the rhetorical effect of revelatory encounters that are mutually reinforcing yet not interdependent, climaxing with Jesus' commission to the witnesses of his resurrection and his departure into heaven. Luke 24 is of foundational importance for the entire two-volume work, for it is here where the 'original eyewitnesses (οἱ ἀπ' ἀρχῆς αὐτόπται) and ministers of the word' (Luke 1:2), the sources for Luke's narrative, are authorized.

Before we explore the relationships between the beginning, middle, and end of Luke, we must comment briefly on the parameters of its beginning and middle. The extent of a narrative's beginning can be notoriously difficult to circumscribe, and Luke's is no exception. Luke 1–2 is indisputably the 'frontline' of the narrative. Yet John's ministry of repentance-baptism (Luke 3) has a preparatory function in the story, previewed earlier in the intertwining nativity scenes (1:16–17, 76–77), and designated later as a 'beginning' point for Jesus' ministry (Acts 1:22; 10:37; cf. 1:5; 13:24; 19:4). After Jesus' baptism, itself a strongly initiatory event (Luke 3:21–22), the beginning of Jesus' ministry is explicitly noted (3:23a), followed by a genealogy extending back to Adam (3:23b–38). The 'Genesis' of his ministry does not yet begin until he experiences the 'Exodus' of testing in the wilderness (4:1–13), at the end of which his nemesis, the devil, departs from him (4:13) and will reappear in dramatic fashion at the commencement of the passion scenes (22:3, 31, 53). Luke 4:14–15 may mark the entrance to the middle of Luke's Gospel. However, the rejection at Nazareth (4:16–30) is widely recognized as the frontispiece for Jesus' mission and destiny. The scene at Nazareth is a fitting capstone to the beginning of Luke when seen as a microcosm of the climactic events of the Gospel itself:

---

[43] See Joseph Plevnik, 'The Eyewitnesses of the Risen Jesus in Luke 24,' *CBQ* 49 (1987): 90–103.

mounting hostility toward Jesus (4:28), expulsion from the city (4:29a; cf. 20:9–19), death (4:29b), resurrection and ongoing ministry (4:30).[44] Since Luke presents a series of beginnings to Jesus' life and ministry, like a set of Chinese boxes, the prudent approach would be to concentrate on the events in the series with ever-decreasing levels of emphasis. This means that the nativity and early childhood scenes (Luke 1–2) take precedence as the beginning to Luke's Gospel, while the inaugural character of the following scenes should be taken into consideration, but in descending order.

6.3 Resurrection and the Hope of Israel at the End of Luke's Gospel

6.3.1 The Empty Tomb (Luke 24:1–12)

The irony about Luke 24 as the conclusion to the Third Gospel is that its basic thrust is actually anti-closural. Death is the primal, closural event. The death of the main character in a narrative brings finality to most any story.[45] Death functions as the decisive closural event in that it brings the actions of a character to an irreversible end, and bequeaths an unchanging life portrait now open to conclusive evaluation. Tales extending beyond the grave are the stuff of mythical or romantic literature and not biography or historiography, or, in other words, any narrative about matters of certainty (ἀσφάλεια, Luke 1:4). Stories of revival from the dead severely test both credulity and the conventions of nonfictional (and fictional!) emplotment.[46] The empty tomb scene in Luke 24 seems to confront a conscious awareness

---

[44] Jacob W. Elias, 'The Furious Climax in Nazareth (Luke 4:28–30),' in *The New Way of Jesus: Essays Presented to Howard Charles* (ed. William Klassen; Newton, Kans.: Faith and Life, 1980), 87–99; Green, *Luke*, 218–19; Ringe, *Luke*, 71.

[45] Deborah H. Roberts ('Afterword: Ending and Aftermath, Ancient and Modern,' in *Classical Closure*, 255) cites from a short piece by Margaret Atwood ('Happy Endings,' in *Murder in the Dark* [Toronto: Coach House, 1983], 40):

> You'll have to face it, the endings are the same however you slice it. Don't be deluded by any other endings, they're all fake, either deliberately fake, with malicious intent to deceive, or just motivated by excessive optimism if not downright sentimentality. The only authentic ending is provided here:
> John and Mary die. John and Mary die. John and Mary die.

Karris has pointed out how the Third Gospel differs from the biographies of historic persons in that it does not end with the account of Jesus' death, but of his resurrected life; Robert J. Karris, *Invitation to Luke: A Commentary on the Gospel of Luke with Complete Text from the Jerusalem Bible* (Garden City, N.Y.: Image, 1977), 272.

[46] We saw in Chapter 4 how even the ancient Greek novelists felt it necessary to provide rational, natural depictions and explanations of apparent deaths.

of this. Central to the scene is the empty tomb itself, to and from which the women (and later, Peter) return. But the vacant sepulchre leaves its visitors baffled about what has become of Jesus.[47] The reality of Jesus' resurrection dawns within the women's consciousness only through an apocalypse of recollection. The meaning and impact of the scene is illuminated by its relationships to the beginning and middle of Luke's Gospel, to which we shall now turn.

6.3.1.1 CIRCULARITY (LUKE 24:1–12)

A point that has been sometimes noted, but less often recognized for its interpretive value, is the sudden reappearance of angels in the Lukan narrative.[48] It has been often suggested that the appearance of 'two men' (ἄνδρες δύο, Luke 24:4) is intended to resemble the ἄνδρες δύο, Moses and Elijah, at the transfiguration (9:30, 32), and the ἄνδρες δύο at Jesus' ascension (Acts 1:10). That the two figures are thereby identified as Moses and Elijah,[49] or as a requisite *pair* of witnesses (as per Deut 17:6; 19:15),[50] is unnecessary, although the recurrence of the expression may well be threading together transfiguration, resurrection, and ascension. Ancient readers familiar with apocalyptic literature would have immediately recognized these 'two personages' as angels. First, in OT and intertestamental literature, when angels appear they may be interchangeably identified as ἄνδρες and ἄγγελοι.[51] Second, the appearance of angels in pairs is an ancient *topos*, reaching back to Canaanite mythology when two 'messengers' would accompany a god on a journey.[52] Third, the vocabulary used to describe their sudden appearance and dazzling apparel is compatible with the

---

[47] Green refers to the tomb's centrality *and* hermeneutical vacuity in the scene as a 'theme of incongruity' (*Luke*, 836).

[48] E.g., Parsons, 'Narrative Closure and Openness,' 207 n.39; Robert H. Smith, *Easter Gospels: The Resurrection of Jesus According to the Four Evangelists* (Minneapolis: Augsburg, 1983), 112. If Luke 22:43 is genuine, it does not constitute a damaging exception, since the angelophany is empowering, not revelatory, and occurs among the climactic scenes of the Gospel.

[49] Jindřich Mánek, 'The New Exodus in the Books of Luke,' *NovT* 2 (1957): 11–12.

[50] Smith, *Easter Gospels*, 108.

[51] E.g., Gen 18:2, 16, 22; 19:5 (ἄνδρες); 19:1, 15 (ἄγγελοι); Zech 1:10, (ἀνήρ); 1:9, 11, etc. (ἄγγελος); cf. Dan 8:15; Tobit 5:4; *2 En.* 1:6; 33:6, 11.

[52] F. I. Andersen, '2 (Slavonic Apocalypse of) Enoch," *OTP* 1:106 n. j (cf. the references to Genesis in the preceding footnote). Two young men, 'gloriously beautiful and splendidly dressed,' appear to Heliodorus in 2 Macc 3:26; they are surely angels. The two angelic figures in *Gos. Pet.* 10.39–40 possess a stature reaching to heaven (cf. *2 En.* 1:4).

description of angels.[53] Finally, the Emmaus pair calls them angels (Luke 24:23). The women at the tomb were participating in a momentous revelatory event, very much like the characters in Luke's prologue (Luke 1–2), who were visited by angels.

In both Luke 24:1-12 and in the prologue we encounter a cluster of similar characters, situations, and actions. We meet not only angels, but women who are receptive to divine revelation, and male figures who are not—at least not initially. Zechariah disbelieves Gabriel's words (1:20), whereas Mary and Elizabeth ecstatically greet the angelic news (1:38, 41–55). So also, the women at the tomb trust implicitly the announcement of the two men at the tomb (24:8–9), while the Eleven and those with them dismiss the women's report as 'an idle tale' (24:11). The narrative lens is focused on the women in Luke 24:1–12, and affirms their credibility as witnesses, by naming them (24:10) and locating them among the followers of Jesus in Galilee (24:6–8). The Lukan prologue similarly focuses on women characters, and particularly on Mary in its final scenes. Mary's hermeneutical function in these scenes is instructive. While others are only amazed at the shepherds' account of angelic heralds to the Messiah's birth (2:17–18), 'Mary treasured all these things and pondered them in her heart' (2:19). Again, after the twelve-year old Jesus was discovered in the temple, 'Mary treasured all these things in her heart' (2:51).[54] Mary is entrusted as a bearer of recollection. Likewise, the women at the tomb are called to remember the words of Jesus concerning his own destiny. However, the women at the tomb are not storing memories, but retrieving them. The act of remembrance acknowledges the fulfilment of promises or prophecies that have been made (cf. 1:54, 72). This was woefully apparent to Peter after he had denied the Lord and 'remembered' Jesus' prediction about his denials (22:61; cf. 22:34). The 'Gentile Pentecost' at Cornelius's house sparked Peter's recognition of a promise coming to fulfilment: 'I remembered the word of the Lord, how he had said, "John baptized with water, but you will

---

[53] Marshall, *Luke*, 885; Green, *Luke*, 837 n. 4.

[54] The discovery of Jesus in the temple contains other possible points of circularity with the first scene of Luke 24. Both incidents happen after the Passover, after three days (2:46; 24:7), involve searching and (not) finding (2:44, 45, 46, 48; 24:2, 3, 5), and authoritative characters who chide others for their vain search attempt (2:49—Jesus: 'Why were you searching for me? Did you not know that I must be in my Father's house?'; 24:5–6a—the two men: 'Why do you search for the living among the dead? He is not here, but has risen'). It is impossible to know whether these points of circularity were *intended* by the author; nevertheless, (re-)readers of Luke have been struck by the pregnant significance of such details (in particular, the time-marker 'after three days') in the account of the twelve-year old Jesus; see James K. Elliott, 'Does Luke 2:41–52 Anticipate the Resurrection?' *ExpTim* 83 (1971): 87–89.

The Resurrection of Jesus and the Hope of Israel (Luke 24)

be baptized with the Holy Spirit'" (Acts 11:16). So the women at the tomb play a significant role within the Lukan pattern of promise and fulfilment. Their power of recollection highlights the essential plot line of the Gospel: 'the Son of Man must be handed over to sinners, and be crucified, and on the third day rise again' (Luke 24:7).

6.3.1.2 PARALLELISM (LUKE 24:1–12)

A pattern begun in the prologue is repeated at key points in the Lukan narrative. In addition to the birth of Jesus being heralded by angels (Luke 1:26–38; 2:9–12), a messenger, John the Baptist, prepared the way for Jesus' ministry (1:17, 76; 3:4, 16; 7:27; cf. Acts 13:24). Moses and Elijah assisted Jesus in foretelling his *exodos* that would take place in Jerusalem (Luke 9:30–32). When Jesus embarked on his fateful journey to Jerusalem he sent messengers ahead of him, evidently James and John (9:52, 54). When Jesus started his ascent toward the Holy City, he sent two disciples ahead of him to prepare for his entry (19:28–34). It is wholly fitting, therefore, that messengers announce Jesus' resurrection.[55]

There is a yet more explicit parallelism in the tomb scene. The words of the angels (Luke 24:7) are reminiscent of Jesus' repeated predictions of his suffering, death, and resurrection. There could not be a more obvious invitation for readers to engage in the discovery of retrospective patterns. On six occasions Jesus makes explicit references to his impending passion and resurrection (9:22; 9:44–45; 13:32–33; 17:25; 18:31–34; 22:15–38). There are four allusions to Jesus' death and resurrection (5:35; 9:31; 11:30; 14:27), as well as four pointers to the fulfilment of the predictions (24:6–8, 20–21, 26, 45–46). Of the predictions, three (possibly only two) directly mention resurrection (9:22; 13:31–33?; 18:31–34). Two of the four allusions (9:31; 11:30) seem to point toward Jesus' resurrection.[56] The passion and resurrection predictions share a preponderance of verbal contacts with the fulfilment logia of Luke 24: 'Son of Man' (9:22, 44; 17:24–25; 18:31 // 24:7); 'must' (9:22; 17:25; 22:37 // 24:26, 44); 'be handed over' (9:44; 18:32; 22:22 // 24:7); 'into the hands of men' (9:44 // 24:7); 'on the third day' (9:22; 13:32?; 18:32 // 24:7; 24:46); 'rise' (ἐγερθῆναι 9:22; ἀναστήσεται 18:33 // ἀναστῆναι 24:7, 46).[57]

---

[55] Most of these parallels have been noted by Maria-Luisa Rigato, '"Remember'...Then They Remembered": Luke 24:6–8,' in *Luke and Acts* (eds. Gerald O'Collins and Gilberto Marconi; New York and Mahwah, N.J.: Paulist, 1991), 101.

[56] Luke does not insert an interpretation of the Jonah saying as Matthew does (Matt 12:40). Perhaps an allusion to the resurrection on the third day seemed transparent enough.

[57] See the collation of these data in Rigato, 'Remember...Then They Remembered,' 100.

The prediction-cum-fulfilment saying in Luke 24:6–8 advances beyond the earlier predictions so as to corroborate and clarify them. First, the saying reminds the women that Jesus spoke in such a way about his destiny while he was still in Galilee. Careful notations have been made in the death and burial scenes about these women as followers of Jesus from his time in Galilee. They saw him die (23:49). They watched as his 'body' was laid in the tomb (23:55). Now they cannot find his 'body' in the tomb (24:3). Contrary to Dillon's disregard for the empirical aspect of the women's recognition that Jesus had been raised from the dead, these data underscore the women's qualifications as persons capable of attesting to Jesus' identity as the same individual who had taught in Galilee and was executed and buried in Jerusalem. To be sure, the actual appearance of Jesus is necessary to fully authorize them as witnesses; but these steps are of indispensable importance, since resurrection in Second Temple Judaism, by definition, concerns bodies being released from the mortality of the grave. These data, coupled with the angelic explanation, reveal for readers the Eleven's unfair presumption that the women were only speaking nonsense. Later, Peter will confirm that Jesus' body was absent from the tomb, but that the expensive burial linen remained (24:12)—confounding any theory that thieves stole away Jesus' corpse while leaving the real loot![58] Second, the saying is unique in its reference to Jesus' having been 'crucified' (24:7; cf. 24:20). In light of the pathos and drama of Luke's crucifixion scene, this is not an unexpected clarification. Finally, one should observe the reaction of the women to the prediction-fulfilment saying, in contrast to the earlier reactions to Jesus' passion predictions. Earlier reactions included misunderstanding, concealment of meaning, and lack of perception (9:45; 18:34). Now the women (and readers, too) are drawing connections between Jesus' predictions and their fulfilment. The reaction of the Eleven to the women's report is in keeping with earlier reactions and exposes their unbelief and need for further revelation from the risen Christ himself.

6.3.1.3 INCOMPLETION (LUKE 24:1–12)

Two descriptive expressions in the tomb scene reveal incompletion in the Third Gospel. (1) Jesus is called 'the Son of Man' in the prediction-fulfilment saying (Luke 24:7). The appearance of this title is not surprising, since it appears regularly in predictions and allusions to Jesus' passion and resurrection (Luke 9:22, 44; 11:30; 17:24–25; 18:31). It is carefully repeated at the Last Supper (22:22), and as Judas approaches the Mount of Olives (22:48). In each of these instances it is connected with Jesus' being 'handed over' (παραδίδωμι). Throughout the Gospel the designation is often

---

[58] Talbert, 'Place of the Resurrection,' 24.

associated with future glory, power, and judgment (9:26; 12:8, 10, 40; 17:22, 24, 26, 30; 18:8; 21:27, 36). This is the association that is still ringing in listeners' ears since Jesus' last vocalization of the title at his trial: 'but from now on the Son of Man will be seated at the right hand of the power of God' (22:69). The allusion to Daniel's vision of the Son of Man in the divine court provides a context for how Jesus' messianic role is to be understood. The assembling of the divine court spells doom and destruction for the world powers opposed to God when the Son of Man appears and is given an everlasting kingdom and the authority to judge the nations (Dan 7:9–28). The portrait of the Son of Man in *1 Enoch* complements that of Daniel in that it portrays the Son of Man as the executor of divine justice on behalf of the righteous. We have already seen how in the 'Similitudes of Enoch' the Son of Man presides in judgment after the resurrection of the dead, when the righteous are granted salvation and everlasting life in paradise, whereas the wealthy landowners and potentates who would not submit to divine rule are destroyed (*1 En.* 46:4–8; 48:8–10; 61:5–13; 62:1–16). The 'sinners' (cf. 62:2), we are told, will be seized with pain 'when they see that Son of Man sitting on the throne of his glory' (62:5).

So when two heavenly figures proclaim that the Christ has risen, and that the prophetic words of the Son of Man have come to pass (Luke 24:6–7), it is not difficult to infer that the time of salvation for God's people has dawned and that their enemies will indeed be brought to destruction (cf. 1:71, 74). Gabriel's announcement to Mary must be truer now than ever: 'He will be great, and will be called the Son of the Most High, and the Lord God will give to him the throne of his ancestor David. He will reign over the house of Jacob forever, and of his kingdom there will be no end' (1:32–33). Yet by the end of Luke 24, or even the end of Luke-Acts as a whole, 'the sinful men' (24:7) responsible for Jesus' death are not dethroned. Yes, the Son of Man has been vindicated by being raised from the dead. From now on he will be seated at the right hand of God. But the final judgment, when the Righteous One and his people experience full vindication in the face of their wealthy and power-hungry oppressors, still lies in the future. Readers will discover how Judas is recompensed for his money-grabbing treachery (Acts 1:18–20), but they are given only a glimpse of the judgment awaiting the murderers of the Righteous One, when Stephen sees the heavens open, and the Son of Man standing at the right hand of God (Acts 7:55–56). At the close of Luke's Gospel, one might say, there is an eschatological aperture that remains open even at the end of Acts. Jesus is the glorified Son of Man by virtue of his resurrection, but he has not yet fully executed the judgment of God over all the earth.

(2) The numerical expression, 'the Eleven' (Luke 24:9), points to a glaring incompletion at the end of Luke's Gospel. This designation will be employed again in 24:33, and it stands in stark contrast to the repeated ref-

erences to 'the Twelve' as the number of disciples chosen by Jesus as his apostles (6:13; cf. 8:1; 9:1, 12; 18:31). The diminution of the Twelve was anticipated earlier by references to Judas as 'belonging to the number of the Twelve' (22:3, 47).[59] Despite his awareness of the satanic opposition that had infiltrated his duodecimal circle (22:21–22), Jesus conferred upon them co-regency with himself (22:29), 'so that you may eat and drink at my table in my kingdom, and you will sit on thrones judging the twelve tribes of Israel' (22:30). The defection of Judas has reduced the number of apostles to eleven, and has therefore ruined the numerical perfection of a twelvefold dominion over Israel. This incompletion is left dangling at the close of the Third Gospel. How will the reign of God now manifest itself through twelve tribal leaders in Israel, in accordance with the ancient promises to Jacob's sons? If Jesus' portfolio as prophet and Messiah included bringing about the long-awaited restoration of Israel, how will it be achieved *now*? This is a question that will be pressed by the Emmaus conversationalists in the next scene.

6.3.2 *The Way to Emmaus (Luke 24:13–32)*

In this account of two disciples' encounter with Jesus en route to Emmaus, there is a concentration of Lukan theological motifs and closural cues. The scene is dominated by journeying, discussion about the Hebrew Scriptures, meal sharing, and recognition of Jesus. These are theological motifs that saturate the Lukan narrative and are skilfully drawn together in one of the most moving and memorable literary portraits in ancient literature. The heaping up of these motifs itself provides a closural movement in the scene. The repeated language of travel boomerangs toward Emmaus and then back again to Jerusalem (24:13, 33), but in the meantime there are teasing notices of Jesus' approach to the Emmaus disciples (24:15), the halting of the two disciples (24:17), and the arrival at their destination (24:28). At Emmaus, Jesus acts as though he is going to part from them, but the disciples offer the stranger hospitality, since twilight is falling and the day will soon be over (24:29). These notations give one the impression that a 'third day' hourglass is running out. Another common closural cue comes in the form of a recapitulation.[60] In 24:19–24 the Emmaus pair provides their travelling companion with a thumbnail sketch of Jesus' entire career all the way up to his death and purported resurrection. Finally, a closural device that would be detected by both Jewish and Greco-Roman readers is

---

[59] On the significance of the number twelve, see Jacob Jervell, *Luke and the People of God* (Minneapolis: Augsburg, 1972), 83–85.

[60] Fowler, 'Second Thoughts on Closure,' 19–20.

The Resurrection of Jesus and the Hope of Israel (Luke 24) 167

the motif of recognition. In the Hebrew Bible a touching recognition scene occurs in Genesis 45 where Joseph reveals his identity to his brothers. Toward the end of Homer's *Odyssey*, Odysseus is not recognized until he accomplishes an unrivalled archery feat. Recognition was a *topos* at the conclusion to many of the Greek romances, when star-crossed lovers were reunited. These theological and closural cues will be analyzed in more detail as we look at how this scene is related to the beginning and middle of Luke's Gospel, and therefore how Jesus' resurrection functions within the first volume of Luke's narrative.

6.3.2.1 CIRCULARITY (LUKE 24:13-32)

When we meet the two disciples who are on their way to Emmaus, we find them walking along and conversing about 'all these things that have happened' (Luke 24:14). This is continuous with 'all these things' that the women reported to the Eleven and those with them (24:9), and hence to these two who were 'from among them' (24:13). The specifics of their conversation are not spelled out until after Jesus joins them on their journey and asks them what they are talking about. Then Cleopas and his companion begin their recital of Jesus' career. The recital itself will concern us under our discussion of the parallelisms in this scene. What we will focus our attention on here is the reason given for the disciples' disappointment and sadness (see 24:17), which forms a negative image of the expectation and joy in Luke's prologue.

The crucifixion of the prophet from Nazareth dashes the disciples' hope of salvation: 'But we had hoped (ἠλπίζομεν) that he was the one to redeem (λυτροῦσθαι) Israel' (24:21a). Luke's prologue is replete with expressions of expectancy concerning God's coming salvation (1:46-55, 67-79; 2:28-32) and the preparation of a people fit to worship God (1:16-17, 74-75). Announcements of God's saving work preface the ministries of John the Baptist (3:4-6) and Jesus (4:18-19). The language of 'redemption' appears at the very beginning of Zechariah's prophecy: 'Blessed be the Lord God of Israel, for he has looked favourably on his people and redeemed (ἐποίησεν λύτρωσιν) them' (1:68). Simeon is 'waiting expectantly for the consolation of Israel' (προσδεχόμενος παράκλησιν τοῦ Ἰσραήλ, 2:25), a reverberation of the Isaianic hope for deliverance of the exiled people of Israel (Isa 40:1-2, 11; 49:9-13; 51:3, 12, 18-19; 57:18; 61:1-2; 66:10-13). Anna praises God and speaks about the infant Jesus 'to all who were looking for the redemption of Jerusalem' (πᾶσιν τοῖς προσδεχομένοις λύτρωσιν Ἰερουσαλήμ, Luke 2:38). These are palpable expectations of liberation rooted in God's redemption of Israel out of Egyptian bondage (Exod 6:6; 13:13-15; 15:13; Deut 7:8; 9:26, etc.) and the corollary hope of restoration from exile (Mic 4:10; 6:4; Isa 63:1-19; Jer 16:14-15; 23:7-8; cf. Bar 2:11-35). The birth of Jesus is greeted with excitement, and Israel's hope of salvation is heralded.

The death of Jesus devastates this hope. Jesus had already anticipated a frustration of Israel's hope for peace in his lament over Jerusalem, in which he predicted her obstinacy and eventual destruction (Luke 19:41–44). The destruction of city and temple, however, does not irreversibly cancel out every prospect of salvation for Israel, since the 'times of the Gentiles,' when Jerusalem remains under foreign domination, will not last forever (21:24). The earth-shaking signs of '"the Son of Man coming in a cloud" with power and great glory' (21:25–27) will ultimately rouse the people of God to their feet, because then their 'redemption (ἀπολύτρωσις) is drawing near' (21:28). Jesus' promises of deliverance for Israel are empty now that he has been crucified and consigned to the grave. The two disciples express the grievous tragedy of how salvation through the prophet Jesus has proven illusory. Jesus' prediction that he would rise from the dead is not taking place, for it is the third day since Jesus was executed (24:21b). True, some women could not find his body in the tomb and claimed to have seen a vision of angels who told them that he was alive (24:22–23). Some other disciples found the tomb just as the women had described—but no one *saw* Jesus (αὐτὸν δὲ οὐκ εἶδον, 24:24).

The hope of Israel's restoration is a scarlet thread that ties the beginning and the end of Luke's Gospel together. But the narrative thread from Jesus' birth to death ought not be construed as a tragic plot, as the Emmaus disciples—and Tannehill—suggest.[61] First, there is an irony in the disciples' rehearsal of how others had not 'seen' Jesus, despite the angelic proclamation of his resurrection, while in the waning hours of the third day these two have met up with the risen Jesus himself (24:15) 'but their eyes were kept from recognizing him' (24:16). Simeon had cradled the baby Jesus in his arms and exclaimed, 'My eyes have seen your salvation' (2:30). John the Baptist declared that 'all flesh will see the salvation of God' (3:6). Yet these two disciples are unable to recognize the risen Jesus who is walking and talking with them! Second, Jesus flatly disavows the Emmaus pair's 'take' on the Easter events. He rebukes them as foolish men, 'slow of heart to believe all that the prophets have declared' (24:25). Jesus' death and resurrection conform to the divine purpose (24:26). Third, it is necessary to observe that the focus of Israel's hope, both in the prologue and in Luke 24, is on the person of Messiah. The interpretation of the Emmaus disciples would be correct if indeed Jesus had *not* been resurrected. If the one who is going to redeem Israel is truly alive, if they can indeed see him alive with their very own eyes, then their hope for Israel's salvation will be rehabilitated. How the resurrection of Jesus is crucial to the continuation of Israel's

---

[61] Tannehill, 'Tragic Story,' 69–85.

hope will be clarified by looking at this scene's parallels to earlier elements in the Gospel.

6.3.2.2 PARALLELISM (LUKE 24:13-32)

The Emmaus disciples' recital of the events of Easter day exhibits their blindness and unbelief. Nevertheless, their recital of Jesus' career as a prophet is remarkably factual. Only their recognition of the risen Jesus and his scriptural role within the divine purpose is necessary for their hope in Israel's salvation to be restored. Several motifs that run through the Gospel intersect on the way to Emmaus to make this scene a miniature of the Gospel narrative's unfolding of Jesus' entire mission. Immediately visible is the journey motif that is signalled frequently in the passage (Luke 24:13, 15, 17, 28). Readers are aware that Jesus had been on a journey to Jerusalem since 9:51 that would terminate with his ἀνάλημψις.[62] He reached Jerusalem in 19:41, and his cleansing of the temple set in motion the events of his passion, death, and resurrection. We find the risen Jesus travelling again, now with two disciples (24:15), after which he will disappear before their eyes (24:31), adumbrating his final departure into heaven (24:51). The journey motif is interwoven with other motifs—such as promise and fulfilment and the responses of misunderstanding or disbelief—all crucial for disclosing Jesus as God's chosen instrument for the salvation of Israel. The encounter with Jesus on the road to Emmaus portrays Jesus as the one who, through rejection, death, and resurrection, embodies the role of the prophet like Moses who is initiating a New Exodus for the people of God.

The travellers from Emmaus are mistaken in their assessment of the Easter events because they cannot bring themselves to believe the indications thus far that Jesus is alive. But they are not mistaken about Jesus' prophetic credentials.[63] They refer to 'the things about Jesus of Nazareth, who was a prophet mighty in deed and word before God and all the people' (Luke 24:19). They speak of Jesus as 'the one who was going to redeem Israel' (24:21). Earlier scenes in the Gospel support their identification of Jesus. Jesus in his inaugural sermon at Nazareth identified himself with Israel's prophets.[64] It was precisely as Nazareth's resident prophet—as the Emmaus pair names him—that Jesus was rejected. And if Jesus the prophet is repudiated in his hometown (4:24), it is not difficult to surmise how he will fare in the city of Jerusalem, which has a reputation for killing prophets (13:33–34). When Jesus resurrects a young man at Nain, a scene reminiscent of

---

[62] Travel notices punctuate the ensuing material up to Jesus' entry into Jerusalem (9:53; 13:22, 33; 17:11; 18:31; 19:11, 28, 41).

[63] Dillon, *Eye-Witnesses*, 117–26; *contra* Plevnik, 'Eyewitnesses,' 95 n. 18.

[64] Smith, *Easter Gospels*, 115.

Elijah the prophet, the townspeople declare that 'a great prophet has risen among us' (7:16). On the heels of this miracle, we learn that it is the full range of Jesus' prophetic words and deeds, in fulfilment of Isaiah's prophecy (cf. Isa 61:1–2 in Luke 4:18–19), that displays his status as 'the Coming One' (7:22; cf. 7:20).[65]

What is remarkable about the description of Jesus in the Emmaus colloquium is that he is spoken of as though he were the promised prophet like Moses. Jesus is called ἀνὴρ προφήτης (24:19) as Moses is in Judges 6:8 (καὶ ἐξαπέστειλεν κύριος ἄνδρα προφήτην πρὸς τοὺς υἱοὺς Ισραηλ). Jesus is 'mighty in word and deed,' as Moses is later described in Acts 7:22. The phraseology is evocative of the epilogue concerning Moses at the close of Deuteronomy. There we are informed that 'there has not yet risen a prophet in Israel like Moses' who relates to God face to face (Deut 34:10), and who performs 'signs and wonders' like Moses did both in Egypt (34:11) and ἔναντι παντὸς Ἰσραήλ (34:12 LXX; cp. Luke 24:19: ἐναντίον τοῦ θεοῦ καὶ παντὸς τοῦ λαοῦ; cf. Exod 4:30; 17:6; 19:11). The anticipated redemption of Israel (Luke 24:21), too, echoes the redemption from Egypt accomplished through Moses, who is later designated in Stephen's speech as 'leader and liberator' (ἄρχοντα καὶ λυτρωτὴν, Acts 7:35). Jesus confirms his prophetic connections when he scolds the Emmaus pair for not believing 'all that the prophets have spoken' (Luke 24:25), and when he interprets what all of the Scriptures have to say about him 'beginning with Moses and all the prophets' (24:27).

Two earlier scenes in the Gospel (and their surrounding co-texts) cast light on the conversation between Jesus and the two travellers and their eye-opening table-fellowship at Emmaus. These two scenes, namely, the transfiguration and the feeding of the five thousand, are not chosen at random. (1) They are truly memorable points in the narrative, and the transfiguration in particular is undoubtedly a revelatory benchmark. (2) They appear strategically before the commencement of Jesus' journey to Jerusalem in 9:51, the mid-point of Luke's first volume. (3) They contain points of contact with the Emmaus scene in that they (a) portray discussions about the identity of Jesus; (b) point toward Jesus' role as the Moses-like leader of a New Exodus; and (c) expose the lack of perception on the part of the disciples. The immediately apparent parallels consist of the appearance of the glorified Jesus at the transfiguration and on the way to Emmaus, and Jesus' actions in distributing bread to the five thousand and to the two at table with him in Emmaus.

---

[65] Jesus' identification with the line of Israel's rejected prophets is further expressed in Luke 6:22–23; 7:39; 11:47–51.

The transfiguration and the feeding of the five thousand are set within a context that highlights the disciples' involvement in the extension of Jesus' kingdom proclamation, and in the increasing speculation about Jesus' identity. The authority and power shared by Jesus with his twelve apostles (Luke 9:1-6) is followed up by suggestions about who Jesus is: a resurrected John the Baptist? a reappearance of Elijah? one of the prophets of old risen from the dead (9:7-8)? When Herod hears these things, he begins a search for Jesus that will not be successful until the time of Jesus' trial (9:9; cf. 13:31; 23:8). Between the feeding of the five thousand and the transfiguration, Jesus asks the Twelve who the crowds think he is. They report the same rumours that had reached Herod (9:19). When Peter confesses that Jesus is the Messiah (9:20), Jesus forbids them to tell anyone (9:21), and delivers his first passion and resurrection prediction (9:22) and a brief discourse on the messianic pattern of discipleship, outlining the Son of Man's path from suffering to glory (9:23-27).

Amidst the speculation concerning Jesus' identity are revelations of Jesus as Israel's awaited prophet like Moses. Despite the echoes of Elisha's multiplication of loaves (9:17; cf. 2 Kgs 4:42-44), the feeding of the five thousand is surely reminiscent of the Lord's provision of manna for Israel 'in the wilderness' (Luke 9:12; cf. Exod 16:4-36). The repetition of the number twelve in connection with the apostles is indicative of the reestablishment of legitimate leadership in Israel (Luke 9:1, 12, 17). Only the prophet like Moses could accomplish this.[66] The exodus and Mosaic imagery is amplified in the transfiguration scene.[67] Moses' ascent to Mt. Sinai, beginning in Exodus 24, is matched by Jesus' ascent onto a mountain (Luke 9:28, 37). Like Moses, Jesus' countenance is transformed (Luke 9:29; Exod 34:29-30, 33-35).[68] As at Sinai, a cloud envelops the mountain (Luke 9:34-35; Exod 24:15, 16, 18).

---

[66] According to Philo, part of God's reasoning for raining down manna was 'to honour the ruler whom He had appointed' (*Moses* 1.198). In Pseudo-Philo the provision of manna was directly associated with Moses' leadership, for it stopped when Moses died (*L.A.B.* 20:8; cf. *T. Mos.* 11:9, 13). Compare also the 'Bread of Life Discourse' (John 6:22-59).

[67] Robert F. O'Toole, 'The Parallels between Jesus and Moses,' *BTB* 20 (1990): 22-23; B. J. Koet, 'Divine Communication in Luke-Acts,' in *The Unity of Luke-Acts* (ed. Joseph Verheyden; BETL 142; Leuven: Leuven University Press), 753-54; Félix Gils, *Jésus Prophète après les Évangiles Synoptiques* (Orientalia et Biblica Lovaniensia 2; Louvain: Publications Universitaires, 1957), 35-39.

[68] This detail is more pointed than the other Synoptics' note that Jesus was 'transfigured' (μετεμορφώθη, Matt 17:2; Mark 9:2).

6.3.2.2.1 The Transfiguration and the Emmaus Scene

Three elements in the transfiguration scene are further indicators that Jesus is the eschatological prophet like Moses, and these may be correlated with the Emmaus scene.

(1) Jesus appears 'in glory' with Moses and Elijah, and the three disciples who are present 'see his glory' (Luke 9:31–32; cf. Exod 24:16–17; Deut 5:24). Neither of the other Synoptics mentions Jesus' glory as Luke does. The expression τὴν δόξαν αὐτοῦ occurs in Luke's Gospel only at 9:32 and 24:26. The earliest point in Luke's narrative where Jesus' glory is mentioned is in Simeon's prophecy that Jesus would be 'glory to your people Israel' (Luke 2:32). On the mount of transfiguration Jesus' inner circle of disciples—as well as Luke's readers—receive their first glimpse of his glory. Both in this co-text (9:26–27) and elsewhere (21:27) the future glory of Jesus is announced, but his glorious kingship over Israel will not be realized, but rather thwarted through crucifixion, until after his resurrection.[69] This is why Jesus is quick to correct Peter's messianic declaration with a passion-resurrection prediction (9:20–22). The disciples speak not a word about what they had seen at the transfiguration (9:36). This cues the reader to the secret of Jesus' pathway from suffering to glory that will remain hidden from the disciples' understanding (9:44–45; 18:31–34), and engenders an expectancy concerning how this course of events will take place. The full disclosure of Jesus to his disciples as Israel's ruler and liberator unfolds only after his resurrection. Jesus tells the Emmaus travellers: 'Was it not necessary that the Messiah should suffer these things and then enter into his glory?' (24:26).

Several points must be made regarding Jesus' saying in Luke 24:26. First, Jesus' entrance into his glory refers to his resurrection from the dead. This is clear from the unmistakable similarities between this saying and other sayings which couple Jesus' suffering with his resurrection:

Luke 24:26: ταῦτα ἔδει παθεῖν τὸν Χριστὸν καὶ εἰσελθεῖν εἰς τὴν δόξαν αὐτοῦ
Luke 9:22: δεῖ τὸν υἱὸν τοῦ ἀνθρώπου πολλὰ παθεῖν...καὶ τῇ τρίτῃ ἡμέρᾳ ἐγερθῆναι
Luke 24:7: δεῖ...σταυρωθῆναι καὶ τῇ τρίτῃ ἡμέρᾳ ἀναστῆναι
Luke 24:46: οὕτως γέγραπται παθεῖν τὸν Χριστὸν καὶ ἀναστῆναι ἐκ νεκρῶν
Acts 17:3: τὸν Χριστὸν ἔδει παθεῖν καὶ ἀναστῆναι ἐκ νεκρῶν
Acts 26:23: εἰ παθητὸς ὁ Χριστός, εἰ πρῶτος ἐξ ἀναστάσεως νεκρῶν[70]

---

[69] Luke 19:37–44; 23:2, 3, 37–38—just as Jesus expected (19:11–27; 20:9–19). Notably, Ps 117:22 LXX, cited in Luke 20:17, is distinctly echoed later in Acts 4:11 as a commentary on Jesus' crucifixion/rejection and resurrection/vindication.

[70] Lohfink, *Die Himmelfahrt Jesu*, 236–39; Dillon, *Eye-Witnesses*, 140–43.

Second, Jesus' entrance into glory signifies his attainment of royal position and authority. In Luke-Acts 'glory,' beyond denoting visual brightness (Luke 2:9; Acts 22:11) or honour (Luke 14:10; 17:18), is usually associated with ascendancy or rulership, or its ascription to God or to those who rightfully participate in it.[71] The precise expression εἰσελθεῖν εἰς τὴν δόξαν αὐτοῦ is unparalleled in our extant literature; however, in Luke-Acts the idea of 'entering the kingdom' occurs a number of times (Luke 13:24; 16:16; 18:17, 24, 25; 23:42; Acts 14:22).[72] Analogous to 'entering into glory' is God's bestowal of 'glory' to persons who assume positions of leadership.[73] At the transfiguration, Moses and Elijah also appear 'in glory' (Luke 9:31), but finally vanish, being eclipsed by the presence of Jesus. This increases the likelihood that the ἔξοδος about which Jesus and the two figures conversed came to pass in Jesus' death and resurrection, when Jesus entered into his glory (24:26–27).[74]

Third, our study of resurrection in the Hebrew Scriptures and Jewish intertestamental literature demonstrated the consistent association of resurrection with exaltation. This exaltation may be expressed through the vocabulary of 'glory' (e.g., *1 En.* 62:14–16; *2 Bar.* 51:5, 10; *T. Benj.* 10:6–9). The wellspring for this concept is Dan 12:1–3 (cf. Dan 12:13 LXX), which envisions a resurrection of the righteous and their concomitant exaltation to star-like (or angel-like) ascendancy (cf. Luke 20:36). Jesus' entrance into his glory fits this pattern. There is no warrant for Lohfink's proposal that Luke 24:26 qualifies as a resurrection text, but not as an exaltation text.[75] Luke has not altered the exaltation kerygma, nor transferred the concept of exaltation from the time of Jesus' resurrection to his ascension. Both the post-resurrection appearances and the ascension are manifestations of Jesus' exalted, royal status after God raised him from the dead.[76] Luke's version of Jesus' exaltation is not novel in its addition of an ascension account, as Lohfink insists.[77] In many of the Jewish sources we

---

[71] Luke 2:9, 14, 32; 4:6; 9:26, 31, 32; 12:27; 19:38; 21:27; Acts 7:2, 55; 12:23. N.B. the textual variant βασιλείαν (in place of δόξαν) in Luke 24:26 $\mathfrak{P}^{75}$.

[72] Luke Timothy Johnson, *The Gospel of Luke* (SP 3; Collegeville, Minn.: Liturgical, 1991), 396.

[73] Such as Moses (Sir 45:2, 3, 7), David (Sir 47:6, 11), Solomon (1 Chron 29:28), Nebuchadnezzar (Dan 4:36), a son of man (Dan 7:14).

[74] Dillon, *Eye-Witnesses*, 143.

[75] Lohfink, *Die Himmelfahrt Jesu*, 236–39.

[76] Luke transitions easily between references to resurrection and ascension when speaking of Jesus' exaltation (Acts 2:32–35; 5:29–30), but otherwise prefers to focus on Jesus' resurrection.

[77] The exceptional aspect of Luke's narrative is that in his ascension accounts he employs the features of the rapture story form, as Lohfink correctly observes. But it is

have studied, exaltation of the righteous into heavenly positions of power is a natural extension of the final resurrection. Consequently, being raised up, not only *from the dead* but *up to the divine throne*, distinguishes Jesus' resurrection as eschatological. It is because his resurrection from the dead issues in exaltation before God that it can be said that he is truly 'the first from the resurrection of the dead' (Acts 26:23; cf. 3:26; 4:2). His resurrection is not merely a precursor to the eschatological resurrection, as are the other resurrection miracles in Luke-Acts (see also Matt 27:52–53), but is itself the genesis of the eschatological resurrection of the dead.

Fourth, the glory of Israel was a preoccupation of the post-exilic prophets. Israel's glory was lost in the exile, but would be restored when the nation repented of its sins and experienced Yahweh's salvation.[78] It is within this context that sense is made of Simeon's expectation for Israel's 'consolation' (Luke 2:25) and his declaration that the Christ-child would be 'the glory of your people Israel' (2:32). Our study of the Jewish conception of resurrection revealed that resurrection is intimately bound up with Israel's remembrance of the exodus and hope for restoration from exile. Time after time, resurrection is integral to the completion of the Sin-Exile-Return pattern. Resurrection from the dead would mean a return to former glory, or rather, greater glory, deliverance from servitude and debasement, and lasting enjoyment of the promised covenant blessings. Although there is no clear portrait of how a suffering and resurrected Messiah would figure into Israel's hope (but see *2 Bar* 30:1–2; *4 Ezra* 7:26–[44]), Luke's perspective is consonant with Israel's resurrection hope. If hope of salvation is heightened when a young man is resurrected (Luke 7:11–17), or when it is speculated that Jesus might be one of the ancient prophets raised from the dead (9:7–8, 19), what if a great prophet had indeed been raised from the dead? This would surely send a strong signal to Israel that God is visiting his people to bring them salvation, in this instance through his servant Jesus, the prophet like Moses. The Messiah's entrance into glory would initiate the restoration of Israel's glory.

(2) In the transfiguration scene Luke alone among the Synoptics includes the note that Moses and Elijah were speaking with Jesus about his ἔξοδος that he was going to accomplish in Jerusalem (Luke 9:31). The term ἔξοδος

---

inaccurate to infer from this that Luke has invested Jesus' ascension with a theological significance that is independent from or competitive with the resurrection. Lohfink's position is based upon a redaction-critical approach that is not supported by the flow of Luke's narrative nor the expositions regarding Jesus' resurrection in the speeches in Acts.

[78] See esp. Isa 40:5; 45:22–25; 46:13; 55:5; 58:8; 60:1–2, 6, 13–14, 19–21; 61:1–2; 62:1–2; 66:11; cf. John J. Kilgallen, 'Jesus, Savior, the Glory of Your People Israel,' *Bib* 75 (1994): 305–28.

has been interpreted variously.⁷⁹ It could refer simply to 'departure' (as opposed to εἴσοδος, 'entrance,' Acts 13:24), and would therefore indicate generally the end-point of Jesus' entire life journey. A specific event at the end of Jesus' life may be in view. The term can be used euphemistically for death (2 Pet 1:15; Wis 3:2; 7:6), and in this case would accord with Jesus' passion prediction in Luke 9:22.⁸⁰ It could anticipate Jesus' ascension or departure previewed in 9:51.⁸¹ The predominant view is that it embraces the whole sweep of Jesus death, resurrection, and ascension. Since the studies by Sharon Ringe and Susan Garrett, scholars have been more attuned to the term as a Mosaic echo in the passage.⁸² Jesus' ἔξοδος is considered the antitype in an exodus typology.⁸³

It is difficult to connect Jesus' ἔξοδος to a single event at the close of his earthly life. Just before the transfiguration, Jesus uttered his first passion and resurrection prediction (Luke 9:22). This tends to support the idea that Jesus' ἔξοδος takes place in connection with his death and resurrection. Charles Talbert sets forth a set of correspondences between Luke 9:1–34

---

⁷⁹ The interpretive options are conveniently listed in Sharon Ringe, 'Luke 9:28–36: The Beginning of an Exodus,' *Semeia* 28 (1983): 92–94; cf. Bock, *Luke*, 869–70.

⁸⁰ Peter M. Renju, 'The Exodus of Jesus,' *BT* 46 (1995): 213–18. Renju correlates Luke 9:31 with 23:39–43.

⁸¹ Luke 9:51 is itself subject to varying interpretations. Jesus' ἀνάλημψις in Luke 9:51 and Acts 1:2 (ἀνελήμφθη) was viewed by van Stempvoort as referring broadly to 'the whole process of his passing away and being taken up' ('The Interpretation of the Ascension in Luke and Acts,' 33). Many interpreters espouse the similar, expansive view that Jesus' ἀνάλημψις includes the whole course of his death, resurrection, and ascension; see Lohfink, *Die Himmelfahrt Jesu*, 212–17; Parsons, *Departure*, 130–33; Bovon, *Lukas*, 2:27; Ellis, *Luke*, 152; Johnson, *Luke*, 162; Tannehill, *Luke*, 168; Evans, *Luke*, 435–36. Dupont, in his critique of van Stempvoort, conceded that in Luke 9:51 ἀνάλημψις may encompass death, resurrection, and ascension because of the appearance of the plural 'days' in the expression ἐν τῷ συμπληροῦσθαι τὰς ἡμέρας τῆς ἀναλήμψεως αὐτοῦ; but in Acts 1:2 the verb ἀνελήμφθη refers specifically to Jesus' ascension (Jacques Dupont, "ΑΝΕΛΗΜΦΘΗ (Act. I.2),' *NTS* 8 [1961–62]: 154–57). Zwiep (*Ascension of the Messiah*, 82–86) has demonstrated why such a concession is unnecessary, since the expression in Luke 9:51 refers to the completion of a period of time *leading up to* the ascension. The retrospective comments in Acts 1:2 and 1:22 distinctly mark Jesus' 'being taken up' (i.e., ascension) as the end-point of his earthly life (cf. 1:11). It is fitting for Luke 9:51, the mid-point of the Gospel narrative, to preview the end-point narrated in the final scene of Luke's first volume (cf. Danker, *Jesus and the New Age*, 208; Green, *Luke*, 403 nn. 7–8).

⁸² Ringe, 'Beginning of an Exodus,' 83–99; Garrett, 'Exodus from Bondage,' 658–80; idem, 'The Meaning of Jesus' Death in Luke,' 11–16.

⁸³ An elaborate (often overly-imaginative) New Exodus typological reading of Luke-Acts is presented in Mánek, 'New Exodus in the Books of Luke,' 8–23.

and Acts 1:1–12 (following J. G. Davies), and the proximity of the reference to the ascension in Luke 9:51, as evidence that Jesus' ἔξοδος takes place at his ascension.[84] However, first, the correspondences are overly general, incidental, or irrelevant.[85] Second, ἔξοδος and ἀνάλημψις cannot be strictly equated. The former term, unlike the latter, is not attested as a rapture term.[86] Although Moses and Elijah were both believed to have ascended into heaven, the term ἔξοδος in 9:31, among other Mosaic elements, more likely reminds one of Israel's exodus from Egypt than an ascent into heaven.[87] This does not mean that we can exclude the ascension from Jesus' exodus experience foreshadowed at the transfiguration, but Jesus' statement to the Emmaus disciples in 24:26 indicates that his death and resurrection already embodies the fulfilment of Jesus' conversation with Moses and Elijah. At the transfiguration, Jesus appeared 'in glory' (9:31–32), previewing his entrance 'into his glory' after his suffering (24:26). Moses and Elijah's conversation about his exodus is a vivid characterization of Jesus' own interpretation of what the Scriptures say about him 'beginning with Moses and all the prophets' (24:27). It is the resurrected Jesus who exemplifies and inaugurates a new exodus for the people of God and who revives the hope for Israel's ultimate redemption.

(3) Finally, the climactic moment of the transfiguration scene occurs with the divine pronouncement over Jesus: 'This is my Son, my Chosen; listen to him!' (Luke 9:35). The concluding command unambiguously harks back to Deut 18:15.[88] The prophetic role of the expected figure in

---

[84] Charles H. Talbert, *Literary Patterns, Theological Themes, and the Genre of Luke-Acts* (SBLMS 20; Missoula, Mont.: Scholars Press, 1974), 61–62, 114–15; Davies, 'Prefigurement of the Ascension,' 229–33.

[85] Talbert (*Literary Patterns*, 61–62) thinks it is significant that Luke uses the verb ἀνέβη (Luke 9:28) instead of the Markan ἀναφέρει (Mark 9:2). But if Luke 9:1–34 and Acts 1:1–12 are correlated, then why is ἀναβαίνω absent from Acts 1:1–12? There is a reasonable explanation for Luke's use of ἀνέβη in Luke 9:28: it is a suitable verb to indicate 'going up' a mountain (cf. Matt 5:1; 14:23; 15:29; Mark 3:13). The appearance of two men in dazzling apparel and a cloud in both passages proves nothing more than that apocalyptic imagery is being employed, just as it is in the empty tomb scene in Luke 24:4–5.

[86] Zwiep, *Ascension of the Messiah*, 86.

[87] The suggestion by Mánek ('New Exodus in the Books of Luke,' 19–20) that the heavenly Jerusalem is the final goal of Jesus' Exodus is not an impossible construal within the confines of Jewish and early Christian apocalyptic thought (cf. Gal 4:25–27; Heb 12:22; Rev 3:12; 21:2, 10), but it is an imaginative leap that does not find any support within the Lukan narrative itself.

[88] The link to Deut 18:15 is forged more strongly in Luke through word order identical to the LXX's (αὐτοῦ ἀκούετε), not similarly found in the other Synoptics (cp. ἀκούετε αὐτοῦ, Matt 17:5; Mark 9:7); David P. Moessner, 'Luke 9:1–50: Luke's Preview of the

Deuteronomy is Moses-like in that it consists of his being the mouthpiece of Yahweh, in lieu of direct contact between God and Israel from which the latter shrank away at Mt. Sinai (Deut 18:16-18). The prophet like Moses will succeed (and supersede) Moses as the authoritative medium and interpreter of God's communication to Israel. This is precisely the role Jesus steps into with every footfall towards Emmaus: 'Then beginning with Moses and all the prophets, he interpreted to them the things about himself in all the Scriptures' (Luke 24:27).

The Hebrew Bible, intertestamental literature, and later rabbinic sources attest to Moses' stature within Judaism as the archetypal leader of Israel.[89] The reigning title applied to Moses is 'prophet.' But he is not just any prophet. In Philo every other appellation given to Moses may be subsumed under the title ἀρχιπροφήτης.[90] There have been many prophets, but Moses is *the* prophet, 'proto-prophet' (προτοπροφήτης,),[91] or 'the prophetic genius' (τὸ προφητικὸν γένος).[92] The idea is not peculiar to Philo, for he claims that Moses is 'everywhere hymned as prophet.'[93] For Luke, the resurrected Jesus is the apex in this prophetic line (cf. 10:24; 11:49-51; 16:16; 18:31; Acts 3:24; 7:52). The manner in which Luke expresses Jesus' fulfilment of the Scriptures is stunning: 'Moses and all the prophets' point to him (Luke 24:27). Luke's preference for the expression 'all the prophets' is characteristic (Luke 11:50; 13:28; 24:25, 27; Acts 3:18, 24, 25; 10:43), and shows how the Scriptures are viewed not simply as texts, but as vital witnesses to God's continuing action in Israel's prophetic history.[94] The interpretive function of Moses as prophet is borne out by Philo's interchangeable references to him as ἑρμηνεύς and προφήτης.[95] This prophetic role is accented in the Emmaus scene, where there is a constellation of hermeneutical termi-

---

Journey of the Prophet Like Moses of Deuteronomy,' *JBL* 102 (1983): 589 n. 61. The concluding echo is striking in contrast to the earlier revelatory benchmark at Jesus' baptism (Luke 3:22), which is substantively the same except for the final command.

[89] On Moses and the prophet like Moses, see Howard M. Teeple, *The Mosaic Eschatological Prophet* (Journal of Biblical Literature, Monograph Series 10; Philadelphia: Society of Biblical Literature, 1957); Wayne A. Meeks, *The Prophet-King: Moses Traditions and the Johannine Christology* (NovTSup 14; Leiden: Brill, 1967), chs. 3-5.

[90] Philo, *Mut.* 103, 125; *Somn.* 2.189; *QG* 4.8.

[91] Philo, *QG* 1.86.

[92] Philo, *Fug.* 147.

[93] Philo, *Her.* 262.

[94] That the centre of Scripture for Luke resides in its prophetic message about Jesus the Christ has been ably argued by Jacob Jervell, 'The Center of Scripture in Luke,' in *The Unknown Paul: Essays on Luke-Acts and Early Christian History* (Minneapolis: Augsburg, 1984), 122-37.

[95] Philo, *Praem.* 55; *Her.* 213; cf. *Mut.* 126; *Spec.* 3.6; *Post.* 1; *Mos.* 1.1.

nology. In response to the disciples' 'conversing' (ὁμιλέω, 24:14–15), 'debating' (συζητέω, 24:15), and 'tossing ideas back and forth' (ἀντιβάλλω, 24:17), Jesus 'interprets' (διερμηνεύω, 24:27) or 'opens' (διανοίγω, 24:32, 45; cf. 24:31) what all the Scriptures say about himself.[96]

There are four implications of Jesus' role as the prophet like Moses. (a) As with Moses, Jesus' prophetic role dovetails with his position as the new leader of Israel. Prophetic and royal categories are not competitive in Luke-Acts. Moses was a prophet, but he was also leader, liberator, and judge (Acts 7:27, 35). The leaders of Israel who follow in the train of Moses are a succession of prophets (3:24). David was a celebrated king, yet Luke views him equally as a prophet (1:16; 2:25, 31, 34; 4:25). (b) While Jesus stands in continuity with all the prophets of old, he nevertheless supersedes them, as is dramatized at the transfiguration with the disappearance of Moses and Elijah and with Peter's awkward proposal. Particularly through death and resurrection, God brings all of the prophets' words to fulfilment in Jesus (Luke 24:25–27; Acts 3:18, 24–25; Acts 10:34). The supercession of all the prophets is evident in Luke's *via negativa* principle of interpretation, in which the various prophetic utterances come to fruition *not* in the lives of the prophets who spoke them, but in Jesus (cf. Acts 2:29–31, 34; 8:34–35; 13:36–37). (c) As such, Jesus is the *eschatological* prophet. Not only does he fulfil in his person the 'living oracles' passed down from Moses onward (Acts 7:38), but he is positioned to authoritatively interpret and order them in their proper christological and ecclesiological configuration. This is crucial for the appointment of legitimate witnesses to his life, death, and resurrection, since the witnesses must not only be qualified to offer empirical validation of what happened, but must be properly equipped to explain the meaning of what happened. (d) There are significant christological and ecclesiological ramifications of the death and resurrection of Jesus for Israel. The risen Jesus is God's authoritative voice in Israel. Those who reject him stand in relationship to those who persecuted all of the prophets (Luke 6:22–23; 11:47–51; Acts 7:52; 13:27). Those who accept him are the descendants of all the prophets (Luke 10:23–24; Acts 3:25). Jesus' life conforms to the prophetic template exemplified throughout Israel's history (exhibited *in extenso* in Stephen's speech, Acts 7:1–53). Moses in particular prefigures the destiny of Jesus, the prophet like Moses (7:37). Moses, though endowed with wisdom and charismatic power to be Israel's deliverer (7:22, 36), was misunderstood (7:25) and rejected by his own people (7:27, 35, 39). Jesus' career follows this same path of misunderstanding and

---

[96] See further, B. J. Koet, 'Some Traces of a Semantic Field of Interpretation in Luke 24,13–35,' in *Five Studies on Interpretation of Scripture in Luke-Acts* (SNTA 14; Leuven: Leuven University Press, 1989), 56–72.

repudiation. But his resurrection from the dead distinguishes him as the one who is bringing Israel, and indeed the whole world, to a critical juncture. One's rejection or acceptance of all the prophets culminates in response to the resurrected Jesus. To misunderstand and reject Jesus and his mission is to misunderstand and reject Moses and all the prophets who spoke about him.[97] This is why Luke coordinates the 'opening' of the Emmaus disciples' eyes with his 'opening' of the Scriptures to them. The words of Abraham in Luke 16:31 gain renewed force: 'If they do not listen to Moses and the prophets, neither will they be convinced even if someone rises from the dead.' The Emmaus disciples represent in miniature God's design for the people of Israel. The risen Jesus offers a blind, uncomprehending, and unbelieving people the opportunity to see the light of salvation, repent, and experience all of the blessings of a renewed covenant with God.

6.3.2.2.2 The Feeding of the Five Thousand and the Emmaus Scene

This leads us to the moment of recognition in the Emmaus scene. The scriptural persuasion happened on the road, but the breakthrough of revelation occurred at the table when Jesus broke bread before the Emmaus disciples. As the three travellers approach the village of Emmaus, Jesus acts as though he is going to take leave of the two disciples and continue journeying on his own. This action adds an anti-closural touch of suspense. Have the two disciples missed their opportunity to recognize the risen Lord? Will they bid him goodbye, or will they extend hospitality to him? At this point there are correspondences with the feeding of the five thousand.

(1) The Emmaus disciples act in a way that contrasts with the Twelve's action in the feeding story. In both scenes it is late in the day (ἡ δὲ ἡμέρα ἤρξατο κλίνειν, Luke 9:12; κέκλικεν ἤδη ἡ ἡμέρα, 24:29), but the Twelve wanted to send the crowds away, whereas the Emmaus pair strongly encourages the stranger to stay with them. The pair follows the proper course of hospitality indicated in Jesus' instruction to the Twelve: 'You give them something to eat' (9:13).[98] Perhaps, not incidentally, the note that Jesus 'stayed with them' has salvific overtones, since the acceptance of hospitality by Jesus and his disciples is a characteristic of success in preaching the kingdom of God (9:4; 10:7; 19:5). Happily, in this instance, Jesus is warmly welcomed and need not shake the dust off his feet and depart from Emmaus (cf. 9:5).

---

[97] The Scriptures put the nation of Israel in 'an accountable position'; Darrell Bock, 'Scripture and the Realisation of God's Promises,' in *Witness to the Gospel: The Theology of Acts* (eds. I. Howard Marshall and David Peterson; Grand Rapids: Eerdmans, 1998), 58.

[98] Anne Thurston, *Knowing Her Place: Gender and the Gospels* (New York and Mahwah, N.J.: Paulist, 1998), 114.

(2) Table fellowship or eating is a typical motif in Luke's Gospel. The Emmaus table scene is reminiscent of both the feeding of the five thousand and the Last Supper, although it is with the feeding that it has the closest affinity. Jesus' actions are nearly identical in 24:30 and 9:16: 'he took bread, blessed and broke it, and gave it to them.' To a slightly lesser degree, these actions approximate what Jesus did at the Last Supper (22:19). This cannot be by accident, as the feeding of the five thousand occurs toward the climax of Jesus' Galilean ministry, and the Last Supper at the end of Jesus' Jerusalem ministry. How appropriate it is for there to be a meal after Jesus' resurrection, too. Their strategic placement within Luke's narrative makes them the three most significant meal scenes in the entire work.[99]

The repetition of the series of actions in 24:30 is what triggers the two disciples' recognition of Jesus. Although we should not dismiss the possibility that a mystical process takes place in which a diabolical veil of darkness has been lifted from their eyes,[100] the dramatic actions possess a power of their own—a power that modern cinematographers would exploit by employing close-up shots, slow-motion, and flashbacks to previous meal scenes. The closure-effect of repetition would not have been lost on ancient readers who were familiar with it as a common feature in recognition scenes. In Chariton, early on in the story, Callirhoe recognizes that it is her husband, Chaereas, who is entering a darkened room merely by the sound of his breathing. He, thinking that she has been unfaithful to him, kicks her in the diaphragm and stops her breathing (1.4.12). Later, the separated couple is drawn together when Chaereas notices Callirhoe by the way she is breathing (8.1.7–8). Even as the simple act of breathing could function as a recognition trigger in Chariton, so an ordinary table blessing in Luke reveals an extraordinary host. The reversal of the two disciples' visual impairment is significant (cp. Luke 24:16 with 24:31), given Cleopas's report that the women could not 'find' Jesus' body, and that others who had inspected the tomb did not 'see' him (24:22–24). The combination of Jesus' interpretation of Scripture and his ritual action causes the identity of the stranger to dawn on the Emmaus disciples. They have truly seen Jesus, resurrected from the dead. He was revealed to them both 'on the road' and 'in the breaking of bread' (24:35). Jesus' prophetic roles as authoritative interpreter and banquet host manifest his identity as the prophet like Moses who is the new leader and liberator of Israel.

---

[99] Arthur A. Just, Jr., *Ongoing Feast: Table Fellowship and Eschatology at Emmaus* (Collegeville, Minn.: Liturgical, 1993), 156-57.

[100] Nolland (*Luke*, 3:1207) takes this position, while a number of commentators are content to observe a divine passive.

6.3.2.3 INCOMPLETION (LUKE 24:13–32)

The parallel imagery, phraseology, and motifs in the Emmaus scene and in earlier scenes in the Third Gospel are sufficient to provide a portrait of the risen Jesus as the promised liberator of Israel. Yet the Emmaus scene could have been even more specific in the way it supports this characterization. This points up a surprising incompletion. While Jesus is said to have explained what Moses and all the prophets have to say about himself, not one text is specifically cited or explained. Listeners will have to wait until they hear the speeches in Acts before they learn the specifics of Jesus' scriptural case. Neither are we provided with details about how Jesus' ἔξοδος will effect the restoration of God's people. When and how will the execution of Jesus' mission as the prophet like Moses be completed? Only in the next scene, but especially in the second part of Luke's narrative (Acts), will the salvific meaning of Jesus' resurrection be more fully expressed. Later we will learn that the resurrection of Jesus is significant as a liberating event because it is a harbinger of the eschatological deliverance that all the people of God will experience in the general resurrection when Messiah-Jesus returns to judge the world. It is then that the redemption of the people of God will be complete, and the final reversal will take place when the enemies of God's people are definitively overturned.

6.3.3 The Final Appearance of the Risen Jesus (Luke 24:36–53)

Luke 24:36–49 and 24:50–53 shall be viewed together, since the elevation of Jesus into heaven properly caps off his final appearance before the assembled disciples. Although 24:50 marks a change in venue, there is no time marker (as in 24:1, 13) or grammatical shift (such as the genitive absolute in 24:36) to signal a new scene. There is a movement within the passage from Jesus' appearance (ἔστη ἐν μέσῳ αὐτῶν) and greeting (24:36), to his farewell meal and instructions (24:44–49), parting benediction (24:50–51a), and disappearance into heaven (διέστη ἀπ' αὐτῶν, 24:51b).[101] Additionally, there exists a symmetry among all three scenes in this chapter in that they share the 'return' motif. The women return from the tomb to the Eleven and those gathered around them (24:9).[102] The Emmaus disciples return to Jerusalem to meet up with the Eleven after they recognize the risen Jesus and he vanishes before their eyes (24:33).[103] So also, after Jesus'

---

[101] Smith (*Easter Gospels*, 128) has pointed out the verbal *inclusio* (ἔστη—διέστη).

[102] Peter, too, 'went home' after his dash to the tomb (24:12).

[103] Schubert ('Structure and Significance of Luke 24,' 168 n. 13) draws a comparison between ἄφαντος ἐγένετο ἀπ' αὐτῶν (24:31) and διέστη ἀπ' αὐτῶν (24:51).

final appearance and departure, all the disciples return to Jerusalem, but this time on an undisturbed note of joy (24:52).

The scenic continuity in 24:36–53 is theologically significant, since it shows how easily Luke moves from post-resurrection appearances to ascension. He telescopes the events of Luke 24 into the time frame of a single day, not because he is ignorant of a protracted elapse of time (viz., forty days between resurrection and ascension, Acts 1:3), but because this allows him to theologically integrate the post-resurrection events. From empty tomb to ascension, Jesus is revealed as the resurrected and exalted Lord, Son of Man, Liberator, and Messiah.[104] Jesus, through his resurrection, has entered into a new life with God, so that he can already speak from the perspective of a sphere of existence set apart from the one he formerly shared with his disciples: 'These are my words that I spoke to you *while I was still with you*' (Luke 24:44).[105] The resurrected Jesus will inexorably take his place at the right hand of God, for it is only appropriate for righteous persons who take part in the eschatological resurrection to enter forevermore into the divine presence. Thus, the ascension is not a theological novelty or a unique redactional element in Luke's work that trumps Jesus' resurrection. Rather, the empty tomb, post-resurrection appearances, and ascension are characteristics of the fact that Jesus is the first individual to take part in the eschatological resurrection.

The final scene of Luke 24 properly functions as the climax to both its own chapter and the Gospel as a whole.[106] There are elements of circularity and parallelism between this scene and the entire foregoing narrative, as well as a crescendo of motifs that have developed in the immediately preceding scenes. This scene is also a hinge-piece with the first chapter of Luke's second volume. For this reason, we need not discuss matters related to incompletion (which have already been touched upon in previous sections), but rather elements of linkage that are prominent in this scene.

---

[104] Cf. Acts 2:29–36 in which both empty tomb and ascension are key indicators that Jesus has fulfilled the prophetic prediction that the Davidic Lord and Messiah would be resurrected from the dead.

[105] Johnson, *Luke*, 405.

[106] Just (*Ongoing Feast*, 1–2) inaccurately views the Emmaus scene as the climax to the whole Gospel. Despite its length and vividness of detail, it is clearly a bridge to the scene of Jesus' final appearance, commissioning, and farewell to all of the assembled disciples.

6.3.3.1 CIRCULARITY (LUKE 24:36-53)

6.3.3.1.1 Extension of Salvation to All Nations

A crucial element of circularity in this final scene is apparent once one recognizes the alteration of a pattern of parallelism that winds through the Gospel, as well as a continuation of that altered pattern henceforth in Luke's work. In the previous two scenes the dominical and scriptural prophecies about Jesus' resurrection were recalled (Luke 24:6-7, 26-27), as they are here (24:44, 46-47). All of these rehearsals have two points in common: (1) an authoritative basis in the words of Jesus and in the plan of God (the divine δεῖ);[107] and (2) the necessary events of (a) the death of the Messiah and (b) his resurrection on the third day. Jesus' restatement of these divine necessities is most emphatic in the final scene. The risen Jesus categorically links his passion-resurrection predictions with the prophecies in the Hebrew Scriptures (cf. 24:27). The Scriptures are unambiguously designated as the threefold Hebrew canon: Law of Moses, Prophets, and Psalms (24:44). But here the words that Jesus formerly uttered, in accordance with 'everything written' about him,[108] include not only (a) his death and (b) his resurrection on the third day (24:46), but (c) 'that repentance and forgiveness of sins is to be proclaimed in his name to all nations' (24:47).[109]

The difficulty with Jesus' final words is that the third element cannot be recalled as an explicit directive from any of Jesus' earlier pronouncements, let alone from his passion-resurrection predictions. Neither is there an immediately identifiable scriptural support for this addition. Although Jesus' ministry was undertaken primarily among 'the people' (i.e., Israel), its universal scope is anticipated early in the Gospel. Simeon called Jesus 'a light

---

[107] All of these passages include δεῖ. The language of dominical speech and presence in 24:6 and 24:44 is strikingly similar: 'Remember how he told (ἐλάλησεν) you, while he was still (ἔτι ὤν) in Galilee' // 'These are my words that I spoke (ἐλάλησα) to you while I was still (ἔτι ὤν) with you'; so observes Jacques Dupont, 'La portée christologique de l'évangélisation des nations d'après Luc 24,47,' in *Neues Testament und Kirche: Für Rudolf Schnackenburg* (ed. Joachim Gnilka; Freiburg: Herder, 1974), 128.

[108] Note the correspondences between 24:27 and 24:44: 'Then beginning with Moses and all the prophets, he interpreted to them the things about himself (τὰ περὶ ἑαυτοῦ) in all the Scriptures (ἐν πάσαις ταῖς γραφαῖς)' // 'These are my words that I spoke to you while I was still with you—that everything written (πάντα τὰ γεγραμμένα) about me (περὶ ἐμοῦ) in the law of Moses, the prophets, and the psalms must be fulfilled.'

[109] The elements are coordinated by three infinitives: παθεῖν...ἀναστῆναι...κηρυχθῆναι.

for revelation to the Gentiles' (2:30-32). John the Baptist announced that 'all flesh will see the salvation of God' (3:6). In Jesus' inaugural sermon he indicated that his prophetic ministry of deliverance was intended to spill over beyond Israel's borders (4:25-27). Other passages reflect a positive approach toward Gentiles (7:1-10; 10:1-16; 13:28-29; and perhaps 14:16-24). Nevertheless, Luke 24:46-47 contains Jesus' first explicit directive regarding the universal mission. The worldwide reach of salvation is previewed toward the beginning of the Gospel, but not fully enacted until after Jesus' resurrection at the end of the Gospel.

That a declaration about the universal extent of salvation appears at the terminal stage of the Gospel narrative may be accounted for by the fact that Jesus is enlisting the Eleven and company under his messianic assignment. The preaching of repentance and forgiveness of sins, begun by John the Baptist and embodied in Jesus' ministry of deliverance, will be carried forward by Jesus' disciples 'in his name' (i.e., as his representatives) unto all the nations. Although earlier Jesus had not specifically articulated the contours of a worldwide mission, his selection of twelve apostles was part of his preparation for it. The apostolic preaching in Acts consistently includes testimony to Jesus' death and resurrection, followed by the offer of repentance and/or forgiveness of sins (cf. Acts 2:22-39; 3:18-19; 5:30-31; 10:39-43; 13:27-39; 26:17-18). The offer is intended not only for Israel, but for 'everyone who believes' in Jesus, in accordance with the testimony of 'all the prophets' (10:43).[110] Exact scriptural support for the extension of salvation to all nations derives from an Isaianic passage, appropriated at three critical junctures in Luke-Acts. Isaiah 49:6 is used by Simeon (Luke 2:32), echoed by Jesus in the witness itinerary ('to the ends of the earth,' Acts 1:8), and cited by Paul at his first explicit turn to the Gentiles (13:47; cf. 26:23).[111]

Therefore, in Luke 24:46-47 Jesus sets forth a messianic triad, that is to say, the three essential components delineating his scripturally requisite actions and identity as Messiah: death, resurrection, and universal mission. Jesus will continue to fulfil his messianic destiny through chosen, Spirit-empowered witnesses in Acts who will preach 'to the ends of the earth.' The previews of universal salvation toward the beginning of the Gospel do not come to full expression or implementation until the close of the Gospel—after Jesus has been raised from the dead!—and throughout Acts. The words of Paul in Acts 26:23 indicate how crucial the resurrection of Jesus is for the universal mission, for it is Jesus himself, who has died and is 'the

---

[110] Dupont, 'La portée christologique,' 131.

[111] Jacques Dupont, *The Salvation of the Gentiles: Studies in the Acts of the Apostles* (New York: Paulist, 1979), 17-19.

The Resurrection of Jesus and the Hope of Israel (Luke 24) 185

first from the resurrection of the dead,' who 'proclaims light to the people and to the Gentiles.' The *risen* Jesus, working through his witnesses by the power of the Spirit, is fulfilling Simeon's vision of universal salvation.

6.3.3.1.2 Devout People Awaiting God's Salvific Action

The final scene contains characters, settings, and actions that are reminiscent of the opening scenes of the Gospel. The nativity scenes are filled with characters whose piety and obedience are exemplary, and who are waiting anxiously for God to bring salvation to his people. As they see the fulfilment of God's promises approaching on the horizon, they break forth into ecstatic joy and praise to God. These characters are attracted to Jerusalem, and especially to its temple. By the end of the Gospel, the story has come full circle. The Galilean prophet, whose most consequential childhood experience took place in the temple, has been drawn to the city of Jerusalem and to the temple, where his destiny begins to play out in his passion, death, and resurrection. After his departure, his disciples obediently follow his command to await the promise of the Father. They joyously return to Jerusalem and are continually in the temple blessing God.[112] The initial celebrants of God's saving action, Zechariah, Elizabeth, Mary, Simeon and Anna, give way to the resurrection witnesses who have even more reason to be joyful and expectant. This circular pattern evokes a sense that a major portion of God's salvific plan has been accomplished, even though strategic aspects of the divine enterprise await completion.

6.3.3.2 PARALLELISM (LUKE 24:36–53)

The final scene contains a concentration of linkages with Acts, particularly with Acts 1, many of which possess parallels within the Gospel. Therefore, in this section we shall treat one parallel that finds its terminal point only here in Luke 24. Along with the passion-resurrection predictions dotting the middle of the Gospel, there are notations about how the disciples were unable to understand Jesus' words about his death and resurrection (9:45; 18:34). The Emmaus disciples suffered from the same condition of incomprehension, for they could not recognize the risen Jesus who was travelling with them. Only in Jesus' interpretation of the Scriptures 'on the road' and 'in the breaking of the bread' were their eyes 'opened' in recognition. A similar chain of events occurs in the final scene of Luke, but in reverse

---

[112] Only toward the beginning (1:64; 2:28) and at the end of the Gospel (24:53) are there characters who 'bless God.' One must say of Jesus' blessing of the disciples with uplifted hands (24:50–51), that while it may qualify as an element of circularity which completes the action of Zechariah (1:22; cf. Parsons, *Departure*, 74–75), it is nevertheless difficult to see how a *priestly* blessing from Jesus contributes to Luke's Christology.

order. First, Jesus appears to a startled and frightened gathering who mistakes him for a ghost. Jesus invites verification of his physicality through palpation[113] and witnessing his consumption of a meal. Second, Jesus 'opens their minds to understand the Scriptures' (24:45). What had once been closed or 'hidden' from them (παρακεκαλυμμένον, 9:45; κεκρυμμένον, 18:34) was now 'open' to them. What they were formerly unable to perceive or understand (μὴ αἴσθωνται, 9:45; οὐδὲν τούτων συνῆκαν...οὐκ ἐγίνωσκον, 18:34), now they could understand (συνιέναι, 24:45).[114] What is it that they were enabled to understand? The Scriptures, to wit (οὕτως, 24:46–47): that it is written that the Messiah is to suffer, rise again on the third day, and that the message of repentance and forgiveness of sins is to be proclaimed to all nations.

The question arises as to the purpose of this final 'opening of their minds,' since a confession of the reality of Jesus' resurrection was already voiced in 24:34. The central thesis of Dillon's dissertation on Luke 24 is that there is a dialectic between the material evidence (visual or tactile) and the revealed truth (the self-disclosing words uttered by Jesus) of the resurrection. According to Dillon, Luke reintroduces the motif of non-recognition at the final post-resurrection appearance of Jesus in order to sustain this dialectic, and to highlight the pre-eminence and vitality of Jesus' interpretive words over his inert and ineffectual physical displays.[115] Several points speak against this reading.

(1) The third scene does not begin in a contrived manner, as though nothing had occurred previously, so as to continue a dialectical pattern.[116] The fear and doubt experienced by the disciples are due to an immediate cause: when Jesus appears to them they think he is a spirit (24:37).

---

[113] The verb ψηλαφάω ('touch, handle,' BDAG 1097) used in Luke 24:39 is something of a *terminus technicus* meaning 'to verify by touching' (Marguerat, 'Luc-Actes: La résurrection à l'œuvre dans l'histoire,' 198; cf. 'ψηλαφάω,' *EDNT* 499–500) or 'examine closely' ('ψηλαφάω,' MM 697). The same verb occurs in 1 John 1:1, in a context that similarly stresses the (post-resurrection?) physicality of Jesus Christ (1:1–3; cf. 4:2).

[114] For a broad treatment of the motif of misunderstanding, see Brigid Curtin Frein, 'The Literary and Theological Significance of Misunderstanding in the Gospel of Luke,' *Bib* 74 (1993): 328–48. See also, Dennis Hamm, 'Sight to the Blind: Vision as Metaphor in Luke,' *Bib* 67 (1986): 457–77; idem, 'Paul's Blindness and Its Healing: Clues to Symbolic Intent (Acts 9; 22 and 26),' *Bib* 71 (1990): 63–72.

[115] Dillon, *Eye-Witnesses*, 204 and *passim*. Dillon's thesis is challenged mightily by Plevnik, 'Eyewitnesses,' 90–103; and Stephen D. Moore, 'Luke's Economy of Knowledge,' *SBL Seminar Papers, 1989* (SBLSP 28; Atlanta: Scholars Press, 1989), 38–56, esp. 39–45.

[116] *Contra* Dillon, *Eye-Witnesses*, 155.

(2) There is no indication in the text that the physical demonstrations are *in toto* ineffectual. To be sure, after Jesus' initial invitation for the disciples to touch and inspect his body, they can scarcely believe their eyes. And after he shows them his hands and feet, they have mixed feelings of joy and incredulity: 'They were still incredulous, still astounded, for it seemed too good to be true' (24:41 REB). So Jesus provides yet another physical demonstration by eating a piece of broiled fish (24:42–43). The physical demonstrations cannot have been designed to reveal the disciples' *inability* to believe that Jesus had been raised from the dead, but rather to dispel any further doubts they had.

(3) Although the reader is apprised of the fact that Jesus 'opened their minds to understand the Scriptures,' there is no added note that it was only at this precise moment that the disciples recognized and believed that he had risen from the dead.[117] It is another matter to say, as we are, that the disciples still needed to understand fully how Jesus' death and resurrection related to the divine plan of salvation. This leads to a final point.

(4) The physical demonstrations *and* the interpretive words of Jesus have a specific aim: to qualify the Eleven and their companions as witnesses (24:48).[118] If the apostolic circle, whose number will be replenished to twelve in Acts 1:12–26, is to be populated by 'eyewitnesses *and* servants of the word' (Luke 1:2), then its members must see for themselves the reality of Jesus' resurrection *and* hear from his very lips the explanation of the dominical and scriptural prophecies. Only then may they legitimately bear witness to what they have both 'seen *and* heard' (Acts 4:20).[119] As witnesses, they are called to work toward the actualization of Jesus' messianic assignment, i.e., in the advancement of the word into all nations. The prerequisites are that they must have a firm grasp of the reality of Jesus' resurrection *and* its meaning within the context of God's saving purpose, conveyed to them by the Risen One himself.[120] Both of these are achieved during Jesus' final appearance to the Eleven and their associates.

---

[117] Moore ('Luke's Economy of Knowledge,' 43) makes this point in conjunction with the observation that the opening of the Scriptures on the Emmaus road did not solely prompt recognition without Jesus' action of breaking bread.

[118] Plevnik, 'Eyewitnesses,' 100–101.

[119] Cf. Luke 2:20; 7:22; Acts 22:14–15; and further on seeing and hearing: Luke 9:9; 10:24; 23:8; Acts 7:34; 28:26–27.

[120] See Jacques Dupont, 'L'Apôtre comme intermédiaire du salut dans les Actes des Apôtres,' *RTP* 112 (1980): 350–51. In addition, Dupont mentions the divine initiative in designating individuals as witnesses, which in the case of the apostles may be traced particularly in connection with the resurrection (Luke 24:48; Acts 1:8, 22; 10:41–42; 22:15; 26:16).

6.3.3.3 LINKAGE (LUKE 24:36–53)

Within a small compass at the close of Luke, there are numerous links with the beginning of Acts. Since it would be impossible to do justice to all of these linkages, we shall mention each of them and comment briefly on those that are paralleled by material earlier in the Gospel, reserving detailed comments for those that illuminate more directly the significance of Jesus' resurrection. The linkages include: (1) Jesus' post-resurrection appearance(s) to his disciples; (2) Jesus' final instructions about the global extension of the message of salvation; (3) the designation of witnesses who begin their mission in Jerusalem; (4) the promise of the Spirit; and (5) Jesus' departure into heaven.

6.3.3.3.1 Jesus' Post-Resurrection Appearances

In both Luke 24:36–43 and Acts 1:3–4a we read of the appearance of the risen Jesus to his disciples. The appearances serve two related functions: one evidentiary, the other restorative and authorizing. (1) The physical demonstrations are evidentiary. They are comprised of an exhibition of Jesus' corporeality, first by an invitation to examine his body visually and tactually; and second, by his consumption of food before them. Jesus intends to establish that his post-resurrection identity is continuous with his previously observable embodied existence (Luke 24:38). Jesus negates any speculation that he is a 'spirit,' as the disciples at first suppose (24:36).[121] Unlike a spirit, he has flesh and bones.[122] It is unnecessary to posit an anti-gnostic tendency at work here, since there existed within the Greco-Roman world a widespread notion, perpetuated on the authority of Homer, that persons could return from the dead in a spiritual form which is in appearance indistinguishable from their prior mortal frame, but ethereal to the touch.[123] The issue in Luke 24 is not whether Jesus' resurrection was spiritual or corporeal, but whether he was resurrected at all. That Jesus was not reappearing as a spirit, but had risen from the dead, is further supported by his act of eating (24:41–43), since spirits cannot eat.[124]

---

[121] Luke 24:36 D reads φάντασμα.

[122] Ignatius, *Smyrn*. 3.2 reads like a periphrastic citation of Luke 24:39: Λάβετε, ψηλαφήσατέ με καὶ ἴδετε, ὅτι οὐκ εἰμὶ δαιμόνιον ἀσώματον.

[123] Homer, *Il*. 23.104–17; *Od*. 11.219. On the soul as an image of the human person in Homer, see above p. 95 n. 14. Similarly (*contra* Talbert, *Luke and the Gnostics*), see Marguerat ('Luc-Actes: La résurrection à l'œuvre dans l'histoire,' 197), who cites Lucian, *Ver. hist*. 2.12.

[124] *T. Ab*. 4:9: 'all the heavenly spirits are incorporeal, and they neither eat nor drink'; cf. Tob 12:19; *2 En*. 56:2 A. Honeycomb, however, can be a food source for angels (*Jos. Asen*. 16:14), and the textual variant in Luke 24:42 (καὶ ἀπὸ μελισσίου

The evidentiary value of the post-resurrection appearances of Jesus is explicated in Acts. According to Acts 1:3, Jesus 'presented himself alive to them by many convincing proofs (ἐν πολλοῖς τεκμηρίοις).' Τεκμήρια refers to 'evidential proof credible on its own merits,'[125] and reflects the formal Aristotelian definition of a necessary proof over against other more questionable forms of evidence.[126] Dillon has made an abortive attempt to overturn this reading. First, he posits that the 'proper antonym' of πνεῦμα in Luke 24:37, 39 is 'not physical one, material one, palpable one, but *living one!*'—as in, 'he presented himself *alive.*'[127] But clearly, in Luke 24:39 πνεῦμα is being contrasted with a body possessed of hands and feet, flesh and bone. The phraseology in Acts 1:3, moreover, is mirrored in Peter's presentation of the resurrected Tabitha:

Acts 1:3   [Jesus] παρέστησεν ἑαυτὸν ζῶντα
Acts 9:41 [Peter] παρέστησεν αὐτὴν ζῶσαν

Excluding the permanence and incomparable theological significance of Jesus' resurrection, this suggests that there is a commonality with respect to how one would attest to the vitality of either previously dead individual. Second, Dillon views the two succeeding participial clauses, δι' ἡμερῶν τεσσεράκοντα ὀπτανόμενος αὐτοῖς and λέγων τὰ περὶ τῆς βασιλείας τοῦ θεοῦ, as epexegetical to τεκμήρια. Hence, the 'convincing proofs' consist of both his forty-day appearance and his instruction. This explanation is on its face plausible, because τεκμήρια can refer not only to material evidence, but verbal testimony as well, and its precise referent must be sought for within context; but we know that the ancients were perfectly capable of distinguishing between reliable descriptions (πιστὰ τεκμήρια) and visible proofs (ἐμφανῆ τεκμήρια).[128] The first subordinate clause could easily function as an explanatory enlargement of the main clause, because Jesus' presentation of himself included 'appearing' to his disciples.[129] The second clause, however, cannot be epexegetical, for 'speaking about the kingdom of God' is a rather vague proof that someone, even someone who made messianic

---

κηρίου) might stem from a tradition that viewed the resurrected Jesus as angelomorphic, or perhaps is symbolical of the promised land or paradise (Evans, *Luke*, 920–21).

[125] 'τεκμήριον, ου, τό,' *EDNT* 3:340; cf. Thucydides 2.39; Plato, *Leg.* 10.886d.

[126] 'τεκμήριον, τό,' II.3, LSJ 1768; cf. Aristotle, *Rhet.* 1.2.16–18.

[127] Dillon, *Eye-Witnesses*, 198.

[128] Irene J. F. de Jong, 'Πιστὰ τεκμήρια in Soph. *El.* 774,' *Mnemosyne* 5 (1994): 679–81; cf. David L. Mealand, 'The Phrase "Many Proofs" in Acts 1,3 and in Hellenistic Writers,' *ZNW* 80 (1989): 134–35.

[129] Haenchen (*Acts*, 140 n. 5) observes that ὀπτάνομαι (cognate ὀπτασία) means 'appear' or 'show oneself,' but not in the sense of a 'vision'; cf. 1 Kgs 8:8 LXX; Tob 12:19. In the papyri οὐκ ὀπτανόμενος is used of missing persons (Lake and Cadbury, *BC* 4:4).

claims, has been raised from the dead. To say 'we should have to understand the instruction as the decisive τεκμήριον'[130] is to make this clause bear far more weight than it can. The main clause stands well on its own. The aorist verb παρέστησεν is used transitively, as it is elsewhere in Acts (9:39, 41; 23:33), to denote that an object or person is being displayed or produced for examination. In Acts 1:3 it is Jesus who presents 'himself' (ἑαυτόν), and this corresponds with the Gospel account of the risen Jesus bidding his disciples to view and touch his body in order to confirm that 'it is I myself' (ἐγώ εἰμι αὐτός, Luke 24:39).[131] That the evidence was 'visible' is reinforced by Acts 10:40 and 13:31.[132] It is preferable, therefore, to interpret the main clause in Acts 1:3 as a flashback to the physical demonstrations of Luke 24:39–43, followed by two participial clauses that provide additional information about Jesus' appearances and instruction to the apostles.

(2) Correlated to the evidentiary aspect, secondly, the post-resurrection appearances have a restorative and authorizing function. The reinstatement of Peter as a devoted follower of Jesus was already hinted at in the previous scene, when an appearance of the risen Jesus to Simon was announced (Luke 24:34). The last time Jesus addressed Peter, he called him 'Simon, Simon,' and urged him to strengthen his companions after his own faithfulness had been tested (22:31–32). This was spoken immediately after Jesus had promised the Twelve co-regency (22:25–30). Now, in the closing scene of Luke's Gospel, the scattered and varied experiences related to Jesus' resurrection are consolidated as the Risen One appears in the midst of the disciples assembled round the Eleven.[133] The first chapter of Acts clarifies the purpose of this gathering. It is embryonic for the promised restoration of Israel. That Jesus appeared to 'the apostles' or 'the eleven apostles' is highlighted (Acts 1:2, 13, 26). We are told that Jesus appeared to them over the

---

[130] Dillon, *Eye-Witnesses*, 199.

[131] The 'Western non-interpolation' in Luke 24:40, if it be authentic on the authority of $\mathfrak{P}^{75}$, reiterates the demonstrative action: ἔδειξεν αὐτοῖς τὰς χεῖρας καὶ τοὺς πόδας.

[132] *Contra* Dillon (*Eye-Witnesses*, 199), Acts 10:40 (ἔδωκεν αὐτὸν ἐμφανῆ γενέσθαι) emphasizes divine agency, not as to the *mode* of Jesus' appearance, but regarding the *choice* of witnesses to whom he would appear (cf. 10:41). The combination δίδωμι + acc. + inf. has a distinctive Semitic flavour (cf. 2:27; 14:3), but the expression ἐμφανῆ γενέσθαι is thoroughly Hellenistic (e.g., Plato, *Leg.* 914c; Josephus, *Ant.* 15.3.3 §52). It is impossible to assert (as Dillon does) that ἐμφανής means 'revealed,' as opposed to 'visible,' so that the means of revelation is mysteriously contrasted with 'empirical availability.' In fact, the word was used 'esp. of the gods *appearing bodily* among men' ('ἐμφανής, ές,' II.a in LSJ 549).

[133] On the pattern of dispersal and gathering, see Luke Timothy Johnson, 'Luke 24:1-11: The Not-So-Empty Tomb,' *Int* 46 (1992): 58.

course of forty days, which may allude to a New Exodus period of preparation under the prophet like Moses.[134] Yet there is an incongruity in the existence of a group of one hundred twenty disciples (a multiple of twelve) clustered around a nucleus of only eleven apostles. Therefore, Matthias is chosen to occupy the twelfth position among the apostles that had been vacated by Judas (1:12–26). The restoration of the Twelve is intimately related to the post-resurrection appearances of Jesus, even though the actual election takes place afterward. To qualify as a member of the Twelve one had to have been present during Jesus' Galilean ministry, when he first began to foretell his destiny (Luke 24:6–7, 44, 46), all the way up to the point of his ascension into heaven, in order to be a witness to *Jesus' resurrection* (Acts 1:21–22). In this way, Jesus' resurrection is fundamental to a restored and authorized leadership in Israel.

In Luke 24:41–43, Jesus eats 'in front of' his disciples, and this is to be interpreted primarily as a further evidence of his corporeal resurrection.[135] But the linkage of this meal with later references to Jesus' eating 'with' his disciples reveals that its evidentiary function was only one aspect of Jesus' post-resurrection meal (cf. Acts 10:41). The significance of Jesus' act of eating in the presence of his disciples is further nuanced in the first chapter of Acts. In Acts 1:4 we learn that Jesus 'was being salted together with' or 'was eating salt with' (συναλιζόμενος) his apostles. The Greek participle in this verse has had a tangled textual and translational history. The same participle with a long *ā* commonly means 'collect' or 'assemble' in Classical and Hellenistic Greek. The major textual variant (συναυλιζόμενος) refers to 'staying with' or 'spending the night with' someone. Modern English translations reflect these variations.[136] The lexical construal of συναλιζόμενος (short *ă*), meaning 'eating salt with,' has been widely rejected in the past because the verb is not attested in extant Greek literature until the second century A.D.[137] Nevertheless, an increasing number of translators and commentators have adopted this meaning.[138] Several points can be made in support of this translation:

---

[134] Mánek, 'New Exodus in the Books of Luke,' 19.

[135] However, the fact that Jesus ate a piece of broiled fish may hark back to his feeding of the multitude (Luke 9:16); cf. Johnson, *Luke*, 402; Nolland, *Luke*, 3:1214. Green (*Luke*, 855 n. 9) lays stress on the fact that Jesus ate *in front of* his followers, not *with* them, and so downplays any connection with table fellowship.

[136] E.g., ESV, NRSV: 'while staying with them'; REB: 'while he was in their company'; NAB: 'while meeting them'; NASB: 'gathering them together.'

[137] See Bruce Metzger's discussion of the UBS Committee's deliberations (*TCGNT* 242).

[138] Translations: NIV, NJB, NLT; cf. MOFFATT. Commentators: C. K. Barrett, *A Critical and Exegetical Commentary on the Acts of the Apostles* (2 vols.; ICC; Edinburgh:

(a) Text-critically, the variant συναυλιζόμενος bears only meagre attestation, and is in any case a more readable clarification (*lectio facilior*).[139]

(b) If συναλιζόμενος (long $\bar{a}$) were the proper reading, whose usage and sense are well-attested in Classical and Hellenistic Greek, then it is strange that it reads so awkwardly here. The appearance of the word is syntactically clumsy, since it should be in the aorist or perfect tense,[140] and in the passive voice it would more naturally be plural.

(c) συναλιζόμενος (short $\breve{a}$) fits grammatically, but it has been open to two objections: first, that it is exceedingly rare; second, that its meaning does not fit well within its co-text. The first objection turns out to be a possible indication of its originality, because this would explain the puzzlement of later scribes who may have been trying to make sense of or correct what they thought was the more familiar but awkward long $\bar{a}$ form. More importantly, though the verb is not attested until the second century, it is not often enough observed that many of the older versions speak with one voice in favour of the reading 'to eat' (Old Latin, Vulgate, Syriac Peshitta and Harklean, Armenian, Ethiopic, Georgian, Coptic).[141] The second objection is addressed by pointing to Luke 24:36–48 and Acts 10:41. A remark about Jesus eating in Acts 1 fits within the pattern of appearance, presentation of convincing proofs, eating, and final charge.[142]

Against the second objection, we shall further propose that it fits perfectly within its immediate co-text. Among Near Eastern peoples, even into modern times, partaking salt together during a meal symbolized a bond of trust between friends.[143] According to the Law of Moses, all sacrifices were

---

T. & T. Clark, 1994–1998), 1:71–72; Bruce, *Acts of the Apostles*, 101; Haenchen, *Acts*, 141 n. 3; Luke Timothy Johnson, *The Acts of the Apostles* (SP 5; Collegeville, Minn.: Liturgical, 1992), 25; I. Howard Marshall, *The Acts of the Apostles: An Introduction and Commentary* (TNTC; Grand Rapids: Eerdmans, 1980), 58; Rudolf Pesch, *Die Apostelgeschichte* (2 vols.; EKKNT 5. Zürich: Benziger; Neukirchen-Vluyn: Neukirchener, 1986), 1:65–67.

[139] Cadbury's proposal that συναλιζόμενος is an orthographical variant of συναυλιζόμενος is conjectural; Henry J. Cadbury, 'Lexical Notes on Luke-Acts: III. Luke's Interest in Lodging,' *JBL* 45 (1926): 310–17.

[140] Clayton Raymond Bowen, 'The Meaning of συναλιζόμενος in Act 1,4,' *ZNW* 13 (1912): 254–55; Bruce, *Acts of the Apostles*, 101.

[141] Bowen, 'Meaning of συναλιζόμενος,' 248–49; *TCGNT* 242; *EDNT* 3:297. Recently it has been pointed out that Ephrem of Syria, one of our best witnesses to the Old Syriac version of Acts, has 'he was salted' (differing from the Peshitta's 'he ate bread'); see Daniel L. McConaughy, 'An Old Syriac Reading of Acts 1:4 and More Light on Jesus' Last Meal before His Ascension,' *OrChr* 72 (1988): 63–67.

[142] Bowen, 'Meaning of συναλιζόμενος,' 256–59; Johnson, *Acts*, 25. Note the presence of the verb παρήγγειλεν immediately following the eating in Acts 1:4 and 10:42.

[143] Everett Gill, 'Jesus' Salt Covenant with the Eleven,' *RevExp* 36 (1939): 197–98.

The Resurrection of Jesus and the Hope of Israel (Luke 24) 193

to be seasoned with salt as a 'covenant of salt' between the Lord and his people (Num 18:19).[144] Apropos of the co-text of Acts 1 is the comment in 2 Chron 13:5 that the Lord granted kingship over Israel to David and his sons via a 'covenant of salt.' In Acts 1:3 Jesus' appearance is paired with his discoursing about the kingdom of God. The ensuing meal is accompanied by Jesus' command to await the promise of the Father in Jerusalem (1:4–5). The implication is clear to the apostles: this solemn meal confirms the covenant that Jesus had initiated at the passion meal. There Jesus' participation in the divine rule was being conferred upon them, too (Luke 22:29–30). Now, after the paschal meal has reached its fulfilment in the death of Jesus, the resurrected Jesus is again eating with his apostles (cf. 22:15–16), speaking to them about the reign of God. No wonder they ask him, 'Lord, is this the time when you will restore the kingdom to Israel?' (Acts 1:6). Jesus cautions them about being presumptuous concerning the timing of this restoration (1:7), but goes on to predict their future empowerment to carry out a worldwide witness to him (1:8). After he has ascended into heaven, two heavenly figures assure them that he will return just as he left (1:11). Thus, the inauguration of the universal dominion of the Messiah, in which his chosen witnesses will participate, is communicated in the first chapter of Acts through the symbolism of salt shared at table.

6.3.3.3.2 The Universal Reach of the Message of Salvation

We have already mentioned the third element in the messianic triad of Luke 24:47: the proclamation of repentance and forgiveness of sins 'to all nations.' This is repeated in Jesus' prediction that the apostolic witness will extend 'to the ends of the earth' (Acts 1:8).

6.3.3.3.3 Witnesses Appointed Whose Activity Originates in Jerusalem

Another link pertains to Jesus' appointment of witnesses whose activity originates in Jerusalem. Starting with Luke 24:47b–48, the remainder of Luke's narrative pinpoints Jerusalem as the point of origin for Christ's witnesses. In Luke 24:47b–48 the participial phrase ἀρξάμενοι ἀπὸ Ἰερουσαλήμ is associated with the following words (ὑμεῖς μάρτυρες τούτων) and not with the foregoing messianic triad.[145] The participle matches the noun μάρτυρες in gender and number. The origination of Jesus' witnesses in Jeru-

---

[144] This practice continued into the Second Temple period (*Jub.* 21:11; 1 Esd 2:29–30; *T. Levi* 9:14). For a comprehensive study, see James E. Latham, *The Religious Symbolism of Salt* (ThH 64; Paris: Beauchesne, 1982).

[145] NA[27]/UBS[4]; Johnson, *Luke*, 403; *pace* Dupont, 'La portée christologique,' 126–27; Giuseppe Betori, 'Luke 24:47: Jerusalem and the Beginning of the Preaching to the Pagans in the Acts of the Apostles,' in *Luke and Acts* (eds. Gerald O'Collins and Gilberto Marconi; New York and Mahwah, N.J.: Paulist, 1991), 107–8.

salem is borne out by his command for them to remain in Jerusalem (Luke 24:49; Acts 1:4). The itinerary outlined in Acts 1:8 clearly marks Jerusalem as the point of departure, and it will remain the geocentric point for witnessing activity throughout the remainder of the narrative until Paul reaches Rome.[146] Roughly the first third of Acts is set in Jerusalem, from which the testimony to the whole house of Israel is launched centripetally into the entire world. The Jerusalem setting for the earliest apostolic witness is mentioned repeatedly (e.g., Acts 8:25; 10:39; 13:31). After his conversion, Paul is drawn to Jerusalem (9:26–31), and later before a mob in Jerusalem he reports how he was urged by Jesus in a vision while praying in the temple: 'Hurry and get out of Jerusalem quickly, because they will not accept your testimony about me' (22:18). Jesus assures Paul in another visitation, 'Keep up your courage! For just as you have testified for me in Jerusalem, so you must bear witness also in Rome' (23:11). The principal witnesses to Jesus' resurrection, as Jesus foretold, would begin their witnessing activity in Jerusalem.[147]

6.3.3.3.4 The Promise of the Father

The promise of the Father is specifically mentioned in such terms only in Luke 24:49 and Acts 1:4 (cf. Acts 2:33). Some readers may recall that Jesus had earlier spoken of the Holy Spirit as a gift from the Father (Luke 11:13). At the close of Luke the promise is closely associated with the agency of the risen Jesus, for it is sent by him ('I am sending upon you...,' 24:49) and, as 'power from on high,' is bestowed only after he has been exalted to the right hand of God (Acts 2:33). Not until Acts 1:5, however, do we learn that this Spirit-empowerment is the fulfilment of John the Baptist's prophecy (Luke 3:16–17). Only the Servant of the Lord, who has been anointed with the Spirit (4:18; cf. 4:1, 14; cf. Acts 10:38) and who fulfils the divine purpose by being killed at the hands of sinful men, raised up from the dead, and exalted before God, can pour out the executive power of God upon his people. Only he can initiate the restoration of Israel through God's cleansing and dynamic Spirit. And only he can extend the Father's promise to those outside of ethnic Israel (Acts 11:15–16; 15:8). It is he who, by virtue of his resurrection from the dead, has been designated as the agent of divine salvation and fulfiller of all of God's promises to his ancient people, Israel (Acts 3:18–26; 13:23, 32–33), as well as the judge over all humankind (10:42; 17:31).

---

[146] Acts 11:2; 12:25; 15:2; 18:22; 19:21; 20:16, 22; 21:13.

[147] See Marie-Eloise Rosenblatt, *Paul the Accused: His Portrait in the Acts of the Apostles* (Collegeville, Minn.: Liturgical, 1995), 7–10.

6.3.3.3.5 The Ascension of Jesus

The ascension of Jesus is undoubtedly the most discussed linkage between Luke 24 and Acts 1, largely due to lingering textual and historical questions that need not detain us here. Both accounts augment readers' perceptions that Jesus was raised *bodily* from the dead, and is now being raised *bodily* into heaven.[148] Both accounts have a future orientation, though one differs from the other. Luke 24:50–53 highlights the obeisance and obedience of the disciples who joyfully return to Jerusalem and spend their time in the temple, waiting for the promise of the Father. Acts 1:9–11 accents the promise that Jesus will return from heaven. There is a step parallelism, with one set of expectations building upon another, progressing towards the culmination of God's rule over all the earth, already inaugurated in the life, death, and resurrection of Messiah-Jesus.

6.4 Conclusion

The final chapter of Luke's Gospel concludes triumphantly with the resurrection of Jesus. Jesus' resurrection is a crucial event in the fulfilment of God's promises to Israel that were prophesied in the Hebrew Scriptures, heralded in Luke's prologue, and inaugurated in the life and ministry of Jesus. Regarding the nature of Jesus' resurrection, we observed Luke's narration of it as a concrete event in which the crucified and buried body of Jesus was released from the mortality of the grave. The resurrection event itself is not recounted, but the emptiness of the tomb and his appearances to his disciples attest to its reality. While the sudden disappearance of Jesus at the meal with the Emmaus disciples may have given the impression that his appearance was like an angelophany, his physical demonstrations before the Eleven affirm the flesh-and-bone nature of his resurrected body. At the same time, Jesus' resurrection is presented as an exaltation, an entrance into a new sphere of dignity and authority as God's appointed leader over Israel. His ascension into heaven completes this idea.

The salvific character of Jesus' resurrection is evident throughout Luke 24. *Theologically*, Jesus' resurrection is an integral part of the plan of God, which is repeatedly emphasized through references to its necessity and conformity to the Scriptures. *Christologically*, it reveals Jesus as the Son of Man, Messiah, Lord, and the great prophet like Moses. As such, Jesus is Israel's promised leader and liberator. However, the final chapter of Luke does not clarify how Jesus will redeem Israel, apart from the proclamation of repentance and forgiveness of sins that accompanies his death and resur-

---

[148] Particularly in Acts 1:9–11 it is stressed that the disciples *see* him being elevated into heaven; see Talbert, *Luke and the Gnostics*, 29–30.

rection in the messianic triad. *Ecclesiologically*, the Jewish people are the initial focus of God's salvation promises, since Jesus' coming aroused hopes that he would redeem Israel. The death of Jesus dashed those hopes, but his resurrection revives them. The witness to Jesus' resurrection will begin at the epicentre of the ancient Jewish faith, Jerusalem. However, it will also be proclaimed to all nations. The Eleven will participate in the restoration and expansion of God's people, and the promise of the Spirit will play a role in the accomplishment of their mission; but readers will have to proceed to Luke's second volume to see how this will all take place. *Eschatologically*, Jesus' resurrection bears the marks of a glorious, apocalyptic event, complete with an opened tomb, the appearance of angels, a reference to his identity as the Son of Man, and his claim that he has 'entered into his glory.' The question of when and how this could effect the eschatological renewal of Israel within God's kingdom is left unexplained. In Acts 1:6 the disciples question Jesus on this very point. The major concern in Luke 24 and in Acts 1 is the worldwide mission of his disciples. With Jesus' resurrection from the dead and ascension into heaven, coupled with the commissioning of Spirit-empowered witnesses to carry the message of repentance and forgiveness of sins throughout the world, one may surmise that both the Jewish people and all humankind are being called to prepare for the definitive salvation and judgment from God that is going to come upon the world.

Chapter 7

Peter's Resurrection Speeches (Acts 2–3)

In Chapter 6 we looked at the pivotal function of resurrection in Luke's plot. Jesus' resurrection and concomitant ascent into heaven form the dénouement for Luke's first volume, and the point of departure for his second. In Chapter 9 we will explore how Jesus' resurrection continues to be of key significance as Luke brings his two-volume work to a close. Thus, Chapters 6 and 9 comprise an *inclusio* for our discussion. Two intervening chapters (7 and 8) will examine the proclamation of Jesus' resurrection in the programmatic speeches by Peter and Paul respectively. We shall preface this part of our study with a few general remarks about our approach to the speeches in Acts.

7.1 The Speeches in Acts and the Resurrection of Jesus

7.1.1 The Resurrection of Jesus: A Unifying Element in the Speeches

Not only does the resurrection of Jesus function pivotally in the plot of Luke-Acts, but it is the theological focus of the message of salvation in the speeches in Acts. This is as it should be, in accordance with Jesus' scriptural (p)review of God's plan that the Messiah must suffer, be raised from the dead, and that repentance for the forgiveness of sins be preached to all nations (Luke 24:46–47). The first chapter of Acts, moreover, sets the stage for the global witness to the risen Jesus. We may confidently label the two great programmatic speeches by Peter and Paul (Acts 2:14–40 and 13:16–41) as 'resurrection speeches.' Jesus' resurrection is a recurring feature in most of the other speeches by the two main characters in Acts. Peter's temple speech (Acts 3:12–26) is bounded by references to Jesus as glorified and risen; and in the ongoing conflict between the temple authorities and the apostles in chapters 4–5 the resurrection of Jesus is repeatedly affirmed by the apostles (4:1–2, 10–11, 33; 5:20, 30–32). The resurrection of Jesus is not mentioned in Stephen's speech (7:1–53), but its focus on Israel's history of rejecting the prophets, including Jesus, culminates in Stephen's vision of the risen Son of Man (7:56). Peter's speech at the house of Cornelius issues in another landmark outpouring of the Spirit precisely while Peter is recounting Jesus' resurrection and its implications (10:34–43; cp. 10:40–43 with 10:44). As for the speeches following Paul's Pisidian Antioch speech, Paul and Barnabas's brief speech at Lystra does not mention Jesus' resurrection (14:15–17). However, it is not evangelistic preaching so much as apologetic for Jewish monotheism. It illustrates the preparatory instruction foundational for the proper understanding of the gospel and its attendant works of power.[1] The transition from monotheistic apologetic to Christian proclamation appears in the Areopagite speech (Acts 17:22–31), which climaxes with Paul's declaration that Jesus is God's appointed judge over the world by virtue of his resurrection. Paul's defence speeches in Acts 22–26 continue to underscore Jesus' resurrection, as we shall see in Chapter 9.

The repeated element of Jesus' resurrection serves to unify the message of the speeches in Acts. Of course, this element recurs with a cluster of others that make up the christological kerygma and the offer of salvation. This repetition is even more striking if Luke is deploying speeches in accordance with Polybius's dictum that 'the whole genus of orations...may be regarded as summaries of events and as the unifying element in historical writing' (*Histories* 12.25a–b).[2] We are not concerned with the perennial debate over whether the repeated pattern of preaching in the speeches is reflective of the primitive kerygma or simply a Lukan schema. What is important is that the authorial audience is undoubtedly given the impression that the message repeated in the speeches is the apostolic kerygma, and that one of its primary unifying components is the resurrection of Jesus, to which the apostles are bearing witness.[3]

7.1.2 The Resurrection of Jesus and Particular Narrative Settings

The principal contribution of narrative criticism to the analysis of the speeches in Acts is its emphasis upon interpreting them within their narrative settings.[4] Collectively the speeches reinforce Luke's theological interpretation of history, but this cumulative effect does not cancel out the individual role each speech plays within the Lukan narrative. 'The speeches are also complementary,' writes Tannehill, 'for they supplement each other,

---

[1] Cf. G. Walter Hansen, 'The Preaching and Defence of Paul,' in *Witness to the Gospel: The Theology of Acts* (eds. I. Howard Marshall and David Peterson; Grand Rapids: Eerdmans, 1998), 314–15. The absence of any reference to resurrection in the Miletus speech (Acts 20:18–35) is understandable because it is not a mission speech.

[2] Cf. Marion L. Soards, 'The Speeches in Acts in Relation to Other Pertinent Ancient Literature,' *ETL* 70 (1994): 90; Witherington, *Acts*, 33.

[3] For a detailed study of Luke's complement of repeated elements in the speeches, see Marion L. Soards, *The Speeches in Acts: Their Content, Context, and Concerns* (Louisville, Ky.: Westminster John Knox, 1994).

[4] Robert C. Tannehill, 'The Functions of Peter's Mission Speeches in the Narrative of Acts,' *NTS* 37 (1991): 400–14.

one expanding a particular theme and providing supporting detail, another expanding a different theme.'[5] Different speeches also present the same theme from different angles within various narrative settings. This conforms to standard historiographical practice. Ancient historians would do well to craft speeches that were literarily appropriate to their surrounding narrative settings, as well as historically appropriate to the speech-events they represent.[6] So amidst the repetition in Acts, each speech adds nuance and particularity to the panoramic vision of God's saving action in history that has come to a mighty watershed in the death and resurrection of Jesus.

The particularities of each speech's presentation of Jesus' resurrection are modulated by varying literary and historical factors. The speaker, audience, and occasion contribute to each speech's unique message and function. The subtleties of a given speech are also due to its function as a singular event within the development of the plot.[7] With regard to Luke's description of Jesus' resurrection in the speeches we may observe at least three kinds of differences. First, there is the use or non-use of Scripture. When the resurrection of Jesus is proclaimed to ethnic Jews, such as those in Jerusalem or Pisidian Antioch, one finds Jewish forms of scriptural citation and interpretation. In contrast, there is only a hint of scriptural exegesis in Peter's speech at the house of Cornelius, the Gentile God-fearer (cf. 10:41, 43); and in Paul's speech before the Athenians at the Areopagus, scriptural argumentation is replaced by philosophical discourse more accessible to Greek listeners. Second, there are differences in language. Especially in Peter's speeches in Jerusalem we find specialized expressions and titles applied to the risen Jesus, such as παῖς θεοῦ (3:13, 26) or ἀρχηγός (3:15; 5:31). Such archaisms appear less frequently as the mission extends outward from Jerusalem.[8] A third set of variations includes differences in emphasis. (a) Peter's Pentecost and temple speeches, for example, as well as Paul's synagogue speech at Pisidian Antioch, accentuate the role of the risen Jesus as the leader of Israel at the climax of the nation's history, while speeches before Gentile audiences (e.g., at Cornelius's household or the

---

[5] Tannehill, 'Functions of Peter's Mission Speeches,' 401.

[6] On the literary and historical appropriateness of ancient speeches, see Conrad Gempf, 'Public Speaking and Published Accounts,' in *The Book of Acts in Its Ancient Literary Setting* (eds. Bruce W. Winter and Andrew D. Clarke; AICS 1; Grand Rapids: Eerdmans; Carlisle: Paternoster, 1993), 259–303.

[7] For a narrative-critical analysis of speeches as actions within the plot of Acts, see Tannehill, 'Functions of Peter's Mission Speeches,' 400–14.

[8] On archaizing in Greco-Roman historiography and in the speeches in Acts, see Soards, 'Speeches in Acts,' 70–71; Eckhard Plümacher, *Lukas als hellenistischer Schriftsteller: Studien zur Apostelgeschichte* (SUNT 9; Göttingen: Vandenhoeck & Ruprecht, 1972), 72–78.

Areopagus) stress Jesus' universal lordship within world history and his appointment as judge over all humankind (10:36, 42; 17:31; cf. 24:25). It is worth mentioning that we observed this same distinction in intercanonical Jewish texts. Resurrection passages directed toward Jewish listeners tend to possess the rich theological complex (resurrection, new creation, covenant renewal, exaltation), whereas those directed toward Gentiles typically focus on the rewards and punishments of final judgment. (b) Luke shows that Paul recognizes the privileged nature of the Twelve's witness to Jesus' resurrection alongside his own exceptional commission as a witness (13:31). (c) While the offer of repentance for forgiveness of sins is a consistent follow-up to the death and resurrection of Jesus, it is expressed in ways that suit particular situations or speakers. For example, Peter speaks to the crowd in Solomon's Portico about their sins being 'wiped out' (3:19) or about Jesus 'turning each of you from your wicked ways' (3:26), while Paul's words sound like the justification language found in his NT letters (13:38–39). These differences, and others, bring verisimilitude and depth to Luke's resurrection theology. They suggest that our theological understanding of Jesus' resurrection must be attuned to the particularities of individual speeches as well as the overall portrait painted by all of the speeches.

7.2 Peter's Speech at Pentecost (Acts 2:14–36)

7.2.1 The Speech in Its Narrative Setting

Peter's Pentecost speech is arguably the 'keynote address' of Acts, 'a summary statement of the theological viewpoint of the author from which the subsequent unfolding of the book is to be understood.'[9] The scene and speech are also linked in a number of ways with the preceding scenes in Acts 1. First, Pentecost is the day of fulfilment, foretold by Jesus, when the promised Holy Spirit would be poured out (cp. 2:1 with 1:5, 8; Luke 24:49).[10] Second, the score and one hundred believers who were 'together…in the same place' on the occasion of Matthias's election to apostolic office (Acts 1:14–15) are still 'together in the same place' at Pentecost (2:1). Third, Peter stood up among those in the upper room to conduct the election of a replacement for Judas, so that someone could be 'added to the eleven apostles' (1:26; cf. 1:13) and become a witness with

---

[9] Richard F. Zehnle, *Peter's Pentecost Discourse: Tradition and Lukan Reinterpretation in Peter's Speeches in Acts 2 and 3* (SBLMS 15; Nashville: Abingdon, 1971), 17.

[10] This thought is expressed well in the KJV of 2:1: 'And when the day of Pentecost was fully come.'

them to the resurrection of Jesus (1:22). At Pentecost, Peter 'stood up with the Eleven' (2:14; cf. τοὺς λοιποὺς ἀποστόλους, 2:37), and for the first time spoke on behalf of the apostles as a witness to Jesus' resurrection (2:32).

The Pentecost speech is linked to its immediate narrative setting. First, it is directed to 'all the residents of Jerusalem,' (2:14), that is to say, Jews from every nation under heaven who were dwelling in Jerusalem (2:5). Second, the speech begins with a rebuttal of the charge that the multi-lingual phenomenon is the effect of intoxication (2:15). Rather, Peter asserts, it is the realization of Joel's prophecy that in the last days God would pour out his Spirit on all flesh (2:16–20). Third, the next link with the narrative setting appears in 2:33 when Peter identifies the exalted Jesus as the efficient cause of 'that which you see and hear.'

Because Peter's quotation from Joel pertains to the outpouring of the Spirit, the bulk of the argumentative portion of the speech (2:22–36) looks at first glance like a change in subject matter. The focus of the speech shifts dramatically to a discussion of Jesus' resurrection. The 'shift in subject matter' is not unexpected, however. This first public announcement of Jesus' resurrection—complete with scriptural argumentation, indictment of Jesus' murderers, and call for repentance—is appropriate to the narrative setting.[11] It also meets a narrative need, since readers have anticipated a more thorough unfolding of the scriptural case for the Messiah's death and resurrection than was merely encapsulated in Luke 24:27, 44–47. The shift, in fact, reveals the internal consistency of the speech. Peter's focus on Jesus of Nazareth turns out to be a clarification of the identity of the κύριος whom anyone may call upon and be saved (Acts 2:21).[12]

7.2.2 The Structure of the Speech

Peter's Pentecost speech extends from 2:14b–40. The response to the speech and Peter's instructions (2:38–40) are included because they are integral to the speech-event. The speech is carefully wrought with three structural features.

(1) There are double (or triple) vocatives, threaded by the word ἄνδρες, that head the three major sections of the speech (2:14, 22, 29).[13] This form of address builds rapport between Peter and his (i.e., the intradiegetic)

---

[11] Tannehill, 'Functions of Peter's Mission Speeches,' 402.

[12] Donald Juel, 'Social Dimensions of Exegesis: The Use of Psalm 16 in Acts 2,' *CBQ* 43 (1981): 544–45.

[13] The use of ἄνδρες with a national designation is Hellenistic (not Jewish) in origin, as it does not appear in Jewish literature, save in Josephus; see C. F. Evans, '"Speeches" in Acts,' in *Mélanges Bibliques en homage au R. P. Béda Rigaux* (eds. Albert Descamps and R. P. André de Halleux; Gembloux: Duculot, 1970), 291–92.

audience.[14] Peter begins by limiting his address to Jews who have been dwelling in Jerusalem, and who may be legitimately held responsible for the death of Jesus.[15] As the speech progresses to its conclusion, however, it is clear that the recent events that have occurred in Jerusalem have universal ramifications for 'the whole house of Israel' scattered throughout the *oikoumenē* (cp. 2:36 with 2:9–11) and even for Gentiles ('all who are afar off,' 2:39).

(2) The speech is structured around three scriptural quotations: Joel 3:1–5 in Acts 2:17–21; Ps 15:8–11 LXX in 2:25–28; and Ps 109:1 LXX in 2:34–35. The passages are interconnected via verbal analogy (Hillel's *gĕzērâh šāwâh*).[16] All three Scriptures have the hookword κύριος. The latter two are linked by the phrase ἐκ δεξιῶν μου. The vocatives and Scripture citations function together to signal divisions within the speech. Cadbury points out that in Acts the end of a quotation may be marked by the introduction of a new vocative (cf. 7:51; 13:25; 26:19), and such is the case in 2:22 and 2:29.[17] The imperatival address to 'the whole house of Israel' may function similarly to close the quotation from Ps 109:1 (2:36).

(3) Scholars have overlooked the fact that the final section of the argumentative portion of the speech contains three conclusive statements marked by the inferential particle οὖν (2:30, 33, 36). Each of these statements draws conclusions about the fact that Jesus has been raised from the dead.

Our comments will concentrate on the two major argumentative sections of the speech in 2:22–28 and 2:29–36 that focus upon the resurrection of Jesus.

7.2.3 The Eschatological Breakthrough of Jesus' Resurrection (Acts 2:22–28)

7.2.3.1 THE CHRISTOLOGICAL KERYGMA (2:22–24)

After disposing of the accusation that the Spirit-filled disciples are drunk with wine, citing the Joel passage for support, Peter launches into a discussion of the true source of the Pentecost phenomena. While God is the grammatical subject of 2:22–24, Jesus occupies the focal point of the discussion, as can be seen by the emphatic placement of Ἰησοῦν τὸν

---

[14] Cf. Zehnle (*Peter's Pentecost Speech*, 26–27) for the rapport aspect.

[15] Tannehill ('Functions of Peter's Mission Speeches,' 403) rightly observes: 'Peter's accusation is appropriate neither to humanity in general nor to Jews in general.'

[16] Richard N. Longenecker, 'Acts,' *ExpBC* 9:75.

[17] Henry J. Cadbury, 'Note XXXII. The Speeches in Acts,' *BC* 5:426.

Ναζωραῖον in 2:22, as well as the resumptive τοῦτον at the beginning of 2:23, and ὅν in 2:24. The course of Jesus' divinely-appointed ministry and death is rapidly but pregnantly described. The mention of God's performance of 'miracles and wonders and signs' through Jesus (2:22) interlaces with the mention of 'wonders' and 'signs' in the Joel citation (2:19), but the public nature of the mighty works (ἐν μέσῳ ὑμῶν καθὼς αὐτοὶ οἴδατε) is reminiscent of the description of the prophet like Moses in Deut 34:10–12.[18] This eschatological figure is handed over by his own people into the hands of lawless men to be crucified, yet in accordance with the determined plan and foreknowledge of God (Acts 2:23). The divine answer to the rejection of Jesus is stated in 2:24, and will occupy the greater part of the remainder of the speech. The contrast between the human rejection of Jesus (crucifixion) and the divine response (resurrection or exaltation) is repeated in Peter's conclusion (2:36).[19] The simple relative clause ὃν ὁ θεὸς ἀνέστησεν (not ὃν ὁ θεὸς ἀνέστησεν ἐκ νεκρῶν) is qualified by a curious participial clause, followed by a comparative (or causative) clause (2:24) and a scriptural quotation from 'David' (2:25–28).

7.2.3.2 'HAVING BROUGHT THE BIRTH PANGS OF DEATH TO AN END' (2:24)

The participial clause λύσας τὰς ὠδῖνας τοῦ θανάτου has long puzzled scholars. Commentators choose from two major interpretations, or take an agnostic or confused position on the matter.[20] The first interpretation diachronically traces the words ὠδῖνες θανάτου to three LXX passages for which the corresponding Hebrew text reads 'cords of death.'[21] The second interpretation views the whole clause as an idiomatic reference to the cessation of death's birth pangs. Representative of the first interpretation is the study by Robert Bratcher.[22] The prime exponent of the second is Frederick Field.[23] The second interpretation is to be preferred, but has not been suf-

---

[18] This squares with the Emmaus pair's recital (Luke 24:19).

[19] The contrast scheme reappears in Acts 3:13–15; 4:10–11; 5:30–31; 10:39–40; 13:27–30.

[20] See, for example, Lake and Cadbury (*BC* 4:23) for a positively indecisive discussion. Haenchen (*Acts*, 180), on one hand, refers to the LXX mistranslation of the Hebrew radical (see our next footnote) and vaguely comments on 'deathpangs' as 'a mysterious expression for the power of death' (followed by Pesch, *Apg.* 1:121–22). On the other hand, he wants to preserve the rope imagery of the Hebrew text by stating that 'λύσας relates to death's power to bind man fast' (181).

[21] The Hebrew radical חבל may be vocalized to mean 'cord' (חֶבֶל) or 'pang, pain' (חֵבֶל); cf. BDB 286.

[22] Robert G. Bratcher, 'Having Loosed the Pangs of Death,' *BT* 10 (1959): 18–20.

[23] Frederick Field, *Notes on the Translation of the New Testament* (Cambridge: Cambridge University Press, 1899; repr. Peabody, Mass.: Hendrickson, 1994), 112. We

ficiently defended. Our contention is that the first view is not likely to have been 'heard' by the authorial audience. We shall demonstrate that the second interpretation conforms to Greek idiom, makes sense within Second Temple Jewish thought about the final resurrection, and is upheld among several Greek Fathers in the history of biblical interpretation.

What has complicated the interpretation of this clause is an appeal to the Hebrew text underlying three LXX passages in which the phrase ὠδῖνες θανάτου appears (2 Kgdms 22:6; Pss 17:5; 114:3 LXX; cf. ὠδῖνες ᾅδου, Ps 17:6 LXX). Bratcher, despite his admission that the word ὠδίν is consistently used in the LXX to mean 'birth pangs,'[24] insists upon translating the phrase in line with its Hebrew *Vorlage*: 'the bonds of death.' He argues that the metaphor of death's birth pangs encompassing or entangling its victim is forced, and does not fit the Hebrew parallelism in any of the passages.[25] However, in the Hebrew text of Ps 116:4 (114:3 LXX), the encirclement of 'the cords of death' is paired with seizure by 'the pangs of Sheol' (שְׁאוֹל מְצָרֵי).[26] The psalmist, whether read from the MT or the LXX, is evidently not averse to mixing metaphors, as Bratcher would have us think.[27] The argument from Hebrew parallelism fares no better, since the translators of the Septuagint muddle Hebrew poetry often enough. Bratcher's argument amounts to pleading that the expression in the Septuagint *ought to* convey the same meaning as the Hebrew phrase it translates. It is quite another thing to ask how ancient Greeks would have comprehended the passages in the LXX. One example will suffice to show that the birth metaphor would have been unavoidable for them. Origen comments on our phrase in Ps 17:5 LXX: Ὠδῖνες θανάτου, ἤτοι αἱ τὸν θάνατον τίκτουσαι, ἢ αἱ συνειλημμέναι

---

reject the view that ὠδῖνες refers here to pain in general, resulting in a translation such as 'having freed him from the agony of death'; cf. Gerhard Schneider, *Die Apostelgeschichte* (2 vols.; HTKNT 5; Freiburg: Herder, 1980–1982), 1:272 n. 77; Strauss, *Davidic Messiah*, 136–37; and numerous English translations (JB, NAB, NASB, NET, NIV, NLT; cf. NRSV, TEV, CEV). This view ungrammatically inserts 'him' (i.e., Jesus) in place of ὠδῖνες θανάτου as the direct object of λύσας. More accurate translations include KJV and ESV.

[24] Even in the three instances where the word is used in a general sense of pain or anguish (Exod 15:14; Deut 2:25; Job 21:17), Bratcher acknowledges, 'the allusion to the sudden and cruel seizure of labor pains is easy to detect' ('Pangs of Death,' 18).

[25] Bratcher, 'Pangs of Death,' 18.

[26] מֵצַר ('straits, distress,' BDB 865) is derived from the verb צרר which is used to denote binding, tying up, restricting, or making narrow. The Hiphil participle is used in Jer 48:41 and 49:22 to refer to a woman in labour (*TWOT* 2:779).

[27] On the mixed metaphors in these passages, see 'θάνατος,' 1.b.β, BDAG 443; Darrell L. Bock, *Proclamation from Prophecy and Pattern: Lucan Old Testament Christology* (JSNTSup 12; Sheffield: Sheffield Academic Press, 1987), 171–72.

ἐκ τοῦ θανάτου.²⁸ Even if Bratcher's analysis were sound, his application of it to Acts 2:24 still proceeds from several questionable assumptions. First, he assumes that in 2:24 there is an allusion to one of the three LXX passages. We do not want to discount entirely the possibility, since there may already be a Davidic undertone at work (cf. 2:25), especially if 2 Kgdms 22:6 or Ps 17:5 LXX is being echoed. Nevertheless, the volume of this allusion is not particularly strong. The expression could just as easily evoke a prevalent eschatological concept than a specific scriptural text.²⁹ Second, he assumes that Luke's readers will not perceive the phrase as a natural Greek expression. We will repudiate this notion below. Third, he assumes that they will interpret it not only as a Septuagintism, but in conformity with the meaning of the Hebrew text. It is doubtful that the authorial audience would be expected to listen to Acts while dutifully comparing scrolls of the Septuagint with the Hebrew Bible.

The first step toward clarifying the meaning of Luke's difficult participial clause is to recognize it as a specimen of perfectly idiomatic Greek. Interpreters have struggled with the participle λύσας. The verb λύω is customarily understood here, in accordance with its entry in elementary Greek textbooks, to mean 'to loose.'³⁰ But forms of λύω with the direct object ὠδίν (usually plural, ὠδῖνας) form an idiomatic expression referring to the cessation of labour pains. This is not merely supported by the lone Septuagintal occurrence in Job 39:2 (ὠδῖνας δὲ αὐτῶν ἔλυσας), which aptly renders a Hebrew phrase denoting the moment of birth (עֵת לְדְתָּנָה).³¹ In fact, the idiom was in use as early as the Classical period,³² throughout the Hellenistic period,³³ and later among the Greek Fathers.³⁴ There is every

---

²⁸ Origen, *Sel. Ps.* 17 (PG 12.1225.31–32).

²⁹ Strauss (*Davidic Messiah*, 136 n. 6) asserts that Luke incorporated this unusual phrase due to an awareness of its LXX context, and reasons: 'If he had simply found it in his source (and was unaware of its Old Testament significance), he would probably have altered it.' Whether or not there is 'a clear if unconscious echo of the Septuagint' (Johnson, *Acts*, 51) is uncertain; but the notion that, if not, Luke would have 'altered it' can only be true on the assumption that Luke would have found the expression foreign to Greek ears. That, as we shall see, is not likely to be the case.

³⁰ Bratcher, 'Pangs of Death,' 19; Haenchen, *Acts*, 181. Barrett (*Acts*, 1:143) calls '*loosing the pangs of death*, a strange expression (since pangs are not normally said to be loosed)'; and Marshall (*Acts*, 75) writes: 'The verb *loosed* goes oddly with this object.'

³¹ Cf. William K. L. Clarke, 'The Use of the Septuagint in Acts,' *BC* 2:97. Field's conclusion about the meaning of the idiom is correct, but his assertion that it could only have originated from the LXX is mistaken (*Notes on the Translation of the NT*, 112).

³² E.g., Plato, *Symp.* 206e; cf. *TDNT* 9:667–68.

³³ See the references s.v. 'λύω' (4), BDAG 607.

³⁴ See 'λύω' (B.3.e.), *PGL* 817 and 'ὠδίν' (1.b.), *PGL* 1555.

reason to believe that the authorial audience of Acts would have immediately grasped the birth imagery inherent in the idiom. This precludes explanations which posit a Semitic source for the turn of phrase.[35] This also undercuts any pressing need to look only to the LXX for an understanding of the expression's meaning.

That the expression would not have violated an ancient Greek's grammatical sensibilities does not yet explain why it is the birth pangs *of death* that have been brought to an end. 'Birth pangs' are identified as the cause of death in many funerary inscriptions, but this is hardly relevant.[36] More appropriately, the halting of birth pangs was associated with Jewish ideas concerning resurrection. The first explicit resurrection text in the Hebrew Bible pictures the earth giving birth to the dead (Isa 26:19).[37] The next verse (26:20) mentions 'chambers' where, according to Jewish apocalyptists and Christians, the righteous dead remained in anticipation of the resurrection.[38] A typical feature in Judeo-Christian resurrection texts is the concept that the earth, Sheol/Hades, or Death will give back the dead who have been deposited in them.[39] Although the legal metaphor of returning something that has been entrusted is most prominent, the birth metaphor—perhaps derived from Isa 26:19—also appears. In *4 Ezra* the souls of the righteous cry out from their chambers for release and final reward, and Ezra the seer is likewise inquisitive about the time of their resurrection (4:33–39). The angelic guide responds (4:40–42):

> He answered me and said, 'Go and ask a woman who is with child if, when her nine months have been completed, her womb can keep the child within her any longer.'
>
> 'No, my lord,' I said, 'it cannot.'
>
> He said to me, 'In Hades the chambers of the souls are like the womb. For just as a woman who is in travail makes haste to escape the pangs of birth, so also do

---

[35] *Contra* Charles C. Torrey, *The Composition and Date of Acts* (HTS 1; Cambridge, Mass.: Harvard University Press, 1916), 28–29; Max Wilcox, *The Semitisms of Acts* (Oxford: Clarendon, 1965), 46–48. Torrey (28) could not have been more wrong when he wrote: 'No writer composing Greek would ever have chosen this unsuitable word [λύσας], and there is nothing in the Old Testament that could have led him to employ it.'

[36] Cf. 'ὠδίν,' MM 701 and *TDNT* 9:668.

[37] The Hiphil form of נָפַל ('to fall') applies to a newborn being 'dropped' out of the womb (BDB 658).

[38] Isa 26:20 and Ezek 37:12 are conflated in *1 Clem.* 50:4.

[39] *1 En.* 51:1; *4 Ezra* 7:32; Rev 20:13; *L.A.B.* 3:10; 33:3; *2 Bar.* 21:23; 42:8; 50:2; *Apoc. Pet.* 4:3–4, 10–12; apocryphal quotation in Tertullian, *Res.* 32.1; *Midr. Ps.* 1:20; *Cant. Rab.* 2:1–2; *Pirqe R. El.* 34; *Pesiq. Rab.* 21:4; see Richard Bauckham, 'Resurrection as Giving Back the Dead,' in *The Fate of the Dead: Studies on the Jewish and Christian Apocalypses* (NovTSup 93; Leiden: Brill, 1998), 271–75.

the places hasten to give back those things that were committed to them from the beginning.'[40]

Birth imagery is appropriate in light of the fact that Israel's return from exile could be expressed as a rebirth.[41] In Chapter 3 we encountered the collocation of resurrection with the restoration of Israel viewed in terms of a woman receiving her dead sons back (esp. 2 Macc 7:22–23). In the NT birth pangs are associated with 'the beginning of sorrows' (Matt 24:8; cf. 1 Thess 5:3; Rev 12:2) that will culminate in the emergence of a new creation (Rom 8:22). In Matt 19:28 the establishment of God's kingdom, involving Israel's restored twelve tribes, occurs at the 'rebirth' (παλιγγενεσία). Thus, birth imagery is apropos of eschatological scenarios and in connection with resurrection.

The use of the distinctive expression in Acts 2:24 resonates within this eschatological context. The eschatological prophet like Moses, Jesus of Nazareth, is unjustly killed; but God raises him up, stopping the birth pangs of death, and bringing death's pregnancy to term, so that death can no longer hold him.[42] This is an eschatological breakthrough within God's plan to bring salvation to Israel and the world. Jesus' resurrection initiates and adumbrates the final resurrection of the dead in which all of the righteous will experience God's ultimate salvation.

The history of the interpretation of this passage among the Greek Fathers is instructive. Ancient interpreters, like some of their modern counterparts, observe in Luke's words a christological statement about Jesus as the first to take part in the eschatological resurrection of the dead. Luke's phrasing resembles the titles Paul ascribes to the resurrected Jesus: 'first fruits (or "firstling") of those who have fallen asleep' (1 Cor 15:20; cf. 15:23) and 'firstborn from the dead' (Col 1:18; cf. Rev 1:5). Commenting on Acts 2:24, Barrett sees a linkage between Jesus' resurrection and the resurrection of others (notwithstanding his rejection of Field's view), but states that the point is developed by Paul rather than Luke.[43] It is worth noting, however, that a Lukan-Pauline nexus has been observed at all on this point. John Chrysostom clearly perceives the birth metaphor in Luke's wording (*Hom.*

---

[40] The grave is again likened to the womb in *b. Sanh.* 92a; cf. Bauckham, 'Giving Back the Dead,' 277–78.

[41] Cf. Isa 66:7–11. In Hos 13:13 the demise of Ephraim is characterized as a stillbirth, followed by the famous words of 13:14 (quoted by Paul in 1 Cor 15:54–55). The restoration/resurrection of Israel is described in Ezek 37:6, 8 in a fashion suggestive of the formation of a foetus in the womb (cf. Job 10:11; Ps 139:13; Eccl 11:5).

[42] καθότι οὐκ ἦν δυνατὸν κρατεῖσθαι αὐτὸν ὑπ' αὐτοῦ may be causal ('because...') or quite possibly comparative ('inasmuch as...' or 'according as...').

[43] Barrett, *Acts*, 1:143.

Act. 6 [PG 60.57.23–30]),⁴⁴ though only elsewhere relates the halting of death pangs in Christ's case to the resurrection of others (*Hom. 1 Cor.* 24 [PG 61.204.17]). Gregory of Nyssa strings Pauline christological appellations together with our Lukan clause: Ἀπαρχὴ τῶν κεκοιμημένων ἐγένετο καὶ Πρωτότοκος ἐκ τῶν νεκρῶν Λύσας τὰς ὠδῖνας τοῦ θανάτου (*Illud tunc et ipse filius* [PG 44.1313.39–41]).⁴⁵ Theodoret freely combines Pauline and Lukan designations for the resurrected Christ, but in one passage brings in more of the Lukan language. He introduces first a composite quotation from Acts—Τὸν δὲ ἀρχηγὸν τῆς ζωῆς ἀπεκτείνατε, ὃν ὁ θεὸς ἤγειρεν ἐκ νεκρῶν, λύσας τοῦ θανάτου τὰς ὠδῖνας—and then the Pauline titles πρωτότοκος πάσης κτίσεως and πρωτότοκος ἐκ τῶν νεκρῶν (*Comment. Dan.* 9 [PG 81.1476.37–42]).⁴⁶

It is remarkable that the Lukan and Pauline phraseology can be so effortlessly paralleled. However, the christological and soteriological inferences could be drawn from Acts 2:24 solely in relation to Luke's language elsewhere regarding the risen Jesus, without imposing Paul's thinking or language on him. Jesus is ἀρχηγὸς τῆς ζωῆς (3:15; cf. 5:31), the one in whom the resurrection from the dead is proclaimed for others (4:2), the one to whom God said (in reference to his resurrection), 'You are my son, today I have begotten you' (13:33), and πρῶτος ἐξ ἀναστάσεως νεκρῶν (26:23). Jesus' resurrection exhibits his appointment by God as Israel's Leader and Saviour, and his role as the precursor to the full manifestation of God's dominion over creation, indeed, over death itself. The resurrection of Jesus, as a divine signal for the coming new creation, heightens the urgency of repentance for the forgiveness of sins (covenant formation or renewal) in view of his installment (exaltation) as God's agent of final salvation and judgment.

7.2.3.3 THE QUOTATION FROM 'DAVID' (2:25–28)

Luke's terse statement about Jesus' resurrection segues into a quotation from a psalm of David (Ps 15:8–11 LXX). This portion of the psalm lends easily to a resurrectional interpretation in at least six ways.⁴⁷ (1) The cita-

---

⁴⁴ Cf. John Chrysostom, *Hom. Jo.* 79 (PG 59.427.41–42); *Remiss. pecc.* (PG 60.759.70).

⁴⁵ Cf. Gregory of Nyssa, *Hom. Cant.* 13 (PG 44.1053.40–43) ; *C. Eunomium*, Book 2 (PG 45.501.46–51) ; Book 4 (PG 45.636.33–35).

⁴⁶ Cf. Theodoret, *Eranistes* 262.1: Ὡς ἄνθρωπος οὖν ἄρα πρωτότοκος ἐκ νεκρῶν. Πρῶτος γὰρ τὰς ὠδῖνας ἔλυσε τοῦ θανάτου, καὶ πᾶσιν ἔδωκε τῆς ἀναβιώσεως τὴν γλυκεῖαν ἐλπίδα (from *TLG*); *Int. ep. Col.* 1 (PG 82.600.44–601.1).

⁴⁷ While it is not impossible that the psalm is chosen because it embraces not only resurrection motifs but the portraiture of a suffering righteous one, the focus is clearly upon resurrection, and any suffering aspect is latent in the psalm but not emphasized by

tion is introduced with pesher understanding, 'David says concerning him' (2:25).⁴⁸ (2) The verb προοράω may be construed temporally instead of spatially (hence, 'I foresaw,' 2:25) as indicated by its use in Acts 2:31.⁴⁹ These first two features enhance the eschatological orientation of the psalm. (3) On the exclamation 'my flesh will dwell in hope' (2:26), Haenchen comments: 'This alone enabled the Christians to hear at this point an echo of the hope of resurrection.'⁵⁰ Israel's 'hope' and 'resurrection' are intimately associated in Luke-Acts (Luke 24:21; Acts 23:6; 24:15; 26:6–8, 29; 28:20). (4) Acts 2:27 is the segment of the psalm spotlighted in Peter's remarks (2:31), which we shall consider below. (5) Knowledge of 'the paths of life' (2:28) is significant since *aliveness* is crucial to the Lukan representation of resurrection (Luke 20:38; 24:5, 23; Acts 1:3; 9:41; 20:12; 25:19). (6) Finally, the passage contains the kind of joy and rejoicing characteristic of those who live in the resurrection age (2:26, 28).⁵¹

7.2.4 Jesus Enthroned as Lord and Messiah (2:29–36)

As one might expect, Peter's explication of the psalm incorporates Jewish interpretive technique and Hellenistic rhetorical argument. His pesher style of interpretation concentrates on the person who spoke the scriptural words (viz., David) and argues that the patriarch could not have fulfilled them. This interpretation is buttressed by indisputable rhetorical proofs. Three interrelated conclusions are made concerning the risen Jesus in 2:30, 33, and 36, around which we will structure our discussion.

7.2.4.1 JESUS' INSTALLMENT ON DAVID'S THRONE (2:29–32)

The first conclusion is prefaced by a refutative enthymeme.⁵² Peter asserts with boldness (παρρησία, common to Greek rhetoric and philosophy) that David is dead and buried. The tomb of David stands as a necessary sign

---

Luke; *pace* David P. Moessner, '*Two* Lords "at the Right Hand"? The Psalms and an Intertextual Reading of Peter's Pentecost Speech (Acts 2:14–36),' in *Literary Studies in Luke-Acts: Essays in Honor of Joseph B. Tyson* (eds. Richard P. Thompson and Thomas E. Phillips; Macon, Ga.: Mercer University Press, 1998), 215–32.

⁴⁸ Richard Longenecker, *Biblical Exegesis in the Apostolic Period* (Grand Rapids: Eerdmans, 1975), 100.

⁴⁹ Lake and Cadbury, *BC* 4:24; Armin Schmitt, 'Ps 16,8–11 als Zeugnis der Auferstehung in der Apg,' *BZ* 17 (1973): 245.

⁵⁰ Haenchen, *Acts*, 181.

⁵¹ Cf. Isa 26:19; *1 En.* 51:4–5; *T. Sim.* 6:77;06\:07; *T. Jud.* 25:4–5; *T. Zeb.* 10:22.

⁵² On the use of rhetoric in Acts, see William S. Kurz, 'Hellenistic Rhetoric in the Christological Proof of Luke-Acts,' *CBQ* 42 (1980): 171–95.

(*tekmērion*) that cannot be gainsaid.[53] There is also a positive basis for the conclusion. Three facts, coordinated by three participles (ὑπάρχων, εἰδώς, προϊδών), introduce the first conclusion (indicated by inferential οὖν).[54] First, David was a prophet. Second, David was aware of his covenant relationship to God. Those who approach the Hebrew Scriptures with faith will regard this aspect of Peter's argument to be just as solid and irrefragable as the presence of David's tomb. God made an oath to David that one of his descendants would sit upon his throne. This oath echoes Ps 131:11 LXX, which restates the divine promise to David in 2 Sam 7:12–13.[55] So, third, David was looking ahead into the future (προϊδών) for the fulfilment of God's promise.

The conclusion is stated simply: David 'spoke concerning the resurrection of the Messiah' (Acts 2:31). A loosely quoted excerpt from Psalm 15 serves as the focal point for this assertion. The repeated words vary in several ways from the preceding citation in 2:27.[56] First, the couplet is forged together by a pair of correlative negative particles (οὔτε...οὔτε). Second, the first person verbs of the citation are converted to third person. Third, in the first clause the words τὴν ψυχήν μου are omitted. This may downplay the image of a disembodied soul flitting in and out of Hades (cf. Luke 24:39). The subject is not merely the return of a dead person, which could be construed variously in the Hellenistic world, but resurrection from the dead. Fourth, in the second clause ἡ σὰρξ αὐτοῦ replaces τὸν ὅσιόν σου. This exchange does not minimize the christological impact of the psalm citation, given the inclusion of the term ὅσιος in the quote from Ps 15:10 LXX in Acts 13:35, and since it is evidently a messianic title that would provide an

---

[53] A necessary sign is inextricably linked to what it signifies (Aristotle, *An. pr.* 2.27). For example, a child born to a widow a year after her husband's death is a *tekmērion* that it cannot be his child (Kurz, 'Christological Proof,' 183).

[54] Dana and Mantey write: 'When οὖν is inferential, that inference is expressed by the main verb in the sentence and not by a verb in a subordinate clause nor by an infinitive nor a participle'; H. E. Dana and Julius R. Mantey, *A Manual Grammar of the Greek New Testament* (Toronto: Macmillan, 1955), 253. So Acts 2:30–31 should not be translated, 'Being therefore a prophet...,' but, 'Therefore [inferential οὖν], being a prophet..., he spoke [main verb ἐλάλησεν]....' An improper understanding of the use of οὖν produces the sort of puzzlement expressed by Lygre ('Exaltation,' 103): 'In vs. 30 οὖν is used to describe David. But the οὖν in vs. 30 does not flow naturally out of vs. 29, for vs. 30 relates more to the content of the quotation from Ps. 16 than to vs. 29.'

[55] Strauss (*Davidic Messiah*, 138) points out the corresponding language in Acts 2:30 and Ps 131:11 LXX: ὤμοσεν, ἐκ καρποῦ, and θρόνον.

[56] For further comments on the variations between 2:27 and 2:31, see Traugott Holtz, 'Geschichte und Verheißung: "Auferstanden nach der Schrift,"' *EvT* 57 (1997): 183–84.

additional explanation of why the psalm concerns the resurrection *of the Christ*. The insertion of ἡ σάρξ could have been influenced by its appearance in the previous verse of the psalm (see 2:26), but in any case underscores the corporeal nature of resurrection. The fact that the Messiah would not be abandoned to the netherworld, nor would his flesh be allowed to experience decay, stands in stark contrast to the prophet David whose body has decomposed in the grave (cf. 13:36).[57]

What remains to be proven is that *Jesus* is the Christ prophesied by David. This fact will not be stated explicitly until the final conclusion of Peter's argument in 2:36; but it will be a certitude, nonetheless, once it has been established that Jesus was indeed raised from the dead. Before we consider this step in Peter's argument, we must ponder the argument we have already met in 2:29–31. First, David is eliminated as a candidate for the fulfilment of the psalm. Second, the fulfilment of the psalm is envisioned within the context of God's oath to David about the enthronement of one of his successors. Third, the manner in which God's promise will be achieved is indicated by the psalm's prophecy concerning the Messiah's *resurrection*. The movement from the second to the third point assumes *a priori* that there is a linkage or equation between enthronement and resurrection. The relationship is spelled out in several textual variants of 2:30 which insert ἀναστήσειν (-σαι) τὸν Χριστόν before καθίσαι ἐπὶ τὸν θρόνον αὐτοῦ (cf. NA[27]). This is unnecessary, since the progression of Peter's logic is evident without such interpolations. The NT attests to early Christian belief in a close association between Christ's resurrection and enthronement.[58] In Chapter 3 we also learned that the language of 'killing' and 'raising to life' was employed in the ancient Near East to refer respectively to the deposition and installment of kings.[59] The combination of both the

---

[57] The expression εἶδεν διαφθοράν is uncommon (comparable expressions do not occur in the LXX) yet not difficult to grasp. Luke uses a similar expression in Luke 2:26 (ἰδεῖν θάνατον) where the sense is 'experience death' (cf. Heb 11:5). Since it is the 'flesh' of Jesus that will not undergo 'destruction' (διαφθορά), there is no reason to balk at the idea that bodily decomposition is in view (*contra EDNT* 1:316). Putrefaction and decay would have been graphically real for first-century Jews who practiced secondary burial; cf. Eric M. Meyers, *Jewish Ossuaries: Reburial and Rebirth. Secondary Burials in Their Ancient Near Eastern Setting* (BibOr 24; Rome: Biblical Institute, 1971); idem, 'Secondary Burials in Palestine,' *BA* 33 (1970): 2–29; Rachel Hachlili, 'Burials, Ancient Jewish,' *ABD* 1:790; idem, *Ancient Jewish Art and Archaeology in the Land of Israel* (HO 7.1; Leiden: Brill, 1988), 93–94.

[58] This is a truism of NT scholarship, but see esp. Dennis C. Duling, 'The Promises to David and Their Entrance into Christianity—Nailing Down a Likely Hypothesis,' *NTS* 19 (1973): 55–77.

[59] See above, pp. 53–54.

literal and figurative meanings of resurrection is illustrated well in the *Testaments of the Twelve Patriarchs*. There, in several instances, the restoration of Israel's primeval leadership coincides with their resurrection from the dead (*T. Sim.* 6:7; *T. Zeb.* 10:2; *T. Jud.* 25:1; *T. Benj.* 10:6–7). The last reference merits quoting: 'Then you will see Enoch, Noah, and Shem and Abraham and Isaac and Jacob being raised up at the right hand (ἀναστα-μένους ἐκ δεξιῶν)[60] in gladness. Then we [i.e., the twelve patriarchs] also shall be raised up (ἀναστησόμεθα) each one over our tribe.' Resurrection and regal exaltation go hand-in-hand. We can see, then, how it would have been perfectly natural for the fulfilment of God's promise to David to be actualized in the 'raising up' of the Messiah. The almost mythical contrast between 'killing' and 'raising up' a ruler plays out dramatically in Peter's speech: 'You killed/crucified' (2:23, 36b); 'God raised up' (2:24, 32; cf. 2:36a).

The resurrection of Jesus is confirmed by the testimony of the twelve apostles in Acts 2:32. The use of τοῦτον τόν Ἰησοῦν resumes the discussion in 2:22–25 (cf. the τοῦτον in 2:23) in order to demonstrate that the Davidic prophecy from Psalm 15 applies to *Jesus*. 'This Jesus, God raised from the dead.' Barrett claims that it cannot be determined whether the following relative clause οὗ πάντες ἡμεῖς ἐσμεν μάρτυρες refers back to Jesus specifically (as per Acts 1:8, μου μάρτυρες; cf. 13:31) or to the entire preceding clause (i.e., the resurrection of Jesus; cf. 1:22, μάρτυρα τῆς ἀναστάσεως αὐτοῦ).[61] Three points speak in favour of the latter construal. First, the cross-reference to 1:22 should be weighted more heavily than 1:8 because of its closer proximity to the Pentecost speech, the appearance of the reconstituted Twelve in both scenes (1:26 and 2:14), and the emphasis in both places upon resurrection witnesses.[62] Second, the parallel in 3:15 (not mentioned by Barrett) most likely refers to both the execution and resurrection of Jesus in the antecedent clause, furnishing a comparative use of the relative pronoun.[63] Finally, and definitively, at this point Peter's argument requires witnesses not simply to Jesus, but to his resurrection. The emphatic ἡμεῖς represents a sudden intrusion of the speaker (and those he represents) into the speech. Peter has been and will continue to appeal to his audience, often emphatically, in the second person (e.g., ὑμεῖς ὑπολαμβάνετε, 2:15; ἐν μέσῳ ὑμῶν καθὼς αὐτοὶ οἴδατε, 2:22; ὑμεῖς καὶ βλέπετε καὶ ἀκούετε, 2:33; ὑμεῖς ἐσταυρώσατε, 2:36; cf. 2:38–39). Doubtless, Peter is at this point

---

[60] Cf. Acts 2:25, 34.

[61] Barrett, *Acts*, 1:148–49.

[62] But even Acts 1:8 is spoken by the risen Jesus who has 'presented himself alive with many convincing proofs' and has appeared to his disciples for forty days (1:3; cf. Luke 24:48).

[63] Cf. Lake and Cadbury, *BC* 4:25.

singling out the 'we,' which now includes Matthias, who are qualified to be witnesses of Jesus' resurrection (cf. μάρτυρα τῆς ἀναστάσεως αὐτοῦ σὺν ἡμῖν, 1:22). The conclusion is inescapable. God promised to David that he would seat one of his descendants on his throne, and that this enthronement would take place in the form of the Messiah's resurrection. Since Jesus has been raised from the dead, he must be the resurrected Messiah foreseen in Psalm 15. The statement of this conclusion, however, is still delayed until the close of Peter's argument in Acts 2:36.

7.2.4.2 THE EXALTED JESUS POURS OUT THE HOLY SPIRIT (2:33–35)

The second conclusive statement brings the argument full circle to explain the events which occasioned the speech in the first place—'that which you yourselves both see and hear' (2:33).[64] Again, an inferential οὖν is couched with circumstantial participial clauses (ὑψωθείς..., λαβών...), but should be taken with the controlling verb in the sentence, 'poured out' (ἐξέχεεν), which harks back to Joel's prophecy (cf. 2:17). The exaltation of Messiah-Jesus has eventuated in his having received from the Father the promised Holy Spirit, which he has therefore poured out upon his expectant disciples. The outpouring of the Spirit has been repeatedly anticipated in the Lukan narrative, particularly in post-resurrection settings (Luke 24:49; Acts 1:5, 8; cf. Luke 3:16). It is the exalted Jesus who bestows God's executive power for Israel's covenant renewal and salvation (cf. ἐξ ὕψους δύναμιν, Luke 24:49; Acts 5:31–32).

How is the exaltation and ascension related to Jesus' resurrection? In Chapter 1 we outlined a number of perspectives on this issue, dwelling particularly on three major positions.[65] A *crux interpretum* in this matter is Acts 2:33 (and its companion text, 5:31). The first view, held by Lohfink and Franklin, posits that Luke drew a sharp separation between Jesus' resurrection and exaltation as distinct events, the latter occurring at Jesus' ascension. In 2:33 Luke has switched the discussion from talking about Jesus' resurrection to talking about his exaltation-ascension. Several items are called forth in support of this interpretation. (1) Lohfink takes the οὖν as consecutive ('then') rather than inferential, so that the exaltation in 2:33 is distinguished temporally from Jesus' resurrection.[66] (2) The structure of the speech lends itself to this bifurcation, because this portion of Peter's argu-

---

[64] Acts 2:33 is not a digression, but essential to answering the question provided in the narrative setting, 'What does this mean?' Cf. John J. Kilgallen, 'A Rhetorical and Source-traditions Study of Acts 2,33,' *Bib* 77 (1996): 178–96. We would add that one of the functions of speeches in ancient historiography involved commentary on events in order to explain their cause(s).

[65] See pp. 5–10 above, since what is written here builds on that earlier discussion.

[66] Lohfink, *Himmelfahrt Jesu*, 228–29.

ment divides into two different sections, the first treating resurrection (2:25–32) and the second exaltation-ascension (2:33–35), with each containing a scriptural citation (Ps 15:8–11 LXX; Ps 109:1 LXX).[67] (3) Jesus' exaltation is linked to his ascension through the negative remark about David *not* ascending into the heavens (2:34a). (4) Acts 5:31 seems to make the same distinction between Jesus' resurrection and exaltation. (5) Foundational to Lohfink's position is his contention that Luke has transformed the primitive exaltation kerygma by narrating the ascension as a separate, observable event.

Let us consider the merits of this position. (1) Lohfink's interpretation of οὖν as continuative or successive is unlikely within an argumentative context. The particle is certainly inferential in 2:30 and 2:36, so a shift to the continuative use in 2:33 would be unnatural. (2) To mark a major break at 2:33, claiming that Peter has switched abruptly from the subject of Jesus' resurrection to that of his exaltation, is artificial.[68] We have already seen that the enthronement of one of David's descendants is foreseen in Psalm 15 as 'the resurrection of the Messiah' (2:30–31). The enthronement or exaltation of Jesus does not in some way exclude his resurrection.[69] The language of exaltation builds upon Peter's discussion of the resurrected Christ. The verb ὑψόω carries forward the Davidic concept of enthrone-

---

[67] Franklin, *Christ the Lord*, 33.

[68] This perception is widespread. Strauss (*Davidic Messiah*, 141; following Jürgen Roloff, *Die Apostelgeschichte übersetzt und erklärt* [17th ed.; NTD 5; Göttingen: Vandenhoeck & Ruprecht, 1981], 51, 58–59; Schneider, *Apg.*, 1:275; et al.) writes: 'The exaltation is presented as a separate act which naturally followed the resurrection,' but adds that 'the smooth transition suggests that Luke is still operating in the context of Davidic promises.' Haenchen (*Acts*, 183) writes: 'With οὖν we are led imperceptibly from the Resurrection to the Exaltation "to the right hand of God" (corresponding to καθίσαι ἐπὶ τὸν θρόνον αὐτοῦ in verse 30: Jesus, sitting on God's right, shares his throne).' Tannehill's analysis (*Narrative Unity*, 1:37) is too tidy, delineating two different subjects (resurrection, 2:24–32; exaltation, 2:33–35), two corresponding scriptural texts (Pss 15 and 109), and two christological titles (Christ and Lord). In response, first, Luke does not so cleanly differentiate between resurrection and exaltation. Second, the psalm citations do not function equally, but Ps 109:1 complements the citation from Ps 15:8–11, further identifying the 'Lord' concerning whom David has prophesied (cp. 2:34–35 with 2:25). Third, the title 'Lord' is distributed throughout Peter's speech and cannot be linked with 2:33–35 as though it were especially associated with exaltation while 'Messiah,' relates more closely to his resurrection.

[69] For a defence of the terms 'enthronement' and 'exaltation' as interchangeable, see Lygre, 'Exaltation,' 151–54. Pesch (*Apg.*, 1:124) observes: 'Da die Auferweckung des Christus in 30 schon mit dem Sitzen auf Gottes Thron in Zusammenhang gebracht war, kann die Erhöhung Jesu zur Rechten Gottes (vg. 5,31) folgernd (οὖν) zur Sprache gebracht werden.' Later (1:125) he equates 'Erhöhung' with 'Himmelfahrt.'

ment.[70] 'Having been exalted to/at the right hand of God' clarifies whose throne (viz., God's) that the resurrected Jesus has been installed upon.[71] (3) The explanatory statement (with γάρ, 2:34a) that David did not ascend into heaven, it must be acknowledged, may well call to readers' minds the ascension accounts in Luke 24:50-53 and Acts 1:9-11 (cp. the word οὐρανός in Luke 24:50, repeated four times in Acts 2:10-11). The authorial audience will probably perceive a contrast between Luke's vivid portrayal of Jesus' ascent into heaven and David's continued entombment. However, they will not inevitably adopt Lohfink's interpretation that the ascension, but *not* the resurrection, is therefore identified with Jesus' exaltation. Lohfink begins by equating exaltation and ascension, and then interprets Acts 2:33 with this preconception in mind. (4) Acts 5:31, if anything, effectively links Jesus' resurrection and exaltation. Here there is no ascension vocabulary. The verb ὑψόω can suggest spatial movement upward, but accents a dignified (i.e., exalted) status. The contrast is not simply between Jesus being killed and then brought back to life. The contrast is between Jesus being murderously humiliated ('hung upon a tree') and his being 'raised up,' indeed, 'exalted to the right hand of God.' To the extent that ascension enters the picture, it is complementary and not competitive with resurrection. (5) The fact that Luke has twice recounted the ascension of Jesus as a separate event from his resurrection does not *ipso facto* point to a Lukan revision of the exaltation kerygma. We reject Lohfink's perpetuation of the idea that Jesus' resurrection-exaltation was originally conceived of as an invisible event which was gradually historicized and concretized. Such an evolutionary model is incompatible with the way resurrection from the dead was expressed within Second Temple Judaism. While there are texts which may be ambiguous about the nature of resurrection, none presents it as a purely spiritual event, and many more depict it as distinctly physical, suggesting that a spiritual resurrection is an oxymoron. Lohfink compares Luke's narrative, not with a primitive Christian understanding of resurrection, ascension, and exaltation, but with a schema developed by nineteenth-

---

[70] This verb is used of David's exaltation to the throne (1 Chron 17:16-17; Ps 88:4-5, 20-21, 25, 28-30 LXX; cf. Isa 52:13); cf. O'Toole, 'Davidic Covenant of Pentecost,' 248-49.

[71] Whether τῇ δεξιᾷ (here or in 5:31) is instrumental or locative cannot be determined on grammatical grounds alone. The locative makes best sense in light of the appearance of ἐκ δεξιῶν in 2:25, 34. It may also recollect the final clause in Ps 15:11 ('delights are in your right hand forever') left out in the aposiopesis of Acts 2:28 (cf. Johnson, *Acts*, 52). In support of the locative, see also Fitzmyer, *Acts*, 259; Haenchen, *Acts*, 183; and most other interpreters. For the instrumental, see esp. Barrett, *Acts*, 149; Jacques Dupont, 'L'Interprétation des Psaumes dans les Actes des Apôtres,' in *Études sur les Actes des Apôtres* (LD 45; Paris: Les Éditions du Cerf, 1967), 302-304.

century liberal Protestants. More damaging to this position, however, is the fact that it makes a judgment concerning the dual-recounting of Jesus' ascension, and then brings that judgment to bear upon its interpretation of the speeches in Acts. We will have more to say about this below.

The second view, represented by such names as Fitzmyer and Zwiep, considers the exaltation statement in Acts 2:33 to be in conformity with the primitive idea of Jesus' transit into heaven at his resurrection. Any hints of 'the ascension' are dismissed. Fitzmyer, for example, handles the mention of David's non-ascension in 2:34a by pointing to the fact that nowhere in the Old Testament is there an 'assumption' of David.[72] Neither the first nor second view preserves the complexity of Luke's narrative. The first view interprets the two Lukan ascension accounts as evidence that Luke is placing special emphasis upon the ascension over against the resurrection; this, despite the fact that the ascension accounts do not provide details that exclusively link them to exaltation or enthronement.[73] Then Acts 2:33 and 5:31 are viewed as supportive of Luke's theology, while statements to the contrary are considered vestiges of traditional formulae. Luke could have done a much better job of imposing his allegedly unique exaltation kerygma in the speeches. The second view has Luke endorsing the traditional resurrection-exaltation theology and adding the ascension accounts merely as theologically negligible appendages. So the one gives preference to a particular interpretation of the Lukan narrative which overshadows the message of the speeches, while the other prefers the (primitive) message in the speeches to the neglect of Luke's narrative. We doubt that authorial readers would take either approach. The reading (or listening) process would involve a dialectical relationship between narrative and speech. The Lukan resurrection and ascension accounts give rise to certain judgments about how Jesus' resurrection, ascension, exaltation are to be understood, but the speeches present the authorized interpretation of the narrated events, and expand, correct, or perhaps even complicate the reader's judgments.

Our own view is that the Lukan material on resurrection, ascension, and exaltation provides the reader with telescoping or overlapping images. A dynamism exists in the relationship between the three theological concepts that defies precise schematization. This is not uncharacteristic of Luke's narrative. In fact, Luke-Acts is renowned for its redundant narration that provides variety, perspective, and even dissonance to the reportage of an event. The accounts of the ascension (Luke 24:50–53; Acts 1:9–11) and

---

[72] Fitzmyer, *Acts*, 260.
[73] Such as in Mark 16:19: ἀνελήμφθη εἰς τὸν οὐρανὸν καὶ ἐκάθισεν ἐκ δεξιῶν τοῦ θεοῦ.

Paul's conversion-commission (Acts 9:1–19; 22:1–16; 26:1–23) are celebrated examples.[74] Yet we contend that the resurrection of Jesus stands as the controlling theological element in Luke's message of salvation. Yes, Luke anticipates the ascension in Luke 9:51, and narrates the ascension once at the end of Luke and once again at the beginning of Acts. The ascension provides a literary link between the two volumes. But to argue that Luke has thereby elevated the ascension of Jesus to a theologically dominant and controlling position cannot be substantiated. Beyond the first chapter of Acts, Jesus' ascension is mentioned again in 3:21, and referred to obliquely in 2:34a. Two exaltation texts (2:33 and 5:31) can probably prompt a mental image of Luke's ascension accounts, but cannot tie Jesus' exaltation exclusively to his ascension. Elsewhere in Luke's work it is the resurrection which occupies the theological focus or climax of God's salvific work through Jesus. This, however, does not displace or distort the reality of Jesus' physical removal into heaven or heavenly session. The resurrection may be broadly conceived to embrace both of the other concepts (exaltation and ascension), but not vice versa. Therefore, it can be employed as an inclusive cipher for the whole string of post-resurrection events (exit from the tomb, appearances, ascent into heaven) and related theological concepts (triumph over death, exaltation, status as Lord, Messiah, Saviour, etc.). Consequently, Luke-Acts preserves the rich complexity of narrative while incorporating theological utility and integrity. A key text for our position is Acts 1:21–22. Here the qualifications for becoming an apostolic witness include being present at Jesus' ascension, yet it is the selection of a witness to Jesus' *resurrection* that is specified. Acts 2:32, following 2:30–31 and followed by 2:33–35, signifies witnessing to more than just post-resurrection appearances, but to the fact that Jesus has been exalted to the right hand of God. Similarly, 5:30–32 involves the witness of the apostles and the Holy Spirit to the death, resurrection, and exaltation of Jesus. Other passages focus on the post-resurrection appearances to the apostles (10:39–41; 13:30–31) yet characterize the risen Jesus as cosmic judge (10:42) or exalted Davidic king (13:33–37). The constraints of narrative disallow Luke from maintaining a temporal unity for Jesus' resurrection, ascension, and exaltation, regardless of whether they once formed a unity or not. It is incorrect, however, to infer that this narrative chronology restricts the meaning of resurrection in Luke-Acts only to Jesus' victory over death.[75] Because Jesus is the primary participant in the *eschatological* resurrection from the dead, his resurrection involves more than just a return from the dead (in contradistinction to, say, Tabitha or Eutychus). Jesus' res-

---

[74] Cf. O'Toole, 'Resurrection-Ascension-Exaltation,' 111–12.
[75] *Contra* Talbert, 'Place of the Resurrection,' 24.

urrection from the dead, never to die again, entails his exaltation to the right hand of God, the mediation of salvation to Israel and the world through appointed witnesses, and his role as universal Lord and judge over creation.

It is the resurrected and exalted Jesus who stands behind the phenomena attendant to the outpouring of the Holy Spirit. Peter says that the gift of the Spirit granted by the Father via the risen Jesus will be offered to whomever the Lord calls (Acts 2:39; a play upon Joel's words cited in 2:21). Salvation also means separation from 'this crooked generation' (2:40). Specifically, within the context of Peter's speech, this implies revoking one's alliance with those who are responsible for the death of Jesus (2:23, 36b). The need to get out from under the guilt for crucifying Jesus (cf. 2:37) is intensified by Jesus' subsequent possession of absolute sovereignty. This is articulated by the citation from Ps 109:1 (2:34b–35), which guarantees the conquest of Jesus over his enemies. It is a truism among NT scholars that Jesus' resurrection constitutes God's vindication of him in the face of his opponents. This claim requires some modification with respect to the Lukan narrative. The complete vindication of Jesus has not been fully accomplished, nor will it be within Luke-Acts. Jesus' resurrection affords not only the opportunity for repentance and forgiveness of sins, but also further resistance. The apostolic preaching of Jesus' resurrection will be the catalyst for conflict from the same Jerusalem authorities who condemned Jesus to death (Acts 3–5). The conflict will reach a flash-point with the martyrdom of Stephen, when the Christ-like saint reports his vision of Jesus standing at the right hand of God (7:55–56). The image of the Son of Man, who holds universal lordship and avenges the people of God who are oppressed by the powerful, could not have been lost on Stephen's murderers. Ironically, even the Way's chief persecutor, Saul, will end up as the persecuted Paul who will share in Jesus' sufferings unto the very end of the Lukan narrative, where we find him chained and awaiting execution in Rome. Jesus' vindication and the hope of Israel will be ultimately realized when the resurrected Jesus exercises his authority as judge of the living and the dead. Then the words of Ps 109:1 will be utterly fulfilled, when God makes all of the Messiah's enemies his footstool.

7.2.4.3 GOD HAS MADE JESUS BOTH LORD AND MESSIAH (2:36)

The final conclusive statement seals the identification of Jesus as the 'Lord' and 'Messiah' who was the subject of several Scriptures previously quoted. A controversial aspect of this verse is its reference to the fact that God 'made' him Lord and Messiah. We need not review the avalanche of literature on this question, but will only point to a recent attempt to argue that Jesus' messiahship, which was announced in Luke 1:35, is not achieved until his resurrection.[76] Mainville's case should not be faulted for the data that it includes, but for what it leaves out. While there is truth in the claim that Jesus enters into the full exercise of his messiahship at his resurrection (understanding messiahship in the royal sphere), Jesus' messianic status is not initiated, but confirmed and legitimated by his resurrection. Jesus is already the Messiah prior to his resurrection. Peter says that Ps 15:10 LXX pertains to 'the resurrection of the Messiah' (Acts 2:31). Jesus spoke of how suffering and resurrection were part of the divine plan for the Messiah (Luke 24:26, 46). Jesus' resurrection from the dead clinches his identification as the promised Messiah of the Scriptures.[77]

7.3 Peter's Speech at Solomon's Portico (Acts 3:12–26)

7.3.1 The Speech in Its Narrative Setting

Peter's speech at Solomon's Portico is directly related to the preceding healing of a crippled man. As Peter begins his remarks, the healed man who had gone with Peter and John into the temple (Acts 3:8) is clinging to them (3:11a), and 'all the people' who were overcome with wonder and amazement at the healing (3:10) have rushed into the portico, still utterly astonished (3:11b). The speech opens, much like the Pentecost speech did, with reference to the people's reaction to the miracle (3:12). Peter dismisses the thought that the healing was performed on account of his own or John's power or piety, and in 3:16 declares that the man's 'wholeness' was granted to him through faith in the name of Jesus. The importance of 'the name' was first introduced in the Pentecost speech (2:21, 38), but becomes a leitmotif of Acts 3–5.

The healing and the speech set the stage for the ongoing conflict between the apostles and the temple authorities in Acts 4 and 5. The conflict is over who possesses legitimate authority or leadership among the people of Israel. According to Luke's account, the fundamental issue is soteriological. The one capable of bringing healing or salvation to Israel is God's appointed leader over Israel. Four constants are involved in the debate. First, there is the presence of the healed man from Acts 3:1–10. Particularly

---

[76] Odette Mainville, 'Le messianisme de Jésus: Le rapport annonce/accomplissement entre Lc 1,35 et Ac 2,33,' in *The Unity of Luke-Acts* (ed. Joseph Verheyden; BETL 142; Leuven: Leuven University Press, 1999), 313–27.

[77] We agree with Longenecker ('Acts,' *ExpBC* 9:76–77) that Acts 2:36 should be interpreted in terms of function or accomplishment, not ontology. Helpful is Tannehill's reference to the stages in a king's life, from birth as heir to the throne, and anointing, to his assumption to the throne (*Narrative Unity*, 1:38–39; cf. Luke 19:12; 22:69).

in Acts 4, the healed man stands with the apostles as an unassailable confirmation of their message (4:9–10, 14). Twice the healing of the lame man is called a 'sign' (σημεῖον, 4:16, 22). Although the healed man does not appear again after chapter 4, healing continues to operate in tandem with the apostles' bold preaching in the temple (4:30–31; 5:12–16). Three other elements are even more pervasive. Second, there is emphasis upon 'the name' of Jesus. The healing of the lame man was accomplished in the name of Jesus (3:6, 16; 4:10), as are other healings (4:30), thus signifying the efficacy of Jesus' name for the salvation of anyone on earth (4:12).[78] The name of Jesus is the power energizing the apostles' ministry of healing and teaching, and something which the temple authorities repeatedly attempt to suppress (4:7–8, 18; 5:28, 40). Third, at every opportunity the apostles bear witness to the resurrection of Jesus (3:13, 14–15, 26; 4:10–11; 5:30–31). According to one summary, the apostles were 'proclaiming in Jesus the resurrection of the dead' (4:2). According to another, 'with great power the apostles gave testimony to the resurrection of the Lord Jesus' (4:33). Fourth, there is the presence of 'the people (of Israel).' The people (ὁ λαός) play a multifaceted role within this part of the Lukan narrative. They are at once spectators (3:9–12; 4:10; 5:12–13) and possible recipients of God's saving work (3:22–25). They are in one sense passively caught up in the debate concerning who legitimately represents God's rulership over them (4:1–5, 8, 10, 17; 5:19–20, 25, 28), but in another sense actively empowered to swing the pendulum of public approval for the apostles and against the temple authorities (4:16–17, 21; 5:13, 26) or against the apostles in favour of their temple leadership (4:25–27). Peter's sermon draws all of these elements together in presenting God's plan of salvation for Israel. Jesus' resurrection is integral to the christological and ecclesiological axes of Lukan soteriology.

The healing of the lame man is not merely an occasion for Peter's temple speech. The healing is itself paradigmatic for God's salvation of Israel by way of his servant Jesus. The speech connects the healing of the lame man with God's action of raising up Jesus from the dead (3:12–15). In turn, Jesus' resurrection is also linked to the restoration of Israel to her proper covenantal relation with God (3:22–26). There may be hints within the healing account that tie it to both resurrection and national restoration. Danielle Ellul observes the occurrence of the verb προσδοκάω in 3:5, and notes that it appears within primitive Christianity to denote hope, i.e., the expectation that the Messiah will bring deliverance.

---

[78] The relationship between the healing of the lame man and the larger compass of God's salvation through Jesus is indicated by Luke's application of salvation vocabulary (σῴζω, σωτηρία) to both the healing and to salvation more generally (Acts 4:9, 12).

Peter's Resurrection Speeches 221

> On est donc sorti du domaine financier (au v. 3 il s'agissait d'obtenir une aumône), pour celui de l'espérance, de la vie: il s'agit maintenant d'«obtenir quelque chose»—une délivrance.[79]

A link between release from the temple-related system of assistance to the poor and the resurrection of Jesus is not far-fetched, considering the powerful apostolic witness to Jesus' resurrection (4:33) in the midst of a summary of the early church's economic *koinōnia* (4:32–35).[80] Luke Timothy Johnson believes that the allusion to Jesus' resurrection in 3:6–7 is 'unmistakable.'[81] This is perhaps so only in retrospect, however, because the identical word ἤγειρεν occurs in 3:7 and 3:15.[82] In light of the enthronement language so prevalent in the Pentecost speech, one might also be struck by the curious detail that Peter took him 'by the right hand.' The repetitious description of the healed man 'leaping and walking' (3:8–9) increases the amplitude of an echo from Isa 35:6 LXX (as well as the whole of Isa 35:1–10) in which Israel's release from exile is described as a healing from paralysis.[83] Not all of these clues bear equal weight, but the collocation of the healing, Jesus' resurrection, and Israel's restoration within the speech tends to strengthen any connection that might be hinted at in the healing story.

7.3.2 The Structure of the Speech

The basic outline of the temple speech is fairly obvious, even though the syntax and logic of its parts are far from clear at every point. Like the Pentecost speech, direct addresses to the audience (incorporating the word ἄνδρες, 3:12, 17) mark the two main divisions of the speech.[84] The first division (3:12–16) explains the healing in relation to the cruel rejection and subsequent resurrection of Jesus. The second division (3:17–26) explains how Jesus' death and resurrection fit into God's plan for Israel's restoration, and emphasizes the repentance afforded to them by the resurrected Jesus. The importance of Jesus' resurrection for Israel's salvation is highlighted by the *inclusio* that frames the speech. In 3:13 Peter speaks of how

---

[79] Danielle Ellul, 'Actes 3/1–11,' *ETR* 64 (1989): 97.

[80] Cf. Green, 'Witnesses of His Resurrection,' 241.

[81] Johnson, *Acts*, 66; cf. the remark of Daniel Marguerat ('Le premier Historien du Christianisme (Luc-Actes),' *FoiVie* 96 [1997]: 30): 'Le miracle selon Luc est donc une continuation de la résurrection dans l'histoire.'

[82] Hamm, 'Acts 3:12–26: Peter's Speech and the Healing of the Man Born Blind,' *PRSt* 11 (1984): 203; Ellul, 'Actes 3/1–11,' 97.

[83] Cf. Hamm, 'Acts 3:12–26,' 201; Johnson, *Acts*, 66; Marguerat, 'Luc-Actes: La résurrection à l'œuvre dans l'histoire,' 207–8.

[84] Soards, *Speeches in Acts*, 39.

God 'glorified his servant Jesus,' and in 3:26 he speaks of how God 'raised up his servant.' We shall, of course, have to further support the resurrectional orientation of this frame below.

7.3.3 Resurrection, Repentance, and Restoration in Peter's Temple Speech (Acts 3:12–26)

Peter's temple speech is probably the bloodiest battleground in the history of Lukan studies. Therefore, we shall concentrate on how Jesus' resurrection is integral to the offer of repentance, and thus restoration, for Israel. The focus of our own discussion, and the magnitude of the discussions of Christology and eschatology in connection with this passage, preclude us from being able to present a definitive or exhaustive treatment of many issues. We believe that the resurrection of Jesus is crucial for the bestowal of God's salvation in the present, such as in his concrete act of healing the lame man; but the resurrection of Jesus also paves the way for the ultimate restoration of Israel at the final resurrection of the dead. Jesus' resurrection establishes him as God's agent of salvation for Israel who provides an opportunity for covenant renewal with God via repentance. The resurrected Jesus, in his role as the prophet like Moses, also portends a decisive division within Israel. Jesus' resurrection places Israel in a state of accountability, and the response of individual ethnic Jews to the resurrected Jesus will determine whether they will participate in Israel's restoration or be expatriated. We will explore the significance of Jesus' resurrection in Peter's temple speech under several headings. First, we shall look at the resurrectional frame of the speech. Second, we shall consider an important christological title (ἀρχηγὸς τῆς ζωῆς). Finally, we shall inquire about the possible relationship between the resurrected Jesus and the final resurrection of repentant Israel by looking at the difficult passage in 3:20–21 concerning the eschatological outcomes of repentance, and the identification of Jesus as the resurrected prophet like Moses in 3:22–26.

7.3.3.1 THE RESURRECTIONAL FRAME OF THE SPEECH (3:13, 26)

The opening and closing of Peter's speech reveal an emphasis upon the resurrection of Jesus. In 3:13 Peter speaks of how Israel's covenant God 'glorified his servant Jesus.' In 3:26—after rehearsing significant features of Israel's covenantal heritage related to Moses (3:22–23), the prophets (2:24), and Abraham (2:25)—Peter speaks of how God 'raised up his servant.' These features form a framing device that communicates the major theme of the speech: the foundation of Jesus' resurrection for God's saving action toward Israel. In the first part of the speech Jesus' resurrection is shown in its relation to the healing of the lame man. In the second part it is shown in relation to the restoration of Israel.

The opening bracket of the frame is the easier to establish. After Peter denies that the healing of the lame man was due to the apostles' own power or piety (3:12), he sets about explaining the source of the healing. His explanation begins with two reverberations of God's covenant faithfulness to Israel. First, there is God's self-designation from Exod 3:6, 15, 'The God of Abraham and Isaac and Jacob' (Acts 3:13). In one of Jesus' own teachings in the temple he uttered these words not only in their obvious connection to Moses at the burning bush (cf. Acts 7:32), but in their more novel connection to the claim that 'the dead are raised' (Luke 20:37). Second, in saying that Israel's ancestral God 'glorified his servant (παῖς) Jesus,' Peter may be echoing the words of Isa 52:13. If so, the fourth Servant Song's depiction of the servant's suffering and humiliation and subsequent vindication and glorification is being appropriately recalled. That it is the 'God of our ancestors' who has glorified Jesus may be compared with Acts 5:30 ('The God of our ancestors raised Jesus'). There is a functional equivalence between the resurrection and glorification of Jesus.[85] What the glorification of the servant does *not* refer to is the healing of the lame man.[86] As Luke is wont to do, he is providing a background discussion of God's past saving deeds in order to better interpret God's present saving action.[87] The cause of the lame man's healing is not explained until 3:16, after Peter has rehearsed in some detail the injustice of Jesus' trial and execution, and the apostolic witness to his resurrection (3:13–15). The first part of Peter's speech indicates that Jesus' resurrection is the *conditio sine qua non* of God's present saving action.[88]

---

[85] N.B. Luke 24:26 where Jesus speaks of the Messiah suffering and entering into his glory.

[86] *Contra* Haenchen, *Acts*, 205. It is also unnecessary to take a mediating position that the glorification of the servant indicates both Jesus' resurrection and the healing of the lame man, as we shall further explain; *contra* Hamm, 'Acts 3:12–26,' 202; O'Toole, 'Some Observations on *anistēmi*,' 86–87.

[87] Cf. Kilgallen ('Acts 2,33,' 182–83) for this pattern in the speeches. The cause of the Pentecost phenomena, e.g., is not disclosed until Jesus' ministry, death, and especially his resurrection have been summarized and interpreted.

[88] Hans F. Bayer, 'Christ-Centered Eschatology in Acts 3:17–26,' in *Jesus of Nazareth: Lord and Christ—Essays on the Historical Jesus and New Testament Christology* (eds. Joel B. Green and Max Turner; Grand Rapids: Eerdmans, 1994), 241. Bayer further comments (242): 'Peter bridges the two known factors of present healing and past death with the hitherto unknown or rejected fact of Jesus' resurrection (v 15) as the "missing link." Without the witness (μάρτυς, v 15b) to the resurrection of Christ the present healing and past rejection and death of Christ remain virtually unrelated factors to the hearers.'

The resurrectional thrust of the closing bracket has been debated. The participle ἀναστήσας in 3:26 is thought by some scholars to refer to Jesus' arrival on the world scene or to the onset of his public ministry. This would accord, so it is asserted, with ἀναστήσει in 3:22.[89] Robert O'Toole has cogently argued in favour of a resurrectional interpretation in his study of 3:26.[90] Before enumerating his most persuasive of arguments, we should point out that Luke has already demonstrated a penchant for employing ἀνίστημι multivalently. He has used the verb without the additional phrase ἐκ τῶν νεκρῶν to refer to both Jesus' victory over death (2:24) and his accession to the Davidic throne (2:32). We have also pointed out how death and resurrection language have a long history of usage encompassing literal and figurative meanings within a regal context. Luke's authorial audience would have probably had public access to this wordplay. We might also note that the same participle appears in 13:33 (without ἐκ τῶν νεκρῶν) where it almost certainly refers to Jesus' resurrection (cf. 13:34). O'Toole's most forceful points include the following. (1) Whenever Jesus' life is referred to in one of the speeches, it appears at the beginning of the speech, never at the end (cf. 2:22; 10:37-39). Luke customarily speaks of Jesus' resurrection at the end of speeches (2:32; 4:10; 5:30; 10:40; 13:30, 34, 37; 17:31; 26:23). (2) The parallels between 3:26 and 3:13 tend to support a resurrectional interpretation ('glorified his servant' = 'raised his servant').[91] (3) The condition in 3:23 forces Israel into a hopeless situation if it only applies to Jesus' earthly life, and not his post-resurrection life. (4) The parallel passage in 26:23 predicates Jesus' proclamation of light 'to the people and to the nations' upon his being the first to suffer and be raised from the dead. It is not odd, then, for 3:26 to refer to the post-resurrection ministry of Jesus to Israel. We should add that it is the resurrected Jesus who grants the opportunity for repentance, especially in Acts (cf. Luke 24:46-47; Acts 5:31; 17:30; 26:20). We may conclude, therefore, that Peter's speech at Solomon's Portico is bounded by corresponding pointers to the foundational truth of Peter's message of salvation for Israel: Jesus' resurrection from the dead.

7.3.3.2 JESUS THE AUTHOR/LEADER OF LIFE (3:15)

Three christological titles are applied to Jesus in 3:14-15. The first two emphasize Jesus' holiness and righteousness (τὸν ἅγιον καὶ δίκαιον, 3:14). The third is more difficult to interpret (τὸν ἀρχηγὸν τῆς ζωῆς, 3:15). The

---

[89] Barrett, *Acts*, 1:213; Bruce, *Acts of the Apostles*, 146; Haenchen, *Acts*, 209-10.

[90] O'Toole, 'Some Observations on *anistēmi*,' 85-92.

[91] Emilio Rasco ('La gloire de la résurrection et ses fruits,' *AsSeign* 24 [1969]: 11) thinks that the glorified servant coincides precisely with the prophet like Moses.

word ἀρχηγός has a broad semantic range, as displayed in the definitions 'leader,' 'ruler,' 'prince,' 'one who begins,' 'instigator,' 'originator,' 'founder.'[92] The word has a classical flavour which conjures up impressions about ancient founders of cities, patrons, or heroes.[93] The nuance of source or origin makes better sense with the genitive τῆς ζωῆς (hence, 'author of life'), unless the genitive signifies direction ('leader to life').[94] The phrase appears in the incongruous statement: 'You killed the author of life'; but the incongruity is softened by the follow-up clause, 'whom God raised from the dead.' The title should be interpreted within the context of Jesus' resurrection. We have argued on the basis of 2:24 that Jesus was the first person to take part in the eschatological resurrection of the dead. Conzelmann has compared the title with the description of Jesus as 'first from the resurrection of the dead' in 26:23.[95] These parallels suggest that Jesus is God's appointed originator or champion of resurrection life. The resurrection of Jesus guarantees the resurrection of those who believe in him.[96] This interpretation is further supported by the summary of the apostles' preaching that immediately follows Peter's sermon: 'they were teaching the people and proclaiming in Jesus the resurrection of the dead' (4:2).[97] The fact that 'leader' (rather than 'author') is a more fitting translation in 5:31 simply demonstrates the subtlety of the word. One may easily slide from the archaic nuance of founder or originator to the idea that such an individual is the eponymous leader of an institution, people, etc. The contrast in 3:15, however, is between Jesus who gives life, and murderers who take it away.[98] Later, the preaching of the apostles will be appropriately called 'the words of this life' (5:20).

---

[92] 'ἀρχηγός, οῦ, ὁ,' BAGD 112; BDAG 138–39.

[93] G. Delling, 'ἀρχηγός,' *TDNT* 1:487–88; Barrett, *Acts*, 1:197–98; Bruce, *Acts of the Apostles*, 141–42. Lake and Cadbury (*BC* 4:36) observe that the word was 'literary, colourful, and far from commonplace. It was applicable to the mythical or historical founders of institutions, to pioneers who bestowed blessings on mankind.' This Hellenistic flavouring influences Lane's translation 'champion' in Heb 2:10; William L. Lane, *Hebrews* (2 vols.; WBC 47a–b; Dallas, Tex.: Word, 1991), 1:56–57.

[94] The latter is advocated by Barrett, *Acts*, 1:198. Fitzmyer (*Acts*, 186) and Johnson (*Acts*, 68) construe the phrase as 'author of life.'

[95] Hans Conzelmann, *Acts of the Apostles: A Commentary on the Acts of the Apostles* (Hermeneia; Philadelphia: Fortress, 1987), 28.

[96] Cf. Donald L. Jones, 'The Title "Author of Life (Leader)" in the Acts of the Apostles,' *SBL Seminar Papers, 1994* (SBLSP 33; Atlanta: Scholars Press, 1994), 631, 636; Eckstein, "Bodily Resurrection in Luke," 122–23.

[97] See our discussion of the significance of Acts 4:2 below pp. 230 and 281–84.

[98] Johnson, *Acts*, 68.

7.3.3.3 JESUS' RESURRECTION, REPENTANCE, AND ISRAEL'S RESTORATION

In the first part of Peter's speech he vigorously implicates his audience in the unjust trial and execution of Jesus. The life-giving power of Jesus' resurrection, on exhibit in the healing of the lame man, stands in stark relief to the people's egregious crime. The second part of the speech outlines the basis for Israel's opportunity for repentance. Peter acknowledges, first, the people's ignorance in their wrongdoing (3:17). Then he reminds them that the Messiah's suffering had to happen in accordance with the words of the prophets (3:18). The command to repent (3:19) is followed by a complex result clause detailing the possible eschatological outcomes if Israel returns to the Lord (3:20–21). The relationship of the resurrected Jesus (as the prophet like Moses) to Israel's return to proper covenant status with God is crucial to the closing part of the speech (3:22–26).

7.3.3.3.1 Repentance and Israel's Resurrection and Restoration (3:20–21)

Two central issues dominate the extensive debate over the interpretation of 3:20–21. First, there is a lack of consensus regarding the meanings of καιροὶ ἀναψύξεως and ἄχρι χρόνων ἀποκαταστάσεως. Second, there is the question of chronology. The conventional view has been to interpret the καιροί and χρόνοι as coordinate expressions related to the eschatological age of salvation.[99] A second view places the two in succession. William Lane believes the καιροὶ ἀναψύξεως characterize the present age of the Spirit, and though participating in some measure with the eschaton, the period remains distinct from the coming consummation, the χρόνοι ἀποκαταστάσεως.[100] A third view has become increasingly popular, which regards the two expressions as coordinate, but temporally prior to the Parousia, and hence indicative of the present age of mission.[101]

---

[99] Oepke, 'ἀποκατάστασις,' *TDNT* 1:391; Schweizer, 'ἀνάψυξις,' *TDNT* 9:664; H. N. Ridderbos, *The Speeches of Peter in the Acts of the Apostles* (London: Tyndale, 1961), 14; Haenchen, *Acts*, 208; Johnson, *Acts*, 74; Marshall, *Acts*, 93–94.

[100] William L. Lane, 'Times of Refreshment: A Study of Eschatological Periodization in Judaism and Christianity (Th.D. diss., Harvard University, 1962), 171–72, 177–80; cf. Lake and Cadbury, *BC* 4:37; C. K. Barrett, 'Faith and Eschatology in Acts 3,' in *Glaube und Eschatologie: Festschrift für Werner Georg Kümmel zum 80. Geburtstag* (eds. Erich Gräßer and Otter Merk; Tübingen: Mohr-Siebeck, 1985), 9–17.

[101] William S. Kurz, 'Acts 3:19–26 as a Test Case of the Role of Eschatology in Lukan Christology,' *SBL Seminar Papers, 1977* (SBLSP 11; Missoula, Mont.: Scholars Press, 1977), 309–23; Hamm, 'Acts 3:12–26,' 207–12; John T. Carroll, *Response to the End of History: Eschatology and Situation in Luke-Acts* (SBLDS 92; Atlanta: Scholars Press, 1988), 141–48; Witherington, *Acts*, 187.

The traditional chronology is to be preferred. First, the coming of the καιροὶ ἀναψύξεως and the sending of the Messiah are correlated results (ὅπως ἄν ἔλθωσιν...καὶ ἀποστείλῃ). Second, heaven must receive the Messiah ἄχρι χρόνων ἀποκαταστάσεως πάντων. Both the καιροί and χρόνοι are thus related to the sending of the Messiah. This does not unquestionably suggest that the start of both time periods is concurrent with the sending of the Messiah—it is possible that the καιροὶ ἀναψύξεως precede the other events—but this chronology seems to make the best sense of the passage's tangled syntax. Barrett's contention that ἀνάψυξις is used to refer only to temporary (but not final) relief is too restrictive.[102] Whether relief is transitory or permanent can only be determined within context. For example, according to Josephus, the Essenes believed in a habitation (like the Isles of the Blessed) for good souls in the afterlife. This place is 'refreshed' (ἀναψύχει) by a gentle breeze that perpetually flows from the ocean (*J. W.* 2.8.11 §155).[103] That aside, the plural καιροί can denote a span of time, such as a season (Acts 14:17; 17:26; cf. Luke 21:24). Yet this does not mean that the time periods in Acts 3:20–21 must precede the sending of the Messiah. There is nothing to preclude the possibility that the Messiah's coming could initiate a period of time during which creation will be restored and prepared for the eternal state. William Kurz has argued that a comparison with Acts 20:6 (ἄχρι ἡμερῶν πέντε) supports his view that ἄχρι χρόνων ἀποκαταστάσεως indicates that the Messiah will be sent *after* this period of time.[104] But the fact that ἄχρι is followed by a plural genitive in only these two instances in Luke-Acts counts for little. There is no evidence to suggest that ἄχρι functions differently with the plural genitive than with the singular. The meaning in 20:6 is that Paul's missionary party travelled from Philippi to Troas *within* five days' time. If the trip had taken more than five days, Luke could have reported ἄχρι ἡμερῶν ἕξ. We already know one example of how Luke would express (with ἄχρι) the idea of an occurrence happening, or in this case ceasing, *after* a period of time: ἄχρι οὗ πληρωθῶσιν καιροὶ ἐθνῶν (Luke 21:24).[105]

---

[102] Barrett, 'Faith and Eschatology,' 10–13.

[103] Euripides (*Suppl.* 615–17) speaks of the gods providing relief from evils (κακῶν δ' ἀναψυχὰς θεοί) for they are capable of bringing them all to an end (πάντων τέρμ' ἔχοντες αὐτοί).

[104] Kurz, 'Acts 3:19–26,' 311; followed by Carroll, *Response to the End of History*, 145 (but see his reservations in n. 111).

[105] Examples of ἄχρι with the plural genitive may be adduced against Kurz's interpretation: Plutarch (*Thes.* 23.1) reports how a famous Athenian warship was preserved ἄχρι τῶν Δημητρίου τοῦ Φαληρέως χρόνων. In *Lys.* 23.5 he relates how Lysander was demoted to second rank (ἄχρι δευτερείων). Josephus (*Ant.* 3.8.2 §196) says the Jewish

Acts 1:6–11 presents some interesting parallels with 3:20–21. The disciples ask Jesus whether he is 'at this time (ἐν τῷ χρόνῳ τούτῳ) restoring (ἀποκαθιστάνες) the kingdom to Israel' (1:6). Jesus tells them that it is not for them to know the χρόνους καὶ καιρούς which have been determined by the Father (1:7). Jesus then promises them empowerment from the Spirit for their worldwide witness (1:8). The outpouring of the Spirit upon the reconstituted Twelve and the nucleus of one-hundred twenty disciples probably signals the beginning of a new stage in God's salvific plan to restore Israel. Yet it seems unlikely that Jesus is saying out of one side of his mouth that his disciples are forbidden to know the specific timetable for God's restoration of Israel, and out of the other that the promise of the Spirit marks the commencement of the final restoration itself. It is more appropriate to speak of the outpouring of the Spirit and the apostolic witness as parts of a necessary preparation for the 'times of restoration.' The subsequent ascension account closes with the two angels explaining how Jesus, who has been taken up into heaven, will return in like manner (1:11). This anticipates what Peter says in 3:20–21. Our contention is that Jesus' return from heaven, according to Acts 1 and 3, will be the time when he fully executes God's ancient plan to restore not only Israel but all creation.

What, then, are the καιροὶ ἀναψύξεως? There are two major proposals,[106] to which we will add a third:

(1) Gerhard Lohfink has advocated an *apocalyptic* perspective.[107] He points to *4 Ezra* 11:46 where the messianic deliverance ushers in a period depicted with the words *uti refrigeret omnis terra*. Lohfink translates part of this clause ἵνα ἀνάψυξαι. While Ezra's eagle vision might provide an illuminating apocalyptic background for our expression, any correlation is nonetheless based on a conjectural retroversion.

(2) William Lane detects a *pneumatic* reference.[108] He bases his view on Symmachus's version of Isa 32:15 which replaces the pouring out of the Spirit from on high (MT, LXX) with the pouring out of ἀνάψυξις. Lane thus sees the 'seasons of refreshing' as coterminous with the present time when God is pouring out his Spirit and granting repentance and forgiveness of

---

temple tax was required of free men between twenty and fifty years old (οἱ ἀπὸ εἴκοσι ἐτῶν ἄχρι πεντήκοντα).

[106] Bayer ('Christ-Centered Eschatology,' 246–47) catalogues three possibilities, but we do not think that the third view in his list, a Sabbath-rest reference, warrants our consideration. Hamm ('Acts 3:12–26,' 207–8) lists the same first two major views as we do. The most comprehensive treatment is Augusto Barbi, *Il Cristo celeste presente nella Chiesa* (AnBib 64; Rome: Biblical Institute, 1979), 46–68.

[107] Gerhard Lohfink, 'Christologie und Geschichtsbild in Apg 3,19–21,' *BZ* 13 (1969): 223–41.

[108] Lane, 'Times of Refreshment,' 171–72, 178–80.

sins. The Parousia and the times of universal restoration will follow this period. The fundamental weakness of Lane's position is the remoteness of this reference to ἀνάψυξις.[109] Actually, any proposal (including our own) is fraught with difficulties because of the paucity of corroborating evidence (biblical or extra-biblical), and the lack of a distinct point of reference in Acts.

(3) A third proposal posits a *resurrectional* reference. The word ἀνάψυξις, and its cognates ἀναψυχή and ἀναψύχω, often refer to cooling, relief, or refreshment.[110] The same form occurs only once in the LXX (Exod 8:15) where it refers to the respite experienced by Pharaoh after one of the plagues had ceased. This can be of no help in interpreting Acts 3:20a. A definition that is not usually highlighted is that of 'revival.'[111] The various forms can refer to revival or reinvigoration associated with human respiration. This is natural since ψυχή (i.e., breath or air) is as intrinsic to breathing as it is to the refreshment of a cool breeze. Plato explains why ψυχή is so-called by saying that when it is present in the body it is the cause of its living, 'giving it the power to breathe and reviving it (ἀναψῦχον), and when this revivifying force (ἀναψύχοντος) fails, the body perishes and comes to an end' (*Crat.* 399d–e).[112] The association of ἀνάψυξις with respiration is common among ancient medical writers.[113] In one passage Galen remarks on how living beings immediately die when deprived of ἀνάψυξις, since it assists in the regulation of heartbeat.[114] It is therefore more than a means to cool the inside of the body or the heart;[115] it is a vital principle without which the body stops functioning and dies.

We would like to propose, with Augustin George, that καιροὶ ἀναψύξεως may be a period of revitalization for Israel that could encompass resurrec-

---

[109] Bayer ('Christ-Centered Eschatology,' 246) questions the presupposition that the term was used pneumatically before Symmachus.

[110] Cf. LSJ 127; *TLNT* 1:120–21; and the commentaries ad. loc.

[111] Lake and Cadbury (*BC* 4:37) translate 'times of revival,' but provide no more explanation than that ἀναψύχειν ('to revive') contrasts with ἀποψύχειν ('to faint').

[112] For other references in Plato to the importance of respiration for bodily function and life, cf. *Tim.* 70c–d, 78e, 84d.

[113] William K. Hobart, *The Medical Language of St. Luke* (Dublin: Hodges, Figgis & Co., 1882), 167. N.B. that our utilization of Hobart is not an endorsement of his thesis regarding the authorship of Luke-Acts.

[114] Galen, *Usu part.* 7.9 (3.544) : δι' ἣν καὶ παραχρῆμα διαφθείρεσθαι τὰ ζῶα στερούμενα τῆς ἀναψύξεως—κατὰ τοῦτο μὲν ὡς ἀνάψυξιν συνεχῆ τῇ καρδίᾳ παρασκευάσασαν αὐτὴν ἐπαινεῖσθαι δίκαιον.

[115] Cf. n. 112 above, and Galen, *Usu part.* 7.5 (3.528); *Diff. febr.* 1.4 (7.287).

tion from the dead.[116] George translates 'les moments de respirer.' He compares ἀνάψυξις to Luke's usage of two terms: (a) ἀποψύχω, used of people fainting (Luke 21:26);[117] and (b) ἐκψύχω, used of people dying (Acts 5:10; 12:23; cp. ἐκπνέω, Luke 23:46). Both words graphically represent a halt in breathing that is either life-threatening or fatal. The comparison with these words suggests that ἀνάψυξις could have the sense of 'breathing again,' 'return of breath,' or 'return to life.' George concludes: 'Par ce verbe, Luc veut sans doute marquer le retour à la vie, la "réanimation."' We would add to George's argument the fact that the return (or presence) of ψυχή / πνεῦμα is noted in two of Luke's accounts of resurrection (Luke 8:55; Acts 20:10).[118] We know, too, that Israel's hope of final salvation is repeatedly linked with their hope in the resurrection of the dead (Acts 23:6; 24:14–15; 26:6–7), and that this hope is based upon what is written in their prophets (cp. 3:21 with 24:14) and what was promised to them by the God of their ancestors (cp. 3:13, 25 with 26:6). Moreover, the time of Israel's ultimate redemption is clearly associated with the coming of the Son of Man (Luke 21:27–28). If the expression καιροὶ ἀναψύξεως refers to a time of revivification for Israel, it would explain the summary of the apostolic preaching in Acts 4:2, which probably cannot be justified solely on the basis of the christological title ἀρχηγὸς τῆς ζωῆς in 3:15. John Chrysostom's comment on our phrase in 3:20a furnishes a confirmation of this interpretation: 'Here he speaks indirectly concerning the resurrection' ('Ἐνταῦθα περὶ τῆς ἀναστάσεως διαλέγεται ἀμυδρῶς, *Hom. Act.* 9 [PG 60.80.13–14]; my translation).

An additional piece of corroborative evidence, though coming some time after Luke-Acts, is tantalizing and insightful. In the *Acts of John* we find the apocryphal tale of how the Apostle John is instrumental in the resurrection of two individuals. When John reaches the home of the deceased, he prays before the gathered crowd: 'Now the time of refreshing (καιρὸς ἀναψύξεως) and confidence has come with you, O Christ; now is the time for us weary ones to have help from you, physician, who heal [sic] freely' (*Acts John* 22). He continues with a prayer, in which he pleads for Christ to bring the knowledge of salvation to the heathen observers by raising up the two dead persons. 'For many of them shall be saved, after they have known your power through the resurrection of the departed (διὰ τοῦ ἐγηγέρθαι τοὺς ἀποψύξαντας).' It is remarkable that the Apostle associates καιρὸς ἀνα-

---

[116] Augustin George, 'L'eschatologie,' in *Études sur l'œuvre de Luc* (SB; Paris: Gabalda, 1978), 329.

[117] Most translations (such as NRSV) have 'faint with fear' or the like (MOFFATT: 'swooning with panic'), but NAB has 'die of fright.' BDAG (125) includes either rendering; however, Luke 21:27 tips the scales in favour of fainting.

[118] Cf. 2 Macc 7:23; 14:46.

ψύξεως with his request for Christ to raise up two people from the dead. This association is strengthened by the fact that the deceased are designated as 'those who have expired' (τοὺς ἀποψύξαντας).[119]

7.3.3.3.2 Resurrected Prophet Like Moses and Israel's Repentance (3:22–26)

Jesus, as the prophet like Moses that God has raised up, is the vital link between Israel and her participation in the eschatological deliverance described in 3:20–21. The present opportunity to prepare for the consummation of God's salvific action has been foretold by Israel's ancient prophets. The necessity of the Messiah's suffering was 'announced beforehand (προκατήγγειλεν) through the mouth of all the prophets (διὰ στόματος πάντων τῶν προφητῶν)' (3:18). God 'spoke (ἐλάλησεν) through the mouth of his holy prophets of old (διὰ στόματος τῶν ἁγίων ἀπ' αἰῶνος αὐτοῦ προφητῶν)' about Israel's future restoration (3:21). Now in 3:22–26 Israel's present accountability is explicitly tied to the prophetic tradition, which has come to its summit in the resurrected Jesus, the prophet like Moses. Two pairs of statements express this.

1.1 Moses spoke (note the μέν) about the prophet like Moses whom God 'will raise up (ἀναστήσει)' (3:22–23).
1.2 For that matter (note the δέ), 'all the prophets (πάντες οἱ προφῆται)' in succession since Samuel 'spoke (ἐλάλησαν) and announced (κατήγγειλαν)' these days (3:24).
2.1 'You (ὑμεῖς)' are the sons of the prophets and the people of Israel's covenant God, the seed of Abraham in whom all families of the earth 'will be blessed (ἐνευλογηθήσονται)' (3:25).
2.2 'To you (ὑμῖν) first' God, 'having raised up (ἀναστήσας) his servant,' sent him to in order to 'bless you (εὐλογοῦντα ὑμᾶς)' by turning each of you from your wicked ways (3:26).

(1.1) The prophetic words from Moses are comprised of a composite citation from Deut 18:15–20 and Lev 24:27. Three points from this prophecy may be highlighted. First, Moses predicted that the Lord God will 'raise up' a Moses-like prophet. The appropriation of the word ἀνίστημι is sufficiently polyvalent to imply being 'raised up' as Israel's prophetic leader and being 'raised up' from the dead.[120] The nuance of resurrection is supported by the flow of the speech up to this point, which does not mention Jesus' entrance into public ministry, but rather his death and resur-

---

[119] We prefer our translation 'those who have expired' to Elliott's 'the departed' (*Apocryphal New Testament*, 312). The Greek text is from Corpus Christianorum: Series apocryphorum (eds. Eric Junod and Jean-Daniel Kaestli; Turnhout, 1983–), 1:169.

[120] Marguerat ('Luc-Actes: La résurrection à l'œuvre dans l'histoire,' 205) also notes the play on words here.

rection. Second, the prophecy indicates the Mosaic prophet's status as the authorized communicator of God's will ('listen to whatever he tells you'). Third, those who do not heed the prophet will be utterly destroyed or uprooted from among the people. The eschatological leader of God's people—Jesus, who has been raised up—creates a division within Israel. As Simeon had prophesied, he is 'destined for the falling and rising of many in Israel' (Luke 2:34). The obverse of repenting and taking part in the καιροὶ ἀναψύξεως and full restoration of Israel is for every ψυχή that does not listen to the prophet to be totally rooted out from among the λαός.[121]

(1.2) This statement follows upon the previous prophecy (μέν, 3:22—δέ, 3:24) by invoking the entire prophetic tradition that followed in Moses' train, beginning with Samuel. The doubling up of ἐλάλησαν and κατήγγειλαν seems repetitive of λαλέω in 3:22 and προκαταγγέλλω in 3:18.[122] Peter says that the age-old prophecies apply to 'these days.' Israel *now* lives at a decisive moment. Each person's present response to the prophet like Moses will determine his or her involvement in God's saving purpose for Israel.

(2.1) Peter appeals to his listeners as privileged heirs of the prophets and of the covenant made by 'the God of your ancestors' with Abraham. His sermon began with a reference to 'the God of Abraham and Isaac and Jacob, the God of our ancestors' who 'glorified his servant Jesus' (2:13). This presses the necessity for his listeners to maintain (or adjust) their alignment with God's purposes as these have been and continue to be expressed through his prophets. Peter cites the crowning promise to Abraham (Gen 22:18; cf. 26:4) that all the families of the earth will be blessed (ἐνευλογηθήσονται) through the patriarch's descendants. These words prepare for the conclusion to the sermon in 3:26.

(2.2) We have already considered the resurrectional frame of Peter's speech. It suggests that the risen Jesus brings to fulfilment or is the key to the future fulfilment of promises made to Israel. God sent his servant first to Israel in order to 'bless' them (εὐλογοῦντα). The Abrahamic covenant, invoked in the nativity canticles of Luke's Gospel (Luke 1:54–55, 72–73), is coming to fruition through the resurrected Jesus. The servant whom God raised up from the dead 'was sent' (ἀπέστειλεν) to offer the blessings of salvation to Israel first. This is the grant of repentance and forgiveness of sins that was heralded during Jesus' ministry, but has now taken on new eschatological urgency since his resurrection (Luke 24:46–47), and is being

---

[121] Michael Wolter, 'Israel's Future and the Delay of the Parousia, According to Luke,' in *Jesus and the Heritage of Israel: Luke's Narrative Claim upon Israel's Legacy* (ed. David P. Moessner; LII 1; Harrisburg, Pa.: Trinity Press International, 1999), 319.

[122] TR has προκατήγγειλαν in 3:24.

mediated to the people of God through Jesus' appointed witnesses. The blessing is defined in Acts 3:26 as 'turning each of you from your wicked ways.' Israelites will reject this blessing at their own peril, or accept it so that God will 'send' (ἀποστείλῃ) the Messiah from heaven to bring to completion God's purposes for the resurrection and restoration of Israel (3:20–21). Implicit in the Abrahamic promise is the extension of salvific blessings to people throughout the world. Only in Peter's sermon at the house of Cornelius will this be explicitly identified as a blessing available to Gentiles (10:43).

7.4 Conclusion

Peter's first two sermons in Acts are critical to our understanding of the function of Jesus' resurrection from the dead within Lukan soteriology. Both sermons present the Christ-event within a *theological* matrix in which God is working out his purposes in accordance with divine foresight revealed through his prophets. The resurrection of Jesus has the *christological* function of establishing Jesus as the divinely appointed ruler over Israel, whether as Lord, Davidic Messiah, or prophet like Moses. This christological function is intimately connected with a set of *ecclesiological* consequences. The resurrected Jesus brings the possibility for every person in Israel to repent and receive forgiveness of sins. The offer, however, requires allegiance to Jesus as the risen and exalted sovereign over Israel and God's definitive prophetic spokesman. This inevitably causes a division within Israel and will be a continued source of conflict in the narrative of Acts. Those who accept the lordship of Jesus will experience the true achievement of God's purposes for the nation, while those who reject him will be excluded from the people of God. The continuation of Luke's narrative will progressively reveal that the salvation through Jesus creates division in Israel, but expands the people of God through the inclusion of Gentiles. The complete salvation of God's people through Jesus, finally, is paradigmatically instanced in Jesus' resurrection. The resurrection of Jesus constitutes a powerful *eschatological* dimension of salvation, because he is the first to take part in the eschatological resurrection of the dead. Jesus' resurrection adumbrates and guarantees that those who call upon him as Lord, and accept his outpouring of the Spirit and forgiveness of sins, will also participate in the total restoration of God's kingdom to Israel at the final resurrection.

Chapter 8

Paul's Resurrection Speech at Pisidian Antioch (Acts 13)

8.1 The Resurrection of Jesus in Paul's Speeches

Paul's role as a witness to the risen Jesus is featured in the defence speeches in Acts. These final speeches are crucial for the movement of Luke's narrative toward its conclusion. In Chapter 9 we will look at relevant portions of these speeches that touch upon the interrelated subjects of Jesus' resurrection and Israel's hope. But before Paul's arrest in Jerusalem, and subsequent detainments in Caesarea and Rome, there are three speeches that provide us with distinctive perspectives on Paul's ministry. Paul's farewell address in Acts 20:18–35 reveals him as a servant of God and caring pastor who has faithfully discharged his duties, 'testifying to both Jews and Gentiles about repentance toward God and faith toward our Lord Jesus' (20:21). Paul characterizes his message broadly as 'testifying to the good news of God's grace' (20:24), 'proclaiming the kingdom' (20:25), 'declaring the complete purpose of God' (20:27), and commending his listeners 'to God and the message of his grace' (20:32). The pastoral setting of the speech sufficiently explains why there was no need to detail the Christian kerygma, which typically culminates with an announcement of Jesus' resurrection. Yet the emphasis upon God's grace, kingdom, and purpose can scarcely be divorced from his action in raising Jesus from the dead. Paul's speech before the Areopagus in Athens gives readers a sample of his preaching to cultivated Gentiles (17:22–31). The speech is sparked by curiosity over Paul's 'proclaiming good news about Jesus and the resurrection' (17:18). The gist of the speech is easily summarized. Paul begins by speaking of pagan ignorance about the true nature of God, and how this ignorance has been overlooked in times past. But now God has issued a command for 'all people everywhere to repent' in view of the final day of judgment. One man has been divinely appointed to judge all the inhabitants of the world, and God has certified this by raising him from the dead (17:30–31). The Areopagite speech is a good example of how the message about Jesus' resurrection can be translated into a digestible form for educated Greeks. But it is Paul's synagogue speech at Pisidian Antioch that constitutes his most comprehensive exposition of the importance of Jesus' resurrection within God's saving purposes (13:16–41).

8.2 Setting and Structure of Paul's Speech at Pisidian Antioch (Acts 13:16–41)

8.2.1 The Narrative Setting of the Speech

The synagogue speech at Pisidian Antioch represents a critical juncture in Luke's narrative, as well as in the life of Paul. By all accounts, this speech is as equally programmatic as Peter's Pentecost speech and Jesus' Nazareth sermon.[1] Paul, or rather Saul, who had been a vicious persecutor of people belonging to the Way, becomes the movement's most ardent proponent. Soon after his commissioning by the risen Jesus he begins to proclaim that Jesus is the Son of God (Acts 9:20) and the Messiah (9:22). Yet his bold preaching is hampered by persecution and suspicion, and his participation in the life and ministry of the church is facilitated by Barnabas (9:27; 11:25–26). He continues to be overshadowed by Barnabas up until the time of the Pisidian Antioch speech. He is repeatedly given second billing behind Barnabas ('Barnabas and Saul,' 11:30; 13:2, 7), and his name shows up last in the list of prophets and teachers at Syrian Antioch (13:1), a list in which Barnabas's name appears first. But after Barnabas and Saul have been commissioned and have set out on their first missionary venture, the focus shifts to Paul. During their ministry on the island of Cyprus, Saul (who, we learn for the first time, is also called Paul, 13:9), is the only character who speaks directly. Then the travelogue, which moves swiftly from Paphos to Pisidian Antioch, is detailing the movements of 'Paul and his companions' (οἱ περὶ Παῦλον, 13:13), and at the synagogue in Antioch it is Paul who rises to address the people (13:16). After the speech we read of 'Paul and Barnabas' (13:43, 46, 50).[2] The speech at Pisidian Antioch is presented as *Paul's* speech, and it is the *first* recorded speech in Luke's recounting of the *first* missionary venture.[3]

---

[1] For a comparison of the three speeches, see Tannehill, *Narrative Unity*, 2:160.

[2] But the order of names does not remain consistent: 'Barnabas and Paul' (14:14; 15:12, 25); 'Paul and Barnabas' (15:2 [2x], 22). The instance in 14:14 may result from the order of the names in 14:12, where Barnabas is called Zeus, while Paul is called Hermes because he was the leading spokesman (Haenchen, *Acts*, 428 n. 3; Bruce, *Acts of the Apostles*, 338). This leaves the alternating order in Acts 15. 'Barnabas and Paul' may stem from an Antiochene source (so Fitzmyer, *Acts*, 549), or the precedence of Barnabas may suit a Jerusalem setting. The oscillation in Acts 15 could be merely stylistic, attributable to Luke's penchant for variety (Haenchen, *Acts*, 447 n. 4), but in any case might not strike listeners as particularly significant.

[3] For a survey of reasons for the speech's programmatic importance, see Strauss, *Davidic Messiah*, 148–49.

The speech stands in continuity with the previous speeches in Acts. The opening retrospective of Israel's history in 13:17-25 is complementary to the main part of Stephen's speech (7:12-45).[4] The speech's *via negativa* argument involving David (13:36-37) is reminiscent of Peter's in 2:29-35, complete with the key text cited from Ps 15:10 LXX (Acts 2:27, 31; 13:35). The speech overlaps with Peter's speech at the house of Cornelius in a number of ways: (1) the address to God-fearers (10:35; 13:16, 26); (2) the reference to John the Baptist (10:37; 13:24-25); (3) Peter's statement in 10:36 (τὸν λόγον [ὃν] ἀπέσταλκεν τοῖς υἱοῖς Ἰσραήλ) resembles Paul's in 13:26 (ἡμῖν [as children of Abraham] ὁ λόγος τῆς σωτηρίας ταύτης ἐξαπεστάλη) without parallels elsewhere; (4) additional detail about the apostolic witness to Jesus' resurrection (10:40-41; 13:31) rather than the simple designation which occurs elsewhere; (5) 'πάντα τὸν πιστεύοντα εἰς αὐτόν receives forgiveness of sins' (10:43) parallels 'ἐν τούτῳ πᾶς ὁ πιστεύων is justified' (13:39); (6) each speech results in controversy over the mission to the Gentiles (10:44-11:18; 13:44-47).[5] The description of Jesus' unjust trial and execution under Pilate (13:28) also resembles that in 3:13-14; but there is the broader parallel of the *Kontrastschema* shared by 13:28-30 with 2:24; 3:13-15; 4:10; 5:30-31; 10:38-40.

The immediate setting for the speech is the least elaborate of any major speech in Acts,[6] but is of no less significance. The concise description of the setting contains three important components:

(1) *Location*. The speech takes place after Paul and Barnabas enter a synagogue ([εἰσ]ελθόντες εἰς τὴν συναγωγήν, 13:14; cf. ἐξιόντων...λυθείσης δὲ τῆς συναγωγῆς, 13:42-43). Immediately after Paul's conversion, the natural place for him to 'proclaim Jesus' was in the synagogues of Damascus (9:20). Paul and Barnabas make it their custom to preach the word of God in the synagogues of the Jews from the very outset of their first missionary venture (13:5; cf. 14:1), and Paul continues this practice (17:1-2, 10, 17; 18:4, 19; 19:8). Yet in none of these other synagogue settings do we have more than a brief summary of Paul's preaching (14:7; 17:2-3; 19:8). Only in Pisidian Antioch, at the earliest stage of Paul's mission, does Luke record a major speech at a Jewish synagogue. The speech, therefore, stands as a model of Paul's preaching and argumentation with Jews elsewhere in the narrative.

---

[4] Cf. Marshall, *Acts*, 221; Paul Schubert, 'The Place of the Areopagus Speech in the Composition of Acts,' in *Transitions in Biblical Scholarship* (ed. J. Coert Rylaarsdam; Essays in Divinity 6; Chicago and London: University of Chicago Press, 1968), 245.

[5] Schubert, 'Place of the Areopagus Speech,' 245.

[6] Schubert, 'Place of the Areopagus Speech,' 244.

(2) *Time and circumstances*. It occurred on the day of the Sabbath (13:14), and as part of the synagogue program. After the 'reading of the Law and the Prophets' the leaders of the synagogue request a 'word of exhortation' from the visiting missionaries (13:15). Aspects of this setting are woven into the speech itself. The synagogue officials ask for a λόγος παρακλήσεως; Paul delivers ὁ λόγος τῆς σωτηρίας ταύτης (13:26). After the speech, Paul and Barnabas are importuned (παρεκάλουν) to speak τὰ ῥήματα ταῦτα again the next Sabbath (13:42). On the following Sabbath nearly the whole city turns out to hear τὸν λόγον τοῦ κυρίου (13:44, 48; τὸν λόγον τοῦ θεοῦ, 13:46). The Jerusalem residents and their rulers are said to have condemned Jesus out of ignorance, not only of his identity, but of 'the voices of the prophets that are read every Sabbath' (13:27), so that they unwittingly 'carried out everything written about him' (13:29). The rhythm of Sabbath day readings forms a common thread between the people of Jerusalem and those who attend synagogue in Antioch of Pisidia. Paul's audience—unlike their Jerusalem counterparts (cf. 13:27)—can be 'in the know' (γνωστὸν οὖν ἔστω ὑμῖν) about the forgiveness of sins afforded to them through Jesus, and about how this salvation relates to the Law of Moses (13:38–39). Paul also relays to them a warning 'spoken by the Prophets' (13:40).

(3) The *addressees* of the speech are 'the people' (τὸν λαόν, 13:15). This could be a generic designation for any assembly of people, but it is more likely a reference to 'the people of God.' Paul's apostrophes make this clear: 'Israelites' (13:17), 'brothers' (13:26, 38; cf. 13:15), and 'descendants of Abraham's family' (13:26). Paul acknowledges 'those who fear God' in his audience (13:16, 26), yet he expresses continuity between 'this people of Israel' (13:17a) whom he is addressing and 'the people' with whom they are historically linked (13:17b; cf. 13:23, 24, 31). The luminaries of Israelite history are identified as 'our ancestors' (τοὺς πατέρας ἡμῶν, 13:17), and the promise made 'to the ancestors' (πρὸς τοὺς πατέρας, 13:32) has been fulfilled 'for us, [their] children' (τοῖς τέκνοις [αὐτῶν] ἡμῖν, 13:33). These data substantiate Tannehill's assertion that the speech is 'by a Jew to Jews.'[7] There is a progression in Acts 13 from 'the people' and 'those who fear God' who are addressed in the speech, and the 'many Jews and devoted proselytes' who follow Paul and Barnabas after the speech (13:43), to the gathering of 'almost the entire city' and 'the crowds' (13:44–45), and τὰ ἔθνη to whom Paul and Barnabas turn (13:36).[8] The Jewish prerogative to receive the message of salvation first, followed by division

---

[7] Tannehill, *Narrative Unity*, 2:166.

[8] On this progression, see Danielle Ellul, 'Antioche de Pisidie: Une Prédication... Trois Credos? (Actes 13,13–43),' *FilNT* 5 (1992): 4.

among Jews, and then the extension of the gospel to the Gentiles, is a pattern replicated throughout Paul's ministry up to the very end of Luke's narrative (18:6; 19:9; 26:20; 28:28).

The location of the speech at such a strategic point in Acts, and its programmatic function for the flowering of Paul's mission to both Jews and Gentiles (cf. 9:15–16), accent its importance within the Lukan narrative. The contents of the speech read like a summation and improvement upon the very best rhetorical arguments that have been developed in earlier speeches. The speech combines historical perspective, apostolic testimony, scriptural argumentation, and personal appeal to forge perhaps the most persuasive case to date for the resurrection of Jesus. Furthermore, it more explicitly defines how the benefits of salvation proceed from God's act of raising Jesus up from the dead. The resurrection of Jesus constitutes the fulfilment of God's promise to 'the ancestors' (13:32–33), and to David in particular (13:22–23, 33–37); and forgiveness of sins is bestowed through the personal agency of the Risen One himself (διὰ τούτου / ἐν τούτῳ, 13:38, 39). So integral is Jesus' resurrection to this paradigmatic speech, that we can confidently state that the resurrection of Jesus is the theological focus of its message of salvation.[9]

8.2.2 The Structure of the Speech

Paul's speech has been outlined in various ways, ranging from a loosely structured 'temporal dynamic' between past and present,[10] or a topical arrangement,[11] to a more rigid rhetorical structure.[12] The most straightforward division of the speech is signalled by the repeated apostrophes in 13:16, 26, and 38 (all of them, as in the Pentecost speech, opening with the

---

[9] Hansen ('Preaching and Defense of Paul,' 300) calls Jesus' resurrection the 'theological focal point' of the speech.

[10] John J. Kilgallen, 'Acts 13,38–39: Culmination of Paul's Speech in Pisidia,' *Bib* 69 (1988): 485–96.

[11] C. A. Joachim Pillai (*Apostolic Interpretation of History: A Commentary on Acts 13:16–41* [New York: Exposition University Press, 1980], 8) offers the following topical division of the speech: introduction (13:16–23); account of John the Baptist (13:24–26); the Christian kerygma (13:27–31); scriptural proofs (13:32–37); call to repentance (13:38–41). Soards (*Speeches in Acts*, 80) outlines the speech around both topical shifts and the repeated addresses in 13:16, 26, and 38.

[12] (a) *Exordium* or proem (13:16); (b) *narratio* (13:17–25); (c) *propositio* (13:26); (d) *probatio* or the setting forth of explanatory proofs (13:27–37); (e) *peroratio* or final exhortation (13:38–41). Cf. George A. Kennedy, *New Testament Interpretation through Rhetorical Criticism* (Chapel Hill: University of South Carolina Press, 1984), 124–25; Witherington, *Acts*, 407.

word ἄνδρες).[13] Danielle Ellul segments the speech according to the repeated addresses, and discerns parallels between the three divisions: OT credo—John the Baptist disqualified as Messiah (13:16–25); NT credo—David disqualified as Messiah (13:26–37); Pauline credo—risk for the people of Israel to be disqualified (13:38–41).[14] This kind of threefold structure, which detects verbal and thematic contacts between the divisions, is preferable to temporal or topical approaches. At the same time, we need not neglect rhetorical cues within the speech. Josef Pichler's structural analysis appreciates the shaping force of the three addresses, yet is attentive to rhetorical indicators. He outlines the speech as follows: (1) *narratio* (13:16b–25); (2) *argumentatio* (13:26–37), noting the 'Grundthese' in 13:26, the commencement of the argument in 13:27 with the word γάρ, and the ὅτι / διότι statements in 13:33–35; (3) *peroratio* (13:38–41).[15] The advantage of this approach is that it rightly sees the influence of rhetoric within the speech, yet recognizes the speech's unique structural development without straitjacketing it into a precise form found in the ancient rhetorical handbooks.

8.3 Paul's Resurrection Speech at Pisidian Antioch (Acts 13:16–41)

8.3.1 Narratio *(13:16b–25): Historical Survey Culminating in Israel's Saviour, Jesus*

Paul opens his speech with an address to his audience (ἄνδρες Ἰσραηλῖται καὶ οἱ φοβούμενοι τὸν θεόν) and an appeal for their attention (13:16b). Then he launches into a rapid survey of Israel's history.

Paul immediately denotes his audience's intimate relationship to God's actions throughout Israel's history. The central actor in the following history is 'the God of this people Israel' (ὁ θεὸς τοῦ λαοῦ τούτου Ἰσραήλ, 13:17a). The demonstrative pronoun τούτου suggests that Paul is pointing to the current embodiment of God's people, Israel, in Jewish communities throughout the world (cp. 'the entire house of Israel,' 2:36). Josef Pichler correctly states: 'Faßt man das τούτου als Demonstrativpronomen auf, wird

---

[13] Cf. David A. deSilva, 'Paul's Sermon in Antioch of Pisidia,' *BibSac* 151 (1994): 35; Strauss, *Davidic Messiah*, 153, 156–57; Schneider, *Apg.*, 1:130.

[14] Ellul, 'Une Prédication...Trois Credos,' 3–14.

[15] Josef Pichler, *Paulusrezeption in der Apostelgeschichte: Untersuchungen zur Rede im pisidischen Antiochien* (ITS 50; Innsbruck and Vienna: Tyrolia, 1997), 132–34 (for a synopsis), 135–206 (for a complete structural analysis).

die synagogale Versammlung als Volk Israel bezeichnet.'[16] Paul's listeners, 'the people' (13:15) or 'Israelites' (13:16), stand in continuity with 'the people' delivered from Egypt by God (13:17), 'all the people of Israel' to whom John the Baptist preached a baptism of repentance (13:24), and 'Israel' to whom God has brought 'a Saviour, Jesus' (13:23). What God has promised or accomplished for 'our ancestors' (13:17) is organically related to what God is bringing to pass among 'us, their children' (13:33).

'God' is the subject of ten aorist verbs in this section of the speech: ἐξελέξατο, ὕψωσεν, ἐξήγαγεν, ἐτροποφόρησεν, κατεκληρονόμησεν, ἔδωκεν (2x), ἤγειρεν, εἶπεν, ἤγαγεν. The historical actions are succinctly described.

(1) One long sentence chronicles God's election of Israel's ancestors (13:17a), his exaltation and later deliverance of his people from Egypt (13:17b), the forty years in the wilderness (13:18), and the grant of Canaan for an inheritance (13:19), all accounting for 450 years of Israel's history (13:20).

(2) The phrase καὶ μετὰ ταῦτα marks the next stage of Israel's history in which the nation was ruled by judges, until the time of Samuel (3:20).

(3) Then (κἀκεῖθεν) they asked for a king, and God gave them Saul (13:21). With the introduction of Israel's monarchy, the summary expands somewhat in the provision of basic lineal information about Israel's first king. After removing Saul, God 'raised up' (ἤγειρεν) David as king. The historical survey seems to be reaching toward a climax, since David's installation as king is accompanied by a solemn, divine pronouncement (εἶπεν μαρτυρήσας): 'I have found David, son of Jesse, a man after my own heart, who will do all my wishes (θελήματα)' (13:22).

(4) Without any intervening history (e.g., the rest of Israel's united monarchy, the period of divided monarchy, Babylonian captivity, or the return from exile), God's climactic act in Israel's history is described in its relation to king David: 'From this man's seed, according to promise, God has brought to Israel a Saviour, Jesus' (13:32). Three key terms emerge from this declaration. (a) 'Promise' (ἐπαγγελία) in all likelihood refers to God's promise to David in 2 Sam 7:12 that one of his descendants would be established in a permanent kingship (cf. 2 Sam 22:51; Ps 17:51 LXX). (b) 'Jesus' is introduced for the first time in the speech.[17] He will not be referred to by that name again until the equally climactic announcement in 13:32–33 (he is referred to only as τοῦτον in 13:27). (c) Jesus is called 'Saviour.' Strauss emphasizes the fact that Jesus was dubbed 'Saviour'

---

[16] Pichler, *Paulusrezeption*, 143. Marshall ('"Israel" and the Story of Salvation,' 356) says '"this people Israel" encompasses past and present members.'

[17] Jesus' name is positioned last in the main clause for emphasis, while reference to David (τούτου) occupies a correspondingly emphatic first position.

even before his birth (cf. Luke 2:11) and that salvation vocabulary is applied to him during his earthly ministry.[18] This is true, but the nearest identification of Jesus as Saviour is in Acts 5:31, which points to his post-resurrection saving activity, and there is no hint of Jesus' earthly ministry in the present speech. The David-Jesus nexus will be capitalized on later in the speech in terms of Jesus' resurrection. F. F. Bruce writes: 'In the present homily it is David who provides the transition from the kerygma of days gone by to the kerygma of the new age. The mighty acts of God in history have culminated in the mightiest act of all, the resurrection of Jesus.'[19] However, the typological circuit will not be closed until 13:32–37, so that the comparison of David (whom God 'raised up') and Jesus (whom he 'has brought') here anticipates further development.[20]

(5) The final element within the historical survey, John the Baptist, is closely associated with, and subservient to, the introduction of Jesus. First, John is introduced in a genitive absolute that describes his function as one who preaches a repentance-baptism to all Israel in preparation for Jesus, who was named in the previous independent clause (note the repetition of πρό: προκηρύξαντος Ἰωάννου πρὸ προσώπου, 13:24).[21] Second, John is said to have been 'finishing his course' (13:25a). Third, he disclaims any identification as Israel's coming deliver (13:25b). Finally, he expresses self-abasement in connection with the One who is coming after him (13:25c). This thumbnail sketch of John is in perfect accord with the Lukan *synkrisis* in the nativity scenes (Luke 1–2),[22] the account of John's ministry (3:1–18), and Jesus' encounter with two of John's disciples (7:18–35). It is not a digression or afterthought.[23] John's prophetic ministry is a necessary prelude

---

[18] Strauss, *Davidic Messiah*, 159.

[19] F. F. Bruce, 'Paul's Use of the Old Testament in Acts,' in *Tradition and Interpretation in the New Testament: Essays in Honor of E. Earle Ellis for His 60th Birthday* (eds. Gerald F. Hawthorne with Otto Betz; Grand Rapids: Eerdmans, 1987), 72; cf. Johnson, *Acts*, 232.

[20] Scribes have refined the symmetry by altering ἤγαγεν to ἤγειρε (13:23), ostensibly to match the same verb used of David in 13:22 (cf. NA^{27}). It is unlikely (*pace* Strauss, *Davidic Messiah*, 159 n. 1) that the change was due to scribes thinking that God's 'bringing' Jesus to Israel as Saviour is equivalent to his 'raising up' Jesus (in the sense of introducing him onto the world stage). It is more probable that 'bringing' was considered inadequate or incorrect, diminishing the parallelism between David being 'raised up' and Jesus being 'raised up (from the dead)' (13:30, 32–33, 36–37; cf. 5:30–31).

[21] Ellul, 'Une Prédication...Trois Credos,' 7.

[22] Cf. Green, *Luke*, 51.

[23] *Pace* Barrett (*Acts*, 1:637) who says 13:24 is added 'almost in the form of an afterthought'; Marshall (*Acts*, 224), 'something of a digression'; Haenchen (*Acts*, 415), 'a short excursus.'

to Jesus' (cf. Acts 1:5; 19:4), and here John's statements serve as testimony undergirding the claim that God has brought forth Jesus as Israel's Saviour.[24]

8.3.2 Argumentatio *(13:26–37): Kerygma and Scriptural Proof*

A new division within the speech is indicated by a renewed address to the audience. This time Paul addresses 'brothers,' 'descendants of Abraham's family,' and 'those among you who fear God.' Even as Paul began by associating his listeners with Israel's history, he now associates them with the culmination of that history. Paul articulates the main proposition of the speech: 'to us the word of this salvation has been sent' (13:26b).[25] Whereas in the first section of the speech Paul began by speaking of 'the God of *this* (τούτου) people, Israel' (13:17), now he announces 'the word of *this* (ταύτης) salvation' that has been sent 'to us' (ἡμῖν). One can hardly miss the contact between this statement about the arrival of the word of 'salvation' (σωτηρία) and 13:23, which heralded the fact that God has brought to Israel 'a Saviour (σωτήρ), Jesus.' The history of God's activity in Israel, climaxing with David and his heir *par excellence*, Jesus, is directly relevant to an understanding of God's present message of salvation to his people. This part of Paul's speech will focus first on the story of Jesus (the kerygma) before demonstrating its correlation with the Davidic promise.

8.3.2.1 THE CHRISTIAN KERYGMA (13:27–31)

The message of salvation is encapsulated in the story of Jesus. The conjunction γάρ leads into the argumentative section of the speech, which substantiates Paul's proposition that the message of salvation has indeed been sent to Israel. What follows is a presentation of the kerygma. The presentation bears similarities to previous rehearsals. Like 3:13–15 and 5:30–31, but unlike 2:22–24 and 10:36–42, Paul's summary does not include information about Jesus' prophetic ministry of teaching and healing, but concentrates on his trial, execution, and resurrection. The account sounds out a pair of characteristic motifs found in earlier reflections on the death and resurrection of Jesus. First, Paul observes the ignorance of the Jerusalem residents and their rulers who are responsible for condemning Jesus to death. This failure to recognize Jesus, and lack of understanding about the prophets, is coupled with an unwitting fulfilment of 'all the things written concerning him' (13:27, 29; cf. 3:17–18). A leitmotif of Luke's post-resurrection

---

[24] Soards, *Speeches in Acts*, 83–84.

[25] NIV and NAB inaccurately render 'this message of salvation' instead of 'the message of this salvation.' The demonstrative ταύτης clearly agrees with σωτηρίας.

scenes was the conjunction of recognizing Jesus with understanding the Scriptures (Luke 24:13–48). Second, the death and resurrection of Jesus form the heart of the scriptural message about him (τὰ περὶ αὐτοῦ γεγραμμένα, Acts 13:29; cf. Luke 22:37; 24:27, 44). It is this message that the people of Jerusalem failed to grasp (despite hearing the Prophets every Sabbath), and that Paul is conveying to his listeners; but the scriptural demonstration will not be set forth until the basic elements of the kerygma have been summarized.

There is a possible parallel between the ancient Israelites' misguided request for a king (Acts 13:21) and the Jerusalemites' request to Pilate that Jesus be put to death (13:28). If so, God's contrasting action was, in the first case, to eventually remove Saul and 'raise up' David as king (13:22), and in the second, to 'raise up' Jesus from the dead. Be that as it may, the contrast scheme is appropriated here as elsewhere (cf. the close parallels in 3:15; 4:10; 10:40). Human ignorance is overruled by divine action: *God raised Jesus from the dead* (13:30).

The final element of the kerygma has to do with the witness to the resurrection of Jesus. Paul's statement coheres with everything that has been written so far in Luke-Acts about the apostolic witness to Jesus' resurrection (13:31). (1) Jesus' appearance over many days (ὃς ὤφθη ἐπὶ ἡμέρας πλείους) reads like a stylistic variation of 1:3 (δι' ἡμερῶν τεσσαράκοντα ὀπτανόμενος).[26] (2) Those to whom he appeared are precisely they who came up with him to Jerusalem from Galilee. A person's continuous presence with Jesus throughout his ministry up until the time of his resurrection (or ascension) has been consistently set forth as the litmus test for being a witness to Jesus' resurrection (1:21–22; 10:38–42; cf. Luke 23:49, 55; 24:6–7; Acts 4:10–13). (3) These persons are called 'his witnesses to the people' (cf. Luke 24:48; Acts 1:8, 22; 2:32; 3:15; 5:32; 10:41). Acts 10:41 records the fact that Jesus did not appear to all the people, but only to witnesses selected by God, namely 'us' (says Peter, representing the Twelve), those who ate and drank with Jesus after his resurrection (cf. Luke 24:41–43; Acts 1:4). The Lukan Paul does not enter into evidence his own encounter with the risen Jesus, because it would not have had the same probative value in this setting. Even the Paul of the NT letters recognized a difference between the appearance of Jesus to him and to the other apostles (1 Cor 15:8). Both the Twelve and Paul saw Jesus after his resurrection. Both were specially selected by God (προχειροτονέω, Acts 10:41; προχειρίζω, 22:14; 26:16). Both testified to what they had 'seen and heard' (Acts 4:20; 22:15; 26:16). Yet *what* they had seen and heard were not identical. The Twelve could personally attest to the fact that the same Jesus

---

[26] Lake and Cadbury, *BC* 4:154.

who lived and ministered in Galilee was killed and raised to life in Jerusalem. In this strict sense, only they could be witnesses to the *resurrection* of Jesus. Paul, like Stephen, had beheld the risen and exalted Jesus, and so both of them could be designated witnesses of the *resurrected* Jesus (Paul: 22:14–15; 26:16; Stephen: 22:20). Paul's witness may also be distinguished from the Twelve's by the fact that their witness was directed primarily to 'the people' (10:42; 13:31) while Paul's more successfully extended to the Gentiles (9:15; 22:21; 26:17, 20, 23; 28:28).[27]

8.3.2.2 DEMONSTRATION FROM THE SCRIPTURES (13:32–37)

The καὶ ἡμεῖς ὑμᾶς at the head of 13:32 signals a transition from the kerygmatic testimony to Jesus' resurrection to the scriptural demonstration of its significance.[28] Paul announces that the promise made to Israel's ancestors has been fulfilled 'for us, their children' by raising up Jesus (13:32–33a).[29] The language of announcement (εὐαγγελιζόμεθα) hints at the salvific character of the message ('the word of this salvation,' 13:26).[30] However, it is Paul's reference to 'the promise' (ἐπαγγελίαν) that traces the trajectory backwards to the climax of his recital of Israel's history, when he spoke of God bringing a Saviour, Jesus, to Israel 'according to promise' (κατ' ἐπαγγελίαν, 13:23). The promise made to the ancestors must be summed up in the promise to David in 2 Sam 7:12.[31] Since the concept of fulfilment was closely correlated with 'the voices of the prophets' and 'what has been written' in 13:27–28, one may naturally expect a scriptural grounding for the claim that God has fulfilled the ancestral promise in Jesus. Indeed, that is exactly what we find in 13:33b–37. But before we consider these scriptural data, we must first inquire into the means by which the ancestral promise has been achieved.

The referent of ἀναστήσας Ἰησοῦς in 13:33 is not universally agreed upon. The majority of scholars read it as a reference to Jesus' resurrection, while a few others think it refers to his entrance onto the world scene. Martin Rese holds the latter position, and lists six arguments in support of

---

[27] Cf. Marshall, *Acts*, 225; Tannehill, *Narrative Unity*, 2:169.

[28] The two pronouns are clearly emphatic. The καί may function as a simple connective (or may be pleonastic) as most translators understand, but could possibly function adjunctively, as Fitzmyer translates: 'we too are proclaiming to you' (*Acts*, 506).

[29] On the textual difficulty with [αὐτῶν] ἡμῖν, see *TCGNT* 362.

[30] Cf. Pichler, *Paulusrezeption*, 240.

[31] That 2 Sam 7 is the subtext for Paul's discussion of God's fulfilment of the promise in Jesus, see Dale Goldsmith, 'Acts 13:33–37: A *Pesher* on II Sam 7,' *JBL* 87 (1968): 321–24. The application of the Davidic promise to Jesus was announced to Mary in Luke 1:32–33.

it.³² (1) The application of the historical account in 13:23–31 begins with 13:32, and 13:33 (ἀναστήσας) sums up the entire historical appearance of Jesus, while 13:34–37 concerns his resurrection. (2) The parallel between 13:22–23 and 13:33.³³ (3) In contrast to 13:30 and 13:34, the phrase ἐκ νεκρῶν is omitted in 13:33. (4) ἀνίστημι has this meaning in 3:22, 26; 7:37. (5) There are no examples of Ps 2:7 used to refer to the resurrection. (6) In Acts 17:18 the content of Paul's preaching is 'Jesus and the resurrection.' Arguments (5) and (6) are the least forceful. As to (5), even if Ps 2:7 were not used elsewhere of Jesus' resurrection (which is debatable, as we shall see), it would not prove that it is not being used in that way here. The force of (6) is difficult to comprehend. There is nothing to suggest that what is meant is a sequence, such as '(the appearance of) Jesus and (then) the resurrection.' Number (1) proceeds from a faulty outline of the speech, and is really only an instance of question-begging. It states what needs to be proven, namely that 13:33 refers to the whole life of Jesus. Number (2) assumes that 13:22–23 has in mind the whole life of David and of Jesus respectively. But the 'raising up' of David refers to the commencement of his kingship, and the 'bringing' of Jesus is too vague to be applied either broadly to his whole life or narrowly to his resurrection. The meaning of this comparison between David and Jesus awaits further development in 13:32–37. Number (3) is of no great consequence because Luke clearly uses ἀνίστημι elsewhere of Jesus' resurrection without the additional qualifier ἐκ νεκρῶν (2:24, 32). Argument (4) is not decisive. Acts 3:22, 26 cannot be unambiguously applied to Jesus' whole life, because that speech does not focus on Jesus' pre-resurrection life (cf. 3:13, 15). The quotation from Deut 18:15 in Acts 7:37 probably applies typologically to Jesus, but the application is not clarified in Stephen's speech, except probably with respect to his rejection by his own people (cf. 7:52). Other allusions to Jesus as the prophet like Moses do not seem to be efficacious without the accompanying reality of Jesus' resurrection from the dead (cf. Luke 24:19–26; Acts 2:22–24).

Several arguments may be advanced in favour of ἀναστήσας Ἰησοῦς as a reference to Jesus' being raised up from the dead. (1) The segment leading up to this point is concerned with Jesus' trial, execution, and resurrection (13:27–31), with 13:30 referring explicitly to God raising Jesus from the dead, and 13:31 speaking of Jesus' post-resurrection appearances. Jesus' resurrection is clearly the topic of discussion in 13:34–37. If ἀναστήσας

---

³² Martin Rese, *Alttestamentliche Motive in der Christologie des Lukas* (SNT 1; Gütersloh: Mohn, 1969), 83–84.

³³ For this argument, see also Bruce, *Acts of the Apostles*, 309; and Strauss (*Davidic Messiah*, 163) who thinks this is the most cogent argument for this position.

Ἰησοῦς in 13:33 were a general reference to Jesus' earthly life, it would interrupt the flow of thought in the passage.³⁴ (2) If on the other side of the argument it is argued that the qualifier ἐκ νεκρῶν is absent, it may be argued obversely that neither is there a modifier suggesting that Jesus' earthly life is meant (e.g., 'horn of salvation,' Luke 1:69; 'a prophet,' Acts 3:22; 7:37; 'David as king,' 13:22).³⁵ But even if such a qualifier were present, it would not rule out resurrection as the occasion of the 'raising up.' Without indications to the contrary, there seems to be no reason for ἀνίστημι to have one frame of reference in 13:33 ('raised'=brought onto the public scene) and another in 13:34 ('raised...from the dead').³⁶ (3) The 'promise' in 13:23 does not unequivocally point to a mode of fulfilment, beyond the introduction of a saviour, and so the fulfilment of the 'promise' announced in 13:33 should clarify the earlier reference, and not vice versa, particularly since Paul is in this section articulating 'the word of this salvation' in terms of Jesus' death and resurrection. We do know that the fulfilment of the Davidic promise (God's oath to David that he would put one of his descendants on the throne) is expressly identified as 'the resurrection of the Messiah' in 2:30–31. O'Toole has pointed to the description of 'the promise made by God to our ancestors' (26:6–8), which is the hope in the resurrection of the dead that has been realized first in Jesus, just as Moses and the prophets had foretold (26:22–23).³⁷ That Jesus' resurrection embodies in large measure God's covenant faithfulness to Israel can be seen from the fact that 'the God of our ancestors raised up Jesus' (5:30; cf. 3:13). Additional arguments can be marshalled on the basis of the following citation from Ps 2:7, but we think that the above points adequately establish Jesus' resurrection as the means by which the ancestral promise (culminating in the Davidic promise) has been fulfilled. Moreover, we think that the meaning of ἀναστήσας Ἰησοῦς, as well as the flow of logic in the presentation of scriptural proofs, determines the usage of Ps 2:7, and not vice versa. Thus, Ps 2:7 contributes to Paul's overall scriptural argument that God's promise to David has been accomplished through the resurrection of Jesus.

---

³⁴ Haenchen, *Acts*, 411 n. 3; Evald Lövestam, *Son and Saviour: A Study of Acts 13,32–37. With an Appendix: 'Son of God' in the Synoptic Gospels* (ConBNT 18; Lund: Gleerup; Copenhagen: Ejnar Munksgaard, 1961), 9; O'Toole, 'Christ's Resurrection in Acts 13,13–52,' 366. Huub van de Sandt, 'The Quotations in Acts 13,32–52 as a Reflection of Luke's LXX Interpretation,' *Bib* 75 (1994): 30 n. 12.

³⁵ Jacques Dupont, 'Filius meus es tu. L'interprétation de Ps. II,7 dans le Nouveau Testament,' *RSR* 35 (1948): 530.

³⁶ Lövestam, *Son and Saviour*, 10.

³⁷ O'Toole, 'Christ's Resurrection in Acts 13,13–52,' 366; cf. deSilva, 'Paul's Sermon in Antioch of Pisidia,' 41.

8.3.2.2.1 The First Scriptural Witness: Psalm 2:7 (Acts 13:33b)

Psalm 2 is a royal psalm portraying the installation of a king on the Davidic throne. There is little doubt that the psalm was interpreted messianically in Second Temple Judaism, and related intertextually to 2 Sam 7:10–14.[38] What is in question is the psalm's application to the resurrection of the Messiah. The heavenly pronouncement, 'You are my Son,' uttered at Jesus' baptism is probably an echo of Ps 2:7 (Luke 3:22, esp. in D), but it is difficult to see how a reference to Jesus' baptism would be applicable here in Paul's speech.[39] Bock has proposed the ingenious suggestion that the introductory clauses in 13:32–33 divide neatly into three parts, with each part corresponding sequentially to one of the following Scripture citations: proclamation of promise to the ancestors (//13:33b=Ps 2:7); reference to its fulfilment for their children (//13:34b=Isa 55:3); the raising up of Jesus (//13:35=Ps 15:10 LXX).[40] This means ἀναστήσας 'Ιησοῦς refers to the resurrection of Jesus, but is supported primarily by the quotation from Ps 15:10. Psalm 2:7, within this configuration, refers to the promise of sonship, and relates to resurrection only through its connection to Ps 15:10.[41] The Achilles' heel of this interpretation is the introductory ὡς clause in Acts 13:33b. This clause indisputably ties Ps 2:7 to the *whole* preceding statement that the promise to the ancestors has been fulfilled for their children by God's raising up Jesus.[42]

The appearance of Ps 2:7 in Heb 1:5 tends to confirm its usage as a resurrection text in Acts 13. The preacher to the Hebrews quotes Ps 2:7 after

---

[38] 4QFlor; *Pss. Sol.* 17:26; cf. Bock, *Proclamation*, 246; Bruce, *Acts of the Apostles*, 309. Lövestam (*Son and Saviour*, 15–23) documents the psalm's messianic usage in post-biblical Judaism, including rabbinic literature.

[39] *Contra* Barrett, *Acts*, 1:645–46; F. F. Bruce, *Commentary on the Book of Acts: The English Text With Introduction, Exposition and Notes* (NICNT; Grand Rapids: Eerdmans, 1956), 260. However, Bruce (in 'Paul's Use of the Old Testament in Acts,' 72) is more amenable to a resurrectional interpretation of Ps 2:7, noting that it is quoted 'in a resurrection context, and the next two quotations are expressly linked to the resurrection.'

[40] Bock, *Proclamation*, 244–45.

[41] Bock (*Proclamation*, 248) views the ὅτι clause in 13:34a, not as an introductory formula for Isa 55:3, but as an explanatory comment on Ps 2:7 that forges a link with Ps 15:10 LXX.

[42] Bock (*Proclamation*, 248) is forced to repunctuate the passage in order to accommodate his proposal. He claims that his repunctuation reveals a structural parallelism: ὡς (13:33), οὕτως (13:34b), διότι (13:35). The manoeuvre is unconvincing, and actually obscures the symmetry: ὅτι...ὡς (13:33), ὅτι...οὕτως (13:34), διότι (13:35). Furthermore, to insert a full stop before ὡς in 13:33 contradicts the usage of ὡς/καθὼς γέγραπται elsewhere in Luke-Acts (Luke 2:23; 3:4; Acts 7:42; 15:15). Cf. the critique of Bock in Strauss, *Davidic Messiah*, 163 n. 1; Hansen, 'Preaching and Defense of Paul,' 303.

he has spoken of how God's Son 'sat down at the right hand of the Majesty on high,' thus placing the psalm citation squarely within an exaltation context. Following the citation, he quotes 2 Sam 7:14, which is at the heart of the Davidic promise tradition. While Psalm 2 is not quoted in Peter's Pentecost speech, the Davidic promise tradition is invoked in Acts 2:30, and linked explicitly with the resurrection of the Messiah in 2:31. Jesus, who is exalted to God's right hand in 2:33, receives the Spirit from the Father. This allusion to a Father-Son relationship is important in view of the previous reference to Jesus' resurrection, and in light of Gabriel's words in Luke 1:32–33 ('he shall be great and shall be called Son of the Most High'). The final conclusion of Peter's speech in Acts 2:36, where Jesus is hailed as both Lord and Messiah, points to the regal power and dignity achieved by God for Jesus by raising him from the dead and seating him at his right hand. The image of coronation/exaltation pictured in Heb 1:5 and Acts 2, along with the accompanying elements from the Davidic promise tradition, make a resurrectional application of Ps 2:7 in Acts 13:33b entirely appropriate.[43] Romans 1:1–3 is an important corroborative text because it draws together the essential components that lie before us in Acts 13: scriptural promise, descent from David, and the declaration of sonship on the basis of resurrection.

Psalm 2:7, therefore, is not out of place as a support for Jesus' resurrection. But does the citation of this psalm in Acts 13:33b indicate an even more direct reference to Jesus' resurrection? Psalm 2:1–2 is quoted in Acts 4:25–26, and interpreted in 4:27–28 as having been played out in the actions of Herod, Pilate, the Gentiles, and the people against Jesus, likely with regard to his trial and crucifixion. In 13:27–29 we may not have a clear allusion to Psalm 2, but it is of no little interest that the residents of Jerusalem and their 'rulers' (cf. 4:26) hand Jesus over to Pilate for execution in accordance with Scripture and in unknowing conformity to the divine purpose. According to the quotation and explanatory comments in 4:25–28, this unjust treatment of Jesus was predicted by David (Ps 1:1–2).[44] In the psalm, the sequel to opposition is God's establishment of his anointed one as king. The drama is paralleled in the life of Jesus in Acts 13. The one who had been crucified and buried, God raised from the dead.[45] If

---

[43] Jacques Dupont, 'L'interprétation des Psaumes,' 295–97; Lövestam, *Son and Saviour*, 26–37.

[44] Cf. W. J. C. Weren, 'Psalm 2 in Luke-Acts: An Intertextual Study,' in *Intertextuality in Biblical Writings: Essays in Honour of Bas van Iersel* (ed. Sipke Draisma; Kampen: J. H. Kok, 1989), 198–99.

[45] deSilva ('Paul's Sermon in Antioch of Pisidia,' 42–43) argues similarly, but does not note the comparison between 4:25–28 and 13:27–29.

the earlier part of the psalm may be applied to the trial and execution of Jesus, Ps 2:7 could easily be applicable to his resurrection from the dead.

One may go one step further in identifying Ps 2:7 as a resurrection prophecy. Lövestam has observed the birth imagery in the expression 'today I have begotten you,' and has sought to connect this expression with the description of Jesus' resurrection in Acts 2:24, as well as with NT passages that combine the birth motif with the idea of resurrection.[46] Since we have already discussed at length the interpretation of 2:24, we need not trace all the contours of Lövestam's discussion, which intersect with ours at many points. The image of God putting an end to the travail of death in the description of Jesus' resurrection in 2:24 may present a useful analogy to the concept of God 'begetting' a son in 13:33 (Ps 2:7). Lövestam is cautious about pressing the birth imagery too far in phrases such as πρωτότοκος ἐκ τῶν νεκρῶν (Col 1:18) and πρωτότοκος τῶν νεκρῶν (Rev 1:5), since they may only be indicative of priority in time and rank (i.e., Jesus is the *first* to take part in the final resurrection).[47] What is nevertheless remarkable is that, although the concept of birth may not be uppermost in these expressions, the *language* or *figure* of begetting is clearly present,[48] and it is associated with the idea of resurrection or enthronement. Revelation 1:5 is significant because it alludes to Old Testament passages that belong within the Davidic promise tradition, such as Isa 55:4, Ps 88:36–38 LXX, and Ps 88:29 LXX. Jesus fulfils the divine promise to David in his capacity as πρωτότοκος τῶν νεκρῶν. One thing Lövestam does not notice is how the description of Jesus' resurrection in Acts 2:24 ('having brought the birth pangs of death to an end') is followed by the introduction to Ps 15:8–11 LXX in Acts 2:25a, 'For David speaks about him....' The psalm citation is then interpreted as a Davidic prophecy concerning the enthronement/ resurrection of the Messiah (2:29–36). We may conclude that at least the *figure* of begetting is associated with the resurrection in the NT, so that God's declaration in Ps 2:7 ('today I have begotten you') may be naturally interpreted within the co-text of Acts 13 as a scriptural proof that God raised Jesus from the dead.

8.3.2.2.2 The Second Scriptural Witness: Isaiah 55:3 (Acts 13:34)
The citation of Isa 55:3 in Acts 13:34 is truly the *crux interpretum* of Paul's speech. The welter of interpretations defies neat classification. The diverse explanations approach the problem differently and are unevenly pre-

---

[46] Lövestam, *Son and Saviour*, 42–48.
[47] Bock (*Proclamation*, 246–48) vigorously opposes Lövestam's interpretation.
[48] Cf. the occurrence of πρωτότοκος in Heb 1:6, following the citations of Ps 2:7 and 2 Sam 7:14.

sented.⁴⁹ We shall divide the interpretive options into three categories, based upon the differences in approach to the citation's relationship to its immediate co-text within the speech. (1) The first set of approaches have in common an emphasis upon the relationship between Isa 55:3 in Acts 13:34 and Ps 15:10 LXX in Acts 13:35. There is no question that the two passages are related to each other after the fashion of the rabbinic interpretive technique of verbal analogy:

13:34 δώσω ὑμῖν / τὰ ὅσια Δαυὶδ / τὰ πιστά
13:35 οὐ δώσεις / τὸν ὅσιόν σου / ἰδεῖν διαφθοράν

How they are related is debated. (a) Lake and Cadbury propose that τὰ ὅσια was unintelligible and therefore needed to be explained by the use of the term in another passage.⁵⁰ The following psalm citation, introduced by διότι, is produced as a verbally parallel explanation of Isa 55:3. The depiction of the 'holy one' not seeing decay furnishes the meaning for 'the holy things': the resurrection. The ὑμῖν in 13:34 is crucial to the argument, because in 13:36 it is noted that another besides David experiences the promise that he will not see corruption. The chief difficulty with this view is that it remains unclear how Ps 15:10 LXX (with its reference to the ὅσιος not seeing decay) shows that τὰ ὅσια means resurrection. It would make better sense for ὅσιος ('holy one') to indicate that τὰ ὅσια, too, refers to the Messiah, and that the entire statement, δώσω ὑμῖν τὰ ὅσια Δαυὶδ τὰ πιστά, should be interpreted as a reference to his resurrection.⁵¹ Another difficulty is that it views the 'holy one' as the referent of ὑμῖν, though the plural pronoun seems to be directed toward Paul's audience (cf. 13:33, 38). (b) Haenchen appears to take both of these criticisms into consideration in his comments on how Ps 15:10 elucidates Isa 55:3: 'In the light of verse 35 the Isaiah text implies: "I will give you Christians the scion of David together

---

⁴⁹ Dupont comments, 'En fait, ces différentes solutions se présentent rarement à l'état pur'; Jacques Dupont, 'ΤΑ ΟΣΙΑ ΔΑΥΙΔ ΤΑ ΠΙΣΤΑ (Actes 13,34=Isaïe 55,3),' in *Études sur les Actes des Apôtres* (LD 45; Paris: Les Éditions du Cerf, 1967), 338. Dupont (339–42) summarizes the positions of five representative interpreters. Bock (*Proclamation*, 252–53) follows this classification, as does Strauss (*Davidic Messiah*, 168–73), but the latter pares the list down to four categories.

⁵⁰ Lake and Cadbury, BC 4:155–56. Williams essentially agrees with this interpretation; C. S. C. Williams, *The Acts of the Apostles*, (HNTC; New York: Harper & Brothers, 1957), 164–65. Bauer ('ὅσιος,' BAGD 585) presents a similar interpretation, but takes τὰ ὅσια to mean 'divine decrees' (in contrast to 'human statutes,' τὰ δίκαια).

⁵¹ Strauss (*Davidic Messiah*, 169) proposes this more consistent application of rabbinic analogy, but rejects this interpretation because the neuter plural τὰ ὅσια probably cannot refer to a person. This, however, is not beyond the bounds of possibility. Lövestam (*Son and Saviour*, 79 n. 4) draws attention to the Greek usage of the neuter plural for persons.

with the immortal life of the Resurrection.'"[52] (c) Wendt rejects interpretations of Acts 13:34 based upon the context of Isa 55:3, and which therefore understand τὰ ὅσια Δαυὶδ τὰ πιστά as 'the holy salvation blessings promised to David' ('die dem David verheissenen heiligen Heilsgüter').[53] Like the others in this category, Wendt insists upon interpreting the expression in connection with the quotation from Ps 15:10. He deduces from the correlation of ὅσιος and τὰ ὅσια that David's personal holiness or piety is meant by τὰ ὅσια Δαυὶδ. The fact that David 'served the purpose of God' is indicative of his holy character (13:36). But the oracle from Isaiah points to a permanent (πιστά) holiness, which David could not achieve, since he died with his own generation. Therefore, only a holy one with an imperishable life, such as the resurrected Jesus, could realize the constant holiness predicated of David. The problem with this view is that it is difficult to understand how τὰ ὅσια, the personal character or active piety of David, may be given to another.

(2) A second approach emphasizes the relationship between 13:34 and 13:26, 38–39. Jacques Dupont begins by defining ὅσιος within the moral sphere, using 13:36 (like Wendt did) to point to David's service to God's will.[54] Another key text for Dupont is Luke 1:75 which speaks of service to God 'in holiness (ἐν ὁσιότητι) and justice.' Dupont advances beyond Wendt, however, in observing that the 'holy things of David' are promised 'to you' (ὑμῖν) in Acts 13:34, and he proceeds to show how Paul repeatedly applies the fulfilment of the Davidic promise to his audience (13:26, 32–33, 38).[55] These 'holy things'—or 'holiness' (Dupont's word is 'la sainteté')—may be considered in their concrete manifestations as the purification of sins or justification (13:38–39).[56] These may not be granted by David, because his holy service to God occurred only during his own lifetime. But the Son of David can make forgiveness of sins and justification available, because he is the 'holy one' whom God has preserved from corruption.

Dupont's contribution has influenced a number of scholars.[57] Yet it is not without difficulties. First, it apprehends Isa 55:3 not as a direct prediction of Jesus' resurrection, as the introductory clause in Acts 13:34a seems to

---

[52] Haenchen, *Acts*, 412.

[53] H. H. Wendt, *Die Apostelgeschichte* (9th ed.; Göttingen: Vandenhoeck & Ruprecht, 1913), 213–15. For summaries of Wendt's view, cf. Lövestam, *Son and Saviour*, 51–52; Strauss, *Davidic Messiah*, 168–69; Bock, *Proclamation*, 253.

[54] Dupont, 'TA 'ΟΣΙΑ ΔΑΥΙΔ ΠΙΣΤΑ,' 347.

[55] Dupont, 'TA 'ΟΣΙΑ ΔΑΥΙΔ ΠΙΣΤΑ,' 351–54.

[56] Dupont, 'TA 'ΟΣΙΑ ΔΑΥΙΔ ΠΙΣΤΑ,' 357.

[57] deSilva, 'Paul's Sermon in Antioch of Pisidia,' 43; Kilgallen, 'Acts 13,33–38,' 497–501; Hansen, 'Preaching and Defence of Paul,' 303; Sandt, 'Quotations in Acts 13,32–52,' 33–42.

suggest, but as an expression of the benefits of that resurrection. Dupont anticipated this criticism, and argued that the focus of 13:34–35 is not on the resurrection itself but on the immortality that results from it.[58] Second, defining τὰ ὅσια within the sphere of moral action does not comport with the meaning of the phrase in Isaiah, where it seems to refer to blessings or benefits of God's covenant with David. However, even if we accept Dupont's definition, there is a problem with his understanding that the 'holiness' of the 'holy one' is somehow communicated or transferred to those who believe in him.[59] There is no indication in the Jewish Scriptures, or even in 13:38–39, that the Davidic deliverer would be the *cause* of the people's holiness, at least not in Dupont's sense.[60] The missing link in this mediation of holiness, not mentioned by Paul in the speech or by Dupont, would probably be the risen Jesus' authority to pour out the gift of the Holy Spirit (Acts 1:5; 2:33; etc; cf. 15:7–9). A third, more fundamental, criticism is that Dupont's interpretation does not adequately account for the *Davidic* nature of the salvation blessings ('the holy things *of David*').[61] In particular, how does God's giving of τὰ ὅσια Δαυίδ fulfil the promises made *to* David?

(3) A third approach interprets the phrase as a reference to God's covenant promises to David.[62] This view recognizes the citation of Isa 55:3 in Acts 13:34 as the *primary* scriptural witness (i.e., in relation to Ps 15:10 LXX which follows) to the fact that God raised Jesus from the dead, and takes seriously the Davidic promise tradition evoked by the expression τὰ ὅσια Δαυίδ τὰ πιστα. Lövestam rejects the notion that the expression was obscure, and would have required explanation.[63] Although the whole expression διαθήσομαι ὑμῖν διαθήκην αἰώνιον, τὰ ὅσια Δαυὶδ τὰ πιστά (Isa 55:3 LXX) has been abridged in Acts 13:34 to δώσω ὑμῖν τὰ ὅσια Δαυὶδ τὰ πιστά (the δώσω probably added to strike a stylistic balance with 13:35), it is difficult to believe that the quotation was simply plucked out of obscurity and paired with Ps 15:10 to clarify its meaning and effect a clever wordplay. The brevity and peculiarity of the expression, and its apparent

---

[58] Dupont, 'ΤΑ ὍΣΙΑ ΔΑΥΙΔ ΠΙΣΤΑ,' 358.

[59] Dupont, 'ΤΑ ὍΣΙΑ ΔΑΥΙΔ ΠΙΣΤΑ,' 358. Dupont has in mind the Pauline idea of participation 'in' Christ's holiness, as evidenced by his quotation from 1 Cor 1:30 (356 n. 72).

[60] Kilgallen, 'Acts 13,33–38,' 502; cf. Rese, *Alttestamentliche Motive*, 88.

[61] For this criticism, see Strauss, *Davidic Messiah*, 170.

[62] This position was championed by Lövestam, *Son and Saviour*, 48–81; followed by Strauss, *Davidic Messiah*, 170–73; Fitzmyer, *Acts*, 517; and expressed in the NRSV ('the holy promises made to David'), NAB ('the benefits assured to David under the covenant'), and ESV ('holy and sure blessings of David').

[63] Lövestam, *Son and Saviour*, 54, 56.

relationship to the Davidic promise tradition, suggest that it was a terse and easily recognizable reference to the covenant promises made to David. These promises, as Strauss summarizes them, are comprised of 'an heir, perpetual favour from God (for that heir), an eternal house, throne and kingdom, and rest and protection from enemies.'[64]

Despite the attractiveness of Dupont's exegesis, this third approach is superior for four reasons. (a) It interprets the scriptural citation in relation to its Isaianic co-text, as well as against the background of the Davidic promise tradition throughout the LXX and within Second Temple Judaism. This precludes any necessity to define 'the holy things of David' within the sphere of morality, since the phrase already operates appropriately within the sphere of God's covenantal relationship with David. (b) It engages directly with the Davidic promise tradition that has already been recalled in Luke's narrative. God's promise to provide David with an heir was noted in 13:23, and explicitly linked with resurrection in 2:30–31. Early on in the Lukan narrative, readers were reminded of the promises to David in the angelic announcement of Jesus' birth (Luke 1:32–33):

> This one will be great and will be called the Son of the Most High, and the Lord God will grant to him the throne of his father David, and he will reign over the house of Jacob forever, and there will be no end to his reign.

Here we can see the promise of sonship, enthronement for David's heir, and the perpetuity of the heir's kingship. These elements of the Davidic promise predominate the discussion of the scriptural witness to Jesus' resurrection in Acts 13:32–37. (c) It is consonant with the flow of the argument within the speech. In order to demonstrate that the promises made to Israel's ancestors have been fulfilled 'by raising up Jesus' from the dead, Paul first presents the quotation from Ps 2:7 (13:33). This Scripture advances the idea that through the resurrection of Jesus, God has raised up the promised Davidic heir (cf. 13:23). The next Scripture from Isa 55:3 is prefaced by the introduction: 'but that he raised him up from the dead, never to return to corruption, he has spoken as follows,...' (13:34). The contrast between the two steps in the argument (ὅτι δὲ ἀνέστησεν αὐτὸν ἐκ νεκρῶν) does not mean that Ps 2:7 refers to Jesus' being 'raised up' onto the world scene, while Isa 55:3 is the first witness to his resurrection from the dead. The contrast, rather, is between God's declaration of Jesus' sonship by virtue of resurrection, and the additional emphasis on Jesus' resurrection *to immortal life* (μηκέτι μέλλοντα ὑποστρέφειν εἰς διαφθοράν), which reinforces the reliability and permanence (τὰ πιστά) of the promises made to David (τὰ

---

[64] Strauss, *Davidic Messiah*, 171. Cf. the survey of the Davidic promise tradition in Strauss (35–74) and Lövestam (*Son and Saviour*, 54–71) as it relates more particularly to Isa 55:3.

ὅσια Δαυίδ).⁶⁵ The Davidic promise of a kingdom which shall not fail cannot be maintained under a king who can be 'killed' (i.e., dethroned). In 13:35 the quote from Ps 15:10 LXX will take this aspect of the argument one step further. (d) That the salvific benefits accrue to the people of Israel (ὑμῖν, 13:34) was characteristic of the Davidic promise tradition within ancient Judaism (2 Sam 7:10; Jer 23:6; Ezek 34:22–31; 37:24–28; 4QFlor; *Pss. Sol.* 17:21) and in Luke-Acts (Luke 1:68–73).⁶⁶ Forgiveness of sins and justification no doubt play an integral part in God's bestowal of salvation blessings upon his people (Acts 13:38–39), but they ought not to be equated with the 'holy things of David,' as Dupont does. The forgiveness or release from sins is 'the Way' to become a true descendant of Abraham (i.e., a member of the people of God; Luke 3:8; 19:1–10), escape 'the coming wrath' (Luke 3:7; cf. Acts 2:38, 40), and participate in the future realization of God's reign that has already drawn near in the life, death, and resurrection of Jesus (Acts 3:18–20; 26:18; cf. Luke 13:28–29; Acts 1:3–11; 20:25, 32; 28:23, 31). The 'holy things of David' pertain to that larger complex of salvation blessings (i.e., life in the kingdom of God) which includes God's 'raising up' a promised heir to David and the establishment of an eternal kingship and dominion and inheritance for the people of God, as was promised to Israel's ancestral leaders.

8.3.2.2.3 The Third Scriptural Witness: Ps 15:10 LXX (13:35)

The introductory formula for the third Scripture presents Ps 15:10 LXX as the conclusion to the scriptural testimony. We read διότι καὶ ἐν ἑτέρῳ λέγει—an unusual way of prefacing scriptural citations as divine speech, almost exactly paralleled only in the *other* 'word of exhortation'⁶⁷ in the NT, the Book of Hebrews (Heb 5:6). The 'therefore' (διότι) subordinates this divine pronouncement to the previous two as a logical result. The pledge, 'You will not let your holy one experience decay,' is predicated on God's fulfilment of his promise to 'raise up' Jesus as the Davidic king and to bring about all of the covenant blessings sworn to David (Acts 13:32–34). The quotation (13:35) and the accompanying explanation (13:36–37) mirror Peter's argument in the Pentecost speech. First, the psalm is applied not to David, 'on one hand' (μέν, 13:36), who had served God's purpose in his generation (cp. 'the purpose [βουλή] of God' here with 'all my [i.e.,

---

⁶⁵ *Contra* Strauss (*Davidic Messiah*, 165) who thinks the stress should be placed on 'but that he raised him *from the dead*.' On the other hand, Strauss (171) helpfully notes the verbal correspondence between τὰ πιστά in Isa 55:3 and the promise to David in 2 Sam (Kgdms) 7:16 that his house and kingdom 'will be made sure' (πιστωθήσεται) forever.

⁶⁶ Lövestam, *Son and Saviour*, 81; Strauss, *Davidic Messiah*, 172 n. 1.

⁶⁷ Note λόγος παρακλήσεως found only in Acts 13:15 and Heb 13:22 in the NT.

Paul's Resurrection Speech at Pisidian Antioch 255

God's] wishes [θελήματα]' in 13:22), then 'fell asleep and was laid with his ancestors and experienced decay (εἶδεν διαφθοράν).' It is applied, 'rather' (δέ), to 'the one whom God raised up,' Jesus, who 'did not experience decay' (οὐκ εἶδεν διαφθοράν). Likewise, Peter appealed to the publicly known fact that David was dead and buried in a tomb (2:29), but that the resurrected Jesus 'did not experience decay' (2:31–32). Secondly, in Peter's speech, God's oath to David that he would place one of his descendants on the throne is explained as a prophecy about the resurrection of the Messiah. Paul's speech follows the same logic. The firmness and durability of the covenant promises to David make the resurrection of Jesus inevitable (διότι). God has brought to Israel a Saviour 'according to promise' (cf. 13:23, 32).

8.3.2 Peroratio (13:38–41): Options of Belief or Unbelief in the Risen One

The final section of the speech consists of a pair of conclusive statements (one an announcement, the other a warning), each beginning with inferential οὖν. Again, a new (in this instance, final) division of the speech is indicated by an address to the audience ('brothers'). The introduction to this twofold conclusion (γνωστὸν οὖν ἔστω ὑμῖν) resembles Peter's words in 2:14, 36 (cf. 28:28), and functions as a purportedly incontrovertible assertion. The first conclusion is an announcement that forgiveness of sins is 'proclaimed through/by this [Jesus] (διὰ τούτου),' and that 'everyone who believes in this [Jesus] (ἐν τούτῳ)' is justified from everything that one was not able to be justified by the Law of Moses (13:38–39). This offer of justification has a distinctively Pauline ring.[68] The connection with Jesus' resurrection reminds one of Paul's discussion of justification in Romans, and in particular his statement that Jesus was 'raised for our justification' (Rom 4:25). The Lukan Paul draws the conclusion that it is through belief in 'this one,' that is, the Jesus who was the object of the resurrection texts just previously cited, that one may receive forgiveness of sins. Knowledge of the Scriptures places Paul's audience (and Luke's readers) in a position different from the Jerusalem people who called for Jesus' execution (τοῦτον ἀγνοήσαντες καὶ τὰς φωνὰς τῶν προφητῶν, 13:27).[69] John Chrysostom perceptively asks why additional scriptural testimony was not brought forth here to persuade the audience that there is forgiveness of sins through this Jesus; but then he answers his own query by saying that the object of the

---

[68] On the echo from Paul's theology, see Haenchen, *Acts*, 412; Kilgallen, 'Acts 13,38–39,' 503; Marshall, *Acts*, 228; Witherington, *Acts*, 414.

[69] Ellul, 'Une Prédication...Trois Credos,' 11.

speech up to this point has been to demonstrate that Jesus is risen, and that once this is acknowledged the other fact is indisputable, namely, that 'through this man, indeed, by him there is forgiveness of sins' (*Hom. Act.* 29 [PG 60.217.20–25]; my translation).

The second part of the conclusion (Acts 13:40–41) *is* buttressed by a scriptural citation. It is a warning quoted from Hab 1:5. In Habakkuk the warning related to God's bringing destruction upon Israel by marshalling the dreaded Chaldeans against them. At Qumran a *pesher* on Habakkuk directed this warning to those who rejected the Teacher of Righteousness and had become unfaithful to God's covenant (1QpHab 2.1–10). A *pesher* style of interpretation appears in Paul's speech, as well. It puts detractors on notice that they should be aghast, and should expect to be obliterated,[70] because of their refusal to believe 'the work' that God is doing (13:41). The key idea of God's 'work' is thrice-repeated in the text: 'because of the work (ἔργον) I am doing (ἐργάζομαι) in your days, a work (ἔργον) which you will not believe.' This raises the question of what this work or deed is. God's ἔργον has been most widely interpreted as an allusion to the Gentile mission. Proponents of this view point to the sequel to the speech as evidence. Paul and Barnabas react to Jewish rejection of their message by turning to the Gentiles (Acts 13:45–47).[71] Some interpreters also refer to the commissioning of Paul and Barnabas to 'the work' (τὸ ἔργον) which God had called them (13:2).[72] The second point is easily dispensed with. The ἔργον in 13:2, 14:26, and 15:38 is Paul and Barnabas's missionary work, generally conceived.[73] It goes without saying that Paul's mission involved being sent to Gentiles, kings, and the people of Israel (9:15), and that the Gentile

---

[70] The verb θαυμάζω should be translated with a negative connotation in this judgmental context ('be aghast,' or perhaps 'be alarmed'), and not in the neutral or even positive sense of most English translations ('be amazed,' 'be astonished,' 'wonder'). The image conveyed by the passive form of ἀφανίζω is one of sudden disappearance, in the negative sense of being swiftly eliminated or destroyed (cf. Barrett, *Acts*, 1:652).

[71] Haenchen, *Acts*, 413; Fitzmyer, *Acts*, 519; Roloff, *Apg.*, 208; Schneider, *Apg.*, 2:141; Dupont *Salvation to the Gentiles*, 140; deSilva, 'Paul's Sermon in Antioch of Pisidia,' 47–48; Sandt, 'Quotations in Acts 13,32–52,' 45–50; cf. Wolter, 'Israel's Future and the Delay of the Parousia,' 324. Barrett's opinion (*Acts*, 1:652–53) is more nuanced, since he distinguishes between God's work accomplished in Christ and the Jewish rejection that follows.

[72] Fitzmyer, *Acts*, 519; Sandt, 'Quotations in Acts 13,32–52,' 45. Sandt points to the three places (13:2; 14:26; 15:38) where ἔργον indicates the mission to the Gentiles. He also notes the only other place where the verb ἐκδιηγέομαι occurs (15:3), viz., in a reporting of the conversion of the Gentiles. The latter point is exceedingly feeble. There is no compelling reason why readers would consider this verb especially associated with the recounting of the Gentile mission.

[73] Cf. Pillai, *Apostolic Interpretation of History*, 72.

mission is a signature concern throughout Luke's entire narrative (from Luke 2:32 to Acts 28:28). The issue, however, is whether that 'work' is the referent in 13:41. It cannot be, because, as even deSilva acknowledges, 'This "work" is in fact not "told" to the hearers in the sermon.'[74] The aftermath of the sermon does not bolster this position either. A closer examination reveals that the immediate response to the speech was positive (13:42–43). Moreover, the speech itself is pervasively Jewish with regard both to its content and target audience. The identity of the God-fearers, and whether they are being accounted among the 'Israelites' or 'children of Abraham' (13:16, 26), is difficult to determine.[75] The positive reception by 'many Jews and devoted proselytes' (13:43) is not symptomatic of any initial Jew-Gentile rift resulting from the speech. It is not until 'nearly the whole city' turns out on the following Sabbath, and the Jews see 'the crowds,' that there is a Jewish backlash against Paul and Barnabas (13:44–45). One may suppose that the authorial audience already understands the universal ramifications of Jesus' resurrection even at the outset of Paul's speech, but the intradiegetic Jewish characters do not fully realize it until they see the throng of Gentiles assembling to hear Paul and Barnabas. Finally, Paul and Barnabas clarify the divine necessity for them to speak the word of God 'first to you [Jews],' and then to turn to the Gentiles after there has been Jewish rejection (13:46–47). This more nuanced reading of the speech's aftermath should caution us about confusing 'the work' itself with the anticipated results of its being rejected that are previewed in the prophetic text.

Some interpreters think 'the work' refers broadly to God's work of salvation (cf. 5:38),[76] while others define it more narrowly as what God has done in Christ.[77] Joachim Pillai identifies it specifically with Jesus' resurrection.[78] He presents four reasons. (1) The entire speech is devoted to God's saving action in Israel's history, which has reached its climax in the resurrection of Jesus. God fulfilled the promise made to Israel's ancestors 'by raising up Jesus' (13:32–33). (2) The temporal indicator, 'in your days' (13:41), suggests a recent event. (3) This event is pivotal for both the salvation and judgment of humankind. The response of human beings to

---

[74] deSilva, 'Paul's Sermon in Antioch of Pisidia,' 48. N.B. that deSilva supports the view we are rejecting.

[75] On this whole question, see Witherington, *Acts*, 341–44.

[76] Soards, *Speeches in Acts*, 87.

[77] Marshall, *Acts*, 228–29; Longenecker, 'Acts,' *ExpBC* 9:223; Barrett, *Acts*, 1:652–53.

[78] Pillai, *Apostolic Interpretation of History*, 71–73. This interpretation is followed by Hansen, 'Preaching and Defence of Paul,' 306. Tannehill (*Narrative Unity*, 2:172) takes a hybrid view that both Jesus' resurrection and the Gentile mission are meant.

God's action in raising Jesus from the dead issues in forgiveness of sins or justification for those who believe, and judgment for those who do not. (4) 'The work' is mentioned as an object of faith: 'a work which you will never believe (οὐ μὴ πιστεύσητε) if someone relates it to you.' God's deed must be the very thing around which Paul's speech revolves. The history of Israel culminates in God's saving act of raising Jesus from the dead. The scriptural witnesses in 13:33-37 are set forth for the express purpose of demonstrating this. Pillai brings in for comparison Paul's statement before Agrippa that he is on trial 'on account of my hope in the promise made by God to our ancestors' (26:6), to which Paul follows up with the question, 'Why is it thought incredible (ἄπιστον) by any of you that God raises the dead?' (26:8).[79] John Chrysostom is again insightful in his comments on 13:41: 'Do not be surprised that it seems incredible (ἄπιστον). Indeed, it was foretold from the first. This may even be aptly said to us, "Beware, scoffers"—concerning those who disbelieve in the resurrection (περὶ τῶν τῇ ἀναστάσει διαπιστούντων)' (*Hom. Act.* 29 [PG 60.217.34-37]; my translation).

The resurrection of Jesus, therefore, is the goal of God's saving purpose for Israel. It is the fulfilment of the promises to Israel's ancestors that have been summed up in God's covenant with David that he would enthrone one of his descendants as head of an eternal kingdom. Consequently, belief in 'this one' (i.e., the risen Jesus) will result in forgiveness of sins and justification apart from the Law of Moses. Rejection will result in eschatological destruction. This explains the way in which the outcome of acceptance or rejection of the word of God is described in 13:46, 48. The Jews who reject it are said to consider themselves 'unworthy of eternal life,' whereas the Gentiles who believe are 'destined for eternal life.' These are the only two occurrences of the expression αἰώνιος ζωή in Acts. The few instances in the Gospel (Luke 10:25; 18:18, 30) refer to Israel's inheritance of eternal life in the coming kingdom of God. The depiction of unbelievers as persons who are 'unworthy of eternal life' (οὐκ ἀξίους...τῆς αἰωνίου ζωῆς, Acts 13:46) is reminiscent of Jesus' characterization of 'those who are worthy (οἱ καταξιωθέντες) to attain to that age and the resurrection of the dead' as persons who are 'no longer able to die,' and who, 'being children of the resurrection, are children of God' (Luke 20:35-36). The theological foundation for this immortal resurrection life proceeds from the fact that

---

[79] deSilva ('Paul's Sermon in Antioch of Pisidia,' 47) demurs, saying that 'the work' in 13:41, as well as the resurrection of the dead in 26:8, are not objects of faith 'in a soteriological sense.' I find this objection incredible. Disbelief in the resurrection of the dead undercuts Israel's connection to her past (Luke 20:37-38) and all hope of future salvation (Acts 23:6; 24:14-15; 26:6-8). We should add that the resurrection of Jesus was initially difficult for the Eleven to believe in Luke 24:11 (cf. 24:25, 41).

God 'is not the God of the dead, but of the living (ζώντων), for all live (ζῶσιν) to him' (20:38). In Acts, the risen Jesus is the one who has been shown 'the paths of life' (2:28), and is described as ἀρχηγὸς τῆς ζωῆς (Acts 3:15). The message of salvation is called 'the words of this life' (5:20), and the response to it, 'repentance that leads to life' (10:18). In Paul's Pisidian Antioch speech, Jesus' resurrection is itself, in a manner of speaking, described as life eternal, because he was raised from the dead 'never again to return to corruption' (13:34). These data suggest that in Luke-Acts, eternal life cannot be disconnected from the resurrection from the dead. They also imply a connection between Jesus, who was the first to participate in the eschatological resurrection from the dead, and those who believe in him who, as a result, are slated to participate as well in the ancient inheritance of eternal life spoken of by the prophets.

8.4 Conclusion

The Pisidian Antioch speech is arguably the most comprehensive presentation of the message of salvation in Luke-Acts. At the heart of the speech is the argument that God's mighty act to bring a Saviour to Israel consists in his raising up Jesus from the dead. The portrayal of Jesus' resurrection conforms quite well to the theological pattern that we have traced in ancient Judaism. The resurrection of Jesus is the act by which God enthrones him as the leader *par excellence* over Israel (exaltation). It constitutes the fulfilment of God's covenant promises to Israel, and provides a way for the people to renew their covenant relationship with God through the forgiveness of sins granted through the risen Jesus (covenant renewal). While there is no explicit reference to a new creation, it is clear that with the resurrection of Jesus an everlasting kingship is established in accordance with God's pact with David. In addition, those who believe in the risen Jesus are granted eternal life, which, in the context of Luke's work, implies participation in the resurrection age when they will experience a deathless existence as God's children.

As to the nature of resurrection, in this speech Jesus' resurrection is set in contrast to David's death. Jesus was crucified and buried. David, too, 'fell asleep and was laid with his ancestors.' But Jesus was raised from the dead. Barrett is correct when he explains Luke's idea of resurrection as 'the reanimation of a dead body, and its emergence from the grave as a reanimated body.'[80] However, in this speech Jesus' resurrection is described also as his permanent deliverance from death, 'never again to return to decay.'

---

[80] Barrett, *Acts*, 1:649.

The resurrection of Jesus is integral to the Lukan presentation of salvation. *Theologically*, it is the mightiest salvific act of the ancestral God of Israel. God's raising Jesus from the dead is the climactic outworking of his salvific work in the history of Israel. *Christologically*, the resurrection of Jesus definitively establishes him as the leader over Israel. Jesus assumes the role of Israel's Saviour. He is the promised son of David, and as the Risen One he holds the position as the enthroned Son of God. This is how the son of David can simultaneously be David's Lord (cf. Luke 20:41–44). Finally, Jesus transcends the leadership of Moses in his capacity to procure forgiveness of sins. This augments the earlier description of the risen Jesus as the prophet like Moses, whom God raised up first for Israel to turn each of them from their sins (Acts 3:22–26). *Ecclesiologically*, the resurrection of Jesus constitutes the achievement of God's salvific purposes for the people of God, Israel. The message of salvation has been sent first to them. But the fulfilment of God's covenant promises to David also initiates an eternal kingdom not only on behalf of Israel, but over the whole world, and God's salvation blessings are extended to all people. 'Everyone who believes' in the risen Jesus may receive forgiveness of sins. The resurrection, as a potentially incredible event for many who count themselves among the people of God, is a source of division within Israel. Therefore, while 'many Jews and devout proselytes' eagerly receive the message of salvation, others reject it. According to God's purpose, spoken of by the prophets (Acts 13:41, 47; cf. Luke 2:29–35), the division caused within Israel opens the way of salvation also to the Gentiles. *Eschatologically*, belief or disbelief in the resurrected Jesus is determinative of eternal destinies. Those who scoff and disbelieve will be destroyed. Those who believe will inherit eternal life, i.e., they will be accounted worthy of the age of resurrection. An implication of the fact that God has fulfilled the promise to Israel's ancestors 'for us' by raising Jesus from the dead, is that the people of God will realize the ultimate hope of salvation at the resurrection of the dead (cf. Acts 26:6–8, 23). At the very least, there is a link of faith between the resurrection of Jesus and the resurrection of all those who believe in him.

Chapter 9

Reading with the End in Mind (2): The Resurrection of Jesus and the Hope of Israel (Acts 28)

The ending of Acts has raised several unavoidable questions which (to borrow from Don Fowler's criteria) are related to readers' perceptions about the degree to which the ending is satisfyingly final, as well as 'the degree to which the questions posed in the work are answered, tensions released, conflicts resolved.'[1] The finality of the work has been questioned because it closes without narrating Paul's legal proceedings before Caesar, nor revealing their outcome. Does Paul stand before Caesar? If so, what was the verdict? Was Paul executed at Rome?[2] In terms of Luke's theological message, there is no consensus either as to whether the closing scenes express a 'final word' about the fate of ethnic Israel. Does the mixed response to Paul, followed by his appropriation of a quotation from Isaiah, signal an irreparable fissure between Christianity and Judaism? In light of this ending, what do we make of the divine promises to Israel, celebrated so enthusiastically in the nativity canticles? Such questions cannot escape our attention, yet our present inquiry proceeds under a different focus than do most studies of Acts 28. We shall be more broadly concerned with how 'the hope of Israel' contributes to Lukan thought. How does the hope of Israel figure within Luke's two-volume work, whose first volume is taken up with the life, death, and resurrection of Jesus, and whose second is devoted most prominently to the missions of Peter and Paul? We shall uncover how the resurrection of Jesus is integral to the hope of Israel proclaimed by Paul on the last page of Luke's narrative.

We will follow the same method of narrative closure for Acts as we did for the Gospel, but we will adjust our procedure due to two exigencies. First, because the final episode in Acts 28 is compressed, by comparison to the lengthier narrative in the three scenes of Luke 24, it will be less cumbersome to consider the closural features (circularity, parallelism, and

---

[1] Fowler, 'Second Thoughts,' 3.

[2] On these questions see, e.g., Colin J. Hemer, *The Book of Acts in the Setting of Hellenistic Historiography* (ed. Conrad H. Gempf; Winona Lake, Ind.: Eisenbrauns, 1990), 390–404, 406–8; Jacques Winandy, 'La finale des Actes: Histoire ou théologie,' *ETL* 73 (1997): 103–6.

incompletion) aggregately from the two scenes and final summary instead of treating each section separately. Second, since the finale of Acts forms the conclusion to all of Luke's work, we may expect to discover, in addition to circularity and parallelism within volume two, circularity and parallelism between the end of Acts and the beginning and end of the Gospel. As in our previous discussion of Luke 24, we will begin by analyzing the parameters of the beginning, middle, and end of Acts.

9.1 The Parameters of the Ending, Middle, and Beginning in Acts

While there is unanimity about the basic skeleton of Luke's Gospel (preface, prologue, Jesus' Galilean ministry, journey to Jerusalem, and final events in Jerusalem), there is virtually no agreement regarding the segmentation of Acts. A geographical organization developed from Acts 1:8 forms the basis for a general outline of Acts: testimony in Jerusalem (Acts 1–8); testimony in Judea and Samaria (9–12); testimony to the end of the earth (13–28).[3] But this simple organization does not command the assent of most commentators.[4] For our purposes it is unnecessary to settle upon a precise plan for Acts. We need only roughly delineate the beginning, middle, and end. Fortunately, it is widely agreed that the conclusion to Acts, though tightly connected to the dramatic account of Paul's shipwreck and arrival in Rome, consists of the final episode in Acts 28:16/17–31.[5] As of 19:21 Paul begins journeying from the eastern edge of Europe, heading towards Jerusalem, and ultimately on to Rome (cf. 20:22; 21:4, 11–13; 23:11). After the harrowing sea voyage and shipwreck on the semi-exotic

---

[3] Philippe Rolland, 'L'organisation du Livre des Actes et de l'ensemble de l'œuvre de Luc,' *Bib* 65 (1984): 81–83.

[4] For a survey of outlines, see Jacques Dupont, 'La question du plan des Actes des Apôtres à la lumière d'un texte de Lucien de Samosate,' *NovT* 31(1979): 220–21. Dupont (221) reports that he himself advanced at one time a five-part and at another a two-part division.

[5] H. J. Hauser, *Strukturen der Abschlusserzählung der Apostelgeschichte (Apg 28,16–31)* (AnBib 86; Rome: Biblical Institute, 1979); Charles B. Puskas, 'The Conclusion of Luke-Acts: An Investigation of the Literary Function and Theological Significance of Acts 28:16–31' (Ph.D. diss., The Graduate School of Saint Louis University, 1980); Jacques Dupont, 'La conclusion des Actes et son rapport à l'ensemble de l'ouvrage de Luc' in *Les Actes des Apôtres: Traditions, rédaction, théologie* (BETL 48; ed. J. Kremer; Leuven: Leuven University Press, 1979), 359–404; see also the commentaries on Acts by Bruce, Fitzmyer, Haenchen, Johnson, Lake and Cadbury, Marshall, Schneider et al. Alexander stresses the connectedness of 28:17–31 to 27:1–28:16; Loveday C. A. Alexander, 'Reading Luke-Acts from Back to Front,' in *Unity of Luke-Acts* (ed. Verheyden, Joseph; BETL 142; Leuven: Leuven University Press, 1999), 424.

island of Malta, his arrival in the Eternal City is punctuated with the announcement: 'And that's how we got to Rome' (28:14).[6] Acts 28:11–15 provides a transition between Paul's departure from Malta and the final scene in 28:16–31.[7] As for discovering the middle of Acts, unlike the Gospel, there exists no pivotal announcement like Luke 9:51 at its mid-point. But Acts 12:25–13:5, though positioned spatially before the middle of the book, comprises a transition into the missionary itinerary of Paul, whose travels and trials will dominate the remainder of the book. Furthermore, in 13:16–41 Luke records Paul's first major speech delivered at Pisidian Antioch, whose archetypal function is comparable to Peter's Pentecost speech. These literary cues, when examined in relation to Acts as a whole, provide the sense of a major shift in which the witness to Jesus is advancing beyond Jerusalem, Judea, and Samaria unto the ends of the earth (cf. 13:46–47).

Defining the transition from the beginning to the middle of Acts is an even more difficult task. Steve Walton, in a recent study of this issue, observes no clear indications of 'where the beginning ends and Acts "proper" starts.'[8] After summarizing six different views on the delimitation of the first major narrative unit in Acts, he settles upon 1:1–2:47 as the 'introduction' to Acts. His two supports for this are (1) the narrative summary in 2:42–47 and (2) a collection of themes common to Acts 1 and 2 that are characteristic of Luke-Acts as a whole. The first support is nullified by the fact that narrative summaries do not appear to demarcate major literary units in Acts.[9] Summaries are not used to indicate breaks in the text, but rather to provide continuity between scenes. They compress events from the story level in order to speed up tempo at the discourse level. They expand focalization to give the impression of extended or repeated action within an open-ended time frame.[10] The second support, a correlation of language and

---

[6] For this translation, see Alexander, 'Reading Luke-Acts from Back to Front,' 425 n. 19.

[7] See Dupont's close reading of literary features which identify Acts 28:16–31 as a distinct literary unit ('La conclusion des Actes,' 361–80).

[8] Walton, 'Where Does the Beginning of Acts End?' 450.

[9] This was argued by J. de Zwaan ('Was the Book of Acts a Posthumous Edition?' *HTR* 17 [1924]: 101–6) against C. H. Turner's interpretation of the summaries as markers for six panels in Acts. Zwaan observed that the summaries do not actually 'summarize' preceding narrative, so he preferred to call them 'stops' rather than summaries (103). They often do not occur 'at the natural end of pericopes' (104). He concluded: 'Accordingly, as in the Gospel, it seems inadvisable to regard these phrases as keystones to Luke's edifice' (106). His position was upheld by Henry J. Cadbury, 'Note XXXI. The Summaries in Acts," *BC* 5:400.

[10] Cf. Maria Anicia Co, 'The Major Summaries in Acts: Acts 2,42–47; 4,32–35; 5:12–16—Linguistic and Literary Relationship,' *ETL* 68 (1992): 56–57; S. J. Noorda,

themes in Acts 1 and 2, is not particularly strong without distinct structural indicators. If Dupont has correctly detected in Acts specimens of Lucian's prescribed literary technique, interlacement, then the discovery of definable breaks within Luke's narrative is all the more difficult.[11] Thus it will be advantageous for us to operate within a couple of dotted lines that may serve as loose boundaries between the beginning of Acts and Acts proper: Acts 1:12 or 1:26.

Giuseppe Betori views 1:12–8:4 as the first part of Acts after the introduction in 1:1–11.[12] Four types of markers delimit the structural unit 1:12–8:4. First, there are several inclusions clustering around the geographical location, Jerusalem. The action in both 1:12 and 8:1 is reset in Jerusalem after a short withdrawal from the city. In 1:12 the apostles return from the Mount of Olives 'into Jerusalem' after Jesus' ascension; and in 8:1 the focus returns to the church 'in Jerusalem' in the aftermath of Stephen's martyrdom 'outside the city' (7:58).[13] A contrast is made between the early Christian community surrounding the apostles who 'entered' Jerusalem (εἰσῆλθον, 1:13) and the church forced to 'pass through' other regions outside the city (διῆλθον, 8:4), leaving the apostles behind in Jerusalem (8:1). The return εἰς Ἰερουσαλήμ (1:12) is counterpoised by a dispersion κατὰ τὰς χώρας τῆς Ἰουδαίας καὶ Σαμαρείας (8:1). Persecution alters the settlement of believers who ἦσαν καταμένοντες (1:13) and πάντες ἦσαν... ὁμοθυμαδόν (1:14) to a community that has been diffused: πάντες δὲ διεσπάρησαν (8:1) and οἱ...διασπαρέντες (8:4). Second, this line of progression is anticipated by Jesus' programmatic statement in 1:8. Third, Betori sees in Stephen a continuation of the pre-eminent wisdom that characterized the apostles.[14] Fourth, 1:12–14 and 8:1–4 are formally similar in that they are 'summary transitions' or 'transitions having the character of summaries.'[15]

'Scene and Summary: A Proposal for Reading Acts 4,32–5,16,' in *Les Actes des Apôtres: Traditions, rédaction, théologie* (BETL 48; ed. J. Kremer; Leuven: Leuven University Press, 1979), 475–83.

[11] Dupont, 'La question du plan des Actes,' 220–31.

[12] Giuseppe Betori, *Perseguitati a causa del Nome: Strutture dei racconti di persecuzione in Atti 1,12–8,4* (AnBib 97; Rome: Biblical Institute, 1981), 21–25.

[13] Might Stephen's vision of the exalted Son of Man (7:55–56) be loosely parallel to the ascension of Jesus (1:9–11)?

[14] More importantly, Stephen's speech—the longest in Luke-Acts—brings the ongoing confrontation between the apostles and Jerusalem's religious leadership to a head.

[15] Betori does not appear to be using the term 'summary' in the technical sense of a 'narrative summary' we discussed earlier. That a major transition is taking place in 8:1–4 may find support in Dupont's identification of interlacement in these verses; Dupont, 'La question du plan des Actes,' 225–26.

These are compelling indicators of a major literary unit starting at Acts 1:12. Betori defines 1:1–11 as the introduction to the Book of Acts, pointing to an inclusio in 1:1–2 and 1:11: ὁ 'Ιησοῦς...ἀνελήμφθη (1:1–2) and ὁ 'Ιησοῦς ὁ ἀναλημφθείς (1:11). However, all of Acts 1 is tightly stitched together, providing a backdrop for the commencement of the apostolic witness at Pentecost (2:1–41).[16] The entire chapter is occupied with the preparedness of resurrection witnesses of Jesus' own choosing. The preface sums up Jesus' teaching activity in relation to 'the apostles' (1:1–2), who are listed in 1:13, and designated at the close of the chapter as 'the eleven apostles' (1:26). The apostles whom Jesus had chosen (οὓς ἐξελέξατο, 1:2) have had exposure to the totality of his ministry from its beginning (περὶ πάντων...ὧν ἤρξατο ὁ 'Ιησοῦς ποιεῖν τε καὶ διδάσκειν, 1:1) up to the point of his ascension (ἄχρι ἧς ἡμέρας...ἀνελήμφθη, 1:2). These same persons are named in 1:13 as the nucleus of witnesses who return to Jerusalem after the ascension (ἀναλημφθείς, 1:11). Later, the Lord Jesus is called upon to point out whom he has chosen (ὃν ἐξελέξω, 1:24) among two candidates who have been present during the totality of his ministry (ἐν παντὶ χρόνῳ ᾧ εἰσῆλθεν καὶ ἐξῆλθεν ἐφ' ἡμᾶς, 1:21) from its beginning (ἀρξάμενος ἀπὸ τοῦ βαπτίσματος 'Ιωάννου) until the time of his ascension (ἕως τῆς ἡμέρας ἧς ἀνελήμφθη ἀφ' ἡμῶν, 1:22).[17] In both Acts 1:1–8 and 1:21–26 the express purpose for the selection of persons who have been present throughout all of Jesus' ministry is that they may act as *witnesses to his resurrection* (1:3–8, 22).

Therefore it seems advisable to consider the beginning of Acts as extending at least to 1:11, while there are indications that the whole of 1:1–26 is an introductory unit emphasizing the necessary replenishment of twelve apostolic witnesses to Jesus' resurrection. Acts 1:1–11 will receive priority as the 'beginning' of Acts, with 1:12–26 receiving close secondary consideration. The middle expanse of Acts stretches out to the final episode in Rome (28:16–31), though a major transition happens nearly midway through the book when Paul's ministry launches westward (12:25–13:5), and his career winds down toward a fateful conclusion in Rome, starting with his final journey back to Jerusalem (Acts 19:21).

---

[16] Acts 2:1, with its note of fulfilment (cf. 1:5b), seems to mark a major development within the narrative, extending beyond the preceding introductory or preparatory matters of Acts 1.

[17] For most of these points of contact between the beginning and end of Acts 1, see Lohfink, *Die Himmelfahrt Jesu*, 218–20.

9.2 Hope of Israel, Resurrection, and Jesus at the End of Acts

9.2.1 Circularity between the End and Beginning of Acts

One need not be surprised at the paucity of closural patterns circumscribing the beginning and end of Acts. First, notwithstanding the secondary preface starting at Acts 1:1, the beginning of Acts is intricately interlaced with the end of the Gospel in order to almost seamlessly link the two volumes together.[18] Second, since Acts 28:16–31 contains Paul's final apology for his association with the Way, we might expect to be able to hear more clearly the reverberations of his apologetic which began as early as 20:18–35. Third, Acts 28 may function more effectively to provide closure for Luke's entire two-volume work, and not simply for the second volume.[19]

Of the small number of 'structural, linguistic, and thematic commonalities' between Acts 28 and Acts 1 indicated by Charles Puskas,[20] only a few may strike readers as establishing a circuit connecting beginning and end. Puskas, relying on Dupont's study of Acts 28, identifies seven structural or linguistic links falling under five thematic categories. (1) Teaching: The verb διδάσκω appears in the first and last verses of Acts (1:1; 28:31). (2) The Holy Spirit: The phrase πνεῦμα ἅγιον occurs in both passages (1:2, 8; 28:25). Puskas sees the Holy Spirit as actively involved in Jesus' instruction in 1:2 and Isaiah's prophecy in 28:25. He presupposes that a comparison can be drawn between the fulfilment of a worldwide mission in Acts 28 and the Spirit-empowerment for its execution promised in 1:8. (3) The kingdom of God: Four of the eight occurrences in Acts of the phrases τῆς βασιλείας τοῦ θεοῦ and τὴν βασιλείαν are equally distributed in Acts 1:3, 6 and 28:23, 31. (4) What is known: There is a contrast between οὐχ ὑμῶν ἐστιν γνῶναι χρόνους ἢ καιρούς (1:7) and γνωστὸν οὖν ἔστω ὑμῖν (28:28).[21] (5) Worldwide mission: (a) Witness terminology appears in Acts 1:8 (μάρτυρες) and 28:23 (διαμαρτυρόμενος). (b) There is a geographical progression from Jerusalem to the ends of the earth, outlined in 1:8 and accomplished in Acts 28. (c) Acts 1:8 represents the last words of Jesus, whereas 28:28 are the last words of Paul; and both touch upon the theme of worldwide mission.

---

[18] Kurz, *Reading Luke-Acts*, 28.
[19] Alexander, 'Reading Luke-Acts from Back to Front,' 419.
[20] Puskas, 'Conclusion of Luke-Acts,' 92–93.
[21] Cf. Dupont, 'La conclusion des Actes,' 390.

The Resurrection of Jesus and the Hope of Israel (Acts 28) 267

We regard numbers (2) and (4) as tenuous,[22] and number (1) collapses into number (3) as part of the description of Paul's delivery of the Christian message, leaving two definite thematic connections between the beginning and end of Acts: the kingdom of God and the worldwide mission. Kurz's brief analysis of closure in Acts 28 delineates three common themes: preaching the kingdom of God (28:23, 31 and 1:3); witnessing (28:23 and 1:8); and the Gentile mission (28:28 and 1:8).[23] No matter how one divides up these commonalities, it is of critical importance to recognize with Kurz that they are 'not peripheral' to Luke's narrative. The book of Acts begins and ends with features that are central to Luke's narrative.

Another common element between the beginning and end of Acts is the apostles' interest in the restoration of the kingdom to Israel (1:6), which finds its counterpart in Paul's confinement for sake of the hope of Israel (28:20).[24] Brawley sees this principal trajectory, the expectation that God will again manifest his supremacy over the world through the people of Israel, mirrored in Acts 1 and 28. But there is also a polemical narrative trajectory at the beginning and end of Acts. At the beginning of Acts, the apostles are poised to take their positions as twelve leaders over Israel; but Judas has turned aside from his heritage (κλῆρος), and it must fall to another so that the apostolic college may be reconstituted. At the end of Acts, Paul claims his heritage among the twelve tribes of Israel, while his Jewish opponents recapitulate Judas' action and forfeit their κλῆρος.[25] Brawley's observance of corresponding polarities at the beginning and end of Acts can be augmented by pointing to the all-important matter of the characters' actions toward Jesus. In the case of Judas, he became the leader of those

---

[22] A link is assumed, not forged, in number (2) between the Spirit's activity in Acts 1 and 28. In 28:25 Paul invokes the Spirit of prophecy operating in the Scriptures, while in 1:8 Jesus is referring to the Spirit-empowerment of his witnesses for worldwide mission. The lexical similarities in number (4) are moot since the same imperative in Act 28:28 (γνωστὸν ἔστω) occurs in 2:14; 4:10; 13:38.

[23] Kurz, *Reading Luke-Acts*, 29.

[24] Puskas ('Conclusion of Luke-Acts,' 94–95) dismisses such a comparison because it assumes (a) that Christ's exaltation involves his resurrection and (b) that Christ's enthronement is presupposed in the concept of the kingdom of God in Acts 28. But we have already observed how resurrection in Second Temple Judaism and the resurrection of Jesus in Luke-Acts involved exaltation before God. The final resurrection of the dead was more than a physiological wonder, but entailed also the restoration of the nation of Israel under the dominion of Yahweh. This means that the resurrection of the Christ would naturally issue in his exaltation as a regent in the eschatological reign of God. So one rather has to object to Puskas's *separation* of the resurrection (of Jesus) from the concept of the kingdom of God.

[25] Robert L. Brawley, 'Paul in Acts: Aspects of Structure and Characterization,' *SBL Seminar Papers, 1988* (SBLSP 27; Atlanta: Scholars Press, 1988), 95–96.

who arrested Jesus (1:16). In the case of the leading Jews at Rome, they must determine whether they are going to align themselves with Paul, who is committed to the kingdom of God and to Jesus (28:23, 31), or with those in Jerusalem who have delivered Paul over to the Romans (28:17; cf. 22:4), and who also had delivered over Jesus into the hands of Gentile sinners (Luke 18:32; 20:20; 22:4, 6, 21, 22; 24:7, 20; Acts 3:13). Strongly implicit in Acts 28 is the cruciality of the response to Paul's testimony about the resurrection of Jesus and its ramifications for Israel and the whole world.

Robert Smith's essay 'The Theology of Acts' is of particular importance for our study, first, because it focuses on the 'much neglected' ending of Acts (28:16–31) as 'a window into the theology of Acts'; and second, because it considers the resurrection of Jesus as central to Luke's theology.[26] Smith argues that the promised restoration of Israel anticipated by the apostles (1:6) is fully realized in Paul's unhindered proclamation of the kingdom of God and teaching about Jesus to all (28:31). There are four steps in Smith's argument. (1) The core of Paul's proclamation concerns the exaltation of Jesus as Davidic king through his resurrection and ascension. (2) The defeat of Satan, inaugurated in Jesus' ministry (Luke 10:1–15), is completed in Jesus' conquest over death and Hades at his resurrection (Acts 2:24). (3) Thus, Jesus is enthroned as universal Lord, and the word of God grows so as to embrace both Jews and Gentiles within the people of God. (4) Finally, the focus on Paul in the final scenes of Acts resolves the problem of geographical and temporal distance from Jesus' earthly ministry. Paul could not have been more distant from the earliest Christian movement, having not been one of the Twelve nor one of the first believers in their witness to Jesus' resurrection, but rather having been a persecutor of the church. Yet at the end of Acts he is preaching Christ at Rome. The answer to the problem of distance may be found in the activity of the risen Jesus, pouring out the Spirit, revealing himself to those whom he has appointed as witnesses, and performing signs and wonders through them.[27]

We are quite sympathetic to Smith's position, despite, on the one hand, our disagreement with part of his thesis and, on the other, the weakness of some of his supporting arguments. The former requires modification; the latter, shoring up. Our major disagreement pertains to his collapsing together of the hope of Israel with the Gentile mission. This is due to his acceptance of the view that the program in Acts 1:8 has come to fulfilment with Paul's preaching at Rome, and his equation of the hope of Israel with Jesus' resurrection. We cannot subscribe to the notion that Rome is coter-

---

[26] Robert H. Smith, 'The Theology of Acts,' *CTM* 42 (1971): 528.

[27] Smith, 'Theology of Acts,' 530–35.

minous with 'the ends of the earth.'[28] Neither do we equate the resurrection of Jesus with the hope of Israel, although it will be necessary to demonstrate that the two are vitally related to each other. We disagree with Smith, then, insofar as his position sets forth a kind of over-realized eschatology in which the hope of Israel and the worldwide mission are fully accomplished by the end of Acts. We agree with him that the resurrection of Jesus lies at the heart of Paul's proclamation of the kingdom of God, but find his argumentation for this point to be less than adequate.[29] We agree that the restoration of Israel, as well as the expansion of the people of God among the Gentiles, does not begin to take shape until after Jesus has been raised from the dead, for only then is he exalted as Israel's Messiah and universal Lord, who pours out the Spirit on 'all flesh.' The full realization of Israel's hope for restoration, however, will not be complete until the final resurrection of the dead, which has been prefigured and guaranteed by God's act of raising Jesus from the dead.

9.2.2 Parallelism between the End of Acts and Earlier Passages

If one were to read Acts 28:16–31 all by itself, without recourse to the preceding narrative, much of it would be difficult to decipher. This final episode could not have been composed so compactly and succinctly without its summations of earlier scenes, actions, and concepts. (1) In his first interview with the leading Jews at Rome (28:17–22), Paul recaps the salient points regarding the legal or quasi-legal proceedings in Acts 23–26: (a) his innocence of any charges that he has acted contrary to 'the people' or their ancestral customs (28:17; cf. 21:28; 24:5; 25:7); (b) the Romans' desire to dismiss Paul's case because he has committed no crime deserving death (28:18; cf. 23:29; 25:25; 26:31–32); (c) his appeal to Caesar in the face of unrelenting Jewish opposition (28:19; cf. 25:11–12, 21; 26:23); and (d) the root cause of his confinement, namely, 'the hope of Israel' (28:20; cf. 23:6; 24:15; 26:6–7).

---

[28] Cf. W. C. van Unnik, 'Der Ausdruck ἕως ἐσχάτου τῆς γῆς (Apostelgeschichte I 8) und sein alttestamentlicher Hintergrund,' in *Sparsa Collecta: The Collected Essays of W. C. van Unnik* (part 1: *Evangelia, Paulina, Acta*; NovTSup 29; Leiden: Brill, 1973), 386–401; James M. Scott, 'Luke's Geographical Horizon,' in *The Book of Acts in Its Graeco-Roman Setting* (eds. David W. J. Gill and Conrad Gempf; A1CS 2; Grand Rapids: Eerdmans, 1994), 525–27, 541.

[29] Puskas's difficulty with Smith's thesis stems from the latter's failure to establish this point ('Conclusion of Luke-Acts,' 94 n. 4). In a later study, however, Smith clarifies the connection between Jesus' resurrection and the preaching of the kingdom of God (*Easter Gospels*, 132–33).

(2) The reception of Paul by the Roman Jews at this initial interview is at best cool. To be sure, they report that they have not received letters from Judea (reminiscent, ironically, of Paul's own epistolary orders from Jerusalem to persecute followers of the Way, cf. 9:2; 22:5), nor have any arriving Jews spoken ill of Paul (28:21). However, the motive for their interest to hear Paul stems from knowledge about universal Jewish antagonism toward 'this sect' (28:22). During his hearing before Felix, Paul was accused of being an 'agitator among all the Jews throughout the world (πᾶσιν τοῖς Ἰουδαίοις τοῖς κατὰ τὴν οἰκουμένην)' and a 'ringleader of the sect of the Nazarenes (τῆς τῶν Ναζωραίων αἱρέσεως)' (24:5). At that time Paul flatly rejected the outsider designation of the Christian movement as a 'sect,' preferred to call it 'the Way,' and defined its scriptural foundation for worship as the hope in the resurrection (24:14–15; cf. 26:6–7).[30] Now, at the end of Acts, Paul's claim that he is enchained because of 'the hope of Israel' (28:20) is counterbalanced by his interlocutors' reference to 'this sect' that is 'denounced everywhere' (28:22).[31]

(3) The fundamental reason for Paul's imprisonment—'the hope of Israel'—cannot be understood apart from previous discussions of this hope in Acts, as well as a wider knowledge of Jewish expectations about Israel's destiny. This obtains, too, for the précis of Paul's message in 28:23, 31. The references to Paul's testimony about 'the kingdom of God' and his persuasive discourse 'concerning Jesus' assume a great deal about the authorial audience's comprehension of these concepts in light of the foregoing narrative. It is reasonable to suppose that this summation is an accurate characterization of the Christian message that has already been presented both at length and in summary form. Philip's preaching was summarized as 'proclaiming good news about the kingdom of God and the name of Jesus Christ' (8:12; cf. 19:8). Peter's Pentecost speech and Paul's Pisidian Antioch speech, in particular, best fit the description of discourse from the Scriptures about God's kingdom and Jesus. One might also safely infer that Paul, in continued obedience to the heavenly vision (cf. 26:19), shared with his audience his Damascus-road encounter with the risen Jesus, already thrice recounted in Acts. There was no need to spell out Paul's preaching in detail yet again when two packed phrases would suffice.

---

[30] Desjardins correctly observes that when αἵρεσις is used by others to refer to the Christian movement in Acts (as in 24:5, 14; 28:22) it seems to carry the negative connotative meaning, 'a non-legitimate sect or cult'; Michel Desjardins, 'Bauer and Beyond: On Recent Scholarly Discussions of Αἵρεσις in the Early Christian Era,' *SecCent* 8 (1991): 74.

[31] Dupont, 'La conclusion des Actes,' 368; Darryl W. Palmer, 'Mission to Jews and Gentiles in the Last Episode of Acts,' *RTR* 52 (1993): 63.

(4) The response to Paul's preaching is divided (28:24–25a). Paul, in turn, issues a prophetic warning from Isa 6:9–10 that provides a negative prognosis for Jews who reject the message of salvation. As Volker Lehnert has suggested, the Isaianic prophecy (28:26–27) and the declaration of Gentile reception of God's salvation (28:28) may function not as a wholesale repudiation of ethnic Israel but as an inducement for recalcitrant Jews to do an about-face.[32] The close of Acts does not 'write off' the Jews as a collective unity.[33] However, we do not think this means that the Lukan narrative simply leaves open the issue of whether or how ethnic Jews will participate in the ancient promises of salvation,[34] or that it assumes an inevitable future restoration for ethnic Israel.[35] Jewish rejection of the gospel in Luke-Acts should not be interpreted as the grounds for a dismissal of all Jews for all time; but neither should it be trivialized so that no long-term consequences for disbelieving Jews are envisioned. Toward the beginning of Luke's Gospel, Simeon had predicted both a division within Israel and an extension of salvation among the Gentiles (Luke 2:32, 34–35). The question of Israel's salvation, furthermore, is complicated by the question of Israel's identity. The Lukan proclamation of the kingdom of God simultaneously offers salvation to Israel while also probing and reshaping the definition of Israel itself (cf. Luke 3:8; 13:28–30; 19:9–10). The people of God are now taking shape around the promised Saviour whom God has 'raised up.' Those who reject God's appointed Lord and Messiah over Israel—the prophet like Moses, Jesus—stand in continuity with ancient Israelites who had opposed God's purposes (Acts 7:51–52). Such persons will be ultimately uprooted from the people of God if they continue in their unbelief (3:23; cf. 13:40–41), for they are thereby counting themselves 'unworthy of eternal life' (13:46). Those who welcome the good news,

---

[32] Volker Lehnert, 'Absage an Israel oder offener Schluß? Apg 28,25–28 als paradoxe Intervention,' *TBei* 29 (1998): 315–23.

[33] *Contra* Jack T. Sanders, 'The Jewish People in Luke-Acts,' in *Luke-Acts and the Jewish People: Eight Critical Perspectives* (ed. Joseph B. Tyson; Minneapolis: Augsburg, 1988), 51–75.

[34] *Contra* Marguerat, 'Enigma of the Silent Closing,' 301; Lehnert, 'Absage an Israel oder offener Schluß,' 323; Palmer, 'Mission to Jews and Gentiles,' 73.

[35] *Contra* Tannehill (*Narrative Unity*, 2:357), e.g., who writes: 'Because God is God, hope remains that God's comprehensive saving purpose will somehow be realized, but there is no indication of how that can happen.' See also David L. Tiede, '"Glory to Thy People Israel": Luke-Acts and the Jews,' in *Luke-Acts and the Jewish People: Eight Critical Perspectives* (ed. Joseph B. Tyson; Minneapolis: Augsburg, 1988), 21–34; Vittorio Fusco, 'Luke-Acts and the Future of Israel,' *NovT* 38 (1996): 1–17.

whether Jews or Gentiles, enter into that trajectory of Israelite history oriented toward complete restoration and salvation (3:19–21; 15:14–17).[36]

The divided response of the Jews in 28:24 is not without precedent in Luke's narrative (cf. 13:45–51; 14:1–6; 17:12–14; 19:9). While the final episode in Acts cannot support the notion that Jews as a collective unity are being disenfranchised, Paul's note about the success of the Gentile mission in 28:28 echoes two previous decisive points in the narrative when Paul turned from the Jews to the Gentiles (13:46; 18:6). We agree with Jervell that by the end of Luke's narrative the mission to the Jews has been completed.[37] However, this is not because Israel has already been restored, but because Paul has faithfully reached all of his own people as of this final episode of Luke's work. Paul has already been accused of causing trouble among 'all the Jews in the *oikoumenē*' (24:5), and the Jews at Rome have said that 'this sect' is contested 'everywhere' (28:22). Paul's mission to ethnic Jews has finally been accomplished by the end of Luke's narrative, opening the way for the light of salvation to shine with full force among the nations (3:25; 9:15; 13:46; 18:6; 22:21; 26:23).[38] According to God's scriptural plan, ethnic Israel has been given priority in the proclamation of salvation through Jesus, and the resulting division among them that Simeon prophesied has come to pass, instanced one last time in 28:24. What remains is the continuing extension of the people of God among the Gentiles that has already been underway ('this salvation of God *has been sent* [ἀπεστάλη] to the Gentiles'). 'The hope of Israel' is the hope of *Israel*, but it is also becoming the hope of the nations.

This leads us to the central question that shall occupy our attention in the remainder of this chapter: the meaning of 'the hope of Israel.' It is remarkable that so few studies have been devoted to this issue,[39] and discussion in the commentaries is limited and uneven, if not inconsistent. There are three views regarding 'the hope of Israel' in Acts 28:20 (and 23:6; 24:15; 26:6–8). (1) First, there is the minimalist view that the hope of Israel is simply

---

[36] Wolter's comments on Israel's identity are incisive ('Israel's Future,' 322–23).

[37] Jervell, *Luke and the People of God*, 68, 174.

[38] Note the appearance of the distinctive word τὸ σωτήριον in Luke 2:30 (cf. 2:32); 3:6; and Acts 28:28; i.e., at roughly the beginning and end of Luke-Acts.

[39] We are aware of only three studies. The first is well known: Klaus Haacker, 'Das Bekenntnis des Paulus zur Hoffnung Israels nach der Apostelgeschichte des Lukas,' *NTS* 31 (1985): 437–51. The second is universally overlooked, but is of signal importance: Robert J. Kepple, 'The Hope of Israel, the Resurrection of the Dead, and Jesus: A Study of Their Relationship in Acts with Particular Regard to the Understanding of Paul's Trial Defense,' *JETS* 20 (1977): 231–41. A third is focused on the connection of the 'hope of Israel' to the intra-Jewish debate regarding the Gentile mission: Anton Deutschmann, 'Die Hoffnung Israels (Apg 28,20)' *BN* 105 (2000): 54–60.

equivalent to the Pharisaic belief in the resurrection of the dead.[40] This is supported by placing emphasis on the hendiadys in 23:6 in which Paul first speaks concerning ἐλπίδος καὶ ἀναστάσεως νεκρῶν as the reason for his being on trial. Subsequently in 24:15 Paul refers to his 'hope in God' as the expectation for the resurrection of both the righteous and unrighteous. In 26:6–8 the hope is characteristic not only of Pharisaism (cf. 26:5), but also of the twelve tribes of Israel who hope to attain the ancestral promise from God, which is once again associated with the resurrection from the dead. (2) Second, there is the view that the hope of Israel is equivalent to Messiah-Jesus and/or his resurrection.[41] This perspective is reflected in the NLT of 28:20: 'I am bound with this chain because I believe that the hope of Israel—the Messiah—has already come.' (3) Finally, there is the mediating view that the phrase expresses a double entendre. The hope of Israel is, in Pesch's words, Paul's 'messianisch-eschatologischen Hoffnung,' or as Marshall puts it, 'the coming of the Messiah and the resurrection.'[42] A clearer articulation of this view posits a hope in the final resurrection of the dead that has found initial actualization in the resurrection of Jesus.[43]

The first view is the simplest and least complicated. It seems to take Paul's expressions of hope at their face value without imposing a christological interpretation where none is necessitated.[44] The difficulties with this view begin with its reductionism. 'Hope' and 'the resurrection of the dead' in 23:6 are not so much equivalent as they are mutually enriching. The resurrection of the dead is a concrete realization of Israel's hope for restoration as twelve tribes (26:6–7), and it will be the occasion when God will definitively execute his judgment on the righteous and the unrighteous (24:15; cf. 10:42; 17:31–32). Hope and resurrection conjure up a complex of images related to God's eschatological salvation for Israel (cf. Luke 1:68; 2:25, 38; 7:11–16; 21:28; 24:21). Our Chapter 3 was devoted to showing the theological richness of Jewish ideas concerning resurrection. Resurrection cannot be reduced to belief in the physiological reality of God's reanimation of

---

[40] Lake and Cadbury, *BC* 4:289; Williams, *Acts*, 249; Fitzmyer, *Acts*, 793. Fitzmyer enlists others, such as Wikenhauser, Weiser, and Johnson, in agreement with his position; but this does not appear to be the case.

[41] Haenchen, *Acts*, 683, 722; Schneider, *Apg.*, 2:415; Kistemaker, *Acts*, 959.

[42] Pesch, *Apg.*, 2:309; Marshall, *Acts*, 423.

[43] Cf. Bruce, *Acts of the Apostles*, 539; Longenecker, 'Acts,' *ExpBC* 9:366; Johnson, *Acts*, 469; Barrett, *Acts*, 2:1240; Marguerat, 'Enigma of the Silent Closing,' 298; and Wikenhauser, who writes, '…es ist die "Hoffnung Israels," d.h. die Auferstehung der Toten, die in Jesus seine erste Verwicklichung gefunden hat (vgl. 23,6; 24,15.21; 26,6–8)'; Alfred Wikenhauser, *Die Apostelgeschichte übersetzt und erklärt* (RNT 5; Regensburg: Pustet, 1961), 288.

[44] Cf. Lake and Cadbury, *BC* 4:289.

corpses. Rather, it is part and parcel with God's fulfilment of his promises to redeem his people, establish his kingdom among them, and shower his covenant blessings upon them. A messianic component to Israel's hope is not abundantly in evidence in connection with the resurrection in Jewish literature, but it is not wholly absent.[45] To disavow any messianic component in Paul's expressions about Israel's hope presents a problem for making sense of his explanation of the cause for his trial. How can Paul be on trial merely on account of his Pharisaic belief in the resurrection of the dead? Fitzmyer is inconsistent in his answer. His interpretation of 23:6 explains Paul's reference to hope and resurrection as a calculated distraction that cleverly avoids any mention of Jesus' resurrection.[46] But in his treatment of 24:21 he sees in the explicit reference to the Pharisaic belief in the resurrection of the dead an implicit reference to Paul's own belief in '"the resurrection of the Dead [One]," i.e., of Jesus Christ, his risen Lord.'[47] Fitzmyer's second explanation, we think, is the better one, and we shall see why as we proceed.

The second view is deficient in that it displaces any future Jewish hope with a Christian hope that has already come to fruition through the resurrection of Messiah-Jesus. According to Haenchen, this displacement comes from Luke himself, who has 'fudged' the Christian message for apologetic purposes. Luke inaccurately draws an equation between the Pharisaic and Christian doctrines of resurrection. 'The Pharisees expect the resurrection of the dead at the *end* of this aeon; a resurrection in the *middle* of this aeon—and such, according to Luke, was that of Jesus—has nothing in common with the Pharisaic expectation.'[48] Moreover, Luke has avoided the real point of contention between Jews and Christians: Paul's teaching regarding the Law. Luke's reframing of the issue, claims Haenchen, certainly would not have rung true for one of Paul's fellow workers, nor would it have con-

---

[45] Cf. *2 Bar.* 30:1–5, esp. 30:1 in which the appearance of the Messiah is followed by the resurrection of 'all who sleep in hope of him'; see also *4 Ezra* 7:28–32; 12:31–34. There is, of course, an exceedingly strong christological component in Paul's teaching on the resurrection (Rom 5:10, 17, 21; 6:5; 8:11, 29; 14:8; 1 Cor 15:16–26; Phil 1:20; 3:8–11, etc.). On the central importance of the resurrection of Jesus for Paul, see Geerhardus Vos, *The Pauline Eschatology* (Grand Rapids: Eerdmans, 1961); Richard B. Gaffin, Jr., *The Centrality of the Resurrection: A Study in Paul's Soteriology* (Grand Rapids: Baker, 1978).

[46] Fitzmyer, *Acts*, 718. Roloff (*Apg.*, 328) calls it a 'taktische Manöver.' Note that in Fitzmyer's treatment of 28:20 (*Acts*, 793) he states categorically that the hope of Israel 'has nothing to do with a "Messianic hope,"…or with a double hope, "the Messiah and the resurrection."'

[47] Fitzmyer, *Acts*, 737.

[48] Haenchen, *Acts*, 115.

The Resurrection of Jesus and the Hope of Israel (Acts 28)

vinced Jews in Luke's own day. But the argument was not designed to win over Jews, but to persuade Roman authorities of the ancient Judaic pedigree of Christianity.[49] There are several problems with this construal of Paul's defence.[50] First, to assert that the trial speeches are specimens of political apologetic ignores their primary function as Christian proclamation. In the progression of the legal proceedings the juridical aspects continue to recede, while Paul's witness to Jesus crescendos (cf. 26:27–29).[51] Secondly, that Paul is running roughshod over Jewish beliefs in order to appeal to Roman officials does not comport with the Lukan representation of the hearings, in which Paul only once in four appearances directly addresses a Roman official, and in this instance it is the Roman governor, Felix, who we are told is well-informed about the Way (24:22), and whose wife is a Jewess (24:24). Felix's successor, Festus, is at a loss as to how to investigate the religious controversies (ζητήματα) surrounding Paul's case (25:19–20; cf. 23:29), so he arranges a hearing before King Agrippa, who is particularly familiar with 'all the Jewish customs and controversies (ζητημάτων)' (26:3). In the conclusion to his speech before Agrippa, Paul appeals to the king's belief in the Prophets (26:27). Then, in the final episode of Acts, Paul summons the leading Jews of the Eternal City to discuss the matter of his trial and his testimony about the kingdom of God and Jesus. The evidence points in the direction that the Lukan work is tailored for authorial readers who are Jewish insiders, able to appreciate subtle distinctions within Judaism,[52] rather than for uncomprehending outsiders, least of all Roman authorities.[53] Third, Haenchen has mischaracterized the Lukan conception of the resurrection. Both the Pharisees *and* Paul, according to Luke's narrative, believe in the *future* resurrection (ἀνάστασιν μέλλειν ἔσεσθαι, 24:15), which is a promise that all twelve tribes of Israel

---

[49] Haenchen, *Acts*, 115–16.

[50] For a thorough refutation of Haenchen's interpretation of 'the hope of Israel,' see Haacker, 'Bekenntnis des Paulus,' 439–43.

[51] N.B. the progression from ἕστηκα κρινόμενος (26:6; cf. ἐγὼ κρίνομαι, 23:6; 24:21) to ἕστηκα μαρτυρόμενος (26:22).

[52] This has been cogently argued by Marilyn Salmon, 'Insider or Outsider? Luke's Relationship with Judaism,' in *Luke-Acts and the Jewish People: Eight Critical Perspectives* (ed. Joseph B. Tyson; Minneapolis: Augsburg, 1988), 76–82. Salmon helpfully observes how Luke's readers would be expected to appreciate not only distinctions within Judaism (e.g., between Sadducees and Pharisees) but even within Jewish sects (e.g., between believing and non-believing Pharisees, Acts 15:5).

[53] C. K. Barrett's classic statement still stands (*Luke the Historian in Recent Study*, 63): 'No Roman official would ever have filtered out so much of what to him would be theological and ecclesiastical rubbish in order to reach so tiny a grain of relevant apology.'

'hope to attain' (ἐλπίζει καταντῆσαι, 26:7). Haenchen's contention that Luke has blurred the difference between Pharisaic and Christian conceptions of the resurrection is wildly simplistic, and his suggestion that this is a product of sub-apostolic naïveté is unsupportable. Luke's representation of the resurrection is deeply embedded in Jewish hopes of salvation, voiced from the outset of his narrative; and his expression of Israel's hope—more than that of any other NT author—is supported by mention of the Hebrew Scriptures (e.g., 24:14; 26:22, 27; 28:23). Paul's confession of the hope of Israel cannot be read merely as a doctrinal tenet over which Jewish sectarians may squabble, but as the very foundation for God's people as a hopeful, worshipping community awaiting ultimate salvation (24:14–15; 26:6–7). 'Paulus tritt hier an die Seite von Maria und Zacharias, Simeon und Hanna und gesellt sich zu den Jüngern auf dem Weg nach Emmaus'![54] The resurrection of Jesus, finally, does not pertain to 'the middle of this aeon,' but is an inaugural event in the end-time preparation of a people who will inhabit the kingdom of God (the resurrection of Jesus is critical for the commencement of 'the last days' when God pours out the Spirit, 2:17). Haenchen unfairly assumes that Luke-Acts does not reflect a nuanced perspective on the relationship between the Christian understanding of Jesus' resurrection and the hope in the general resurrection of the dead inherited from Judaism. To be sure, Luke was no systematician, but we think Haenchen has purportedly discovered logical inconsistencies where none need be found.

The third view appears to be the most commonly accepted, but is usually articulated with the least clarity or detail, and nearly always with the paltriest substantiation. Most exponents of this perspective offer little more than the bare assertion that the hope of Israel refers at once to Israel's hope for the resurrection of the dead and its fulfilment in the resurrection of Jesus.[55] Nevertheless, this view is on its face advantageous because it best explains how Paul can claim that he is on trial because of 'the hope of Israel' or 'the resurrection of the dead,' when the more obvious reason seems to be his belief in the risen Jesus. Roughly a century ago Adolf von Harnack set forth a most plausible explanation for Paul's line of defence:

> Whenever the Resurrection was spoken of, our Lord, as a matter of course, formed for St Paul, for St Luke, and for the listeners the efficient cause. We may even believe that St Paul, at the beginning of his discourse, said roundly, 'Touching the Resurrection of the dead I stand here called in question'; for Luther also

---

[54] Haacker, 'Bekenntnis des Paulus,' 442.
[55] E.g., Bruce, *Acts of the Apostles*, 498; Johnson, *Acts*, 398; Wikenhauser, *Apg.*, 250–51; Schneider, *Apg.*, 2:332; Pesch, *Apg.*, 2:243; Barrett, *Acts*, 2:1064; cf. Haenchen, *Acts*, 683.

declared a hundred times that he was called in question touching the merits and honour of Jesus Christ, while his opponents asserted that these things did not come at all into the question.[56]

F. F. Bruce writes in a similar vein: 'The hope of Israel, for Paul, was bound up with the resurrection of Christ (cf. 13:32–39) and therefore with the hope of resurrection as such (cherished by the Pharisees), "for if the dead are not raised, then Christ has not been raised" (1 Cor. 15:16).'[57] We believe these statements are intuitively correct, and qualify as reasonable and logical inferences from readings of Luke-Acts. However, they offer little in the way of evidence or argumentation for the claim that there is a linkage between Jesus' resurrection and the hope of Israel or the resurrection of the dead.[58] The problem of explaining any connection that might exist between these elements presents itself in their scattered and elliptical occurrences throughout Luke's narrative; and this raises also the question of why, if it is the case that Paul's hope in the resurrection of the dead is related to the reality of Jesus' resurrection, it is not more clearly expressed in his defence speeches.

Two general lines of argument may be pursued to address these issues. First, the terse expressions about Israel's hope and resurrection appear to presuppose authorial readers who are already familiar with key Jewish eschatological concepts.[59] These expressions are loaded with significance when viewed against the Jewish background concerning resurrection that we explored in Chapter 3.[60] Second, a comparative analysis of three interlocking theological concepts in Luke-Acts—the hope of Israel, the resurrection of the dead, and Jesus' resurrection—can elucidate the relationships between them. Robert Kepple, whose seminal study on this question has not attracted proper attention, first advanced this approach.[61] Although I have seen fit to modify, expand, or otherwise fortify Kepple's arguments, on the whole his approach is sound. These two general lines of argument will be

---

[56] Adolf von Harnack, *The Date of the Acts and the Synoptic Gospels* (Crown Theological Library 33; trans. John Richard Wilkinson; New York: G. P. Putnam's Sons; London: Williams and Norgate, 1911), 87.

[57] Bruce, *Acts of the Apostles*, 290.

[58] Indeed, Barrett (*Acts*, 2:1240) registers some doubt as to whether in Luke-Acts (as in Paul) Israel's hope of messianic salvation is 'guaranteed and anticipated by the resurrection of Jesus.'

[59] Even 23:8, for example (cf. Luke 20:27), informs readers about insider distinctions between two Jewish sects, but affords little, if any, additional information about resurrection itself.

[60] Haacker ('Bekenntnis des Paulus,' 443–46) has also pursued this angle, but on a more modest scale than our own.

[61] Kepple, 'Hope of Israel, Resurrection of the Dead, and Jesus,' 235–41.

forged together in the following discussion, in which we shall look at the interplay between Paul's statements about the hope of Israel and parallel statements regarding both the general resurrection and the resurrection of Jesus in Luke's narrative.

Three theological propositions reveal the interrelation of the hope of Israel, the resurrection of the dead, and the resurrection of Jesus. (1) The hope of Israel and the resurrection of the dead are spoken of in the Law and the Prophets, and they are expressed as God's promise to Israel's ancestors. (2) The resurrection of Jesus is also predicted in the Law and the Prophets, and it is 'the key fulfilment'[62] of God's promise to Israel's ancestors. (3) Finally, the resurrection of Jesus is vitally connected to the final resurrecttion of the dead.

9.2.2.1 THE SCRIPTURAL PROMISE OF HOPE AND RESURRECTION

There is no coincidence in the fact that Paul's declaration about his imprisonment on account of 'the hope of Israel' in 28:20 is followed by a second meeting with the Jews at Rome in which he argues his position from the Law of Moses and from the Prophets (28:23). Paul, at his hearing before Agrippa, stated that his hope resided in 'the promise made by God to our ancestors,' a promise that the twelve tribes of Israel 'hope to attain' (26:6–7).[63] The following verse (26:8) makes it clear that this hope most certainly involves the resurrection of the dead. The hope for the resurrection of the dead is a fundamental reason for Israel's existence as a worshipping community. Paul expressed this same thought before Felix.[64] The defining characteristic of the Way (i.e., authentic Judaism) is its hope in God for the resurrection of the dead (24:15), a hope that stems from 'believing everything that is in accordance with the Law, and that is written in the Prophets' (24:14). Jesus himself, we will recall, grounded belief in the resurrection of the dead in the covenant formula, 'The God of Abraham, the God of Isaac, and the God of Jacob' (Luke 20:37). In Luke-Acts the hope in the resurrection of the dead is above all *theo*centrically based. The hope is in God, the promise is from God, and this has been communicated to God's people via the Law and the Prophets as a promise that will come to realization for the covenant faithful, even of Israel's ancient past.

---

[62] Kepple employs this expression, albeit not with our same emphasis.

[63] Observe the three forms (two nominal, one verbal) of the word 'hope' in this passage.

[64] The mention of worship or service in 24:14 and 26:7 is reminiscent of the covenant faithful at the beginning of Luke's Gospel who are awaiting the fulfilment of God's salvific promises and are anticipating (Zechariah, Luke 1:74) or actively participating in worship (Anna, λατρεύουσα νύκτα καὶ ἡμέραν, 2:37; cp. νύκτα καὶ ἡμέραν λατρεῦον, Acts 26:7).

Luke's 'hope of Israel' accords with and is enriched by the expressions of hope in the resurrection that emerged within Second Temple Judaism. In our Chapter 3 we demonstrated, among other things, that the hope in resurrection stemmed from deep-seated trust in God's covenant faithfulness to his people (see esp. 2 Macc 7:9, 11, 14, 36). The resurrection of the dead is the concrete, eschatological actualization of God's complete restoration of Israel, when God (in the words of Acts 1:6) 'restores the kingdom to Israel.' Again and again, resurrection—whether understood metaphorically or literally—is linked to the idea of Israel's ultimate salvation or restoration (Hos 6:1–3; Ezek 37:1–14; Isa 25:8–9; 26:19; Dan 12:1–3, etc.). The *Testaments of the Twelve Patriarchs* vividly depict all historical Israel, including the patriarchs of old, and particularly the primeval twelve tribal leaders, taking part in the resurrection (*T. Jud.* 25:1, 3–5; *T. Benj.* 10:6–9). These pictures of resurrection cohere nicely with Luke's expression of belief in the resurrection as a 'hope' or 'promise' made by God to Israel's ancestors, and espoused by the twelve tribes of Israel. Paul's stance before the Jewish leaders in Rome is that he is not at odds with the ancestral faith of Israel, but that he shares in the same hope that they do. Why, then, does Paul's teaching continue to elicit so much controversy among Jews? A second theological proposition answers this question.

9.2.2.2 THE KEY FULFILMENT OF THE PROMISE: THE RESURRECTION OF JESUS

The climax of Paul's defence is in Acts 26:22–23: 'To this day I have had help from God, and so I stand here, testifying to both small and great, saying nothing but what the Prophets and Moses said would take place: that the Messiah must suffer, and that, by being the first to rise from the dead, he would proclaim light both to our people and to the Gentiles.' Here the resurrection of Jesus is of central importance for the proclamation of salvation, and this is in full accord with the Scriptures. The resurrection of Jesus has already been associated with Israel's hope of salvation. The pair of disciples on the road to Damascus related their disappointment concerning the death of Jesus: 'We had hoped (ἠλπίζομεν) that he was the one to redeem Israel' (Luke 24:21). Jesus subsequently undertook the rehabilitation of the disciples' hope through personally revealing himself as the Risen One and explaining the Scriptures to them (24:25–27; cf. 24:44–47). Peter's quotation of Ps 15:8–11 LXX (Acts 2:25–28) includes the expression, 'my flesh will dwell in hope (ἐπ' ἐλπίδι), because you will not abandon my soul to Hades, nor allow your Holy One to experience corruption' (2:26b–27). Since we have already explored Peter's resurrection speech at Pentecost, we shall do no more than note: (1) that Peter uses Scripture to support the idea that Jesus' resurrection was foreordained by God; (2) that his argument singles out the patriarch David as the recipient of God's oath that through his progeny a perpetual kingship would be established; and (3) that David envisioned the fulfilment of God's promise through the resurrection of the Messiah (2:29-31). The resurrection of Jesus, therefore, stands as the key fulfilment of the promise to Israel's ancestors (lit. 'fathers,' 26:6; cf. 24:14), or in this case to the patriarch, David. This conclusion is supported by Paul's Pisidian Antioch speech, wherein he specifically mentions that God has brought to Israel a Saviour, Jesus, 'according to promise' (κατ' ἐπαγγελίαν, 13:23), and that 'we are announcing to you the good news regarding the promise (ἐπαγγελίαν) made to the ancestors,' namely, 'that God fulfilled this [promise] for us, their children, *by raising up Jesus*' (13:32-33). We must recall that Paul has emphasized how God's fulfilment of his promise to David forms the climax to Israel's history, which began with 'the God of this people Israel' electing 'our ancestors' (13:17). Again, the resurrection of Jesus is shown to be predicted in the Scriptures, and in particular it is viewed as the realization of God's covenant promises to David (note especially τὰ ὅσια Δαυὶδ τὰ πιστά, 13:34). The resurrection of Jesus demonstrates God's covenant faithfulness toward Israel, for it is the God of Abraham and Isaac and Jacob who exalted his servant Jesus (3:13), raising him from the dead as Author/Leader of Life (3:15; 5:31) and as the expected prophet like Moses (3:22-23). Hence, Israel's resurrection/ restoration and Jesus' resurrection are each prophesied in the Scriptures and regarded as a covenant promise made to the ancestral people of God; and the resurrection of Jesus is the key fulfilment of the promise. We say *key* fulfilment, because the hope of Israel remains a future hope at the end of Acts.[65] The resurrection of Jesus does not exhaust the divine plan for the people of God. It is only the beginning of God's salvation through the pouring out of the Spirit, the offer of repentance and forgiveness of sins, and ultimately the resurrection of the dead and the final judgment. Jesus' resurrection adumbrates and guarantees God's final salvific act of resurrecting and restoring and vindicating his covenant people.

9.2.2.3 THE RESURRECTION OF JESUS AND THE RESURRECTION OF THE DEAD

At the climax of Paul's apologetic speeches he proclaims the Messiah as πρῶτος ἐξ ἀναστάσεως νεκρῶν (26:23). This is remarkable since Paul, having previously designated 'the resurrection of the dead' as the reason for his trial (23:6; 24:15, 21), now declares the Messiah as 'the first from the resurrection of the dead.' This suggests a relationship between the resurrection of Jesus and the final resurrection of the dead. Such a relationship has already been indicated earlier in the narrative.

---

[65] Recall Paul's words in Rom 8:24-25: 'For in hope we were saved. Now hope that is seen is not hope. For who hopes for what is seen? But if we hope for what we do not see, we wait for it with patience.'

9.2.2.3.1 Proclaiming 'in Jesus the Resurrection of the Dead' (Acts 4:2)

Paul was not the first to be arrested or imprisoned because of the hope of Israel. The narrator informs us in Acts 4:2 that the apostles were taken into custody by the temple coalition for two reasons: first, they were teaching 'the people'; and second, they were 'proclaiming that in Jesus there is the resurrection of the dead' (καταγγέλλειν ἐν τῷ Ἰησοῦ τὴν ἀνάστασιν τὴν ἐκ νεκρῶν). The precise meaning of the latter statement is difficult to ascertain. There are two principal interpretations. (1) As in the NRSV, the phrase ἐν τῷ Ἰησοῦ may be taken to be instrumental, meaning that the eschatological resurrection of the dead is in some way effected through Jesus.[66] (2) A number of commentators understand the general sense to be that the apostles were proclaiming (*contra* the Sadducees, cf. Luke 20:27–40; Acts 23:8) that the validity of the resurrection of the dead has been confirmed 'in the case of Jesus' or 'by means of (the story of) Jesus.'[67] Fitzmyer's variation on this interpretation, which apprehends τὴν ἀνάστασιν τὴν ἐκ νεκρῶν in the abstract ('there was "resurrection from the dead" in the case of Jesus of Nazareth'), can scarcely be accurate.[68] During Jesus' debate with the Sadducees he employs an identical syntactical construction to refer to the eschatological resurrection (τῆς ἀναστάσεως τῆς ἐκ νεκρῶν, Luke 20:35).[69] From a grammatical standpoint, there is little question that in 4:2 a relationship is being expressed between the person of Jesus and the final resurrection of the dead. The issue is how to characterize this relationship. Our contention is that the relationship cannot merely concern the pedantic

---

[66] Conzelmann, *Acts*, 32; O'Toole, *Christological Climax*, 113–14; Schneider, *Apg.*, 1:343–44; Nigel Turner, *Grammatical Insights into the New Testament* (Edinburgh: T. & T. Clark, 1965), 155–56; and Chrysostom (as per Barrett, *Acts*, 1:220).

[67] Barrett, *Acts*, 220; Bruce, *Acts of the Apostles*, 148; Marshall, *Acts*, 98; Pesch, *Apg.*, 1:164; Gottfried Schille, *Die Apostelgeschichte des Lukas* (THKNT 5; Berlin: Evangelische Verlaganstalt, 1983), 131.

[68] Fitzmyer, *Acts*, 298. Haenchen's interpretation (*Acts*, 214) is similar, for he seems to take the whole expression as a periphrastic way of saying that the apostles simply taught that Jesus was raised from the dead; cf. O'Toole's rebuttal on the basis of Greek syntax (*Christological Climax*, 113).

[69] The usage of ἀνάστασις in this pericope is instructive. In Luke 20:27 the Sadducees are said to deny any 'resurrection' (anarthrous, generic/abstract), but in their example they speak of 'the resurrection' (articular, definite), to which Jesus also refers in 20:35–36. Acts 17:32 and 23:8 may also present examples of an anarthrous form referring to 'resurrection' in the abstract. The anarthrous form in 24:15 is possibly indefinite, while anarthrous ἀναστάσεως νεκρῶν with περί or ἐκ is naturally definite (23:6; 24:21; 26:23), in accordance with the common parlance of truncating definite articles in prepositional phrases (in accord with the Canon of Apollonius). Elsewhere, whether speaking of the general resurrection or Jesus' resurrection, articular (definite) constructions are used (Luke 14:14; Acts 1:22; 2:31; 4:33; 17:18).

question of whether or not the dead may be raised or, more appositely, whether there will be a resurrection of the dead at the end of the age. Several points may be argued in favour of the view that the resurrection of Jesus is being vitally linked to the final resurrection.

(1) Ever since Jesus worsted the Sadducees in debate on this issue, there has not, will not, nor need be any other polemic for the reality of resurrection than the testimony that already stands in the Scriptures (Luke 20:37; Acts 26:8, 27). Even in Acts 17:31, Paul does not argue for a belief in the resurrection of the dead from Jesus' resurrection. Rather, Jesus' resurrection certifies his position as righteous judge at the final judgment. Belief in the Scriptures is fundamental, because those who refuse to listen to Moses and the prophets would not be convinced even if someone were raised from the dead (Luke 16:31). Both the general resurrection and Jesus' resurrection are to be believed, first and foremost, on the basis of the words of Scripture (cf. Acts 24:14; 26:23, 27).

(2) If Sadducees and their sympathizers were rankled by evidence for resurrection from the dead, this still does not sufficiently explain their course of action against the apostles. William Baird perceptively notes, 'Pharisees, who were talking about resurrection all the time, ran no danger of being imprisoned.'[70]

(3) The other resurrection miracles in Luke-Acts do not share the same direct and intimate connection with the eschatological resurrection. They may be regarded as tokens of the final resurrection and, like the healing of the lame man in Acts 3, may be indicative of the in-breaking of God's kingdom (cf. Luke 7:16, 22). But Jesus' resurrection issues in a new, indestructible life with God (Acts 2:27, 31; 13:35–37). When God raised up Jesus, he loosed the pangs of death (2:24), and thereby effected the first instance of the eschatological resurrection of the dead. Jesus was exalted as ὁ ἀρχηγός τῆς ζωῆς (3:15; cf. 5:31). Conzelmann correctly points out that in 4:2 ἐν τῷ Ἰησοῦ belongs with τὴν ἀνάστασιν τὴν ἐκ νεκρῶν and is positioned before it for emphasis. Further, for the meaning of the expression he refers to 26:23, a verse which he in turn compares with 1 Cor 15:20; Rom 1:3–4; and Col 1:18.[71] In Acts 26:23 πρῶτος ἐξ ἀναστάσεως νεκρῶν is inadequately translated 'the first to rise from the dead' in virtually every English version. The expression cannot mean that Jesus was the first person ever to rise from the dead, since the ministries of Elijah, Elisha, and Jesus

---

[70] William Baird, 'The Acts of the Apostles,' in *Acts & Paul's Letters* (Interpreter's Concise Commentary 7; ed. Charles M. Laymon; Nashville: Abingdon, 1983), 13; cf. O'Toole, *Christological Climax*, 113.

[71] Conzelmann, *Acts*, 32, 211. On Acts 26:23, see also Haenchen, *Acts*, 688 n. 1; Johnson, *Acts*, Fitzmyer, *Acts*, 761, O'Toole, *Christological Climax*, 117; and Eckstein, "Bodily Resurrection in Luke," 122–23.

himself should disabuse any reader of that notion; and in any case, that would be better expressed: πρῶτον ἀναστῆναι ἐκ νεκρῶν. Luther's translation best captures the sense: 'der Erste sein aus der Auferstehung von den Todten.' Jesus is the first to take part in the eschatological resurrection of the dead. Jesus is not 'first' in terms of temporal priority only, but in rank or dignity, and hence in salvific causality. As 'the first from the resurrection of the dead' he proclaims light to the people and to the Gentiles, for in his capacity as ἀρχηγὸς καὶ σωτήρ he grants 'repentance to Israel and forgiveness of sins' (5:31). Therefore, to reject the risen Jesus means also to reject the Messiah whom God has appointed to usher in the blessings of the resurrection age (3:18–21). Jesus' resurrection is not merely a precursor to the eschatological resurrection of the dead. It is a guarantee of it. Jesus' resurrection is vitally connected with that of others, so that those who refuse the apostolic proclamation 'in Jesus of the resurrection of the dead' are refusing 'the message of this life' (5:20). They have excluded themselves from 'those who are considered worthy of a place in that age and in the resurrection from the dead' (Luke 20:35). They have judged themselves 'unworthy of eternal life' (Acts 13:46). They have been cut off from the people of God (3:23).

(4) Finally, since Acts 4:2 constitutes 'a wonderfully concise characterization of the kerygma,'[72] it should be interpreted within the context of the eschatological, messianic, and ecclesiological claims made in the apostles' saving message. The action taken against the apostles is in response to the miracle of healing and Peter's message in Acts 3. The proclamation concerning Jesus' resurrection comports with what we know about the fourfold theological pattern of Jewish hope in the resurrection. Resurrection opens the way to exaltation, covenant renewal, and participation in God's new creation. The death and resurrection of Jesus are decisive for setting in motion God's eschatological timetable (3:18–21), but it is the messianic and ecclesiological ramifications that are most disturbing to the temple elite. Jesus' resurrection demonstrates his identity as Holy and Righteous One, ἀρχηγός, Messiah, and prophet like Moses—in short, God's appointed ruler over Israel. Particularly vexing is the identification of Jesus as the Suffering Servant (3:13, 26) whose rejection and death, for which Israel's present leadership is responsible, have been reversed through resurrection (3:15; 4:10; 5:30; cf. 5:28).[73] According to Peter's quotation of Ps 117:22

---

[72] Johnson, *Acts*, 76.

[73] Recently, O'Toole ('How Does Luke Portray Jesus as Servant of YHWH?' 342–44) has argued that Jesus' resurrection is associated with his being the Servant of Yahweh (Acts 3:13–15; 8:33), and that he is active as the Servant after his resurrection (3:22, 26; 4:30; 13:47; 26:23).

LXX in Acts 4:11, Israel's present leadership has been rejected in favour of Jesus and those who were 'with Jesus' (4:13), who now speak and act 'in his name' (4:7, 10, 12, 17–18; 5:28, 40–41) in obedience to God (5:29, 32). The 'nation-building' connotation of the psalm citation is corroborated in its appearance earlier on the lips of Jesus (Luke 20:16 // Matt 21:42; Mark 12:10), as well as in 1 Pet 2:6.[74] Jesus, 'the stone repudiated by *you*, the builders' (Acts 4:11 // '*you* crucified,' 4:10) 'has become the cornerstone' (4:11 // '*God* raised from the dead,' 4:10). Jesus' resurrection is essential to the reconstitution of Israel, which began with 120 believers, and made numerical gains of 3,000, then 5,000, then a myriad of others (Acts 2:41; 4:4; 5:14; 6:7; 21:20). Luke hints at the triumph of the resurrected Jesus as Israel's leader, although by ironic contrast, through the character of Gamaliel. Gamaliel cites the example of two revolutionary movements among the people, which died out once their leaders were killed (5:36–37). By contrast, Jesus has been raised from the dead, and thus the restoration of Israel will advance toward its completion, because Messiah-Jesus is alive. The parallels between the apostles' experience and that of Paul before the Sanhedrin are unmistakable. Both the Twelve and Paul stand on trial because of the hope of Israel, which embraces the resurrection/restoration of the people of God that has been initiated in the resurrection of Jesus.

9.2.2.3.2 Proclaiming 'Jesus and Anastasis' (Acts 17:18)

Prior to Paul's arrival in Athens, his preaching in Thessalonica is outlined as scriptural exposition and demonstration that 'the Christ had to suffer and be raised from the dead,' and that Jesus is the Christ (17:2–3). The believers in Berea are commended because they readily accept the message, but also examine the Scriptures for verification (17:11). Then, at Athens, Paul's message captures the attention of certain Epicurean and Stoic philosophers. Some of Paul's Greek listeners thought him to be a messenger of 'strange deities.'[75] The reason for this misunderstanding is explained in a narrative aside: ὅτι τὸν Ἰησοῦν καὶ τὴν ἀνάστασιν εὐηγγελίζετο (17:18). This reflects how a Greek audience could mistake Paul's teaching about 'Jesus and the resurrection' for an introduction of two new deities, analogous to other familiar pairings such as Isis and Osiris, or Adonis and Aphrodite: Jesus and his consort Anastasis (note the feminine gender of the latter term in Greek).[76] At the close of Paul's Areopagus speech, he asserts that God

---

[74] Fitzmyer, *Acts*, 301.

[75] There may be a foreboding allusion here and in 17:19 ('new teaching') to the trial of Socrates (Plato, *Apol.* 24b–c; Xenophon, *Mem.* 1.1.1); cf. Pesch, *Apg.*, 2:135; Lake and Cadbury, *BC* 4:212.

[76] Howard Clark Kee, *To Every Nation Under Heaven: The Acts of the Apostles* (New Testament in Context; Harrisburg, Pa.: Trinity Press International, 1997), 214.

authorized Jesus as the righteous judge over humankind, and that God exhibited proof of this by raising him from the dead (17:31). Significantly, it is noted in 17:32 that some of the listeners poked fun, not at the claim that God raised Jesus from the dead, but at resurrection of the dead generally. 'Jesus *and* the resurrection' aptly sums up Paul's message, and both parts of the equation are essential. Belief in one implies belief in the other.

We may conclude that in Luke-Acts the hope of Israel, the resurrection of the dead, and Jesus' resurrection are inextricably bound together, so that each of them involves the others. (1) The hope of Israel will be completely actualized through the final resurrection of the dead. (2) This hope of resurrection was predicted in the Law and the Prophets, and constitutes a principal component of God's covenant promise to Israel's ancestral leaders. (3) Jesus' resurrection, too, was predicted in the Law and the Prophets, and was foreseen as the key fulfilment of God's covenant promise to the patriarch, David—not to mention, Moses, who foretold of a coming prophet like himself whom God would 'raise up.' (4) Finally, the resurrection of Jesus is vitally linked with the final resurrection of the dead. Consequently, to repudiate Paul's witness to the resurrected Jesus means also to reject Israel's hope of restoration that will be finalized at the resurrection of the dead. A trilogy of beliefs emphasizes different aspects of God's salvific action: ecclesial (hope of Israel), eschatological (the resurrection of the dead), and christological (resurrection of Jesus). While Luke's chosen medium, narrative, does not lend itself to a tidy schematization of these beliefs like the one we have provided, Paul's apologetic cannot be apprehended clearly without a pre-understanding about the interdependence of these three theological concepts. Before demonstrating this further (see 9.3 below), we shall briefly comment on elements of incompletion at the very end of Luke's narrative project.

9.2.3 Incompletion in Acts 28

The primacy of the hope of Israel, and the kernel of the gospel as a message about the kingdom of God and about Jesus, is what readers are left with at the end of Luke's narrative. The fate of Paul was foreshadowed earlier in the story (20:25, 38), and it seems nearly certain that Paul had to have appeared before Caesar (25:8, 11, 12, 21; 26:23; 27:24). Yet it is surprising that the Lukan narrative does not provide us with the high drama of a trial scene before Caesar (such as we would find, for example, in Philostratus's account of Apollonius of Tyana). Instead we read about two meetings with Jewish leaders at Rome, and then a final summary about Paul's two-year residency in Rome. Writers could be compared to sculptors or painters in the ancient world, since they could verbally create a scene or picture in the listener's mind. This final picture of Paul, living two years in Rome, welcoming all who came to see him, and 'proclaiming the kingdom of God and teaching about the Lord Jesus Christ with all boldness and without hindrance' (28:30–31), might have reminded listeners of a stock scene from funerary art in the ancient world. In funerary reliefs, the deceased is pictured at home or at work, greeting family members and/or visitors.[77] Is this the sort of image of Paul that we find at the end of Acts? If so, Paul is remembered, not as a martyr, or as a political apologist for Christianity, but as an evangelist who lived and died for the hope of Israel, which had been invested with new meaning for him because of the reality of God's kingdom, revealed to him by the resurrected Jesus. The story of Paul is cut short, but the story of the risen Jesus goes on. The ends of the earth await.

9.3 The Focus of Paul's Apology: Hope of Israel, the Resurrection, and Jesus' Resurrection

The main plank of Paul's defence—the hope of Israel and the resurrection of the dead—has presented a difficulty for scholars. In Haenchen's mind, as we have seen, it is a Lukan misconception that does not accurately represent the true controversy in which Paul was embroiled. For others, Paul is cleverly employing a diversionary measure or tactical manoeuvre. Calvin found it necessary to acquit Paul of dissembling by magnifying the hypocrisy of the unholy alliance against him.[78] How can Paul say that he is on trial because of the hope of Israel when the real issue revolves around his belief in the risen Jesus? O'Toole's literary analysis of the defence speeches suggests that Paul's speech in Acts 26 constitutes the christological climax of the series, for it articulates Paul's witness to the resurrected Christ with a clarity not found in the earlier speeches, and is designed chiefly to defend Christianity and its claim that the resurrection of the dead finds its realization in Christ's resurrection.[79] Tannehill has taken a similar route, but argues that interpreters have tended to overlook 'Paul's Christological reticence' in the defence speeches.[80] The christological component of Paul's message is 'concealed' in the defence speeches leading up to Acts 26 in order to advance the narrator's rhetorical strategy, not only to defend Paul against alleged anti-Jewish activity, but also to serve an evangelistic

---

[77] Garland, *Greek Way of Death*, 65.

[78] John Calvin, *Commentary upon the Acts of the Apostles* (2 vols.; trans. Henry Beveridge; Grand Rapids: Eerdmans, 1949), 2:319–20.

[79] O'Toole, *Christological Climax*, 156–60.

[80] Robert C. Tannehill, 'The Narrator's Strategy in the Scenes of Paul's Defense,' *Foundations and Facets Forum* 8 (1992): 261. Schneider (*Apg.*, 2:348) claims that the christological components have been sublimated under the banner of the general resurrection of the dead.

The Resurrection of Jesus and the Hope of Israel (Acts 28)   287

purpose. By mentioning only the Jewish hope in the resurrection of the dead in the beginning stages of his defence, the Lukan Paul is establishing common ground with Jewish listeners. Not until Paul's speech before Agrippa is the narrator's missionary strategy revealed, and the connection between Israel's hope, the resurrection, and Jesus disclosed.[81]

The difficulty of Paul's defence vanishes if Luke's authorial audience is already prepared to perceive a relationship between the hope of Israel, the resurrection of the dead, and Jesus' resurrection. The Lukan Paul, then, is not being coy, clever, or dishonest. He is simply highlighting one aspect, then another, of the message of salvation. While it is true that on the literary level (or more properly, the discourse level), as O'Toole has demonstrated, the defence speeches work toward a christological climax in Acts 26, it is quite another thing to argue for a developing missiological strategy, as Tannehill does. A developmental explanation of Paul's defence is rendered unnecessary if it is the case that characters within the narrative, and hence the readers of the narrative, recognize an association between the hope of Israel, the resurrection of the dead, and Jesus' resurrection. This connection, which others have recognized intuitively,[82] is borne out by a number of clues in Luke's narration of Paul's defence proceedings.

(1) The frontispiece to Paul's defence is his address to the Jerusalem mob in 22:1–21. This address sets the stage for the following scenes by detailing Paul's former adversarial stance toward the Way, and showing how he was transformed into a follower of Jesus when he was encountered by the Risen One on the road to Damascus. The purpose of this first encounter was explained to Paul by Ananias: 'The God of our ancestors has chosen you to know his will, to see the Righteous One and to hear his voice; for you will be his witness to all the world of what you have seen and heard' (22:14–15). Paul reports how Jesus appeared to him a second time in a vision while he was praying in the temple. He saw Jesus saying to him, 'Hurry, leave Jerusalem at once, because they will not receive your testimony about me' (22:18). The obstacles to Paul's function as a witness are compared with his own opposition to Jesus' witness, Stephen (22:20). Paul's defence is initially framed in terms of his one time opposition to the Way, which the God of Israel's ancestors reversed by selecting him as a witness. Paul's role as a witness to the risen Jesus is neither concealed nor suppressed. It is rather the overarching function of Paul within the defence

---

[81] Tannehill, 'Narrator's Strategy,' 260.
[82] See the quotes from Harnack and Bruce above (pp. 276–77), as well as Kepple ('Hope of Israel, Resurrection of the Dead, and Jesus,' 240): 'Admittedly Luke could have presented this so that it would have been more obvious to us, but it probably was obvious to Luke and to those for whom he wrote.'

speeches, as the repetition of Paul's Damascus road experience before King Agrippa underscores (26:9–18). There, Paul's commission as a witness is all the more emphatic, issuing directly from the risen Jesus (26:16–18; cp. 9:13–16). It is impossible to think that Luke's authorial audience is expected to keep in check the christological thrust of Paul's defence as they listen in on the succeeding hearings in chapters 23–26.

(2) When Paul stands up in the Jerusalem Sanhedrin and shouts out that he is on trial because of 'hope and the resurrection of the dead' (23:6), the response of certain scribes is revealing. Their response is prepared for in the narrative aside in 23:8, in which we learn that the Sadducees say there is no resurrection, nor angel or spirit, while the Pharisees acknowledge both (or all of them). What relationship, if any, exists between belief in angels or spirits and belief in the resurrection is difficult to determine. But it is important to note that some scribes of the Pharisees protest Paul's innocence, and indicate that at issue is the possibility of 'whether a spirit or angel has spoken to him' (23:9). There is no dissent among commentators that a direct correlation is being made here between Paul's standing trial and his report that Jesus had appeared to him on the road to Damascus. Jesus' resurrection is very much alive as an issue. Some of the scribes have come to Paul's defence, perhaps because they fear that the inquisition of Paul is being used by the Sadducees to discredit their theological position by making Paul's claim a *reductio ad absurdum* of their belief in the resurrection;[83] or perhaps the scribes are deflecting criticism of resurrection faith by reinterpreting Paul's Damascus experience as an angelic visitation. In either case, Paul's role as a witness to the resurrected Jesus is ostensibly viewed in tandem with his declaration concerning 'the hope and the resurrection of the dead.' This is confirmed by an appearance of the Lord Jesus to Paul, the very night of the tumultuous events in the Sanhedrin. The Lord stood by him and said, 'Take heart! For just as you solemnly testified about the things concerning me (διεμαρτύρω τὰ περὶ ἐμοῦ) in Jerusalem, so you must testify (μαρτυρῆσαι) in Rome, as well' (23:11).

(3) In Paul's speech before the Roman governor, Felix, and the opposing counsel from Jerusalem, he refutes the civil charge that he is a disturber of the Jews, and the religious charge that he is the ringleader of an illegitimate sect or heresy. Rather than being out of step with Judaism, Paul argues that the Way preserves its essence by worshipping the ancestral God of Israel[84] and by possessing the hope in God for a resurrection of both the righteous and the unrighteous (24:14–15). Paul defies any of his accusers, either his

---

[83] Longenecker, 'Acts,' *ExpBC* 9:328.

[84] Paul notes in 24:11 that he had come to Jerusalem only twelve days earlier for the express purpose of worshipping.

opponents from Asia or those from within the Sanhedrin, to charge him with anything other than what he called out in the Sanhedrin: 'It is about the resurrection of the dead that I am on trial before you today' (24:21). The legitimacy of the Way as the authentic expression of ancient Jewish faith is lashed to its fundamental hope for the resurrection of the dead. Yet readers of Luke's second volume know that the man who is on trial once opposed 'this Way' (22:4; cf. 9:2), and that this was tantamount to persecuting the risen Jesus himself (9:5; 22:8; 26:15). Opposition to the Way meant to oppose also 'the name of Jesus' (9:21; 26:9) and the kingdom of God (19:8-9; cf. 8:12; 28:23, 31). The mention of 'the Way' and 'the resurrection *of both the righteous and the unrighteous*' are not incidental to Paul's apology before Felix. Luke notes that Felix was 'rather well-informed about the Way' (24:22), and that his wife, Drusilla, was a Jewess (24:24). Felix takes it upon himself to decide Paul's case (24:22; cf. 24:10), and so the vignette about Paul's private appearance before Felix and Drusilla cannot be of marginal significance. It contributes to Paul's divinely ordained purpose to stand as a witness to Jesus. Paul speaks to Felix 'concerning faith in Christ Jesus' (24:24). His discussion of 'justice' and 'self control' carry a Hellenistic philosophical flavour, but his talk of 'the coming judgment' is distinctively Jewish (24:25), and melds with Paul's earlier testimony concerning hope in the resurrection *of both the righteous and the unrighteous*. It is this juridical aspect of Jewish hope in the resurrection, as we have noted previously, that is commonly presented to Gentile ears (cf. 10:42; 17:31). Felix's rejection of the Way is evidenced by an ironic contrast with Paul. While Paul stands confidently and with a clear conscience before Felix's judgment seat, Felix is frightened by Paul's preaching about justice, self control, and the coming judgment. While Paul hopes for the resurrection of the dead, Felix hopes to receive a bribe from Paul (24:26). It is worth noting that boldness and economic equity characterize the community of faith in which testimony to the resurrection of the Lord Jesus is given (4:31–34).

(4) That the christological component of Paul's defence was being concealed or suppressed from Paul's intradiegetic audience, or from Luke's authorial audience who has already heard the preaching about Jesus in the major speeches of Acts, cannot be sustained in light of Festus's synopsis of the troublesome case left to him by his predecessor. Festus condenses the issue down to two points: a controversy (a) about matters pertaining to the Jewish religion, and (b) about a certain Jesus who had died, whom Paul claimed to be alive (25:19). According to Festus, one of the principal points of contention had to do with the resurrection of Jesus. No doubt, Festus expressed this in a way that an outsider to Judaism would be expected to understand it, yet the description is perfectly consonant with Luke's phraseology elsewhere regarding resurrection (Luke 20:38; 24:5, 23; Acts 1:3;

9:41; 20:12). It would be awkward, indeed, for the narrator to (prematurely) unveil the christological aspect of Paul's message through a character so utterly uninformed about such matters. Such an unlikely source for this explicit statement suggests that it should be obvious to all that the resurrection of Jesus was a fundamental reason for Paul's trial.[85] But Festus's outsider perspective also reflects his myopia concerning the theological significance of Jesus' resurrection. Neither Jesus' resurrection nor Israel's hope in the resurrection of the dead is merely about individual survival after death. In this we agree with Tannehill, who writes: 'It is a hope for the Messiah's promised rule, which is established through resurrection and characterized by resurrection life corporately shared.'[86] The resurrection of Jesus and the expectation of the final resurrection of the dead are bound up with 'the hope of Israel,' which encompasses the entire complex of prophetic dreams and promises for the restoration of God's people, Israel.

(5) Paul again states before King Agrippa that he is on trial because of his solidarity with the twelve tribes of Israel in their hope in God's promise (26:6–7). The connection between this promise and the resurrection of Jesus is then skilfully articulated by way of an interrogative: 'Why is it deemed incredible by any of you that God raises the dead?' (26:8). It is striking that Paul, after speaking of a promise which Israel obviously hopes to attain sometime in the future, employs the present tense in his question (ὁ θεὸς νεκροὺς ἐγείρει). But it is the collocation of these opening statements with Paul's segue-way into the account of his former life as a persecutor of Christians that is truly significant. 'Indeed (μὲν οὖν), I myself thought I had to do many things against the name of Jesus' (26:9). There is a natural progression from the hope of Israel, to the belief that God raises the dead, to Paul's former opposition to Jesus. The connection between 26:8 and 26:9 lies in the fact that Paul cannot mention the resurrection of the dead without

---

[85] Bruce (*Acts*, 492) writes: 'The puzzled allusion of the pagan Festus contains the crux of the dispute. Paul's insistence (ἔφασκεν) on the resurrection as the hope of Israel and in particular on the resurrection of Jesus as the validation of this hope had impressed itself on the governor's mind. In Paul's earlier appeals to the resurrection hope as the core of his faith (23:6; 24:15) the resurrection was probably affirmed and not simply implied, as might be inferred from the narrative; otherwise Festus would not have grasped the point so accurately.' Calvin (*Acts*, 2:367), too, surmises that Paul must have had occasion to speak forthrightly about the death and resurrection of Jesus in other unrecorded hearings before Festus. The real point, however, is that authorial readers have had the benefit of the entire preceding narrative, and understand the association of the three theological concepts we have been discussing, so that Festus's words do not come as a revelation to them.

[86] Tannehill, 'Narrator's Strategy,' 266.

having the resurrection of Jesus uppermost in mind.[87] The battle line against those who belong to the Way was established early on in Luke's second volume, and it developed around the healing and saving authority of the name of Jesus Christ of Nazareth, whom God raised from the dead.[88]

Thus, from beginning to end, Paul's defence is coherent only if one perceives an unbreakable link between the hope of Israel, the eschatological resurrection of the dead, and Jesus' resurrection. This linkage is implicit, but not suppressed or concealed. Paul may therefore freely highlight one or another of these components of Israel's ultimate salvation without distortion or dishonesty. Acts 26 illustrates the ease with which Paul can transition from the eschatological and ecclesiological hope of Israel to the christological reality that had broken into his own life. The christological component comes to the fore in Acts 26 in order to elicit an immediate and direct response to the resurrected Jesus, who is personally present in Paul's ministry, proclaiming the light of salvation to Jews and Gentiles (26:22–23). Festus viewed Paul's proclamation of Jesus as 'the first from the resurrection of the dead' as madness (26:23–24). King Agrippa, however, understood the evangelistic aim of Paul's testimony: 'Do you think you can persuade me to become a Christian so quickly?' (26:28). Belief in the prophets (26:27), belief in the resurrection of the dead (26:8), belief in the key fulfilment of Israel's hope, Jesus' resurrection (26:22–23), and repentance (26:20) are essential for participation in the final salvation of God's people (cf. κλῆρος, 'inheritance,' 28:18).

9.4 Conclusion

Paul's defence speeches convey the resurrection of Jesus as the focus of the message of salvation in Luke-Acts. Paul's final exchanges with the Jews at Rome are extensions of his earlier witness to Christ in the defence speeches, though in compact summary form. The final episode in Acts assumes Luke's exposition of the Christian message throughout the speeches in Acts. By standing for 'the hope of Israel' and 'testifying about the kingdom of God' and 'persuading them concerning Jesus' from the Law and the Prophets, the Lukan Paul encapsulates the good news that climaxed

---

[87] Cf. O'Toole, *Christological Climax*, 47–48; Bruce, *Acts of the Apostles*, 499; Longenecker, 'Acts,' *ExpBC* 9:348; Johnson, *Acts*, 433; Conzelmann, *Acts*, 210; Pesch, *Apg.*, 2:277.

[88] Cf. 3:15–16; 4:7, 10, 12, etc., where the name of Jesus indicates the authority and presence of Jesus himself. In the controversy between the apostles and the temple authorities in Acts 3–5, the authority of Jesus' name is specifically linked to the reality of Jesus as the risen and exalted Saviour who is able to heal and perform signs and wonders through the apostles.

in the resurrection of the Christ. Points of circularity between the beginning and ending of Luke's narrative show that Paul is preaching the same message about the kingdom of God that the risen Jesus taught the disciples in Acts 1:3.

The hope of Israel, paralleled in Paul's defence speeches, is part of a theological 'iron triangle': the hope of Israel, the resurrection of the dead, and the resurrection of Jesus. Israel's hope for restoration, viewed as coming to ultimate fulfilment at the final resurrection of the dead, is intimately associated with Jesus as 'the first from the resurrection of the dead.' Any one of these naturally implies the others. Each of them highlights a different aspect of salvation: hope of Israel (ecclesiological); resurrection from the dead (eschatological); and the resurrection of Jesus (christological).

The Lukan theology of Jesus' resurrection in Paul's defence speeches is consonant with what we have encountered in the course of our entire study. *Theologically*, the hope of resurrection and its key fulfilment in the resurrection of Jesus originate from God. They are part of God's covenant promises made to ancestral Israel, and are communicated through Moses and the Prophets. *Christologically*, Jesus' resurrection is a principal component in the messianic triad: death, resurrection, and the proclamation of salvation to the people of Israel and to the Gentiles. *Ecclesiologically*, Jesus' resurrection, as the key fulfilment of Israel's hope, affords the Jews a primary opportunity to respond to the message of salvation, as instanced one last time in the final episode of Acts. But it also places Israel at a point of decision. In accordance with Simeon's prophecy, the offer is greeted with a divided response, followed by the extension of salvation to the Gentiles. *Eschatologically*, Jesus is the first person to participate in the final resurrection of the dead, and this stands as a paradigm and guarantee of the ultimate restoration of God's people that will take place at the final resurrection of the dead.

Bibliography

1. Commentaries on Luke and Acts

Baird, William. 'The Acts of the Apostles.' In *Acts & Paul's Letters*. Edited by Charles M. Laymon. Interpreter's Concise Commentary 7. Nashville: Abingdon, 1983.

Barrett, C. K. *A Critical and Exegetical Commentary on the Acts of the Apostles*. 2 vols. International Critical Commentary. Edinburgh: T. & T. Clark, 1994–1998.

Bock, Darrell L. *Luke*. 2 vols. Baker Exegetical Commentary on the New Testament 3a–b. Grand Rapids: Baker, 1994.

Bovon, François. *Das Evangelium nach Lukas*. Evangelisch-katholischer Kommentar zum Neuen Testament 3. Zurich: Benziger; Neukirchen-Vluyn: Neukirchener, 1989.

Bruce, F. F. *The Acts of the Apostles: Greek Text with Introduction and Commentary*. 3d rev. and enl. ed. Grand Rapids: Eerdmans, 1990.

———. *Commentary on the Book of Acts: The English Text With Introduction, Exposition and Notes*. New International Commentary on the New Testament. Grand Rapids: Eerdmans, 1956.

Calvin, John. *Commentary upon the Acts of the Apostles*. Translated by Henry Beveridge. 2 vols. Grand Rapids: Eerdmans, 1949.

Conzelmann, Hans. *Acts of the Apostles: A Commentary on the Acts of the Apostles*. Hermeneia. Philadelphia: Fortress, 1987.

Danker, Frederick W. *Jesus and the New Age: A Commentary on St. Luke's Gospel*. Rev. ed. Philadelphia: Fortress, 1988.

Dunn, James D. G. *The Acts of the Apostles*. Narrative Commentaries. Valley Forge, Pa.: Trinity Press International, 1996.

Ellis, E. Earle. *The Gospel of Luke*. Rev. ed. New Century Bible. Grand Rapids: Eerdmans, 1975.

Evans, C. F. *Saint Luke*. TPI New Testament Commentaries. London: SCM; Philadelphia: Trinity Press International, 1990.

Fitzmyer, Joseph A. *The Acts of the Apostles: A New Translation with Introduction and Commentary*. Anchor Bible 31. Garden City, N.Y.: Doubleday, 1998.

———. *The Gospel According to Luke*. 2 vols. Anchor Bible 28–28a. Garden City, N.Y.: Doubleday, 1981.

Green, Joel B. *The Gospel of Luke*. New International Commentary on the New Testament. Grand Rapids: Eerdmans, 1997.

Grundmann, Walter. *Das Evangelium nach Lukas*. Theologischer Handkommentar zum Neuen Testament 3. Berlin: Evangelische, 1971.

Haenchen, Ernst. *The Acts of the Apostles: A Commentary*. Philadelphia: Westminster; Oxford: Basil Blackwell, 1971.

———. *Die Apostelgeschichte*. 12th ed. Göttingen: Vandenhoeck & Ruprecht, 1959.
Johnson, Luke Timothy. *The Acts of the Apostles*. Sacra Pagina 5. Collegeville, Minn.: Liturgical, 1992.
———. *The Gospel of Luke*. Sacra Pagina 3. Collegeville, Minn.: Liturgical, 1991.
Karris, Robert J. *Invitation to Luke: A Commentary on the Gospel of Luke with Complete Text from the Jerusalem Bible*. Garden City, N.Y.: Image, 1977.
Kee, Howard Clark. *To Every Nation Under Heaven: The Acts of the Apostles*. New Testament in Context. Harrisburg, Pa.: Trinity Press International, 1997.
Kistemaker, Simon J. *Exposition of the Acts of the Apostles*. New Testament Commentary. Grand Rapids: Baker, 1990.
Lake, Kirsopp, and Henry J. Cadbury. *The Acts of the Apostles: English Translation and Commentary*. Vol. 4 of *The Beginnings of Christianity*. Edited by Jackson F. J. Foakes and Kirsopp Lake. 5 vols. London: Macmillan, 1920–1933.
Longenecker, Richard N. 'Acts.' In vol. 9 of *Expositor's Bible Commentary*. Edited by Frank Gaebelein. 12 vols. Grand Rapids: Zondervan, 1986.
Marshall, I. Howard. *The Acts of the Apostles: An Introduction and Commentary*. Tyndale New Testament Commentaries. Grand Rapids: Eerdmans, 1980.
———. *The Gospel of Luke*. New International Greek Testament Commentary. Exeter: Paternoster; Grand Rapids: Eerdmans, 1978.
Meyer, Heinrich August Wilhelm. *Critical and Exegetical Handbook to the Acts of the Apostles*. Translated from the 4th ed. by Paton J. Gloag. Rev. and ed. William P. Dickson. New York: Funk & Wagnalls, 1889.
Nolland, John. *Luke*. 3 vols. Word Biblical Commentary 35a–c. Dallas, Tex.: Word, 1989–1993.
Pesch, Rudolf. *Die Apostelgeschichte*. 2 vols. Evangelisch-katholischer Kommentar zum Neuen Testament 5. Zürich: Benziger; Neukirchen-Vluyn: Neukirchener, 1986.
Plummer, Alfred. *A Critical and Exegetical Commentary on the Gospel According to St. Luke*. International Critical Commentary. New York: Charles Scribner's Sons, 1901.
Polhill, John B. *Acts*. New American Commentary 26. Nashville: Broadman, 1992.
Ringe, Sharon. *Luke*. Westminster Bible Companion. Louisville: Westminster John Knox, 1995.
Roloff, Jürgen. *Die Apostelgeschichte übersetzt und erklärt*. 17th ed. Das Neue Testament deutsch 5. Göttingen: Vandenhoeck & Ruprecht, 1981.
Schille, Gottfried. *Die Apostelgeschichte des Lukas*. Theologischer Handkommentar zum Neuen Testament 5. Berlin: Evangelische Verlaganstalt, 1983
Schneider, Gerhard. *Die Apostelgeschichte*. 2 vols. Herders theologischer Kommentar zum Neuen Testament 5. Freiburg: Herder, 1980–1982.
Schweizer, Eduard. *The Good News According to Luke*. Translated by David E. Green. Atlanta: John Knox, 1984.
Stein, Robert H. *Luke*. New American Commentary 24. Nashville: Broadman, 1992.
Talbert, Charles H. *Reading Luke: A Literary and Theological Commentary on the Third Gospel*. New York: Crossroad, 1982.

Bibliography

Tannehill, Robert C. *Luke*. Abingdon New Testament Commentaries. Nashville: Abingdon, 1996.

———. *The Narrative Unity of Luke-Acts: A Literary Interpretation*. 2 vols. Foundations and Facets. Philadelphia: Fortress, 1986.

Wendt, H. H. *Die Apostelgeschichte*. 9th ed. Göttingen: Vandenhoeck & Ruprecht, 1913.

Wikenhauser, Alfred. *Die Apostelgeschichte übersetzt und erklärt*. Regensburger Neues Testament 5. Regensburg: Pustet, 1961.

Williams, C. S. C. *The Acts of the Apostles*. Harper's New Testament Commentaries. New York: Harper & Brothers, 1957.

Witherington, Ben III. *The Acts of the Apostles: A Socio-Rhetorical Commentary*. Grand Rapids: Eerdmans; Cambridge: Paternoster, 1998.

2. Texts and Translations

Greek texts and English translations are from the Loeb Classical Library unless noted.

Black, Matthew. *The Book of Enoch or 1 Enoch: A New English Edition with Commentary and Textural Notes*. Studia in Veteris Testamenti pseudepigrapha 7. Leiden: Brill, 1985.

Cathcart, Kevin J., and Robert P. Gordon. *The Targum of the Minor Prophets: Translated, With a Critical Introduction, Apparatus, and Notes*. The Aramaic Bible 14. Wilmington, Del.: Michael Glazier, 1989.

Charles, R. H. *The Apocalypse of Baruch*. London: Adam and Charles Black, 1896.

Corpus Christianorum: Series apocryphorum. Edited by Eric Junod and Jean-Daniel Kaestli, eds.. Turnhout, 1983.

Elliott, J. K., ed. *Apocryphal New Testament*. Oxford: Clarendon, 1993.

Grene, David, and Richmond Lattimore, eds. *The Complete Greek Tragedies*. 4 vols. Chicago: University of Chicago Press, 1992.

Latte, Kurt, ed. *Hesychii Alexandrini Lexicon*. 3 vols. Hauniae: Ejnar Munksgaard, 1953.

Montefiore, C. G., and H. Loewe. *A Rabbinic Anthology*. Cleveland, Ohio: Meridian, 1963.

Nauck, August, ed. *Tragicorum Graecorum Fragmenta*. Hildesheim: Georg Olms, 1964.

Patrologia graeca. Edited by J.-P. Migne. 162 vols. Paris, 1857–1886.

Reardon, B. P., ed. *Collected Ancient Greek Novels*. Berkeley: University of California Press, 1989.

Sommerstein, Alan H., ed. *The Comedies of Aristophanes*. 10 vols. Warminster: Aris and Phillips, 1996.

Wehrli, Fritz, ed. *Die Schule des Aristoteles: Texte und Kommentar*. 10 vols. Basel: Benno Schwabe, 1948.

3. Reference Works

Balz, Horst, and Gerhard Schneider, eds. *Exegetical Dictionary of the New Testament*. 3 vols. Grand Rapids: Eerdmans, 1990–1993.

Bauer, Walter, William F. Arndt, F. Wilbur Gingrich, and Frederick W. Danker. *A Greek-English Lexicon of the New Testament and Other Early Christian Literature*. 2d ed. Chicago: University of Chicago Press, 1979.

Bauer, Walter, Frederick W. Danker, William F. Arndt, and F. Wilbur Gingrich. *A Greek-English Lexicon of the New Testament and Other Early Christian Literature*. 3d ed. Chicago: University of Chicago Press, 2000.

Brown, Colin, ed. *New International Dictionary of New Testament Theology*. 4 vols. Grand Rapids: Zondervan, 1975–1985.

Brown, Francis, S. R. Driver, and Charles A. Briggs. *A Hebrew and English Lexicon of the Old Testament*. Oxford: Clarendon, 1907.

Charlesworth, James H., ed. *Old Testament Pseudepigrapha*. 2 vols. Garden City, N.Y.: Doubleday, 1983.

Dana, H. E., and Julius R. Mantey. *A Manual Grammar of the Greek New Testament*. Toronto: Macmillan, 1955.

Holladay, William L., ed. *A Concise Hebrew and Aramaic Lexicon of the Old Testament*. Leiden: Brill, 1988.

Kittel, Gerhard, and Gerhard Friedrich, eds. *Theological Dictionary of the New Testament*. Translated by Geoffrey W. Bromiley. 10 vols. Grand Rapids: Eerdmans, 1964–1976.

Liddell, H. G., R. Scott, and H. S. Jones. *A Greek-English Lexicon*. 9th ed. Oxford: Clarendon, 1996.

Patristic Greek Lexicon. Edited by G. W. H. Lampe. Oxford, 1968.

Spicq, Ceslas. *Exegetical Dictionary of the New Testament*. Translated and edited by James D. Ernest. 3 vols. Peabody, Mass.: Hendrickson, 1994.

Turner, Nigel. *Grammatical Insights into the New Testament*. Edinburgh: T. & T. Clark, 1965.

4. Other Works

Abel, Félix Marie. *Les Livres des Maccabées*. Etudes bibliques. Paris: Gabalda, 1949.

Achtemeier, Paul J. 'The Lukan Perspective on the Miracles of Jesus: A Preliminary Sketch.' Pages 153–67 in *Perspectives on Luke-Acts*. Edited by Charles H. Talbert. Perspectives in Religious Studies, Special Studies Series 5. Danville, Va.: Association of Baptist Professors of Religion, 1978.

Alexander, Loveday C. A. 'The Preface to Acts and the Historians.' Pages 79–82 in *History, Literature, and Society in the Book of Acts*. Edited by Ben Witherington III. Cambridge: Cambridge University Press, 1996.

Bibliography

———. 'Reading Luke-Acts from Back to Front.' Pages 419–46 in *The Unity of Luke-Acts*. Edited by Joseph Verheyden. Bibliotheca ephemeridum theologicarum lovaniensium 142. Leuven: Leuven University Press, 1999.

Alsup, John E. *The Post-Resurrection Appearance Stories of the Gospel-Tradition*. Calwer Theologische Monographien 5. London: SPCK, 1975.

Argyle, A. W. 'The Ascension.' *Expository Times* 66 (1954–1955): 240–42.

Atwood, Margaret. *Murder in the Dark: Short Fictions and Prose Poems*. Toronto: Coach House, 1983.

Auvray, P. *Isaïe 1–39*. Sources bibliques. Paris: Gabalda, 1972.

Baltzer, Klaus. *The Covenant Formulary in Old Testament, Jewish, and Early Christian Writings*. Translated by David E. Green. Oxford: Basil Blackwell, 1971.

Bamberger, Bernard. 'The Saducees and Belief in Angels.' *Journal of Biblical Literature* 82 (1963): 433–35.

Barbi, Augusto. *Il Cristo celeste presente nella Chiesa*. Analecta biblica 64. Rome: Biblical Institute, 1979.

Barclay, John M. G. 'The Resurrection in Contemporary New Testament Scholarship.' Pages 13–30 in *Resurrection Reconsidered*. Edited by Gavin D'Costa. Oxford: Oneworld, 1996.

Barclay, William. *Crucified and Crowned*. London: SCM, 1961.

Barrett, C. K. 'Faith and Eschatology in Acts 3.' Pages 1–17 in *Glaube und Eschatologie: Festschrift für Werner Georg Kümmel zum 80. Geburtstag*. Edited by Erich Gräßer and Otter Merk. Tübingen: Mohr-Siebeck, 1985.

———. *Luke the Historian in Recent Study*. Facet Books, Biblical Series 24. Philadelphia: Fortress, 1970.

Barth, Christoph. 'Theophanie, Bundschließung und neuer Anfang am dritten Tage.' *Evangelische Theologie* 28 (1968): 521–33.

Bartlett, John R. *The First and Second Books of the Maccabees*. Cambridge Bible Commentary. Cambridge: Cambridge University Press, 1973.

Barton, Stephen C. 'Can We Identify the Gospel Audiences?' Pages 173–94 in *The Gospels for All Christians*. Edited by Richard Bauckham. Grand Rapids: Eerdmans, 1998.

Bauckham, Richard. 'Life, Death, and the Afterlife in Second Temple Judaism.' Pages 80–95 in *Life in the Face of Death: The Resurrection Message in the New Testament*. Edited by Richard N. Longenecker. McMaster New Testament Studies. Grand Rapids: Eerdmans, 1998.

———. 'Resurrection As Giving Back the Dead.' Pages 269–89 in *The Fate of the Dead: Studies on the Jewish and Christian Apocalypses*. Novum Testamentum Supplements 93. Leiden: Brill, 1998.

———. 'The Rich Man and Lazarus: The Parable and the Parallels.' *New Testament Studies* 37 (1991): 225–46.

———. 'Visiting the Places of the Dead in the Extra-Canonical Apocalypses.' *Proceedings of the Irish Biblical Association* 18 (1995): 78–93.

Bayer, Hans F. 'Christ-Centered Eschatology in Acts 3:17–26.' Pages 236–50 in *Jesus of Nazareth: Lord and Christ—Essays on the Historical Jesus and New Testament Christology*. Edited by Joel B. Green and Max Turner. Grand Rapids: Eerdmans, 1994.

———. *Jesus' Predictions of Vindication and Resurrection*. Wissenschaftliche Untersuchungen zum Neuen Testament 20. Tübingen: Mohr-Siebeck, 1986.

Benoit, Pierre. 'L'Ascension.' *Revue biblique* 56 (1949): 161–203.

———. 'The Ascension.' Pages 209–53 in vol. 1 of *Jesus and the Gospel*. Translated by Benet Weatherhead. 2 vols. New York: Herder and Herder, 1973.

Bertram, G. 'Die Himmelfahrt Jesu vom Kreuz aus und der Glaube an seine Auferstehung.' Pages 187–217 in *Festgabe für Adolf Deissmann zum 60. Geburtstag*. Edited by K. L. Schmidt. Tübingen: Mohr-Siebeck, 1927.

Betori, Giuseppe. 'Luke 24:47: Jerusalem and the Beginning of the Preaching to the Pagans in the Acts of the Apostles.' Pages 103–20 in *Luke and Acts*. Edited by Gerald O'Collins and Gilberto Marconi. New York and Mahwah, N.J.: Paulist, 1991.

———. *Perseguitati a causa del Nome: Strutture dei racconti di persecuzione in Atti 1,12–8,4*. Analecta biblica 97. Rome: Biblical Institute, 1981.

Bickermann, E. 'Das leere Grab.' *Zeitschrift für die neutestamentliche Wissenschaft* 23 (1924): 281–92.

Boccaccini, Gabriele. *Middle Judaism: Jewish Thought, 300 B.C.E. to 200 B.C.E.* Minneapolis: Fortress, 1991.

Bock, Darrell L. *Proclamation from Prophecy and Pattern: Lucan Old Testament Christology*. Journal for the Study of the New Testament: Supplement Series 12. Sheffield: Sheffield Academic Press, 1987.

———. 'Scripture and the Realisation of God's Promises.' Pages 41–62 in *Witness to the Gospel: The Theology of Acts*. Edited by I. Howard Marshall and David Peterson. Grand Rapids: Eerdmans, 1998.

Bolt, Peter G. 'Life, Death, and the Afterlife in the Greco-Roman World.' Pages 51–79 in *Life in the Face of Death: The Resurrection Message in the New Testament*. Edited by Richard N. Longenecker. McMaster New Testament Studies. Grand Rapids: Eerdmans, 1998.

———. 'What Were the Sadducees Reading? An Enquiry into the Literary Background of Mark 12:18–23.' *Tyndale Bulletin* 45 (1994): 369–94.

Bolton, J. D. P. *Aristeas of Proconnesus*. Oxford: Clarendon, 1962.

Bonner, Stanley F. *Education in Ancient Rome: From the Elder Cato to the Younger Pliny*. Berkeley: University of California Press, 1977.

Bovon, François. *Luc le théologien. Vignt-cinq ans de recherches (1950–1975)*. 2d ed. Monde de la Bible 5. Geneva: Labor et Fides, 1988.

———. *Luke the Theologian: Thirty-Three Years of Research (1950–1983)*. Translated by Ken McKinney. Pittsburgh Theological Monograph Series. Allison Park, Pa.: Pickwick, 1987. Translation of *Luc le théologien. Vignt-cinq ans de recherches (1950–1975)*. Neuchâtel: Delachaux; Paris: Niestlé, 1978.

———. 'Le salut dans les écrits de Luc.' *Revue de théologie et de philosophie* 23 (1975): 296–307.
Bowen, Clayton Raymond. 'The Meaning of συναλιζόμενος in Act 1,4.' *Zeitschrift für die neutestamentliche Wissenschaft* 13 (1912): 247–59.
Bowersock, G. W. *Fiction as History: Nero to Julian*. Berkeley: University of California Press, 1994.
Brändle, Max. 'Auferstehung Jesu nach Lukas.' *Orientierung* 24 (1960): 85–89.
Bratcher, Robert G. 'Having Loosed the Pangs of Death.' *The Bible Translator* 10 (1959): 18–20.
Braun, Willi. *Feasting and Social Rhetoric in Luke 14*. Society for New Testament Studies Monograph Series 85. Cambridge: Cambridge University Press, 1995.
Brawley, Robert L. *Luke-Acts and the Jews: Conflict, Apology, and Conciliation*. Society of Biblical Literature Monograph Series 33. Atlanta: Scholars Press, 1987.
———. 'Paul in Acts: Aspects of Structure and Characterization.' Pages 90–96 in *SBL Seminar Papers, 1988*. Society of Biblical Literature Seminar Papers 27. Atlanta: Scholars Press, 1988.
Breech, Earl. 'These Fragments I Have Shored Against My Ruins: The Form and Function of 4 Ezra.' *Journal of Biblical Literature* 92 (1973): 267–74.
Bremmer, Jan. *The Early Greek Concept of the Soul*. Princeton: Princeton University Press, 1983.
Brodie, Thomas L. 'Towards Unravelling Luke's Use of the Old Testament: Luke 7.11–17 As an *Imitatio* of 1 Kings 17.17–24.' *New Testament Studies* 32 (1986): 241–67.
Brown, Andrew L. 'Protesilaus.' Page 1265 in *The Oxford Classical Dictionary*. Edited by Simon Hornblower and Antony Spawforth. 3d ed. Oxford: Oxford University Press, 1996.
Bruce, F. F. 'Paul's Use of the Old Testament in Acts.' Pages 71–79 in *Tradition and Interpretation in the New Testament: Essays in Honor of E. Earle Ellis for His 60th Birthday*. Edited by Gerald F. Hawthorne and Otto Betz. Grand Rapids: Eerdmans, 1987.
———. *The Time Is Fulfilled: Five Aspects of the Fulfillment of the Old Testament in the New*. Grand Rapids: Eerdmans, 1978.
Brueggemann, Walter. 'Amos iv 4–13 and Israel's Covenant Worship.' *Vetus Testamentum* 15 (1965): 1–15.
———. 'From Dust to Kingship.' *Zeitschrift für die alttestamentliche Wissenschaft* 84 (1972): 1–18.
Bückers, H. 'Das "ewige Leben" in 2 Makk 7:36.' *Biblica* 21 (1940): 406–12.
Bultmann, Rudolf. *History of the Synoptic Tradition*. Translated by John Marsh. Oxford: Basil Blackwell, 1963.
Burkert, Walter. *Greek Religion: Archaic and Classical*. Translated by John Raffan. Oxford: Basil Blackwell, 1985.
Byrne, Brendan. 'Sons of God.' Pages 156–59 in vol. 6 of *Anchor Bible Dictionary*. Edited by David N. Freedman. Garden City, N.Y.: Doubleday, 1991.

———. *'Sons of God'–'Seed of Abraham': A Study of the Idea of the Sonship of God of All Christians in Paul Against the Jewish Background*. Analecta biblica 83. Rome: Biblical Institute, 1979.

Cadbury, Henry J. 'Appendix C: Commentary on the Preface of Luke.' Pages 489–510 in *Prolegomena II: Criticism*. Edited by Jackson. F. J. Foakes and Kirsopp Lake. Vol. 2 of *The Beginnings of Christianity*. Part 1: *The Acts of the Apostles*. London: Macmillan, 1920–1933.

———. *The Book of Acts in History*. London: Adam and Charles Black, 1955.

———. 'Lexical Notes on Luke-Acts: III. Luke's Interest in Lodging.' *Journal of Biblical Literature* 45 (1926): 305–22.

———. *The Making of Luke-Acts*. 2d ed. London: SPCK, 1959. Repr., Peabody, Mass.: Hendrickson, 1999.

———. 'Note XXXI. The Summaries in Acts.' Pages 392–401 in *Additional Notes to the Commentary*. Edited by Jackson. F. J. Foakes and Kirsopp Lake. Vol. 5 of *The Beginnings of Christianity*. Part 1: *The Acts of the Apostles*. London: Macmillan, 1920–1933.

———. 'Note XXXII. The Speeches in Acts.' Pages 402–27 in *Additional Notes to the Commentary*. Edited by F. J. Foakes Jackson and Kirsopp Lake. Vol. 5 of *The Beginnings of Christianity*. Part 1: *The Acts of the Apostles*. London: Macmillan, 1920–1933.

Carroll, John T. 'Jesus as Healer in Luke-Acts.' Pages 269–85 in *SBL Seminar Papers, 1994*. Society of Biblical Literature Seminar Papers 33. Atlanta: Scholars Press, 1994.

———. *Response to the End of History: Eschatology and Situation in Luke-Acts*. Society of Biblical Literature Dissertation Series 92. Atlanta: Scholars Press, 1988.

Casey, Robert P. 'Note V. Μάρτυς.' Pages 30–37 in *Additional Notes to the Commentary*. Edited by F. J. Foakes Jackson and Kirsopp Lake. Vol. 5 of *The Beginnings of Christianity*. Part 1: *The Acts of the Apostles*. London: Macmillan, 1920–1933.

Cavallin, H. C. C. *Life After Death: Paul's Argument for the Resurrection of the Dead in 1 Cor 15*. Part 1: *An Enquiry into the Jewish Background*. Coniectanea biblica, New Testament Series 7.1. Lund: Gleerup, 1974.

Cerfaux, L. 'Témoins du Christ d'après le livre des Actes.' *Angelicum* 20 (1943): 166–83.

Chance, J. Bradley. *Jerusalem, the Temple, and the Salvation of Israel*. Macon, Ga.: Mercer University Press, 1988.

Charlesworth, James H. 'Baruch, Book of 2 (Syriac).' Pages 620–21 in vol. 1 of *Anchor Bible Dictionary*. Edited by David N. Freedman. 6 vols. Garden City, N.Y.: Doubleday, 1992.

Clark, Andrew. 'Role of the Apostles.' Pages 169–90 in *Witness to the Gospel: The Theology of Acts*. Edited by I. Howard Marshall and David Peterson. Grand Rapids: Eerdmans, 1998.

Bibliography

Clarke, William K. L. 'The Use of the Septuagint in Acts.' Pages 66–105 in *Prolegomena II: Criticism*. Edited by Jackson. F. J. Foakes and Kirsopp Lake. Vol. 2 of *The Beginnings of Christianity*. Part 1: *The Acts of the Apostles*. London: Macmillan, 1920–1933.

Clements, Ronald E. *Isaiah 1–39*. New Century Bible. Grand Rapids: Eerdmans, 1980.

Co, Marie Anicia. 'The Major Summaries in Acts: Acts 2,42–47; 4,32–35; 5:12–16—Linguistic and Literary Relationship.' *Ephemerides theologicae lovanienses* 68 (1992): 49–85.

Cohen, Shaye J. D. *From the Maccabees to the Mishnah*. Edited by Wayne A. Meeks. Library of Early Christianity 7. Philadelphia: Westminster, 1987.

Cohn-Sherbok, D. M. 'Jesus' Defense of the Resurrection of the Dead.' *Journal for the Study of the New Testament* 11 (1981): 64–73.

Collins, John J. *The Apocalyptic Imagination: An Introduction to Jewish Apocalyptic Literature*. 2d ed. Biblical Resources Series. Grand Rapids: Eerdmans, 1998.

———. *Daniel*. Hermeneia. Minneapolis: Fortress, 1993.

———. *Daniel, First Maccabees, Second Maccabees with an Excursus on the Apocalyptic Genre*. Old Testament Message 16. Wilmington, Del.: Michael Glazier, 1981.

———. 'Testaments.' Pages 325–55 in *Jewish Writings of the Second Temple Period: Pseudepigrapha, Qumran Sectarian Writings, Philo, Josephus*. Edited by Michael E. Stone. Compendia rerum iudaicarum ad novum testamentum 2. Assen: Van Gorcum, 1984.

Conzelmann, Hans. *The Theology of St. Luke*. Translated by Geoffrey Buswell. London: Faber and Faber, 1960.

Cook, John G. 'Some Hellenistic Responses to the Gospels and Gospel Traditions.' *Zeitschrift für die neutestamentliche Wissenschaft* 84 (1993): 233–54.

Croy, N. Clayton. 'Hellenistic Philosophies and the Preaching of the Resurrection (Acts 17:18, 32).' *Novum Testamentum* 39 (1997): 21–39.

Cullmann, Oscar. *Immortality of the Soul or Resurrection of the Dead? The Witness of the New Testament*. London: Epworth, 1958.

Dahood, Mitchell. *Psalms*. 3 vols. Anchor Bible 16–17a. Garden City, N.Y.: Doubleday, 1965–1970.

Darr, John. *Herod the Fox: Audience Criticism and Lukan Characterization*. Journal for the Study of the New Testament: Supplement Series 163. Sheffield: Sheffield Academic Press, 1998.

Daube, David. 'On Acts 23: Sadducees and Angels.' *Journal of Biblical Literature* 109 (1990): 493–97.

Davies, J. G. *He Ascended into Heaven*. London: Lutterworth, 1958.

———. 'The Prefigurement of the Ascension in the Third Gospel.' *Journal of Theological Studies* 6 (1955): 229–33.

Davies, W. D., and Dale C. Allison. *The Gospel According to Matthew*. 3 vols. International Critical Commentary. Edinburgh: T. & T. Clark, 1988–1991.

Davis, Christopher A. *The Structure of Paul's Theology*. Lewiston, N.Y.: Edwin Mellen, 1995.

Dawsey, James M. 'Confrontation in the Temple: Luke 19:45–20:47.' *Perspectives in Religious Studies* 11 (1984): 153–65.
Delcor, M. *Le Livre de Daniel.* Sources bibliques. Paris: Gabalda, 1971.
Denis, Albert-Marie. *Introduction aux pseudépigraphes grecs d'Ancien Testament.* Studia in Veteris Testamenti pseudepigrapha 1. Leiden: Brill, 1970.
Derrett, J. Duncan M. *The Anastasis: The Resurrection of Jesus as an Historical Event.* Warwickshire: Drinkwater, 1982.
deSilva, David A. 'Paul's Sermon in Antioch of Pisidia.' *Bibliotheca Sacra* 151 (1994): 32–49.
Desjardins, Michel. 'Bauer and Beyond: On Recent Scholarly Discussions of Αἵρεσις in the Early Christian Era.' *Second Century* 8 (1991): 65–82.
Deutschmann, Anton. 'Die Hoffnung Israels (Apg 28,20).' *Biblische Notizen* 105 (2000): 54–60.
Dewald, Carolyn. 'Wanton Kings, Pickled Heroes, and Gnomic Founding Fathers: Strategies of Meaning at the End of Herodotus's *Histories*.' Pages 62–82 in *Classical Closure: Reading the End in Greek and Latin Literature.* Edited by Deborah H. Roberts, Francis M. Dunn, and Don Fowler. Princeton: Princeton University Press, 1997.
Di Lella, Alexander A. 'Wisdom of Ben-Sira.' Pages 931–45 in vol. 6 of *Anchor Bible Dictionary.* Edited by David N. Freedman. Garden City, N.Y.: Doubleday, 1991.
Dibelius, Martin. *From Tradition to Gospel.* Translated by Bertram Lee Woolf. London: Iver Nicholson and Watson, 1934.

———. *Studies in Luke-Acts.* London: SCM; New York: Charles Scribner's Sons, 1956.
Dillon, Richard J. 'Easter Revelation and Mission Program in Luke 24:46–48.' Pages 240–70 in *Sin, Salvation, and the Spirit.* Edited by Daniel Durken. Collegeville, Minn.: Liturgical, 1979.

———. *From Eye-Witnesses to Ministers of the Word: Tradition and Composition in Luke 24.* Analecta biblica 82. Rome: Biblical Institute, 1978.
Doble, Peter. *The Paradox of Salvation.* Society for New Testament Studies Monograph Series 87. Cambridge: Cambridge University Press, 1996.
Dömer, M. *Das Heil Gottes: Studien zur Theologie des lukanischen Doppelwerkes.* Bonner biblische Beiträge 51. Köln and Bonn: Peter Hanstein, 1978.
Downing, F. Gerald. 'Theophilus' First Reading of Luke-Acts.' Pages 91–109 in *Luke's Literary Achievement: Collected Essays.* Edited by C. M. Tuckett. Journal for the Study of the New Testament: Supplement Series 116. Sheffield: Sheffield Academic Press, 1995.
Dreyfus, F. 'L'argument scripturaire de Jésus en faveur de la résurrection des morts (Marc, XII, 26–27).' *Revue biblique* 66 (1959): 213–24.
Drinkard, Joel F. Jr. 'Right, Right Hand.' Page 724 in vol. 5 of *Anchor Bible Dictionary.* Edited by David N. Freedman. Garden City, N.Y.: Doubleday, 1991.
Duling, Dennis C. 'The Promises to David and Their Entrance into Christianity— Nailing Down a Likely Hypothesis.' *New Testament Studies* 19 (1973): 55–77.

Dupont, Jacques. 'L'Apôtre comme intermédiaire du salut dans les Actes des Apôtres.' *Revue de théologie et de philosophie* 112 (1980): 342–58.

———. 'La conclusion des Actes et son rapport à l'ensemble de l'ouvrage de Luc.' Pages 359–404 in *Les Actes des Apôtres: Traditions, rédaction, théologie*. Edited by J. Kremer. Bibliotheca ephemeridum theologicarum lovaniensium 48. Leuven: Leuven University Press, 1979.

———. 'Filius meus es tu. L'interprétation de Ps. II, 7 dans le Nouveau Testament.' *Recherches de science religieuse* 35 (1948): 522–43.

———. 'L'interprétation des Psaumes dans les Actes des Apôtres.' Pages 283–307 in *Études sur les Actes des Apôtres*. Lectio divina 45. Paris: Les Éditions du Cerf, 1967.

———. 'La portée christologique de l'évangélisation des nations d'après Luc 24,47.' Pages 125–43 in *Neues Testament und Kirche: Für Rudolf Schnackenburg*. Edited by Joachim Gnilka. Freiburg: Herder, 1974.

———. 'La question du plan des Actes des Apôtres à la lumière d'un texte de Lucien de Samosate.' *Novum Testamentum* 31 (1979): 220–31.

———. *The Salvation to the Gentiles: Studies in the Acts of the Apostles*. New York: Paulist, 1979.

———. 'ΤΑ ὍΣΙΑ ΔΑΥΙΔ ΤΑ ΠΙΣΤΑ (Actes 13,34=Isaïe 55,3).' Pages 337–59 in *Études sur les Actes des Apôtres*. Lectio divina 45. Paris: Les Éditions du Cerf, 1967.

———. "ΑΝΕΛΗΜΦΘΗ (Act. I.2).' *New Testament Studies* 8 (1961–1962): 154–57.

Eckstein, Hans-Joachim. 'Bodily Resurrection in Luke.' Pages 115–23 in *Resurrection: Theological and Scientific Assessments*. Edited by Ted Peters, Robert John Russell, and Michael Welker. Grand Rapids: Eerdmans, 2002.

Eliade, Mircea. *Zalmoxis, the Vanishing God: Comparative Studies in the Religions and Folklore of Dacia and Eastern Europe*. Translated by Willard R. Trask. Chicago: University of Chicago Press, 1972.

Elias, Jacob W. 'The Furious Climax in Nazareth (Luke 4:28–30).' Pages 87–99 in *The New Way of Jesus: Essays Presented to Howard Charles*. Edited by William Klassen. Newton, Kans.: Faith and Life, 1980.

Elliott, James K. 'Does Luke 2:41–52 Anticipate the Resurrection?' *Expository Times* 83 (1971): 87–89.

Ellis, E. Earle. 'Jesus, the Sadducees and Qumran.' *New Testament Studies* 10 (1964): 274–79.

Ellis, John M. *Against Deconstruction*. Princeton: Princeton University Press, 1989.

Ellul, Danielle. 'Actes 3/1–11.' *Etudes théologiques et religieuses* 64 (1989): 95–99.

———. 'Antioche de Pisidie: Une Prédication…Trois Credos? (Actes 13,13–43).' *Filologia Neotestamentaria* 5 (1992): 3–14.

Evans, C. F. *Resurrection and the New Testament*. Studies in Biblical Theology 12. London: SCM, 1970.

———. '"Speeches" in Acts.' Pages 287–302 in *Mélanges Bibliques en homage au R. P. Béda Rigaux*. Edited by Albert Descamps and R. P. André de Halleux. Gembloux: Duculot, 1970.

Feldman, Louis H. 'Josephus.' Pages 981–98 in vol. 3 of *Anchor Bible Dictionary.* Edited by David N. Freedman. Garden City, N.Y.: Doubleday, 1991.

Ferguson, John. *Greek and Roman Religion: A Source Book.* Noyes Classical Studies. Park Ridge, N.J.: Noyes, 1980.

Field, Frederick. *Notes on the Translation of the New Testament.* Cambridge: Cambridge University Press, 1899. Repr., Peabody, Mass.: Hendrickson, 1994.

Finkelstein, Louis. 'The Pharisees: Their Origin and Their Philosophy.' *Harvard Theological Review* 22 (1929): 185–261.

Fish, Stanley. *Is There a Text in This Class? The Authority of Intrepretive Communities.* Cambridge, Mass.: Harvard University Press, 1980.

Fitzmyer, Joseph A. 'The Ascension of Christ and Pentecost.' Pages 265–94 in *To Advance the Gospel.* 2d ed. Biblical Resource Series. Grand Rapids: Eerdmans, 1998.

———. 'The Resurrection of Jesus According to the New Testament.' Pages 369–81 in *To Advance the Gospel.* 2d ed. Grand Rapids: Eerdmans, 1998.

———. '"Today You Shall Be with Me in Paradise" (Luke 23:43).' Pages 203–33 in *Luke the Theologian: Aspects of His Teaching.* New York and Mahwah, N.J.: Paulist, 1989.

Flanagan, Neal. 'The What and How of Salvation in Luke-Acts.' Pages 203–13 in *Sin, Salvation, and the Spirit.* Edited by Daniel Durken. Collegeville, Minn.: Liturgical, 1979.

Fohrer, Georg. *Das Buch Jesaja.* 2d ed. Zürcher Bibelkommentare. Zurich and Stuttgart: Zwingli, 1967.

Forbes, Peter Barr Reid, and Robert Browning. 'Hesychius.' Pages 701–2 in *The Oxford Classical Dictionary.* Edited by Simon Hornblower and Antony Spawforth. 3d ed. Oxford: Oxford University Press, 1996.

Fowler, Don. 'Second Thoughts on Closure.' Pages 3–22 in *Classical Closure: Reading the End in Greek and Latin Literature.* Edited by Deborah H. Roberts, Francis M. Dunn, and Don Fowler. Princeton: Princeton University Press, 1997.

Franklin, Eric. 'The Ascension and Eschatology of Luke-Acts.' *Scottish Journal of Theology* 23 (1970): 191–200.

———. *Christ the Lord: A Study in the Purpose and Theology of Luke-Acts.* Philadelphia: Westminster, 1975.

Frein, Brigid Curtin. 'The Literary and Theological Significance of Misunderstanding in the Gospel of Luke.' *Biblica* 74 (1993): 328–48.

Fuller, Daniel P. *Easter Faith and History.* Grand Rapids: Eerdmans, 1965.

Fuller, Reginald H. *The Formation of the Resurrection Narratives.* New York: Macmillan, 1971.

———. 'Luke and the *Theologia Crucis.*' Pages 214–20 in *Sin, Salvation, and the Spirit.* Edited by Daniel Durken. Collegeville, Minn.: Liturgical, 1979.

Fusco, Vittorio. 'Luke-Acts and the Future of Israel.' *Novum Testamentum* 38 (1996): 1–17.

Gaffin, Richard B. Jr. *The Centrality of the Resurrection: A Study in Paul's Soteriology.* Grand Rapids: Baker, 1978.

Gardner-Smith, P. *The Narratives of the Resurrection.* London: Methuen, 1926.

Garland, Robert. *The Greek Way of Death.* Ithaca, N.Y.: Cornell University Press, 1985.

Garland, Robert S. J., and John Scheid. 'Death, Attitudes to.' Pages 433–34 in *The Oxford Classical Dictionary.* Edited by Simon Hornblower and Antony Spawforth. 3d ed. Oxford: Oxford University Press, 1996.

Garrett, Susan R. 'Exodus From Bondage: Luke 9:31 and Acts 12:1–24.' *Catholic Biblical Quarterly* 52 (1990): 656–80.

———. 'The Meaning of Jesus' Death in Luke.' *Word and World* 12 (1992): 11–16.

Gaster, T. H. 'Resurrection.' Pages 39–43 in *Interpreter's Dictionary of the Bible.* Edited by George A. Buttrick. Nashville: Abingdon, 1976.

Gaston, Lloyd. *Horae Synopticae Electronicae: Word Statistics of the Synoptic Gospels.* Sources for Biblical Studies 3. Missoula, Mont.: SBL, 1973.

Geisler, Norman L. *The Battle for the Resurrection.* Nashville: Thomas Nelson, 1989.

———. *In Defense of the Resurrection.* Lynchburg, Va.: Quest, 1991.

Gempf, Conrad. 'Public Speaking and Published Accounts.' Pages 259–303 in *The Book of Acts in Its Ancient Literary Setting.* Edited by Bruce W. Winter and Andrew D. Clarke. Vol. 1 of *The Book of Acts in Its First Century Setting.* Grand Rapids: Eerdmans; Carlisle: Paternoster, 1993.

Genette, Gérard. *Narrative Discourse: An Essay in Method.* Translated by Jane E. Lewin. Ithaca, N.Y.: Cornell University Press, 1980.

George, Augustin. 'Les anges.' Pages 149–83 in *Études sur l'œuvre de Luc.* Sources bibliques. Paris: Gabalda, 1978.

———. 'L'Eschatologie.' Pages 321–47 in *Études sur l'œuvre de Luc.* Sources bibliques. Paris: Gabalda, 1978.

———. 'Les récits de miracles. Caractéristiques lucaniennes.' Pages 67–84 in *Études sur l'œuvre de Luc.* Sources bibliques. Paris: Gabalda, 1978.

———. 'Le sens de la mort de Jésus.' Pages 185–212 in *Études sur l'œuvre de Luc.* Sources bibliques. Paris: Gabalda, 1978.

———. 'Le vocabulaire de salut.' Pages 307–20 in *Études sur l'œuvre de Luc.* Sources bibliques. Paris: Gabalda, 1978.

Giles, Kevin. 'Ascension.' Pages 48–50 in *Dictionary of Jesus and the Gospels.* Edited by Joel B. Green and Scot McKnight. Downers Grove, Ill.: InterVarsity, 1992.

———. 'Salvation in Lukan Theology (1).' *Reformed Theological Review* 42 (1983): 10–16.

———. 'Salvation in Lukan Theology (2).' *Reformed Theological Review* 42 (1983): 45–49.

Gill, Everett. 'Jesus' Salt Covenant with the Eleven.' *Review and Expositor* 36 (1939): 197–98.

Gillman, Neil. *The Death of Death: Resurrection and Immortality in Jewish Thought.* Woodstock, Vt.: Jewish Lights, 1997.

Gils, Félix. *Jésus Prophète après les Évangiles Synoptiques*. Orientalia et Biblica Lovaniensia 2. Louvain: Publications Universitaires, 1957.

Ginsberg, H. L. 'The Oldest Interpretation of the Suffering Servant.' *Vetus Testamentum* 3 (1953): 400–4.

Glöckner, Richard. *Die Verkündigung des Heils beim Evangelisten Lukas*. Walberberger Studien, Theologische Reihe 13. Mainz: Matthias-Grünewald, 1975.

Goldingay, John E. *Daniel*. Word Biblical Commentary 30. Dallas, Tex.: Word, 1989.

Goldsmith, Dale. 'Acts 13:33–37: A *Pesher* on II Sam 7.' *Journal of Biblical Literature* 87 (1968): 321–24.

Goldstein, Jonathan A. *II Maccabees*. Anchor Bible 41a. Garden City, N.Y.: Doubleday, 1983.

Goppelt, Leonhard. 'The Easter Kerygma in the New Testament.' Pages 27–58 in *The Easter Message Today*. Edited by Leonhard Goppelt, Helmut Thielicke, and Hans-Rudolf Müller-Schwefe. London: Thomas Nelson, 1964.

———. *Theology of the New Testament*. Translated by John Alsup. 2 vols. Grand Rapids: Eerdmans, 1981.

Gottschalk, H. B. *Heraclides of Pontus*. Oxford: Clarendon, 1980.

Goulder, M. D. *Type and History in Acts*. London: SPCK, 1964.

Gowan, Donald E. *Theology of the Prophetic Books: The Death and Resurrection of Israel*. Louisville, Ky.: Westminster John Knox, 1998.

Graß, Hans. *Ostergeschehen und Osterberichte*. Göttingen: Vandenhoeck & Ruprecht, 1964.

Green, Joel B. 'Acts of the Apostles.' Pages 7–24 in *Dictionary of the Later New Testament and Its Developments*. Edited by Ralph P. Martin and Peter H. Davids. Downers Grove, Ill.: InterVarsity, 1997.

———. 'The Death of Jesus, God's Servant.' Pages 18–28, 170–73 in *Reimaging the Death of the Lukan Jesus*. Edited by Dennis D. Sylva. Bonner biblische Beiträge 73. Frankfurt am Main: Anton Hain, 1990.

———. 'The Message of Salvation in Luke-Acts.' *Ex Auditu* 5 (1989): 21–34.

———. '"Witnesses of His Resurrection": Salvation, Discipleship, and Resurrection in the Acts of the Apostles.' Pages 227–46 in *Life in the Face of Death: The Resurrection Message in the New Testament*. Edited by Richard N. Longenecker. McMaster New Testament Studies. Grand Rapids: Eerdmans, 1998.

Green, Joel B., and Michael C. McKeever. *Luke-Acts and New Testament Historiography*. Institute for Biblical Research Bibliographies 8. Grand Rapids: Baker, 1994.

Grogan, G. 'Isaiah.' In vol. 6 of *Expositor's Bible Commentary*. Edited by Frank Gaebelein. 12 vols. Grand Rapids: Zondervan, 1986.

Guillaume, Jean-Marie. *Luc Interprète des anciennes traditions sur la résurrection de Jésus*. Etudes biblique. Paris: Librairie Lecoffre, 1979.

Gundry, Robert H. 'The Essential Physicality of Jesus' Resurrection According to the New Testament.' Pages 204–19 in *Jesus of Nazareth: Lord and Christ. Essays on the Historical Jesus and New Testament Christology*. Edited by Joel B. Green and Max Turner. Grand Rapids: Eerdmans, 1994.

Guthrie, W. K. C. *The Greeks and Their Gods*. Boston: Beacon, 1962.
Haacker, Klaus. 'Das Bekenntnis des Paulus zur Hoffnung Israels nach der Apostelgeschichte des Lukas.' *New Testament Studies* 31 (1985): 437–51.
Hachlili, Rachel. *Ancient Jewish Art and Archaeology in the Diaspora*. Handbuch der Orientalistik 1.35. Leiden: Brill, 1998.
———. *Ancient Jewish Art and Archaeology in the Land of Israel*. Handbuch der Orientalistik 7.1. Leiden: Brill, 1988.
———. 'Burials, Ancient Jewish.' Page 790 in vol. 1 of *Anchor Bible Dictionary*. Edited by David N. Freedman. Garden City, N.Y.: Doubleday, 1991.
Haenchen, Ernst. 'Judentum und Christentum in der Apostelgeschichte.' *Zeitschrift für die neutestamentliche Wissenschaft* 54 (1963): 155–87.
Haight, Elizabeth Hazelton. *Essays on the Greek Romances*. Port Washington, N.Y.: Kennikat, 1943.
Halpern-Amaru, Betsy. *Rewriting the Bible: Land and Covenant in Postbiblical Jewish Literature*. Valley Forge, Pa.: Trinity Press International, 1994.
Hamm, Dennis. 'Acts 3:12–26: Peter's Speech and the Man Born Lame.' *Perspectives in Religious Studies* 11 (1984): 199–217.
———. 'Paul's Blindness and Its Healing: Clues to Symbolic Intent (Acts 9; 22 and 26).' *Biblica* 71 (1990): 63–72.
———. 'Sight to the Blind: Vision as Metaphor in Luke.' *Biblica* 67 (1986): 457–77.
Hansen, G. Walter. 'The Preaching and Defence of Paul.' Pages 295–324 in *Witness to the Gospel: The Theology of Acts*. Edited by I. Howard Marshall and David Peterson. Grand Rapids: Eerdmans, 1998.
Harnack, Adolf von. *The Date of Acts and the Synoptic Gospels*. Translated by John Richard Wilkinson. Crown Theological Library 33. New York: G. P. Putnam's Sons; London: Williams and Norgate, 1911.
Harris, Murray J. *From Grave to Glory: Resurrection in the New Testament*. Grand Rapids: Zondervan, 1990.
———. *Raised Immortal: Resurrection and Immortality in the New Testament*. Grand Rapids: Eerdmans, 1983.
Harris, William V. *Ancient Literacy*. Cambridge, Mass.: Harvard University Press, 1989.
Hasel, Gerhard F. 'Resurrection in the Theology of Old Testament Apocalyptic.' *Zeitschrift für die alttestamentliche Wissenschaft* 92 (1980): 267–84.
Hauser, H. J. *Strukturen der Abschlusserzählung der Apostelgeschichte (Apg 28,16–31)*. Analecta biblica 86. Rome: Biblical Institute, 1979.
Hawkins, John C. *Horae Synopticae*. Oxford: Clarendon, 1909.
Hemer, Colin J. *The Book of Acts in Its Setting of Hellenistic Historiography*. Edited by Conrad H. Gempf. Winona Lake, Ind.: Eisenbrauns, 1990.
Hengel, Martin. *Judaism and Hellenism: Studies in Their Encounter in Palestine During the Early Hellenistic Period*. 2 vols. Minneapolis: Fortress, 1974.

Henten, Jan Willem van. *The Maccabean Martyrs As Saviours of the Jewish People: A Study of 2 and 4 Maccabees*. Journal for the Study of Judaism Supplement 57. Leiden: Brill, 1997.

Hobart, William K. *The Medical Language of St. Luke*. Dublin: Hodges, Figgis & Co., 1882.

Hollander, H. W., and M. de Jonge. *The Testaments of the Twelve Patriarchs: A Commentary*. Studia in Veteris Testamenti pseudepigrapha 8. Leiden: Brill, 1985.

Holtz, Traugott. 'Geschichte und Verheißung: "Auferstanden nach der Schrift."' *Evangelische Theologie* 57 (1997): 179–96.

Hooker, Morna D. *Beginnings: Keys That Open the Gospels*. Harrisburg, Pa.: Trinity Press International, 1997.

Horst, P. W. van der. *Ancient Jewish Epitaphs*. Kampen: Kok Pharos, 1991.

———. *The Sentences of Pseudo-Phocylides with Introduction and Commentary*. Studia in Veteris Testamenti pseudepigrapha 4. Leiden: Brill, 1978.

Hoskyns, Edwyn Clement, and Francis Noel Davey. *Crucifixion-Resurrection: The Pattern of the Theology and Ethics of the New Testament*. London: SPCK, 1981.

Hubbard, David Allan. *Hosea: An Introduction and Commentary*. Tyndale Old Testament Commentaries 22a. Downers Grove, Ill.: InterVarsity Press, 1989.

Jackson, F. J. Foakes, and Kirsopp Lake, eds. *The Beginnings of Christianity*. 5 vols. Part 1: *The Acts of the Apostles*. London: Macmillan, 1920–1933.

Jacob, Edmond, Carl-A. Keller, and Samuel Amsler. *Osée, Joël, Amos, Abdias, Jonas*. 3d ed. Commentaire de l'Ancien Testament 11a. Geneva: Labor et Fides, 1992.

Janzen, J. Gerald. 'Resurrection and Hermeneutics: On Exodus 3.6 in Mark 12.26.' *Journal for the Study of the New Testament* 23 (1985): 43–58.

Jervell, Jacob. 'The Center of Scripture in Luke.' Pages 122–37 in *The Unknown Paul: Essays on Luke-Acts and Early Christian History*. Minneapolis: Augsburg, 1984.

———. 'The Future of the Past: Luke's View of Salvation History and Its Bearing on His Writing of History.' Pages 104–26 in *History, Literature, and Society in the Book of Acts*. Edited by Ben Witherington III. Cambridge: Cambridge University Press, 1996.

———. *Luke and the People of God*. Minneapolis: Augsburg, 1972.

Johnson, Dan G. *From Chaos to Restoration: An Integrative Reading of Isaiah 24–27*. Journal for the Study of the Old Testament: Supplement Series 61. Sheffield: Sheffield Academic Press, 1988.

Johnson, Luke Timothy. *The Literary Function of Possessions in Luke-Acts*. Society of Biblical Literature Dissertation Series. Missoula, Mont.: Scholars Press, 1977.

———. *Living Jesus: Learning the Heart of the Gospel*. San Francisco: HarperSanFrancisco, 1999.

———. 'On Finding the Lukan Community: A Cautious Cautionary Essay.' Pages 87–100 in volume 1 of the *SBL Seminar Papers, 1979*. 2 vols. Society of Biblical Literature Seminar Papers 16. Missoula, Mont.: Scholars Press, 1979.

———. 'The Social Dimension of *Sōtēria* in Luke-Acts and Paul.' Pages 520–36 in *SBL Seminar Papers, 1993*. Society of Biblical Literature Seminar Papers 32. Atlanta: Scholars Press, 1993.

Jones, Donald L. 'The Title "Author of Life (Leader)" in the Acts of the Apostles.' Pages 627–36 in *SBL Seminar Papers, 1994*. Society of Biblical Literature Seminar Papers 33. Atlanta: Scholars Press, 1994.

Jong, Irene J. F. de. 'Πιστὰ τεκμήρια in Soph. *El*. 774.' *Mnemosyne* 5 (1994): 679–81.

Jonge, Marinus de. 'Patriarchs, Testaments of the Twelve.' Pages 182–84 in vol. 5 of *Anchor Bible Dictionary*. Edited by David N. Freedman. Garden City, N.Y.: Doubleday, 1991.

Juel, Donald. 'Social Dimensions of Exegesis: The Use of Psalm 16 in Acts 2.' *Catholic Biblical Quarterly* 43 (1981): 543–54.

Just, Arthur A. Jr. *The Ongoing Feast: Table Fellowship and Eschatology at Emmaus*. Collegeville, Minn.: Liturgical, 1993.

Kaiser, Otto. *Isaiah 13–39*. Old Testament Library. Philadelphia: Westminster, 1974.

Kany, Roland. 'Der lukanische Bericht von Tod und Auferstehung Jesu aus der Sicht eines hellenistischen Romanlesers.' *Novum Testamentum* 28 (1986): 75–90.

Karris, Robert J. *Luke: Artist and Theologian. Luke's Passion Account as Literature*. Theological Inquiries. New York: Paulist, 1985.

Käsemann, Ernst. 'Das Problem des historischen Jesus.' *Zeitschrift für Theologie und Kirche* 51 (1954): 125–53.

———. *Der Ruf der Freiheit*. 5th ed. Tübingen: Mohr-Siebeck, 1972.

———. 'Ministry and Community in the New Testament.' Pages 63–134 in, *Essays on New Testament Themes*. London: SCM, 1964.

Kegel, Günter. *Auferstehung Jesu–Auferstehung der Toten: Eine traditionsgeschichtliche Untersuchung zum Neuen Testament*. Gütersloh: Mohn, 1970.

Kellermann, Ulrich. *Auferstanden in den Himmel*. Stuttgarter Bibelstudien 95. Stuttgart: Katholisches Bibelwerk, 1979.

Kennedy, George A. *New Testament Interpretation through Rhetorical Criticism*. Chapel Hill: University of South Carolina Press, 1984.

Kepple, Robert J. 'The Hope of Israel, the Resurrection of the Dead, and Jesus: A Study of Their Relationship in Acts with Particular Regard to the Understanding of Paul's Trial Defense.' *Journal of the Evangelical Theological Society* 20 (1977): 231–41.

Kilgallen, John J. 'Acts 13,38–39: Culmination of Paul's Speech in Pisidia.' *Biblica* 69 (1988): 485–96.

———. 'Jesus, Savior, the Glory of Your People Israel.' *Biblica* 75 (1994): 305–28.

———. 'A Rhetorical and Source-Traditions Study of Acts 2,33.' *Biblica* 77 (1996): 178–96.

———. 'The Sadducees and Resurrection From the Dead: Luke 20,27–40.' *Biblica* 67 (1986): 478–95.

Kimball, Charles A. *Jesus' Exposition of the Old Testament in Luke's Gospel*. Journal for the Study of the New Testament: Supplement Series 94. Sheffield: Sheffield Academic Press, 1994.

Kingsbury, Jack Dean, ed. *Gospel Interpretation: Narrative-Critical and Social Scientific Interpretation*. Harrisburg, Pa.: Trinity Press International, 1997.

Knibb, Michael A. 'The Exile in Intertestamental Literature.' *Heythrop Journal* 17 (1976): 253–72.

Knight, W. F. Jackson. *Elysion*. New York: Barnes & Noble, 1970.

Kodell, Jerome. 'Luke's Theology of the Death of Jesus.' Pages 221–30 in *Sin, Salvation, and the Spirit*. Edited by Daniel Durken. Collegeville, Minn.: Liturgical, 1979.

Koet, B. J. 'Divine Communication in Luke-Acts.' Pages 745–57 in *The Unity of Luke-Acts*. Edited by Joseph Verheyden. Bibliotheca ephemeridum theologicarum lovaniensium 142. Leuven: Leuven University Press, 1999.

———. 'Some Traces of a Semantic Field of Interpretation in Luke 24,13–35.' in *Five Studies on Interpretation of Scripture in Luke-Acts*. Studiorum Novi Testamenti Auxilia 14. Leuven: Leuven University Press, 1989.

Kohler, Kaufmann. 'Sadducees.' Pages 630–33 in vol. 10 of *Jewish Encyclopedia*. Edited by I. Singer. 12 vols. New York: Funk & Wagnalls, 1903.

Kolarcik, Michael. *The Ambiguity of Death in the Book of Wisdom 1–6*. Analecta biblica 127. Rome: Biblical Institute, 1991.

Kränkl, Emmeram. *Jesus der Knecht Gottes: Die heilsgeschichtliche Stellung Jesu in den Reden der Apostelgeschichte*. Regensburg: Pustet, 1972.

Kurz, William S. 'Acts 3:19–26 as a Test Case of the Role of Eschatology in Lukan Christology.' Pages 309–23 in *SBL Seminar Papers, 1977*. Society of Biblical Literature Seminar Papers 11. Missoula, Mont.: Scholars Press, 1977.

———. 'Hellenistic Rhetoric in the Christological Proof of Luke-Acts.' *Catholic Biblical Quarterly* 42 (1980): 171–95.

———. *Reading Luke-Acts: Dynamics of Biblical Narrative*. Louisville, Ky.: Westminster/John Knox, 1993.

Ladd, George Eldon. *I Believe in the Resurrection of Jesus*. Grand Rapids: Eerdmans, 1975.

Lake, Kirsopp. *The Historical Evidence for the Resurrection of Jesus Christ*. New York: G. P. Putnam's Sons, 1907.

Lane, William L. *Hebrews*. 2 vols. Word Biblical Commentary 47a–b. Dallas, Tex.: Word, 1991.

———. 'Living a Life of Faith in the Face of Death: The Witness of Hebrews.' Pages 247–69 in *Life in the Face of Death: The Resurrection Message in the New Testament*. Edited by Richard N. Longenecker. McMaster New Testament Studies. Grand Rapids: Eerdmans, 1998.

———. 'Times of Refreshment: A Study of Eschatological Periodization in Judaism and Christianity.' Th.D. diss., Harvard University, 1962.

Lang, Bernhard. 'Afterlife—Ancient Israel's Changing Vision of the World Beyond.' *Bible Review* 4 (1988): 12–23.

Latham, James E. *The Religious Symbolism of Salt*. Theologie historique 64. Paris: Beauchesne, 1982.

Lattimore, Richard. *Themes in Greek and Latin Epitaphs*. Illinois Studies in Language and Literature 28.1–2. Urbana, Ill.: University of Illinois Press, 1942.
LaVerdiere, Eugene A. 'The Ascension of the Risen Lord.' *The Bible Today* 95 (1978): 1553–59.
Le Moyne, Jean. *Les Sadducéens*. Etudes bibliques. Paris: Gabalda, 1972.
Lehnert, Volker. 'Absage an Israel oder offener Schluß? Apg 28,25–28 als paradoxe Intervention.' *Theologische Beiträge* 29 (1998): 315–23.
Lesêtre, H. 'Résurrection de la chair.' Columns 1063–76 in *Dictionnaire de la Bible*. Edited by F. Vigouroux. 5 vols. Paris, 1895–1912.
Lichtenberger, Hermann. 'Resurrection in the Intertestamental Literature and Rabbinic Theology.' Pages 23–31 in *Reincarnation or Resurrection?* Edited by Hermann Häring and Johann-Baptist Metz. Concilium 5. London: SCM, 1993.
Lohfink, Gerhard. 'Christologie und Geschichtsbild in Apg 3,19–21.' *Biblische Zeitschrift* 13 (1969): 223–41.
———. *Die Himmelfahrt Jesu: Untersuchungen zu den Himmelfahrts- und Erhöhungstexten bei Lukas*. Studien zum Alten und Neuen Testament 26. Munich: Kösel-Verlag, 1971.
Longenecker, Richard N. *Biblical Exegesis in the Apostolic Period*. Grand Rapids: Eerdmans, 1975.
Lövestam, Evald. *Son and Saviour: A Study of Acts 13,32–37. With an Appendix: 'Son of God' in the Synoptic Gospels*. Coniectanea biblica, New Testament 18. Lund: Gleerup; Copenhagen: Ejnar Munksgaard, 1961.
Lygre, John G. 'Exaltation: Considered with Reference to the Resurrection and Ascension in Luke-Acts.' Ph.D. diss., Princeton Theological Seminary, 1975.
MacAlister, Suzanne. *Dreams and Suicides: The Greek Novel From Antiquity to the Byzantine Empire*. London: Routledge, 1996.
MacDonald, Dennis R. 'Luke's Eutychus and Homer's Elpenor: Acts 20:7–12 and *Odyssey* 10–12.' *Journal of Higher Criticism* 1 (1994): 4–24.
MacIntosh, A. A. *Hosea*. International Critical Commentary. Edinburgh: T. & T. Clark, 1997.
MacMullen, Ramsay. *Christianizing the Roman Empire (A.D. 100–400)*. New Haven: Yale University Press, 1984.
Maddox, Robert. *The Purpose of Luke-Acts*. Forschungen zur Religion und Literatur des Alten und Neuen Testaments 126. Göttingen: Vandenhoeck & Ruprecht, 1982.
Maile, J. F. 'The Ascension in Luke-Acts.' *Tyndale Bulletin* 37 (1986): 29–59.
Mainville, Odette. 'Le messianisme de Jésus: Le rapport annonce/accomplissement entre Lc 1,35 et Ac 2,33.' Pages 313–27 in *The Unity of Luke-Acts*. Edited by Joseph Verheyden. Bibliotheca ephemeridum theologicarum lovaniensium 142. Leuven: Leuven University Press, 1999.
Mánek, Jindřich. 'The New Exodus in the Books of Luke.' *Novum Testamentum* 2 (1957): 8–23.
Mangatt, G. 'The Gospel of Salvation.' *Bible Bhashyam* 2 (1976): 60–80.

Marguerat, Daniel. 'The Enigma of the Silent Closing of Acts (28:16–31).' Pages 284–304 in *Jesus and the Heritage of Israel: Luke's Narrative Claim Upon Israel's Heritage*. Edited by David P. Moessner. Luke the Interpreter of Israel 1. Harrisburg, Pa.: Trinity Press International, 1998.

———. 'Le premier Historien du Christianisme (Luc-Actes).' *Foi et Vie* 96 (1997): 19–34.

———. 'Luc-Actes: La résurrection à l'œuvre dans l'histoire.' Pages 195–214 in *Résurrection: L'àpres-mort dans la monde ancient et le Nouveau Testament*. Edited by Odette Mainville and Daniel Marguerat. *Le Monde de la Bible* 45. Montreal: Médiaspaul; Geneva: Labor et Fides, 2001.

Marshall, I. Howard. *The Acts of the Apostles*. New Testament Guides. Sheffield: Sheffield Academic Press, 1997. 1992.

———. 'How Does One Write on the Theology of Acts?' Pages 3–16 in *Witness to the Gospel: The Theology of Acts*. Edited by I. Howard Marshall and David Peterson. Grand Rapids: Eerdmans, 1998.

———. '"Israel" and the Story of Salvation: One Theme in Two Parts.' Pages 340–57 in *Jesus and the Heritage of Israel: Luke's Narrative Claim Upon Israel's Legacy*. Edited by David P. Moessner and David L. Tiede. Luke the Interpreter of Israel 1. Harrisburg, Pa.: Trinity Press International, 1999.

———. *Luke: Historian and Theologian* . 3d ed. New Testament Profiles. Downers Grove, Ill.: InterVarsity Press, 1988.

———. 'The Resurrection in the Acts of the Apostles.' Pages 92–107 in *Apostolic History and the Gospel*. Edited by W. Ward Gasque and Ralph P. Martin. Grand Rapids: Eerdmans, 1970.

———. 'The Resurrection of Jesus in Luke.' *Tyndale Bulletin* 24 (1973): 55–98.

Martin-Achard, Robert. *From Death to Life: A Study of the Development of the Doctrine of the Resurrection in the Old Testament*. Edinburgh and London: Oliver and Boyd, 1960.

———. 'Résurrection dans l'Ancien Testament et le Judaïsme.' Columns 437–87 in vol. 10 of *Supplément au Dictionnaire de la Bible*. Edited by L. Pirot et al. Paris, 1928–.

Martin, Luther H. *Hellenistic Religions: An Introduction*. New York and Oxford: Oxford University Press, 1987.

Martin, Ralph P. 'Salvation and Discipleship in Luke's Gospel.' *Interpretation* 30 (1976): 366–80.

Martinez, Florentino Garcia. *Qumran and Apocalyptic: Studies on the Aramaic Texts From Qumran*. Studies on the Texts of the Desert of Judah 9. Leiden: Brill, 1992.

Mason, John P. *The Resurrection According to Paul*. Lewiston, N.Y.: Edwin Mellen, 1993.

Mason, Steve. *Flavius Josephus on the Pharisees: A Composition-Critical Study*. Studia post-biblica 39. Leiden: Brill, 1991.

Mauchline, John. *Isaiah 1–39: Introduction and Commentary*. Torch Bible Commentaries. New York: Macmillan, 1962.

McCasland, Selby Vernon. 'The Scripture Basis of "On the Third Day."' *Journal of Biblical Literature* 48 (1929): 124–37.
McConaughy, Daniel L. 'An Old Syriac Reading of Acts 1:4 and More Light on Jesus' Last Meal before His Ascension.' *Oriens christianus* 72 (1988): 63–67.
McCready, Wayne O. 'Sadducees and Ancient Sectarianism.' *Religious Studies and Theology* 12 (1992): 79–97.
McKeating, Henry. *The Books of Amos, Hosea, and Micah*. Cambridge Bible Commentary. Cambridge: Cambridge University Press, 1971.
Mealand, David L. 'The Phrase "Many Proofs" in Acts 1,3 and in Hellenistic Writers.' *Zeitschrift für die neutestamentliche Wissenschaft* 80 (1989): 134–35.
Meeks, Wayne A. *The Prophet-King: Moses Traditions and the Johannine Christology*. Novum Testamentum Supplements 14. Leiden: Brill, 1967.
Menoud, Philippe H. 'Jesus and His Witnesses: Observations on the Unity of the Work of Luke.' Pages 149–66 in *Jesus Christ and Faith*. Translated by Eunice M. Paul. Pittsburgh: Pickwick, 1978.
Metzger, Bruce M. 'The Ascension of Christ.' Pages 77–87 in *Historical and Literary Studies*. New Testament Tools and Studies 8. Grand Rapids: Eerdmans, 1968.
———. *A Textual Commentary on the Greek New Testament*. 2d ed. Stuttgart: Deutsche Bibelgesellschaft/United Bible Societies, 1994.
Meyers, Eric M. *Jewish Ossuaries: Reburial and Rebirth. Secondary Burials in Their Ancient Near Eastern Setting*. Biblica et orientalia 24. Rome: Biblical Institute, 1971.
———. 'Secondary Burials in Palestine.' *Biblical Archaeologist* 33 (1970): 2–29.
Moessner, David P. 'The Appeal and Power of Poetics: Luke's Superior Credentials (παρακολουθηκότι), Narrative Sequence (καθεξῆς), and Firmness of Understanding (ἡ ἀσφάλεια) for the Reader.' Pages 84–123 in *Jesus and the Heritage of Israel: Luke's Narrative Claim Upon Israel's Heritage*. Edited by David P. Moessner. Luke the Interpreter of Israel 1. Harrisburg, Pa.: Trinity Press International, 1999.
———. '"The Christ Must Suffer": New Light on the Jesus–Peter, Stephen, Paul Parallels in Luke-Acts.' *Novum Testamentum* 28 (1986): 220–56.
———. 'Good News for the "Wilderness Generation": The Death of the Prophet Like Moses According to Luke.' Pages 1–34 in *Good News in History: Essays in Honor of Bo Reicke*. Edited by Ed. L. Miller. Atlanta: Scholars Press, 1993.
———. *Lord of the Banquet: The Literary and Theological Significance of the Lukan Travel Narrative*. Harrison, Pa.: Trinity Press International, 1989.
———. 'Luke 9:1–50: Luke's Preview of the Journey of the Prophet Like Moses of Deuteronomy.' *Journal of Biblical Literature* 102 (1983): 575–605.
———. 'The "Script" of the Scriptures in Acts: Suffering as God's Plan (βουλή) for the World for the "Release from Sins."' Pages 218–50 in *History, Literature, and Society in the Book of Acts*. Edited by Ben Witherington III. Cambridge: Cambridge University Press, 1996.
———. '*Two* Lords "at the Right Hand"? The Psalms and an Intertextual Reading of Peter's Pentecost Speech.' Pages 215–32 in *Literary Studies in Luke-Acts: Essays in*

Honor of Joseph B. Tyson. Edited by Richard P. Thompson and Thomas E. Phillips. Macon, Ga.: Mercer University Press, 1998.

Moessner, David P., and David L. Tiede. 'Introduction: *Two* Books but *One* Story?' Pages 1–4 in *Jesus and the Heritage of Israel: Luke's Narrative Claim Upon Israel's Legacy.* Edited by David P. Moessner and David L. Tiede. Luke the Interpreter of Israel 1. Harrisburg, Pa.: Trinity Press International, 1999.

Moore, George Foot. *Judaism in the First Centuries of the Christian Era: The Age of Tannaim.* Cambridge, Mass.: Harvard University Press, 1927–1930. Repr. Peabody, Mass.: Hendrickson, 1997.

Moore, Stephen D. *Literary Criticism and the Gospels: The Theoretical Challenge.* New Haven and London: Yale University Press, 1989.

———. 'Luke's Economy of Knowledge.' Pages 39–45 in *SBL Seminar Papers, 1989.* Society of Biblical Literature Seminar Papers 28. Atlanta: Scholars Press, 1989.

Moore, Stephen D., and Janice Capel Anderson. 'Taking It Like a Man: Masculinity in 4 Maccabees.' *Journal of Biblical Literature* 117 (1998): 249–73.

Morgan, J. R. 'Make-Believe and Make Believe: The Fictionality of the Greek Novels.' Pages 175–229 in *Lies and Fiction in the Ancient World.* eds. Christopher Gill and T. P. Wiseman. Austin, Tex.: University of Texas Press, 1993.

Motyer, Alec. *The Prophecy of Isaiah: An Introduction and Commentary.* Downers Grove, Ill.: InterVarsity Press, 1993.

Moulton, J. H. '"It Is His Angel."' *Journal of Theological Studies* 3 (1902): 514–27.

Nellessen, E. *Zeugnis für Jesus und das Wort. Exegetische Untersuchungen zum lukanischen Zeugnisbegriff.* Köln: Peter Hanstein, 1976.

Neyrey, Jerome H. *The Passion According to Luke: A Redaction Study of Luke's Soteriology.* Theological Inquiries. New York: Paulist, 1985.

———, ed. *The Social World of Luke-Acts: Models for Interpretation.* Peabody, Mass.: Hendrickson, 1991.

Nickelsburg, George W. E. Jr. 'Enoch, First Book of.' Pages 512–13 in vol. 2 of *Anchor Bible Dictionary.* Edited by David N. Freedman. 6 vols. Garden City, N.Y.: Doubleday, 1992.

———. *Resurrection, Immortality, and Eternal Life in Intertestamental Judaism.* Harvard Theological Studies 26. Cambridge: Harvard University Press, 1972.

Noorda, S. J. 'Scene and Summary: A Proposal for Reading Acts 4,32–5,16.' Pages 475–83 in *Les Actes des Apôtres: Traditions, rédaction, théologie.* Edited by J. Kremer. Bibliotheca ephemeridum theologicarum lovaniensium 48. Leuven: Leuven University Press, 1979.

North, Helen F. 'Death and the Afterlife in Greed Tragedy and Plato.' Pages 49–64 in *Death and the Afterlife: Perspectives of World Religions.* Edited by Hiroshi Obayashi. New York: Praeger, 1992.

North, John A. 'The Afterlife: Rome.' Pages 997–1007 in vol. 2 of *Civilization of the Ancient Mediterranean: Greece and Rome.* Edited by Michael Grant and Rachel Kitzinger. 3 vols. New York: Charles Scribner's Sons, 1988.

Ó Fearghail, Fearghus. *The Introduction to Luke-Acts: A Study of the Role of Lk 1,1–4,44 in the Composition of Luke's Two-Volume Work*. Analecta biblica 126. Rome: Biblical Institute, 1991.

O'Donnell, James J. *Augustine: A New Biography*. New York: HarperCollins, 2005.

Oepke, A. 'Auferstehung II (des Menschen).' Pages 930–38 in vol. 1 of *Reallexikon für Antike und Christentum*. Edited by Theodor Klauser et al. Stuttgart: Anton Hiersemann, 1950–.

Ollenburger, Ben C. 'If Mortal Die, Will They Live Again? The Old Testament and Resurrection.' *Ex Auditu* 9 (1993): 29–44.

Osborne, Grant R. *The Resurrection Narratives: A Redactional Study*. Grand Rapids: Baker, 1984.

Oswalt, John N. *The Book of Isaiah: Chapters 1–39*. New International Commentary on the Old Testament. Grand Rapids: Eerdmans, 1986.

O'Toole, Robert F. 'Activity of the Risen Jesus in Luke-Acts.' *Biblica* 62 (1981): 471–98.

———. 'Acts 2:30 and the Davidic Covenant of Pentecost.' *Journal of Biblical Literature* 102 (1983): 245–58.

———. 'Christ's Resurrection in Acts 13,13–52.' *Biblica* 60 (1979): 361–72.

———. *The Christological Climax of Paul's Defense (Ac 22:1–26:32)*. Analecta biblica 78. Rome: Biblical Institute, 1978.

———. 'How Does Luke Portray Jesus As Servant of Yhwh?' *Biblica* 81 (2000): 328–46.

———. 'Luke's Understanding of Jesus' Resurrection-Ascension-Exaltation.' *Biblical Theology Bulletin* 9 (1979): 106–14.

———. 'The Parallels Between Jesus and Moses.' *Biblical Theology Bulletin* 20 (1990): 22–29.

———. 'Some Observations on *anistēmi* "I Raise," in Acts 3:22, 26.' *Science et esprit* 31 (1979): 85–92.

———. *The Unity of Luke's Theology: An Analysis of Luke-Acts*. Good News Studies 9. Wilmington, Del.: Michael Glazier, 1984.

———. 'Why Did Luke Write Acts (Lk-Acts)?' *Biblical Theology Bulletin* 7 (1977): 66–76.

Palmer, Darryl W. 'Mission to Jews and Gentiles in the Last Episode of Acts.' *Reformed Theological Review* 52 (1993): 62–73.

Parker, Floyd. 'The Terms "Angel" and "Spirit" in Acts 23,8.' *Biblica* 84 (2003): 344–65.

Parsons, Mikeal C. *The Departure of Jesus in Luke-Acts: The Ascension Narratives in Context*. Journal for the Study of the New Testament: Supplement Series 21. Sheffield: JSOT Press, 1987.

———. 'Narrative Closure and Openness in the Plot of the Third Gospel: The Sense of an Ending in Luke 24:50–53.' Pages 201–23 in *SBL Seminar Papers, 1986*. Society of Biblical Literature Seminar Papers 25. Atlanta: Scholars Press, 1986.

Parsons, Mikeal C. and Richard I. Pervo. *Rethinking the Unity of Luke-Acts*. Minneapolis: Fortress, 1993.

Pelling, Christopher. 'Is Death the End? Closure in Plutarch's *Lives*.' Pages 228–50 in *Classical Closure: Reading the End in Greek and Latin Literature*. Edited by Deborah H. Roberts, Francis M. Dunn, and Don Fowler. Princeton: Princeton University Press, 1997.

Perkins, Pheme. *Resurrection: New Testament Witness and Contemporary Reflection*. Garden City, N.Y.: Doubleday, 1984.

Pervo, Richard I. *Profit with Delight: The Literary Genre of the Acts of the Apostles*. Minneapolis: Fortress, 1987.

Pichler, Josef. *Paulusrezeption in der Apostelgeschichte: Untersuchungen zur Rede im pisidischen Antiochien*. Innsbrucker theologische Studien 50. Innsbruck and Vienna: Tyrolia, 1997.

Pilch, John J. 'Sickness and Healing in Luke-Acts.' Pages 181–209 in *The Social World of Luke-Acts: Models for Interpretation*. Edited by Jerome Neyrey. Peabody, Mass.: Hendrickson, 1991.

Pillai, C. A. Joachim. *Apostolic Interpretation of History: A Commentary on Acts 13:16–41*. Hicksville, N. Y.: Exposition University Press, 1980.

Plevnik, Joseph. 'The Eyewitnesses of the Risen Jesus in Luke 24.' *Catholic Biblical Quarterly* 49 (1987): 90–103.

Plümacher, Eckhard. *Lukas als hellenistischer Schriftsteller: Studien zur Apostelgeschichte*. Göttingen: Vandenhoeck & Ruprecht, 1972.

Porter, Stanley E. 'Resurrection, the Greeks and the New Testament.' Pages 52–81 in *Resurrection*. Edited by Stanley E. Porter, Michael A. Hayes, and David Tombs. Journal for the Study of the New Testament: Supplement Series 186. Sheffield: Sheffield Academic Press, 1999.

Powell, Mark Allan. 'Luke's Second Volume: Three Basic Issues in Contemporary Studies in Acts.' *Trinity Seminary Review* 13 (1991): 69–81.

———. 'Salvation in Luke-Acts.' *Word and World* 12 (1992): 5–10.

Price, Robert M. *The Widow Traditions in Luke-Acts: A Feminist-Critical Scrutiny*. Society of Biblical Literature Dissertation Series 155. Atlanta: Scholars Press, 1997.

Puskas, Charles B. 'The Conclusion of Luke-Acts: An Investigation of the Literary Function and Theological Significance of Acts 28:16–31.' Ph.D. diss., The Graduate School of Saint Louis University, 1980.

Rabinowitz, Peter J. *Before Reading: Narrative Conventions and the Politics of Interpretation*. Ithaca, N. Y. and London: Cornell University Press, 1987.

———. 'Reader-Response Theory and Criticism.' Pages 606–9 in *The Johns Hopkins Guide to Literary Theory and Criticism*. Edited by Michael Groden and Martin Kreiswirth. Baltimore and London: Johns Hopkins University Press, 1994.

Rabinowitz, Peter J. and Michael W. Smith. *Authorizing Readers: Resistance and Respect in the Teaching of Literature*. New York and London: Teachers College Press, 1998.

Rad, Gerhard von. *Old Testament Theology*. 2 vols. San Francisco: Harper & Row, 1965.
Radl, Walter. *Das Lukas-Evangelium*. Erträge der Forschung 261. Darmstadt: Wissenschaftliche, 1988.
Ramsey, A. Michael. 'What Was the Ascension?' Pages 135–44 in *Historicity and Chronology in the New Testament*. Dennis E. Nineham et al. London: SPCK, 1965. Repr. from *SNTS Bulletin* 2 (1951): 43–50.
Rasco, Emilio. 'La gloire de la résurrection et ses fruits, Acts 2,14.22–28; 3,13–15.17–19; 5,17b–32.40b–41.' *Assemblées du Seigneur* 24 (1969): 6–14.
Reardon, B. P. *The Form of Greek Romances*. Princeton: Princeton University Press, 1991.
Reese, James M. *Hellenistic Influence on the Book of Wisdom and Its Consequences*. Analecta biblica 41. Rome: Biblical Institute, 1970.
Reiling, J., and J. L. Swellengrebel. *A Translator's Handbook on the Gospel of Luke*. UBS Helps for Translators 10. Leiden: Brill, 1971.
Reimer, Ivoni Richter. *Women in the Acts of the Apostles: A Feminist Liberation Perspective*. Translated by Linda M. Maloney. Minneapolis: Fortress, 1995.
Renju, Peter M. 'The Exodus of Jesus.' *The Bible Translator* 46 (1995): 213–18.
Rese, Martin. *Alttestamentliche Motive in der Christologie des Lukas*. Studium zum Neuen Testament 1. Gütersloh: Mohn, 1969.
Rétif, A. 'Témoinage et prédication missionaire dans les Actes des Apôtres.' *La nouvelle revue théologique* 73 (1951): 152–65.
Richardson, N. J. 'Early Greek Views About Life After Death.' Pages 50–66 in *Greek Religion and Society*. Edited by P. E. Easterling and J. V. Muir. Cambridge: Cambridge University Press, 1985.
Ridderbos, H. N. *The Speeches of Peter in the Acts of the Apostles*. London: Tyndale, 1961.
Rigato, Maria-Luisa. '"'Remember'...Then They Remembered": Luke 24:6–8.' Pages 93–102 in *Luke and Acts*. Edited by Gerald O'Collins and Gilberto Marconi. New York and Mahwah, N.J.: Paulist, 1991.
Riley, Gregory J. *Resurrection Reconsidered: Thomas and John in Controversy*. Minneapolis: Fortress, 1995.
Ringe, Sharon. 'Luke 9:28–36: The Beginning of an Exodus.' *Semeia* 28 (1983): 83–99.
Robbins, Vernon K. 'The Claims of the Prologues and Greco-Roman Rhetoric: The Prefaces to Luke and Acts in Light of Greco-Roman Rhetorical Strategies.' Pages 89–92 in *Jesus and the Heritage of Israel: Luke's Narrative Claim Upon Israel's Heritage*. Edited by David P. Moessner. Luke the Interpreter of Israel 1. Harrisburg, Pa.: Trinity Press International, 1999.
Roberts, Deborah H. 'Afterword: Ending and Aftermath, Ancient and Modern.' Pages 251–73 in *Classical Closure: Reading the End in Greek and Latin Literature*. Edited by Deborah H. Roberts, Francis M. Dunn, and Don Fowler. Princeton: Princeton University Press, 1997.

Roddy, Nicolae. '"Two Parts: Weeks of Seven Weeks": The End of the Age as *Terminus ad Quem*.' *Journal for the Study of Judaism in the Persian, Hellenistic and Roman Period* 14 (1996): 3–14.

Rohde, Erwin. *Psyche: The Cult of Souls and Belief in Immortality among the Ancient Greeks*. Translated by W. B. Hillis. 8th ed. London and New York: Harcourt Brace, 1925. Repr., Chicago: Ares, 1985.

Rolland, Philippe. 'L'organisation du Livre des Actes et de l'ensemble de l'œuvre de Luc.' *Biblica* 65 (1984): 81–86.

Rosenblatt, Marie-Eloise. *Paul the Accused: His Portrait in the Acts of the Apostles*. Collegeville, Minn.: Liturgical, 1995.

Sabourin, Leopold. 'The Miracles of Jesus (III): Healings, Resuscitations, Nature Miracles.' *Biblical Theology Bulletin* 5 (1975): 146–200.

Salmon, Marilyn. 'Insider or Outsider? Luke's Relationship with Judaism.' Pages 76–82 in *Luke-Acts and the Jewish People: Eight Critical Perspectives*. Edited by Joseph B. Tyson. Minneapolis: Augsburg, 1988.

Sanders, Jack T. 'The Jewish People in Luke-Acts.' Pages 51–75 in *Luke-Acts and the Jewish People: Eight Critical Perspectives*. Edited by Joseph B. Tyson. Minneapolis: Augsburg, 1988.

Sandt, Huub van de. 'The Quotations in Acts 13,32–52 as a Reflection of Luke's LXX Interpretation.' *Biblica* 75 (1994): 26–58.

Sawyer, John F. A. 'Hebrew Words for the Resurrection of the Dead.' *Vetus Testamentum* 23 (1973): 218–34.

Schmitt, Armin. 'Ps 16,8–11 als Zeugnis der Auferstehung in der Apg.' *Biblische Zeitschrift* 17 (1973): 229–48.

Schneider, Gerhard. 'Der Zweck des lukanischen Doppelwerks.' *Biblische Zeitschrift* 21 (1977): 45–66.

Schubert, Paul. 'The Place of the Areopagus Speech in the Composition of Acts.' Pages 235–61 in *Transitions in Biblical Scholarship*. Edited by J. Coert Rylaarsdam. Essays in Divinity 6. Chicago: University of Chicago Press, 1968.

———. 'The Structure and Significance of Luke 24.' Pages 165–86 in *Neutestamentliche Studien für Rudolph Bultmann, zu seinem siebzigsten Geburtstag am 20. August 1954*. Edited by Walther Eltester. Beihefte zur Zeitschrift für die neutestamentliche Wissenschaft 21. Berlin: Töpelmann, 1954.

Schürer, Emil. *The History of the Jewish People in the Age of Jesus Christ (175 B.C.–A.D. 135)*. Edited by Geza Vermes, Fergus Millar, and Matthew Black. 3 vols. Edinburgh: T. & T. Clark, 1979.

Scott, James M. 'Luke's Geographical Horizon.' Pages 483–544 in *The Book of Acts in Its Ancient Graeco-Roman Setting*. Edited by David W. J. Gill and Conrad Gempf. Vol. 2 of *The Book of Acts in Its First Century Setting*. Grand Rapids: Eerdmans; Carlisle: Paternoster, 1994.

Sharples, Robert William. 'Hermippus (2).' Page 692 in *The Oxford Classical Dictionary*. Edited by Simon Hornblower and Antony Spawforth. 3d ed. Oxford: Oxford University Press, 1996.

Smith, Barbara Herrnstein. *Poetic Closure: A Study of How Poems End*. Chicago: University of Chicago Press, 1968.

Smith, Robert H. *Easter Gospels: The Resurrection of Jesus According to the Four Evangelists*. Minneapolis: Augsburg, 1983.

———. 'The Theology of Acts.' *Concordia Theological Monthly* 42 (1971): 527–35.

Soards, Marion L. 'The Speeches in Acts in Relation to Other Pertinent Ancient Literature.' *Ephemerides theologicae lovanienses* 70 (1994): 65–90.

———. *The Speeches in Acts: Their Content, Context, and Concerns*. Louisville, Ky.: Westminster John Knox, 1994.

Sourvinou-Inwood, Christiane. 'To Die and Enter the House of Hades: Homer, Before and After.' Pages 15–39 in *Mirrors of Mortality: Studies in the Social History of Death*. Edited by Joachim Whaley. Social History of Human Experience. New York: St. Martin's, 1981.

Spronk, Klaas. *Beatific Afterlife in Ancient Israel and in the Ancient Near East*. Alter Orient und Altes Testament 219. Neukirchen-Vluyn: Neukirchener, 1986.

Squires, John T. *The Plan of God in Luke-Acts*. Society for New Testament Studies Monograph Series 76. Cambridge: Cambridge University Press, 1993.

Stemberger, Günter. 'Auferstehung, I/2. Judentum.' Pages 443–50 in vol. 4 of *Theologische Realenzyklopädie*. Edited by Gerhard Krause and Gerhard Müller. Berlin: Walter de Gruyter, 1977–.

———. *Der Leib der Auferstehung*. Analecta biblica 56. Rome: Biblical Institute, 1972.

———. *Jewish Contemporaries of Jesus: Pharisees, Sadducees, Essenes*. Translated by Allan W. Mahnke. Minneapolis: Fortress, 1995.

Stempvoort, P. A. van. 'The Interpretation of the Ascension in Luke and Acts.' *New Testament Studies* 5 (1958): 30–42.

Stone, Michael E. 'Esdras, Second Book of.' Pages 611–12 in vol. 6 of *Anchor Bible Dictionary*. Edited by David N. Freedman. 6 vols. Garden City, N.Y.: Doubleday, 1992.

———. *Features of the Eschatology of IV Ezra*. Harvard Semitic Studies 35. Atlanta: Scholars Press, 1989.

———. *Fourth Ezra: A Commentary on the Book of Fourth Ezra*. Hermeneia. Minneapolis: Fortress, 1990.

———. 'Reactions to Destructions of the Second Temple.' *Journal for the Study of Judaism in the Persian, Hellenistic and Roman Period* 12 (1981): 195–204.

Strauss, David F. *The Life of Jesus Critically Examined*. Translated by George Eliot. Lives of Jesus Series. Philadelphia: Fortress, 1972.

Strauss, Mark L. *The Davidic Messiah in Luke-Acts: The Promise and Its Fulfillment in Luke's Christology*. Journal for the Study of the New Testament: Supplement Series 110. Sheffield: Sheffield Academic Press, 1995.

Stuart, Douglas. *Hosea-Jonah*. Word Biblical Commentary 31. Waco, Tex.: Word, 1987.

Sutcliffe, Edmund F. *The Old Testament and the Future Life*. 2d ed. London: Burns Oates & Washbourne, 1947.

Talbert, Charles H. *Literary Patterns, Theological Themes, and the Genre of Luke-Acts*. Society of Biblical Literary Monograph Series 20. Missoula, Mont.: Scholars Press, 1974.

———. *Luke and the Gnostics*. Nashville: Abingdon, 1966.

———. 'The Place of the Resurrection in the Theology of Luke.' *Interpretation* 46 (1992): 19–30.

———. Review of Joseph A. Fitzmyer, *The Gospel According to Luke (X–XXIV)*. *Catholic Biblical Quarterly* 48 (1986): 336–38.

———. 'Shifting Sands: The Recent Study of the Gospel of Luke.' *Interpretation* 30 (1976): 381–95.

Tannehill, Robert C. '"Cornelius" and "Tabitha" Encounter Luke's Jesus.' Pages 132–41 in *Gospel Interpretation: Narrative-Critical and Social Scientific Approaches*. Edited by Jack Dean Kingsbury. Harrisburg, Pa.: Trinity Press International, 1997.

———. 'The Functions of Peter's Mission Speeches in the Narrative of Acts.' *New Testament Studies* 37 (1991): 400–14.

———. 'Israel in Luke-Acts: A Tragic Story.' *Journal of Biblical Literature* 104 (1985): 69–84.

———. 'The Lukan Discourse on Invitations (Luke 14,7–24).' Pages 1603–16 in vol. 2 of *The Four Gospels 1992: Festschrift Frans Neirynck*. Edited by F. Van Segbroeck et al. 3 vols. Bibliotheca ephemeridum theologicarum lovaniensium 100. Leuven: Leuven University Press, 1992.

———. 'The Narrator's Strategy in the Scenes of Paul's Defense.' *Foundations and Facets Forum* 8 (1992): 255–69.

———. 'Rejection by the Jews and Turning to the Gentiles: The Pattern of Paul's Mission in Acts.' Pages 83–101 in *Luke-Acts and the Jewish People: Eight Critical Perspectives*. Edited by Joseph B. Tyson. Minneapolis: Augsburg, 1988.

———. 'The story of Israel within the Lukan Narrative.' Pages 325–39 in *Jesus and the Heritage of Israel: Luke's Narrative Claim Upon Israel's Heritage*. Edited by David P. Moessner. Luke the Interpreter of Israel 1. Harrisburg, Pa.: Trinity Press International, 1998.

Teeple, Howard M. *The Mosaic Eschatological Prophet*. Journal of Biblical Literature, Monograph Series 10. Philadelphia: Society of Biblical Literature, 1957.

Throckmorton, B. H. 'Σῴζειν, σωτηρία in Luke-Acts.' *Studia Evangelica* 6 (1973): 515–26.

Thurston, Anne. *Knowing Her Place: Gender and the Gospels*. New York and Mahwah, N.J.: Paulist, 1998.

Tiede, David L. '"Glory to Thy People Israel": Luke-Acts and the Jews.' Pages 21–34 in *Luke-Acts and the Jewish People: Eight Critical Perspectives*. Edited by Joseph B. Tyson. Minneapolis: Augsburg, 1988.

Toon, Peter. *The Ascension of Our Lord*. Nashville: Thomas Nelson, 1984.

———. 'Resurrected and Ascended: The Exalted Jesus.' *Bibliotheca Sacra* 140 (1983): 195–205.

Torgovnick, Marianna. *Closure in the Novel*. Princeton: Princeton University Press, 1981.

Torrey, Charles C. *The Composition and Date of Acts*. Harvard Theological Studies 1. Cambridge, Mass.: Harvard University Press, 1916.

Toynbee, J. M. C. *Death and Burial in the Roman World*. Aspects of Greek and Roman Life. Ithaca, N.Y.: Cornell University Press, 1971.

Trémel, Bernard. 'À propos d'Actes 20,7–12: Puissance du thaumaturge ou du témoin?' *Revue de théologie et de philosophie* 112 (1980): 359–69.

Trites, Allison A. *The New Testament Concept of Witness*. Society for New Testament Studies Monograph Series 31. Cambridge: Cambridge University Press, 1977.

Tromp, Nicholas J. *Primitive Conceptions of Death and the Nether World in the Old Testament*. Bibliotheca orientalis 21. Rome: Biblical Institute, 1969.

Turner, Max. *Power From on High: The Spirit in Israel's Restoration and Witness in Luke-Acts*. Journal of Pentecostal Theology Supplement Series 9. Sheffield: Sheffield Academic Press, 1996.

Unnik, W. C. van. 'The "Book of Acts" the Confirmation of the Gospel.' Pages 340–73 in *Sparsa Collecta: The Collected Essays of W. C. Van Unnik*. Part 1: *Evangelia, Paulina, Acta* Novum Testamentum Supplements 29. Leiden: Brill, 1973.

———. 'Der Ausdruck ἕως ἐσχάτου τῆς γῆς (Apostelgeschichte I 8) und sein alttestamentlicher Hintergrund.' Pages 386–401 in *Sparsa Collecta: The Collected Essays of W. C. Van Unnik*. Part 1: *Evangelia, Paulina, Acta* Novum Testamentum Supplements 29. Leiden: Brill, 1973.

———. 'L'Usage de ΣΩΖΕΙΝ "sauver" et des dérivés dans les Évangiles synoptiques.' Pages 16–34 in *Sparsa Collecta: The Collected Essays of W. C. Van Unnik*. Part 1: *Evangelia, Paulina, Acta* Novum Testamentum Supplements 29. Leiden: Brill, 1973.

VanderKam, James C. 'Exile in Jewish Apocalyptic Literature.' Pages 89–109 in *Exile: Old Testament, Jewish, and Christian Conceptions*. Edited by James M. Scott. Journal for the Study of Judaism: Supplement 56. Leiden: Brill, 1997.

Varneda, Pere Villalba I. *The Historical Method of Flavius Josephus*. Arbeiten zur Literatur und Geschichte des Hellenistischen Judentums 19. Leiden: Brill, 1986.

Verheyden, Joseph, ed. *The Unity of Luke-Acts*. Bibliotheca ephemeridum theologicarum lovaniensium 142. Leuven: Leuven University Press, 1999.

Vermeule, Emily. 'The Afterlife: Greece.' Pages 987–96 in vol. 2 of *Civilization of the Ancient Mediterranean: Greece and Rome*. Edited by Michael Grant and Rachel Kitzinger. 3 vols. New York: Charles Scriber's Sons, 1988.

Viviano, Benedict T., and Justin Taylor. 'Sadducees, Angels, and Resurrection (Acts 23:8–9).' *Journal of Biblical Literature* 111 (1992): 469–98.

Vos, Geerhardus. *The Pauline Eschatology*. Grand Rapids: Eerdmans, 1961.

Walton, Steve. 'Where Does the Beginning of Acts End?' Pages 447–67 in *The Unity of Luke-Acts*. Edited by Joseph Verheyden. Bibliotheca ephemeridum theologicarum lovaniensium 142. Leuven: Leuven University Press, 1999.

Wanke, Joachim. *Die Emmauserzählung: Eine redaktionsgeschichtliche Untersuchung zu Lk 24,13–35*. Erfurter theologische Studien 31. Leipzig: St. Benno-Verlag, 1973.

Wasserberg, Gunter. *Aus Israels Mitte—Heil für die Welt*. Beihefte zur Zeitschrift für die neutestamentliche Wissenschaft 92. Berlin and New York: Walter de Gruyter, 1998.

Wedderburn, A. J. M. *Baptism and Resurrection: Studies in Pauline Theology Against Its Graeco-Roman Background*. Wissenschaftliche Untersuchungen zum Neuen Testament 44. Tübingen: Mohr-Siebeck, 1987.

Weren, W. J. C. 'Psalm 2 in Luke-Acts: An Intertextual Study.' Pages 189–203 in *Intertexutality in Biblical Writings: Essays in Honour of Bas Van Iersel*. Edited by Sipke Draisma. Kampen: J. H. Kok, 1989.

Wifall, Walter. 'The Status of "Man" As Resurrection.' *Zeitschrift für die alttestamentliche Wissenschaft* 90 (1978): 382–94.

Wijngaards, J. 'Death and Resurrection in Covenantal Context (Hos. VI 2).' *Vetus Testamentum* 17 (1967): 226–39.

Wilckens, Ulrich. 'Interpreting Luke-Acts in a Period of Existential Theology.' Pages 60–83 in Leander E. Keck and J. Louis Martyn, *Studies in Luke-Acts*. Nashville: Abingdom, 1966.

Wilcox, Max. *The Semitisms of Acts*. Oxford: Clarendon, 1965.

Wildberger, Hans. *Jesaja 13–27*. Biblischer Kommentar: Altes Testament 10.2. Neukirchen-Vluyn: Neukirchener, 1978.

Wilder, Amos N. 'In Memoriam: Henry Joel Cadbury, 1883–1974.' *New Testament Studies* 21 (1975): 313–17.

———. 'Variant Traditions of the Resurrection in Acts.' *Journal of Biblical Literature* 62 (1943): 307–18.

Winandy, Jacques. 'La finale des Actes: Histoire ou théologie.' *Ephemerides theologicae lovanienses* 73 (1997): 103–6.

Witherington, Ben III. 'Salvation and Health in Christian Antiquity: The Soteriology of Luke-Acts in Its First Century Setting.' Pages 145–66 in *Witness to the Gospel: The Theology of Acts*. Edited by I. Howard Marshall and David Peterson. Grand Rapids: Eerdmans, 1998.

Wolff, Hans Walter. *Hosea*. Hermeneia. Philadelphia: Fortress, 1974.

Wolter, Michael. 'Israel's Future and the Delay of the Parousia, According to Luke.' Pages 307–24 in *Jesus and the Heritage of Israel: Luke's Narrative Claim Upon Israel's Legacy*. Edited by David P. Moessner and David L. Tiede. Luke the Interpreter of Israel 1. Harrisburg, Pa.: Trinity Press International, 1999.

Wright, N. T. *The New Testament and the People of God*. Minneapolis: Fortress, 1992.

———. *The Resurrection of the Son of God*. Minneapolis: Fortress, 2003.

York, John O. *The Last Shall Be First: The Rhetoric of Reversal in Luke*. Journal for the Study of the New Testament: Supplement Series 46. Sheffield: Sheffield Academic Press, 1991.

Young, Edward J. *The Book of Isaiah*. 3 vols. Grand Rapids: Eerdmans, 1969.

Zehnle, Richard F. *Peter's Pentecost Discourse: Tradition and Lukan Reinterpretation in Peter's Speeches in Acts 2 and 3*. Society of Biblical Literature Monograph Series 15. Nashville: Abingdon, 1971.

———. 'The Salvific Character of Jesus' Death in Lucan Soteriology.' *Theological Studies* 30 (1969): 420–44.

Zeitlin, Solomon. 'The Sadducees and the Belief in Angels.' *Journal of Biblical Literature* 83 (1964): 67–71.

———, ed. *The Second Book of Maccabees*. Jewish Apocryphal Literature. New York: Harper & Brothers, 1954.

Zwaan, J. de. 'Was the Book of Acts a Posthumous Edition?' *Harvard Theological Review* 17 (1924): 95–153.

Zwiep, A. W. *The Ascension of the Messiah in Lukan Christology*. Novum Testamentum Supplements 77. Leiden: Brill, 1997.

Index of Modern Authors

Abel, Félix Marie 64, 65, 296
Achtemeier, Paul J. 121, 296
Alexander, Loveday C. A. 45, 157, 262, 263, 266, 296
Allison, Dale C. 143, 301
Alsup, John E. 4, 297
Amsler, Samuel 53, 308
Argyle, A. W. 6, 297
Atwood, Margaret 160, 297
Auvray, P. 56, 297
Baird, William 282, 293
Baltzer, Klaus 82, 297
Balz, Horst 296
Bamberger, Bernard 141, 297
Barbi, Augusto 228, 297
Barclay, John M. G. 4, 297
Barclay, William 6, 297
Barrett, C. K. 6, 191, 205, 207, 212, 215, 224, 225, 226, 227, 241, 247, 256, 257, 259, 273, 275, 276, 277, 281, 293, 297
Barth, Christoph 54, 297
Bartlett, John R. 63, 64, 297
Barton, Stephen C. 20, 297
Bauckham, Richard 70, 138, 206, 207, 297
Bauer, Walter F. 250, 296
Bayer, Hans F. 33, 36, 223, 228, 229, 298
Benoit, Pierre 6, 8, 9, 298
Bertram, G. 7, 298
Betori, Giuseppe 193, 264, 265, 298
Bickermann, E. 7, 298
Black, Matthew 70, 72, 295
Boccaccini, Gabriele 62, 298
Bock, Darrell L. 175, 179, 204, 247, 249, 250, 251, 293, 298
Bolt, Peter G. 34, 93, 98, 131, 298
Bolton, J. D. P. 103, 298
Bonner, Stanley F. 94, 298
Bovon, François 8, 22, 29, 30, 31, 43, 119, 123, 175, 293, 298

Bowersock, G. W. 108, 299
Brändle, Max 2, 299
Bratcher, Robert G. 203, 204, 205, 299
Braun, Willi 133, 299
Brawley, Robert L. 130, 267
Breech, Earl 77, 299
Bremmer, Jan 95, 103, 107, 124, 299
Briggs, Charles A. 296
Brodie, Thomas L. 119, 299
Brown, Andrew L. 101, 299
Brown, Colin 296
Brown, Francis 296
Browning, Robert 104, 304
Bruce, F. F. 8, 37, 87, 140, 143, 192, 199, 224, 225, 235, 241, 245, 247, 262, 273, 276, 277, 281, 287, 290, 291, 293, 299
Brueggemann, Walter 54, 55, 58, 299
Bückers, H. 64, 299
Bultmann, Rudolf 4, 7, 299
Burkert, Walter 94, 299
Byrne, Brendan 135, 136, 299
Cadbury, Henry J. 1, 11, 36, 37, 44, 124, 156, 189, 192, 202, 203, 209, 212, 225, 226, 229, 243, 250, 262, 263, 273, 284, 294, 300
Calvin, John 286, 290, 293
Carroll, John T. 30, 226, 227, 300
Casey, Robert P. 34, 35, 300
Cathcart, Kevin J. 53, 295
Cavallin, H. C. C. 50, 59, 60, 62, 66, 69, 70, 71, 72, 78, 84, 85, 300
Cerfaux, L. 34, 300
Chance, J. Bradley 46, 300
Charles, R. H. 78, 79, 82, 295
Charlesworth, James H. 78, 296, 300
Clark, Andrew 34, 35, 300
Clarke, William K. L. 205, 301
Clements, Ronald E. 56, 301
Co, Marie Anicia 263, 301
Cohen, Shaye J. D. 86, 301

Cohn-Sherbok, D. M. 136, 301
Collins, John J. 49, 59, 60, 63, 67, 69, 82, 301
Conzelmann, Hans 31, 37, 225, 281, 282, 291, 293, 301
Cook, John G. 99, 301
Croy, N. Clayton 112, 301
Cullmann, Oscar 62, 63, 301
Dahood, Mitchell 49, 301
Dana, H. E. 210, 296
Danker, Frederick W. 134, 175, 293, 296
Darr, John 20, 301
Daube, David 141, 142, 143, 301
Davey, Francis Noel 33, 308
Davies, J. G. 6, 176, 301
Davies, W. D. 143, 301
Davis, Christopher A. 50, 81, 301
Dawsey, James M. 130, 131, 302
Delcor, M. 60, 302
Denis, Albert Marie 69, 302
Derrett, J. Duncan M. 100, 302
deSilva, David A. 239, 246, 248, 251, 256, 257, 258, 302
Desjardins, Michel 270, 302
Deutschmann, Anton 272, 302
Dewald, Carolyn 147, 302
Di Lella, Alexander A. 86, 302
Dibelius, Martin 4, 302
Dillon, Richard J. 2, 35, 37, 39, 41, 146, 164, 169, 172, 173, 186, 189, 190, 302
Doble, Peter 39, 302
Dömer, M. 22, 302
Downing, F. Gerald 156, 302
Dreyfus, F. 137, 302
Drinkard, Joel F. Jr. 85, 302
Driver, S. R. 296
Duling, Dennis C. 211, 302
Dunn, James D. G. 121, 293
Dupont, Jacques 175, 183, 184, 187, 193, 215, 246, 248, 250, 251, 252, 253, 254, 256, 262, 263, 264, 266, 270, 303
Eckstein, Hans-Joachim 9, 225, 303
Eliade, Mircea 102, 303
Elias, Jacob W. 160, 303

Elliott, J. K. 125, 128, 231, 295
Elliott, James K. 162, 303
Ellis, E. Earle 123, 138, 293, 303
Ellis, John M. 17, 303
Ellul, Danielle 220, 221, 237, 239, 241, 255, 303
Evans, C. F. 5, 123, 136, 137, 138, 175, 189, 201, 293, 303
Feldman, Louis H. 85, 90, 304
Ferguson, John 92, 304
Field, Frederick 203, 205, 207, 304
Finkelstein, Louis 143, 304
Fish, Stanley 18, 304
Fitzmyer, Joseph A. 8, 9, 10, 11, 41, 45, 121, 124, 132, 134, 137, 138, 142, 215, 216, 225, 235, 244, 252, 256, 262, 273, 274, 281, 282, 284, 293, 304, 320
Flanagan, Neal 23, 29, 304
Fohrer, Georg 56, 304
Forbes, Peter Barr Reid 104, 304
Fowler, Don 147, 148, 150, 158, 166, 261, 304
Franklin, Eric 7, 8, 41, 44, 45, 213, 214, 304
Frein, Brigid Curtin 186, 304
Fuller, Daniel P. 2, 304
Fuller, Reginald H. 5, 38, 304
Fusco, Vittorio 271, 304
Gaffin, Richard B. Jr. 274, 305
Gardner-Smith, P. 5, 305
Garland, Robert 92, 93, 94, 95, 105, 126, 286, 305
Garrett, Susan R. 39, 40, 175, 305
Gaster, T. H. 49, 58, 305
Gaston, Lloyd 124, 305
Geisler, Norman L. 9, 305
Gempf, Conrad 199, 305
George, Augustin 23, 30, 39, 40, 119, 123, 125, 141, 229, 230, 305
Giles, Kevin 8, 23, 30, 305
Gill, Everett 192, 305
Gillman, Neil 50, 305
Gils, Félix 171, 306
Ginsberg, H. L. 60, 306
Glöckner, Richard 23, 39, 306
Goldsmith, Dale 244, 306

Goldstein, Jonathan A. 63, 64, 65, 66, 306
Gordon, Robert P. 53, 295
Gottschalk, H. B. 106, 107, 306
Goulder, M. D. 120, 306
Gowan, Donald E. 61, 306
Graß, Hans 5, 306
Green, Joel B. 3, 11, 16, 23, 24, 30, 37, 38, 41, 120, 123, 127, 130, 131, 132, 134, 138, 158, 160, 161, 162, 175, 191, 221, 241, 293, 306
Grene, David 97, 295
Grogan, G. 55, 56, 306
Grundmann, Walter 123, 293
Guillaume, Jean-Marie 2, 306
Gundry, Robert H. 9, 306
Guthrie, W. K. C. 97, 307
Haacker, Klaus 272, 275, 276, 277, 307
Hachlili, Rachel 55, 211, 307
Haenchen, Ernst 1, 12, 31, 124, 189, 192, 203, 205, 209, 214, 215, 223, 224, 226, 235, 241, 246, 250, 251, 255, 256, 262, 273, 274, 275, 276, 281, 282, 286, 293, 307
Haight, Elizabeth Hazelton 111, 307
Halpern-Amaru, Betsy 77, 307
Hamm, Dennis 186, 221, 223, 226, 228, 307
Hansen, G. Walter 198, 238, 247, 251, 257, 307
Harnack, Adolf von 6, 276, 277, 287, 307
Harris, Murray J. 8, 9, 307
Harris, William V. 94, 307
Hasel, Gerhard 56, 57, 59, 307
Hauser, H. J. 262, 307
Hawkins, John C. 124, 307
Hemer, Colin J. 261, 307
Hengel, Martin 62, 307
Henten, Jan Willem van 66, 67, 308
Hobart, William K. 229, 308
Holladay, William L. 60, 296
Hollander, H. W. 82, 83, 308
Holtz, Traugott 210, 308
Hooker, Morna D. 157, 308
Horst, P. W. van der 74, 109, 308

Hoskyns, Edwyn Clement 33, 308
Hubbard, David Allan 53, 308
Jackson, F. J. Foakes 308
Jacob, Edmond 53, 308
Janzen, J. Gerald 132, 308
Jervell, Jacob 29, 166, 177, 272, 308
Johnson, Dan G. 56, 308
Johnson, Luke Timothy 3, 11, 20, 30, 173, 175, 182, 190, 191, 192, 193, 205, 215, 221, 225, 226, 241, 262, 273, 276, 282, 283, 291, 294, 308
Jones, Donald L. 225, 309
Jones, H. S. 296
Jong, Irene J. F. de 189, 309
Jonge, Marinus de 82, 83, 308, 309
Juel, Donald 201, 309
Junod, Eric 231, 295
Just, Arthur A. Jr. 180, 182, 309
Kaestli, Jean-Daniel 231, 295
Kaiser, Otto 52, 56, 57, 309
Kany, Roland 111, 112, 127, 309
Karris, Robert J. 39, 160, 294, 309
Käsemann, Ernst 37, 38, 309
Kee, Howard Clark 82, 284, 294
Kegel, Günter 2, 309
Keller, Carl-A. 53, 308
Kellermann, Ulrich 65, 309
Kennedy, George A. 238, 309
Kepple, Robert J. 272, 277, 278, 287, 309
Kilgallen, John J. 132, 134, 135, 136, 137, 174, 213, 223, 238, 251, 252, 255, 309
Kimball, Charles A. 134, 136, 138, 309
Kingsbury, Jack Dean 11, 310
Kistemaker, Simon J. 273, 294
Kittel, Gerhard 296
Knibb, Michael A. 75, 310
Knight, W. F. Jackson 92, 310
Kodell, Jerome 38, 39, 310
Koet, B. J. 171, 178, 310
Kohler, Kaufmann 86, 310
Kolarcik, Michael 67, 310
Kränkl, Emmeram 7, 310
Kurz, William S. 11, 44, 209, 210, 226, 227, 266, 267, 310

Index of Modern Authors

Ladd, George Eldon 8, 310
Lake, Kirsopp 5, 7, 124, 189, 203, 209, 212, 225, 226, 229, 243, 250, 262, 273, 284, 294, 308, 310
Lane, William L. 43, 225, 226, 228, 229, 310
Lang, Bernhard 49, 310
Latham, James E. 193, 310
Latte, Kurt 104, 295
Lattimore, Richmond 92, 94, 95, 96, 97, 98, 113, 295, 311
LaVerdiere, Eugene A. 7, 311
Le Moyne, Jean 86, 131, 141, 311
Lehnert, Volker 271, 311
Lesêtre, H. 49, 311
Lichtenberger, Hermann 50, 311
Liddell, H. G. 296
Loewe, H. 79, 295
Lohfink, Gerhard 7, 41, 42, 43, 44, 45, 172, 173, 174, 175, 213, 214, 215, 228, 265, 311
Longenecker, Richard N. 202, 209, 219, 257, 273, 288, 291, 294, 311
Lövestam, Evald 246, 247, 248, 249, 250, 251, 252, 253, 254, 311
Lygre, John G. 10, 44, 46, 210, 214, 311
MacAlister, Suzanne 112, 311
MacDonald, Dennis R. 121, 311
MacIntosh, A. A. 53, 311
MacMullen, Ramsay 99, 311
Maddox, Robert 11, 44, 311
Maile, J. F. 8, 9, 311
Mainville, Odette 219, 311
Mánek, Jindřich 161, 175, 176, 191, 311
Mangatt, G. 23, 311
Mantey, Julius R. 210, 296
Marguerat, Daniel 3, 11, 31, 36, 127, 153, 186, 188, 221, 231, 271, 273, 312
Marshall, I. Howard 2, 11, 12, 16, 23, 25, 28, 30, 31, 34, 133, 135, 136, 137, 162, 192, 205, 226, 236, 240, 241, 244, 255, 257, 262, 273, 281, 294, 312
Martin, Luther H. 96, 312

Martin, Ralph P. 312
Martin-Achard, Robert 52, 54, 55, 60, 65, 312
Martinez, Florentino Garcia 70, 312
Mason, John P. 50, 312
Mason, Steve 88, 90, 312
Mauchline, John 56, 312
McCasland, Selby Vernon 53, 313
McConaughy, Daniel L. 192, 313
McCready, Wayne O. 141, 313
McKeating, Henry 53, 313
Mealand, David L. 189, 313
Meeks, Wayne A. 177, 313
Menoud, Philippe H. 34, 313
Metzger, Bruce M. 6, 75, 191, 313
Meyer, Heinrich August Wilhelm 124, 294
Meyers, Eric M. 211, 313
Migne, J.-P. 295
Moessner, David P. 12, 39, 40, 150, 176, 209, 313, 314
Montefiore, C. G. 79, 295
Moore, George Foot 50, 314
Moore, Stephen D. 11, 66, 186, 187, 314
Morgan, J. R. 110, 314
Motyer, Alec 56, 314
Moulton, J. H. 143, 314
Nellessen, E. 34, 314
Neyrey, Jerome H. 11, 39, 40, 314
Nickelsburg, George W. E. Jr. 50, 59, 60, 62, 63, 68, 69, 71, 72, 80, 84, 314
Nolland, John 123, 134, 138, 180, 191, 294
Noorda, S. J. 263, 314
North, Helen F. 105, 314
North, John A. 92, 314
Ó Fearghail, Fearghus 25, 315
O'Donnell, James J. 93, 315
Oepke, A. 99, 226, 315
Ollenburger, Ben C. 55, 58, 315
Osborne, Grant R. 8, 315
Oswalt, John N. 56, 57, 315
O'Toole, Robert F. 2, 3, 11, 23, 31, 41, 45, 144, 171, 215, 217, 223,

224, 246, 281, 282, 283, 286, 287, 291, 315
Palmer, Darryl W. 270, 271, 315
Parker, Floyd 140, 143, 315
Parsons, Mikeal C. 10, 16, 43, 148, 158, 161, 175, 185, 315, 316
Pelling, Christopher 151, 156, 316
Perkins, Pheme 5, 316
Pervo, Richard I. 16, 121, 316
Pesch, Rudolf 192, 203, 214, 273, 276, 281, 284, 291, 294
Pichler, Josef 239, 240, 244, 316
Pilch, John J. 30, 316
Pillai, C. A. Joachim 238, 256, 257, 258, 316
Plevnik, Joseph 159, 169, 186, 187, 316
Plümacher, Eckhard 199, 316
Plummer, Alfred 137, 294
Polhill, John B. 140, 294
Porter, Stanley E. 116, 316
Powell, Mark Allan 11, 23, 316
Price, Robert M. 126, 316
Puskas, Charles B. 262, 266, 267, 269, 316
Rabinowitz, Peter J. 17, 18, 19, 20, 316
Rad, Gerhard von 52, 317
Radl, Walter 23, 317
Ralph P. Martin 23
Ramsey, A. Michael 8, 317
Rasco, Emilio 224, 317
Reardon, B. P. 109, 111, 295, 317
Reese, James M. 67, 317
Reiling, J. 137, 317
Reimer, Ivoni Richter 125, 126, 317
Renju, Peter M. 175, 317
Rese, Martin 244, 245, 252, 317
Rétif, A. 34, 317
Richardson, N. J. 92, 317
Ridderbos, H. N. 226, 317
Rigato, Maria-Luisa 163, 317
Riley, Gregory J. 92, 96, 112, 317
Ringe, Sharon 160, 175, 294, 317
Robbins, Vernon K. 157, 317
Roberts, Deborah H. 160, 317
Roddy, Nicolae 78, 318

Rohde, Erwin 92, 94, 96, 97, 99, 101, 104, 318
Rolland, Philippe 262, 318
Roloff, Jürgen 214, 256, 274, 294
Rosenblatt, Marie Eloise 194, 318
Sabourin, Leopold 119, 318
Salmon, Marilyn 275, 318
Sanders, Jack T. 271, 318
Sandt, Huub van de 246, 251, 256, 318
Sawyer, John F. A. 57, 59, 318
Schille, Gottfried 281, 294
Schmitt, Armin 209, 318
Schneider, Gerhard 11, 204, 214, 239, 256, 262, 273, 276, 281, 286, 294, 296, 318
Schubert, Paul 2, 146, 181, 236, 318
Schürer, Emil 50, 318
Schweizer, Eduard 138, 226, 294
Scott, James M. 269, 318
Scott, R. 296
Sharples, Robert William 103, 318
Smith, Barbara Herrnstein 151, 319
Smith, Michael W. 17, 316
Smith, Robert H. 161, 169, 181, 268, 269, 319
Soards, Marion L. 198, 199, 221, 238, 242, 257, 319
Sommerstein, Alan H. 100, 295
Sourvinou-Inwood, Christiane 95, 319
Spicq, Ceslas 296
Spronk, Klaas 49, 319
Squires, John T. 26, 319
Stein, Robert H. 136, 294
Stemberger, Günter 50, 58, 63, 64, 66, 72, 78, 79, 81, 85, 87, 319
Stempvoort, P. A. van 9, 10, 44, 175, 319
Stone, Michael E. 75, 76, 77, 78, 319
Strauss, David F. 6, 7, 319
Strauss, Mark L. 40, 41, 204, 205, 210, 214, 235, 239, 240, 241, 245, 247, 250, 251, 252, 253, 254, 319
Stuart, Douglas 53, 319
Sutcliffe, Edmund F. 52, 319
Swellengrebel, J. L. 137, 317

Index of Modern Authors

Talbert, Charles H. 3, 10, 11, 34, 35, 38, 131, 158, 164, 175, 176, 188, 195, 217, 294, 320
Tannehill, Robert C. 11, 20, 23, 24, 38, 46, 47, 122, 123, 124, 133, 150, 168, 175, 198, 199, 201, 202, 214, 219, 235, 237, 244, 257, 271, 286, 287, 290, 295, 320
Taylor, Justin 141, 142, 143, 321
Teeple, Howard M. 177, 320
Throckmorton, B. H. 23, 320
Thurston, Anne 179, 320
Tiede, David L. 12, 271, 320
Toon, Peter 6, 8, 320
Torgovnick, Marianna 148, 149, 150, 151, 156, 321
Torrey, Charles C. 206, 321
Toynbee, J. M. C. 92, 93, 321
Trémel, Bernard 122, 321
Trites, Allison A. 34, 35, 37, 321
Tromp, Nicholas J. 52, 321
Turner, C. H. 263
Turner, Max 36, 40, 321
Turner, Nigel 281, 296
Unnik, W. C. van 22, 23, 45, 269, 321
VanderKam, James C. 75, 321
Varneda, Pere Villalba I. 154, 321
Verheyden, Joseph 16, 321
Vermeule, Emily 92, 94, 95, 96, 321
Viviano, Benedict T. 141, 142, 143, 321

Vos, Geerhardus 274, 321
Walton, Steve 157, 263, 321
Wanke, Joachim 2, 321
Wasserberg, Gunter 11, 146, 322
Wedderburn, A. J. M. 70, 322
Wehrli, Fritz 106, 107, 295
Wendt, H. H. 251, 295
Weren, W. J. C. 248, 322
Wifall, Walter 60, 322
Wijngaards, J. 53, 54, 322
Wikenhauser, Alfred 273, 276, 295
Wilckens, Ulrich 31, 322
Wilcox, Max 206, 322
Wildberger, Hans 56, 322
Wilder, Amos N. 1, 7, 322
Williams, C. S. C 250, 273, 295
Winandy, Jacques 261, 322
Witherington, Ben III 30, 121, 142, 198, 226, 238, 255, 257, 295, 322
Wolff, Hans Walter 53, 322
Wolter, Michael 232, 256, 322
Wright, N. T. 5, 50, 61, 92, 99, 116, 142, 322
York, John O. 134, 322
Young, Edward J. 57, 322
Zehnle, Richard F. 39, 200, 202, 322
Zeitlin, Solomon 63, 64, 141, 323
Zwaan, J. de 263, 323
Zwiep, A. W. 2, 6, 8, 31, 41, 46, 175, 176, 216, 323

Index of Ancient Literature and Scripture

1. Classical and Hellenistic Writings

Achilles Tatius
  Leucippe and Clitophon
    3.15.21 *111*
    3.17.4 *110*
    5.7.4 *111*
    5.18.4 *110*
    5.19.2 *110*
    7.5.3 *110*
    7.6.2 *110*
Aelian
  De natura animalium
    1.51 *94*
Aeschylus
  Agamemnon
    1360–61 *99*
  Eumenides
    94–105 *95*
    647–48 *99*
    649–51 *99*
Apollonius
  Mirabilia
    3 *103*
Apuleius
  Florida
    19 *111*
Aristophanes
  Pax
    832–33 *97*
  Ranae
    170–80 *100*
    178 *100*
    180–270 *95*
Aristotle
  Analytica priora
    2.27 *210*

De anima
  406b 4–5 *107*
Poetica
  7.21–35 *153*
Rhetorica
  1.2.16–18 *189*
Celsus, Aulus Cornelius
  De medicina
    2.6.13–16 *108*, *111*
Chariton
  Callirhoe
    1.5.1 *109, 110*
    1.8.1 *109*
    3.3.1 *109*
    3.3.2 *110*
    3.3.3 *110*
    3.3.4 *110*
    3.8.9 *110*
    5.5.2 *110*
Cicero
  De republica
    6.9–26 *113*
  Tusculanae disputationes
    1.10–11 *98*
    1.11 *94*
    1.17.38–39 *97*
    1.31.7 *113*
    1.37–44 *98*
Diodorus Siculus
  Bibliotheca historia
    1.3.1–8 *155*
    1.3.3 *152*
    1.3.4 *155*
    1.3.5 *152*
    1.3.8 *152, 155*

1.4.6 *154*
1.41.10 *155*
1.42.1–2 *155*
1.5.2 *152*
1.6.1 *155*
1.98.10 *154*
2.1.1 *154*
2.1.3 *154*
2.60.3 *154*
3.1.1–2 *154*
3.1.3 *154*
3.74.6 *154*
4.1.5 *154*
4.85.7 *154*
5.1.1–2.1 *155*
5.84.4 *155*
11.1.1 *154*
11.92.5 *154*
12.2.3 *154*
12.84.4 *154*
13.1.1–3 *155*
13.1.3 *154*
13.114.3 *154*
14.2.4 *154*
14.117.9 *154*
15.1.6 *154*
15.95.4 *154*
16.1.1–2 *154*
16.1.1–3 *154*
16.95.5 *154*
17.1.1 *154*
17.1.2 *154, 155*
17.118.4 *154*
18.1.5 *154*
18.1.6 *154*

18.74.3 *154*
19.1.9–10 *154*
19.1.10 *154*
19.110.5 *154*
20.1.1–5 *155*
20.113.5 *154*
20.2.3 *154*
40.8.1 *152*
Diogenes Laertius
  Lives of Eminent
  Philosophers
    1.9 *49*
    1.109 *102*
    5.87 *106*
    7.156 *113*
    7.157 *113*
    8.31–32 *97*
    8.41 *102*
    8.60–61 *106*
    8.67 *106*
    10.124–25 *112*
    10.139 *112*
    10.63–67 *112*
Dionysius of Haicarnassus
  Antiquitates romanae
    1.8.4 *152*
    1.18.1–2 *152*
  De Thucydide
    10 *153*
    12 *153*
  Epistula ad Pompeium
  Geminum
    3.767 *153*
    3.769 *153*
    4.778 *153*
Euripides
  Alcestis
    1123–25 *100*
    1127 *100*
    1129 *100*
    1131 *100*
    1159–63 *100*
  Fragment 971 *97*

Helena
  1014–15 *97*
Supplices
  533–34 *97*
  615–17 *227*
Galen
  De differentiis febrium
    1.4 (7.287) *229*
  De locis affectus
    6.5 *106*
  De usu partium
    7.5 (3.528) *229*
    7.9 (3.544) *229*
Heraclitus
  Fragment 86 *99*
Herodotus
  Historiae
    3.62 *49, 99*
    4.15 *103*
    4.71 *66*
    4.94 *102*
    4.95–96 *102*
    9.116–20 *101*
Hesiod
  Opera et dies
    171 *96*
  Theogonia
    119 *96*
    311 *95*
    721–35 *96*
    770–73 *95*
Historia Apollonii regis
Tyrii
  26–27 *111*
Homer
  Iliad
    1.3 *95*
    1.3–4 *95*
    2.698–702 *101*
    3.322 *95*
    3.646 *95*
    6.284 *95*
    6.422 *95*
    6.487–89 *95*

    7.131 *95*
    7.330 *95*
    8.13–16 *96*
    8.367–70 *95*
    8.368 *95*
    8.481 *96*
    11.41 *95*
    15.184–93 *95*
    16.856 *95*
    21.56 *95, 99*
    22.482 *95*
    23.104 *95*
    23.104–17 *95, 188*
    23.71–76 *95*
    23.72 *95*
    24.551 *99*
    24.736 *99*
  Odyssey
    4.561–68 *96*
    5.1–268 *99*
    10.492–94 *95*
    10.495 *95*
    10.521 *95*
    10.536 *95*
    11.29 *95*
    11.49 *95*
    11.57 *95*
    11.83 *95*
    11.96–99 *95*
    11.155 *95*
    11.207 *95*
    11.213 *95*
    11.219 *188*
    11.393 *95*
    11.476 *95*
    11.582–600 *96*
    20.355 *95*
    20.356 *95*
    24.14 *95*
Lucian
  A True Story
    2.12 *188*

Dialogues of the Dead
  95
Funerals
  2 *94*
  2–9 *94*
  7–8 *96*
  9 *96*
  10 *95*
Icaromenippus
  1 *97*
The Fly
  7 *103*
The Lover of Lies
  25 *106*
  26 *102*
Lucretius
  De rerum natura
    3.624–33 *112*
Ovid
  Metamorphoses
    15.389–90 *94*
Pausanias
  Description of Greece
    4.32.4 *98*
    10.4.10 *93*
    10.29.1-2 *96*
    10.31.9-11 *96*
Philostratus
  Vita Apollonii
    4.45 *108*, *120*, *126*
Pindar
  Fragment 6 *96*
  Olympianikai
    2.68–84 *96*
  Pythionikai
    3.54–58 *99*
  Threnoi
    6 *96*
Plato
  Apology of Socrates
    24b–c *284*
  Cratylus
    399d–e *229*
    400c *99*

Laws
  10.886d *189*
  914c *190*
Meno
  81b *89*
  81b–c *89*
Phaedo
  111c–114c *96*
  70c *89*
  71e *89*
  72a *89*
Phaedrus
  80e *89*
  81e *89*
  107c *89*
  114c *89*
  133d *89*
Republic
  614b–621d *100*
  621b *98*
Symposium
  206e *205*
Timaeus
  70c–d *229*
  78e *229*
  84d *229*
  91c *107*
Plautus
  Captivi
    5.4.1–2 *96*
Pliny the Elder
  Natural History
    1.52.179 *107*
    2.23.94 *98*
    7.51.171-72 *107*
    7.52.173-79 *106*
    7.52.174 *103*
    7.52.174-75 *106*
    7.52.175 *102*, *106*, *107*, *111*
    7.55.188-90 *107*
    10.86 *94*

Plutarch
  Cleomenes
    39 *94*
  De Iside et Osiride
    47 *49*
  Moralia
    45c–d *121*
    264d–e *105*
    264f *105*, *126*
    264f–265a *105*
    265a–b *106*
    592c–d *103*
    761e–762a *101*
    784a *102*
    973e–974a *111*
    1105b *94*
  On the Soul (Περὶ ψυχῆς)
    Fragment 176 *106*, *107*
    Fragment 177 *107*
  Theseus
    23.1 *227*
Polybius
  Histories
    3.1.4 *152*
    3.1.4–5 *153*
    3.1.4–10 *152*
    12.25a–b *198*
    39.8.3–4 *152*
    39.8.3–8 *152*
    39.8.8 *152*
    39.83–84 *153*
Seneca
  Ad Marciam de consolatione
    19.1 *94*
    26.1–6 *113*
Servius
  Commentary on the Aeneid of Vergil
    5.95 *94*

Sophocles
  Elektra
    137-45 *99*
Suidas
  s.v. 'ἄπνους' *106*
Thucydides
  Peloponnesian War
    4.12 *124*

Valerius Maximus
  1.6.12 *106*
Virgil
  Aeneid
    2.272-73 *95*
    2.277-79 *95*
    6 *95*
    6.548-627 *96*

Xenophon
  Anabasis
    Books 2-5, 7 *44*
  Memorabilia
    1.1.1 *284*
Xenophon (Greek Novelist)
  Ephesian Tale
    3.7.1 *110, 111*

2. Old Testament Pseudepigrapha

2 Baruch (Syriac Apocalypse)
11:4 *79*
11:6 *79*
13:9 *135*
21:23 *206*
21:24 *80*
28:2 *78*
29:1-8 *78*
29:8 *78*
30:1-2a *78*
30:1-5 *274*
30:2 *83*
30:3 *78*
32:6 *81*
42:7 *79*
42:8 *206*
44:5-9 *76*
44:8-15 *81*
48:6 *79*
49:2-3 *79*
49:3 *81*
50:2 *206*
50:2-4 *79*
51:1 *79, 80*
51:2 *79, 80*
51:3 *80, 136*
51:4-6 *80*
51:5 *79, 80, 136, 173*
51:6 *80*
51:7 *80*

51:8 *80*
51:9 *80*
51:9-10 *136*
51:10 *80*
51:10-11 *60*
51:11 *80*
51:12 *80*
51:14 *80*
51:16 *80*
52:3 *79*
54:14 *79*
54:17 *79*
54:22 *80*
57:1-2 *80*
72:1-74:4 *78*
74:4 *78*
83:8 *80*
85:3-5 *76*
85:13 *79*
85:15 *79*

1 Enoch (Ethiopic Apocalypse)
22:13b *69*
25:6 *83*
38:2-3 *72*
39:5 *60, 141*
39:6 *72*
40:6 *72*
45:5 *72*
46:3-4 *72*
46:4-8 *72, 165*

46:6 *71*
48:2 *72*
48:8-10 *72, 165*
48:10 *72*
49:2 *72*
49:3 *72*
51:1 *71, 206*
51:2 *71*
51:3 *71, 72*
51:4-5 *71, 209*
51:4c *71*
51:5 *72, 83*
52:4 *72*
52:6 *72*
52:9 *72*
53:6 *72*
54:1-2 *141*
55:4 *72*
61:1-12 *72*
61:5 *72*
61:5-13 *165*
61:8 *72*
61:10 *72*
62:1-2 *72*
62:1-16 *165*
62:2 *72, 165*
62:5 *165*
62:7 *72*
62:9 *72*
62:13 *72*
62:14 *72*

62:14–16 72, 133, 173
63:1–12 72
63:11 72
69:11 136
69:27–29 72
71:14 72
71:17 72
91:10 59, 70, 73
92:3 59
92:3–5 70, 73
104:2–6 60
4 Ezra
2:1 76
2:1–32 76
2:2–14 76
2:16 76
2:23 76
2:31 76
2:39 73
3:1 75
4:26 76
4:33–39 206
4:33–43 75
4:35 75, 78, 133
4:37 75
4:40–42 78, 206
4:41 79
5:24 76
5:28 135
6:20–24 76
6:25 76
6:58 135
7:26 76, 80
7:26–[44] 76, 174
7:28–32 274
7:30 77
7:31 77
7:31–32 77
7:32 79, 206
7:35 77, 133
7:[36] 77
7:[37] 77
7:[38] 77

7:43 [113] 76
7:[43] 77
7:[46] 77
7:49 [119] 76
7:55 [125] 60, 77
7:[75] 78
7:[78] 78
7:[80] 78, 79
7:[95] 79
7:[97] 60, 77
7:[113] 77
7:[129–30] 75
8:4–12 76
8:13 76
8:52 76
8:54 77
10:1 76
10:4 125
10:14 76
10:15 76
10:16 75, 76
10:27 76
10:42 76
10:44 76
10:54 76
11:46 228
12:31–34 274
13:36 76
14:29 75
14:30 75
14:31–33 75
14:34 75
14:35 75
14:41 76
Joseph and Aseneth
16:14 188
Jubilees
1:25–28 135
2:20 135
21:11 193
22:17 93
23:30–31 59

Liber antiquitatum
  biblicarum (Pseudo-
  Philo)
3:10 206
19:7 76
19:12 77
19:13 77
20:8 171
32:10 135
33:3 206
Lives of the Prophets
3:12 55
Psalms of Solomon
1:5 61
17:21 254
17:26 247
17:30 135
Sibylline Oracles
3:702–4 135
5:248–50 135
Testament of Abraham
4:9 188
Testament of Moses
9:1 131
9:1–7 67
10:3 135
10:9 60
11:9 171
11:13 171
Testaments of the Twelve
  Patriarchs
  Testament of Asher
    6:5–6 85
    7:2 83
    7:7 83
  Testament of Benjamin
    10:6–7 212
    10:6–9 84, 173, 279
  Testament of Dan
    5:4–7 83
    5:9 83
  Testament of Issachar
    6:3–4 83

Testament of Judah	14–17 *83*	5:4–7:3 *82*
9:3 *124*	18:3 *61*	6:2 *82, 83*
24:1 *61*	18:13 *135*	6:5–6 *82*
25:1 *83, 84, 212,*	18:14 *83*	6:7 *83, 84, 209, 212*
279	*Testament of Naphtali*	*Testament of Zebulun*
25:3–5 *83, 133, 279*	1:6–12 *82*	9:1–9 *83*
25:4 *59, 84*	4:3 *83*	9:5–6 *83*
25:4–5 *209*	*Testament of Reuben*	9:7 *83*
25:5 *84*	6:5 *83*	10:2 *83, 84, 209,*
26:4 *84*	*Testament of Simeon*	*212*
Testament of Levi	5:2–3 *83*	
9:14 *193*	5:4–6 *83*	

3. Dead Sea Scrolls

1QIsa^a *56*	4 Second Ezekiel *55*	4QFlor *247, 254*
1QpHab 2.1–10 *256*	4QDibHam^a *58*	
	3:4–6 *135*	

4. Josephus

Against Apion	13.16.6 §432 *154*	1.2.4 §58 *88*
2.1 §1 *44*	14.15.5 §429 *67*	1.33.2 §650 *88*
2.30 §§217–18 *88*	14.16.4 §491 *154*	1.33.9 §673 *154*
2.30 §218 *89*	15.3.3 §52 *190*	2.8.10 §151 *87, 88*
Antiquities of the Jews	15.11.7 §425 *154*	2.8.11 §§154–55 *87*
Proem 2 §7 *152*	17.8.4 §§349–53 *88*	2.8.11 §155 *89, 227*
Proem 2–4 §§5–26 *152*	17.8.5 §354 *88*	2.8.11 §158 *87*
1.22.1 §346 *154*	18.1.3 §14 *90*	2.8.14 §163 *87, 89*
3.8.2 §196 *227*	18.1.3 §16 *142*	2.8.14 §165 *86, 140*
4.8.49 §331 *154*	18.1.4 §16 *86, 140*	2.22.1 §654 *154*
6.14.9 §378 *154*	18.9.9 §379 *154*	3.8.5 §§372–75 *88*
7.15.3 §394 *154*	20.12.1 §259 *152*	3.8.5 §374 *89*
8.15.6 §420 *154*	20.12.1 §260 *152*	6.1.5 §§46–48 *88*
11.8.7 §346 *154*	20.12.1 §261 *152*	6.10.1 §442 *154*
11.8.7 §347 *154*	*Jewish War*	7.8.7 §§341–57 *88*
12.11.2 §§432–33 *154*	Proem 6–12 §§17–26	7.11.5 §454 *152*
12.11.2 §434 *154*	*152*	

5. Philo

De fuga et inventione	*De mutatione nominum*	125 *177*
147 *177*	103 *177*	126 *177*

De posteritate Caini
  1 *177*
De praemiis et poenis
  55 *177*
De sacrificiis Abelis et Caini
  1.5 *134*
De somniis
  2.189 *177*
De specialibus legibus
  3.6 *177*
De vita Mosis
  1.1 *177*
  1.198 *171*
Quaestiones et solutiones in Genesin
  1.86 *177*
  4.8 *177*
Quis rerum divinarum heres sit
  213 *177*
  262 *177*

6. Rabbinic Texts

ʾ*Abot de Rabbi Nathan*
  5 *86*
b. Berakot 54a *86*
Midrash I
  Psalm 1:20 *206*
Pesiqta Rabbati
  21:4 *206*
Pirqe Rabbi Eliezer
  34 *206*
Rabbah
  Genesis
    95.1 *79*
  Canticles
    2:1–2 *206*
b. Sanhedrin
  90a *86*
  91b *79*
  92a *207*
  100b *86*
y. Sanhedrin
  10.1d *86*
  10.8a–b *86*
Tanḥuma
  Wayiggash 104b *79*
Targum of the Prophets
  Hosea 6:2
    10.1d *53*

7. Apostolic Fathers and Church Fathers

Aristides
  Apology
    15 *6*
Barnabas
  15:8–9 *6*
  15:9 *43*
1 Clement
  50:4 *206*
Cyprian
  Ad Quirinum testimonia adversus Judaeos
    2.25 *53*
  Treatises
    3.2.25 *53*
Eusebius
  Contra Hieroclem
    9.35 *108*
  Praeparatio evangelica
    15.20.6 *113*
    9.35 *107*
Gregory of Nyssa
  Contra Eunomium
    2 *208*
    4 *208*
  Homiliae in Canticum Canticorum
    13 *208*
  Illud tunc et ipse filius
    208
Ignatius
  Epistula ad Smyrnaeos
    3.2 *188*
John Chrysostom
  De remissione peccatorum *208*
  Homilae in Joannem
    79 *208*
  Homiliae in Acta Apostolorum
    6 *208*
    9 *230*
    29 *256, 258*
  Homiliae in epistulae primae ad Corinthios
    24 *208*
Lactantius
  Divinarum institutionum libri VII
    4.29 *53*
  Epitome divinarum institutionum
    47 *53*
Origen
  Contra Celsum
    2.16 *106*
    4.57 *94*
    5.14 *99*
    7.32 *101*
    11.55 *108*

Selecta in Psalmos 17
    205
Tertullian
  Adversus Marcionem
    4.43.1 *53*
  De anima
    28 *102*

De resurrectione carnis
    32.1 *206*
Theodoret
  Commentarius in
  Visiones Danielis
    9 *208*

Eranistes
    262.1 *208*
Interpretatio epistolae
  ad Colossenses
    1 *208*

8. New Testament Apocrypha and Pseudepigrapha

Acts of John
  22 *230*
Acts of Peter
  28 *125*, *128*

Apocalypse of Peter
  4:3–4 *206*
  4:10–12 *206*
Epistle to the Apostles
  51 *6*

Gospel of Peter
  10.39 *127*
  10.39–40 *161*
  13.56 *6*

9. Old Testament

Genesis
  2:7 *55*, *65*
  3:19 *55*
  6:1–4 *136*
  6:17 *65*
  7:15 *65*
  7:22 *65*
  11:9 *60*
  13:17 *71*
  15:1–18 *24*
  15:13 *77*
  18:2 *161*
  18:16 *161*
  18:22 *161*
  19:1 *161*
  19:5 *161*
  19:15 *161*
  22:18 *232*
  26:4 *232*
  38:8 *131*
  45:1–28 *167*
  50:13 *52*
Exodus
  2:15–16 *54*

  3:6 *132*, *136*, *137*,
    223, *308*
  3:15 *223*
  3:15–16 *137*
  4:30 *170*
  6:6 *24*
  8:15 *229*
  12:40–41 *77*
  15:13 *24*
  16:4–36 *171*
  17:6 *170*
  19–20 *54*
  19:11 *54*, *170*
  24:4 *54*
  24:15 *171*
  24:16 *171*
  24:16–17 *172*
  24:18 *171*
  34:2 *54*
  34:4 *54*
  34:29–30 *171*
  34:33–35 *171*
Leviticus
  24:27 *231*

Numbers
  16:30 *137*
  16:33 *137*
  18:19 *193*
  24:17 *60*
Deuteronomy
  2:25 *204*
  5:24 *172*
  5:33 *71*, *75*
  7:8 *24*, *167*
  7:12–26 *59*
  8:1 *71*, *75*
  8:4 *73*
  9:26 *24*, *167*
  11:1–25 *59*
  11:9 *71*, *75*
  12:1 *71*
  12:10 *71*
  13:15 *24*
  15:15 *24*
  17:6 *161*
  18:15 *176*, *245*
  18:15–20 *231*
  18:16–18 *177*
  19:15 *161*

24:18 *24*
25:5 *131*
29:5 *73*
30:6 *75*
30:15–20 *75*
30:16 *71*
30:20 *71*
31:21 *68*
31–34 *68*
32:4–9 *68*
32:18 *68*
32:19–26 *68*
32:27–33 *68*
32:35 *68*
32:36 *68*
32:36–39 *68*
32:39 *66, 68*
32:40–43 *68*
32:47 *68, 71*
32:48–51 *40*
34:10 *170*
34:10–12 *203*
34:11 *170*
34:12 *170*
Joshua
  24:32 *52*
Judges
  5:20 *60*
  6:8 *170*
Ruth
  1:6 *24*
  4:15 *67*
1 Samuel
  1:1–2:11 *24*
  1:12 *125*
  2:5 *67*
  2:5b–6 *68*
  2:6–8 *55*
  2:6–10 *84*
  2:21 *24*
  31:31 *125*
2 Samuel
  7:4–17 *24*

7:10 *254*
7:10–14 *247*
7:12 *240, 244*
7:12–13 *210*
7:14 *248, 249*
7:16 *254*
7:23 *24*
12:16–23 *125*
22:51 *240*
1 Kings
  1:21 *123*
  2:10 *52, 123*
  4:25 *24*
  8:8 *189*
  11:21 *123*
  11:43 *123*
  14:20 *123*
  16:2–3 *55*
  17:8–24 *119*
  17:10 *119*
  17:17 *120*
  17:17–24 *8, 52, 66, 299*
  17:19 *120*
  17:21 *120, 123*
  17:22 *119*
  17:23 *119, 120, 126*
2 Kings
  4:10–11 *120*
  4:21 *120*
  4:22–25 *120*
  4:32–37 *8, 52, 66*
  4:33 *120*
  4:34 *125*
  4:34–35 *120*
  4:35 *120*
  4:36 *126*
  4:42–44 *171*
  13:21 *8, 52, 66*
  18:31 *24*
1 Chronicles
  10:11 *125*
  17:16–17 *215*
  29:28 *173*

2 Chronicles
  13:5 *193*
Nehemiah
  1:10 *24*
Job
  1:2 *67*
  10:8–12 *65*
  10:11 *207*
  21:17 *204*
  38:7 *60*
  39:2 *205*
  42:13 *67*
Psalms
  1:1–2 *248*
  2:1–1 *248*
  2:7 *245, 246, 247, 248, 249, 253*
  6:6 *137*
  13:4 *123*
  15:8–11 LXX *202, 208, 214, 249, 279*
  15:10 LXX *210, 219, 236, 247, 250, 251, 252, 254*
  15:11 LXX *215*
  17:4–6 *137*
  17:5 LXX *204, 205, 240*
  17:6 LXX *204*
  22:30 *123*
  37:29 *71*
  48:3 MT *54*
  65:10 *24*
  69:29 *58*
  69:36 *71*
  77:16 *24*
  88:3–12 *137*
  88:4–5 LXX *215*
  88:20–21 LXX *215*
  88:25 LXX *215*
  88:28–30 LXX *215*
  88:29 *249*
  88:36–38 *249*

Index of Ancient Literature and Scripture 339

90:15 *77*
106:4 *24*
109:1 LXX *202, 214, 218*
113:7 *55*
114:3 LXX *204*
114:4 *71*
114:6 *71*
115:17 *137*
116:4 *204*
117:22 LXX *172, 284*
125:1 LXX *24*
131:11 LXX *210*
139:13 *207*

Ecclesiastes/Qoheleth
3:19–21 *62*
11:5 *207*
12:7 *62, 65*

Isaiah
4:3 *58*
6:9–10 *271*
11:1–9 *72*
14:12–14 *60, 61*
25:7 *57*
25:8a *56*
25:8–9 *279*
26:9 *58*
26:14 *57, 61*
26:19 *55, 56, 57, 58, 59, 61, 83, 90, 116, 206, 209, 279*
26:20 *206*
26:20–21 *61*
26:21 *58*
32:15 *228*
35:1–10 *221*
35:6 *221*
35:9–10 *71*
36:16 *24*
38:10–11 *137*
40:1 *24*
40:1–2 *167*
40:2 *24*
40:5 *174*
40:11 *24, 167*
41:27 *24*
42:1 *72*
43:11 *24*
45:22–25 *174*
46:13 *174*
49:6 *184*
49:9–13 *167*
49:10 *24*
49:13 *24*
51:3 *24, 167*
51:10 *24*
51:12 *24, 167*
51:18 *24*
51:18–19 *167*
51:19 *24*
52:1 *73*
52:7 *24*
52:13 *40, 60, 215, 223*
52:13–53:12 *37*
53:5 *24*
53:6 *38, 40*
53:7–8 *37*
53:11 *40, 60*
53:12 *37, 40*
54:10 *24*
54:13 *24*
55:3 *247, 249, 250, 251, 252, 253, 254*
55:5 *249*
55:5 *174*
57:2 *24*
57:18 *24, 167*
57:19 *24*
58:6 *25*
58:8 *174*
59:8 *24*
60:6 *174*
60:1–2 *174*
60:13–14 *174*
60:17 *24*
60:19–21 *174*
61:1–2 *25, 167, 170, 174*
61:2 *24*
61:10 *73*
62:1–2 *174*
63:1–19 *167*
66:7–11 *207*
66:10–13 *167*
66:11 *174*
66:11–13 *24*
66:12 *24*
66:14 *59*
66:24 *59*

Jeremiah
15:9 *67*
15:15 *24*
16:14–15 *167*
23:6 *254*
23:7–8 *167*
27:22 *24*
29:10 *24*
30:7 *58*
48:41 *204*
49:22 *204*
51:39 *123*
51:53 *60*
51:57 *123*

Lamentations
2:1 *60*

Ezekiel
34:22–31 *254*
37 *55, 61, 66*
37:1–14 *55, 57, 58, 61, 90, 279*
37:2–3 *66*
37:5–6 *55*
37:6 *207*
37:8–10 *55*
37:11 *55*
37:12 *206*
37:12–13 *55*
37:15–28 *55*
37:24–28 *254*

Daniel
    4:11 *60*
    4:20 *60*
    4:22 *60*
    4:36 *173*
    7 *72*
    7:9–28 *165*
    7:10 *58*
    7:13 *60*
    7:14 *173*
    8:10 *60*
    8:15 *161*
    8:39 *60*
    10:21 *58*
    11:21–45 *58*
    11:32–33 *59*
    11:33 *60*
    11:35 *60*
    11:36–38 *59*
    11:39 *59*
    11–12 *133*
    12:1 *58*
    12:1–3 *52, 55, 58, 61, 90, 173, 279*
    12:2 *56, 58, 59, 61, 65, 66, 73, 78, 84, 85*
    12:2–3 *70, 81, 142*
    12:3 *60, 83, 91, 116*
    12:13 *173*
    13 *61*

Hosea
    5:13 *54*
    5:14 *54*
    5:15 *54*
    6 *61*
    6:1–3 *52, 54, 61, 90, 279*
    6:2 *54*
    6:3 *54, 83*
    10:6 *54*
    13:13 *207*

Joel
    3:1–5 *202*

Amos
    4:4–13 *54*

Micah
    4:4 *24*
    4:10 *167*
    6:4 *24, 167*

Habakkuk
    1:5 *256*

Zechariah
    1:9 *161*
    1:10 *161*
    1:11 *161*
    3:10 *24*

Malachi
    3:1 *24*
    3:16–18 *58*
    4:5–6 *24*

10. Apocrypha

Additions to Esther
    16:14–16 *135*
Baruch
    2:11–35 *167*
    2:17 *137*
    4:11 *68*
    4:15 *68*
    4:19 *68*
    4:21–23 *68*
    5:1 *73*
    5:5–9 *71*
1 Esdras
    2:29–30 *193*
2 Esdras
    2:15–17 *76*
    2:23 *76*
    2:29–30 *24*
    2:29–31 *76*
Judith
    8:6 *126*
    9:4 *135*
    9:13 *135*
2 Maccabees
    1:5 *68*
    2:19–32 *63*
    3:26 *161*
    6:1–11 *63*
    6:12–17 *63, 67, 68*
    6:16 *69*
    6:18–31 *63*
    6:23 *68*
    6:28 *63, 68*
    6:31 *63, 67*
    7:1–42 *63*
    7:2 *68*
    7:6 *67, 68*
    7:9 *63, 65, 68, 89, 279*
    7:11 *63, 65, 66, 68, 279*
    7:14 *64, 65, 68, 279*
    7:16 *67, 69*
    7:16–17 *68*
    7:18 *68*
    7:18–19 *67, 68*
    7:19 *68*
    7:20 *65*
    7:21 *68, 76*
    7:22 *65*
    7:22–23 *64, 68, 76, 207*
    7:23 *65, 66, 68, 230*
    7:27 *68*
    7:27–29 *64, 68*
    7:28 *68, 76*
    7:29 *66, 68, 76*
    7:30 *68*
    7:30–38 *67*
    7:31 *68*
    7:32 *68*
    7:32–33 *68*
    7:33 *68*

7:34 *68*
7:35–36 *68*
7:36 *64, 68, 279*
7:36–37 *68*
8:5 *63*
9:8 *66*
9:10 *60, 66*
9:29 *66*
12:39 *66*
12:39–45 *66*
12:40 *66*
12:44 *65, 66*
12:44–45 *63*
12:45 *66*
14:45–46 *63*
14:46 *65, 66, 230*
3 Maccabees
  5:7 *135*
  6:3 *135*
  6:8 *135*
  6:28 *135*
  7:6 *135*
  7:6–7 *135*
  7:15–16 *125*
4 Maccabees
  1:11 *69*
  6:28–29 *69*
  7:3 *67*
  7:19 *138*
  9:22 *67*
  14:4–5 *67*
  14:5 *67*

14:6 *67*
16:13 *67*
16:23–24 *67*
16:25 *138*
17:12 *67*
17:21–22 *69*
18:6–19 *66*
18:13–19 *66*
18:23 *67*
Sirach/Ecclesiasticus
  10:11 *62*
  14:12–19 *62*
  14:17 *73*
  16:18 *24*
  16:30 *62*
  17:1 *62*
  17:27–28 *137*
  17:27–30 *62*
  17:30 *62, 67*
  28:6 *62*
  36:17 *135*
  38:21 *62*
  39:9 *86*
  40:1 *62*
  40:11 *62*
  41:4 *62*
  41:10 *62*
  41:13 *86*
  44:8–14 *86*
  44:9 *62*
  45:2 *173*
  45:3 *173*

45:7 *173*
46:12 *86*
47:6 *173*
47:11 *173*
48:5 *62*
48:13–14 *8, 52, 66*
48:14 *62*
Tobit
  5:4 *161*
  12:19 *188, 189*
  13:4 *135*
Wisdom of Solomon
  1:15 *67*
  2:13 *136*
  2:16 *136*
  2:23 *67*
  3:2 *175*
  3:4 *67*
  4:1 *67*
  5:5 *136*
  6:18 *67*
  6:19 *67*
  7:6 *175*
  8:13 *67*
  8:17 *67*
  12:1 *67*
  13:2 *60*
  14:11 *24*
  15:3 *67*
  18:4 *67*
  19:9 *71*

11. New Testament

Matthew
  3:7 *129*
  5:1 *176*
  9:18–19 *8*
  9:23–26 *8*
  12:39–40 *33*
  12:40 *163*
  14:23 *176*

15:29 *176*
16:1 *129*
16:6 *129*
16:11–12 *129*
16:21 *33*
17:2 *171*
17:5 *176*
17:9 *33*

17:23 *33*
18:10 *143*
19:28 *207*
20:18–19 *33*
20:24–28 *37*
21:42 *33, 284*
22:23 *129*
22:23–33 *86*

22:30 *142, 143*
22:32 *137*
22:34 *129*
24:8 *207*
26:29 *33*
26:32 *33*
27:52–53 *174*
27:63–64 *33*
28:1–20 *33*
28:4 *124*

Mark
3:13 *176*
5:21–24 *8*
5:22–24 *123*
5:35–43 *8, 123*
5:39 *124*
8:31 *32, 33*
9:2 *171, 176*
9:7 *176*
9:9 *32*
9:9–10 *33*
9:10 *32*
9:26 *124*
9:31 *32, 33*
10:33–34 *33*
10:34 *32*
10:41–45 *37*
12:8–23 *131*
12:10 *33, 284*
12:18 *129*
12:18–27 *86*
12:25 *143*
12:26 *132*
12:27 *137*
14:25 *33*
14:28 *33*
14:36 *23*
16:1–8 *33*
16:2 *6*
16:9 *6*
16:19 *42, 43, 44, 216*

Luke
1:1 *26*
1:1–4 *1*
1:2 *159, 187*
1:3 *19, 150*
1:4 *19, 160*
1:5–2:52 *24*
1:16–17 *28, 159, 167*
1:17 *163*
1:20 *162*
1:26–38 *163*
1:27 *27*
1:28 *24*
1:30 *24*
1:32 *27*
1:32–33 *165, 244, 248, 253*
1:35 *218*
1:38 *162*
1:41–55 *162*
1:46–55 *167*
1:47 *23, 24, 26, 28*
1:51–55 *84*
1:54 *162*
1:54–55 *28, 232*
1:55 *25, 27*
1:67–79 *167*
1:68 *23, 28, 167, 273*
1:68–73 *254*
1:69 *23, 25, 27, 246*
1:69–75 *27*
1:70 *26*
1:71 *23, 25, 28, 165*
1:72 *162*
1:72–73 *28, 232*
1:73 *27*
1:74 *165, 278*
1:74–75 *28, 167*
1:75 *251*
1:76 *163*
1:76–77 *159*
1:77 *23, 25, 28*
1:78 *23*
1:79 *23*
2:1–2 *19*
2:4 *27*
2:9 *173*
2:9–12 *163*
2:10 *28*
2:11 *23, 25, 27, 72, 241*
2:14 *23, 173*
2:17–18 *162*
2:19 *162*
2:20 *187*
2:23 *247*
2:25 *23, 28, 167, 174, 273*
2:26 *28, 72, 211*
2:28–32 *167*
2:29 *24*
2:29–35 *260*
2:30 *23, 25, 168, 272*
2:30–31 *28*
2:30–32 *184*
2:32 *28, 173, 174, 184, 257, 271, 272*
2:34 *29, 232*
2:34–35 *271*
2:37 *278*
2:38 *23, 28, 167, 273*
2:44 *162*
2:45 *162*
2:46 *162*
2:48 *162*
2:49 *162*
2:51 *162*
3:1–2 *19*
3:1–18 *241*
3:3 *25*
3:4 *163, 247*
3:4–6 *167*
3:6 *23, 26, 29, 168, 184, 272*
3:8 *134, 254, 271*
3:15 *72*
3:16 *163, 213*
3:16–17 *194*

Index of Ancient Literature and Scripture

3:21–22 *159*
3:22 *124, 177, 247*
3:23a *159*
3:23b–38 *159*
3:7 *254*
4:1 *194*
4:1–13 *159*
4:6 *173*
4:13 *159*
4:14 *194*
4:14–15 *159*
4:16–30 *25, 120, 159*
4:18 *194*
4:18–19 *167, 170*
4:21 *26*
4:24 *169*
4:25–27 *184*
4:28 *160*
4:29a *160*
4:29b *160*
4:30 *160*
4:32 *130*
4:36 *130*
4:40–43 *29*
4:41 *72*
4:43 *26*
5:20–24 *25*
5:24 *72, 130*
5:35 *163*
6:5 *72*
6:13 *166*
6:20 *26*
6:22 *72*
6:22–23 *170, 178*
6:35–36 *135*
7:1–10 *184*
7:3 *23*
7:11–16 *273*
7:11–17 *8, 119, 120, 174*
7:12 *66, 120*
7:15 *119, 122, 125*
7:16 *23, 126, 170, 282*

7:18–35 *241*
7:20 *170*
7:22 *29, 170, 187, 282*
7:27 *163*
7:28 *26*
7:29–30 *134*
7:30 *26*
7:34 *72*
7:39 *170*
7:47–49 *25*
8:1 *26, 35, 166*
8:1–3 *29*
8:40–42 *8*
8:41–42 *119*
8:42 *120*
8:43–48 *29*
8:49–56 *8, 119*
8:51 *120*
8:53 *123*
8:55 *120, 123, 230*
8:55–56 *125*
8:56 *124, 126*
9:1 *130, 166, 171*
9:1–6 *171*
9:1–34 *175, 176*
9:2 *29*
9:4 *179*
9:5 *179*
9:7–8 *171, 174*
9:9 *171, 187*
9:11 *29*
9:12 *166, 171, 179*
9:13 *179*
9:16 *180, 191*
9:17 *171*
9:19 *171, 174*
9:20 *72, 171*
9:20–22 *172*
9:21 *171*
9:22 *33, 39, 72, 127, 163, 164, 171, 172, 175*
9:23–27 *171*

9:26 *72, 165, 173*
9:26–27 *172*
9:28 *171, 176*
9:29 *171*
9:30 *161*
9:30–32 *163*
9:31 *40, 163, 173, 174, 175, 176*
9:31–32 *172, 176*
9:32 *161, 172, 173*
9:34–35 *171*
9:35 *72, 176*
9:36 *172*
9:37 *171*
9:44 *40, 72, 163, 164*
9:44–45 *163, 172*
9:45 *164, 185, 186*
9:51 *10, 169, 170, 175, 176, 217, 263*
9:52 *163*
9:54 *163*
9:58 *72*
10:1–15 *268*
10:1–16 *184*
10:3 *124*
10:7 *179*
10:9 *29*
10:18 *124*
10:19 *130*
10:23–24 *29, 178*
10:24 *177, 187*
10:25 *258*
11:4 *25*
11:13 *194*
11:20 *29*
11:29–30 *33*
11:30 *72, 163, 164*
11:47–51 *170, 178*
11:49–51 *177*
11:50 *177*
12:8 *72, 165*
12:10 *25, 72, 165*
12:27 *173*

Luke (continued)
12:40 *72, 165*
13:10–17 *29*
13:24 *173*
13:28 *138, 177*
13:28–29 *133, 184, 254*
13:28–30 *271*
13:29 *73, 139*
13:30 *134*
13:30–31 *163*
13:31 *171*
13:32 *163*
13:32–33 *163*
13:33 *39*
13:33–34 *169*
14:7–14 *133*
14:10 *173*
14:11 *134*
14:13 *133*
14:14 *133, 281*
14:14–15 *139*
14:15 *73, 133*
14:15–24 *133*
14:16–24 *184*
14:21 *133*
14:24 *133*
14:27 *163*
15:18–19 *134*
15:21 *134*
15:24 *134, 139*
15:32 *134, 139*
16:14–15 *133*
16:16 *173, 177*
16:19–31 *138*
16:29 *27*
16:31 *27, 32, 33, 179, 282*
17:3–4 *25*
17:12–19 *29*
17:18 *173*
17:22 *72, 163, 165*
17:24 *72, 165*
17:24–25 *163, 164*

17:25 *39, 163*
17:26 *72, 165*
17:30 *72, 165*
18:8 *72, 165*
18:11–12 *133*
18:13 *134*
18:14 *134*
18:17 *173*
18:18 *258*
18:24 *173*
18:25 *173*
18:30 *258*
18:31 *72, 163, 164, 166, 177*
18:31–33 *33, 36, 39*
18:31–34 *163, 172*
18:32 *163, 268*
18:33 *32, 127*
18:34 *164, 185, 186*
19:1–10 *254*
19:5 *179*
19:9 *23*
19:9–10 *29, 271*
19:10 *72*
19:11–27 *172*
19:12 *219*
19:28–34 *163*
19:37–44 *172*
19:38 *23, 173*
19:41 *169*
19:41–44 *168*
19:42 *23*
19:44 *23*
19:45–48 *130*
19:47 *48, 130*
19:48 *130*
20:1 *130*
20:1–40 *130*
20:6 *130*
20:9 *130*
20:9–19 *160, 172*
20:16 *284*
20:17 *33, 172*

20:19 *130*
20:20 *268*
20:26 *130, 134*
20:27 *130, 277, 281*
20:27–33 *131*
20:27–40 *48, 86, 130, 131, 281*
20:28 *132*
20:33 *132*
20:34 *132*
20:34–36 *132*
20:35 *132, 281, 283*
20:35–36 *258, 281*
20:36 *132, 136, 143, 173*
20:37 *223, 278, 282*
20:37–38 *48, 132, 136, 258*
20:38 *209, 259, 289*
20:39 *130*
20:40 *130*
20:41 *72*
20:41–44 *27, 131, 260*
20:42 *27*
20:45–21:4 *131*
21:12 *35*
21:13 *35*
21:22 *26*
21:24 *26, 168, 227*
21:25–27 *168*
21:26 *230*
21:27 *72, 165, 172, 173, 230*
21:27–28 *230*
21:28 *23, 168, 273*
21:36 *72, 165*
21:37–38 *130*
22:3 *159, 166*
22:4 *268*
22:6 *268*
22:15–16 *193*
22:15–38 *163*
22:16 *73*

22:18 *33*
22:19 *180*
22:19–20 *38*
22:21 *23, 268*
22:21–22 *166*
22:22 *39, 72, 163, 164, 268*
22:24–27 *37*
22:25–30 *190*
22:28 *72*
22:29–30 *193*
22:30 *73, 166*
22:31 *159*
22:31–32 *190*
22:34 *162*
22:36 *31*
22:37 *26, 37, 39, 163, 243*
22:44 *124*
22:47 *166*
22:48 *164*
22:53 *159*
22:61 *162*
22:67 *72*
22:69 *72, 165, 219*
23:2 *72, 172*
23:3 *172*
23:8 *171, 187*
23:27 *30*
23:34 *25*
23:35 *72*
23:37–38 *172*
23:39 *72*
23:39–43 *175*
23:42 *173*
23:43 *9*
23:46 *230*
23:48 *30*
23:49 *35, 127, 164, 200, 243*
23:50–56 *158*
23:54 *158*

23:55 *35, 127, 158, 164, 243*
23:56 *158*
24:1 *120, 158, 181*
24:1–12 *158, 160, 161, 162, 163, 164*
24:1–53 *33, 146, 158*
24:2 *109, 162*
24:2–3 *158*
24:3 *33, 110, 162, 164*
24:4 *110, 161*
24:4–5 *176*
24:5 *32, 33, 162, 209, 289*
24:5–6a *162*
24:6 *158*
24:6–7 *35, 39, 165, 183, 191, 243*
24:6–8 *162, 163, 164*
24:7 *32, 72, 127, 158, 162, 163, 164, 165, 172, 268*
24:8–9 *162*
24:9 *158, 165, 167, 181*
24:10 *158, 162*
24:11 *110, 124, 162, 258*
24:12 *110, 158, 164, 181*
24:13 *120, 158, 166, 167, 169, 181*
24:13–32 *166, 167, 169, 181*
24:13–48 *243*
24:14 *167*
24:14–15 *178*
24:15 *166, 168, 169, 178*
24:16 *168, 180*
24:17 *158, 166, 167, 169, 178*
24:19 *169, 170, 203*
24:19–24 *166*

24:19–26 *245*
24:20 *164, 268*
24:20–21 *163*
24:21 *24, 30, 127, 158, 167, 168, 169, 170, 209, 273, 279*
24:22 *110*
24:22–23 *168*
24:22–24 *180*
24:23 *32, 33, 110, 125, 139, 162, 209, 289*
24:24 *158, 168*
24:25 *168, 170, 177, 258*
24:25–27 *178, 279*
24:26 *9, 39, 40, 41, 43, 45, 47, 72, 163, 168, 172, 173, 176, 219, 223*
24:26–27 *112, 173, 183*
24:27 *27, 36, 170, 176, 177, 178, 183, 201, 243*
24:28 *158, 166, 169*
24:29 *158, 166, 179*
24:30 *180*
24:30–35 *122*
24:31 *169, 178, 180, 181*
24:32 *178*
24:33 *158, 165, 166, 181*
24:34 *159, 186, 190*
24:35 *159, 180*
24:36 *158, 181, 188*
24:36–39 *158*
24:36–43 *188*
24:36–48 *192*
24:36–49 *181*
24:36–53 *182*
24:37 *142, 143, 186*
24:38 *188*

Luke (continued)
  24:39 *142, 143, 186, 188, 189, 210*
  24:39–43 *190*
  24:40 *190*
  24:41 *187, 258*
  24:41–43 *188, 191, 243*
  24:42 *188*
  24:42–43 *187*
  24:43 *161*
  24:44 *26, 27, 39, 182, 183, 191, 243*
  24:44–47 *112, 201, 279*
  24:44–48 *36*
  24:44–49 *181*
  24:45 *178, 186*
  24:45–46 *163*
  24:46 *32, 40, 72, 127, 158, 163, 172, 183, 191, 219*
  24:46–47 *183, 184, 186, 197, 224, 232*
  24:46–48 *35*
  24:47 *25, 34, 183, 193*
  24:47b–48 *193*
  24:48 *187, 212, 243*
  24:49 *36, 194, 213*
  24:50 *158, 181, 215*
  24:50–51a *181*
  24:50–53 *6, 9, 44, 45, 158, 181, 195, 215, 216*
  24:51 *158, 169, 181*
  24:51b *181*
  24:52 *182*
  24:53 *157, 158*
  24:56b *158*
John
  3:4 *104*
  4:22 *23*
  4:42 *23*
  6:22–59 *171*
  6:39 *32*
  6:57 *32*
  11:11 *84*
  11:25 *32*
  11:38–44 *127*
  11:43–44 *8*
  12:1–2 *8*
  14:19 *32*
  20:1–21:25 *33*
  20:9 *32*
Acts
  1:1 *265, 266*
  1:1–2 *157, 265*
  1:1–3 *35*
  1:1–8 *265*
  1:1–11 *44, 45, 264, 265*
  1:1–12 *6, 176*
  1:1–26 *265*
  1:2 *10, 175, 190, 265, 266*
  1:3 *29, 32, 33, 45, 46, 125, 139, 182, 189, 190, 193, 209, 212, 243, 266, 267, 289, 292*
  1:3–4a *188*
  1:3–8 *34, 265*
  1:3–11 *254*
  1:4 *191, 192, 194, 243*
  1:4–5 *36, 193*
  1:5 *159, 194, 200, 213, 242, 252*
  1:5b *265*
  1:6 *193, 196, 228, 266, 267, 268, 279*
  1:6–11 *228*
  1:7 *26, 193, 228*
  1:8 *36, 184, 187, 193, 194, 200, 212, 213, 228, 243, 262, 264, 266, 267, 268*
  1:9–11 *6, 9, 44, 195, 215, 216*
  1:10 *161*
  1:11 *35, 175, 193, 228, 265*
  1:12 *264, 265*
  1:12–14 *264*
  1:12–26 *187, 265*
  1:13 *190, 200, 264, 265*
  1:14 *264*
  1:14–15 *200*
  1:16 *26, 27, 178, 268*
  1:18–20 *165*
  1:21 *265*
  1:21–22 *37, 46, 191, 217, 243*
  1:21–26 *265*
  1:22 *32, 35, 159, 175, 187, 201, 212, 213, 243, 265, 281*
  1:24 *265*
  1:26 *190, 200, 212, 264*
  2:1 *19, 200, 265*
  1:1–13 *36*
  2:1–41 *265*
  2:3 *124*
  2:5 *201*
  2:9–11 *202*
  2:10–11 *215*
  2:13 *232*
  2:14 *201, 212, 255, 267*
  2:14–36 *25, 200*
  2:14–40 *197*
  2:14b–40 *201*
  2:15 *201, 212*
  2:16–20 *201*
  2:17 *213, 276*
  2:17–21 *202*
  2:19 *203*
  2:21 *25, 201, 218, 219*
  2:22 *36, 130, 201, 202, 203, 212, 224*

2:22–24 *202, 242, 245*
2:22–25 *212*
2:22–28 *202*
2:22–36 *131, 201*
2:22–39 *184*
2:23 *26, 39, 41, 203, 212, 218*
2:23–24 *40, 127*
2:23–35 *45*
2:24 *32, 34, 203, 205, 207, 208, 212, 222, 224, 225, 236, 245, 249, 268, 282*
2:24–32 *214*
2:24–36 *27*
2:25 *27, 178, 205, 209, 212, 214, 215, 222*
2:25–28 *202, 203, 208, 279*
2:25–32 *214*
2:25a *249*
2:26 *24, 209, 211*
2:26b–27 *279*
2:27 *33, 128, 190, 209, 210, 236, 282*
2:28 *209, 215, 259*
2:29 *201, 202, 210, 255*
2:29–31 *178, 211, 280*
2:29–32 *209*
2:29–35 *236*
2:29–36 *44, 182, 202, 209, 249*
2:30 *202, 209, 210, 211, 214, 248*
2:30–31 *43, 46, 210, 214, 217, 246, 253*
2:31 *27, 32, 33, 72, 128, 178, 209, 210, 219, 236, 248, 281, 282*
2:31–32 *255*

2:32 *32, 34, 35, 201, 212, 217, 224, 243, 245*
2:32–33 *36*
2:32–35 *46, 173*
2:33 *8, 35, 43, 194, 201, 202, 209, 212, 213, 214, 215, 216, 217, 248, 252*
2:33–34 *46*
2:33–35 *213, 214, 217*
2:34 *27, 178, 212, 215*
2:34–35 *202, 214*
2:34a *214, 215, 216, 217*
2:34b–35 *218*
2:36 *25, 27, 30, 35, 72, 202, 203, 209, 211, 212, 213, 214, 218, 219, 239, 248, 255*
2:36a *212*
2:36b *212, 218*
2:37 *201, 218*
2:38 *25, 219, 254*
2:38–39 *212*
2:38–40 *25, 201*
2:39 *202, 218*
2:40 *218, 254*
2:41 *284*
2:42–47 *122, 263*
2:44–46 *134*
3:1–10 *219*
3:3–11 *157*
3:5 *220*
3:6 *220*
3:6–7 *36, 221*
3:7 *221*
3:8 *219*
3:8–9 *221*
3:9–12 *220*
3:10 *219*
3:11a *219*
3:11b *219*

3:12 *36, 219, 221, 223*
3:12–15 *220*
3:12–16 *221, 222*
3:12–26 *197*
3:13 *27, 40, 139, 220, 221, 222, 223, 224, 230, 245, 246, 268, 280, 283*
3:13–14 *236*
3:13–15 *127, 203, 223, 236, 242, 283*
3:13–16 *40*
3:14 *40, 72, 224*
3:14–15 *35, 40, 46, 220, 224*
3:14–16 *37*
3:15 *27, 34, 35, 36, 128, 208, 212, 221, 224, 225, 230, 243, 245, 259, 280, 282, 283*
3:15–16 *291*
3:16 *30, 219, 220, 223*
3:17 *26, 221, 226*
3:17–18 *41, 242*
3:17–26 *221*
3:18 *26, 35, 39, 40, 41, 72, 177, 178, 226, 231, 232*
3:18–19 *184*
3:18–20 *254*
3:18–21 *283*
3:18–26 *194*
3:19 *226*
3:19–21 *272*
3:20 *72*
3:20–21 *29, 222, 226, 227, 228, 231, 233*
3:20a *229, 230*
3:21 *26, 217, 230, 231*
3:22 *27, 224, 232, 245, 246, 283*
3:22–23 *222, 231, 280*

Acts (continued)
   3:22–25 *220*
   3:22–26 *220, 222,*
      226, 231, 260
   3:23 *224, 271, 283*
   3:24 *26, 29, 177, 178,*
      231, 232
   3:24–25 *178*
   3:25 *27, 177, 178,*
      230, 231, 272
   3:25–26 *27*
   3:26 *32, 34, 174, 220,*
      222, 224, 231, 232,
      233, 245, 283
   4:1–2 *48, 86, 130, 197*
   4:1–5 *220*
   4:2 *32, 37, 122, 174,*
      208, 220, 225, 230,
      281, 282, 283
   4:4 *284*
   4:7 *284, 291*
   4:7–8 *220*
   4:8 *220*
   4:9 *30, 220*
   4:9–10 *220*
   4:10 *30, 34, 36, 37,*
      40, 220, 224, 236, 243,
      267, 283, 284, 291
   4:10–11 *197, 203, 220*
   4:10–13 *243*
   4:11 *172, 284*
   4:12 *23, 30, 220, 284,*
      291
   4:13 *284*
   4:14 *30, 37, 220*
   4:15 *30*
   4:16 *37, 220*
   4:16–17 *220*
   4:17 *220*
   4:17–18 *284*
   4:18 *220*
   4:20 *37, 187, 243*
   4:21 *220*

4:21–22 *37*
4:22 *30, 220*
4:22–23 *30*
4:25 *27, 178*
4:25–26 *248*
4:25–27 *220*
4:25–28 *248*
4:26 *72, 248*
4:27–28 *41, 248*
4:28 *26*
4:29–30 *37*
4:30 *36, 220, 283*
4:30–31 *220*
4:31–34 *289*
4:32 *134*
4:32–35 *221*
4:33 *32, 35, 36, 122,*
   134, 197, 220, 221,
   281
4:34–35 *134*
5:10 *230*
5:12 *36*
5:12–13 *220*
5:12–16 *220*
5:13 *220*
5:14 *284*
5:17 *130*
5:19–20 *220*
5:20 *197, 225, 259,*
   283
5:25 *220*
5:26 *220*
5:28 *220, 283, 284*
5:29 *284*
5:29–30 *173*
5:30 *34, 40, 127, 139,*
   224, 246, 283
5:30–31 *8, 35, 46,*
   184, 203, 220, 236,
   241, 242
5:30–32 *197, 217*
5:31 *23, 25, 27, 30,*
   43, 128, 208, 213, 214,

215, 216, 217, 224,
225, 241, 280, 282,
283
5:31–32 *35, 213*
5:32 *35, 36, 243, 284*
5:36–37 *284*
5:38 *26, 257*
5:40 *220*
5:40–41 *284*
5:42 *35, 72*
6:7 *284*
6:8 *36*
6:15 *124*
7:1–53 *29, 178, 197*
7:2 *27, 173*
7:6 *77*
7:8 *27*
7:12–45 *236*
7:22 *170, 178*
7:25 *23, 178*
7:27 *27, 178*
7:30–36 *136*
7:32 *27, 223*
7:34 *187*
7:35 *27, 170, 178*
7:36 *178*
7:37 *178, 245, 246*
7:38 *178*
7:39 *178*
7:42 *247*
7:45 *72*
7:45–46 *27*
7:51 *202*
7:51–52 *271*
7:52 *40, 72, 177, 178,*
   245
7:55 *8, 173*
7:55–56 *36, 165, 218*
7:56 *72, 197*
7:58 *264*
8:1 *264*
8:1–4 *264*
8:4 *264*

Index of Ancient Literature and Scripture

8:5 *35, 72*
8:6 *36*
8:12 *270, 289*
8:13 *36*
8:22 *25*
8:25 *34, 194*
8:31 *129*
8:32–33 *37*
8:33 *283*
8:34–35 *178*
8:35 *129*
9:1–19 *217*
9:2 *270, 289*
9:5 *289*
9:13–16 *288*
9:15 *244, 256, 272*
9:15–16 *238*
9:20 *235, 236*
9:21 *289*
9:22 *35, 72, 235*
9:26–31 *194*
9:27 *235*
9:31 *24*
9:36–42 *119*
9:36–43 *8*
9:37 *120*
9:38 *120*
9:39 *120, 190*
9:40 *120*
9:41 *33, 125, 139, 189, 190, 209, 290*
10:11 *124*
10:18 *259*
10:34 *178*
10:34–43 *197*
10:34–44 *36*
10:35 *236*
10:36 *23, 236*
10:36–42 *242*
10:37 *159, 236*
10:37–39 *224*
10:37–41 *35*
10:38 *29, 130, 194*

10:38–40 *236*
10:38–42 *243*
10:39 *35, 194*
10:39–40 *40, 127, 203*
10:39–41 *217*
10:39–43 *184*
10:40 *127, 190, 224, 243*
10:40–41 *35, 236*
10:40–43 *46, 197*
10:41 *32, 190, 191, 192, 243*
10:41–42 *187*
10:42 *35, 137, 192, 194, 217, 244, 273, 289*
10:43 *25, 34, 177, 233, 236*
10:44 *197*
10:44–11:18 *236*
11:2 *194*
11:15–16 *194*
11:15–17 *36*
11:16 *163*
11:25–26 *235*
11:28 *19*
11:30 *235*
12:15 *142, 143*
12:23 *173, 230*
12:25 *194*
12:25–13:5 *263, 265*
13:1 *235*
13:2 *235, 256*
13:5 *236*
13:7 *235*
13:9 *235*
13:13 *235*
13:14 *236, 237*
13:15 *237, 240, 254*
13:16 *235, 236, 237, 238, 240, 257*
13:16–23 *238*
13:16–25 *239*

13:16–41 *25, 197, 234, 239, 263*
13:16b *239*
13:16b–25 *239*
13:17 *237, 240, 242, 280*
13:17–25 *29, 236, 238*
13:17a *237, 239, 240*
13:17b *237, 240*
13:18 *240*
13:19 *240*
13:20 *240*
13:21 *240, 243*
13:22 *26, 27, 240, 241, 243, 246, 255*
13:22–23 *238, 245*
13:23 *23, 25, 28, 194, 237, 240, 242, 244, 246, 253, 255, 280*
13:23–31 *245*
13:24 *159, 163, 175, 237, 240, 241*
13:24–25 *236*
13:24–26 *238*
13:25 *202, 241*
13:26 *23, 25, 236, 237, 238, 239, 244, 251, 257*
13:26–37 *239, 242*
13:26b *242*
13:27 *26, 41, 178, 237, 239, 240, 242, 255*
13:27–28 *244*
13:27–29 *248*
13:27–30 *40, 127, 203*
13:27–31 *238, 242, 245*
13:27–37 *238*
13:27–39 *184*
13:28 *236, 243*
13:28–30 *236*
13:29 *41, 237, 242, 243*
13:29–31 *35*

Acts (continued)
  13:30 *34, 224, 241,
    243, 245*
  13:30–31 *46, 217*
  13:31 *35, 46, 190, 194,
    212, 236, 237, 243,
    245*
  13:32 *25, 237, 240,
    244, 245, 255*
  13:32–33 *194, 238,
    240, 241, 247, 251,
    257, 280*
  13:32–33a *244*
  13:32–34 *254*
  13:32–37 *27, 238, 241,
    244, 245, 253*
  13:32–39 *277*
  13:33 *26, 32, 34, 41,
    43, 208, 224, 237, 240,
    244, 245, 246, 247,
    248, 249, 250, 253*
  13:33–35 *239*
  13:33–37 *217, 238,
    244, 258*
  13:34 *32, 33, 34, 224,
    245, 246, 247, 249,
    250, 251, 252, 253,
    254, 259, 280*
  13:34–35 *252*
  13:34–37 *128, 245*
  13:34a *247*
  13:34b *247*
  13:35 *33, 210, 236,
    247, 250, 252, 254*
  13:35–37 *282*
  13:36 *26, 33, 44, 211,
    237, 250, 251, 254*
  13:36–37 *178, 236,
    241, 254*
  13:37 *33, 34, 224*
  13:38 *25, 237, 238,
    250, 251, 267*
  13:38–39 *26, 237, 251,
    252, 254, 255*
  13:38–41 *238, 239, 255*
  13:39 *236, 238*
  13:40 *237*
  13:40–41 *256, 271*
  13:41 *256, 257, 258,
    260*
  13:42 *237*
  13:42–43 *236, 257*
  13:43 *235, 237, 257*
  13:44 *237*
  13:44–45 *237, 257*
  13:44–47 *236*
  13:45–47 *256*
  13:45–51 *272*
  13:46 *134, 235, 237,
    258, 271, 272, 283*
  13:46–47 *257, 263*
  13:47 *23, 184, 260, 283*
  13:48 *237, 258*
  13:50 *235*
  14:1 *236*
  14:1–6 *272*
  14:3 *36, 122, 190*
  14:7 *236*
  14:12 *235*
  14:14 *235*
  14:15–17 *26, 198*
  14:17 *227*
  14:19 *124*
  14:22 *173*
  14:26 *256*
  15:2 *194, 235*
  15:3 *256*
  15:5 *275*
  15:7 *26*
  15:7–9 *252*
  15:8 *36, 194*
  15:12 *36, 235*
  15:14 *23*
  15:14–17 *272*
  15:15 *247*
  15:18 *26*
  15:21 *26*
  15:22 *235*
  15:25 *235*
  15:38 *256*
  16:17 *23, 26*
  17:1–2 *236*
  17:2–3 *236, 284*
  17:3 *32, 34, 35, 39, 40,
    41, 72, 172*
  17:10 *236*
  17:11 *284*
  17:12–14 *272*
  17:16–18 *48*
  17:17 *236*
  17:18 *32, 34, 112, 234,
    245, 281, 284*
  17:19 *284*
  17:19–34 *48*
  17:22–31 *198, 234*
  17:26 *26, 227*
  17:30 *26, 224*
  17:30–31 *29, 234*
  17:31 *32, 34, 35, 122,
    194, 224, 282, 285,
    289*
  17:31–32 *273*
  17:32 *32, 34, 112, 144,
    281, 285*
  17:34 *144*
  18:2 *19*
  18:4 *236*
  18:5 *35, 72*
  18:6 *238, 272*
  18:19 *236*
  18:22 *194*
  18:28 *35, 72*
  19:4 *159, 242*
  19:8 *236, 270*
  19:8–9 *289*
  19:9 *238, 272*
  19:16 *140*
  19:21 *262, 265*

Index of Ancient Literature and Scripture 351

19:22 *194*
20:1-2 *122*
20:6 *227*
20:7 *122*
20:7-12 *119*
20:8 *120*
20:9 *124*
20:9-10 *8*
20:10 *120, 122, 230*
20:11 *122*
20:11-12 *125*
20:12 *33, 122, 125, 139, 209, 290*
20:16 *194*
20:18-35 *198, 234, 266*
20:20 *34*
20:21 *34, 234*
20:22 *194, 262*
20:24 *26, 34, 122, 234*
20:25 *26, 234, 254, 285*
20:27 *26, 234*
20:28 *38*
20:28-32 *122*
20:32 *122, 234, 254*
20:38 *285*
21:4 *262*
21:11-13 *262*
21:13 *194*
21:14 *26*
21:20 *284*
21:28 *269*
22:1-16 *217*
22:1-21 *287*
22:4 *268, 289*
22:5 *270*
22:6-10 *142*
22:8 *289*
22:11 *173*
22:14 *40, 72, 243*
22:14-15 *187, 244, 287*
22:15 *35, 187, 243*
22:17-21 *142*
22:18 *35, 194, 287*

22:20 *36, 244, 287*
22:21 *244, 272*
23:6 *24, 32, 34, 139, 209, 230, 258, 269, 272, 273, 274, 275, 280, 281, 288*
23:6-8 *86, 130*
23:6-10 *48*
23:8 *139, 141, 142, 281, 288*
23:9 *142, 288*
23:11 *35, 194, 262, 288*
23:24 *23*
23:29 *269, 275*
23:33 *190*
24:5 *269, 270, 272*
24:10 *289*
24:14 *230, 276, 278, 280, 282*
24:14-15 *48, 122, 230, 258, 276*
24:15 *24, 34, 139, 209, 269, 270, 272, 273, 275, 278, 280, 281, 288, 290*
24:20-21 *139*
24:21 *32, 34, 144, 274, 275, 280, 281, 289*
24:22 *144, 275, 289*
24:24 *144, 275, 289*
24:24-25 *35*
24:25 *144, 289*
24:26 *289*
25:7 *269*
25:8 *285*
25:11 *285*
25:11-12 *269*
25:12 *285*
25:19 *32, 125, 139, 209, 289*
25:19-20 *144, 275*
25:21 *269, 285*
25:25 *269*

26:1-23 *217*
26:2-3 *144*
26:3 *275*
26:5 *139, 273*
26:6 *230, 258, 273, 275, 280, 290*
26:6-7 *24, 230, 269, 270, 276, 278, 290*
26:6-8 *48, 139, 209, 246, 258, 260, 272, 273*
26:7 *276, 278*
26:8 *34, 258, 278, 282, 290, 291*
26:8-9 *24*
26:9 *289, 290*
26:9-18 *288*
26:15 *289*
26:16 *35, 187, 243, 244*
26:16-18 *288*
26:17 *244*
26:17-18 *184*
26:18 *25, 254*
26:19 *202, 270*
26:20 *134, 224, 238, 244, 291*
26:22 *27, 275, 276*
26:22-23 *35, 246, 279, 291*
26:23 *24, 32, 34, 39, 40, 72, 144, 172, 174, 184, 208, 224, 225, 244, 260, 269, 272, 280, 281, 282, 283, 285*
26:23-24 *291*
26:24 *144*
26:26-27 *144*
26:27 *275, 276, 282, 291*
26:27-29 *275*
26:28 *144, 291*
26:29 *209*

Acts (continued)
- 26:31–32 *269*
- 27:24 *285*
- 27:34 *23*
- 27:43 *23*
- 27:44 *23*
- 28:1 *23*
- 28:4 *23*
- 28:11–15 *263*
- 28:14 *263*
- 28:16–31 *146, 262, 263, 265, 266, 268, 269*
- 28:17 *268, 269*
- 28:17–22 *269*
- 28:18 *269, 291*
- 28:19 *269*
- 28:20 *24, 209, 267, 269, 270, 272, 273, 278*
- 28:21 *270*
- 28:22 *270, 272*
- 28:23 *27, 34, 254, 266, 267, 268, 270, 276, 278, 289*
- 28:24 *272*
- 28:24–25a *271*
- 28:25 *266, 267*
- 28:26–27 *187, 271*
- 28:28 *23, 26, 238, 244, 255, 257, 266, 267, 271, 272*
- 28:30–31 *286*
- 28:31 *254, 266, 267, 268, 270, 289*

Romans
- 1:1–3 *248*
- 1:3–4 *282*
- 1:4 *32*
- 4:24 *32*
- 4:25 *32, 255*
- 5:10 *274*
- 5:17 *274*
- 5:21 *274*
- 6:4 *32*
- 6:5 *32, 274*
- 6:9 *32*
- 6:10 *32*
- 7:4 *32*
- 8:11 *32, 33, 274*
- 8:22 *207*
- 8:24–25 *280*
- 8:29 *274*
- 8:34 *8, 32*
- 10:9 *32*
- 14:8 *274*
- 14:9 *32, 137*

1 Corinthians
- 1:30 *252*
- 4:5 *8*
- 6:1–4 *80*
- 6:14 *32*
- 15 *32*
- 15 *116*
- 15:4 *32*
- 15:8 *243*
- 15:12 *32*
- 15:13 *32*
- 15:14 *32*
- 15:15 *32*
- 15:16 *32, 277*
- 15:16–26 *274*
- 15:17 *32*
- 15:20 *32, 207, 282*
- 15:23 *207*
- 15:35 *79*
- 15:42 *33*
- 15:42–44 *81*
- 15:47 *8*
- 15:50 *33, 79*
- 15:50–53 *81*
- 15:52 *33*
- 15:53 *33*
- 15:54 *33*
- 15:54–55 *207*

2 Corinthians
- 4:10 *33*
- 4:14 *32*
- 5:15 *32*
- 12:2 *97*
- 13:4 *32*

Galatians
- 1:1 *32*
- 3:17 *77*
- 4:25–27 *76, 176*

Ephesians
- 1:3 *8*
- 1:20 *8, 32*
- 2:6 *8*
- 6:9 *8*

Philippians
- 1:20 *274*
- 3:8–11 *274*
- 3:10 *32*
- 3:20 *8*
- 3:21 *33*

Colossians
- 1:18 *207, 249, 282*
- 2:12 *32*
- 3:1 *8*

1 Thessalonians
- 1:10 *8, 32*
- 4:4 *32*
- 4:16 *8*
- 5:3 *207*

2 Thessalonians
- 1:7 *8*

1 Timothy
- 4:18 *8*

2 Timothy
- 2:8 *32*
- 4:1 *137*

Hebrews
- 1:3 *8*
- 1:5 *247, 248*
- 1:6 *249*
- 1:13 *8*
- 4:14 *43*
- 5:6 *254*

Index of Ancient Literature and Scripture

7:16 *43, 128*
7:26 *43*
8:1 *8*
8:1 *43*
9:12 *8*
9:24 *8, 43*
9:25 *32*
10:12–13 *8*
11:5 *211*
12:2 *8*
13:20–21 *43*
13:22 *254*
James
  2:26 *123*
1 Peter
  1:3 *32*

1:4 *33*
1:12 *80*
1:21 *32*
2:4 *32*
2:6 *284*
3:20 *23*
3:21 *32*
3:22 *8*
4:5 *137*
2 Peter
  1:15 *175*
1 John
  1:1 *186*
  1:1–3 *186*
  4:2 *186*

Revelation
  1:5 *207, 249*
  1:12–18 *8*
  1:17 *124*
  1:18 *32, 33*
  2:8 *32, 33*
  3:12 *176*
  3:21 *8*
  6:1–7 *8*
  7:17 *8*
  12:2 *207*
  20:13 *206*
  21:2 *176*
  21:10 *176*

Paternoster Biblical Monographs

(All titles uniform with this volume)
Dates in bold are of projected publication

Joseph Abraham
Eve: Accused or Acquitted?
A Reconsideration of Feminist Readings of the Creation Narrative Texts in Genesis 1–3

Two contrary views dominate contemporary feminist biblical scholarship. One finds in the Bible an unequivocal equality between the sexes from the very creation of humanity, whilst the other sees the biblical text as irredeemably patriarchal and androcentric. Dr Abraham enters into dialogue with both camps as well as introducing his own method of approach. An invaluable tool for any one who is interested in this contemporary debate.

2002 / 0-85364-971-5 / xxiv + 272pp

Octavian D. Baban
Mimesis and Luke's on the Road Encounters in Luke-Acts
Luke's Theology of the Way and its Literary Representation

The book argues on theological and literary (mimetic) grounds that Luke's on-the-road encounters, especially those belonging to the post-Easter period, are part of his complex theology of the Way. Jesus' teaching and that of the apostles is presented by Luke as a challenging answer to the Hellenistic reader's thirst for adventure, good literature, and existential paradigms.

***2005** / 1-84227-253-5 / approx. 374pp*

Paul Barker
The Triumph of Grace in Deuteronomy

This book is a textual and theological analysis of the interaction between the sin and faithlessness of Israel and the grace of Yahweh in response, looking especially at Deuteronomy chapters 1–3, 8–10 and 29–30. The author argues that the grace of Yahweh is determinative for the ongoing relationship between Yahweh and Israel and that Deuteronomy anticipates and fully expects Israel to be faithless.

2004 / 1-84227-226-8 / xxii + 270pp

Jonathan F. Bayes
The Weakness of the Law
God's Law and the Christian in New Testament Perspective

A study of the four New Testament books which refer to the law as weak (Acts, Romans, Galatians, Hebrews) leads to a defence of the third use in the Reformed debate about the law in the life of the believer.

2000 / 0-85364-957-X / xii + 244pp

Mark Bonnington
The Antioch Episode of Galatians 2:11-14 in Historical and Cultural Context

The Galatians 2 'incident' in Antioch over table-fellowship suggests significant disagreement between the leading apostles. This book analyses the background to the disagreement by locating the incident within the dynamics of social interaction between Jews and Gentiles. It proposes a new way of understanding the relationship between the individuals and issues involved.

2005 / 1-84227-050-8 / approx. 350pp

David Bostock
A Portrayal of Trust
The Theme of Faith in the Hezekiah Narratives

This study provides detailed and sensitive readings of the Hezekiah narratives (2 Kings 18–20 and Isaiah 36–39) from a theological perspective. It concentrates on the theme of faith, using narrative criticism as its methodology. Attention is paid especially to setting, plot, point of view and characterization within the narratives. A largely positive portrayal of Hezekiah emerges that underlines the importance and relevance of scripture.

2005 / 1-84227-314-0 / approx. 300pp

Mark Bredin
Jesus, Revolutionary of Peace
A Non-violent Christology in the Book of Revelation

This book aims to demonstrate that the figure of Jesus in the Book of Revelation can best be understood as an active non-violent revolutionary.

2003 / 1-84227-153-9 / xviii + 262pp

Robinson Butarbutar
Paul and Conflict Resolution
An Exegetical Study of Paul's Apostolic Paradigm in 1 Corinthians 9

The author sees the apostolic paradigm in 1 Corinthians 9 as part of Paul's unified arguments in 1 Corinthians 8–10 in which he seeks to mediate in the dispute over the issue of food offered to idols. The book also sees its relevance for dispute-resolution today, taking the conflict within the author's church as an example.

2006 / 1-84227-315-9 / approx. 280pp

Daniel J-S Chae
Paul as Apostle to the Gentiles
His Apostolic Self-awareness and its Influence on the Soteriological Argument in Romans
Opposing 'the post-Holocaust interpretation of Romans', Daniel Chae competently demonstrates that Paul argues for the equality of Jew and Gentile in Romans. Chae's fresh exegetical interpretation is academically outstanding and spiritually encouraging.
1997 / 0-85364-829-8 / xiv + 378pp

Luke L. Cheung
The Genre, Composition and Hermeneutics of the Epistle of James
The present work examines the employment of the wisdom genre with a certain compositional structure and the interpretation of the law through the Jesus tradition of the double love command by the author of the Epistle of James to serve his purpose in promoting perfection and warning against doubleness among the eschatologically renewed people of God in the Diaspora.
2003 / 1-84227-062-1 / xvi + 372pp

Youngmo Cho
Spirit and Kingdom in the Writings of Luke and Paul
The relationship between Spirit and Kingdom is a relatively unexplored area in Lukan and Pauline studies. This book offers a fresh perspective of two biblical writers on the subject. It explores the difference between Luke's and Paul's understanding of the Spirit by examining the specific question of the relationship of the concept of the Spirit to the concept of the Kingdom of God in each writer.
2005 / 1-84227-316-7 / approx. 270pp

Andrew C. Clark
Parallel Lives
The Relation of Paul to the Apostles in the Lucan Perspective
This study of the Peter-Paul parallels in Acts argues that their purpose was to emphasize the themes of continuity in salvation history and the unity of the Jewish and Gentile missions. New light is shed on Luke's literary techniques, partly through a comparison with Plutarch.
2001 / 1-84227-035-4 / xviii + 386pp

Andrew D. Clarke
Secular and Christian Leadership in Corinth
A Socio-Historical and Exegetical Study of 1 Corinthians 1–6

This volume is an investigation into the leadership structures and dynamics of first-century Roman Corinth. These are compared with the practice of leadership in the Corinthian Christian community which are reflected in 1 Corinthians 1–6, and contrasted with Paul's own principles of Christian leadership.

2005 / 1-84227-229-2 / 200pp

Stephen Finamore
God, Order and Chaos
René Girard and the Apocalypse

Readers are often disturbed by the images of destruction in the book of Revelation and unsure why they are unleashed after the exaltation of Jesus. This book examines past approaches to these texts and uses René Girard's theories to revive some old ideas and propose some new ones.

2005 / 1-84227-197-0 / approx. 344pp

David G. Firth
Surrendering Retribution in the Psalms
Responses to Violence in the Individual Complaints

In *Surrendering Retribution in the Psalms*, David Firth examines the ways in which the book of Psalms inculcates a model response to violence through the repetition of standard patterns of prayer. Rather than seeking justification for retributive violence, Psalms encourages not only a surrender of the right of retribution to Yahweh, but also sets limits on the retribution that can be sought in imprecations. Arising initially from the author's experience in South Africa, the possibilities of this model to a particular context of violence is then briefly explored.

2005 / 1-84227-337-X / xviii + 154pp

Scott J. Hafemann
Suffering and Ministry in the Spirit
Paul's Defence of His Ministry in II Corinthians 2:14–3:3

Shedding new light on the way Paul defended his apostleship, the author offers a careful, detailed study of 2 Corinthians 2:14–3:3 linked with other key passages throughout 1 and 2 Corinthians. Demonstrating the unity and coherence of Paul's argument in this passage, the author shows that Paul's suffering served as the vehicle for revealing God's power and glory through the Spirit.

2000 / 0-85364-967-7 / xiv + 262pp

Scott J. Hafemann
Paul, Moses and the History of Israel
The Letter/Spirit Contrast and the Argument from Scripture in 2 Corinthians 3
An exegetical study of the call of Moses, the second giving of the Law (Exodus 32–34), the new covenant, and the prophetic understanding of the history of Israel in 2 Corinthians 3. Hafemann's work demonstrates Paul's contextual use of the Old Testament and the essential unity between the Law and the Gospel within the context of the distinctive ministries of Moses and Paul.
2005 / 1-84227-317-5 / xii + 498pp

Douglas S. McComiskey
Lukan Theology in the Light of the Gospel's Literary Structure
Luke's Gospel was purposefully written with theology embedded in its patterned literary structure. A critical analysis of this cyclical structure provides new windows into Luke's interpretation of the individual pericopes comprising the Gospel and illuminates several of his theological interests.
2004 / 1-84227-148-2 / xviii + 388pp

Stephen Motyer
Your Father the Devil?
A New Approach to John and 'The Jews'
Who are 'the Jews' in John's Gospel? Defending John against the charge of antisemitism, Motyer argues that, far from demonising the Jews, the Gospel seeks to present Jesus as 'Good News for Jews' in a late first century setting.
1997 / 0-85364-832-8 / xiv + 260pp

Esther Ng
Reconstructing Christian Origins?
The Feminist Theology of Elizabeth Schüssler Fiorenza: An Evaluation
In a detailed evaluation, the author challenges Elizabeth Schüssler Fiorenza's reconstruction of early Christian origins and her underlying presuppositions. The author also presents her own views on women's roles both then and now.
2002 / 1-84227-055-9 / xxiv + 468pp

July 2005

Robin Parry
Old Testament Story and Christian Ethics
The Rape of Dinah as a Case Study

What is the role of story in ethics and, more particularly, what is the role of Old Testament story in Christian ethics? This book, drawing on the work of contemporary philosophers, argues that narrative is crucial in the ethical shaping of people and, drawing on the work of contemporary Old Testament scholars, that story plays a key role in Old Testament ethics. Parry then argues that when situated in canonical context Old Testament stories can be reappropriated by Christian readers in their own ethical formation. The shocking story of the rape of Dinah and the massacre of the Shechemites provides a fascinating case study for exploring the parameters within which Christian ethical appropriations of Old Testament stories can live.

2004 / 1-84227-210-1 / xx + 350pp

Ian Paul
Power to See the World Anew
The Value of Paul Ricoeur's Hermeneutic of Metaphor in Interpreting the Symbolism of Revelation 12 and 13

This book is a study of the hermeneutics of metaphor of Paul Ricoeur, one of the most important writers on hermeneutics and metaphor of the last century. It sets out the key points of his theory, important criticisms of his work, and how his approach, modified in the light of these criticisms, offers a methodological framework for reading apocalyptic texts.

2006 / 1-84227-056-7 / approx. 350pp

Robert L. Plummer
Paul's Understanding of the Church's Mission
Did the Apostle Paul Expect the Early Christian Communities to Evangelize?

This book engages in a careful study of Paul's letters to determine if the apostle expected the communities to which he wrote to engage in missionary activity. It helpfully summarizes the discussion on this debated issue, judiciously handling contested texts, and provides a way forward in addressing this critical question. While admitting that Paul rarely explicitly commands the communities he founded to evangelize, Plummer amasses significant incidental data to provide a convincing case that Paul did indeed expect his churches to engage in mission activity. Throughout the study, Plummer progressively builds a theological basis for the church's mission that is both distinctively Pauline and compelling.

2006 / 1-84227-333-7 / approx. 324pp

David Powys
'Hell': A Hard Look at a Hard Question
The Fate of the Unrighteous in New Testament Thought
This comprehensive treatment seeks to unlock the original meaning of terms and phrases long thought to support the traditional doctrine of hell. It concludes that there is an alternative—one which is more biblical, and which can positively revive the rationale for Christian mission.

1997 / 0-85364-831-X / xxii + 478pp

Sorin Sabou
Between Horror and Hope
Paul's Metaphorical Language of Death in Romans 6.1-11
This book argues that Paul's metaphorical language of death in Romans 6.1-11 conveys two aspects: horror and hope. The 'horror' aspect is conveyed by the 'crucifixion' language, and the 'hope' aspect by 'burial' language. The life of the Christian believer is understood, as relationship with sin is concerned ('death to sin'), between these two realities: horror and hope.

2005 / 1-84227-322-1 / approx. 224pp

Rosalind Selby
The Comical Doctrine
The Epistemology of New Testament Hermeneutics
This book argues that the gospel breaks through postmodernity's critique of truth and the referential possibilities of textuality with its gift of grace. With a rigorous, philosophical challenge to modernist and postmodernist assumptions, Selby offers an alternative epistemology to all who would still read with faith *and* with academic credibility.

2005 / 1-84227-212-8 / approx. 350pp

Kiwoong Son
Zion Symbolism in Hebrews
Hebrews 12.18-24 as a Hermeneutical Key to the Epistle
This book challenges the general tendency of understanding the Epistle to the Hebrews against a Hellenistic background and suggests that the Epistle should be understood in the light of the Jewish apocalyptic tradition. The author especially argues for the importance of the theological symbolism of Sinai and Zion (Heb. 12:18-24) as it provides the Epistle's theological background as well as the rhetorical basis of the superiority motif of Jesus throughout the Epistle.

2005 / 1-84227-368-X / approx. 280pp

Kevin Walton
Thou Traveller Unknown
The Presence and Absence of God in the Jacob Narrative
The author offers a fresh reading of the story of Jacob in the book of Genesis through the paradox of divine presence and absence. The work also seeks to make a contribution to Pentateuchal studies by bringing together a close reading of the final text with historical critical insights, doing justice to the text's historical depth, final form and canonical status.
2003 / 1-84227-059-1 / xvi + 238pp

George M. Wieland
The Significance of Salvation
A Study of Salvation Language in the Pastoral Epistles
The language and ideas of salvation pervade the three Pastoral Epistles. This study offers a close examination of their soteriological statements. In all three letters the idea of salvation is found to play a vital paraenetic role, but each also exhibits distinctive soteriological emphases. The results challenge common assumptions about the Pastoral Epistles as a corpus.
2005 / 1-84227-257-8 / approx. 324pp

Alistair Wilson
When Will These Things Happen?
A Study of Jesus as Judge in Matthew 21–25
This study seeks to allow Matthew's carefully constructed presentation of Jesus to be given full weight in the modern evaluation of Jesus' eschatology. Careful analysis of the text of Matthew 21–25 reveals Jesus to be standing firmly in the Jewish prophetic and wisdom traditions as he proclaims and enacts imminent judgement on the Jewish authorities then boldly claims the central role in the final and universal judgement.
2004 / 1-84227-146-6 / xxii + 272pp

Lindsay Wilson
Joseph Wise and Otherwise
The Intersection of Covenant and Wisdom in Genesis 37–50
This book offers a careful literary reading of Genesis 37–50 that argues that the Joseph story contains both strong covenant themes and many wisdom-like elements. The connections between the two helps to explore how covenant and wisdom might intersect in an integrated biblical theology.
2004 / 1-84227-140-7 / xvi + 340pp

Stephen I. Wright
The Voice of Jesus
Studies in the Interpretation of Six Gospel Parables
This literary study considers how the 'voice' of Jesus has been heard in different periods of parable interpretation, and how the categories of figure and trope may help us towards a sensitive reading of the parables today.
2000 / 0-85364-975-8 / xiv + 280pp

Paternoster
9 Holdom Avenue,
Bletchley,
Milton Keynes MK1 1QR,
United Kingdom
Web: www.authenticmedia.co.uk/paternoster

Paternoster Theological Monographs
(All titles uniform with this volume)
Dates in bold are of projected publication

Emil Bartos
Deification in Eastern Orthodox Theology
An Evaluation and Critique of the Theology of Dumitru Staniloae
Bartos studies a fundamental yet neglected aspect of Orthodox theology: deification. By examining the doctrines of anthropology, christology, soteriology and ecclesiology as they relate to deification, he provides an important contribution to contemporary dialogue between Eastern and Western theologians.

1999 / 0-85364-956-1 / xii + 370pp

Graham Buxton
The Trinity, Creation and Pastoral Ministry
Imaging the Perichoretic God
In this book the author proposes a three-way conversation between theology, science and pastoral ministry. His approach draws on a Trinitarian understanding of God as a relational being of love, whose life 'spills over' into all created reality, human and non-human. By locating human meaning and purpose within God's 'creation-community' this book offers the possibility of a transforming engagement between those in pastoral ministry and the scientific community.

***2005** / 1-84227-369-8 / approx. 380 pp*

Iain D. Campbell
Fixing the Indemnity
The Life and Work of George Adam Smith
When Old Testament scholar George Adam Smith (1856–1942) delivered the Lyman Beecher lectures at Yale University in 1899, he confidently declared that 'modern criticism has won its war against traditional theories. It only remains to fix the amount of the indemnity.' In this biography, Iain D. Campbell assesses Smith's critical approach to the Old Testament and evaluates its consequences, showing that Smith's life and work still raises questions about the relationship between biblical scholarship and evangelical faith.

2004 / 1-84227-228-4 / xx + 256pp

Tim Chester
Mission and the Coming of God
Eschatology, the Trinity and Mission in the Theology of Jürgen Moltmann
This book explores the theology and missiology of the influential contemporary theologian, Jürgen Moltmann. It highlights the important contribution Moltmann has made while offering a critique of his thought from an evangelical perspective. In so doing, it touches on pertinent issues for evangelical missiology. The conclusion takes Calvin as a starting point, proposing 'an eschatology of the cross' which offers a critique of the over-realised eschatologies in liberation theology and certain forms of evangelicalism.
2006 / 1-84227-320-5 / approx. 224pp

Sylvia Wilkey Collinson
Making Disciples
The Significance of Jesus' Educational Strategy for Today's Church
This study examines the biblical practice of discipling, formulates a definition, and makes comparisons with modern models of education. A recommendation is made for greater attention to its practice today.
2004 / 1-84227-116-4 / xiv + 278pp

Darrell Cosden
A Theology of Work
Work and the New Creation
Through dialogue with Moltmann, Pope John Paul II and others, this book develops a genitive 'theology of work', presenting a theological definition of work and a model for a theological ethics of work that shows work's nature, value and meaning now and eschatologically. Work is shown to be a transformative activity consisting of three dynamically inter-related dimensions: the instrumental, relational and ontological.
2005 / 1-84227-332-9 / xvi + 208pp

Stephen M. Dunning
The Crisis and the Quest
A Kierkegaardian Reading of Charles Williams
Employing Kierkegaardian categories and analysis, this study investigates both the central crisis in Charles Williams's authorship between hermetism and Christianity (Kierkegaard's Religions A and B), and the quest to resolve this crisis, a quest that ultimately presses the bounds of orthodoxy.
2000 / 0-85364-985-5 / xxiv + 254pp

Keith Ferdinando
The Triumph of Christ in African Perspective
A Study of Demonology and Redemption in the African Context
The book explores the implications of the gospel for traditional African fears of occult aggression. It analyses such traditional approaches to suffering and biblical responses to fears of demonic evil, concluding with an evaluation of African beliefs from the perspective of the gospel.
1999 / 0-85364-830-1 / xviii + 450pp

Andrew Goddard
Living the Word, Resisting the World
The Life and Thought of Jacques Ellul
This work offers a definitive study of both the life and thought of the French Reformed thinker Jacques Ellul (1912-1994). It will prove an indispensable resource for those interested in this influential theologian and sociologist and for Christian ethics and political thought generally.
2002 / 1-84227-053-2 / xxiv + 378pp

David Hilborn
The Words of our Lips
Language-Use in Free Church Worship
Studies of liturgical language have tended to focus on the written canons of Roman Catholic and Anglican communities. By contrast, David Hilborn analyses the more extemporary approach of English Nonconformity. Drawing on recent developments in linguistic pragmatics, he explores similarities and differences between 'fixed' and 'free' worship, and argues for the interdependence of each.
2006 / 0-85364-977-4 / approx. 350pp

Roger Hitching
The Church and Deaf People
A Study of Identity, Communication and Relationships with Special Reference to the Ecclesiology of Jürgen Moltmann
In *The Church and Deaf People* Roger Hitching sensitively examines the history and present experience of deaf people and finds similarities between aspects of sign language and Moltmann's theological method that 'open up' new ways of understanding theological concepts.
2003 / 1-84227-222-5 / xxii + 236pp

John G. Kelly
One God, One People
The Differentiated Unity of the People of God in the Theology of Jürgen Moltmann

The author expounds and critiques Moltmann's doctrine of God and highlights the systematic connections between it and Moltmann's influential discussion of Israel. He then proposes a fresh approach to Jewish–Christian relations building on Moltmann's work using insights from Habermas and Rawls.

2005 / 0-85346-969-3 / approx. 350pp

Mark F.W. Lovatt
Confronting the Will-to-Power
A Reconsideration of the Theology of Reinhold Niebuhr

Confronting the Will-to-Power is an analysis of the theology of Reinhold Niebuhr, arguing that his work is an attempt to identify, and provide a practical theological answer to, the existence and nature of human evil.

2001 / 1-84227-054-0 / xviii + 216pp

Neil B. MacDonald
Karl Barth and the Strange New World within the Bible
Barth, Wittgenstein, and the Metadilemmas of the Enlightenment

Barth's discovery of the strange new world within the Bible is examined in the context of Kant, Hume, Overbeck, and, most importantly, Wittgenstein. MacDonald covers some fundamental issues in theology today: epistemology, the final form of the text and biblical truth-claims.

2000 / 0-85364-970-7 / xxvi + 374pp

Keith A. Mascord
Alvin Plantinga and Christian Apologetics

This book draws together the contributions of the philosopher Alvin Plantinga to the major contemporary challenges to Christian belief, highlighting in particular his ground-breaking work in epistemology and the problem of evil. Plantinga's theory that both theistic and Christian belief is warrantedly basic is explored and critiqued, and an assessment offered as to the significance of his work for apologetic theory and practice.

2005 / 1-84227-256-X / approx. 304pp

Gillian McCulloch
The Deconstruction of Dualism in Theology
With Reference to Ecofeminist Theology and New Age Spirituality

This book challenges eco-theological anti-dualism in Christian theology, arguing that dualism has a twofold function in Christian religious discourse. Firstly, it enables us to express the discontinuities and divisions that are part of the process of reality. Secondly, dualistic language allows us to express the mysteries of divine transcendence/immanence and the survival of the soul without collapsing into monism and materialism, both of which are problematic for Christian epistemology.

2002 / 1-84227-044-3 / xii + 282pp

Leslie McCurdy
Attributes and Atonement
The Holy Love of God in the Theology of P.T. Forsyth

Attributes and Atonement is an intriguing full-length study of P.T. Forsyth's doctrine of the cross as it relates particularly to God's holy love. It includes an unparalleled bibliography of both primary and secondary material relating to Forsyth.

1999 / 0-85364-833-6 / xiv + 328pp

Nozomu Miyahira
Towards a Theology of the Concord of God
A Japanese Perspective on the Trinity

This book introduces a new Japanese theology and a unique Trinitarian formula based on the Japanese intellectual climate: three betweennesses and one concord. It also presents a new interpretation of the Trinity, a co-subordinationism, which is in line with orthodox Trinitarianism; each single person of the Trinity is eternally and equally subordinate (or serviceable) to the other persons, so that they retain the mutual dynamic equality.

2000 / 0-85364-863-8 / xiv + 256pp

Eddy José Muskus
The Origins and Early Development of Liberation Theology in Latin America
With Particular Reference to Gustavo Gutiérrez

This work challenges the fundamental premise of Liberation Theology, 'opting for the poor', and its claim that Christ is found in them. It also argues that Liberation Theology emerged as a direct result of the failure of the Roman Catholic Church in Latin America.

2002 / 0-85364-974-X / xiv + 296pp

Jim Purves
The Triune God and the Charismatic Movement
A Critical Appraisal from a Scottish Perspective

All emotion and no theology? Or a fundamental challenge to reappraise and realign our trinitarian theology in the light of Christian experience? This study of charismatic renewal as it found expression within Scotland at the end of the twentieth century evaluates the use of Patristic, Reformed and contemporary models of the Trinity in explaining the workings of the Holy Spirit.

2004 / 1-84227-321-3 / xxiv + 246pp

Anna Robbins
Methods in the Madness
Diversity in Twentieth-Century Christian Social Ethics

The author compares the ethical methods of Walter Rauschenbusch, Reinhold Niebuhr and others. She argues that unless Christians are clear about the ways that theology and philosophy are expressed practically they may lose the ability to discuss social ethics across contexts, let alone reach effective agreements.

2004 / 1-84227-211-X / xx + 294pp

Ed Rybarczyk
Beyond Salvation
Eastern Orthodoxy and Classical Pentecostalism on Becoming Like Christ

At first glance eastern Orthodoxy and classical Pentecostalism seem quite distinct. This ground-breaking study shows they share much in common, especially as it concerns the experiential elements of following Christ. Both traditions assert that authentic Christianity transcends the wooden categories of modernism.

2004 / 1-84227-144-X / xii + 356pp

Signe Sandsmark
Is World View Neutral Education Possible and Desirable?
A Christian Response to Liberal Arguments
(Published jointly with The Stapleford Centre)

This book discusses reasons for belief in world view neutrality, and argues that 'neutral' education will have a hidden, but strong world view influence. It discusses the place for Christian education in the common school.

2000 / 0-85364-973-1 / xiv + 182pp

Hazel Sherman
Reading Zechariah
The Allegorical Tradition of Biblical Interpretation through the Commentary of Didymus the Blind and Theodore of Mopsuestia

A close reading of the commentary on Zechariah by Didymus the Blind alongside that of Theodore of Mopsuestia suggests that popular categorising of Antiochene and Alexandrian biblical exegesis as 'historical' or 'allegorical' is inadequate and misleading.

2005 / 1-84227-213-6 / approx. 280pp

Andrew Sloane
On Being a Christian in the Academy
Nicholas Wolterstorff and the Practice of Christian Scholarship

An exposition and critical appraisal of Nicholas Wolterstorff's epistemology in the light of the philosophy of science, and an application of his thought to the practice of Christian scholarship.

2003 / 1-84227-058-3 / xvi + 274pp

Damon W.K. So
Jesus' Revelation of His Father
A Narrative-Conceptual Study of the Trinity with Special Reference to Karl Barth

This book explores the trinitarian dynamics in the context of Jesus' revelation of his Father in his earthly ministry with references to key passages in Matthew's Gospel. It develops from the exegeses of these passages a non-linear concept of revelation which links Jesus' communion with his Father to his revelatory words and actions through a nuanced understanding of the Holy Spirit, with references to K. Barth, G.W.H. Lampe, J.D.G. Dunn and E. Irving.

2005 / 1-84227-323-X / approx. 380pp

Daniel Strange
The Possibility of Salvation Among the Unevangelised
An Analysis of Inclusivism in Recent Evangelical Theology

For evangelical theologians the 'fate of the unevangelised' impinges upon fundamental tenets of evangelical identity. The position known as 'inclusivism', defined by the belief that the unevangelised can be ontologically saved by Christ whilst being epistemologically unaware of him, has been defended most vigorously by the Canadian evangelical Clark H. Pinnock. Through a detailed analysis and critique of Pinnock's work, this book examines a cluster of issues surrounding the unevangelised and its implications for christology, soteriology and the doctrine of revelation.

2002 / 1-84227-047-8 / xviii + 362pp

Scott Swain
God According to the Gospel
Biblical Narrative and the Identity of God in the Theology of Robert W. Jenson

Robert W. Jenson is one of the leading voices in contemporary Trinitarian theology. His boldest contribution in this area concerns his use of biblical narrative both to ground and explicate the Christian doctrine of God. *God According to the Gospel* critically examines Jenson's proposal and suggests an alternative way of reading the biblical portrayal of the triune God.

2006 / 1-84227-258-6 / approx. 180pp

Justyn Terry
The Justifying Judgement of God
A Reassessment of the Place of Judgement in the Saving Work of Christ

The argument of this book is that judgement, understood as the whole process of bringing justice, is the primary metaphor of atonement, with others, such as victory, redemption and sacrifice, subordinate to it. Judgement also provides the proper context for understanding penal substitution and the call to repentance, baptism, eucharist and holiness.

2005 / 1-84227-370-1 / approx. 274 pp

Graham Tomlin
The Power of the Cross
Theology and the Death of Christ in Paul, Luther and Pascal

This book explores the theology of the cross in St Paul, Luther and Pascal. It offers new perspectives on the theology of each, and some implications for the nature of power, apologetics, theology and church life in a postmodern context.

1999 / 0-85364-984-7 / xiv + 344pp

Adonis Vidu
Postliberal Theological Method
A Critical Study

The postliberal theology of Hans Frei, George Lindbeck, Ronald Thiemann, John Milbank and others is one of the more influential contemporary options. This book focuses on several aspects pertaining to its theological method, specifically its understanding of background, hermeneutics, epistemic justification, ontology, the nature of doctrine and, finally, Christological method.

2005 / 1-84227-395-7 / approx. 324pp

Graham J. Watts
Revelation and the Spirit
A Comparative Study of the Relationship between the Doctrine of Revelation and Pneumatology in the Theology of Eberhard Jüngel and of Wolfhart Pannenberg

The relationship between revelation and pneumatology is relatively unexplored. This approach offers a fresh angle on two important twentieth century theologians and raises pneumatological questions which are theologically crucial and relevant to mission in a postmodern culture.

2005 / 1-84227-104-0 / xxii + 232pp

Nigel G. Wright
Disavowing Constantine
Mission, Church and the Social Order in the Theologies of John Howard Yoder and Jürgen Moltmann

This book is a timely restatement of a radical theology of church and state in the Anabaptist and Baptist tradition. Dr Wright constructs his argument in dialogue and debate with Yoder and Moltmann, major contributors to a free church perspective.

2000 / 0-85364-978-2 / xvi + 252pp

Paternoster
9 Holdom Avenue,
Bletchley,
Milton Keynes MK1 1QR,
United Kingdom
Web: www.authenticmedia.co.uk/paternoster

www.ingramcontent.com/pod-product-compliance
Lightning Source LLC
Chambersburg PA
CBHW071231290426
44108CB00013B/1376